BILL DAVIS

BILL DAVIS

Nation Builder, *and Not So Bland After All*

STEVE PAIKIN

DUNDURN
A J. PATRICK BOYER BOOK

TORONTO

Editor: Michael Carroll
Interior and cover design: Laura Boyle
Printer: Friesens
Cover image: Archives of Ontario/ C221-0-0-30/ Premier of Ontario, Bill Davis ca. 1960/ Copyright Transferred to Archives of Ontario.

Library and Archives Canada Cataloguing in Publication

Paikin, Steve, 1960-, author
    Bill Davis : nation builder, and not so bland after all / Steve Paikin.

Includes index.
Issued in print and electronic formats.

ISBN 978-1-4597-3175-2 (hardback).--ISBN 978-1-4597-3176-9 (pdf).--ISBN 978-1-4597-3177-6 (epub)

1. Davis, William G., 1929-. 2. Ontario--Politics and government--1943-1985. 3. Premiers (Canada)--Ontario--Biography. 4. Ontario. Legislative Assembly--Biography. 5. Legislators--Ontario--Directories. I. Title.

FC3076.1.D38P35 2016   971.3'04092   C2016-904001-1

Conseil des Arts du Canada   Canada Council for the Arts

Canada

ONTARIO ARTS COUNCIL
CONSEIL DES ARTS DE L'ONTARIO
an Ontario government agency
un organisme du gouvernement de l'Ontario

C2016-904002-X

1 2 3 4 5   20 19 18 17 16

We acknowledge the support of the **Canada Council for the Arts** and the **Ontario Arts Council** for our publishing program. We also acknowledge the financial support of the **Government of Canada** through the **Canada Book Fund** and **Livres Canada Books**, and the **Government of Ontario** through the **Ontario Book Publishing Tax Credit** and the **Ontario Media Development Corporation**.

Care has been taken to trace the ownership of copyright material used in this book. The author and the publisher welcome any information enabling them to rectify any references or credits in subsequent editions.
                                                                — J. Kirk Howard, President

The publisher is not responsible for websites or their content unless they are owned by the publisher.

Printed and bound in Canada.

VISIT US AT
Dundurn.com | @dundurnpress | Facebook.com/dundurnpress | Pinterest.com/Dundurnpress
Dundurn
3 Church Street, Suite 500
Toronto, Ontario, Canada
M5E 1M2

This book is dedicated to
Kathleen Mackay Davis,
who raised five children,
managed a husband,
bore the weight of a province,
and made it all work.
She is the unsung hero of the Bill Davis legacy.

CONTENTS

INTRODUCTION

Election night — June 12, 2014 — was one of the most anticipated in Ontario political history. Because the public opinion surveys were all over the map, none of the so-called experts could predict with any certainty what was about to transpire. Millions of Ontarians would turn on their television sets that night with no clue as to who was going to win.

I got a taste of that uncertainty just a few days earlier. After taping an episode of *The Agenda* on TVO with the provincial finance minister and his opposition critics, and when the cameras were no longer rolling, I asked all of them what they thought would happen on election night. Michael Prue, who was running for re-election for the New Democratic Party in Beaches–East York, forecast another minority government for the Liberals. But Vic Fedeli, a rookie member for the Progressive Conservatives from Nipissing, was feeling so bullish about things that he saw a majority government for his PCs. The finance minister himself, Charles Sousa, whose rejected budget was the cause of the election in the first place, looked down, shook his head, and didn't even dare predict. I confess I was taken aback by his apparent lack of confidence in the Liberal Party's re-election prospects.

On the night of June 12, I anchored TVO's live, four-hour, commercial-free election broadcast. It was the ninth Ontario election I'd covered. After eight elections, you'd think I would have a strong sense of what was about to happen. But I didn't. Sources I've long trusted over the years were all saying different things.

Then the numbers started to come in. The Liberals quickly jumped out to a solid lead. Then they surpassed the all-important 54-seat count — enough for a majority government. And yet none of the other network "Decision Desks" was prepared to declare definitively that the Liberals had indeed won their majority. Everyone was just too skittish and lacked confidence to make the call.

But as the night wore on, as the Liberal numbers firmed up, and as the Tory numbers just fell flat, shock gave way to acceptance: Premier Kathleen Wynne had saved the Liberals' bacon, and thanks to a remarkably efficient vote, captured a solid majority government with just 38.7 percent of the total votes cast. Not only that, she had broken the rookie curse.

Not since 1971 had Ontarians given an unambiguous victory to a first-time leader. In that case, a young 41-year-old rookie leader named William Grenville Davis inherited the PC mantle from Premier John P. Robarts in February, then enlarged the size of the PC majority in the ensuing October election. But for more than four decades after that election, no governing party had figured out how to transfer power from one leader to the next successfully. Until now.

The other big takeaway on election night in 2014 was how thoroughly Ontarians repudiated PC Leader Tim Hudak's unadulterated, unambiguous, "small-*c*" conservative agenda. Seventy percent of them voted against it. Since Bill Davis's departure in 1985, and in almost every general election thereafter, Progressive Conservatives had abandoned the moderate, pragmatic centre that was such a feature of the 42-year-long Tory dynasty (from 1943–85) and had moved harder to the right. The result: just two election wins in nearly 30 years, both by Mike Harris (in 1995 and 1999). While true-blue conservatives interpreted those mandates as Ontarians finally embracing their inner Common Sense Revolutionary zeal, many other observers didn't. They saw those wins as a reaction (maybe overreaction?) to an ineffective and unlucky NDP government — a "market correction," if you like.

And so the 2014 election result crystallized for many what had become increasingly clear over the years. First, in Ontario, there is only about 30 percent of the population that embraces a hard right-wing agenda of deep tax cuts, an increasingly confrontational approach with unions, and a fervent dislike of government in general and the public sector in particular. Second, that right-wing core is simply not big enough to win elections.

The bottom line: it's still Bill Davis's Ontario.

That's right. Almost three decades after he retired from a quarter-century-long career in politics, it's still Bill Davis's Ontario. Despite the influx of millions of people from faraway places, whose customs and religious practices are a million miles removed from the Christian town of Brampton he grew up in, it's still Bill Davis's Ontario.

Why write a book on a man who's been out of public life for 30 years? For so many reasons, the first of which is, incredibly, Bill Davis has *never* sat down with an author to tell his life story for a book. So many lesser politicians have had their biographies written, and yet Davis has always refused. Part of that can be attributed to his own personal modesty, upon which his parents always insisted. "I've never been too attentive to my legacy," Davis told me in 2015. It's astonishing, particularly given his accomplishments. His tenure as premier was nearly 14 years long — he's the second-longest-serving premier in Ontario history. He won four consecutive elections, something that hadn't been done since before the First World War. Had he not retired from politics in 1985 at the height of his personal popularity, no doubt he would have won a fifth mandate as well. "He'd have wiped the floor with David Peterson and me," acknowledged Bob Rae of that 1985 campaign Davis opted not to fight.

Prime Minister Pierre Trudeau gets most of the credit for patriating the Constitution with an accompanying Charter of Rights and Freedoms. But it's no exaggeration to say it never would have happened without Bill Davis, and this book will tell you why. Davis was and is a *progressive* conservative. He understood, particularly during the six years (1975–81) he governed in a minority legislature, how to tack right on some issues, then tack left on others, to ensure the support of one of the other parties in the legislature and keep his government alive for another day. He loved nothing more than a theatrical sparring match with his opposition critics during Question Period. But he understood it wasn't personal, just business, so much so that when Brian Mulroney asked for his advice on whom to appoint as Canada's ambassador to the United Nations, Davis gave a glowing recommendation for that socialist ideologue from the 1970s and his favourite legislative sparring partner, former NDP leader Stephen Lewis.

Even before he became premier in 1971, Davis had already made a massive contribution to getting Ontario's young people ready for the latter half of the 20th century and beyond. He was Premier John Robarts's minister of education *and* minister for universities for almost a decade, overseeing the creation of the entire community college system. How big a player was he during the 1960s? Well, Bill Davis spent more than 40 percent of the Ontario budget. Education back then was like health care today — it's where the money went. He disappointed Trudeau and other francophones by declining to make Ontario officially bilingual, preferring instead to keep the temperature of the Tory core down, and instead, offer public services in French where numbers warranted. It's a policy some people carped about, but no government in the three decades since Davis left office has changed that policy. However, he infuriated that right-wing core of his party when he used the levers of the state to buy a chunk of an oil company named Suncor because he thought the province needed a "window on the industry" during the Arab oil embargo days. He was the target of hundreds of protests over the years, including most memorably some university students, upset at tuition rate increases, who crashed one of his announcements and chanted, "Save us from Davis!" But he also won an award for being the best champion of public transit not in Ontario, or even Canada, but in all of North America.

Davis also demonstrated that when the facts changed, so could his policies. He won the 1971 election, in part, by appealing to the Tory core and refusing to extend further public funding to the Roman Catholic school system, which at that time only received public funding to the end of Grade 10. But 13 years later, seeing immigration swell the Catholic population of Ontario and no longer able to explain why the final two years of high school weren't publicly funded, as well, he did one of the most astonishing *volte-faces* in Ontario history, suddenly becoming the champion of full funding for separate schools and in the process becoming a turncoat to that same Tory core.

The conservative journalist Claire Hoy wrote a book about Davis three decades ago. That's the only book on Davis's life that's ever been written. Hoy never cared for Davis's more pragmatic, moderate brand of conservatism, and as a result, the book is, if I may say, a particularly churlish account of those years. For about a decade, I've teased Ontario's 18th premier: "Are you really going to give Claire Hoy the last word on your life?" I've reminded him that, as someone first elected in 1959, his institutional memory of this province and country is virtually unparalleled in today's Canada. I told him he owed it to history and himself to let someone tell his story. "I don't even care if it's me," I told him numerous times. "You must let someone get these stories on the record for posterity."

Finally, in June 2014, a month shy of his 85th birthday, Davis invited me to his home on Main Street in Brampton for a chat. After (for him) surprisingly little small talk, he got to the point.

"All right, let's do it," he said. For a man whose governing style was often teased for "never putting off until tomorrow what you can avoid doing altogether," the former premier apparently ran out of excuses for further delay.

William Davis has always claimed that how the public regarded his legacy was never important to him. It may be one of the reasons why he's never been in a rush to have his biography written. And while modesty is one of his best-known characteristics, I've also believed you don't get that successful for that long in politics without having a healthy ego and some abiding interest in how history will treat you. It's one of the more interesting paradoxes about Bill Davis: his parents raised him to avoid the spotlight, and for heaven's sake, don't brag about yourself. "Moderation in all things," his mother would drum into his head. Davis took the admonition to heart so fervently that he could barely bring himself to using the first-person-singular pronoun when campaigning. But he is now, as I type this, 86 years old. His mind is still sharp as a tack, even if his body and health occasionally fail him. Physically, he is a very frail octogenarian. So while he is modest, he has apparently come to the realization, late in life, that he has an enviable record — not without its controversies or failures — and maybe it wouldn't be such a bad thing if people knew a little more about it. No doubt seeing the constant parade of books by and about premiers whose accomplishments paled in comparison to his finally gnawed away at him, as well.

Having gotten the green light from Brampton, Ontario's most famous acolyte to begin this project, I next expected to hear a long list of dos and don'ts from him.

It never came. Davis told me, "This is your book. You handle it how you want. My only request is that I'd like to talk some about my father and the Constitution. The rest is up to you."

When I expressed my surprise at this short list of conditions, Davis offered up the smile of someone who is comfortable with his place in history, and secure in the knowledge that an objective analysis of his era would result in a fair, mostly positive book.

"You know, Steven," he finally said, "I think it's fair to say, and that history will show, that as a province, Ontario did not do badly at all during the time we were there."

Note: not the time "*I* was there," but rather the time "*we* were there." He's 86 years old and he still can't use the first-person-singular pronoun because he knows his parents wouldn't approve.

Pierre Trudeau is dead. Alberta's Peter Lougheed, Ralph Klein, and Don Getty are gone. Tommy Douglas and Allan Blakeney of Saskatchewan and Howard Pawley and Sterling Lyon of Manitoba are, too. Same with Quebec's Jean Lesage, Robert Bourassa, and René Lévesque. Likewise both Premier Bennetts of British Columbia — W.A.C. and his son, Bill, and New Brunswick's Richard Hatfield.

Bill Davis, thankfully, is still with us. He is the last of his generation's legendary first ministers, and finally, as I hope will be revealed in these pages, at a point in his life where he can be more open, revealing, and introspective about his public and private lives. Davis has had good reason to be so sphinx-like over the years. He has suffered his share of tragedies in his private life, which for five decades he could never speak about publicly. Only lately has he let his guard down a bit about that tragedy. Furthermore, despite so much time in public life, he was and is a very private man, always keeping his political cards close to his chest. One of the most enduring images of Davis is the premier sitting back in his chair, chewing hard on his pipe, and listening to his advisers debate an issue while he betrays no hint of what his position on the issue in question might be. Davis always felt if he took a position on an issue at the beginning of the debate, it would adversely influence what his ministers or advisers might say. So he stayed sphinx-like to encourage the most open, honest conversation.

Thirty years ago Bill Davis agreed to give me an interview for the CBC supper-hour newscast on his life after politics. Ironically, the most memorable thing he said came after the formal interview had ended and the cameras were turned off. I observed that his new job as a corporate lawyer, serving on boards, making much more money, working much saner hours, and seeing more of his grandchildren than he ever saw of his own children, must be the best job he'd ever had.

"Steven, let me tell you," he retorted. "This job on its most fascinating day can't touch being premier of Ontario on its dullest."

That one quote transformed my own thinking about public life and begat my first book, *The Life: The Seductive Call of Politics*. This book on Ontario's 18th premier is now my seventh book, and frankly, the one I think I was destined to write. Mr. Davis, I'm glad you finally said yes.

I've watched Ontario politics pretty closely for almost 35 years now. I've always maintained it's still Bill Davis's Ontario.

This book will tell you what that truly means.

Steve Paikin
May 2016
Toronto, Ontario

I

The Early Years

1

BILLY

Brampton, Ontario, today is a profoundly multicultural, dynamic city of more than 524,000 people, nearly two-thirds of which is comprised of visible minorities. The largest single ethnic group is South Asians, who make up 40 percent of the city's population. In 2015 the *Financial Times* of Great Britain ranked Brampton number one in foreign direct investment strategy among 16 mid-sized North American cities. More than 800 businesses employing nearly 7,000 people are active in the life sciences sector. Sheridan College has a Brampton campus with both an applied engineering centre and a robotics centre. Algoma University has a Brampton campus offering business degrees. The city has three GO Train stations and a bus rapid transit system. The Brampton Civic Hospital is a 600-bed health-care facility with 4,100 employees on staff and can accommodate 80,000 emergency patient visits every year. Canon Canada Inc., the company that makes cameras, office equipment, scanners, and medical digital imaging machines, is building its new five-storey, 180,000-square-foot Canadian headquarters in Brampton.

All of which is to say, this is *nothing* like the Brampton, Ontario, that William Grenville Davis was born into on July 30, 1929.

That Brampton had a population of about 5,500 souls, and they were virtually all descended from immigrants of the British Isles. It was (and is) nicknamed The Flower City because in the 1850s an immigrant from England named Edward Dale established what became the largest cut flower business in North America. Ever wonder how Brampton's Rose Theatre got its name? That's how. It's all about flowers in Brampton.

The first thing you need to know about young William Davis is that he loved his mother but idolized his father and still does. His mother, born Vera Mildred Hewetson, was one of six children from a family that came to Brampton in 1914. She was extremely active in local church affairs and was head of the Women's Christian Temperance Union, which goes a long way toward understanding why Bill Davis, to this day, isn't much of a drinker. In fact, Tom Kierans, his long-time friend, jokes that the first drink Davis probably ever took in his life was at the meeting of his advisers and those of the candidate he'd just defeated for the Ontario PC Party leadership in 1971. They clinked glasses to celebrate burying the hatchet after the convention and a pledge to bring the party together. Davis was 41 years old.

"Was he really a teetotaler?" I asked Kierans.

"Oh, yeah," he said.

"You almost never saw him take a drink?" I asked again skeptically.

"I *never* saw him drink," Kierans insisted.

That was Davis's mother's influence. Officially, alcohol was never in the house, or if it was, young William was told it wasn't alcohol, but rather "antibiotics."

Albert Grenville Davis might have been a rising star in politics himself had he not been unlucky enough to contract tuberculosis, which left him in below-average health for much of his adult life. He actually had to leave his family and move to a sanatorium in Gravenhurst for a year to recover. As a young man, he worked for the Department of Agriculture for a couple of summers, earning enough money to attend Osgoode Hall Law School, which he did right out of high school. He never did attend an undergraduate university program.

Vera and Grenville (who actually went by "A. Grenville Davis") were married on June 26, 1923. The wedding was supposed to take place the day before, but perhaps in a most appropriate harbinger for the life one of the Davis children would one day lead, the wedding had to be postponed for a day because an Ontario general election had been called for June 25. In another example of a good omen, the Conservative Party of G. Howard Ferguson defeated the only United Farmers of Ontario government ever elected in the province's history, returning the Tories to power with a majority government after a four-year hiatus. The Davises approved.

The family would have three children, all perfectly spaced apart. In 1925 they welcomed a daughter, Peggy. Four years later came William, whose mother actually wanted to give him "Grenville" as a first name. But given that his father and grandfather already had Grenville as a middle name, Vera apparently relented. The tradition would continue and Grenville would be the child's middle name. It's amusing to note that for a man whose future political philosophy would best be described as "bland," there is actually some controversy about when Bill Davis was actually born. His birth certificate says July 29, 1929. But his mother always maintained he was born on July 30. The family's official line is that the registrar in Brampton made a mistake. Bill Davis's views may have been bland on many issues in the future, but on this one he firmly backs his mother: "She should know better than the registrar," he told the *Toronto Star* on his 42nd birthday. "She was there."

In any event, four years after Bill's birth, another sister, Molly, came along.

Young "Billy" as the family called him never knew his maternal grandfather, John Hewetson, who died when William was only a year old. But he knew his maternal grandmother, Eliza, much better, since the Davis clan lived in the Hewetsons' home for 30 years. It was called "The Castle," and Eliza lived with the Davises until her death when William was 15 years old.

Bill Davis's home life was plenty busy. Growing up as the middle child between two sisters explains so much about how, later in his political life, he was able to so skillfully find the sweet spot among competing societal interests. However, there were also plenty of stories in the Davis home about what a pest that middle child was.

Peggy Davis (now Dale) once told a local archivist about a time when she and some of her girlfriends were meeting in the family dining room when she was 12 and Billy was eight. Her brother apparently wanted in on the meeting and began pestering his sister to allow him through a locked glass door. "I don't know whether he was just pushing against the glass door or whether he deliberately smashed it," Peggy told the historian. "He shoved his fist through the door and it bled so badly I was afraid he would die and that it would be all my fault because I hadn't let him in." Fortunately, repairs were made both to the door and the younger brother. (Sadly, Peggy Dale died on March 15, 2016, at age 90.)

For a while there was actually another child in the home, as well. After the outbreak of the Second World War, a cousin from Manchester, England, named Russell Crompton moved into the Davis home for four years for safekeeping. William was 11, Russell was 12, and the boys got on well enough that Russell was always referred to as "the adopted brother."

The Davises seem to have had a blessedly normal upper-middle-class family life. A. Grenville Davis set an example of public service that his only son clearly admired and came to emulate. Davis, the father, chaired the local hospital board, chaired the district high school board, chaired the library board, was recording steward at Grace United Church, was a member of the Lions Club Rotary Club, and that was just in his "spare" time. His real job was, for nearly 31 years — from 1928 to 1959 — to be a Crown attorney in Peel County.

"He was in public life in his own way" is how his son describes it. "You'll not meet a better Crown attorney no matter how long you live," Bill Davis says. "I was lucky to have parents who were very community-minded."

Before he took sick, A. Grenville Davis loved sports, something he clearly passed down to his son. Davis, the father, was the youngest player on his Brampton Excelsiors lacrosse team, which managed to make it to the national championships in 1914 before falling to the Vancouver Athletic Club in the Mann Cup finals. A. Grenville was such a good player that he was enshrined in the Canadian Lacrosse Hall of Fame. In fact, his son was so proud that he chose to interrupt his campaign for the Ontario PC leadership in 1971 to see his father honoured.

This father-son tandem clearly had a deep and special relationship. "Dad didn't play favourites," Bill Davis insists, "but he and I had interests the girls simply didn't have." One of those interests was politics. A. Grenville Davis, while not a card-carrying Conservative because of his job, was clearly conservative in his philosophical orientation, as were most folks in Brampton in those days. From 1900 until 1962, Peel sent the Tory candidate to Ottawa in every single federal election. Young William was no doubt influenced by his father's political leanings. Once, before William was even 10 years old, he raced home from school to tell his father about something incredible he'd just seen. The younger Davis said he'd been to the local train station and with his own eyes had seen R.B. Bennett, the former prime minister, who was still the national Conservative Party leader.

"He spoke to me!" Davis told his father.

"What did he say?" Grenville Davis inquired.

"He told me to get the hell out of the way," young Billy replied. It wouldn't be the last time Bill Davis would have a run-in with a federal Conservative Party leader.

From the age of eight, William knew he wanted to be a lawyer because his father was. The story is evocative of Davis's father's own experience. Grenville Davis apparently visited the Peel County courthouse a couple of times at the age of 14 and also decided the law was for him. Predictably enough, when the son did become a lawyer, the two men worked together in the same law firm, argued cases together, and apparently a couple of dozen times argued against each other, as well, although the son insists he never kept score of who bested whom more.

Bill Davis loved his father so much, not only because they shared a love of sports and politics, and for most of their lives were the only males in the house, but also because William came to see what a fair and decent man his father was. He was the kind of man who didn't go for the jugular when he saw an accused with inadequate defence counsel. "He was not seeking a conviction for the sake of the conviction," says his son. "He wanted to see what was done was right."

That passion for justice eventually led the senior Davis to oppose the death penalty. On one occasion he was required to witness a hanging at the Brampton Jail.

"He said to me that he was sure that the conviction was right," Bill Davis recalls. But A. Grenville Davis always worried that someday the conviction might not be right. "That never happened, thank goodness, but he said that sort of thing *could* happen. Life imprisonment does not satisfy everybody, but he thought then it was better than what we were doing." Canada abolished capital punishment in 1962.

Bill Davis admires his father so much that when it came time to build a new courthouse in Brampton and the Mike Harris government wanted to name it after the former premier, Bill Davis demurred. He told the government his father worked in the courts of Brampton more than he ever did, and therefore it didn't make much sense to name it after him. So the compromise was to name it after *both* of them, which is why since the year 2000 the building at 7755 Hurontario Street in Brampton is called the A. Grenville and William Davis Courthouse.

Bill Davis went to Central Public School in Brampton, not McHugh Public School, with whom there was quite a rivalry back in the day. A well-known part of Davis's academic record is that he was smart enough to skip Grade 5. What's less well known is that he took two years to do Grade 13. More on that later.

Music was a big part of the Davis family's life. Billy was forced to take piano lessons, which he chafed at. One day he was supposed to play at a women's church meeting but refused to show up. When he could do music on his own terms, however, he enjoyed it. He helped form a school band during his teenage years and was the band's piano player.

The Davises were able to afford private school educations for all their children and, in fact, Peggy attended Bishop Strachan School and Molly went to Havergal. But despite visits to Trinity College School, St. Andrew's College, and Appleby College, William refused to go to private school. He loved Brampton High, in particular the sports teams he was on, and he was on a lot of them. Davis appears to have inherited his father's athletic ability, and certainly a passion for winning, which would come in handy during his years in politics. That may also partly explain why William opted to do Grade 13 for a second time. Having skipped a grade, he could afford to put off university for another year. And he champed at the bit to continue playing high school football.

It might be hard to envision the avuncular Bill Davis of the 1980s smoking his pipe in a three-piece suit having a temper. The fact is that he could display one when he wanted to and one day, when he was 16, he wanted to. In a football game between the Brampton Wildcats and Mimico, the record will show that the quarterback for Brampton, Bill Davis, and Mimico's Al Doyle were ejected for fist fighting.

Davis was discovering that he hated to lose. He had a nasty competitive streak that lay just under his calm surface. There was another time when Davis was quarterbacking Brampton and getting his butt kicked. The score was 50–0 for Port Credit. Late in the game, with Brampton moving toward Port Credit's end of the field, Davis called for a "quick kick" (essentially, punting the ball into the end zone for a single point, but on an earlier down, not on a third down, when everyone expects a punt). "They beat us 50–1," an old Davis high school friend named Ted White says while laughing. "Bill was damned if we'd be shut out."

Like his father, Davis also played for the Brampton Excelsiors lacrosse team. One time during a game in Maple, Ontario, in 1949, Elmer Harris slashed Billy across the face, cutting him for 11 stitches along his hairline. Unlike his father, Billy decided that was enough lacrosse. He subsequently dropped the sport.

But the younger Davis also enjoyed basketball and, in fact, played guard for Brampton High in a game at Maple Leaf Gardens before a Toronto Huskies game. (The Huskies were Toronto's team in the Basketball Association of America, a forerunner of today's National Basketball Association. The team only lasted from 1946 to 1947, then disbanded. Professional basketball returned to Toronto in 1995 when the NBA awarded the expansion Raptors to the city.) Davis also loved baseball, playing first base for Brampton's team. Even as premier, he loved to play in the "MPPs vs. the Press Gallery" baseball games. There he'd be at first base with a Toronto Blue Jays jacket on and, of course, smoking his pipe.

Despite the respect Davis held for his father, there was one wish of his dad's he fought. His father wanted him to enter a public-speaking contest, but the son refused, insisting such events were "only for girls." The father persisted and eventually prevailed, but only after the younger Davis convinced three of his buddies to join him to "give him cover." Sure enough, Bill Davis won the contest.

No doubt partly because he grew up in fear of crossing his mother and disappointing his father, Davis was, most of the time, a pretty serious young man. While most of his friends were off sneaking cigarettes and beer during their high school years, Davis never did. Despite coming from a family of relatively decent financial means, Davis always got himself a summer job. He washed cans at the Brampton Dairy. He performed job evaluations in the personnel department at A.V. Roe Canada Ltd., an organization that would come to have a profound impact on his political future. He was a councillor at Woodeden, a camp for handicapped kids near London, Ontario. He didn't care for summer camp himself and instead enjoyed spending some of the summer break at the family cottage on Townsend Island, about eight miles out from Honey Harbour on

Georgian Bay. He took up boating, and it became one of his favourite pastimes. He bought his first car with some friends at age 16 for $100. But when he couldn't afford the insurance payments and his father wouldn't give him the money for that insurance, he sold it.

While Bill Davis loved his dad, he also enjoyed being an annoyance to his father, particularly at football games. Hard to believe for someone who has since become one of the country's biggest boosters of the Toronto Argonauts, but 70 years ago Davis attended the Argo games at Varsity Stadium with his father and cheered for every team *except* the hometown club. Yes, he only did it to spite his father. "I just had to be different," he says today.

It got so annoying for Argo fans that one sitting nearby the Davises complained, "Grenville, can't you keep your son quiet?" That angry fan's name was Roy McMurtry, whose son of the same name would become Bill Davis's attorney general three decades later. Eventually, once the Argos started to lose a lot, the younger Davis became sympathetic to their plight and became one of their biggest fans.

Here's a story that demonstrates Bill Davis's idea of getting into trouble. One night he and some friends snuck a portable organ out of someone's cottage. They took it on a boat and went for a joyride as Billy played and sang songs to the gang.

Now, back to Grade 13 — why would an ambitious young man such as Bill Davis want to repeat his final year of high school? As Davis tells the story, he says the first time he did Grade 13 Brampton High's football team had a particularly bad year. So Davis and four of his fellow students returned for a Grade 13 victory lap during which things improved dramatically on the football field.

"We managed to beat Runnymede Collegiate, which for Brampton was a major accomplishment!" Davis chortles when thinking about it today. "It was almost worthwhile taking a further year just to be able to do that."

So there were sports, music, boating, public speaking, school, family, friends, and yes, one more significant interest in young Bill's life, as well: politics.

Everybody seems to agree that Bill Davis's first significant brush with politics came courtesy of a man named Gordon Graydon, the Conservative MP for the riding of Peel, which included the town of Brampton. Graydon had three daughters, one of whom was the same age as Davis, and they went through elementary and secondary school together. Kids today would say the two students "hung out together" but didn't date. Graydon, the father, inculcated in young William an interest in federal politics and the national Conservative Party. So, at age 12, Davis visited Parliament for the first time and saw Gordon Graydon in action. At 13 he joined the Young Progressive Conservatives. At 16 he attended the party's national convention. By the time he was 20, he was already president of the Peel Progressive Conservative Association, which represented both the federal and provincial parties' interests. He now clearly had political aspirations, but not the ones you might think.

"I can now say that I was interested in those days in becoming the minister of state for external affairs," Davis says today.

In 1951 Davis went off to University College at the University of Toronto where some smart registrar noticed his interest in foreign affairs and therefore asked Davis whether he'd consider spending a summer at a United Nations–run school in Connecticut called the Institute of World Affairs.

"Out of nowhere he asked me if I wanted to go, and I think I hesitated about one-tenth of a second before saying yes," Davis recalls.

He rubbed shoulders with some impressive American academics, including Harvard University's William Y. Elliott, best known for being part of President Franklin D. Roosevelt's foreign affairs brain trust in the 1930s and 1940s.

"It was, for me, a very rewarding experience," Davis says.

Perhaps his most enduring legacy that summer was helping to save the life of a man who was one of America's foremost political scientists, academics, and diplomats. Ralph Bunche had helped establish the United Nations and had recently won the Nobel Peace Prize, the first African American ever to do so. But he never would have been awarded the Medal of Freedom by President John F. Kennedy in 1963 had Bill Davis and some of his friends not been close by during that summer in Connecticut.

"He tipped his canoe," Davis remembers. "We made sure he didn't drown."

One of the interesting things about looking back on Bill Davis's life is to try to find those moments in his long-ago past that in hindsight now reveal a leader in the making. His first year at University College provided one of those moments. Davis played in two or three exhibition games for the University of Toronto Varsity Blues football team. But clearly he wasn't going to be as big a star on the Blues as he had been at Brampton High. The level of play was significantly higher.

Davis recalls playing one game against Balmy Beach, laughs, and says, "I almost left the field. Someone who tackled me must have been three times bigger than me." So the coach offered him a choice: play full-time with the Blues (with the understanding that he'd probably be setting himself up for a massive case of hurt), or instead, run the U of T Literary and Athletic Society. That latter job was akin to being commissioner of the U of T's intramural sports league. The idea was to get as many students as possible playing intramural sports and have the colleges and faculties compete against one another in as many sports as possible. The more participants and victories, the more points the college or faculty got, and therefore, campus bragging rights.

It wasn't a tough call. Davis enjoyed the gig tremendously. He helped lead the junior basketball team at University College to a title, played a few games of water polo, and even came out of "retirement" to play some lacrosse. It looked as if his University College might win the whole thing, but near the season's end the forestry faculty won a football game, giving them enough points to take the title.

It was a great time to be a U of T student. There was a terrific rivalry among the colleges. Innes College and New College were created while Davis was there. The Varsity Blues football squad played in front of packed houses in a 20,000-seat stadium. (By comparison, when I went to U of T, we were lucky to have 500 fans at the games. Eventually, the university gave up hoping for bigger crowds, tore down the old stadium, and replaced it with one that seats only 5,000 spectators.)

The takeaway here is that Bill Davis was put into a position of significant leadership. Not only did he excel as head of the Literary and Athletic Society, but he also discovered he enjoyed it. Those two qualities would come in very handy later in the 1950s when a potential political career beckoned.

In 1955, after graduating from the U of T, Davis followed in his father's footsteps by attending the Osgoode Hall Law School, then located in downtown Toronto (the law school was still almost a decade and a half away from relocating to its current premises at York University). One of his classmates was Donald S. Macdonald, a future federal Liberal cabinet minister.

As president of the Peel Progressive Conservative Association, Davis not only made an important connection with the local MP Gordon Graydon but was also taken under the wing of Thomas Laird Kennedy, the local MPP of Ontario's legislature. With the exception of the three years during which the Liberals' Mitchell Hepburn swept the province (1934–37), Kennedy had been the MPP since 1919 and was a much-liked agriculture minister — the only portfolio he ever had and ever wanted. He actually became the "caretaker" premier of Ontario for seven months, from October 1948 to May 1949, after Premier George Drew left Queen's Park to become leader of the federal Progressive Conservatives. Once Leslie Frost took over the premiership in 1949, he sent Kennedy back to agriculture, a post the Peel MPP kept until he was 75 years old.

Kennedy had a homespun way about him that made him hard to dislike. As agriculture minister, he would often be interviewed by CFRB Radio whenever Southern Ontario got a decent rainfall.

"That rain was worth X millions of dollars to the farmers of Ontario," he would tell the listeners. One day Bill Davis got up the temerity to ask the minister how he could know, with such precision, the value of any rainfall.

"I don't," Kennedy told him, "but it sounds good."

Kennedy (whose nephew Douglas Kennedy would become a Tory MPP from 1967 to 1985 and whose grandson, Ted Chudleigh, would also become a Tory MPP from 1999 to 2014) had a significant influence on Davis's interest in politics, but only to a point. The reality was that Bill Davis had his eye on federal, meaning national, politics, and that meant keeping an eye on Gordon Graydon's prospects.

Graydon was a bit of a star in national Tory circles. When the Liberals under William Lyon Mackenzie King were winning seats everywhere in their 1935 federal election landslide win, Graydon took Peel riding, even though he wasn't quite yet 40 years old. He actually became the opposition leader in the House of Commons from 1943 to 1945 because the PC Party leader, John Bracken, didn't have a seat.

Bracken was actually a person of some historic significance in Canadian political history. He was the highly successful premier of Manitoba under the Progressive Party banner from 1922 to 1943. When the federal Conservative Party recruited him to become its leader in 1942, he agreed only on the condition that the national party incorporate his provincial party's name into its moniker. So desperate were the federal Tories for this highly regarded provincial politician to come their way, they agreed. And that's why from 1942 until Stephen Harper and Peter MacKay merged their parties in 2003, the federal Tories were known as the Progressive Conservative Party of Canada.

In any event, when Bracken was the federal leader after 1943, a young Bill Davis and his cousin, Russell Cooper — who would go on to chair three of Davis's local election campaigns — went to Ottawa to hear Bracken speak at a hotel.

"He was so exciting that the windows behind him sort of turned reddish," Davis remembers.

Actually, that had less to do with Bracken's barnburner of a speech and more to do with a massive fire engulfing the E.B. Eddy pulp mill across the Ottawa River in Hull. Davis and Cooper ran to the windows to watch the blaze, "which was far more exciting than John Bracken's speech," Davis admits. Canadians apparently shared Davis's opinion, since Bracken was done as PC Party leader by 1948 after losing an election to the Liberals' Louis St. Laurent. Bracken never became prime minister.

Davis saw a lot of Bracken's successor as national PC leader, as well. Premier George Drew had resigned from Queen's Park to take the federal position. One time, Davis was driving Drew around Galt in Southwestern Ontario during a campaign tour. It was hot, and Davis offered to help Drew take his jacket off. "Thanks very much, but no," came the leader's reply. Davis later learned that Drew had injuries from serving in the First World War and didn't want people to see them. (In fact, Drew, Frost, and John Robarts, all of whom preceded Davis as Ontario premier, served in the war; Davis became the first postwar premier never to wear a military uniform. He was 10 years old when the war broke out.)

Bill Davis had always hoped to succeed his political hero Gordon Graydon as the MP for Peel and then chase his dream to become the country's external affairs minister. But in September 1953 Graydon suddenly died. Normally, the death of an opposition MP, while sad for his or her family and friends, doesn't have ripples beyond that. Graydon's death did. It changed the course of Ontario political history. Davis was only 24 years old and not ready yet to run for Parliament. The timing just wasn't right. John Pallett, who was eight years older than Davis and was biding his time waiting for Tom Kennedy to retire so he could run provincially, turned his sights instead to the federal arena and became the next MP for Peel. He held that job until 1962 when the Liberals took the seat for the first time since 1896.

But the point was: it was this game of political musical chairs that eventually prompted Davis to run *provincially*. The seat at Queen's Park opened up because Tom Kennedy, one of Davis's biggest boosters, decided in 1958 at the age of 80 to finally pack it in. Going provincial wasn't Davis's first choice as an entree into politics. But unlike in 1953, the timing was right. He sought his father's advice and his father suggested he go for it.

Did he seek his mother's advice?

"She said it was okay as long as I didn't have too much 'antibiotics' in the house," Davis says, laughing as he remembers the conversation more than five and a half decades later.

And so, at age 29, William Grenville Davis took his first real steps into big-league politics. He ran for the Progressive Conservative Party's nomination in the provincial riding of Peel against the reeve of Toronto Township, which actually wasn't in Toronto but rather in present-day Mississauga. While Davis remembers his competitor, who was a professor of architecture at the University of Toronto, as an educated, intelligent man, he actually remembers the candidate's charming wife better.

Laughing, he says, "I always look back and say, thank heavens I wasn't running against his wife because I think she would've won."

Davis did have many things going for him, but in particular, one significant factor — geography. There was a kind of unspoken rule at this time that because Peel riding was so big, encompassing present-day Brampton, Mississauga, and more, the federal and provincial members shouldn't both come from the same part of the riding. Gordon Graydon was from the Brampton (north) end when he served in Parliament, while Tom Kennedy was from the Mississauga (south) end when he served at Queen's Park. John Pallett, the MP who took over after Graydon's death, was a past chair of the Mississauga Hospital board of directors and president of the Port Credit Lions Club — in other words, from the south end of the riding. That meant Davis, who was from the north end, had a distinct advantage, which he used to his benefit. The nominating meeting was held in December 1958 at Brampton High School, and

Davis won it. He would carry the Tory banner into the next provincial election, widely expected to take place some time the next year, and so without delay, he began campaigning.

However, two things would soon transpire that nearly ruined Davis's electoral prospects before he barely got out of the starting gate. On February 13, 1959, his mentor and champion, Thomas Kennedy, died while still representing Peel in the legislature. All these years later Davis says, not quite facetiously: "Tom Kennedy wanted to go to heaven, and he did. I forgave him for this, but it took me a while." Besides the loss of a personal friend and mentor, Kennedy's death at age 80 also meant this local legend wouldn't be around to help Davis campaign and navigate the treacherous waters of the next shoe that was to fall.

They called it "Black Friday" in Peel. On Friday, February 20, 1959 — exactly one week after Tom Kennedy's death — Prime Minister John Diefenbaker announced he was killing the Avro Arrow fighter jet. To most Canadians, the cancellation of that plane was a blow to our national prestige. To the 47,000 people at A.V. Roe Canada Ltd., its sister plant, or its 30 suppliers and 650 subcontractors (including quite possibly the greatest collection of aviation engineers ever assembled at a Canadian factory), it meant instant unemployment. And since it was estimated at the time that fully a quarter of Brampton's workforce owed their jobs, in some way, to the Arrow's existence, for Bill Davis it meant his election in a typically safe Tory seat was now in real jeopardy. There were now tens of thousands of employees, and their families, who were furious with Prime Minister John Diefenbaker and by extension the Progressive Conservative Party.

Even relating the story 55 years later, Bill Davis doesn't smile. He says he was in utter shock when the announcement came down, and so he went to the legislature the following day to talk to Premier Leslie Frost to see what could be done.

"Mr. Frost was very sympathetic," Davis recalls. "He picked up the phone and called Mr. Diefenbaker. I had come from a fairly modest background and was somewhat surprised to hear the discussion that went on." That's Bill Davis's way of saying the prime minister and the premier had a hell of a shouting match on the phone.

Frost allowed Davis to stay in the room to hear the conversation. Did Premier Frost use profanity?

"He used some colourful language!" is all Davis will say about it today. "He used language we didn't use in our dining room at home."

Frost was in the fourth year of his second mandate and was no doubt already thinking about when to call his next election. Despite Diefenbaker's having won the biggest majority government in Canadian history less than a year earlier, a tarnished PC Party brand wasn't going to help Frost. The premier was understandably concerned not only about his candidate in Peel but about his own general election prospects, as well.

The premier called the next Ontario general election for June 11, 1959, and Davis could instantly tell that holding the seat for the Progressive Conservatives was going to be a tall order. People from Brampton who knew him and his family for years refused to shake his hand while he was campaigning. It was just as bad in neighbouring Streetsville and Malton. This was light years away from the experience Davis would enjoy two decades later when he campaigned jovially and with ease wherever he went in Ontario. This campaign was brutal.

Davis and his campaign manager Russell Cooper decided to concentrate their efforts in parts of the riding that were farther away from the Avro Arrow debacle. They went to Caledon, Albion, and Bolton in the north part of the riding, and Port Credit, Lakeview, and Cooksville in the south, hoping to find friendlier audiences. And they found some.

However, one night Davis and Cooper drove past the Peel Junior Farmers Building in Brampton. "I've never seen so many cars in Brampton in one place," Davis says today. The Liberals were having a public meeting. Who was the guest speaker that could draw such a crowd? Was it the local Liberal candidate? It wasn't. Was it the leader of the Liberal Party, John Wintermeyer? No again. It was a test pilot for the Avro Arrow, expressing his unhappiness at the cancellation of the fighter jet. The issue wasn't going away.

Before Davis officially became the Tory candidate, a photographer for the *Cooksville Gazette* snapped what would turn out to be a historic picture of Davis with both Premier Leslie Frost and former Premier Thomas Kennedy. The caption of the photo read: "Past, Present, and The Future." People in Peel and in the Progressive Conservative Party had big plans for Bill Davis.

The problem was that it looked as if Davis was going to lose.

So much for "The Future."

2

HELEN

As we have learned, William Davis seemed to have all the things a happy university student needs: good friends, an active social life, interesting academic courses, a chance to shine in the university's extracurricular world, and professors who took an interest in his future.

There was one more element we haven't mentioned that completed this happy picture.

Her name was Helen Louise MacPhee.

Helen followed in her older brother Neil's footsteps by enrolling in the U of T's University College, coincidentally, also Bill Davis's college. She was born in Walkerville, had graduated from Walkerville Collegiate in Windsor, and was such a good student that she won the Paul Martin Medal, named not after the 21st prime minister of Canada but rather after his father of the same name, who was a legendary Liberal cabinet minister.

After moving to Toronto, Helen lived in residence at the corner of Hoskin Avenue and St. George Street in the heart of the U of T's downtown campus. Davis lived a five-minute walk away in an elegant old fraternity house where the university's law faculty now stands, just south of the Royal Ontario Museum. Bill was a couple of years older than Helen but only one year ahead of her at university. "She got through high school one year sooner because she didn't go back and play football for a year!" Davis says, laughing. The two met and evidently hit it off, discovering in the process they had much in common. Both of their fathers were lawyers.

And in echoes of Davis's own future professional relationship with his father, Helen's brother, Neil, would also become a lawyer and also work with his father, whose name was also Neil.

The couple's relationship started while both were U of T students but continued even after Davis switched to Osgoode Hall, from which he eventually graduated in 1955. It was during Davis's law school years that the couple decided to marry.

Knowing how shy Bill Davis is with women, I wondered who proposed to whom?

"I think I did, but she was ready!" is how Davis remembers it. He did go through the formality of asking Helen's father for his blessing and permission, and with that, a wedding date was set. The blessed event would take place at St. Mary's Anglican Church in Windsor on June 20, 1955. It was a hot and steamy day. Each family had its respective clergyman overseeing the service: the Reverend F.C. McRitchie for the MacPhees; and Richard H.N. Davidson, the reverend at the Grace United Church in Brampton, for the Davises. William Grenville Davis was 23 years old; Helen Louise MacPhee was 22. They were young and in love and life was grand. The ceremony was followed by a reception at the Essex Golf and Country Club, where Helen's father, mother, and brother were all club champions.

From the outset, Helen understood that she was going to have to share her husband with the world of politics. Davis had been very active with a Progressive Conservative U of T campus group called the Macdonald-Cartier Club. The outfit was run by Thomas Symons, who would go on to become the founding president of Trent University in Peterborough. Once the couple moved to Brampton, Davis was hip-deep in becoming a lawyer, in Peel County politics, and in one more thing: children.

Almost immediately, the couple began to have kids. The Davises welcomed their first-born, Neil Grenville Davis, into the world on January 8, 1956. He was named after Helen's father and brother, and of course became the fourth generation of Davises to be given the middle name Grenville. Twenty months later their second child arrived: Nancy Louise Davis on September 28, 1957 (Nancy was just a name they liked; Louise was both Helen's and Helen's mother's middle name).

As the 1950s were coming to a close, it was a great time to be an Ontario Tory. Premier Leslie Frost, at age 63, was known as the "Silver

Fox," suggesting a very sharp political acumen, and as "Old Man Ontario," connoting he was as deep a part of the political firmament of the province as anyone ever had been. If he wasn't at the top of his game, he was still pretty close to the summit. Frost called his final election for June 11, 1959, having just passed his 10th anniversary as prime minister of Ontario. (No, that's not a misprint. While people generally referred to the province's first minister as "premier," the official job title was actually "prime minister of Ontario.")

The voters didn't disappoint. While Frost didn't reach the nearly unprecedented heights of the 1955 election, in which he captured more than 48 percent of the votes and nearly 86 percent of the seats, he still won a big majority government. The Tories dropped only 2 percent in the total vote but lost 12 seats, thanks to some difficult vote splits. Still and all, it was hard to be upset. The PCs took 71 seats compared to just 22 for the Liberals and five for the Co-operative Commonwealth Federation (CCF), the forerunner of the New Democratic Party. It was also Frost's third consecutive majority government, something no party had done in 30 years, and something no party has been able to replicate since.

That was the good news province-wide for the Tories. But what about in the riding of Peel where 29-year-old Bill Davis was desperately trying to break into the big leagues and fend off anti-Tory sentiment, thanks to Diefenbaker's cancellation of the Avro Arrow jet? June 11 was a long nail-biter of a night in Brampton. There would be no Tom Kennedy–like landslide for the Progressive Conservative candidate this time. In fact, Bill Davis would be up well past his normal bedtime before learning that he had prevailed by a scant 1,203 votes over the Liberal candidate, Bill Brydon, then a Brampton town councillor and future mayor of Brampton. It would be the second toughest campaign in Peel in a century, only behind Tom Kennedy's 1934 loss in the Liberals' sweep under Mitchell Hepburn.

"The Future" was apparently back on track.

Five weeks later the news got even better when Helen Davis delivered the couple's third child, Helen Catherine Davis (named after her mother, but henceforth known as Catherine), on July 17, 1959.

That tense election night behind him, there seemed little question but that Davis was now seen as a rising star in the Progressive Conservative galaxy. Premier Frost wasted little time in giving him a bit of the spotlight.

But a little background here first. Before every new session in Parliament the government of the day has the Queen's representative (in this case, the lieutenant governor) read the Speech from the Throne. The speech is usually a vague, lofty-sounding checklist of the government's priorities. A member from the government benches then has to move the motion to enable MPPs to vote on the speech. Given that the Frost government had a majority, there was never any question of the speech's adoption — the Tories had the numbers to get it passed. What was in question was which MPP would be given the honour of moving that motion and making the first speech in the legislature on behalf of the new government.

The answer was Bill Davis. The question was what did he actually have to do?

"I didn't know what he [Frost] meant by that," Davis admits. "I thought he meant move the chair or something."

Eventually, they figured it out and Davis was told that in the course of praising the government's far-sighted, brilliant agenda, he could also refer to as many as two of his own local pet projects. And so he did. He talked about the need to create a new park at the Forks of the Credit River in Peel, and the necessity of improving conditions in the public school system for what were then called students who were "trainably mentally retarded." That expression certainly wouldn't hold up today, but it did demonstrate that Davis was preparing to plant his flag on issues around education. It would be the beginning of a lifelong connection to that part of Ontario life.

Davis then did what ambitious backbenchers did. He wasn't elevated to Premier Frost's cabinet, so he got himself appointed to nearly every committee he could. From January to April 1960, Davis served simultaneously on the legislative committees for education, travel and publicity, private bills, public accounts, privileges and elections, municipal law, mining, legal bills, labour, health and welfare, highways and highway safety, government commissions, game and fish, energy, agriculture, and conservation. That's right: 16 different committees. He also established a lifestyle habit he would follow for the rest of his days in politics — he went home and slept in his own bed every night.

It wasn't unusual for MPPs who represented ridings outside of the provincial capital simply to stay at a hotel in Toronto after a long day of politicking. Certainly, Premier Frost did it. His Victoria riding was a good two hours or more east of Queen's Park, so he kept a room at the Royal York Hotel. Many of the other Tory MPPs did *not* therefore keep a room at the Royal York, lest the premier see them traipsing in after a night of overindulging in "antibiotics." John Robarts, for example, stayed at the Westbury Hotel near Maple Leaf Gardens. His love of and need for late-night carousing meant he didn't want to be anywhere close to Frost's hotel. But this wasn't an issue for Bill Davis. He was simply too square to be one of the guys out partying into the night on a regular basis. It's no doubt one of the reasons why, when he lived in a fraternity house while attending the U of T, the boys put him in charge of running the bar. They knew he wouldn't drink the profits away, and they trusted him with the money. And so, when he wasn't on the road for politics, it was home to Brampton every night.

Two years into Leslie Frost's last term the "Silver Fox" announced he was stepping down as premier of Ontario. At 12 years and 188 days he was the second-longest-serving premier of all time, and number one on the list was Oliver Mowat at 24 years, so clearly, there was no chance of hanging around long enough to challenge that. It was 1961, Frost was now 66, and he no doubt looked south of the border to see a dynamic 43-year-old just-elected president of the United States and sensed it was time to renew the Progressive Conservative Party. The leadership contest to come would help catapult two current MPPs into the headlines: one was a candidate, the other a campaign manager for another candidate.

But just before the PC Party could renew itself, the Davis family was doing likewise. Helen Davis delivered her fourth child — Robert Ian William on October 7, 1961. The couple just liked the first two names and, of course, William was for the baby's father.

Three days before Tories gathered in Toronto to select Leslie Frost's replacement, something happened about 60 miles away that would come to influence Bill Davis's political life for the next decade and a half. In St. George, Ontario, near Brantford, the longest-serving MPP of all time was driving his car when he suddenly slumped over the steering wheel and died. Harry Nixon was 70 years old and had served in Ontario's legislature since 1919, a remarkable 42 years as an MPP and still *the* record for longevity at Queen's Park. That wasn't the only noteworthy thing about Nixon's political career. He actually represented four different parties during his time in the legislature: the United Farmers of Ontario, the Progressives, the Liberal-Progressives, and the Liberals. He was also the last Liberal premier of Ontario before the Progressive Conservative dynasty began in 1943 and was highly respected by all sides of the legislature. However, because the PC leadership convention was occurring, almost no Tories were able to attend Nixon's funeral, with one significant exception: the outgoing premier Leslie Frost.

Harry Nixon's 33-year-old son, Robert, remembered meeting Premier Frost five or six years earlier when he, Nixon, was in his twenties. There was a ceremony at the legislature and Harry had brought his wife, Alice, and son Robert to meet the lieutenant governor and premier.

"I hope you remember that your grandfather was a Conservative," Frost said to young Robert.

"Yeah, but my dad's a Liberal," Robert Nixon answered back, and everyone had a good chuckle over the exchange.

Harry Nixon was Robert Nixon's hero. The father had taken his son to numerous political meetings over the years, introduced him to innumerable politicians and constituents, and while the son eventually became a teacher and farmer, he was definitely interested in his father's business. But now that Harry Nixon was dead, his son, through his grief, also knew two things were a certainty: first, a by-election would have to be called in Brant riding; and second, he wanted to contest that nomination to represent the Liberal Party in that by-election.

First, however, the Nixon family had to perform the sad duty of burying their patriarch. There is one story associated with that funeral that speaks volumes about the Nixon family. Because so many people attended the church where Harry Nixon's funeral took place, there were barely enough prayer books to go around, and some of the books were very old and fraying badly. Out of the corner of her eye, Harry's widow, Alice, glanced over to see the condition of the prayer book Leslie Frost was using. She called Robert over and said, "Please make sure Mr. Frost's prayer book is in good condition." It wasn't the worst week of her life. After all, Alice's oldest son, Jackson, was killed during the Second World War. But it was surely *one* of the worst weeks of her life, and at that moment her biggest concern was making sure the premier of Ontario felt respected at the funeral of one of his political rivals.

As Liberals were burying a former premier of Ontario in St. George, Tories were gathering at Varsity Arena in Toronto on October 25, 1961, to choose the next premier of Ontario. It would turn out to be one of the most competitive and exciting of any leadership conventions in Canadian political history. After the first ballot, the top four candidates were astonishingly within just 20 votes of one another. Attorney General Kelso Roberts from the downtown Toronto riding of St. Patrick and with the most Bay Street support led the ballot with just 20.5 percent of the delegates' votes. In second place was London's John Robarts, the education minister, with 20.1 percent. Robert Macaulay, the brilliant but mercurial energy resources minister from Toronto's Riverdale riding, was third with 19.8 percent. And Haldimand-Norfolk's James Allan, Premier Frost's treasurer, who had introduced the province's first sales tax (nicknamed the "Frost Bite") was in fourth place with 19.4 percent. There were seven candidates altogether, but the race came down to those four.

After five ballots, delegates were still unable to crown a winner. As if further magnifying the closeness of the race, the final ballot came down to the two contenders whose names were practically the same: Robarts (who moved into the lead on the second ballot) and Roberts. As the third-place candidate forced to drop off the ballot, Bob Macaulay would play kingmaker. Macaulay's campaign manager was none other than 32-year-old William Davis, who convinced his candidate his best play was to back Robarts. And so Macaulay marched over to the box of John P. Robarts, took one of the Londoner's buttons, pinned it on his jacket lapel, and ensured the education minister's victory on the *sixth* ballot, with 61 percent of the votes. The marathon was over, but the convention delivered two important and historic outcomes. First, John Robarts would be sworn in two weeks later as Ontario's 17th prime minister; and second, he would never forget the important part Bill Davis played in making sure that would happen. "The Future" continued to look bright.

In fact, Davis didn't have to wait long for his first big break in politics. Before the behemoth Ontario Hydro ran Ontario's electricity generation and transmission system, there was something called the Hydro-Electric Power Commission (HEPCO), created by Adam Beck in 1906. Beck has a statue on University Avenue in downtown Toronto that appropriately looks north at Queen's Park, presumably to keep an eye on what politicians do with the energy file. Neil B. Freeman, in his book *The Politics of Power*, describes HEPCO as a "unique hybrid of a government department, crown corporation and municipal cooperative that coexisted with the existing private companies." In December 1961, Premier Robarts gave the second vice-chairman's position at HEPCO to Davis — the equivalent of a junior cabinet minister's rank. Robarts made the appointment on the recommendation of Robert Macaulay as a kind of "thank-you-for-making-me-prime-minister" appointment. It got Davis going up the political ladder early in his career, and perhaps more important, added $10,000 a year to his annual MPP's salary, which was a whopping $7,000 a year.

One of the first duties Premier Robarts had to perform was calling a by-election for Harry Nixon's Brant riding, which he did for January 18, 1962. The winner was Robert Nixon. He couldn't have known it then, but for the next decade and a half, the new member for Brant and the new member for Peel would go on to lead their respective parties, fight two titanic, bruising elections against each other, and dominate Ontario politics for a generation.

You could be forgiven for thinking that at this moment in his life Bill Davis had the world by the tail. His fellow MPPs saw him as a rising star. The new premier liked him and owed him. He was in love with his university sweetheart, now his wife, and the couple had a wonderfully symmetrical boy-girl-girl-boy family. Davis's parents were still alive, and Grenville had just retired as the highly respected Crown attorney for Peel after three decades in the job. It was all too good to be true.

And tragically it was.

No one could quite figure out why, but for some time Helen Davis just wasn't herself. She had actually started manifesting signs of ill health in university, but the problems came and went. Eventually, her health took a marked downturn. The diagnosis: she was suffering from cancer and colitis, and worst of all, they were both caught too late.

The Davises took Helen to New York City to have surgery performed, and at first, she seemed to rally after the operation. But then, in early 1962, not long after Ian's birth, Bill, Helen, and the four children went to Windsor to visit the MacPhees. Something went terribly wrong and Helen began to suffer internal bleeding. She was rushed to the hospital, but doctors simply couldn't stop the bleeding.

Helen MacPhee Davis died in hospital in Windsor on March 5, 1962. She was 31 years old. Her husband, William Grenville Davis, age 32, was now a widower with four children, the oldest of whom was only six.

The Davis family brought Helen's body back to Brampton for the funeral. "It was the largest service I had seen, or probably anyone had seen in Brampton," Bill Davis now recalls sombrely. Helen herself was liked by so many people in the community. Plus, the fact that she was the daughter-in-law of the town's best-known Crown attorney and the wife of the riding's MPP all combined to create a set of circumstances in which so many people simply wanted and needed to pay their respects.

Bill Davis didn't have the luxury of taking the time to grieve over his wife's death, although he surely did but in his own private way. Even to this day, his family doesn't quite know how he got through this chapter of his life. His future political adviser, Norman Atkins, once told me: "I don't think he's ever really gotten over her." Lending credence to Atkins's claim is that, to this day, Davis still has difficulty talking about Helen, even with his children. Catherine Davis, the couple's third child, now says her father "never talked about the tragedy, but he worked really hard to raise our spirits and ward off the sadness he must have known we were feeling."

Suffice to say, the children were Davis's immediate concern. The youngest, Ian, wasn't even a year old yet, and so he remained in Windsor with Helen's mother. Then Bob Macaulay said he knew a governess from England who could come over, move into the Davis home in Brampton, and manage the household.

"She was very good with the kids," Davis now says.

When he next met with Premier Robarts, Davis acknowledged that with the addition of the governess, there was more stability brought to his home life. But he also admitted to the premier that, perhaps for the first time in his life, he was adrift. The man once seen as "The Future" of the Progressive Conservative Party of Ontario told his premier his life had fallen apart and he thought he simply needed to quit politics.

3

KATHLEEN

Premier John Robarts was a dozen years older than Bill Davis — not quite old enough to be a father figure to him, but certainly more mature in years than, say, a big brother would be. It was something in between. Robarts had the look of a man in charge and a gruff, gravelly voice lending an additional sense of gravitas to his character. It's why his nickname, the "Chairman of the Board," suited him so well. Although he fancied himself a modern-day "management man" for the go-go 1960s, Robarts was very much a people person, and at this moment in his premiership he could tell that one of his people was in trouble.

Robarts and Davis met after Helen's death, and the premier couldn't have been more understanding. He had a genuine sympathy for Davis's plight, and with two adopted children of his own living back in London with his wife, Norah, he certainly had first-hand experience with the tug of war between politics and family life.

Davis laid it out there: as much as he loved politics and respected the premier, his kids needed him closer to home, and a political life just wouldn't allow that. Robarts listened carefully, then did something extraordinary. Davis didn't know this at the time, but in later years it would emerge that the new premier wanted Bill Davis to be in his first cabinet when it was sworn in on November 8, 1961. But Robarts could see that his first choice for education minister — Bill Davis — was in no condition to take the job. In late 1961 it was apparent that Helen Davis's health was failing and her husband simply couldn't do what he needed to do on the home front *and* take on the responsibilities of a senior cabinet post at the same time. So, in an almost unprecedented move, Robarts held on to the education portfolio while being sworn in as premier. He'd already been the education minister for two years under Leslie Frost and figured he could do both jobs until Davis was ready. So when Davis told the premier he thought he might need to quit, Robarts, in his *Father Knows Best* way urged Davis to hang in there.

Davis agreed.

Robarts's advice turned out to be prescient. By the fall of 1962, Davis's life had evidently settled down enough that both he and Robarts thought he was ready to assume greater responsibilities. And so, on October 25, 1962, almost a year to the day after winning the PC Party leadership, Robarts handed his biggest-spending ministry over to his youngest cabinet minister. It was clearly a match made in heaven. Davis loved and cared about education. It would turn out to be the only cabinet job he would ever want or have, and he would have it for more than eight years.

How was it that Bill Davis's life went from utter tragedy to making sense again over the course of a year? Several factors were involved. He had a remarkably understanding boss and many sympathetic colleagues. His parents and his late wife's parents did their part. And, yes, the governess from England brought stability into his home. But there was one person who saw what a disaster Davis's life had become, and she made a decision, in effect, to devote her life to improving his.

Her name was Kathleen Mackay, and it's no exaggeration to say that she saved Bill Davis's life. She saved Bill and Helen's four children from, possibly, a childhood without a mother, and in doing so, allowed Davis to pursue the political dreams he'd had since he was a teenager.

Kathleen Mackay (pronounced *Mc-KYE*) was born in Chicago on September 10, 1933, to Roland Parks Mackay of Atlanta, Georgia, and Margaret Pomeroy of Rochester, Minnesota. Her father was a much-published, highly regarded neurologist who would eventually testify at the murder trial of Jack Ruby, the man who gunned down President John F. Kennedy's assassin, Lee Harvey Oswald. Kathleen's mother was a nurse at the renowned Mayo Clinic. Kathleen, like Bill, was a middle child. She had an older sister, three years her senior, and a younger brother three years her junior. When she was five or six years old, she and the family moved from

Chicago to a small, well-to-do suburb called Hinsdale, Illinois. Hinsdale may have the distinction of being the only small town in America connected to two legendary baseball owners: Charles Comiskey, who owned the Chicago White Sox, plus a taxi company in Hinsdale; and Bill Veeck, who grew up in Hinsdale and became one of the most colourful and outlandish baseball owners ever. Like Comiskey, he also owned the White Sox, but also the Milwaukee Brewers, Cleveland Indians, and most memorably, the St. Louis Browns, where he had what society then called a "midget" go to the plate for an at-bat. The midget walked (pretty small strike zone) and Major League Baseball then passed a new rule saying no more midgets.

Like Bill, Kathleen appears to have had a Norman Rockwell–like childhood. She loved spending time in her father's splendid den with its vast array of books. He taught her an appreciation for music, poetry, and reading. Her father also took her to the odd baseball game at Wrigley Field, where she fell in love with centre fielder Andy Pafko, who played for the Cubs from 1943 to 1951. Even today Kathleen gets giddy when recalling her affection for the man who made the Cubs all-century team and just died a few years ago at age 92. "He was *soooo* attractive," she coos.

Kathleen says her mother "was a peach of a woman with a gentle nature" who, given the times, was the more significant presence in the children's lives. "Because of her gentle nature and good sense of humour," Kathleen now says, "I made it through childhood to adulthood."

After graduating from Hinsdale Township High School, Kathleen made her way to Ann Arbor to study English literature and art history at the University of Michigan. With her bachelor of arts secured, she did something rather unusual for a young girl in the mid-1950s: she and four other girlfriends travelled all through Europe in a couple of cars, one of them a Volkswagen Beetle, visiting Germany, France, Italy, and the Scandinavian countries.

When the trip ended, the other girls returned to the United States, but Kathleen remained in Germany to continue her studies in art history at the University of Munich. Her German was improving, and she adored immersing herself in European culture. But it all came to an abrupt end after a skiing accident in Austria. Kathleen busted up a knee, after which her father brought her home to Hinsdale where she suffered for weeks. "I had a cast on for a while and it drove me insane," she says. "I could get around, but it was a big nuisance." Kathleen eventually recovered but acknowledges some regrets over "that year of unfinished business."

Kathleen's next move was to San Francisco where she got a job in California's state-run nursery system, which had been created during the Second World War. The idea was, Dad went off to war, Mom went to the factory to build warplanes and ships, and their children were cared for in this early version of a child-care system. The great discovery for Kathleen Mackay was that she absolutely adored children. In fact, today she admits: "I didn't know I liked children that much." Unlike most women of the time, she felt no urge to get married or have children of her own. "I never had such good days," she says. "San Francisco was a wonderful city, so open to everyone." She decided the Golden State was the place to be, so she also enrolled at the University of California at Berkeley to earn her teaching degree.

"I remember standing in one schoolyard and thinking to myself, I didn't have to get married. I just loved these children so much. I'll just stay here all my life," she recalls.

She got a job as a kindergarten teacher and felt a purposefulness in her life she hadn't felt before. She does, however, remember getting a strange call from someone at the school asking if she minded teaching black children. "Having never met a black person, I said no, of course I didn't mind," she recalls, still clearly uncomfortable more than five decades later that someone would ask such a question. But that became her job: kindergarten teacher to a class of almost all-black middle-class kids.

Kathleen Davis now admits there was a man interested in her in San Francisco and the two "came close to an engagement." But for whatever reason, the relationship never made it to the next level.

So how did a member of the Ontario legislature from Brampton, Ontario, and a kindergarten teacher in San Francisco, California, manage to have their lives intersect? The answer is: Georgian Bay. The Davises and the Mackays both had cottages close to each other on Georgian Bay. Coincidentally, both Bill's and Kathleen's grandparents built their respective cottages. The families knew each other, and Kathleen was actually a good friend of Molly Davis, Bill's younger sister. Because of the age gap (almost four and a half years), Kathleen and Bill had hardly had any interaction during those summers, although they were aware of each other. In fact, during their teenage years, Kathleen admits to being terrified in Bill's presence.

"Billy was sort of an idol in Georgian Bay," she says. "He was definitely the leader of the pack. I couldn't even imagine speaking to him." Yes, there was a bit of a schoolgirl crush happening, but tempered by the reality that the two really only saw each other for five weeks in the summer, and even then, they didn't exactly pal around together.

Once Bill and Helen started dating, Kathleen and Helen also became summertime acquaintances, although not close friends. Today Kathleen remembers Helen as "the most beautiful woman you'll ever see."

Bill and Helen married, four kids and politics soon followed, and Kathleen got to know the older Davis children a little bit. The main connection was still her friendship with Davis's younger sister, Molly.

And then Helen died.

"I remember calling Billy's mother and asking if there was anything I could do," recalls Kathleen, who says her thoughts at this time were overwhelmingly for the four Davis children who were now without a mother. She saw Bill on Georgian Bay in the summer of 1962 but never discussed how he was coping with Helen's loss. It was something Bill Davis didn't, or couldn't, talk about then, or frankly, for decades thereafter.

But somehow, during the rest of 1962, the relationship between Bill Davis and Kathleen Mackay changed. She had reached out to Davis with a letter, probably because of advice she had received from her mother, who had told her: "He's never going to need you more than now." Kathleen went from the girl Bill Davis noticed hanging around with his kid sister to a woman in whom he was now taking a special interest. In fact, Davis began to pursue her. He made two trips to San Francisco to "court" Kathleen. The two even took a side trip to Las Vegas to see the great Judy Garland sing. Davis was apparently burning up the phone lines to San Francisco on a regular basis, as well. And remember, these were the days long before free video calls around the world on Skype. Long-distance phone calls were extremely expensive. Davis's lifelong political confidant Clare Westcott remembers seeing a phone bill of $200 for one call alone. "He was wooing her over the phone for hours at a time," Westcott says. Then he catches himself and rephrases his reply. "I once told Davis: 'You weren't wooing her, you were interviewing her for a job.'"

Clare Westcott, now 92 years old, still has all his marbles and loves to tell stories about the old days, which he remembers with astonishing clarity. While his description of the Davis courtship might seem a bit blunt, the fact was, if Kathleen Mackay and Bill Davis were going to become "an item," she was going to be required to give up a life in California where she was the decision-maker, enjoying somewhat of a carefree existence as a single woman and teacher in San Francisco, for the life of a political wife where *her* agenda was never *the* agenda, and who was inheriting four young children to boot. If it was, in effect, a job interview, the job was incalculably more difficult than anything Kathleen was accustomed to.

For some reason, however, she wasn't daunted by the assignment. "I didn't worry about being accepted by the children because I'd had all that training," Kathleen now says. "I felt very comfortable with what I was signing up for. It didn't scare me. I knew I could do some good."

And Bill Davis continued to pursue her. The two eventually talked about making their union more permanent.

"When he asked me to get married, I was so swept away, I just said, 'Yes, yes, yes!'" Kathleen says. "I was aware of what need he was in. I couldn't think of saying no."

She said goodbye to San Francisco and drove her Volkswagen back to Hinsdale, Illinois. Eventually, she sold the car for $100 to Clare Westcott, even though Westcott says it was virtually falling apart.

William Davis, 33, and Kathleen Mackay, 29, were married on January 29, 1963, at the Union Church of Hinsdale. It was a small affair, maybe just 50 people, and no political guests from Ontario. Westcott knows this will sound less than romantic when he describes his friend as "an executive who has to make a fast decision that's good for the company. It has to be done. And she happens to be a beautiful girl."

As she looks back on those heady days, Kathleen does acknowledge one thing for which she wasn't prepared. "I didn't know anything about the political part!" she admits. Kathy Davis understood she was joining the Davis family, marrying Bill, embracing the role of stepmother to four kids, but "I don't even remember [politics] being a part of my thinking," she now says. "I didn't really know what part I'd play, but it all became quite evident." It was a huge learning curve, particularly because as an American, Kathleen had no knowledge of any of the players on the Ontario political scene.

Kathleen took her place in the Davis family's home. She now describes her mother-in-law, Vera, as "authoritarian, although very good to me. She was always watching me, and fortunately I didn't make too many mistakes!" Vera was known as "Gramsy" and Grenville as "Grandfather." "Billy's father was just one of the nicest people I can remember ever knowing," she says. "A very gentle and sweet person."

She never called either of her in-laws by their first names. "Even Billy called them 'Mother' and 'Father,'" she says.

By this point, Davis had been education minister for three months, and now that Kathleen had brought stability to his home and personal life, his career was in a position to blossom. In fact, Bill Davis was about to preside over what was probably the most important decade for educational expansion in Ontario history. His workload and travel schedule increased exponentially. Davis's job kept him out of the house almost every night of the week. There were Tory party functions, late-night sittings in the legislature, activities in the riding, and many other must-attend events that were a routine part of every cabinet minister's life. He routinely didn't make it home until 11:00 p.m. or midnight. And so Kathleen tried to create a routine for herself. The kids were to be in bed by 9:00 p.m., after which it was her time. She had a little television set, chesterfield, and desk set up outside the kitchen, which she referred to as "my spot." She loved nothing more than to watch comedies featuring Bob Hope or Lucille Ball or curl up with a good book. "I was always reading," she says. Bill's older sister had moved to Sudbury by now, but the Davis parents were still around, as was Bill's younger sister, Molly, Kathleen's original summertime friend.

Given the demands of her husband's job, Kathleen Davis insisted on only one thing: her husband had to be there having breakfast with his children every morning he possibly could. She understood dinners just weren't going to happen. But breakfast was a must. "That was when the kids could have access to Bill," she says. Remember, these were the early 1960s in Brampton. Almost universally, husbands worked outside the home, women worked inside the home, kids expected their mothers to be there and expected their fathers wouldn't be. Even with their father being a high-profile politician, the Davis children, in that respect, led a fairly normal life.

Kathleen Davis hadn't come from a very political family in Illinois. The Mackays were interested in politics but not involved in it. They did know this: they were staunch Democrats in a wealthy suburb that was overwhelmingly Republican. In fact, when Kathleen's friends learned she was marrying a conservative, they weren't amused. "Jesus," one of them said to her, "you're marrying a Republican?"

"No!" Kathleen corrected her. "He's a *Progressive* Conservative."

Davis's profile throughout the 1960s went in only one direction: up and up and up. Ontario was neck-deep in a school-building boom as the population increased and as the revenues flowed into the treasury. There were many days when Davis and his predecessor as education minister, Premier Robarts, opened literally three new schools in one day. It was a great time to be the education minister. Davis travelled all over the province, making good-news announcement after good-news announcement and establishing a ton of political contacts that would pay dividends in the future. The teachers never went on strike (they wouldn't get that right until 1975). And the best part: it was the federal government that paid most of the cost of building these new schools through a new "dominion-provincial" cost-sharing program. Financially, the Feds might have been on the hook for the majority of the expenditures, but politically, Bill Davis was reaping most of the rewards.

From time to time, Kathleen accompanied Bill to an event, even though she wasn't much of a fan of politics. But she understood that part of her job as his wife was to be present, smile admiringly when he spoke, and humanize a politician who could from time to time be dull, technocratic, and very shy.

"I didn't mind going to events when I knew people there," Kathleen now says. "And he made things easier by being by my side. He didn't just leave me alone."

Roy McMurtry, a future attorney general and Ontario Superior Court chief justice, told the writer Erna Paris for a magazine article five decades ago: "You meet so many political wives who are scheming, manipulative, uptight broads. I know very few whose human warmth and genuineness can match hers."

The education minister's advisers might not have told him this to his face, but they certainly believed Kathleen projected warmth that he wasn't capable of showing at this point in his political career. In fact, one handwritten memo from an unnamed Tory operative from London stated it bluntly in the first line of the missive: "Dear Kathleen — a lot more photogenic than Billy." Kathleen didn't know about the memo, but when I showed it to her, she said: "Well, if that's true, I'm very glad to hear it!"

When Davis succeeded Robarts as premier of Ontario, Kathleen's value became still more apparent. Even Conn Smythe, the founder of the Toronto Maple Leafs, noticed. Writing a "Dear Mrs. Davis" letter to her, the Leafs' owner complimented her because, "Knowing that behind every successful man is a wonderful woman."

If she ever felt that politics was dominating her husband's life too much and the family was getting too short shrift, she kept those thoughts to herself. "I didn't think I had the right to say that," she says. "This was his work, and it was important work."

Kathleen Davis saw herself as a traditional 1960s housewife. She can't recall a single example in her husband's entire political career where he sought her advice on an issue, or where she offered it unsolicited. That simply wasn't this couple's modus vivendi.

Less than 10 months after the Davises married, Kathleen gave birth to her first child, Bill's fifth: Sarah Margaret Davis was born on October 22, 1963. Margaret was Kathleen's mother's name, but the child would go by "Meg." The pregnancy wasn't planned, but Kathleen today describes it as "the best thing that ever happened to me." Meg's birth came at a particularly happy time for the family. Unlike the first time he stood for election in 1959 and barely scraped through, Davis was re-elected easily on September 25, 1963, as John Robarts won his first mandate after taking over from Leslie Frost.

All families, of course, have their issues, but the Davises seem to have had fewer problems than many, integrating a second mother and a new baby into their operation. Having said that, there was one odd story.

"After we married," the new Mrs. Davis told Erna Paris more than 50 years ago, "they were still calling me 'Aunty Kathy' until one day Bill's mother took them aside and told them I wasn't their aunt anymore."

No doubt Kathleen's constant presence and love for the four children she inherited contributed significantly to making the transition easier than it might have been. The fact that the four kids were still very young also probably helped.

"I have nothing but the greatest admiration for Kathleen Davis," said Norman Atkins, who would go on to become one of the most important election campaign advisers in Ontario history. "She is just one of those special, special people. She didn't take a specific interest in politics, but she was such a tremendous asset to Billy Davis through a period in his life that could have been far more difficult if it hadn't been for her."

But that's not to say there weren't difficult moments.

One time at the Davis family cottage on Georgian Bay, Bill and Kathleen got into a fight about something, the subject of which Kathleen can't even remember anymore, even though it led to one of the most memorable exchanges she ever had with one of her stepchildren. Kathleen says her husband made "some caustic remark," after which she walked out the front door of the cottage and headed for the rocks on the waterfront in tears. Ian, the fourth Davis child, who would have been in high school at this point, was at the water's edge and had heard the exchange. Kathleen was "half in tears." Seeing this, Ian said, "Sorry, Mom."

Kathleen then said something that to this day she regrets saying. "I shouldn't have said it, but I was upset," she now says of the outburst.

"Well, I'm not your real mother," she told Ian, "so you don't have to worry about me."

Ian, who was still in a crib and diapers when his mother died, responded, "You're the only mother I've ever known and I don't want any others."

What a moment!

"You could never have five nicer children," Kathleen Davis marvels today.

4

EDUCATION

One of the best things Bill Davis had going for him when he became minister of education was the fact that the premier of the day had also held the same portfolio. So Davis never had to do what a lot of ministers had to do, namely, convince the boss of the importance of the work he was doing. Robarts was a huge champion of building up Ontario's education system, and unlike a lot of conservative thinkers of the time, saw a role for deep involvement by the government. His education minister shared that view.

The 1960s were a new decade of seemingly infinite possibilities, and both Robarts and Davis had a goal to make Ontario a laboratory for all sorts of educational experiments and investments. Fortunately for them, the economy was such that the revenues were there to make it all happen. Not only that, but the federal government took a big interest, as well. The Feds said if the provinces wanted to expand their technical and vocational schools, they'd pick up 75 percent of the construction costs and also a big chunk of the operational costs. Robarts and Davis didn't have to be geniuses to understand what the implications for the Ontario economy could be, and not just in education. This would surely be a boon for the construction industry, as well. Robarts, as education minister, also led the reorganization of the high school curriculum and "branches" of high school study (arts and science; business and commerce; and science, technology, and trades), which had the positive effect of keeping more students in school longer. Throughout the 1960s the student participation rate for 15- to 19-year-olds went from 62 to 77 percent.

As a former teacher, Liberal MPP Robert Nixon took a keen interest in Ontario's educational development during this time. He recalls there being a lot of debate in the legislature over many of Davis's initiatives, but frankly not much opposition. "It's pretty hard to strike many sparks when the financing is practically unlimited and everybody is quite enthused about what's going on," Nixon says today about that decade.

While Ontario urbanized further throughout the 1960s, school boards changed significantly. The big were getting bigger and the small were getting smaller. More than 200 school boards had an average student body of 1,000 students. However, more than 1,000 school boards had fewer than 30 kids. By 1964, in one of his most controversial early decisions, Davis was determined to put those tiny rural school boards on more equal financial footing with the bigger boards. And so he ultimately forced the amalgamation of 1,500 rural school boards into 130 more centralized and, he hoped, more efficient operations. Messing with local autonomy has always been fraught with danger in Ontario history, and Davis would run into a wall of local anger a decade later when he tried to amalgamate smaller municipalities into regional governments. But for now he was satisfied offering a better organized, more equal system of educational governance across counties, including more French instruction, kindergarten for everyone, and special classes for what were then called "the handicapped" and the gifted.

As the 1960s motored on, education boomed along with the province's population. In 1950, the year before John Robarts was first elected as an MPP, there were 25,000 schoolteachers in Ontario. By the time Robarts retired from politics in 1971, there were 93,000, most of them getting their jobs during Davis's time as education minister. Despite that explosion in numbers, there were actually teacher shortages for some of that time, having the effect of bringing salaries up. Class sizes also went down. Who was an Ontario teacher's best friend? Why, Bill Davis, of course.

Davis would be the first person to tell you that, while he got all the attention as education minister, he was actually half of a dynamic partnership. The other half was his deputy minister, Dr. Ed Stewart, one year his junior, who would eventually follow Davis to the premier's office and become his deputy minister and secretary to the cabinet. Frank Miller, Ontario's 19th premier, said of Stewart: "He was as good as it was possible to be regarding political and policy advice."

Roy McMurtry, one of only two men in Ontario history to be both attorney general and chief justice of the province's highest court, went even further: "There has never been a more distinguished public servant in the history of Ontario than Ed Stewart."

Davis's deputy minister was as expert at assembling facts, crystallizing what was important, weighing options, and advising his minister as anyone who has ever served in that capacity at Queen's Park. Like so many people attracted to public life, Stewart, son of a United Auto Workers man in Windsor, started as a teacher, a local superintendent of education, assistant deputy minister, then a deputy minister advising Davis. He was plain-spoken, down-to-earth, unimpressed by political hotshots, and told it like it was. His maxim was: "Good, honest, and simple government is the very best politics, whatever the affiliation of the government of the day."

Sally Barnes, who started in the press gallery before moving into Davis's premier's office, called Stewart "a breath of fresh air that lasted till the end of the Davis days. Ed had no enemies. He was a truly remarkable man."

Both Davis and Stewart quickly realized how extraordinary their partnership was, which lasted nearly a quarter century.

In 1965, not quite halfway through his tenure as minister, Davis commissioned a report about education that a half century later people still vigorously debate. Some think the report was a brilliant addition to the overarching question of the mission of education. Others see it as typical 1960s gobbledygook, very touchy-feely, and taking the province's education system in exactly the wrong direction. The official title of the report was *Living and Learning: The Report of the Provincial Committee on Aims and Objectives of Education in the Schools of Ontario*. But it became better known by the names of its two chairmen: Supreme Court of Canada Justice Emmett Hall and former school principal Lloyd Dennis.

The Hall-Dennis Report was unlike anything that had preceded it. For example, the titles of some of its chapters were "The Truth Shall Make You Free," "The Search for Truth in a Democratic Society," and "Today's

Child." This was a report that eschewed typical bureaucratic language and attempted to make the case that the child should be at the centre of the educational experience. So rote, regimented learning was out, and the child's individual needs and interests were in. Walter Pitman was the NDP's education critic at the time and would become a future director at the Ontario Institute for Studies in Education (OISE) and president of Ryerson Polytechnical Institute. He read the Hall-Dennis Report, hoping to get some ammunition with which to clobber Davis. Instead, he became captivated by its vision and 258 recommendations.

"Its impact can still be seen directly in the foundations of education today," says Dr. Karen Grose, TVO's vice-president of digital education and a former principal and school superintendent. "We see a broader range of practices that reflects a more student-centred approach to learning, as well as practices that nurture health, well-being, and the emotional needs of children in learning. We see the impact strong, positive relationships between home and school can have on student success."

However, the report had its share of critics, as well. A quarter century after the report came out in 1968, another MPP from Brampton, testifying before the public accounts committee of the legislature, cited Hall-Dennis as part of the reason he got into politics in the first place.

"We ruined one entire generation of kids with that process," said Robert Callahan, the Liberal MPP for Brampton South from 1985 to 1995. Callahan ran against Davis twice in Brampton in 1977 and 1981, losing both times. He liked to joke that he "scared Bill Davis out of politics."

"You couldn't flunk a kid," Callahan continued. "That was an absolute no-no. You might throw their nose out of joint. The net result was that kids kept getting moved from one grade up to the next one and they hadn't even learned what they had to learn in the grade below. We wondered why these kids were dropping out or why we found an inability to spell or to write." Callahan and many others came to blame Hall-Dennis for everything that ailed the education system.

At that same committee meeting the province's deputy minister of education, Charles Pascal, took issue with Callahan's interpretation of the report: "It's important to know that some of what Hall-Dennis wanted in terms of lifelong learning and independent learning skills is not mutually exclusive of a back-to-basics curriculum."

Whether Hall-Dennis was the beginning of an educational revolution or a U-turn in the wrong direction will no doubt be debated forever. That's the kind of impact the report had. And Bill Davis commissioned it. Sadly, the report was so controversial in its time that, according to an obituary in the *Globe and Mail* after Lloyd Dennis's death, Davis summoned him to a fancy Toronto restaurant in late 1968 and dismissed him. The move embittered Dennis toward Davis for four decades until he received a short letter from Davis in 2009, supporting a bid to have a new school in Orillia named after the former principal. The bid, alas, failed.

It was in the mid-1960s that Davis met someone with whom he would also have a quarter-century-long relationship in politics. Nick Lorito was an Italian-Canadian kid who lived at Keele Street and Eglinton Avenue in the west end of Toronto and who one day marched into the Ministry of Transportation headquarters at Keele and Highway 401, looking for a job. He was told there might be an opening down at Queen's Park driving ministers around.

"I was so naive," he recalls. "I didn't know what Queen's Park was. And ministers? I asked them, 'Does it matter if I'm Catholic?'"

Lorito ended up at the garage at Queen's Park, washing cars, and eventually became the driver for Agriculture Minister William Stewart, who was the MPP for Middlesex North near London. One day he took Stewart to an important event near his riding — the first classes to be held in September 1964 at the Ontario Vocational Centre, which three years later would become Fanshawe College. Also in attendance were three other heavy hitters from cabinet: Premier John Robarts; Charles MacNaughton, the treasurer (today known as the minister of finance); and Bill Davis, the education minister. Since Stewart was staying in the area, he asked Lorito if he'd mind driving Davis back to his home in Brampton. That was the first time Davis and Lorito met, but it wasn't the beginning of anything permanent, at least not yet. Lorito left the driving corps shortly thereafter to pursue something else.

But in 1966 he dropped into the garage at Queen's Park to say hello to the old gang when Charles MacNaughton happened by, telling Lorito: "I've got the perfect job for you. Bill Davis is looking for a driver."

Lorito's immediate reaction was: "I'm not driving him." The word was apparently out that the "Davis assignment" was a tough one. There were five kids who occasionally needed schlepping around the province, including frequent visits to Windsor to see the parents of their late mother. "I don't want the job," Lorito told the treasurer.

MacNaughton wouldn't listen. He forced Lorito to meet with Davis the following day, and for some reason Lorito showed up at room 369 in the Legislative Assembly building the next day to meet with the minister of education.

"I hear you want this crazy job," Davis said to him after some requisite small talk.

"Not necessarily," responded Lorito, demonstrating abundant moxie for a 27-year-old.

The two men started talking turkey. "I'm not a babysitter," Lorito told Davis. "And I've got a serious girlfriend. So I'll consider this, but I'm not driving five little kids to Windsor every weekend."

Davis demonstrated his typical poker face. "I understand," he said. "We'll come back to that."

Lorito wasn't finished. "I'm only going to work for you, and only when you work. When you're on vacation, I'm on vacation, too." He was trying to make it clear that driving Clare Westcott all over Toronto wasn't going to be part of the job description.

"No problem," replied Davis, who then brought his legendary skills of finding compromise to bear. "How would you feel if you took the children to the gas station at Number 4 Highway in London and I'll get the grand-parents to meet you there?" And then, as if to close the deal, Davis added, "And you can bring your girlfriend along with you."

And so began a relationship that became much more than a politician and his driver. Nick Lorito became one of those people Bill Davis spent hours and hours with, driving all over the province. "It was just him and me, and I'd tell him exactly what I thought," Lorito now recalls. "When he was wrong, I'd tell him so."

For example, one day the cabinet was debating whether to force Ontarians to buy fishing licences for every provincial park. Lorito weighed in: "If I'm in a park and my three-year-old suddenly wants to fish, you're telling me I'm going to need a licence for that? That's stupid. That'll cost you votes."

Davis left the cabinet meeting and told Lorito, "I brought your con-cerns to cabinet and lots of people agreed with you Nick. I think I got it stalled for two years." That became a regular conversation piece for the minister and the driver. Lorito loved to bowl, and Davis would frequently ask him: "So, Nick, what do the boys at the bowling alley think of …?" and fill in the blank depending on the hot issue of the day.

Lorito drove Davis to so many new school openings that he jokes: "I used to go to bed counting the blocks in the walls." Another indication of their unusual relationship happened in 1968 when Davis had an event in Georgetown, a community in Halton Region. Lorito checked out some model homes nearby, liked what he saw, and decided to put an offer in on one. But when he went to seek a mortgage at the bank that his family had done business at for years, he was turned down. His wife, Pat, was pregnant, and the bank feared the loss of her income would make Lorito a bad risk.

Some days later Davis asked his driver when he was putting an offer down on the house. "I'm not, boss," he replied. "I was denied." And he explained why.

"Put an offer in," Davis said quietly and calmly to him.

"I can't," Lorito answered.

"Nick, we'll get you a mortgage," Davis said. And that was that. The education minister arranged everything, and the Loritos got their house.

"He liked me," Lorito says. "We were friends."

Lorito became an increasingly important part of what made the Davis family click. In 1967 he drove the kids all the way to Montreal for Expo 67. And when Davis's father started to show signs of dementia, Lorito was the only guy who could coax him into a car to take him to the family cottage at Honey Harbour on Georgian Bay, or into the boat there, as well.

"It became more than a job," Lorito says. "I mean, I had a key to his house. I'd walk in and put on the coffee every day."

The two men talked mostly about politics and sports. Lorito never heard Davis raise his voice or swear — ever. But Lorito could always tell when Davis was angry with him.

"He'd call me Nicholas!" Nick laughs. "One day he wanted me to drive him home by another route. So I questioned him. 'Why would you want to go that way?'"

Lorito remembers an irritated Davis answering, "Because, Nicholas, I'm the premier and I want to go that way. I have my reasons."

To this day Lorito doesn't know why Davis wanted the route changed, and he's never asked.

More typical, however, were stories such as this one, in which Davis's family was vacationing in Vermont, waiting for the education minister to arrive. Davis had to give "one last speech" in Toronto before heading out. But the weather worsened, and eventually all flights in and out of the city were grounded.

"Mrs. Davis is going to kill me if I don't get to Vermont," Lorito remembers Davis saying. "Nick, can you get me to Kingston tonight and at least I'll get halfway there?"

Lorito reached for the car phone — primitive by today's standards, but more sophisticated than a CB radio — and told Davis, "You call my wife and tell her why I'm not coming home tonight."

Davis made the call. "Pat," he began, "I'm wondering if I could borrow Nick for the night."

"We drove all night long," Lorito recalls. Davis actually drove from Toronto to the U.S. border while his driver napped, then Lorito picked up the drive in New York State and on to Vermont. The pair made it in one piece through a blizzard, but Davis avoided Kathleen's wrath.

The 1960s were tumultuous times on university and college campuses in the United States. Students began protesting against an increasingly unpopular war in Vietnam, which ultimately saw hundreds of thousands of American kids sent halfway around the world and more than 58,000 not come home. Officially, Canada didn't participate in that war, although some Canadians volunteered to fight, and as a result, our post-secondary campuses experienced nothing close to what transpired in the United States. But that's not to say there were no protests north of the border.

In October 1968, about 30 students at a secondary school in Welland, Ontario, set up a picket line to demand their student council be free from interference by the school's administration. The students wanted such things as the right to dress and wear their hair the way they wanted; to have the school flag flown at half-mast after Martin Luther King was assassinated; and to distribute anti–Vietnam War pamphlets the school authorities had confiscated.

The president of the student council was a headstrong 16-year-old who showed impressive leadership and oratorical skills. As he mobilized support for his views, more students joined the demonstration. The school began calling parents, asking them to come to the school and help. The father of the student council president showed up. A scuffle with his son ensued, and the son was knocked to the ground in plain view of the assembled crowd, which included members of the local media. The plan to break up the demonstration failed. The next day there were 80 students out there. The day after that there were 150, following a meeting with the school's superintendent that failed to resolve the issue. Eventually, the Board of Education was called in and struck a special panel, which included students, aimed at settling the situation. The student body president was even given a chance to address the school's assembly, which he did, and declared a partial victory.

But then the school principal demanded that the student council president bring a note from home explaining why he missed classes due to the strike. The student refused, saying he was no longer living at home and had no legal guardian. Everyone had already seen how toxic the student's relationship with his father was. With no note from a parent forthcoming, the principal suspended the student. The student refused to leave. The principal called in the police to remove the student forcibly and have him charged with assault and trespassing. "I am here to get an education and I will not leave," said the student, who was then suspended indefinitely. The case actually made it to court. The *Globe and Mail* heard about it and urged in an editorial that the minister of education intervene to prevent this use of "arbitrary school authority."

That minister of education was named Bill Davis. That student body president was named Peter Kormos, who 20 years later would become the MPP for Welland. According to Larry Savage's book *Socialist Cowboy*, Davis initially agreed to meet with Kormos to resolve the issue but then changed his mind. As a result, the two never met. Kormos never did return to school but did end up serving 23 years in the Ontario legislature, almost as many as Davis.

May 21, 1965, turned out to be a pretty significant day in the history of the Province of Ontario. For starters, the province got its own flag that day. Ontario didn't actually have an official flag before then. After a vituperative and historic debate in Parliament in Ottawa, culminating with the choice of the red maple leaf as Canada's national flag in February 1965, John Robarts thought it would be good politics for Ontario to have its own flag. So he took the old Red Ensign, removed the Canadian coat of arms, put Ontario's on instead, and voila, the province had its own flag. It turned out not to be that big a deal, and more than a half century later it's doubtful the majority of Ontarians either know we have a flag or could even recognize it.

However, there was another milestone event that happened on that day in May 1965 that has much better stood the test of time and has been an unambiguous success story. If there's one thing Bill Davis is known for during his tenure as Ontario's education minister, it's the creation of the community college system. It was on May 21, 1965, that Davis introduced Bill 153, which established new alternatives to university in Ontario — 20 colleges of applied arts and technology. They were considered a revolutionary development in post-secondary education that would offer a new vocational training option and lead much more directly into the labour force.

The colleges were built in literally every corner of the province from St. Clair College in Windsor to Algonquin College in Ottawa, and from four colleges in Toronto (Centennial, George Brown, Humber, and Seneca) to Confederation College in Thunder Bay and Northern College in Timmins. It was a massive investment in the educational infrastructure of the province. The first one opened in Scarborough. It was called Centennial College and provided post-secondary education for 430 full-time day students. More than 40 percent of the students were from nearby secondary schools, another 14 percent were adults over age 19 who had been out of school for at least a year and were coming back, and a further 160 students took courses part-time in the evenings.

To give an indication of how much simpler it was to get things done 50 years ago, consider this tale of how Centennial College came into being. Reg Stackhouse, the future Scarborough MP in the 1970s and 1980s but at this point a local school board trustee, hoped to locate one of the new community colleges in his home borough. Stackhouse, who was also a professor at the University of Toronto, got in his car with his brother-in-law, Sheldon Lush, a Scarborough businessman, and drove all over the borough to find a potential site. The pair found an old munitions building no longer in use by the federal government and thought, bingo, here's our site.

In May 1966, Stackhouse went to Ottawa with Anson Taylor, the director of public education in Scarborough, and Ewart Prudhomme, the municipal treasurer, to meet the minister of public works, who was responsible for the munitions building in question. While waiting to see the minister, a bureaucrat told the trio they were wasting their time, that there was no chance they'd get the building. Undaunted, Stackhouse began his pitch to Public Works Minister George McIlraith. He barely got the words "We'd like to open Scarborough's first community college" out of his mouth when McIlraith cut him off. The minister began to wax on about how much he loved Scarborough, that he'd started his legal career as a solicitor when Scarborough was still a township, and that he'd do anything to repay the people. McIlraith called his bureaucrats and said, "Arrange a lease."

Next, Stackhouse had to sell the education minister on the plan, since Davis was also eyeing a proposal for Toronto's west end. In the days before email, Stackhouse marshalled everyone he knew to the cause, got them to write letters to their MPPs promoting the Scarborough option, and copied Davis on all the letters.

It worked. Davis opted for Centennial and insisted the college be open by the fall of 1966. In today's complicated political world, Davis would have been pilloried for setting such a ridiculous target. But this was 1966 and life was a lot less complicated. Stackhouse figured the college would need $5 million as an initial budget and asked the Ministry of Education for that allocation. Again, he was rebuffed, but again he wouldn't take no for an answer. "Your minister has announced his plans in the legislature and will be very embarrassed, I suspect, if the money doesn't come through," he told the bureaucrat.

The official called back later in the day, asking, "How much did you say you needed?"

On October 17, 1966, Centennial College opened its Warden Woods Campus. Professor Stackhouse was on the inaugural board of regents and took the hint from John Robarts that the premier wouldn't mind receiving a little recognition associated with the college. And that's how Ontario's premier managed to get Centennial College's first "honorary diploma," presented by Reg Stackhouse. The incident reflected a little professional jealousy by Robarts of his education minister, who was scoring a lot of positive ink with the creation of the college system. It was Robarts, as education minister, who made Grade 13 optional and worried that too many students would miss out on a post-secondary education. But, he told Stackhouse, "we created a void and now it's filled."

Today Centennial College has four campuses, 18,000 full-time students, and another 20,000 part-timers. The whole college system has grown to 24 institutions today, including two French-language colleges added in the 1990s. And in a development no one would have imagined 50 years ago, one of the largest growing cohorts attending the college system today are *university* graduates, who want to continue their education in a more career-focused direction.

Before the creation of the college system, the educational alternatives for high school graduates who didn't want to go to university were quite slim. The college system changed all that. As he looks back on it today, Davis considers it one of his proudest achievements, although he won't quite put it that way.

"There are very few people who won't acknowledge that it was one of the better things that the government did" is how he now puts it.

Davis's connection to the college system has lasted for more than five decades. Many of the colleges have given him honorary diplomas, including Seneca College, whose chairman of the board at the time was another former education minister, Dave Cooke, who had the job from 1993 to 1995. He introduced Davis at the ceremony. As Cooke marvelled at all the colleges that were created on Davis's watch, the former education minister from Brampton teased the former education minister from Windsor by saying, "Don't forget about all the universities, too!" In fact, of Ontario's current 23 universities, six of them have their origins during the time Davis was Ontario's inaugural minister responsible for university affairs, a new portfolio Robarts added to Davis's responsibilities in 1964.

The list includes Trent University in Peterborough (established in 1963, opened in 1964) whose first chancellor was former premier Leslie Frost and whose first president was Davis's University of Toronto friend, Tom Symons. Brock University in St. Catharines and the University of Guelph came in 1964. Laurentian University in Sudbury was established in 1959 but didn't get its current campus until 1964. Lakehead University in Thunder Bay opened in 1965. And York University, which was established in 1959, didn't open its vast campus at the corner of Keele Street and Steeles Avenue in northwest Toronto until 1965. Davis was particularly involved in the creation of that one.

Is it fair to say that regardless of who was the minister of education and university affairs in the 1960s, he would have come up with all those new universities and the college system? Maybe. The baby boomers needed educating.

"But if you take a look at how it was done and how much was going on all at the same time, I sit back in amazement," Dave Cooke says. Cooke recalls his own experience in government and the hundreds of hoops he had to jump through before making infinitely less significant announcements than what was on Davis's plate 30 years earlier. "The management and the decisions that they made on how they were to get through this was pretty amazing," he says.

Bill Davis has often been referred to as the father of Ontario's community college system, and as such he continues to take an interest in the welfare of his 24 children. Ontario's 21st premier, Bob Rae, with whom Davis has a close personal friendship, says it wasn't unusual when he occupied the premier's office to hear from his predecessor if he had concerns about the colleges.

"He built, as minister of education, an extraordinary infrastructure for education in the province," says Rae, who was tasked in 2004 with reviewing the province's post-secondary sector. He signed up Davis to be one of seven members of his advisory panel. "He did so without any deep sense of narrow partisanship, and he did it with a broad sense of what was good for the community as a whole."

By 1967 Davis's star was shining very brightly, and so he actually allowed himself to contemplate running for the leadership of the Progressive Conservative Party — but not of the *Ontario* Progressive Conservative Party. The *federal* PCs were set to replace John George Diefenbaker as their leader in September at Maple Leaf Gardens, and Labatt Breweries executive Don McDougall was putting together a "Bill Davis for national leader" movement. When Davis's friend, Eddie Goodman, learned of the effort, he met with Davis and made his position on the movement clear: "For what earthly reason" would you want to run for this job, he asked Davis.

Of course, Bill Davis's original interest in politics was at the federal level, and eight years of representing Peel County at Queen's Park had done nothing to change that. He told Goodman that McDougall was convinced he could put together a good organization for Davis and they could pull a respectable vote.

Goodman was having none of it. "This would be a major mistake in your career and you will not do well," he said bluntly. He told the education minister he might pull 100 to 150 votes and would look opportunistic in light of some of the genuine heavy hitters who were contesting the leadership — candidates such as Nova Scotia Premier Robert Stanfield, Manitoba Premier Duff Roblin, and former Diefenbaker cabinet ministers Davie Fulton, George Hees, Donald Fleming, Michael Starr, and Alvin Hamilton, not to mention Dief himself. Goodman told Davis that John Robarts would probably run one more time later in the year and that Davis would have a first-class opportunity to get the Ontario premier's job if he cooled it and kept his nose clean.

Finally, Goodman told Davis if he was truly interested in federal politics, he ought to become chairman of the upcoming "Thinkers Conference" in August in Montmorency Falls, Quebec. And that's exactly what happened. Davis stood down from the national leadership, which was won by Stanfield, and as chairman of the policy sessions, played an influential role in getting the national party to embrace the so-called *deux nations* vision of the country ("Canada is composed of the original inhabitants of this land and the two founding peoples (*deux nations*) with historic rights, who have been, and continue to be, joined by people from many lands").

By the end of 1970, Davis was coming up on eight years as minister of education. He was the longest-serving minister in that portfolio since Conservative MPP Robert Pyne held the job from 1905 to 1914. He was trying his best not to think about what might come next in his career. But the reality was that he had to. The rumours were just everywhere that something big was about to transpire.

II

PREMIER OF ONTARIO

5

LEADER

John Parmenter Robarts had always told his closest friends that should he be successful in winning two general elections his plan was to step down as prime minister of Ontario after a decade on the job. By the winter of 1970, the end of that decade was fast approaching. Robarts won the PC Party leadership in October 1961, scored the highest percentage of the total votes cast in a postwar general election in 1963 — 48.9 percent, a record that still stands to this day — then kept the PC dynasty alive in 1967 by winning another majority government.

But a number of things were on Robarts's mind by the winter of 1970. First, he knew he wouldn't be contesting a third general election as party leader in a year's time, and so, as a good leader must, he needed to start thinking about who would succeed him and when. Given his desire to ensure that his successor would have almost a full year as premier under the belt before having to call the next election meant retirement needed to happen soon. Second, other things that had less to do with politics and more to do with the rest of his life were gnawing at Robarts with some urgency. He was approaching his 54th birthday and realized the window for a post-political career in the private sector would never be more open. (In fact, when Robarts did retire from public life, a plethora of law firms and corporate boards chased after him in a way that probably no other public figure in Canadian political history had to this point experienced.)

And then there was his health. By the winter of 1970, Robarts was quite grey and overweight and looked (by today's standards) like a man who was about to receive his first pension cheque. Those old football injuries were coming back to haunt him. He was asking a pair of bum knees to support far too much weight. Add to that almost a decade in the second most important job in Canadian politics, and Robarts appeared tired and ready to pack it in.

Actually, Ontario's 17th premier once told his former executive assistant and friend, Richard Rohmer, "Dick, if only I could take a year off and recharge my batteries, I'd love to go on." But, of course, politics doesn't work that way.

The notion that Robarts was considering stepping down wasn't exactly top secret at Queen's Park, either. His cabinet and caucus could do the math just as well as the premier's advisers could, and they suspected a resignation announcement wasn't far off. And so many of those who were considering launching campaigns to succeed Robarts started to get their political ducks in line. Organizations had to be created, supporters lined up, money raised, and campaign platforms written. However, there was one possible candidate for the Ontario PC Party leadership who refused to do any of that.

His name was Bill Davis.

Davis knew many of his cabinet colleagues were beginning to plan their leadership bids, and yet none of his closest friends and advisers could convince Davis that he needed to do likewise. Clare Westcott, who first came to Queen's Park working for Premier Leslie Frost and become one of Davis's closest advisers, remembers his friend, the education minister, nixing any plans to create a leadership organization. "The man's still there!" Davis would tell his people, referring to Premier Robarts. The worst thing you could be called in Bill Davis's political world was disloyal, and he'd be damned (well, of course, he'd never use such language, but you get the idea) if he was going to do a single thing to mount a leadership bid, lest it be interpreted as a lack of loyalty to his friend and premier.

The realists surrounding Davis were telling him that was how the game was played. But the Boy Scout in Davis wouldn't hear of it. His was a principled and loyal stand. It was also naive as hell. Ironically, Robarts seemed convinced Davis would eventually replace him. Near the end of his premiership, when asked privately to weigh in on controversial issues, Robarts would say, "Don't talk to me about it. See Davis. He's going to be premier."

In December 1970, John Robarts called the press conference that Bill Davis's advisers had been awaiting with such anticipation. Robarts uttered one of the truest maxims any political leader has ever said: "I am a product of my time exactly, and my time is finished." And with that the race to become Ontario's 18th premier was now officially on.

It was during this time that Bill Davis made a decision that nearly fatally doomed his leadership prospects. Over the previous decade there developed a group of political organizers who were quite simply the best in the country at what they did. And what they did was band together to win elections and leadership conventions by employing new and unique strategies and tactics never before seen in Canadian political contests. It started with New Brunswicker Dalton Camp, the former president of the Progressive Conservative Party of Canada, who added his brother-in-law, Norman Atkins. The two men had known each other since Atkins was nine years old, and it's not too strong to say that Atkins worshipped the man who had married his sister, Linda. Camp used to joke that Atkins was a Tory because Camp was a Tory. "If I'd have been an NDPer, Norman would have been an NDPer, too," he'd say. Atkins, who would become one of the most important and successful political campaign operators in Ontario history, learned almost everything he knew about the game from Camp. The two started together in 1952, helping Hugh John Flemming defeat the incumbent premier of New Brunswick, John B. McNair, and continued their collaboration through several more elections, both provincial and federal.

Over the years they would add other foot soldiers to the cause. Some were nicknamed "The Spades" because they did the spadework for Camp. They included Chad Bark, the Eglinton PC riding association president; Toronto lawyers Patrick Vernon, Don Guthrie, Pat Patterson, and Roy McMurtry; and Paul Weed, Ross DeGeer, Eric Ford, and future Mike Harris cabinet minister Bill Saunderson. Sometimes they were called "The Eglinton Mafia" after the midtown Toronto riding in which they tried to get Camp elected in the 1965 federal election. Others would be called "The Dirty Dozen" after the 1967 movie set during the Second World War. But their most famous moniker would be "The Big Blue Machine."

Conventional wisdom holds that the Big Blue Machine was so named by journalist Claire Hoy in the mid-1970s. Hoy was a baseball fan who saw the 1975 and 1976 Cincinnati Reds win back-to-back World Series. When he saw the track record of these Tory backroom boys, he nicknamed them the Big Blue Machine in tribute to the Reds. But in his book *The Big Blue Machine*, former PC MP Patrick Boyer points out it was actually Ontario Premier George Drew who first used the expression while campaigning in 1943. Drew promised supporters his party would "build a big blue machine that will advance from one side of this province to the other and roll up a big majority at Queen's Park."

Regardless, that group of expert political practitioners was hoping to find a home in Bill Davis's nascent leadership campaign organization, figuring they'd already helped win several elections for other Progressive Conservative parties in other provinces across Canada, but they now wanted a foothold in Canada's biggest province. For Camp and Atkins, who ran an advertising agency, winning elections was the fun part they did for nothing. The reward came once their victors took office, then steered considerable government advertising work their way. It was a formula that had worked and would work numerous times before the dynamic duo was done with politics.

In any event, the group of Toronto organizers, who at this point were still going by the nickname The Spades, met to decide whom they wanted to back in the race to succeed Robarts. Naturally, with Davis presumed to be the obvious successor, he was their choice. But when their offer was made, it was rebuffed. Clare Westcott told the group: "Thanks, guys, but I don't need any help." The insiders on Davis's team — John Latimer, Hugh Macaulay, Ward Cornell of *Hockey Night in Canada* fame, and chief fundraiser Bill Kelly — probably figured they already had the convention sewn up, so why invite more organizers into the tent with whom they'd eventually have to share power and influence with the new leader? The Spades were shocked at the rejection but resolved to find another candidate to back in hopes of, as Patrick Boyer describes it, "teaching a lesson to the smug bastards around Davis who'd ungraciously turned them down."

Dalton Camp, who was most anxious to break into Ontario politics, wanted to support Robarts's treasurer, 60-year-old Charles MacNaughton.

MacNaughton was a big name who had a great deal of caucus support but didn't want the job and ultimately became chairman of Davis's campaign. So The Spades targeted their second choice. At first he also turned them down, but after further reflection, he gave them the green light. And that's how MPP Allan Lawrence became the biggest threat to what was supposed to be an easy ride to the finish line for William G. Davis.

"We were surprised how many people wanted to be involved in running against the Ontario establishment," Norman Atkins told former *London Free Press* reporter George Hutchison, who taped numerous interviews with significant players in Ontario political history. ("Hutch" had intended to use the interviews for a book of his own but eventually abandoned the project and gave the tapes to me).

It's also fair to say there might have been some concern in the Davis camp about associating themselves too closely with Dalton Camp. In some PC circles, Camp was still radioactive from his championing the leadership review of John Diefenbaker five years earlier. Some of Davis's people no doubt thought they were going to win this thing, anyway, so why bother alienating their supporters who liked Dief? In any event, Camp and his followers were out.

On December 20, 1970, Davis became the first candidate to jump into the race and was the favourite to win it from that moment on. He had fully three-quarters of the PC caucus publicly backing him. John Latimer, who owned Kilcoo Camp near Minden and knew Davis from their time working on Robert Macaulay's 1961 leadership bid, was his campaign manager. William Kelly, a vice-president and director of marketing with Consumers' Gas, and Hugh Macaulay (Robert's brother and a board member at Ryerson Polytechnical Institute, as the university was then called) were his policy and money men. As both minister of education *and* university affairs, Davis's departments controlled a huge chunk of the provincial budget (akin to being the minister of health today), and so plenty of people in Progressive Conservative political circles were anxious to jump on board his team, lest they be left behind.

"The Bill Davis campaign looked at it as a coronation," said Thomas Wells, a Scarborough MPP since 1963, cabinet minister since 1966, and someone who had known Davis since their days playing football together at the University of Toronto. Davis's people kept telling Wells their man was going to win and to get on the bandwagon. "I felt a little uneasy about that," Wells remembered. "The party's interest could be best served by a vigorous campaign and choices. We might drift complacently into having a new leader without having the sense that something had to be done to revitalize the party."

Bill Davis knew the entire province extremely well. Someone figured out that by opening new schools all over Ontario — sometimes at the rate of three a day — Davis's schedule required him to travel almost 125,000 miles a year, giving between four and five speeches a week in the process.

"He's got IOUs he doesn't even know about" was how one of his aides described his political standing in the party and province.

Even Davis's NDP education critic, the MPP for Peterborough, Walter Pitman, recognized his foe's talent. "He's a cool, calculating man with a firm grasp on that monster of an empire he's been running," Pitman said, referring to the Ministry of Education. "He's the only guy with the toughness to organize that cabinet. I regard him as the most able minister the Conservatives have."

(Try to imagine anyone on the opposite side of the legislature floor saying that about a political opponent today. You can't. It's another indication of how vicious politics has become, and how much more collegial it used to be back in the day.)

Even Pitman's former leader, Donald C. MacDonald, who'd been in the legislature since 1953, thought Davis had more going for him than the man he was trying to replace.

"Davis has far more political savvy," MacDonald said at the time. "He's an obviously more adept politician than John [Robarts] was in the beginning, or come to think of it, was at the end. He plays with a lot of the Liberal riff-raff like a cat playing with a mouse."

Davis was only 41 years old, but as he joked when we discussed his leadership bid four decades later, "I was old for my age." In fact, that was sort of true. Davis had held significant cabinet responsibilities since age 33, had been in elective politics since he was 29, but had been around politics for another decade or more before that. Even before John Robarts became leader of the party, people had been telling him Davis was a future premier-in-waiting. Remember the picture of Premier Leslie Frost, former premier Thomas Kennedy, and Davis for the *Cookstown Gazette*? "Past,

Present, and The Future," said the caption. The inference was unmistakable. Frost was the most successful Tory premier in half a century, winning three consecutive majority governments, something that still hasn't been replicated to this day. (Dalton McGuinty fell one seat short of doing so in 2011.) Tom Kennedy was Davis's mentor and the "caretaker premier" between Premiers George Drew and Leslie Frost when Drew left Queen's Park to become the federal PC Party leader. Surely, the picture suggested, Davis would take over the leadership and continue the dynasty without a hiccup. Certainly, his predecessor as the MPP for Peel believed that. Kennedy often introduced Davis to people as "a boy who'll be premier someday."

Having said all that, Davis was also an introvert, at times painfully shy, and at this point in his life still surprisingly weak at working a roomful of people.

"When I first met Billy Davis, he couldn't look at a group and speak to them head-on," recalls Norman Atkins. "He was all over the place."

Still, Davis was the man who created the community college system and TVOntario, the province's new educational broadcaster. Five new universities started on his watch. There was improved funding for the separate school system to the end of Grade 10. True, he did run into some friction when he amalgamated 1,500 rural school boards into 130 more centralized, efficient operations. (Premier Robarts used to tease Davis about the unpopularity of that initiative, saying, "Better they be mad at you than at me!") And there would be some other nagging concerns with the Davis campaign. But as 1970 came to a close, things looked awfully good for the man from Peel County. In fact, after his second week of campaigning, he took the weekend off to watch his father, A. Grenville Davis, be installed in the Ontario Lacrosse Hall of Fame in Toronto.

As much as the deck seemed to be stacked for a Davis win, plenty of other candidates jumped into the race, thinking, if Davis faltered, one of them could take the torch from Robarts. And keep in mind, unlike Davis, they'd all started organizing months earlier and had other qualities on offer that, frankly, Davis didn't.

Davis's toughest opponent turned out to be the candidate backed by The Spades — 45-year-old lawyer Allan Lawrence, who entered politics just one year before Davis did, in 1958. Lawrence had solid support in what was then called Metropolitan Toronto — the old cities of Toronto,

North York, Scarborough, Etobicoke, and the boroughs of York and East York, what people today call "The 416" or the "MegaCity." Lawrence represented the downtown Toronto riding of St. George, but he was also the minister of mines, so he had good support in Northern Ontario, as well. That was a good coalition to start with, and Lawrence intended to build from there. His campaign slogan was "Winning Is Only the Beginning."

If there was a "change" candidate in the race, Lawrence was it. He was the one candidate who tried to shine a spotlight on the education system and the public's concerns "with what's happening inside these buildings." While Davis was the education superstar, constantly opening new schools and travelling all over the province championing his new, modern system, Lawrence was focusing on all the money going out the door to pay for that system. When he jumped into the race two weeks after Davis did, Lawrence suggested the education budget was out of control. He didn't think that the budget should exceed a third of provincial spending, whereas under Robarts and Davis, education was now gobbling up more than 40 percent of provincial expenditures. And money wasn't the only issue. Lawrence also gave voice to those concerned with rising student alienation, drug use, and school dropouts. While he insisted his remarks shouldn't be taken as an attack on Davis, it was hard to see how they could be seen as anything but just that.

Lawrence was once an aggressive, maverick backbencher who referred to himself as "a burr under the saddle of the government" — taking on the traditional but nowadays completely disregarded role of government watchdog from its own backbenches. For example, Lawrence was part of a group of disgruntled government MPPs who stared down their own premier, forcing Robarts to withdraw Bill 99, amendments to the Police Act that were designed to give the police sweeping new powers and take a bite out of organized crime in Ontario. Even the attorney general championing the bill, Fred Cass, admitted, "Yes, these are drastic, draconian measures that in some ways are really unbelievable in a country that has an English common law system." Lawrence's and his colleagues' opposition to the bill was so successful that Cass was forced to resign over the issue. In 1968 Robarts put Lawrence in cabinet, taking a page from U.S. President Lyndon Johnson's famous adage about preferring to have his political opponents "inside the tent pissing out, rather than outside the tent pissing in." Once inside cabinet, Lawrence set out to prove he could be a dynamic, modern, urbane force in politics, equal to the NDP's new firebrand leader Stephen Lewis, who had overwhelmingly won his party's leadership in one ballot back in October 1970 and was garnering a lot of attention.

Sometimes Lawrence's shoot-from-the-hip style got him into trouble. While not confirmed, the story went that Lawrence once told his cabinet colleagues that if he ever got to be the leader, he'd fire 60 percent of them. That's a tough way to win support from your colleagues, but Lawrence seemed to relish his reputation as the blunt-talking bad boy of provincial politics who shot first and aimed later. Claire Hoy, a relatively new journalist at Queen's Park at the time, saw it differently. "I don't think Allan Lawrence was very bright," Hoy recalled. "But he had a great team."

Ah, yes, the Lawrence team. While the candidate might have left much to be desired, his campaign staff was the most talented squad ever assembled in Ontario political history. Along with Camp and Atkins, the team included future cabinet minister and Ontario chief justice Roy McMurtry; strategists Ross DeGeer and Paul Weed; Bill Saunderson, a future cabinet minister in Mike Harris's government; and lawyer Brian Armstrong. So while Davis had the party establishment and most of the cabinet and caucus with him, Lawrence had state-of-the-art polling techniques, campaign literature, and advertising in his corner. As Ross DeGeer told Patrick Boyer in *The Big Blue Machine*, "The Davis campaign organizers wanted to fight the war using the old rules — make two lines to shoot at each other. Well, sorry, we were into guerrilla warfare." Most of that warfare was imported from state-of-the-art techniques from the United States, as opposed to Great Britain, where previous Tory organizers had looked for their inspiration.

For example, Al Lawrence wasn't the greatest speaker. But he looked good at a time when television was starting to become an increasingly important medium for political campaigns. When Norman Atkins skillfully edited together short sound bites of Lawrence's speeches, he created an image of a more commanding presence. It levelled what ought to have been a fairly uneven playing field for the Lawrence team. It was all new and fresh.

"We were looking for a challenge and for some fun," Norman Atkins said. "We had an opportunity to make an impression on the party. But it never occurred to us we could win the thing."

Thomas Wells thought about running for the leadership himself. He was a year younger than Davis, was responsible as health minister for implementing medicare toward the end of Robarts's second term, and was getting some pressure from his supporters to consider running. But he wasn't sure he could raise enough money, hated the notion of going into personal debt to finance a campaign, and so ultimately decided to back Lawrence — the only cabinet minister to do so. He considered Davis a personal friend (not just a political one), so Wells called Davis to break the news to him. Apparently, Davis was a gentleman about it.

"He just said, 'Thank you for letting me know,'" Wells recalled.

Others on the Davis campaign weren't so sanguine about it. Charlie MacNaughton, for one, admonished some of Wells's people, saying, "Tom's making a big mistake. He should be with us."

After Davis and Lawrence and running third in the contest was the original Common Sense Revolutionary, to borrow a term from the Mike Harris years. Darcy McKeough was only 37 years old but ambitious as hell and unabashedly right wing. McKeough was a Robarts loyalist, as well, having been put into cabinet, like Davis, at the tender age of 33. To this day, McKeough organizes an annual John P. Robarts luncheon every December at the Toronto Club, where the former premier's colleagues gather to enjoy several Scotches and thick steaks and hoist a glass in memory of the Chairman of the Board.

McKeough was nicknamed "The Duke of Kent," a rather pompous moniker for such a young guy (he represented the riding of Kent West in Southwestern Ontario). But the name stuck and McKeough didn't mind it at all. He had decent support from rural Ontario, but as municipal affairs minister he also had to carry the can for establishing several regional governments around the province, which didn't make him too popular in parts of the Tory heartland. Still, McKeough came to politics having successfully run his family's plumbing and heating business in Chatham. He had a sharp wit and a profane tongue. If Davis was a bit of an old-timer at 41, McKeough at 37 could relate; friends referred to him as "a new fogey."

Next in popularity was Robert Welch, the 42-year-old minister of citizenship and provincial secretary from the Niagara Peninsula riding of Lincoln. Like McKeough, Welch was first elected in 1963 and everybody liked him. Despite a high, squeaky voice, he could rouse a crowd with his oratory. Robarts also liked Welch a lot but feared he didn't have the horses to compete with the other candidates. So, although officially neutral, he quietly "loaned" one of his top advisers in his office to the Welch campaign. He didn't want to see any of "his boys" embarrassed in the race to succeed him.

There were actually two candidates named Lawrence in this contest. The other was 47-year old Albert Benjamin Rutter Lawrence, the financial and commercial affairs minister, known to everyone as "Bert." This Lawrence was another contrarian. He was considered an ideas man with no chance to win but had a decent base of support in Eastern Ontario. One of his supporters was an 18-year-old student named Maureen McTeer. However, there was a student council president also from Ottawa who bucked the regional trend. His name was Hugh Segal, and he supported Davis. Bert Lawrence warned the Tories that they needed something more than just "a continuation of the old regime." Segal seemed more attracted to the civility of Davis's candidacy, which he thought marked a pretty stark contrast with the style of leadership exhibited by the current prime minister of the country, Pierre Elliott Trudeau.

"I have watched the erosion in our strength over the past two elections and I see no sign that it isn't continuing," Bert Lawrence said in a pretty obvious shot across Davis's bow. And if people missed that one, Lawrence continued by suggesting people didn't want "more of the same, safe, dull, responsible, slow government provided by Mr. Robarts."

Yikes!

Finally, there was one fringe candidate who was a late entrant to the race. Robert Pharand was a 26-year-old graduate student from the University of Ottawa who ran simply to give added attention to a single issue he cared about deeply: funding for the Roman Catholic school system. Separate school students attended many of the leadership campaign events, mostly to heckle the five other cabinet ministers when the issue of Catholic school funding came up, and to cheer for Pharand when he raised it. At this point in Ontario history the province only offered public funding to separate schools to the end of Grade 10, and even doing that had caused the Robarts government some severe political headaches.

Robarts was proud of his government's support for Catholic schools. There were certainly few Tory votes in it for the government — the Liberals overwhelmingly took the Catholic vote. But by offering additional public assistance to the separate school system as he did in 1964 through his so-called "Foundation Tax Plan," Robarts thought he was ensuring the financial viability of the separate school system for generations to come.

"I settled one of the greatest problems we had had in Ontario since before Confederation," Robarts had said, beaming. But his celebration was premature. The Catholic population was increasing, and so were its demands for even more funding. "I see I only settled it for five years," Robarts sadly concluded later. His successor would now inherit "The Bishops' Brief," as the Catholic school funding file was known. Ontario's outgoing premier admitted to considerable disappointment that separate school supporters were, yet again, demanding more.

For his part, Pharand wanted if not full funding to the end of Grade 13, then at least some financial aid for those additional high school years. But this was 1971, and there was absolutely no appetite in the Tory heartland to implement this idea. Davis, because he was education minister, was a particular target for separate school protestors. On February 3 at Cambrian College's Sault Ste. Marie campus, Davis confirmed that government policy opposed any extension of public funding, while students confronted him with a banner saying HAVE A HEART, UNCLE BILL. With astonishing prescience so rare for this era, Pharand predicted a time when public and separate schools would share facilities and exchange courses. Such talk was heretical in the Progressive Conservative circles of the early 1970s, even though virtually everything Pharand campaigned on has come to pass. This wouldn't be the last time Bill Davis had to deal with the issue of separate school funding. In fact, that issue would go on to play a decisive role in two future elections.

So there were six candidates in total in the race to replace Robarts, and frankly, not many were predicting much of a contest. Even the supposedly neutral party president, Alan Eagleson, said, "Davis is certainly cut in the cloth of the Robarts style. He's solid and soft sell."

For the most part, the race was a fairly gentlemanly affair by today's standards. The candidates talked in generalities and mostly avoided attacking one another. But as the February convention date beckoned, Davis found himself more in the crosshairs, particularly on the spending issue, so much so that on January 13, 1971, he offered up his strongest defence to date. Davis told delegates in London that he had no apologies to make when it came to education spending, that the other "have" provinces

— Alberta and British Columbia — both spent more per pupil, as did every neighbouring American state. Davis was clearly feeling the heat on his department's spending but told delegates, "If you think I'm going to apologize for what has been done in education … well, you're wrong."

Davis to this point had been trying to skate through the leadership campaign by being as uncontroversial as possible, speaking in vague platitudes and hoping his opponents would play nice, as well. That worked for a time, but the closer Tories got to convention day, the sharper the comments became. Even Davis, known throughout his career as a Red Tory, couldn't resist tossing some red meat to the more conservative delegates.

"Politics today has to be aggressive," he said. "We have to start calling a spade a spade … such as starting to identify the NDP with socialism, which is what it is."

More than four decades later, readers could be forgiven for wondering whether those words really came out of Davis's mouth. After all, he was hardly known for being the "aggressive" candidate in the race. In fact, he was perhaps best known over his entire political career for his blandness. Furthermore, some of his best and most respected friends in politics would turn out to be those evil "socialists" he railed against while seeking the PC leadership. As we'll come to see, some of Davis's biggest problems in politics were with the hard right wing of his own party, not the left wingers on the other side of the legislature.

In fact, for a candidate trying to burnish his right-wing credentials, Davis occasionally proposed ideas that were quite progressive. In a campaign in which he tried to make as few promises as possible and essentially sit on his lead, he did pledge to appoint Ontario's first-ever minister of the environment should the delegates select him as their champion. In 1971 Ontario had no environment minister. People were only beginning to have an appreciation of how damaging pollution could be to the planet. While Robarts took several important steps to acknowledge the environment's increasing importance (the creation of the Niagara Escarpment Commission, for example), basically every ministry had the responsibility of creating its own pollution control regulations and some weren't that excited about doing so. Davis wanted something more dramatic than that and promised to create, along with a new minister, a pollution control commission made up of government and industry, while at the same time providing financial assistance to environmental citizens' groups such as Pollution Probe, which had just been founded in 1969.

Was Davis really a red-baiting, "small-*c*" conservative? Or was he really a big-spending progressive, as one could easily conclude from his education ministry budgets? Reporters often tried to get to the core of his beliefs, usually without much success. Harold Greer of the *Ottawa Citizen* landed on a major insight into the candidate, calling him "the friendliest and most accessible of politicians, but he does not reveal himself easily." As to Davis's habit of never using the first-person-singular pronoun, always preferring to use "we," Greer wondered whether that was "overpowering modesty," or "the ultimate in political obfuscation." It wouldn't be the first or last time Bill Davis was accused of being as transparent as a sphinx. But Greer did go on to describe what would become the classic Davis modus operandi: he never goes "looking for trouble" and never does or says "more than is absolutely necessary." It was an observation that was bang on. Davis embraced that philosophy of politics after hearing an admonition from one of his mentors, former premier Thomas Kennedy, who once told him: "Always be humble, even if you don't feel like it. And remember you never get into trouble for the speeches you don't make."

Davis did his best to describe what Progressive Conservatism meant to him: "To retain the productive links with the past while discarding institutions and procedures that have outlived their usefulness." That actually sounded like Davis — a bit technocratic, a bit bland, but pretty solid.

With three weeks to go until convention day, conventional wisdom suggested Davis still had a commanding lead. And so Allan Lawrence got tougher. In a speech in Thornhill to delegates from York Region (one of Darcy McKeough's new regional governments that had just come into existence on January 1), Lawrence said education costs "were out of control." He pledged to put a three-year freeze on education spending, then only let it increase commensurate with the growth of the province's economy. Lawrence wanted the freeze to determine whether Ontario was getting its money's worth. One alternate delegate, a former Vaughan Township trustee named Terry Goodwin, said Lawrence's comments were "insulting" and insisted the candidate take them back. Lawrence refused and so Goodwin stormed out. (Being a proper, polite Tory, he later returned and apologized.)

The truth was, as much as Davis still was the front-runner, there were plenty of Tories who were concerned about his spending. Compared to the finances of today where ministry budgets are either flatlined, or at the most, raised at the rate of inflation, the government's finances in the 1960s were simply astounding. In 1968 Bill Davis's education budget increased by almost 20 percent. In one year! In 1969, when spending was reduced somewhat, his budget still went up by nearly 15.5 percent. And in 1970 it was still expected to rise by almost 14 percent. While those numbers are astonishing by today's standards, it's worth remembering that Ontario was experiencing boom times. The revenues were flying in as never before, and despite huge spending increases, the Robarts government balanced its budget every year.

It's an indication of how genteel the candidate debates were at this point in Ontario political history that Allan Lawrence took some heavy flak for something he said about the unemployed. Lawrence liked to give quick, snappy, chippy answers that could get him headlines, so he talked about creating some incentives in the welfare system that "would get these people off their butts and back into the mainstream of working life."

While the line drew enthusiastic applause, media observers immediately speculated on whether the words would come back to haunt Lawrence. Later in the same debate the candidate seemed concerned about that, too, as he tried to walk back the comments.

By the third week of January, 1971 — with the convention only three weeks away — the rhetoric became even more heated. Bert Lawrence said Bill Davis just wasn't "that fresh, that new, that invigorating, that inspiring a man that the party and public are expecting." He then took a shot at one of Davis's proudest achievements — the Ontario Institute for Studies in Education — saying the institute was overextended and showing "the signs and smells of waste."

Bob Welch then gave a speech at a party event in which he threw away his prepared text and freelanced on the need for the PCs to become a more open party, seeking out members from non-traditional quarters, including unions. His audience responded with loud applause.

The traditional Tory strategy on running for the party leadership had been to stake out the right-wing ground to appeal to the party's most conservative elements in the heartland, then move closer to the middle at election time. That was right out of the Nixon playbook (that's American president Richard, not Ontario Liberal leader Robert). This will come as a surprise to those who only think of Bill Davis as a Red Tory, but the reality was, the education minister was following that tried, tested, and true blueprint. Toward the end of January while campaigning in Peterborough, Davis offered, "There is no way this riding should be represented by a socialist," referring to Walter Pitman, who had lost the NDP leadership to Stephen Lewis a few months earlier and had complimented Davis's political acumen earlier in the campaign. Both opposition parties responded with dismay at the education minister's name-calling. The riding's former NDP candidate accused Davis of "lowering the tone of politics," while the nominated Liberal candidate said "it was not a democratic remark," presaging an anti-socialist campaign theme whenever the next election took place.

Bill Davis red-baiting? Ironic for a candidate who in years to come would be the target of opprobrium from his party's right wing for himself being too pink. But this was a leadership campaign. With both Lawrences and Welch staking out the more progressive ground among Progressive Conservatives, and with Darcy McKeough unabashedly all by himself over on the far right, Davis unsurprisingly tried to play that middle ground — tacking left, tacking right — as he surveyed what the situation required. He did have a lot of ideological ground to cover, given that 42 of the Tories' 62 MPPs were supporting him, a number that's even more impressive when you consider four other MPPs were running against him and Robarts was staying neutral.

Davis continued to punch back rather than play punching bag. At an all-candidates debate on January 28 he fired back at the Lawrences, saying, "The politician who caters to human yearning for simple answers to complex questions may make headlines, but he doesn't make satisfactory public policy."

The education minister had tried his best during the campaign to offer as little new substantive policy as possible, partly to avoid being a bigger target than he already was, but also out of loyalty to Robarts. He just didn't think it was appropriate, with the premier still on the job and he still in his cabinet, to be running all over the province contradicting the government's current policy. Davis said it was more important for delegates to get to know him as a man and understand his principles, rather than have him trot out some "instant policies" that could get him through a leadership contest but not stand up to scrutiny thereafter.

"Proposals as such are valueless without the resolve and the stamina to back them up and ... the willingness to make hard decisions in the face of powerful opposition and outraged interests," he told delegates. It was classic, steady-as-she-goes politicking.

As an example, Davis referred to an issue that was quite hot at the time: the proliferation of noisy snowmobiles whose drivers were often the targets of criticism for their reckless driving habits. A few weeks earlier Southern Ontario had been hit hard by a snowstorm, and Davis used the incident to demonstrate why he didn't join the chorus of snowmobile nay-sayers to garner a cheap, temporary headline.

"The maniacs of yesterday were suddenly public-spirited citizens and brave ones at that ... as they went out in a raging blizzard to deliver food and drink to schools," he offered. "The machines that so irritated people were suddenly indispensable tools in a crisis." Davis's message was clear: If you want a headline grabber who'll give you temporary gratification, vote for one of the other guys. If you want strong and steady with a longer view of Ontario's issues, I'm your guy.

Two of Davis's core values were crashing into each other during the campaign. He loved to compete and win. He'd done so since his school days, whether academically or in sports. But throughout his life his parents had also told him to be properly modest and not indulge in attention-seeking behaviour. But how do you win a contest without trying to take the spotlight off the other guy and put it on yourself?

"I hate talking about myself," Davis confessed one day to a group of Hamilton delegates, backing up the revelation with an inability to use the first-person pronoun. "We are relatively young. We have had some political success, and I think we say things when we feel they have to be said though they may be unpopular." And with that the candidate scanned the room quickly, looking for another question.

The 1971 PC leadership campaign will always have a unique place in Ontario political history, not only because of who won it but also because it was the first leadership campaign in which television began to matter a lot. The last time Tories gathered to pick John Robarts as their leader at Varsity Arena in Toronto in 1961, television was in its infancy in Canada. But by 1971 the CBC was giving free airtime to the five main candidates, and the reviews about Davis's performance were harsh.

"On television, the education minister came across like a slightly younger Sydney Greenstreet, though not nearly as interesting," wrote Dennis Braithwaite in the *Toronto Telegram*, referring to the actor who had gained fame playing shady characters in *Casablanca* and *The Maltese Falcon*. "Our boy has put on weight, mostly around the jowls and through the neck.... The net effect of the Davis phiz [*sic*] was not pretty or rugged or intelligent or inspiring, or any of the things politicians hope to project."

And Braithwaite wasn't finished ripping the front-runner. "William Davis' image needs a lot of work. He is no great shakes as an orator, his manner is wooden and that face, well, it's fat, there's no other word for it."

Conversely, Braithwaite loved Allan Lawrence, who he described as "lean, trim, fair-headed, energetic, decisive, nice, decent, and every other pleasurable adjective you want to throw in." And in case you missed his point the first time, Braithwaite ended his column with: "[Davis] better get himself some new clothes, not just duds that fit the new frame, but something designed after World War II."

Meanwhile, the Duke of Kent was looking for a way to gain some traction for his campaign, so he decided to play the unity card. "I do not propose to divide our party between establishment and dissenters — two arbitrary and artificial groupings which, if they really existed, would not be strong enough, either of them, to win an election in Ontario," said Darcy McKeough. "I will unite, not divide. I want the leadership, but I do not want it so badly that I would weaken, undermine, or destroy this party."

McKeough might have had trouble getting more delegates on board, but he had no trouble attracting the admiration of one of the rising stars of journalism of the day. "I wanted Darcy to win," admits Claire Hoy, then writing for the *Toronto Star*, but who's also written for plenty of other Ontario newspapers, including the *Toronto Telegram* and *Toronto Sun*. "He was fiscally to the right of Davis," where Hoy thinks every thinking politician ought to be.

By the time the candidates and delegates made their way to Maple Leaf Gardens at the corner of Church and Carlton Streets in downtown Toronto, the race was truly on. If anyone had thought this would be a simple coronation of the front-runner, they were about to be disabused of that notion in dramatic fashion.

Maple Leaf Gardens had seen its share of remarkable political events since its construction in 1931 as the new home for Toronto's beloved hockey team. In 1932 Sir Winston Churchill spoke at the Gardens during his "wilderness years." At the time his political career seemed over.

Not quite.

In 1967 the Progressive Conservative Party of Canada held its leadership convention aimed at replacing John Diefenbaker there and chose Nova Scotia Premier Robert Stanfield as their new standard-bearer. And perhaps the most famous political rally in Canadian history happened there when 18,000 rabid Liberal supporters packed the Gardens to hear Pierre Trudeau make a last-ditch passionate plea for constitutional renewal. With echoes of the Trudeaumania that captivated Canadians a decade earlier ringing through the hall, the prime minister took to the stage in rock star–like fashion, only to be defeated by Joe Clark less than two weeks later in the 1979 general election. But like Churchill, Trudeau wasn't quite done with public life, either.

One of the most historically significant events ever to take place at Maple Leaf Gardens was the selection of Ontario's first-ever female premier, Kathleen Wynne, who won the Ontario Liberal leadership there in three dramatic ballots on January 26, 2013. Perhaps the wildest leadership convention in Canadian history also took place there when a relatively unknown MPP from Ottawa named Dalton McGuinty came from fourth place on the second ballot to capture the Ontario Liberal leadership at 4:30 in the morning on December 1, 1996, after three more marathon-like ballots. That convention was so long that it not only started on one day and ended on another, but it also actually began in one month and ended in another.

While these conventions clearly have their place in the Canadian political firmament, it was the Ontario Progressive Conservative Party's 1971 leadership convention that had more than its share of wild and crazy occurrences. The convention took place over three days from February 10 to 12, and yes, by the time it was over, the candidate who was expected to win did, in fact, win. But nothing went according to script in one of the strangest conventions ever held. The apparent closeness of the race also contributed to what was now a not at all disguised bitterness between the two principal candidates' campaign teams. Lawrence himself said there was "no middle road" between him and Davis, "no compromise. That's the stark reality." Davis's campaign manager, John Latimer, said his workers were spending their time "trying to combat the anti-Davis feeling Al Lawrence's people are trying to generate…. It's not at all healthy for the party to harbour bitterness among individuals involved in it."

Lawrence's campaign manager, Ross DeGeer, might have rued the "inevitable" bitterness that accompanied tough leadership campaigns. "But a lot of us who work hard in the party felt the need to rock the boat and we've knocked Davis off from his position of sure victory." Lawrence was blunter: "I think some people [in the Davis camp] have been too damn touchy … about my criticism of education costs."

Pity the poor Godfrey family. Paul, at this time a municipal councillor in North York but a future Metro Toronto chairman and city power broker, was backing Davis. His wife, Gina, was a proud Lawrence acolyte. How was the couple handling the situation?

"We smirk at each other when we pass in the hall," Paul Godfrey joked. (The couple seems to have figured out how to disagree amicably. They're still married after 48 years.)

On February 10, 1971, an estimated 10,000 Tory supporters — almost 2,000 of whom were official voting delegates — began to gather at the Royal York Hotel for the prelude to the leadership selection itself. As predicted, the Big Blue Machine's superior organization made the hotel look as if Lawrence was the favourite to win. "We had that place covered with signs before the others even arrived," Ross DeGeer said in *The Big Blue Machine*. There were policy sessions the candidates had to attend, hospitality suites galore for the evening entertainment, and a testimonial dinner in Robarts's honour, to thank the Chairman of the Board for keeping the dynasty alive for another nine years and 113 days.

The convention speeches proceeded as anticipated. Davis spoke first, was nervous, and actually had to deal with hecklers, an oddity at a leadership event of any party. Lawrence was confident and relaxed and delivered his well-written speech with polish. Welch was rousing. But the best speech belonged to Darcy McKeough, who brought a mixture of passion, partisanship, and piss and vinegar to the occasion.

"We need a leader who can beat that sham statesman of 1971, Stephen Lewis," McKeough boomed, referring to the new NDP leader. "And I ask you: can Stephen Lewis really shed his background as waffle-leaning puppet of union leadership, and all that that entails?"

The crowd lapped it up. McKeough then referenced a *Toronto Star* article that suggested if he won the leadership he would conduct a "harsh" campaign against the NDP. The municipal affairs minister picked up on that word. "Ladies and gentlemen, he was right. There is no doubt. It will be harsh where it needs to be harsh. It will have guts…. It will have personality. It will have sweat and strain and effort to the point of exhaustion. But it will have your support. And we will have the victory."

Premier Robarts, who had done his best to stay neutral to this point, was seen in his private box, growling, "Attaboy, Darcy!"

Sadly for McKeough, his barnburner of a speech didn't change any minds on the editorial boards of the province's major newspapers. "If a reasoned consideration of records and positions is what will guide the delegates to their decision, then the man is William Davis," editorialized the *Globe and Mail*.

"He is only 41, a man of proven ability, and has shown that he can accept responsibility with courage, conviction and good sense," added the *Toronto Telegram*. "Mr. Davis is the man to continue the advances made by Ontario under Conservative leaders and administrations."

Demonstrating a savvy about politics he would show during his four decades in journalism, the *Tele*'s political editor, Fraser Kelly, acknowledged Davis would likely win the convention "more by hesitant default than by overwhelming enthusiasm." Kelly noted how close the contest seemed to be and chalked it up to the ineptness of Davis's campaign and the astuteness of Lawrence's.

On February 12, 1971, Tory delegates from across the Province of Ontario gathered at Maple Leaf Gardens to participate in choosing John Robarts's successor. Sprinkled throughout the crowd was the Grade 13 class from South Huron District High School in Exeter, the home riding of Robarts's treasurer, Charles MacNaughton, who was backing Davis in this contest. For some reason the visiting class got off the bus, entered the arena, and immediately had Lawrence campaign signs handed to them. Holding one of them was a student named Janet Ecker.

"I don't recall being interested in politics at the time, but I can remember being quite fascinated about being in Maple Leaf Gardens and the signs and noise and everything," says Ecker four and a half decades later. "It was just a really fascinating experience."

Something must have clicked with young Janet, because four years later she'd work in the communications unit of the Ministry of Consumer and Commercial Relations for her former University of Western Ontario journalism professor Frank Drea, who was parliamentary assistant to the minister. A decade later she'd be deputy press secretary to the premier of Ontario. Three decades later she'd become the first female treasurer in Ontario history to bring in a budget. But it all started on a February day at Maple Leaf Gardens in 1971.

There was another young Progressive Conservative in the arena that night, also holding a sign for Lawrence. He was 16 years old and had been involved in PC Party politics for two years already. The fact that he was one of the many young people supporting the more exciting Lawrence campaign turned out to be somewhat ironic given that he would go on to have a long and deeply meaningful relationship with Lawrence's chief competitor at that leadership convention. That 16-year-old's name was John Tory.

One of the things Bill Davis noticed when he arrived at the Gardens was how many local education officials were actually *not* supporting him. Despite enjoying so much success in the education portfolio, Davis discovered that his reduction of school boards cost him dearly at the convention. Years later he told Liberal MPP Sean Conway, "You know, young Mr. Conway, you'd be surprised how many of those people showed up at Maple Leaf Gardens with Al Lawrence buttons on."

Appropriately, given the venue, Bill Davis was nominated by a fellow Tory MPP who knew the building well — Stanley Cup champion Syl Apps, who played for the Maple Leafs from 1936 to 1948 and had represented Kingston and the Islands in Ontario's legislature since 1963.

However, almost from the get-go, nothing else at this convention went according to Hoyle. Party President Alan Eagleson, the hockey agent and executive director of the National Hockey League Players' Association, explained to the delegates how the party's newfangled voting machines were supposed to work, and at 3:00 p.m. delegates lined up to cast their ballots. But just before 5:00 p.m. as scrutineers were counting that first ballot, someone realized the number of delegates who had voted and the number of votes counted by the voting machines didn't match. In fact, the votes of 140 delegates simply didn't register at all with the machines. That represented nearly 10 percent of the voters. "We got some fantastic errors," said Elmer Bell, the convention's deputy elections officer.

A little background is in order here. The PCs wanted to show Ontarians how modern and progressive they were, so they introduced voting machines at this convention, replacing old-fashioned paper ballots and boxes. The man who won the contract to provide the machines was a fellow named Thomas "Windy" O'Neill, who was actually a card-carrying Liberal Party member. It didn't take long for conspiracy theorists to suggest that O'Neill was attempting to embarrass the Tories by sabotaging their convention. For his part, O'Neill insisted the machines worked when he tested them, and besides, they weren't his, anyway. He was merely the Canadian agent for an American company and was renting them.

A quick "what-the-hell-do-we-do" meeting took place among party organizers and the campaigns, and it was unanimously agreed that the first ballot results needed to be tossed out. When Eagleson announced that decision to the delegates, the Gardens cascaded with boos. At 6:20 p.m. delegates learned they would have to do the first ballot over again, but not right away, since someone had to run to Toronto City Hall and collect metal boxes while others mimeographed new paper ballots with the candidates' names on them. By 7:30 pm, the CBC's Ontario network bailed on covering the convention — there was only so much filling without results that the public broadcaster could do — but returned at 8:15 p.m. and stayed the rest of the way. Robarts, who could be a real curmudgeon when things didn't go to his liking, grumbled about being overburdened by technology.

"I don't mind licking my particular stub of pencil and marking my X as I've done many times before," he said, trying to make the best of an exasperating situation.

The *Timmins Press* agreed, offering this editorial a few days later: "Perhaps it would be a good idea to stay with the tried and true method of simply marking an 'X.'" The PC Party evidently concurs and has used paper ballots and pencils in every subsequent leadership vote, including the one on May 9, 2015, which chose Patrick Brown over Christine Elliott. Apparently, the PCs have raged against the machine.

In the midst of all of this confusion, Darcy McKeough experienced what he has subsequently referred to as "the greatest moment in my life."

You have to remember that McKeough idolized John Robarts — absolutely worshipped him. McKeough's first election was in 1963, also Robarts's first election as premier. It was Robarts who gave him his first cabinet job at age 33. Joyce and Darcy McKeough even named the premier as godfather to their second son, Jamie. So when John Parmenter Robarts walked over to the McKeough box and said to Joyce, "I voted for my godson's father on the first ballot!" the McKeoughs couldn't have been prouder. "I will go to the grave with that!" McKeough says in his memoir, *The Duke of Kent*, about the honour paid to him on that day by the boss.

The significance of the voting machine snafu would prove to be fatal for Allan Lawrence's campaign, even though he didn't realize it yet. It took another hour and 25 minutes for the "second first ballot" voting to take place, and by the time the results were announced, it was already 9:00 p.m.

As expected, Bill Davis led on the first ballot but with what must have been considered a disappointing number, given all the establishment fire-power behind him. Davis captured 548 votes, good for only 33.1 percent. Allan Lawrence was nipping at his heels with 431 votes, good for 26 percent of the votes cast. The rest of the pack seemed too far back to win, but clearly, depending on how long each candidate remained on the ballot or which of the leading candidates they moved to, someone could play kingmaker. Darcy McKeough came third, scoring 273 votes and representing only 16.5 percent of the delegates, while Robert Welch had just missed third place himself with 270 votes or 16.3 percent of the total. Bert Lawrence, as expected, had almost no support with just 128 votes (7.7 percent) and Robert Pharand completed the leader board with seven votes, or 0.4 percent. Canadians were still five years away from Joe Clark's improbable 1976 national PC leadership victory from third place on the first ballot. The fact was, at this point in Ontario's history every convention victor was in either first or second place on the first ballot. So everyone in that arena now knew their next leader would be Bill Davis or Allan Lawrence.

As the last-place finisher on the first ballot, Pharand was obliged to drop out and he did so without endorsing any of the other candidates. Bert Lawrence did the same, despite entreaties from Darcy McKeough's camp to hang in there for another ballot. Since Lawrence surpassed 5 percent of the votes cast, he wasn't obliged to drop off, and McKeough's father-in-law, Senator David Walker, urged him to stay, figuring the longer the contest went on, the better chance McKeough had to work a deal with Bob Welch and become more competitive. But it didn't happen, and Bert Lawrence's night came to an end, with no endorsement in the offing. In fact, when someone from the Allan Lawrence camp threw a campaign kerchief into the Bert Lawrence section of the stands, it was quickly tossed right back out. So, four candidates would remain for the second ballot, which didn't get under way until 10:00 p.m. Again, the campaigns still had no idea how impactful the lateness of the voting would prove to be.

Bob Welch had desperately tried to gain some traction in his campaign by being the guy everyone liked. He loved to toss his script aside and speak from the heart and did so in dramatic fashion. But after the second ballot his campaign was done. Only three votes behind McKeough on the first ballot, Welch found himself further behind after the second ballot, 288 to 271. While McKeough gained nearly 1 percent more votes, Welch saw his tally rise only 0.1 percent. Meanwhile, Davis was now at 595 votes (good for 36 percent), while Allan Lawrence narrowed the gap just a bit more with 498 votes (good for 30.1 percent).

At that moment Welch could have played a significant role by tipping the balance for one of the two front-runners, or by breathing additional life into McKeough's campaign. But he didn't. Despite a 20-minute private conversation between Welch and McKeough, the MPP from Lincoln dropped out without endorsing anyone, insisting it would have gone against the grain of his whole campaign for a more open party and no backroom deals. Davis supporters were warned not to be too overzealous in their courting of Welch's delegates. They didn't want any heavy-handedness backfiring against their candidate. Having said that, when Welch delegate Dr. Matthew Dymond, a former leadership candidate himself in the 1961 contest, pulled a Davis button out of his suit pocket and put it on, a Davis worker got on the phone and yelled, "We need more Davis buttons in the Welch area!" It was getting late, and it was getting tense.

At 20 minutes after midnight the third-ballot results were announced. Again, the order was the same, but the numbers were tightening in excruciating fashion. Davis led with 669 votes, only good for 41.3 percent. Allan Lawrence was now less than 4 percentage points behind: 606 votes, or 37.4 percent. Now all eyes were on Darcy McKeough, who by coming third, was forced off the final ballot. What would the Duke of Kent do? Every other candidate had dropped out without endorsing anyone. With 346 votes (21.3 percent of the total), McKeough had the power and the numbers to be kingmaker. Davis supporters busily pressed their man's buttons into the hands of McKeough delegates. But could they attract enough of them?

Neil MacPhee, president of the Windsor-Walkerville PC Association and a relative of Davis's from his marriage to his first wife, Helen, had told his candidate more than an hour ago that he had it on good authority that McKeough would endorse Davis. "That'll finish it," Davis responded.

At 35 minutes after midnight, the phone in Davis's box rang. The candidate had a brief conversation with someone, then told one of his supporters standing next to him, "Darcy and George Kerr are coming over." (Cabinet Minister Kerr was the only cabinet minister to endorse McKeough.)

At this moment something happened that no one can quite explain, not even the candidate who did it. Observers wrongly assume the choreography of a leadership convention is all set in stone before the first ballot is cast. Surely, deals that have been made before the convention will be executed on the convention floor as planned. Surely, everyone knows what everyone is going to do. Except the dynamics of a leadership convention can be completely unpredictable.

In this same building 25 years into the future, Dwight Duncan finished ahead of Dalton McGuinty on the first ballot. According to the deal Duncan *thought* he had with McGuinty, the latter was supposed to drop off the ballot and endorse him. Duncan was even caught on camera looking across the floor of Maple Leaf Gardens at McGuinty's box, saying, "Come on, Dalton. Come to Papa." But McGuinty didn't move. He was within spitting distance of Duncan's vote total, so he broke the deal (if, in fact, there ever was one) and stayed on to fight again. It turned out to be the right decision, since eventually McGuinty did win.

Similarly, in 2013, in the same building where Liberals gathered to replace McGuinty, cabinet minister Eric Hoskins dropped off after the first ballot and headed for first-place finisher Sandra Pupatello's section of the arena because that was the deal the two of them had made before convention day. But Hoskins stopped, intercepted by Party President Greg Sorbara, who told him something the cameras couldn't hear. Suddenly, Hoskins changed direction and walked toward second-place finisher Kathleen Wynne's box. In both cases the noise, the hoopla, the last-minute intervention, or maybe just the confusion of convention day, brought an unanticipated dynamic to the proceedings.

Darcy McKeough also had that convention-day dynamic affect him, or so it seemed. McKeough marched toward Bill Davis's box. Was he going to endorse him? Davis thought so. The front-runner was there, hand outstretched, ready to welcome the kingmaker to his team. But McKeough kept right on going. He disappeared into the melee as a perplexed Davis wondered what had just happened. McKeough went into a hallway, away from the prying television cameras, for a last-minute confab with his team. The momentum was with Allan Lawrence. Since trailing by 7 percentage points on the first ballot, Lawrence had narrowed the gap with each successive ballot to the point where he and Davis were now less than 4 points apart.

What was McKeough going to do?

It might well be that McKeough needed some time to compose himself because this was the first time he'd ever competed for something and lost. As his mother told *Toronto Star* writer Sally Barnes, "Even as a boy he always won everything he tried." But not this time. The municipal affairs minister returned to the scene of so much bedlam, marched back to Davis's box, and grabbed the education minister's hand.

More than 44 years after this convention, I called Darcy McKeough at his home in Chatham-Kent to ask him what had happened at that moment. Why did he brush past Davis's outstretched hand and delay his endorsement?

"I have no recollection of that at all," McKeough, now 83, says. "Maybe I walked right by him because I just didn't see him."

That's a completely plausible explanation. The chaotic atmosphere of a convention can do that. Plus, there was never any question where McKeough would go if he wasn't successful. To this day he is adamant that there were "no deals" between his camp and Davis's. However, McKeough adds, "I'd always known what I was going to do."

In any other convention, McKeough's move to Davis would have sealed the deal for the front-runner. But, as we've seen, this was no ordinary convention. The lateness of the hour had also become a full-fledged crisis for Allan Lawrence. Some of Lawrence's key supporters were from Northern Ontario and many of them had left the Gardens to get a head start on the trip home. There was a howling blizzard outside the arena. "The snow was so thick you could hardly get to the subway," recalled cabinet minister Tom Wells. None of the northern delegates could have imagined they'd still be at the convention in the wee small hours of the morning, and some had organized late flights or bus trips home. In addition, Darcy McKeough's efforts to be the kingmaker didn't go as well as hoped. It became apparent that fewer than half of his delegates would follow him to Bill Davis. Would the choice of who would lead the nearly three-decades-old Tory dynasty really be determined by some delegates needing to catch a bus?

At two o'clock in the morning the fourth and final ballot results were announced. The evening started with 1,689 registered delegates eligible to vote. Four ballots later more than 100 delegates had left and it was a reasonable supposition that most of them were for Allan Lawrence. Notwithstanding the travel plans of some of his northern delegates, Lawrence's momentum continued. But it just wasn't quite enough. An accountant from Hamilton named Bruno Bragoli mounted a nearly 13-foot-high ladder, stood precariously at the top of it, and swivelled the scoreboard so that it faced the crowd, revealing the final count: Bill Davis, 812 votes, Allan Lawrence, 768 votes. After all was said and done, *it was only a forty-four-vote difference.*

Kathleen Davis put her arms around her husband, who had just won with an underwhelming 51.4 percent of the vote and said, "I'm supposed to give you a kiss," then did so in the only footage I can ever recall seeing of the candidate and his wife kissing each other on the lips in public. While Kathy looked affectionate, the candidate looked dazed, perhaps not sure he'd really won, perhaps astonished at the closeness of a race he was supposed to win going away, or perhaps uncomfortable at the public display of affection.

However, that kiss might not be Kathy Davis's chief recollection of the convention. At one point an overzealous supporter hopped over the railing into the box where the Davis family was gathered and sent Mrs. Davis sprawling backward into her seat. He continued on without an apology in order to shake the hand of the winner. Mrs. Davis first appeared startled, then ticked off, then put the two youngest Davis children (Ian, nine, and Meg, seven) in the row behind her for safety.

Consistent with every other oddity that could have happened on this day, even the announcement of Davis's victory didn't come off cleanly.

"The new prime minister of Ontario is … Bill Davis!" shouted Party President Alan Eagleson from the podium.

Except it wasn't true. And Arthur Harnett, the PC Party's executive director, knew it. He leaned over to Eagleson and reminded him, "Not yet, Alan."

Eagleson tried again. "The new leader of the Progressive Conservative Party of Ontario is Bill Davis. The Honourable John Robarts is still the premier."

Correct.

With all eyes in the Gardens now on Davis, the winner picked up his seven-year-old daughter, Meg, and began addressing a media scrum. Meg had already won plenty of hearts on the day with a homemade sign that read: VOTE FOR DADDY.

When Robarts got to the stage to congratulate all the candidates, the soon-to-be former premier decided this was no time for a long speech. So he made it short, sweet, and memorable. "I've achieved my objective," he told the audience. "I'm a has-been!" And then, in a very touching and very un-Robarts-like fashion, he concluded with, "I love you all." Politicians, even curmudgeons such as Robarts, can get mushy when they realize, it's really over. And for all intents and purposes, for the Chairman of the Board it really was now over.

The immediate postscript to this convention was somewhat predictable. The Liberals, having already predicted Davis's victory, circulated a news release on the floor of the arena congratulating the new leader and calling him "an incoming caretaker of an outgoing government."

Party President Alan Eagleson threatened to sue over the voting machine foul-up. "Windy" O'Neill mused about launching a lawsuit, as well, but put the blame on the delegates. He said American voters had used the same machines for 55 years with no problems. "So I know it's not the machine," he said. "It must have been the delegates' fault." Regardless, those machines cost the PC Party four hours of organizational headaches and might very well have cost Allan Lawrence the leadership.

Perhaps the most unusual postscript of the 1971 Ontario PC leadership convention came from the iconoclastic Dalton Camp. The former national party leader was one of the most polarizing forces in Canadian politics. Some Tories despised him because he'd led the revolt to review

John Diefenbaker's increasingly bizarre leadership. Others praised him for having the guts to stand up to a leader who had become more autocratic, more paranoid, and more out of touch with reality.

Writing in the *Toronto Telegram* at the convention's conclusion, Camp offered the following observation about the man the Tories had just narrowly chosen to lead them into the next election: "The trouble with the campaign was, from its outset, that Bill Davis, believed to be a certain winner, ran under wraps, throwing nothing away, accepting whatever came his way and he passed through the convention still an enigma. Now, it might be asked, will the real Bill Davis please stand up?"

The *real* Bill Davis? It would take years for Davis to feel sufficiently comfortable as premier to show his *real* personality to the public. In the meantime there was a cabinet to pick, a Speech from the Throne to write, a budget to deliver, and some big decisions to be made, including a future election date to select. And the man ultimately responsible for doing all of that would be William Grenville Davis, the 18th premier of the Province of Ontario.

6

TRANSITION

The smartest decision Bill Davis made after winning the leadership of his party was to listen to Roy McMurtry, his friend, who would go on to become one of the most distinguished public servants in Canadian history. In February 1971, though, McMurtry was a 38-year-old lawyer and Progressive Conservative activist who saw his party at a crossroads.

Leadership conventions almost by design create tensions within a political family. Activists who normally work together on issues, and more often than not feel the same way about those policies, are suddenly thrust into the uncomfortable position of having to choose one friend over another. Feelings get hurt. Things get said that can't be taken back. Friends become foes. And when the result of a party's leadership choice is razor-thin, the contest, in effect, never really comes to an end. Unless the runner-up is handled very carefully, bitterness over losing can ensue and the party never really does unite around its new leader.

McMurtry knew all this, which is why he thought it was imperative for the Bill Davis team and the Allan Lawrence team to get together soon after the convention. At this point the Tories had been in power for 28 straight years, but every time the governing party changes leaders, it creates a new dynamic. McMurtry wanted to ensure that nobody's nose got any further out of joint than it already was and that all the convention players now realized "job one" was coming together and winning the next election, which was probably going to take place later that year.

Given his friendship with Bill Davis going back to their University of Toronto days together, you might assume McMurtry had worked on the Davis campaign. But he didn't. McMurtry had suffered a debilitating back injury in the lead-up to the convention, and as a result, was on the sidelines for the whole thing. That turned out to be a very useful thing in terms of his next role: playing peacemaker between the Davis and Lawrence camps.

Fortunately, Progressive Conservative delegates had chosen a leader who didn't hold grudges. Even more than that, Bill Davis quickly realized that the team supporting Allan Lawrence was far superior to his own. He'd had every imaginable advantage going into the leadership race, and yet had barely eked out the win. Whoever these brainiacs were on the Lawrence campaign, Bill Davis knew one thing about them — he wanted them working for him now.

So immediately after the convention, McMurtry went to one of Davis's most trusted confidants, Hugh Macaulay, half of a dynamic brother combination in Ontario politics. His brother, Robert, was a minister in John Robarts's government, and Bill Davis had run Robert's leadership campaign against Robarts 10 years earlier. So the players were close friends and allies. McMurtry urged Hugh Macaulay to convince the new leader to put together a meeting so that both sides could hammer out their differences and move forward. Macaulay made the pitch and Davis readily agreed. "I was out to make peace between the two organizations," Davis recalls more than four decades later. "But the bottom line was, we were all Tories and they wanted to be helpful."

The meeting took place one week after the convention at the National Club on Bay Street in downtown Toronto. To be sure, there was some awkwardness as the confab began. But Davis started the meeting by giving some strong, unifying remarks that hit all the right notes. He was accompanied by confidants Hugh Macaulay and Clare Westcott. Lawrence campaign organizers such as Norman Atkins, Dalton Camp, Ross DeGeer, Paul Weed, and Bill Saunderson all embraced the challenge of working for the new premier of Ontario. After all, as Davis now says, "there wasn't *much* bitterness off the top of the meeting because these were the same people who wanted me to run for the leadership. It would have been hard for them to be mad at me, since six months earlier they all wanted to work on my team."

The meeting by all accounts went extremely well. Davis did what he did best — he listened intently as Atkins laid out how he saw the year ahead. The new party leader was very receptive, even though it was only the second time he'd ever met Atkins. "The first time was in 1963 when he was getting a shoeshine in the Park Plaza," Atkins told the *Toronto Star* all those years ago. After the formal proceedings were over, Davis, Atkins, and McMurtry went out for late-night drinks at Sutton Place Hotel, a rarity for the new PC leader. The hope was that Davis and Atkins would truly hit it off and get more comfortable with each other, and clearly that happened. Eventually, Davis developed a deep and respectful bond with Atkins, even repeatedly teasing him for years to come for nearly torpedoing his political career at Maple Leaf Gardens.

Shortly after their get-together, Davis tapped Atkins to manage the next provincial election campaign, the date of which was still to be determined. After the federal PCs had lost the 1968 election to Pierre Trudeau's Liberals, Atkins and Malcolm Wickson, the party's national director, had developed a new election plan that was ready to go. The next Ontario election would be the guinea pig for that plan. This was, in effect, the beginning of the legendary Big Blue Machine, even if technically it still hadn't been christened as such.

The two campaign teams therefore coalesced well around their new mission, namely, winning the next general election whenever Bill Davis wanted to call it. In the spring, many of them got together one Monday morning at the now long-gone Theodore's restaurant to begin working on the strategy they hoped would lead to another Tory majority. They called themselves the Monday Morning Breakfast Club. Norman Atkins, Clare Westcott, Hugh Macaulay, and Roy McMurtry were all there and agreed on an historic change in emphasis for an Ontario election campaign: it would be focused on television, not the newspapers. It would "sell" the grey Bill Davis as a strong leader in the same way the Republicans sold an unlikeable Richard Nixon as a strong leader in that party's successful presidential campaign three years earlier.

Two weeks after Davis won his party's leadership he was sworn in as Ontario's 18th and last "prime minister." Perhaps some explanation about the title of Ontario's first minister is in order here. Before Confederation, the term *prime minister* was reserved for the head of the government in

the United Kingdom. Canadian first ministers were referred to as *premier*.
Then, from Confederation in 1867 until 1905, it seems the terms *prime
minister* and *premier* were used fairly interchangeably. However, when
James P. Whitney came to office in 1905, he formally changed the title to
prime minister of Ontario. After Whitney's departure in 1914, the next
several first ministers used both titles interchangeably. Even the mercurial
Liberal Mitchell Hepburn apparently employed both titles, although I'd
always heard that he preferred to be called prime minister, so as to seem on
equal footing with arch-nemesis William Lyon Mackenzie King, the prime
minister of Canada. Again, for no particular reason anyone can remember,
once the Tories returned to power in 1943, George Drew preferred to be
known only as "prime minister." Robert Nixon, whose father, Harry, was
the last Liberal premier in 1943 before the 42-year-long Tory dynasty took
hold, once joked in a legislative debate in 1971 about the title change.

"My dad used to be premier of Ontario," Nixon began, "and he said
one time that the biggest change after the election in 1943 was that all
of the stationery that had been imprinted and embossed 'Office of the
Premier' was thrown out by the new incumbent and new stationery was
printed up and embossed 'Office of the Prime Minister.'" Part of the thinking might have related to Quebec where the first minister is called *premier
ministre*. So perhaps Drew thought that if it was good enough for Quebec,
it ought to be good enough for Ontario, as well.

One of the first questions John Robarts got in 1961 after winning the job
was: "Are you officially going to change the title back to premier?" Robarts
didn't seem to care much either way but responded that "prime minister"
was the name that was already on the door of the office, and since it would
cost something to remove it and put a new sign up, he might as well leave it
the way it was. And so he did. Besides, he'd say, "Just call me John."

William Davis, however, believed that Canada ought to have just
one prime minister and that man resided at 24 Sussex Drive and worked
on Parliament Hill. And so he asked the highly respected University of
Toronto historian J.M.S. Careless to research the issue for him. Careless
eventually reported back to Davis, and although there was no official announcement in the legislature, William Grenville Davis became
Ontario's last "prime minister." For almost the first year of his tenure,
the sign on Davis's office door and the salutation the receptionist offered

when answering the phone were "Prime Minister William Davis's Office." But on February 28, 1972, on letterhead emblazoned with "Department of the Prime Minister," James Fleck, Davis's chief executive officer, sent a memo to all staff, saying that all ensuing press releases, speeches, and references coming out of that office would henceforth refer to Davis exclusively as "premier." The "prime minister" letterhead would continue to be used until its stock was exhausted, which happened in September. Interestingly, it wasn't until 1983 that the law was actually changed, relegating "prime minister of Ontario" to the historical anachronism bin and making "premier of Ontario" the legal and official title. The *Hamilton Spectator* approved, but not without taking a bit of a kick at Davis at the same time, saying: "We are glad Mr. Davis cracked down on this growing habit of self aggrandizement before it really got out of hand."

From where he was sitting, it was hard for Davis to have feelings of self-aggrandizement. After all, Nick Lorito, his driver, who had almost become a member of the family over the past five years, brought an urgent problem to Davis's attention.

"Who do I work for?" Lorito asked the new premier.

"You work for me, Nick," Davis replied. "Why?"

"Well, apparently there are a lot of people who worked for the old premier who think I work for them," said Lorito, who was becoming increasingly frustrated at the number of Robarts cronies who wanted him to drive them around.

Without ruffling feathers, Davis found a solution to the driver problem. "Every time they asked me to do something for them, Mr. D would tell me to wait around," Lorito says. "'You may have to get Mrs. Davis soon,' he'd say. They stopped asking after two weeks of that."

On another occasion, Davis saw Lorito at a PC convention at Mansfield in Central Ontario. He told him, "Go hide somewhere for an hour. Quick, get lost." Lorito didn't get it but did as he was told. An hour later the premier explained. Apparently, Darcy McKeough was looking for a ride home to Chatham. Davis, not wanting to disappoint his cabinet colleague, agreed to McKeough's request, but then told Lorito to shoo, so his driver wouldn't have to make the trek to Chatham.

In any event, it was a warm moment for the Davis family on March 1, 1971, when the pride of Brampton, Ontario, was officially sworn into office by Lieutenant Governor William Ross Macdonald. Davis's parents were there on the floor of the legislature to watch the swearing-in, at which the new premier used his father's Bible.

Perhaps surprisingly and maybe with the benefit of four and a half decades of hindsight, Davis now says adjusting from senior cabinet minister to premier wasn't that tall a task. He had spent more than a decade on the government benches, including more than eight as a senior cabinet minister. He had a close relationship with the man he was replacing, so even at age 41 he was well prepared for the job. And he knew his fellow cabinet ministers well, having served with them for so long. In other words, Davis felt quite ready to be premier of Ontario.

Choosing a cabinet is often the most thankless task any first minister has. Everyone in caucus feels they deserve to be in but, of course, most won't get in. Some get in not because of any particular genius on their part but because the premier likes them, or needs that region of the province represented at the cabinet table, or perhaps the MPP won his seat by a narrow margin and the premier wants to help solidify his election prospects for next time. There are myriad considerations. Many of those who get in think they should be in more senior portfolios than what the premier ultimately offered. It is one of the most complicated of all political arts, and Davis has admitted many times over the years that it was the hardest part of his job as premier for two reasons. First, he found it exceedingly painful to have to tell someone, "I am dropping you from cabinet," knowing what that would do to the colleague's self-esteem. And second, losing a seat at the cabinet table also meant taking a large pay cut, no doubt causing added stress to the personal finances of many members.

Of course, when it came to balancing all those competing interests nearly half a century ago, it was much easier than today. For example, in his final cabinet, John Robarts had no representatives from the Italian, Portuguese, South Asian, Asian, or black communities, and for obvious reasons: there were no representatives to choose from in his caucus from those communities. None had ever been elected yet. There was one woman in caucus (Ada Pritchard from Hamilton), but there was certainly no hue and cry to include her in the cabinet ahead of the many more experienced male MPPs. Almost every single cabinet minister was white, male, and Protestant. Diversity in cabinet consisted of two francophone ministers

(Fernand Guindon and René Brunelle), one Jew (Allan Grossman), and the first-ever Ukrainian Canadian elected to the legislature (John Yaremko).

But when Bill Davis took over the responsibilities of cabinet-making, it was a new decade and Ontario was starting to hear the rustlings of a need for more inclusiveness on the executive council. The province was just beginning to become increasingly multicultural, and there were now two women on the Tory backbenches. How would Davis respond?

By the standards of the day, the new premier made a huge splash with his new cabinet. Davis took what John Robarts had left him, completely redesigned it, and according to the youngest member of the new 29th legislature, "The transition from Robarts to Davis was seamless," said Dennis Timbrell four and a half decades later. "Premier Davis was clearly in charge."

Of the 23 members of the first Davis cabinet, only two ministers retained the portfolios they previously held under Robarts. Davis dropped a handful of Robarts ministers, mostly because they had already indicated they wouldn't be running again, and introduced some new faces to the cabinet. For example, Syl Apps, the Stanley Cup champion and former captain of the Toronto Maple Leafs, had been on Robarts's backbench since 1963, so Davis installed him as correctional services minister. Similarly, Kenora's Leo Bernier had been a backbencher since 1966 but won a promotion to a revamped Ministry of Mines and Northern Affairs, which he would hold for 14 years. In fact, Bernier would become such a fixture in the job that he was eventually nicknamed "Emperor of the North." And Jim Snow, who won his first election in 1967 in Halton East by just 164 votes, was elevated to the cabinet as a minister without portfolio. He, too, would subsequently have a long, influential run in cabinet as transportation minister for 10 years and would have a highway in Halton Region named after him.

Again, another indication of how much Davis trusted his driver, Nick Lorito, could be seen in the selection of the cabinet. Lorito was there, at Davis's home in Brampton, when the premier and his closest advisers chewed over possible options. Lorito was at the house and found out who the new ministers were before the ministers themselves did. "I'd be there in the kitchen when they made the cabinet," he says. "Mr. D would tell me, 'Your job is to hook up new ministers with good drivers.' I was treated better than some ministers were," Lorito marvels without an ounce of boasting in his voice.

Of course, the biggest thing observers were looking for was to see how Davis would treat those he had defeated at the leadership convention two weeks earlier, and on that score the new premier was clearly indicating those battles were over and it was time to unify and look forward. Allan Lawrence won a huge promotion from minister responsible for the province's mining industry to minister of justice and attorney general. Darcy McKeough, who had brought just enough delegates over on the fourth ballot to make Davis the winner, also earned a significant promotion — from municipal affairs minister to the new, revamped treasurer, minister of economics, and chairman of the treasury board of cabinet, which approved every government expenditure. Davis clearly held no hard feelings for Robert Welch, since he gave the Lincoln MPP his former job as minister of education. Even Bert Lawrence, who was often critical of Davis during the campaign and got very few delegates to show for his troubles, earned a big bump up from minister of financial and commercial affairs to minister of health. Meanwhile, Charles MacNaughton, Davis's leadership campaign chair who shooed away some of the best talent that could have helped his candidate, was now 60 years old and looked older. MacNaughton was demoted from treasurer to minister for highways and transport, but at least he survived the shuffle. In terms of diversity in the cabinet, there were still two francophone ministers (Tourism Minister Fernand Guindon and Lands and Forests Minister René Brunelle), still one Ukrainian (John Yaremko, moved to the Ministry of Citizenship), and one Jew (Allan Grossman won a major promotion from corrections to trade and development).

But still no women, and that became increasingly problematic.

Yes, Davis won significant kudos for so dramatically re-engineering his cabinet and for being so generous to his leadership rivals. But reporters started inquiring as to why, with two capable women now in his caucus, Davis had decided to appoint neither one to cabinet. The premier said all the things one normally says in these circumstances: "Cabinet-making is difficult, there are many considerations to balance, I'm not saying no forever, but just not yet," et cetera. For their part, both Margaret Scrivener and Margaret Birch demonstrated they were good team players. Neither publicly complained about being excluded and both said all the right things about not expecting to be appointed and needing to learn the job of an MPP first. In a sense, Davis was damned if he did and damned if he didn't. By not putting one of his female MPPs in cabinet, he left himself open to charges that he was behind the times and not in touch with the aspirations of half the Ontario population. However, had he appointed one of the Margarets to cabinet, he'd surely have been accused of tokenism. Regardless, the issue of an all-male cabinet at the dawn of the 1970s wasn't going to go away.

Nineteen seventy-two was a leap year, and the Speech from the Throne took place on February 29. Lieutenant Governor W. Ross Macdonald read the speech opening the second session of the 29th Parliament, and it was not what you'd call a barnburner. Throne speeches are generally supposed to be high on rhetoric and short on detail. They're meant to be an overarching vision of the government's agenda. But the following lines were actually written into the 1972 Speech from the Throne: "The Farm Products Marketing Act and The Ontario Milk Act will be amended to reflect the principles of recommendations contained in the recent report of the Royal Commission Inquiry into Civil Rights. Amendments to The Edible Oil Products Act to permit the blending of certain dairy products with edible oil products will be proposed." With poetry like that it's not hard to understand why the Queen's Park press gallery was often so frustrated at the lack of news the government seemed to go out of its way not to make.

But also tucked into the speech one page later was this: "My Government, in considering the observations and recommendations of the Williston Report, will accelerate its efforts to provide improved treatment and facilities for the mentally ill, and expand the scope and availability of training programs for the retarded within their home communities." Nearly half a century ago, when few other jurisdictions in North America cared about these things, the Davis government had mental health issues on its radar screen.

Soon after Davis became premier, his office received a letter from a young Progressive Conservative who thought Ontario's first minister needed to be a little more in touch with young people's values. The letter writer advised Davis that if he wanted to secure more youth votes in the next provincial election, he'd do well to lower the drinking age to 18 from 21, and while he was at it, why not lower the voting age, as well? A few weeks later the writer got an official reply from the premier. And what so impressed him was that the letter was signed "Bill," *in ink*, not in "autopen." John Tory was so moved at getting a personally signed reply from Ontario's premier that he's kept that letter as a souvenir for the past 45 years. It was only when Tory became Davis's principal secretary a decade later that he came to realize that several staffers in the premier's office made it a point to learn how to replicate the premier's signature *in ink* to lighten Davis's workload. Tory never had the heart to ask Davis whether the "Bill" on that prized letter was legit or just scrawled by someone who knew how to copy Davis's signature well, not that Davis would remember, anyway. But Tory has kept the letter nonetheless.

If you've ever wondered what the first law the new Davis government passed, wonder no more. It was called the "chicken and egg" bill, and reporters had a field day writing about it. The bill empowered local marketing boards to seize any agricultural products marketed in Ontario without a permit. The idea was to curb imports of farm products from other provinces, especially Quebec. The bill passed in the legislature on April 15 "after the opposition had *pecked* away at it for more than six hours," according to the *Toronto Star*.

One of the intriguing things that really emerged during the debate on the throne speech was a budding respect, even affection that was developing between the leader of the Progressive Conservative Party and the leader of the New Democratic Party. Stephen Lewis looked across the floor of the legislature at his opposite number and began his cheery response to the throne speech. "It is a different premier today, is it not?" Lewis began. "A little more sartorial elegance, I may say in the latter weeks, chaperoned as you are by Arthur Harnett and under contract to Alan Eagleson and programmed by Martin Goldfarb."

"You left out my wife!" Davis interrupted, clearly getting into the spirit of the thing.

"I'm going to get to that," Lewis retorted. Then, referring to recent reports that the PC Party president was complaining because Kathleen Davis's skirts were too long, Lewis added, "What right does Alan Eagleson have to comment on the length of Kathy's skirts?" A ripple of laughter went through the legislature.

Lewis was on a roll. Referencing Goldfarb's previous work for a razor company, the NDP leader imagined "Tory commercials with Bill Davis shaving with a Wilkinson blade …"

"Are they made here?" Davis interjected with a laugh.

And so it went. Nowadays it would be unusual for the first minister even to be in the legislature when the leader of the third party was offering his or her response to the throne speech. Davis was not only there but playing off Lewis's shtick as both men thoroughly enjoyed the camaraderie of the moment.

Before April 1971 was over, however, Davis would be reminded in stark fashion about an issue that simply wouldn't go away. The premier met with Pierre Trudeau, his federal counterpart, on April 23 in Ottawa, then borrowed Trudeau's Lockheed JetStar to fly to Windsor for a meet-the-people tour. But the tour got off to a shaky start when 250 Catholic school students lined the driveway leading to the airport, chanting, "Save us, Davis!" The premier required seven police officers to create a cordon to protect him.

But again, in contrast to what you might see in today's brand of politics, rather than ignoring the students, Davis waded right in and met with a delegation of three of them. "Is there anything new you want to tell us?" asked Bill MacDonald, the 17-year-old head of the delegation.

"I quite understand what you are demonstrating for," said Davis, now completely surrounded by the students who had stopped chanting to listen.

"We need money, not talk!" another student shouted from the crowd. "We'll have no schools by the time you're finished," offered another.

Davis would only commit to responding "soon" to an official request for more money from separate school trustees. "You never get too far in talking to Mr. Davis," said MacDonald after the meeting. "But it's nice to talk to him, anyway."

Funding for the Roman Catholic school system was an issue that would never go away for Davis, not in April 1971, not in the election campaign to come, and not 13 years later when it blasted onto the Ontario political stratosphere when least expected. Nevertheless, the last "prime minister" of Ontario was now firmly ensconced in the job. He had moved past the rivalries from the leadership convention. He had dramatically reworked the cabinet that would run the government. Now it was time to *really* change the channel on something big.

7

SPADINA

One of the first meetings Bill Davis had after winning the PC leadership at Maple Leaf Gardens was with the man he was about to replace: John Roberts. The outgoing premier wanted to let his successor know that, in his view, the government was comfortably on top of all of the major issues of the day — with two exceptions.

"I've only left you two issues," Roberts said to Davis. "The Bishop's Brief ... and Spadina."

Davis had to smile. It was as if Roberts was saying, "I've been the starting pitcher and I'm now leaving in the ninth inning with the bases loaded and nobody out in a tie game. Okay, Bill, get us out of this jam, and there's no room for error." Roberts gave Davis no advice on how to decide these matters.

The Bishop's Brief referred to the increasing calls among the province's Catholic leadership for more public funding for the separate school system. Roberts and Davis had thought they'd put this issue to rest for a generation back in 1964 with the province's new so-called "Foundation Tax Plan." The plan obliged school boards across the province to raise a certain amount of money through local property taxes, then the province would step in with additional grants to bring every board up to a "foundation" level, theoretically creating a more equitable system. But boards were allowed to raise and spend funds beyond the foundation level as long as those funds came from local taxes. It was an acknowledgement that richer cities with more needs could spend more if they wanted. Of course, it also had the perverse effect of exacerbating the gap between richer and poorer schools. Catholic schools, for example, felt they were falling farther and farther behind.

And then there was "Spadina."

For a decade the battle over the Spadina Expressway had been *the* most intractable urban affairs battle in the history of Ontario's capital. It was one of those issues that perfectly reflected the differing priorities of those who lived in the "old city" of Toronto and those who lived in the inner suburbs of North York, Etobicoke, and Scarborough. Toronto City Council, representing the old city, was adamantly opposed to Spadina. It didn't want a new expressway coming in from the northwest part of the city and ripping up their inner-city neighbourhoods. Conversely, Metropolitan Toronto Council, the majority of whose members were made up of the suburban municipalities, favoured the expressway and the shorter commute times it supposedly promised. Every planner and engineer at the Metro level of government insisted the highway was essential for Toronto's growth. Building superhighways was a provincial responsibility — all of the so-called "400 series highways" to this point had been built and maintained by the province. But the Spadina Expressway was to be built within the boundaries of Metro Toronto, and as such, Metro Council technically had the final word on the project.

Technically.

Now here were the political realities. Reality number one: the province was expected to kick in for much of the cost of building the expressway. Without that provincial contribution the highway was dead in the water. Both levels of government had already spent a whopping $80 million, and remember those are 1971 dollars. Expressed in today's figures and taking inflation into account, that's nearly $500 million for what at that point was still less than a mile and a half of highway. Reality number two: Ontario's capital was called "Tory Toronto" for a reason. The 1967 election had given 12 seats to the PCs in Metro Toronto, 7 to the NDP, and only 6 to the Liberals. And most significantly, the Spadina Expressway would cut through downtown neighbourhoods that were represented by influential Tories at Queen's Park such as Allan Grossman, John Yaremko, and Leonard Reilly. Grossman and Yaremko were cabinet ministers.

On the first day of March 1971, Bill Davis was sworn in as Ontario's 18th premier. On the last day of May 1971 — just three months into his premiership — Bill Davis made his first truly historic decision. He called one of the members of his new Big Blue Machine, the ad wizard Dalton Camp, and asked him to draft a speech that he, the premier, could deliver in the legislature in three days' time. The subject: overruling the legal decision of another elected level of government and cancelling the Spadina Expressway. Davis knew the decision would unleash a firestorm of criticism, and yet he seemed quite at peace with it all. He told Val Sears of the *Toronto Star* that there was no particular eureka moment when he came to his decision ("not while I was shaving or anything like that"), or any particular relief at making it.

On Thursday, June 3, the record will show Bill Davis gave a noon-hour speech at a Progressive Conservative businessmen's luncheon in Toronto. But his head was definitely elsewhere. At one point he told people he had to get to Queen's Park later that day to make an announcement about "the environment." Reporters started wondering — what could that be about?

That afternoon at the legislature routine proceedings actually started quite routinely. As Lands and Forests Minister René Brunelle rose first to recite the latest forest-fire statistics in the province, there was no hint of the history that was about to be made in such a major way.

Brunelle having finished, Bill Davis rose to his feet. Dalton Camp was watching from the Speaker's Gallery. The speech began innocuously enough: "Mr. Speaker, I should like to inform the House of the Government's decision in the matter of the William R. Allen [Spadina] Expressway." (The highway was to be named after Bill Allen, the Metro Toronto Council chairman from 1962 to 1969.)

Davis spent the next two pages of the speech reminding everyone that Spadina had been debated to death and he had no intention of going through the arguments, for or against, in the legislature today. There was, however, still, no indication of what the premier's announcement was actually going to be.

Then, atop page three, the shocker: "Mr. Speaker, the Government of Ontario does not propose to proceed in support of the plan for the Spadina Expressway." And just like that a decade of planning, politicking, and protesting over Spadina came to an end.

The speech went on for another six pages, but the only part of it anyone remembers was this unforgettable line from the pen of Dalton Camp: "If we are building a transportation system to serve the automobile, the Spadina Expressway would be a good place to start. But if we are building a transportation system to serve people, the Spadina Expressway is a good place to stop." (The full speech is in Appendix 2.)

Spadina was dead. Bill Davis killed it. Four and a half decades later people are *still* debating whether the premier made the right call — that's how monumental a decision this was.

The ramifications of the decision were almost endless:

1. The Democracy: Davis did acknowledge in his speech that the Spadina issue was Toronto's decision to make. "But the Government and Legislature of Ontario have their responsibilities as well, and their interests," he added. In other words, Those of you who think I've subverted the democratic will of the city — not so fast. I've got responsibilities a*nd interests* here, too. One of the politicians his views contravened was his own treasurer, Darcy McKeough, who famously insisted: "This happens to be a matter for local government to determine and we are not about to stick our nose in urban problems."

2. The Power to the People: Davis gave a huge lift to the grassroots protest movements in downtown Toronto, which Metro Council and the majority of members of the Ontario Municipal Board had overruled.

3. The Environment: Davis accepted the arguments of those who said rather than alleviate traffic congestion Spadina would merely encourage more people to get in their cars, further polluting and causing congestion in an already smoggy city.

4. The Politics (I): Davis's Big Blue Machine was in search of an issue that would contrast its man from the (by the end) stodgy, old school John Robarts. With this one decision they positioned Davis as a modern, decisive, ecologically friendly politician. The decision would do

wonders for Davis's political fortunes, although much less for Toronto's traffic woes. The only additional subway capacity added in Toronto by the Davis government was four miles in Scarborough and several underutilized subway stations on the Spadina line from St. George Street north to Wilson Avenue.

5. The Politics (II): Killing Spadina completely took the wind out of the NDP's sails. That party already had the second-largest number of seats in Metro Toronto, and by championing the anti-Spadina forces, the NDP were convinced they would pick up several more seats in the ensuing election. By cancelling the expressway, Davis neutralized the NDP's best urban issue.

Yes, the NDP ultimately got the decision it wanted on Spadina, and ironically, one of the party's apparatchiks helped make it happen. A woman named Ellen Adams, whose title was special assistant to the New Democratic Party caucus, managed to get Davis's executive assistant, Clare Westcott, to come to a secret meeting in the basement of Queen's Park. All the legendary anti-Spadina gang was there, including Colin Vaughan, the architect, future city councillor, Citytv reporter, and father to current Liberal MP Adam Vaughan; Jane Jacobs, author of the hugely influential *The Death and Life of Great American Cities*; and Nadine Nowlan, future city councillor, whose book *The Bad Trip* about Spadina was a big seller. Adams hoped Westcott would take what he learned from the group and go directly back to Davis with his report. And that seems to be exactly what happened. It would cost the NDP in the upcoming election campaign. But the party only had its own operative, Ellen Adams, to blame.

Davis said with a straight face that politics wasn't part of his decision-making calculus. Of course, no one believed that. But he told the *Star*'s Val Sears more than 40 years ago the same thing he told me 40 months ago: "I have never had to make an important decision that went against my personal convictions. I honestly didn't know whether this was good politically or not."

Four months after Davis's announcement Peter Regenstreif, then the head of the Department of Canadian Studies at the University of

Rochester, and soon-to-be well-known Canadian pollster, conducted some surveys on the Spadina issue. He was in the field from October 7 to 11, 1971, and found only 28 percent of Metro Toronto voters endorsed stopping Spadina. Fully 51 percent opposed Davis's decision. For those who believe Bill Davis was only capable of making a big decision once he polled it to death and had the majority of people behind him, these numbers tell a different story.

The Spadina Expressway story didn't end with Bill Davis's decision that day in June 1971. The road was supposed to stop at Lawrence Avenue West in northwest Toronto. But land expropriation and preparation of the highway had already been done farther south, all the way to Eglinton Avenue West. People started calling that unserviced land the "Davis Ditch." So Davis determined in 1975 to allow the expressway to be built to Eglinton. But, he swore, no farther. And he promised to give the "old city" of Toronto a three-foot strip of land at Eglinton to ensure that was where Allen Road would stop forever.

In 1973 Metropolitan Toronto got a new chairman for its council — Paul Godfrey, one of the city's most influential wheeler-dealers. Once upon a time he actually did win an election, that of alderman on North York's council. Somehow he parlayed that relatively junior post into becoming Toronto's most important municipal politician, a job that back then didn't require getting a mandate from the people, but rather simply the majority of the votes of Metro Toronto councillors. And Godfrey almost always had those. Godfrey was pro-Spadina and had a solid relationship but not particularly close friendship with Davis. Still, the Tory Metro chairman and the Tory premier met frequently and worked well together. In 1975 Godfrey took the position that "you can't fight these battles forever," and so he agreed with the compromise to build Spadina only as far as Eglinton to the south. But in exchange he got a concession from Davis to build Highway 400 even farther south to St. Clair Avenue West. Because of the politics involved, the Spadina Expressway was officially renamed the William R. Allen Road. Similarly, so as not to stir up the anti-highway set, Highway 400 south of the 401 is called Black Creek Drive.

In 1982 Godfrey predicted the province would some day extend the Spadina Expressway farther south into downtown Toronto. He speculated it would happen "A.D. — after Davis."

Three decades after Davis it still hasn't happened. But that doesn't mean the 77-year-old Godfrey, who is now president and CEO of Postmedia, has given up. "I'll always hope for the rebirth of the Spadina Expressway," he told me in 2015. "I still think it should have been finished in the 1970s."

If nothing else, you've got to give Godfrey marks for consistency. He said the same thing to Alan Christie of the *Toronto Star* in 1982: "You can't kill Spadina. It's like a time clock that keeps ticking along. One day the alarm will go off."

Forty-five years after Bill Davis stopped the Spadina Expressway the alarm hasn't gone off yet.

8

ELECTION

For some reason at the dawn of the 21st century, it became all the rage in Canadian politics to change one crucial element related to our federal and provincial elections — the timing of them. In the 19th and 20th centuries, one of the most important powers any first minister had was the right to decide when to call an election. And, naturally, those first ministers would make that call when they thought it best advantaged their party and disadvantaged their opponents the most. That required superb political antennae and obviously, even with that built-in advantage, governments were often defeated, anyway.

In the 21st century that all changed. First ministers across Canada voluntarily gave up this power and instead passed fixed-election-date laws. The theory was that never again would elections be held at the capricious whim of a first minister. The moment one election was done the electorate would already know when the next election would happen — for the most part exactly four years from the election that had just transpired. Yes, there were myriad exceptions to this rule. Minority Parliaments could obviously fall at any time, prompting an earlier election, or in the case of Prime Minister Stephen Harper, the four-year waiting period could simply be ignored, which was legal but infuriating to his opponents. But the idea was to give voters the impression that the playing field was now more level and that the party in power couldn't stack the deck in terms of timing for its advantage. (British Columbia was the first province to pass a fixed-election law back in 2001; Quebec was the most recent to do so in 2014; 11 of Canada's 14 jurisdictions now have fixed-election-date laws.)

But back in 1971 there were no fixed-election dates. Governments were elected for five-year terms but traditionally went to the polls after four years. The thinking was: get the hard decisions out of the way in the first two years, spend two years implementing your policies, hope that good things ensued, then get the electorate to judge you. Waiting until the fifth year to have an election has somehow been seen as prime ministers and premiers being afraid to have voters render their verdict on them, so first ministers rarely waited that long. But knowing when to make the election call for a *new* prime minister or premier to take over the mandate of a predecessor has always been a tricky proposition. And in the spring of 1971 those were the circumstances Bill Davis found himself in.

John Robarts had won a majority government on October 17, 1967. So, if one stuck to the four-year tradition, the next election would be sometime in October 1971. But Robarts was gone, and now it was ultimately Davis's decision when to renew the PC government. If the transition from Robarts to Davis went well and Davis renewed Tory fortunes, Davis theoretically could go to the people that spring after just a few months in the premier's office. Some first ministers like to strike when the iron is hot. Or he could take the safer, more traditional route and go to the polls in October, as Robarts surely would have done had he not retired. But if things went amiss, Davis could risk holding out until the following winter or spring with the hope that things would improve for the government during the extra time.

There was a lot riding on Bill Davis's getting this decision right. While he didn't feel it was such a big adjustment going from senior cabinet minister to premier in terms of doing the actual job, he does admit today that he keenly felt the burden of being responsible for the career prospects of 117 Progressive Conservative candidates. The nearly three-decades-long PC dynasty was at stake, not to mention the thousands of public service jobs for Tory supporters and the power of patronage to boot. Party officials were rightly concerned that the electorate would be less interested in nearly three decades of past governance and more interested in: "What are you going to do for me today and tomorrow?" In an admittedly self-serving interview at the time, Arthur Harnett, the party's executive director, said the new premier "can read the mood of the province more accurately than anybody else I've seen." Before Davis's political career was over, it wasn't just Tory partisans who were saying that.

One of the chief criticisms of John Robarts's leadership by the time his premiership was over was the state of disrepair into which the Progressive Conservative Party had fallen. Robarts, frankly, had lost interest in party business. He loved governing and being "centre front," as he called the spotlight of the premier's office, but had grown weary of the rubber-chicken circuit designed to fill the party coffers. "The difference between Davis and Robarts is that Davis was a political animal since he was a kid," said Clare Westcott, Davis's executive assistant.

In fact, Davis was far more attuned than Robarts to the political needs of being the party leader and used all of the advantages of being premier to improve not only Ontario's fortunes but his party's, as well.

"We now have a very political premier who functions very politically and wants to know what the party is doing on a day-to-day basis," said Harnett at the time.

Davis took a much more aggressive and ambitious approach to fundraising. Knowing the weight of the decision that was upon his shoulders, he didn't want that decision to be affected by inadequate financial support or resources. So he barnstormed all over Ontario looking for friendly audiences prepared to support the Tories. And to be sure, there was considerable added interest in meeting or seeing Ontario's new premier. No doubt the advice of his Peel County mentor and predecessor as MPP, Thomas Kennedy, was never far from his mind. Kennedy used to tell him: "You can have all the programs and policies in the world, Billy, but they're not worth a damn if you can't win."

Davis did a Northern Ontario swing toward the end of June that saw 600 local Tories come together in Thunder Bay at a $10-a-plate fundraising dinner. The next night 375 showed up for a $2.50-a-plate luncheon in Timmins where the premier sported a pair of stickers on his jacket lapels proclaiming WE CAMPAIGN HARDER. The dollar figures reflect a much more modest time when it came to political fundraising. Even when factoring inflation into account, a $10 ticket price today would only equal about $60. Ontario's governing Liberals today charge $1,000 a plate for entry to their annual Heritage Dinner.

The northern swing went splendidly for Davis with one minor exception. There were a dozen students from the Thunder Bay Roman Catholic school system protesting his event in that northwest Ontario city. Not a big number to be sure, but the protesters managed to get a comment out of the premier. "A statement will be made on the issue prior to the next election," Davis said, referring to whether the government would extend public funding to separate schools beyond Grade 10. "I'm hopeful it won't be an election issue whatever the decision is." It's hard to know if that was naïveté or wishful thinking, but it certainly didn't reflect reality as the next election date approached.

Meantime, the Big Blue Machine was busily organizing its plans in anticipation of Davis's election call. It divided Ontario into different regions, then fanned out to meet with constituency representatives and local media in each area to get a better sense of the particular issues on the ground in each part of the province. It would turn out to be invaluable legwork, since Davis could drop in anywhere and be current on local issues of significance. Tom MacMillan was a 26-year-old member of the Big Blue team who worked at the Abitibi Paper Company during the week, then on the weekends volunteered to drive all over the province to help the party's machinery do its work. He told Patrick Boyer in *The Big Blue Machine* that he loved "learning a lot about the province, about people, and about politics. And I had to believe in the cause. Bill Davis was a very easy guy to believe in."

One of the innovations that MacMillan contributed to Team Davis was recruiting a band from Northern Ontario called Jalopy, led by Ike Kelneck. This young, hip group revved up crowds as never before — a particular necessity given how charismatically challenged the PC leader was. The party did a dry run of sorts in Sudbury, which included a thousand kids waving flags and singing "A Place to Stand, a Place to Grow" ("Ontari-ari-ari-o") theme song as an impressed Davis arrived. Ross DeGeer told Boyer: "You could see him puff up with new energy and confidence."

Meanwhile, Robert Nixon was eagerly anticipating his second general election as Liberal leader. He hadn't had a prayer of winning the 1967 campaign against a popular premier in John Robarts, and he'd known it. As Nixon himself likes to joke, he was a 39-year-old teacher/farmer who had "basically just fallen off a turnip truck" when he found himself in an election campaign against the Chairman of the Board. He'd been the leader of his party for less than a year, so it had been a pretty tall challenge.

But by 1971 Nixon had been an MPP for almost a decade, party leader for four years, and the son of a former Ontario premier in Harry Nixon, who was the last Liberal premier of Ontario before the Tory dynasty began in 1943. Even one Progressive Conservative backbencher of the day had to acknowledge: "You've got to at least give him credit for keeping together that motley collection he's saddled with in the Liberal caucus." Donald Rosebrugh, the Liberals' campaign chair, was blunt about the party's approach: "We're selling Nixon as he is — honest, forthright, articulate, and able to relate to people." The Liberals as a brand seemed to be in pretty good shape. The federal party had 62 MPs and 23 senators from Ontario, all of whom presumably had organizations and resources that could be enlisted to the cause.

Davis's other opponent in the race was, like him, a rookie leader. After Donald C. MacDonald, Stephen Lewis became just the second-ever leader of the New Democratic Party, capturing his party's title a few months before Davis won his. Lewis was only 33 years old and a true ideological fire-breathing socialist, whose father, David, had become leader of the federal NDP half a year after Stephen won the provincial crown. They were a father-son dynamo. But as calm and cool as Davis was, Stephen Lewis was the opposite. He radiated heat and spoke with a dramatic staccato oratory. Bob Nixon looked on jealously, saying, "Stephen Lewis can read the phone book and make it sound like Shakespeare." But one Liberal strategist claimed to be happy taking on Lewis: "For every person who likes him, he scares off two."

While Nixon was certainly a better prepared, more seasoned leader for his second campaign, so was his opponent. Image-makers, who were just now starting to become superstars in the campaign backrooms, went to work on Bill Davis. They took a 41-year-old dull politician out of his three-piece suits and began dressing him in bolder stripes and bell-bottom pants! Even the headline on the curmudgeonly Claire Hoy's *Toronto Star* column noticed a difference: "A dashing new Premier Bill Davis to woo the city voters," exclaimed the *Star* on July 10. Davis actually consented to a new hairstylist named Stan Anderson getting rid of "that old cowlick and boyish wave."

"He's still rigid," one cabinet minister admitted to Hoy. "But he's improved incredibly in his ability to mix with people. There's room for improvement there, but he's come a long way."

One of the PC Party's most influential backroom advisers was a man much better known for performing the same function for Prime Minister Pierre Trudeau. Martin Goldfarb was one of Canada's first superstar pollsters and focus group guys. Even before Davis became leader, Goldfarb was holding what he called "sensitivity sessions" in hotels across Ontario, each session comprised of only 10 to 15 people. Goldfarb could go in depth on issues and concerns, even offering the new leader a quality of information that could be tailor-made to one region in particular. Those focus groups were complemented with much larger public opinion surveys of 1,500 to 2,000 Ontario voters. This is standard operating procedure today, but back in the early 1970s it was a truly revolutionary approach to campaigning. Goldfarb concluded Davis didn't have an issues problem. "Davis's problem is getting people to feel there is a new breed here even if you handle it in the same old way," he said. "The basic objective of our research is to tell politicians how far [they can] go." It would mark the beginning of Davis's love affair with polling. And he would spend the next decade and a half denying that government decisions were only made because polls told him what to do.

Certainly, the Spadina Expressway decision gave Ontarians the impression there was a dynamic new sheriff in town. But that wasn't the only issue in which Davis seemed not at all like the stereotypical dull Tory. A few weeks before Spadina, Davis announced he was banning commercial logging from Quetico Provincial Park west of Thunder Bay. Then, in the middle of July, less than two months after the Spadina announcement, Davis appointed Halton West MPP George Kerr to be Ontario's first-ever minister of the environment. To be sure, these were all decisions Davis believed in, but they had the added virtue of portraying him as a sensitive environmentalist with a new way of doing business.

Then, in mid-July 1971, hoping to attract a larger chunk of the youth vote, the premier said he would change the law allowing 18-year-olds to vote and drink alcohol legally. The move would create more than 400,000 additional voters — although not John Tory who was still only 16 and who urged the premier to take the step in that much-cherished letter — eligible to cast a ballot in the upcoming election. Hopefully, they wouldn't use their newfound legal rights to become inebriated on election day.

Everything seemed to be rolling out exactly as Davis and the Tory faithful wanted — with one major exception. Davis was in pain.

Literally. He was suffering from debilitating back pain and sciatica that caused shooting pains down his left leg. Every now and then — when he'd get into a car or take a flight of stairs too quickly — his face would betray the secret he was trying to keep and he'd noticeably wince. One day when Davis thought no one was watching, he lifted and shook his leg as if to bring it back to life. *Globe and Mail* reporter Ross H. Munro witnessed what happened, but in typical Davis style the premier refused to talk about his back woes and soldiered on.

One July day Davis toured Camp Petawawa in Eastern Ontario for five hours, allowing local Progressive Conservatives to run him ragged. He even took a few baseball swings at a picnic afterward. Aides were both in awe and furious with him for risking his health that way. The fact was, Davis probably needed an operation to fuse a herniated disc in his spine or at the very least ought to have been wearing a corset or brace for added support. He rejected both options, telling the *Globe and Mail*'s Munro: "I don't like anything which limits my freedom of movement." It was said quietly and firmly with the unmistakable admonition that the reporter had better move on to other subjects.

No one knows for sure, but it was suspected that Davis's back problems probably originated from his football-playing days. Back in 1967, he had to be admitted to Wellesley Hospital in Toronto, suffering from back and leg pains and dizzy spells. Needless to say, the timing of Davis's health woes could hardly have been worse. He was trying to convey an image of youthful vigour while doing this summertime dry run in anticipation of an election call soon to come.

Although the premier's health would be monitored closely for the rest of the summer, his aides almost had a collective heart attack on August 2 in North Bay. It was advertised as "Buffalo Bill Davis Day" by North Bay Mayor Merle Dickerson, the PC Party's nominated candidate for the upcoming election in Nipissing riding. As rain began to fall on the organizers' parade, a skittish horse lurched ahead and flipped the premier off a three-foot-high cart. Onlookers gasped as Davis was thrown backward head over heels and went down hard on all fours. His frantic handlers got him up, and undaunted, Davis got on another horse and continued with the parade. "I'm glad the old reflexes are still in good shape," he said, trying to make light of the incident. He assured onlookers afterward that he wasn't in pain "yet."

On another occasion during the summer of 1971, Davis flew into St. Catharines for another pre-writ regional tour. One member of the Ontario Provincial Police's detail fell off his motorcycle and sustained serious injuries. Davis was so concerned about the man's condition that he had one of his advance people call Norman Atkins to see whether the entire day's events should be cancelled. Atkins said no, that the show must go on.

When the advance man relayed that advice to Davis, the premier got on the phone to Atkins himself. "Are you sure, Norman?"

Atkins was losing patience. "You're goddamn right. Drop in on him at the end of the day." It's an indication of Davis's humanity that he was so conflicted over the issue. The premier ended up buying the cop a watch and visited him at the hospital at the end of the day's events.

Back at Queen's Park, Davis was moving an aggressive agenda through the legislature. By the beginning of August when the legislature was adjourned, the majority government Davis had inherited from Robarts had passed 131 bills into law. Besides the voting and drinking age changes and stopping logging in Quetico Park, there was a toughening of welfare regulations for those 16 to 18 years old, creating a detox centre for chronic alcohol abusers, lowering beer prices, providing a government air service for Northern Ontario residents, stopping the sale of Crown lands and giving preference to Canadians in leasing them, giving preference to Canadian-owned firms seeking government loans and grants, curbing foreign ownership of paperback-distributing companies, suing Dow Chemical Co. for $25 million for allegedly polluting the St. Clair waterways with mercury, and giving citizens greater rights before boards and commissions.

Barnstorming all over Ontario, getting the party back in fighting shape, passing a ton of new legislation, burying the hatchet with his opponents after a tough leadership battle, getting his ducks lined up for an impending election — it all seemed to be going Bill Davis's way. The one item perhaps missing from that list was an opportunity for the new premier to strut his stuff on a national stage — and then that happened.

On August 4, 1971, Davis flew to British Columbia to participate in the annual premiers' conference where he was the new kid on the block. Some of the premiers turned out to be historic figures such as W.A.C. Bennett of British Columbia, Allan Blakeney of Saskatchewan, Richard Hatfield of New Brunswick, Ed Schreyer of Manitoba, and Robert Bourassa of Quebec.

Bourassa, like Davis, was a young rookie premier (only 38 years old), upon whom huge hopes were invested. The conference was making the country's first significant attempt to patriate the Canadian Constitution from Great Britain by agreeing to an amending formula and an entrenched Charter of Rights and Freedoms. In the 1980s and 1990s, Canadian politicians would on three occasions agree to constitutional change, but one agreement was imperfect (the 1982 agreement that lacked Quebec's signature), and the two other efforts ultimately failed (the Meech Lake Accord in 1990 and the Charlottetown Accord in 1992). None of those three efforts might have been necessary had the meeting in Victoria succeeded.

Actually, that requires a bit of a clarification. The meeting in Victoria *did* succeed. All nine premiers who attended (Newfoundland didn't) left British Columbia agreeing on a package of items that could have represented constitutional success. The Victoria Charter enumerated a bill of rights that, while not as extensive as those rights eventually agreed to by nine provinces and the federal government a decade later, were still significant (freedom of expression, religion, voting; no discrimination based on sex, race, or religion). Language rights were included (official bilingualism). Quebec's entitlement to three of the nine judges on the Supreme Court was confirmed. And the first ministers also managed to solve the thorniest problem: how to amend the Constitution. The charter gave veto rights to the federal, Ontario, and Quebec governments. British Columbia wanted but didn't get a veto; however, as a compromise, any future amendments would require the consent of two western provinces, comprising half of the West's population.

Imagine the future constitutional quagmires that could have been avoided had the Victoria Charter taken hold. But it didn't. The premiers left British Columbia with an agreement, but immediately after leaving Victoria, Bourassa started having doubts. He began demanding more for his province, then had second thoughts about his ability to sell the package to an increasingly nationalistic Quebec population. He feared that the separatists and Quebec's student movement would eat him alive. So Bourassa put the kibosh on the plan. Pierre Trudeau later said in his memoirs that he blamed Bourassa for the rise of the Parti Québécois (PQ), its subsequent election win in 1976, and the Meech Lake Accord, which of course Trudeau famously and vehemently opposed.

Forty-four years after Bill Davis left Victoria with an agreement I asked him about his profound disappointment that the agreement reached in British Columbia was fleeting. He, too, was not kind to Bourassa.

"He was not the bravest man in the world" is how he described his Quebec counterpart.

When I tried to suggest that at 38 years old perhaps Bourassa just wasn't politically mature enough to carry it off, Davis wasn't buying.

"Yes, he was young," Davis acknowledged. "But there were several of us who were young."

In fact, Davis had just celebrated his 42nd birthday a few days before the conference started. Nova Scotia's Gerald Regan was 43. Richard Hatfield had just turned 40. Alexander B. Campbell of Prince Edward Island was 37. And Manitoba's Ed Schreyer was only 35. Youth, for Ontario's 18th premier, was no excuse.

There was one more issue, heretofore not mentioned, that could represent a massive wild card in the upcoming election campaign. In tying up all the loose ends of issues that could have been problematic, Davis made one decision that completed the two-item checklist left to him by his predecessor. He had already stopped Spadina. That left the Bishop's Brief.

In the lead-up to the 1971 election, both opposition parties had done a lot of soul-searching on the issue of whether to offer further public funding to the Roman Catholic school system in Ontario. Robert Nixon had authorized his Liberal Party to write a special paper on the issue, reviewing the history and ultimately recommending further funding. Nixon spoke in favour of the policy at the party's annual convention before the election. At the same time the NDP was doing its own formal review, even though its former leader, Donald C. MacDonald, had been a staunch supporter of increasing funds for the Catholic system. Ultimately, the party again arrived at the same conclusion — history and fairness dictated further support for Catholic education. Even though both opposition parties supported the idea, they were also both aware of how controversial their stand could be with a considerable chunk of the electorate. And so, as Nixon recalled four and a half decades later: "This should be done without lighting a partisan match."

By the third week of August, there was still no decision from the premier on the issue. None of the major party leaders seemed to want Catholic school funding to become an election issue, but Nixon accused

Davis of making it one by delaying a decision. Finally, on August 27, Tory MPPs were summoned to a special caucus meeting to consider the matter. It was well known that the majority of caucus was against extending further funds to the Catholic school system, but no one knew where Davis would land. For his part, Robert Nixon couldn't understand the delay. He says the premier had already met with Catholic Church leaders and the opposition leaders and had given them all every impression that some additional public funding would be forthcoming. Finally, on August 31, 1971, Davis made his much-anticipated announcement.

"There are few issues in the realm of public policy where the reconciliation of different views and the possibility of compromise are so difficult to achieve," Davis began, "and few issues which have the potential of creating misunderstanding, stirring prejudice, and inviting recrimination."

The premier went on to give a bit of a history lesson. Catholic education was firmly entrenched as a constitutional right for the elementary years, Catholic families had their choice to send their children either to public or Catholic schools, and no government policy wanted to inhibit that choice. But, he added, the policy of the secondary school years had "been determinedly and deliberately non-denominational and non-sectarian" ever since Confederation and was supported by every governing party since. Davis then reminded everyone that Ontario's first premier, John Sandfield Macdonald, terminated grants to religious universities — a policy that had been in place for three decades — to the point where Ontarians now expected their post-secondary system to be non-denominational. At the same time, Davis added, improvements had been made and would no doubt continue to be made to the separate school system, which no one at the time of Confederation could have imagined. He then gave the example of his own efforts as education minister to give the separate school system additional financial support through Grade 10.

Davis was almost halfway through his speech, and still no one knew what he was going to announce. Then a hint: while the improvements Davis implemented in the 1960s were "a practical and sensible solution for many who would have been otherwise disadvantaged, it was never intended as an encroachment upon the principle of a free, non-denominational and non-sectarian secondary school system, accessible to all and supported by all."

Then the other shoe fell: "The government has therefore concluded that it cannot support the proposals of the Ontario Separate School Trustees Association."

Even though he had already dropped the news bombshell, Davis actually continued his speech for another seven pages. (The full speech is in Appendix 3.) He went on to argue that fully funding the separate school system "would fragment the present system beyond recognition and repair" and would inevitably oblige future governments to fund other religious educational institutions out of fairness to them. Davis said students changed schools all the time, from elementary to secondary, from public to Catholic, from secondary to post-secondary, "without adverse effect on their educational progress."

This speech, more than any other, would dramatically change the dynamic of the pending 1971 election campaign. It's hard to know whether he really believed what he next said, but you can be sure his critics didn't: "I can only say, on behalf of my colleagues, that our decision has been made, as much as is humanly possible, without regard to any political consideration, advantage, or disadvantage."

Davis said his decision didn't preclude making other improvements to the Catholic system, or for that matter, enhancements to the teaching of morals and ethics in the public system. The premier concluded his speech by offering his "profound willingness on the government's behalf to maintain a spirit of goodwill and understanding, regardless of the differences that are obviously profound."

Fat chance.

It's easy to be cynical about decisions such as the Catholic school funding one. You could conclude that Davis was simply pandering to his Tory base, which would have had huge problems with the premier had he extended funding. But that underestimates how deeply Davis personally felt about the issue. He knew anti-Catholic bigots would approve of his decision, and he didn't like the notion that he was helping them indulge in their bigotry. He also knew how rickety the financial foundations of the Catholic system were, that many Catholic parents simply couldn't afford to pay tuition to send their children through to the end of high school, and that many of those Catholic secondary schools would, as a result, be closed. That no doubt explains why, midway through the press conference after his speech, Davis became momentarily lost for words.

You will rarely meet a politician who plays his emotional cards closer to his vest than Bill Davis. Yet, when asked what the decision meant to him *personally*, Davis choked up, had a tremor in his voice, and his eyes began to water. He turned away from the cameras for a moment, then regained his composure and finished his answer. "It's harder to say no," he told reporters in clearly one of the largest understatements so far of his premiership. One of Davis's aides described the scene as "the gloomiest press conference ever … almost solemn, like hearing the death of a close friend." Davis no doubt agonized and struggled with the decision and thought he'd made the right one. But that didn't mean the decision wouldn't haunt him for years to come.

"Everybody was hornswoggled," Robert Nixon told me in 2015 in his St. George, Ontario, living room, still capable at age 87 of getting angry over the issue.

But Davis's distress on the issue wouldn't go away. Back in those days, each party was given an opportunity to tape a seven-and-a-half-minute free-time broadcast. In the dying days of the campaign, Davis was preparing to do his on-camera performance when a call came into the studio for him. Norman Atkins, who was with Davis, wasn't sure who was on the other end of the line, but surmised it was a senior cabinet minister trying to get Davis to soften his opposition to further Catholic school funding, claiming the Tories would lose the election if he didn't. Davis listened, then asked Atkins whether the party should use its broadcast to announce a softening of the position. Atkins firmly shut him down, saying the decision was made and he should use the free-time broadcast to restate his position.

"I have research," Atkins told the premier. "The majority of Ontarians are opposed to full funding. There are even divisions within Catholic ranks." Davis did the broadcast and reiterated the party's position, but as the story demonstrates, he continued to struggle personally with the issue.

All these years later there's still no consensus on whether Premier Davis gave an undertaking to the Catholic Church and the opposition leaders before the election that he would extend further public funds to the separate school system. The Liberal leader insists he did. The premier insists he didn't.

"I don't recall us ever having agreement on the issue," Davis says today of those discussions. "We discussed it. I knew their positions. I know what I discussed with Robert. I may have said, 'I'll think about it,' or 'We'll see.'" But that was it, he insists.

As much as Davis said he *hoped* his decision wouldn't be part of the 1971 campaign, clearly that wasn't going to happen. Funding for separate schools would become a *huge* issue. Which party it would help, however, was still an open question. Bishop Gerald Emmett Carter, who had spent his life trying to improve Catholic education both in Quebec and Ontario, certainly intended to make it an election issue. And his brother, Alexander, who was the bishop in Sault Ste. Marie, expressed even more disappointment, saying, "Leaders should lead, not follow the more ignorant and biased parts of the public."

NDP leader Stephen Lewis, no doubt sensing the issue could explode with incalculable consequences, said he intended to raise the matter "but we're not inclined to make it a major issue because nothing is achieved by provocativeness." He called Davis's delay in making the announcement "irresponsible and I can only assume deliberate." Robert Nixon saw an inconsistency in Davis's decision. How was it, he asked, that Education Minister Davis moved to fix an inequity for Catholic schools up to Grade 10, but Premier Davis wouldn't do it for the rest of the secondary years?

Interestingly, Davis's decision was greeted with widespread support on the province's editorial pages. A few days before Davis's announcement the *Globe and Mail* published an editorial headlined: "The Answer Should Be No." Accompanying the editorial was a cartoon of Davis dressed as a "Queen's Park Academy Headmaster" with an apple on his desk. Written on the apple were the words: "$eparate $chools." After the announcement, the right-leaning *Toronto Telegram* said the premier had chosen "wisely," adding once Catholics had a fully funded system, what prevented other faiths from making their claims? "The resulting strain on the public treasury and democratic fabric of our society could be tragic," the paper editorialized. The *Kingston Whig-Standard* praised him "for being quietly and tenacious capable of adhering to his principles." Even the liberal *Toronto Star* praised Davis's speech and offered: "We endorse this line of reasoning." However, despite the editorial endorsements, one thing was clear: the issue wasn't going away now or more than a decade later.

As the summer progressed, the rumours of an imminent election call became more and more intense. Finally, on Monday, September 13, 1971, Premier William Grenville Davis visited Lieutenant Governor William Ross Macdonald and advised him to draw up the writs sending Ontarians to the polls to elect their 29th legislative assembly. The meeting took place at the end of a busy day, during which Davis had revealed several more policy positions. He announced the abolition of medicare and hospital premiums for old age pensioners, then confessed with a smile that it was "not a complete accident" that this bit of good news was shared with the electorate on the same day as the election call. Frankly, it was the perfect announcement for a Tory government whose base was made up disproportionately of seniors and against whom neither opposition party could object to reaping further pre-election goodies. With the legislature dissolved, 68 Progressive Conservative, 27 Liberal, and 21 New Democrat MPPs all hit the hustings, hoping to hang on to their jobs and have lots of their fellow nominated candidates join them.

Davis told a crammed media studio at the legislature that the time had come for him to seek his own mandate, having inherited the premiership from Robarts. When asked what the election was about, he answered simply: "It is a question of leadership."

The election launch, which had Davis answering reporters' questions for more than an hour, didn't go flawlessly. The premier spent much of the news conference sidestepping questions about a public inquiry that just that day had reported its findings into the government's acquisition of land on the Niagara Escarpment. Police were investigating whether there was a premature leak of a report recommending the government buy more than 54,000 acres of escarpment land for $18.5 million. He also declined to answer numerous questions on how much the Tories intended to spend during the campaign, which didn't sit well with the press gallery. Estimates ranged from $3 to $6 million.

However, Fraser Kelly, the *Toronto Telegram*'s political editor, also noted Davis looked "dapper, brown striped suit, wide lapels, colorful tie with a large knot." He also wondered, in an era of the increasing presidentialization of Canadian politics, whether Liberal leader Robert Nixon's image was "more fuzzy than presidential." If so, Kelly noted, "he's got just over five weeks to change it." Further exacerbating Nixon's problems:

Pierre Trudeau wasn't nearly as popular in 1971 as he was in 1968, and voters often didn't and don't distinguish between the federal and provincial party labels. No one was quite sure whether Trudeau's unpopularity would tamp down the provincial Liberal vote.

As an indication of how times have changed, on the day of the election call, fully 79 of Ontario's 117 ridings still didn't have candidates nominated to run. Thirty-five of those were from the governing PCs. Nowadays, parties pride themselves on getting as full a slate of candidates nominated as possible before an election is actually called. It makes them look organized and eager. Campaigns four decades ago apparently didn't worry about such things. In fact, as shocking as this will sound to modern campaign organizers whose leaders would instantly hit the ground running, Davis's actual campaign itinerary wouldn't begin for another week. He would spend this first week of the campaign with some relatively minor party functions, such as attending candidate-nominating meetings.

The two opposition leaders followed suit in the media studio. Nixon rolled out his preference for the Liberal Party's election slogan: "A Change People Can Trust." Again, as strange as it might sound and in contradistinction to today's campaigns, the Grits on day one still hadn't made the final decision on a campaign slogan. Nixon said he'd be focusing on jobs, the economy, decentralizing government, the environment, and Ontario's role in Confederation. Stephen Lewis said his NDP platform would highlight the need to create jobs, reduce the cost of living, reform the taxation system, protect the environment, and "regain control of the economy." The NDP also indicated it expected to be badly outspent by the Tories. The party had an election war chest of only a quarter of a million dollars. New Democrats were also concerned about polling, which showed Lewis the most untrustworthy of the three leaders. As a result, the party produced a 13-minute documentary showing Lewis at home and at the cottage. Fraser Kelly described Lewis's opening statement as "exuding confidence and optimism."

While things certainly looked promising for the governing Tories, nothing could be taken for granted. There were plenty of irritants across the provincial heartland, any one of which could rise up and catch the Tories off guard. Regional governments (such as York Region north of Toronto) were intended to streamline and modernize the delivery of municipal services but instead became a catchphrase for bureaucratic bungling. Rightly or wrongly, the issue came to be seen as the large provincial government trying to ram unwanted changes down the throats of local governments. Most of those local politicians were Tory sympathizers, which made the self-inflicted wound even worse. Davis brought a temporary halt to establishing more regional governments, but that didn't mean the issue was off the table.

New Democrats were also heartened by a by-election that had taken place two years earlier. In September 1969, voters shocked the Robarts government by handing the riding of Middlesex South, right next door to the premier's hometown of London, to the NDP. It had been a staunchly Tory bastion for decades. In that case, the NDP exploited the PC government's lack of interest in embracing the federal government's new medicare plan. Could the NDP make that same formula work on a wider basis? They hoped so, particularly with a dynamic new leader in Stephen Lewis now in place. Observers also couldn't help but notice that six of the eight provincial governments that had gone to the polls over the past two years had been defeated. There was an anti-incumbency feeling in the air across Canada, and the Ontario Tories were the embodiment of incumbency, having won eight straight elections over 28 years. And how about those 18-year-olds now eligible to vote for the first time? Where would they mark their X?

Ontario's 21st premier, Bob Rae, once said you should never get into a fight with someone who buys newsprint by the ton. By that he meant you never win when you fight the media because they always get the last word. Bob Nixon apparently disagreed. As the campaign progressed, Nixon became increasingly miffed. He accused the media of "an underground holding of hands" with the NDP, suggesting the media preferred the NDP to the Liberals as the *real* alternative to the Tories. Did Nixon feel the media were promoting the NDP at the Liberals' expense? "Yes," he said straight out. "It's an impression I have." It's a truism in politics that if you're complaining about coverage, you're not explaining your platform. Reporters also went after Nixon, as they did Davis, on campaign expenditures. Only the NDP was precise in detailing how much it intended to spend, probably because it had so little to spend it could look virtuous in being so transparent. Conversely, Nixon told the media the Liberals would spend between $450,000 and "an unlimited amount."

The media pounced. One wag blasted Nixon "for not levelling with us."

Nixon retorted, "I am not going to open the books." Again, complaining versus explaining.

Nixon ought not to have felt picked on. A few days later the media had the same confrontation with Davis, who came close to losing his cool when asked how much the Tory campaign would spend. "I won't tell you because I don't know" was the premier's reply, which satisfied no one. Davis also had qualms about making campaign contributors' names public, since no law obliged any party to do so. At this point contributors to all parties made their donations with a presumption that the donation would stay secret. The media kept hounding Davis. How about a commission to study campaign contributions? He wouldn't rule it out. How about "leading the way" by being transparent about the whole thing? "I've thought about it," Davis replied. Could your entourage provide that information? Well, Davis acknowledged, they would know the names, but "I doubt if they'll tell you very much, either." The hounding continued, so much so that Davis uncharacteristically shut it down. "I don't know where the money is coming from … *please!*" And off he went.

Strangely enough, those encounters weren't the biggest media story of the campaign. In a true shocker, the *Toronto Telegram*, Canada's third-largest newspaper, announced it would cease publication after nearly a century of existence. Million-dollar losses year after year forced the hand of the newspaper's proprietor, John Bassett, himself a former two-time Tory candidate, owner of the Canadian Football League's Toronto Argonauts, and a former part owner of the National Hockey League's Maple Leafs. After the *Tele*'s death, the *Toronto Sun* emerged from its ashes and began publishing in November 1971. "It's tragic, but the decision has been made" was the premier's reaction to the news.

For all of the ink that has been spilled over the years describing Bill Davis as calm, cool, dull, patrician, technocratic, shy, and bland, that list omits another feature of the Davis personality that the premier only rarely lets out of the cage. He is competitive as hell and can be a vicious attacker if he feels he needs to be. With still one month to go before election day, Davis apparently felt he needed to be.

"I have been disgusted, but not surprised, by the blatant attempts on the part of the leader of the Ontario Liberals to magnify the already serious plight of companies," Davis said, declining to name his opponent as was his custom. But then he changed his custom. "In his transparent play to make political gains from other people's troubles, Bob Nixon tried to throw us a curve and it turned out to be a boomerang!"

Davis rarely uttered his opponent's name. It was an indication that this campaign wasn't just business as usual or even theatrics as usual. In the judgment of many observers, the 1971 Ontario election campaign was personal, although Davis rejects that conclusion. "I had some respect for Bob's father," Davis says today. "He was a decent person. But Bob and I were competitors and I can't say it was my job to help him with his campaign."

Hearing Davis's comments from back then, Nixon responded in kind, calling Davis "a past master of spending who is just beginning to get his hand into the public till."

Again, by today's standards, Davis was running an unusual campaign insofar as he tried to promise nothing. He accused both of his opponents of promising a billion dollars worth of "wild promises" and assured Ontarians "mine will be few."

"Let them make all the promises they want," Davis taunted his opponents. "I won't be making promises. What we're offering is prudent and decisive management of the people's affairs." It was hardly a dramatic clarion call with which to storm the barricades. But it was accurate. That's exactly what a Davis government was offering in all its marvellous blandness.

An indication that the PC forces were in solid organizational shape came a week and a half into the campaign. The Tories managed to get nearly 3,000 people into a hockey arena in Belleville to hear Premier Davis reiterate he was running on his record, would be making no promises, and unlike his opponents, certainly wouldn't be raising taxes. It was a piping hot night in Belleville, and the premier was dripping in sweat. Still, he waded right into the huge crowd with his wife, Kathy, who was busy shaking hands, as well. Several long-haired youths approached the couple, one asking, "Would you legalize marijuana?" Davis shook his head and continued through the crowd.

Perhaps because of the heat, perhaps because of what party officials called "audience exhaustion" (Davis was nearly two hours late arriving), the event was actually described as a "tactical success" but a "spontaneous failure." It certainly looked impressive: Davis on the stage with his family and 12 cabinet ministers, including "The Four" who had challenged him for the leadership earlier in the year (Allan Lawrence, Bert Lawrence, Darcy McKeough, and Robert Welch). But he was rarely interrupted by applause.

It didn't get any better the next day in Kingston where the father of the community college system visited St. Lawrence College to no cheers, no boos, no applause, nothing. There were a few attempts by the premier to make small talk with the students, but it fell flat. The students — either showing some moxie by thumbing their noses at the establishment, or disrespect by snubbing the highest-ranking politician in the province — lounged around the main hall and essentially ignored Davis. Later in the day at Queen's University before 150 students Davis was finally forced to confront the campaign's most significant sleeper issue: Catholic school funding.

"I'm sorry," a student told him, "you won't get my support because of the separate school issue."

"I'm sorry, too," Davis responded. Then he added, "You have to do what you think is right." The separate school issue soon followed Davis everywhere, but there was still no indication of whether it was a net vote getter or vote loser. The next day at Niagara Community College in Welland, 400 students waited inside the cafeteria for the premier to arrive. But he had to run a gauntlet of more than 700 separate school students wearing their Notre Dame College School blazers outside the college. The school authorities had given the students permission to spend their lunch hour protesting at the premier's event and had bused them to it. But the students weren't permitted into the community college to hear the premier's remarks. They carried placards saying UNCLE BILL WANTS YOU UNLESS YOU'RE CATHOLIC, GOD HELP US, DAVIS WON'T, and YOU GAVE US THE VOTE, BUT YOU WON'T GET IT BACK. Things got nervous-making for a while as two police officers held the doors shut to prevent the Notre Dame students from storming the building. Some pounded at the doors until other students with loudspeakers brought that to an end. For those of you who think Mike Harris, premier from 1995 to 2002, was the first Tory leader to face huge, frightening demonstrations — well, he wasn't.

Inside, Davis again had to face down questions about his separate schools decision. He answered one question with words that would be used against him in dramatic fashion more than a decade later: "I'm in favour of a single high school system for persons of all creeds and religions," he said. "I cannot see laying the groundwork for a fragmentation of the school system in this province."

Then there was something that attracted far less attention but was vintage Bill Davis: after the Welland event was over, the premier invited three of the protesters to join him for a private meeting in his car to discuss the subject further, and in calmer surroundings. Not many leaders would have done that.

But the separate school issue just wouldn't go away. A few days later in Burlington an anxious-sounding 10-year-old girl named Judy Wright approached the premier as he was trying to leave an event at Progressive Conservative candidate George Kerr's campaign headquarters. She asked him, "Mr. Davis, why are you against separate schools?"

Despite aides trying to rush the premier out of the event — he was already an hour behind schedule — Davis stopped and told the girl, "You tell your teachers, your friends, and your parents, Judy, I'm not against separate schools."

Davis undoubtedly believed that, but he was having a tough time convincing others that was true. Days later in Sault Ste. Marie, where once again the father of the community college system wanted positive media coverage related to public education, Davis found himself fending off allegations from Catholic education adherents. Two carloads of separate school students followed Davis's bus to half a dozen different campaign stops. Their sign read: UNCLE BILL WENT ALL UPHILL TO COVER THE CATHOLIC GRANTS; BILL FELL DOWN AND LOST HIS CROWN AND EQUAL RIGHTS CAME AFTER.

Election campaigns four decades ago were different from the ones of today in some very real ways. For example, could you imagine Stephen Harper, the former prime minister, attending so many open events where attendees weren't screened? Back in the day, campaigns weren't solely comprised of closed, exclusive events for party supporters. Leaders, including first ministers, mainstreeted in public, and yes, took the risk that some unpleasantness might occur. One time Davis was campaigning with cabinet minister Robert Welch, the PC candidate for Lincoln. As the two candidates were standing and talking outside their campaign bus, which was blocking traffic, a motorist shouted, "If you want my vote, get your damn bus out of the way!" The premier hopped on and the bus quickly took off. Another time Davis was campaigning outside a smelter in Sudbury. The idea was to meet the workers coming off shift. While a few snubbed the premier and refused to shake his hand ("You've got some nerve" or "You must be joking" were a couple of the comments overheard), most were what you'd expect — polite Canadians who said "Nice to meet you" and that was that. Yes, there were the odd minor embarrassments, but it was important to be seen as accessible to the electorate — *to actually like and mingle with the people you wanted to serve*. Contrast that with, for example, Stephen Harper's 2011 election campaign in which it was doubtful he encountered a single non-Tory supporter during the entire drama. Every event was so tightly scripted and controlled to ensure the prime minister never had to meet someone who wasn't a Progressive Conservative. Not only that, Harper's "media availabilities" with the working press after his events were hopelessly short. Five questions in both official languages were all that the prime minister's staff allowed and that was it. As we already saw from the kickoff of the 1971 election campaign, Premier Davis's first "availability" lasted more than an hour.

Things were even complicated when Davis returned home to Brampton where 2,000 supporters crammed into the local hockey arena to see their favourite son nominated as the PC candidate in the riding of Peel North, which had been renamed for the 1967 election. While uncharacteristically predicting the Tories would increase their seat count from 68 to 80 — quite a boast — Davis discovered the New Democrats had nominated a candidate of their own who could give the premier a major headache. That candidate's name was Neil Davis. The premier had a 15-year-old son by the same name. There was also the concern that with the candidates being listed on the ballot in alphabetical order Neil Davis's name would appear above William Davis's. Might that confuse some people? Bill Davis certainly feared so.

"There is a difference between the Davises," the premier said. "I'm the Davis who was born in Peel North, lives in Peel North, and works in Peel North!"

His opponent, Neil Davis, was a 30-year-old, bearded teacher from Mississauga who insisted, since he'd been nominated by the NDP in March and the premier wasn't nominated until September, "It's the Conservatives who confused the issue by fielding a second candidate named Davis."

It wasn't all doom and gloom on the hustings. In Prescott in Eastern Ontario, Davis signed dozens of small maple leaf flags held by youngsters. "You'd think he was another Bobby Orr," one onlooker commented.

Davis heard the quip. "No, I'm not. The salary is not the same."

Stephen Lewis made his own trek to the Niagara Peninsula shortly after Davis did, but the NDP leader attracted a much larger crowd. About 1,000 community college students gathered in Welland to hear Lewis wonder whether he was running against "Pierre Elliott Davis or William Trudeau." The gist of Lewis's shot was that the premier seemed to be wandering all over Ontario, making no commitments and offering no changes. "I am hard-pressed to believe how any man in 1971 can say nothing to the electorate when there are 140,000 people unemployed in Ontario," Lewis said.

Then the ghost of Spadina reappeared on September 23. Bob Nixon had pledged to continue building the expressway to Eglinton Avenue, given that the land had already been expropriated and was ready for servicing. Davis, at this point, still opposed that view, saying that would create "a greater traffic jam" at Eglinton. He accused Nixon of coming down on the issue "with both feet planted firmly in the air," given that Nixon's caucus was split on the issue. Davis insisted he wouldn't budge from his "difficult decision" to stop Spadina at Lawrence Avenue. Of course, four years from now, the premier more than budged and adopted the Nixon position, allowing the expressway to be built to Eglinton Avenue. But that was the future. For the present the Tories saw the Spadina issue as a drum with which to beat the Liberals.

Davis was adamant about not trying to out-promise his opponents, but there were occasions when he was too cute by half. Toward the end of September in Sudbury he announced that the government would spend $4 to $5 million a year for the next five years purchasing land along the Niagara Escarpment for recreational purposes. When asked whether this wasn't, in fact, an election promise, Davis replied, "No, this is not part of an election announcement." Really?

Later in the campaign Davis promised to triple provincial grants to municipalities for winter works projects and to ask the federal government to move up the personal income tax cuts scheduled for 1974. As a package, the commitments would cost $150 million. Expressed in today's dollars, that's nearly $900 million — in a campaign in which Davis insisted there would be no out-promising the opposition. In fairness Davis wanted one-third of that amount to come from the federal government, but still, even without the federal contribution, it was still a $550 million pledge in today's dollars.

Robert Nixon pounced, telling a large rally of 700 of his own supporters in London that the Tory campaign was failing, and as a result, Davis was now adopting a new "policy-a-day" strategy. But Davis countered, charging his opponents with promising $2 billion in spending promises apiece. Only three weeks ago he was accusing them of promising $1 billion apiece. Reporters pressed the premier for details on how he got to the new higher number. At first he refused. But with more pressing by the media, Davis again uncharacteristically revealed more than he perhaps should have. He said civil servants working for the treasury board of cabinet crunched the numbers and came up with the new $2 billion figure. Civil servants had been pressed into working for the Tory campaign? "I think it is most appropriate," Davis said with a straight face.

When Robert Nixon learned of Davis's statement, he had a fit. "When the premier phones [treasury board officials] and says, 'All right boys, take a look at the Liberal program, find everything that you can, put the most expensive price tags on it, add it up, and give it to me because I've got a press conference Tuesday,' well, I consider that irresponsible and vicious politics." Some campaign rhetoric is theatrics. It rarely was between Davis and Nixon. They just didn't like each other and the rhetoric reflected that.

The *Toronto Star* took Nixon's side on this one. "A civil service can retain the confidence of the people it serves only if it is seen to be impartial," the *Star* editorialized. "Mr. Davis is trying to mislead the voters of Ontario, to distract them from his own government's spending record. He hasn't much confidence in the public's intelligence."

It was hard to know how Davis truly felt about how things were going in the campaign. If his predictions were any indication, not as well as he had hoped. During the third week of September, he predicted more than 80 seats for his Tories, which would have been a big boost over the 68 left to him by Robarts. However, on September 28, he scaled down his forecast to "71 or more" seats. Was it a lack of confidence? Were the polls suggesting his earlier prediction was too bold? There were still more than three weeks to go until election day.

Everyone recognized that Bill Davis had the best "Made in Ontario" campaign team around. What Stephen Lewis wanted the public to know was that wasn't the whole story. Lewis frequently blasted Davis for further "Americanizing" Ontario politics. It was a reference to the Big Blue Machine's hiring of Market Opinion Research Inc., run by Robert Teeter, the Detroit-based polling whiz kid, who was 10 years Davis's junior but a rising star in Republican Party circles. Lewis described Teeter's advising Davis as "the final, ultimate indignity" of the growing U.S. domination of Ontario. "He can't just have a presidential tour. Nobody is rushing to touch the hem of the garment," the NDP leader said.

Yes, Teeter was doing additional state-of-the-art polling for the PCs and had been since the late 1960s. But he was also responsible for warming up the stolid, staid, shy Davis image. Teeter discovered after the PC leadership convention that 75 to 80 percent of Ontarians could name, unaided, the new premier of Ontario — solid name recognition numbers. But they knew hardly anything about him. "It wasn't that he had a bad personality, it was just that he had a kind of lack of a public personality," Teeter said at the time. The consultant advised Davis to travel a lot, to get around the province, meet as many people as possible, and generate local media stories, particularly ones involving his family. Davis, as we have seen, took the advice very much to heart.

Politics is often filled with irony, and this is surely one. When Mike Harris became premier of Ontario in 1995, it was thanks in part to significant involvement from Republican Party consultants from the United States. Harris and his advisers were excoriated by critics for his unprecedented use of right-wing imports. Except it wasn't unprecedented. Bill Davis had already done it a quarter-century earlier. And it wasn't only Tories who did it. Dalton McGuinty, before becoming Ontario's 24th premier, occasionally took trips to Chicago to be tutored by David Axelrod, one of the key advisers behind Barack Obama's presidential bid. In other words, this sort of thing wasn't new.

Meanwhile, to prepare for both the media interviews and the campaign commercials and films to come, Bob Teeter spent hours with Davis, practising his on-camera answers to myriad questions such as why he wanted to be premier, why he preferred "Bill" over "William," or why the family bought Thor, now the province's most famous dog thanks to the power of campaign advertising, for $1.25 (the *Thor* story, believe it or not, made the front page above the fold of the *Brampton and Bramalea Daily Times*).

I've seen the raw tape of these practice sessions (they're in the TVO archives), and Davis comes across flat, flat, flat, even when asked the same question several times over. It's as if he knows how important it is to get these answers right, but intellectually he still can't bring himself to put his heart into this humiliating exercise. However, Donald Haig, president of Film Arts, responsible for making the Tory commercials, said: "Without sounding immodest, I think Davis is looking more human in these films."

Critics harped on the indignity of selling the premier as if he were a bar of soap, or creating a "cult of the leader" style of campaign. But the staff made no apologies for it. They insisted they weren't trying to create an image of Davis that wasn't authentic; rather they were trying to do what Davis hadn't been able to do, namely, tell people what kind of a guy he really was. Furthermore, the PC campaign team thought it was a bit rich for the media to complain about the leader focus, given that their reports often said "Davis did this" or "Davis did that" when, in fact, a minister, the cabinet, or the entire government was actually on the hook for any number of decisions.

Perhaps the most revealing piece of tape in the TVO archives is when Teeter asks Davis: "About separate school funding ... what do you plan to do?" It was a straightforward, innocent-sounding question. Davis paused ... and paused ... and paused. And looked very uncomfortable. There is no answer on the videotape.

As September gave way to October, the Ontario electorate was about to experience something unprecedented for a provincial election campaign. The three leaders agreed to have an hour-long debate televised on CFTO (the Toronto CTV affiliate) and the CBC's Ontario network. Well, actually, it was more of a kaffeeklatsch than a debate. But it was the first of its kind in Ontario history. The three leaders were seated in comfy chairs (no standing on podiums yet) with a coffee table between each leader. The debate was taped in the morning, but not shown until 10:00 p.m. The broadcasters were proud to be showing the debate "unedited, and in colour." Each network provided one moderator (Ken Cavanagh of CBC and Joe Mariash of CFTO) and one reporter (Larry Solway of CBC and Fraser Kelly of CFTO). As viewers watched the program, they saw the social democrat Lewis on the left of the shot, the conservative Davis on the right, and the liberal Nixon in the middle chair. As expected, it was a two-on-one affair for most of the night but interestingly enough, given that it was a new experience for them all, the leaders were all on best behaviour. Lewis was determined not to seem too radical or smug and came off as poised and in control. Nixon went for a firm tone, but no throwing daggers. Davis reportedly looked less comfortable than the other two — perhaps natural considering his and Robarts's records were under attack most of the night — and he did counterattack several times.

What was the verdict on the debate? "We were great," offered Stephen Lewis. "But the format was dull, listless, and ridiculous."

Lewis's wife, Michele Landsberg, called it "boring and pointless — no opportunity for give and take — comparable to Mr. Dressup."

A reporter asked Lewis if he had ever seen any better programs. "Yes, several thousand spring to mind," replied Lewis, always fast with a good quip. Nixon also found the format too rigid and Davis called it "frustrating" because he was occasionally unable to refute what the opposition leaders had said about him.

CFTO received 33 favourable calls after the debate and just 23 unfavourable. The station also received 10 calls at 10:00 p.m., wondering why *Ironside*, the regularly scheduled crime drama starring Raymond Burr, wasn't on.

With less than a week to go, Davis hardly did what could be called playing it safe. He went to a shopping mall in Windsor — not the wasteland for Progressive Conservatives half a century ago that it is today, but hardly friendly Tory territory, either. He then attended pub night at the University of Windsor where 1,000 students were on hand to welcome him. Four female members of a rock group kissed him and one bartender tapped on his arm and told him, "Mr. Davis, sir, you'll have to move along. You're interrupting the bar service." Try to imagine some other political leaders being that accessible in such an uncontrolled environment.

And then the premier of Ontario got a gift from heaven. Well, maybe not heaven, but the next best thing — the Government of Canada. Pierre Elliott Trudeau's Liberals announced that in an effort to stimulate a sluggish economy Canadians would see their income taxes cut retroactively to July 1, 1971. What did Bill Davis do? He said, me, too, and "paralleled" the federal move. It wasn't a huge tax cut. It would only amount to 3 percent of Ontarians' taxable income and represent $42 million more for citizens to have in their pockets. But it represented a big victory for Tory forces, which had been urging the federal Liberals for months to cut income taxes and pledging to match whatever they did.

Two helpful things then followed. First, the newspapers gave huge, front-page play to the tax-cut announcement, and because the plan was unveiled on a Friday, it headlined the Saturday papers — the day of the week with the largest readership. Second, Robert Nixon endorsed the move, saying he'd suggested the same thing himself before the legislative session had ended. "We thought then that it was appropriate and I still feel it is appropriate," he said at the time. The tax cut would modestly increase the size of the deficit, but given the timing of the announcement, no one was making much of a fuss about that. For the Tories it took away a potential selling point for the Liberals, namely, that they were better positioned than the other parties to have more harmonious relations with the federal Liberals than anyone else. Six days before the election the Progressive Conservatives showed when push came to shove they could get along with the federal Liberal government just fine, thank you.

With four days to go, Stephen Lewis looked like a leader about to score a big breakthrough. The NDP attracted 3,000 cheering, singing, and hand-clapping supporters to the O'Keefe Centre to hear their leader refer to the PC campaign as "the ultimate corruption of the political process." Lewis refused to let up on the "Americanization of the Tory" campaign. "I want to tell the Tories in Ontario something," he said. "We're not yet Americans! We're Canadians in this province!" The crowd went wild, interrupting Lewis for nearly a minute with applause and cheers. Of course, there was the obligatory singing of "Solidarity Forever," "We Shall Not Be Moved," and "This Land Is Your Land" — it was an NDP gathering, after all. But the deafening applause for star MPP Morton Shulman and former leader Donald C. MacDonald, not to mention three standing ovations for Lewis, made the event a memorable night.

Meanwhile, at the same time, Bill Davis was having fun heckling some NDPers who had crashed his rally in Dundas, just outside Hamilton. "Enjoy yourself between now and Wednesday," the premier said, "because around nine o'clock Thursday night your party is going to come in either second or third." No Liberal enthusiasts crashed the event, prompting Davis to add,

Bill Davis was the middle of three children, born July 30, 1929, in Brampton, Ontario. *Davis Family*

A young Bill Davis with his hero, his father A. Grenville Davis, who was a Crown attorney for three decades in Peel County. *Davis Family*

Bill Davis with his first wife, Helen, who died tragically in 1962, leaving the MPP a widower with four young children. *Davis Family*

Helen with Neil, their first of four children. *Davis Family*

Bill Davis is rarely happier than when he's on water. He loves driving his boat on Georgian Bay. *Davis Family*

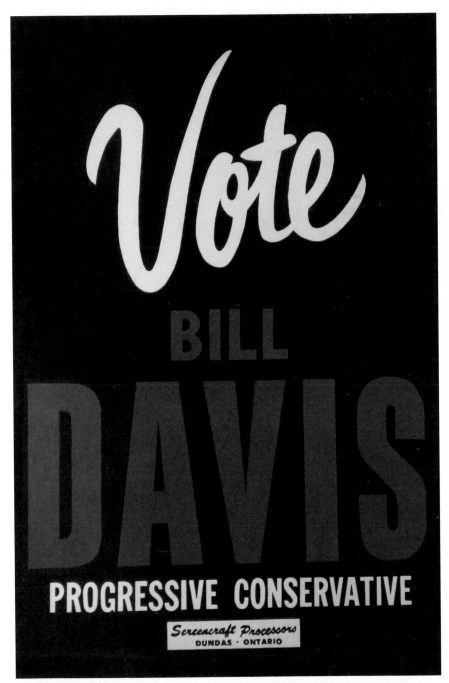

A sign from Bill Davis's first campaign as an MPP for the June 11, 1959, election. He barely squeaked in. *Steve Paikin*

Bill Davis campaigns in his first election in June 1959 for Premier Leslie Frost.
Davis Family

Bill Davis and his first wife, Helen, along with three of their four children.
From left to right: Catherine, Neil, and Nancy. *Davis Family*

Past, present, and future: (left to right) Premier Leslie Frost, former premier Tom Kennedy, and future premier Bill Davis after the rookie MPP's first election win in 1959. *Davis Family*

Bill Davis did Grade 13 twice so he could quarterback his high school football team for another season. Davis is seen here playing catch with his oldest son, Neil, who insists he caught the pass. *Office of the Premier of Ontario*

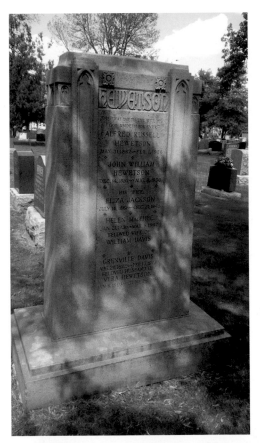

The final resting place in Brampton of Bill Davis's first wife, Helen. *Steve Paikin*

Bill Davis, his second wife, Kathleen, and their five children. From left to right: Catherine, Ian, Neil, Nancy, and Meg in Davis's arms. *Davis Family*

A young Bill Davis enjoys double kisses from daughters Nancy and Catherine. *Office of the Premier of Ontario*

Cartoonists often portrayed Bill Davis as a Tory fat cat in pinstripes. *Office of the Premier of Ontario*

Before he puffed on his more famous pipe, a younger Premier Bill Davis smoked cigars. *Office of the Premier of Ontario*

Bill Davis governed from 1975 to 1981 in minority legislatures and grew
into the role of a trusted, seasoned politician. *Office of the Premier of Ontario*

After the death of his first wife in 1962, Bill Davis courted and married Kathleen Mackay, who was originally from outside Chicago. *Office of the Premier of Ontario*

As Bill Davis settled into his office, he became as comfortable as an old sweater in the job of premier of Ontario. *Office of the Premier of Ontario*

Bill Davis's cottage near Honey Harbour on Georgian Bay, the place where Davis truly bonded with his children. *Steve Paikin*

The Davis family's boat at the cottage on Georgian Bay. Bill Davis's grandchildren call him "Dutch," which was also his father's nickname. *Steve Paikin*

Bill Davis grew into his job as premier, winning back his majority government in 1981. *Steve Paikin*

Margaret Birch was Ontario's first-ever female cabinet minister, having been appointed by Bill Davis in 1972. Now 95 years old, Birch has many pictures of the premier in her home in Pickering, Ontario. *Steve Paikin*

This is the Bill Davis with whom Ontarians became very comfortable, enjoying a big belly laugh. *Office of the Premier of Ontario*

Bill Davis with German Chancellor Helmut Schmidt. *Office of the Premier of Ontario*

"Maybe that is an indication that they have finally given up all hope."

Two days before election day the Silver Fox entered the drama. Davis went to a 600-person event in Lindsay, ostensibly to be photographed with Leslie Frost, premier from 1949 to 1961, and the premier when Davis won his first election in 1959. The *Globe and Mail* did publish a picture of a smiling Davis with Frost, but the story itself was more about how wistful Frost was at how much campaigning had changed. People were no longer interested in long speeches, he observed. Radio and television had changed the public's appetite for serious talk. And he gave Davis the advice his own father had given him: "You can do more with a friendly shake of the hand and pat on the back than by talking politics." Frost would know. In his day he won three straight majority governments — still, as of this publication, the last Ontario premier to achieve that.

In 1971, unlike in 2016, the news media didn't publish public opinion polls every five minutes during election campaigns. There actually was some intrigue and drama over how election night would roll out. But some polling was published and much of it was downright scary for the Tories. On solving unemployment, 79 percent felt the Progressive Conservatives had done only a fair or poor job. Fully 71 percent thought they'd done a fair or poor job of keeping taxes down. On controlling pollution, 65 percent felt Davis had done a fair or poor job — hardly the inspiring kind of numbers the leader wanted to see on the eve of an election. On a range of other issues, the government was also on the wrong side of the charts: the numbers for resisting American economic penetration, encouraging investment, helping farmers, and handling strikes and labour disputes were awful. But there were two numbers the Tories had to love. On providing good education, they enjoyed a favourability of 73 percent. One wonders how much of that number was wrapped up in Davis's decision not to offer public funds to the Catholic system. And on who would make the best premier, it was no contest: Ontarians liked Bill Davis by a three-to-one margin over the other party leaders.

It remained to be seen which set of numbers would prove to be more relevant on October 21, 1971 — Bill Davis's fourth election day, but first as premier of the Province of Ontario. His appointments secretary was very optimistic. In Davis's daily diary, the only entry on that date appears at 8:00 p.m. all in capital letters. It says: RE-ELECTION OF W.G.D.!!!

9

MAJORITY (I)

Although known as a labour town, Hamilton wasn't always a wasteland for the Progressive Conservative Party. In fact, in the lead-up to the 1971 provincial election, the Tories had three of the city's five seats, with the NDP carrying the other two. The Liberals were shut out. So, with three days to go before election day, the *Hamilton Spectator* knew its readership when it endorsed Bill Davis and the PC Party. "Ontario can ill afford to dump a man of such experience, talent, and influence," the *Spectator* editorialized. "In such trying times, this is no time to experiment with any leader who lacks even one of these qualities."

Despite that praise, the newspaper wasn't blindly in love with Davis. "He is capable of buying votes with expensive election-eve promises," the *Spectator* pointed out. "He has a record of spending money on frills and dubious experiments. And he evidently will continue to tolerate a bureaucracy that is surely the Fat Lady of Canada's civil service circus." It seemed there were still plenty of doubts about Ontario's new premier.

And things got off to a rocky start on election day when Davis showed up at the polling station to vote, only to discover he was technically not eligible to do so. Somehow his name had been misspelled on the voters' list as "William David." An embarrassed poll clerk struck out the incorrect spelling and pencilled in the premier's actual name at the bottom of the list. Would it be an omen or something to laugh about later in the evening?

Liberal leader Robert Nixon's day started with some awkward small talk with reporters at his family farm in St. George in Brant County. Someone asked him whether he had his victory speech ready to go, and he assured them he did, which elicited a few chuckles. Then he added, "I've got the other one ready to go, as well," which elicited louder laughs.

One journalist followed up: "C'mon, Bob, what're you going to say if you lose?"

Not missing a beat, the quick-witted Liberal leader stole a page from his American namesake after a failed run for governor of California in 1962 and said, "What I'm going to say is, 'Well, you won't have Nixon to kick around anymore.'" Howls of laughter ensued. Nixon's 82-year-old mother, Alice, joined the festivities and recalled that it was "52 years ago yesterday that Harry was first elected to the legislature." Alice Nixon had seen her share of election days.

Stephen Lewis's election day also started with a laugh. As he went door to door in his Scarborough West riding, he told reporter Warren Gerard: "If we do really poorly, I'll get up before the TV cameras and say, 'F[!@#] you, Ontario!'"

The Big Blue Machine had done everything it could to get Davis to this day. Even in Brampton, the campaign wasn't leaving anything to chance. A full-page ad appeared in the *Brampton Daily Times* with the headline: "Action Speaks Louder Than Words." In case Bramptonians who'd been represented by Davis for 12 years hadn't yet got the message that experienced leadership was the key to their future, the ad gave it one more shot:

> Nobody's saying that words aren't important. Dialogue is, after all, pretty central to our notion of democracy. People talk to other people, and listen to other people talk about the changes that could or should happen to our society. But there's something else that's pretty central to our notion of democracy, and that's leadership. One person must act when all has been said. One person must speak for us. One person must listen, and very carefully, when there are difficult decisions to be made. Bill Davis is not new to the challenge of leadership. During his seven months as Premier, he has acted

to stimulate our economy, to create opportunities for Canadians and for Canadian enterprise. He has acted on a wide front to clean up our environment — air, land and water. He has acted to expand and up-grade a variety of government services, from day care centres to Medicare for those 65 and over. In all, more than 130 pieces of legislation have been introduced, debated, and made law in those seven short months. In the course of the present election campaign, Bill Davis continues to listen and speak out, but his promises are few. Our economy can ill afford the tax increases to which others have freely committed themselves. We may be sure that when action is called for, he will be both wise and decisive. In what he has already done is the true promise of what is to come from the leadership of Bill Davis.

Under that copy was a head-and-shoulders "action" shot of Bill and Kathy Davis, presumably looking down at a child during a rally, although what they're looking at isn't in the shot. But the image conveys concern and gravitas. Neither Davis is smiling. It's a serious moment for a serious election-day decision. The caption under the picture: "Davis is doing things ... for people. He listens, he understands, he acts. On Thursday, re-elect Bill Davis in Peel North."

On October 21, 1971, people all over Ontario and not just in Peel North did just that. Davis captured nine seats more than he inherited from John Robarts for a total of 78. The *Globe and Mail* said it well in its front-page headline: "Landslide for Davis." The rookie premier took 44.5 percent of the total votes cast, an increase of 2.2 percentage points from 1967. And what must have been especially satisfying, the Tories took almost all of those new seats from the Liberals. In fact, both opposition parties were locked in a virtual tie. The Liberals ended up with 20 seats (down from 28), the NDP with 19 seats (down from 20). The Liberals only took 27.8 percent of the total votes cast (down almost 4 points), while the NDP were right on the Liberals' heels with 27.1 percent of the votes (up 1.2 points from 1967). It was about as perfect a result as the PCs could have hoped for. The new premier improved on what he had inherited, he kept the Tory dynasty alive for another four years, and the opposition was evenly divided and hugely disappointed with their respective showings.

"It's like 1963 all over again," said John Robarts, referring to his own majority government win as a rookie leader. Even Davis's Liberal opponent in Peel North, Gary Thaler, conceded: "Davis will be in power as long as he wants to be." He wasn't far off. Vernon Singer, the Liberals' deputy leader, just couldn't seem to get his head around the idea that Davis won so big. "He's not that bright," Singer said. "A new idea is hard for him to grasp. I think he lacks a real depth of knowledge, particularly of the complex operations of government. But as a politician, who can argue? He won 78 seats and that's the test."

Other Liberals were even less charitable with their comments. True Davidson, the 69-year-old mayor of East York who lost in the riding of York East, said she was already laying the groundwork for a rematch. "Somebody has got to save Ontario from these rascals and it's my private mission," she said, adding every vote for her was a vote against the "privilege, patronage, graft, and corruption" of Ontario's Tory governments.

Donald C. MacDonald, the former NDP leader, acknowledged the image-making machine behind Davis was "second to none." But Davis himself? "He's bright without being brilliant," MacDonald said. "I don't think he has any outstanding intellectual qualities. He's often indecisive and he is usually terribly evasive."

But even the fiery former coroner, NDP MPP Morton Shulman, gave Davis his due: "I find him a highly intelligent human being. He's a cut above the average politician in honesty and he does things he thinks are right, regardless of the consequences." It was a generous thing to say about one's adversary so soon after an electoral thrashing — another indication how different the politics of the time were compared to today.

A deeper look inside the numbers showed a province-wide embracing of the Davis-led Progressive Conservatives. The Tories gained 13 seats while losing only three, and in each of those three, local issues were a greater factor than the premier. For example, the Liberals took the riding of York–Forest Hill in midtown and northwest Toronto away from the Tories. The defeated PC candidate Barry Lowes had a simple explanation: "That damn ditch." It was a reference to the Spadina Expressway, whose cancellation put that seat, plus Downsview, into the

Liberal column. Also, Phil Givens, the former Toronto mayor, was the Liberal candidate in York–Forest Hill, which surely didn't hurt, even if he only won by 1,400 votes. What did anti-Spadina champion and Toronto City Councillor William Kilbourn think of the Liberal show-ing in Toronto? "They were humiliated and I'm delighted," he offered. The Liberals took only three of 26 seats in Ontario's capital; the NDP captured 7; Davis's Tories were victorious in a whopping 16. In a capital that today has delivered 20 out of 22 seats to Kathleen Wynne's Liberal Party (with two New Democrats and no PCs at all), it might be hard to fathom, but Toronto was once a true Tory bastion.

Ontario's only husband-wife MPP team was also broken up. The NDP's Jim Renwick held his seat in Riverdale, but former *Toronto Telegram* columnist Frank Drea soundly defeated his wife, Marilyn Renwick, in Scarborough Centre. Interestingly, Drea was the only Roman Catholic PC candidate in Toronto, and he backed Davis's deci-sion *not* to offer public funding to separate schools. He accused his church of "talking against us from the pulpit," despite being "a good strong Catholic and a separate school supporter, and I still can't believe how vicious it got." When Drea was asked how he managed to overcome all that and defeat the popular former sitting member, he said, "Because I'm a hard-nosed son of a bitch." Drea would spend the next 14 years at Queen's Park repeatedly proving the accuracy of his claim.

The PCs even won the downtown Toronto seat of Dovercourt, which used to be so reliably Progressive Conservative, but not since 1955, and they lost a seat they secretly hoped they'd lose. It was 44 years later that Davis told me he was not sorry to see North Bay Mayor Merle Dickerson go down to defeat in Nipissing by just 44 votes, coincidentally, the same number of votes by which Davis won the PC Party leadership. Actually, with 183 of 184 polls reporting, Dickerson was leading *by one vote*. The last poll did him in. Some people thought Dickerson, who was mayor on three different occasions, was "colourful." Others not so much. By the time Dickerson's political career was over, he had spent two weeks in jail for playing poker in an illegal gambling room and faced corruption charges on two separate occasions: first, that he'd bribed ineligible voters, including an underage teenager; and second, that he'd offered a competitor for the mayor's chair a job in exchange for that candidate's dropping out of the race. When found guilty of that second infraction, Dickerson was removed from office and barred from running again for two years. Colourful indeed.

One of the successful Tory candidates was the chairman of the Young Progressive Conservatives, who captured the Don Mills riding. His name was Dennis Timbrell. He would become the youngest of all MPPs elected on that October day — just 24 years old. He was a teacher who gave up his $6,000-a-year job at Don Mills Junior High School the year before to dedicate himself full-time to winning the seat. His teaching certificate was signed by the education minister of the day: Bill Davis.

The 1971 election brought a lot of new Tory MPPs to Queen's Park who would go on to have successful careers in Ontario politics, including Muskoka's Frank Miller, who would eventually succeed Davis as premier; Claude Bennett from Ottawa South; John Clement from Niagara Falls (whose stepson, Tony, would also become a future provincial and federal cabinet minister); Sidney Handleman from Carleton; John Rhodes from Sault Ste. Marie, whose son, Paul, would be a press gallery member and then one of Premier Mike Harris's top campaign advisers; and Gordon Walker in London North, who became one of the more prominent small-c conservative voices in the Davis government, occasionally to the premier's chagrin. Two young candidates managed to buck the province-wide trend to the Tories: Floyd Laughren, a future NDP finance minister, who had just celebrated his 36th birthday a few weeks before election day, took Nickel Belt away from the Tories, who had held the seat since 1955; 32-year-old Albert Roy similarly took Ottawa East away from them for the first time since 1955; and 34-year-old rookie Mike Cassidy, who would soon replace Stephen Lewis as NDP leader, won his first election by the nail-biting margin of 182 votes in Ottawa Centre. He defeated Garry Guzzo, who nearly a quarter of a century later would try again, this time victoriously in the 1995 Mike Harris sweep.

Politics in 1971 was still overwhelmingly a man's game. There were just two female MPPs in the 117-seat Ontario legislature. One of them was retiring, and the other, the NDP's Marilyn Renwick, lost. Only 20 women were on the ballot at all in 1971, and just two of them won: Margaret Birch in Scarborough East and Margaret Scrivener in the downtown Toronto riding of St. David. Immediately, there was speculation as to whether Davis would appoint one of them to the cabinet, making that

MPP the first female cabinet minister ever. That's right — in 104 years of Confederation, there had still never been a woman appointed to an Ontario cabinet. John Diefenbaker had appointed the first federal female cabinet minister (Ellen Fairclough of Hamilton) in 1957.

In his analysis of the election results, *Telegram* reporter Eric Dowd wrote that Davis won so big because he offered "reassurance, restraint, and confidence in troubled times, when the Opposition parties suggested only stridency and uncertainty." But Dowd also expressed concern about the way Davis and his Big Blue Machine won, noting the "mammoth, personality-centred advertising campaign that leaves behind some disturbing questions for Ontario politics." It wouldn't be the first or last time observers would excoriate the Tories for campaigns that sold the premier "like soap." The *Globe and Mail*'s George Bain very much disliked a campaign that "pitched uncomfortable close" to ads for protection against untidy underarms, jungle mouth, and itching feet.

The Liberals countered with advertising, too, of course, but it just didn't work. Their radio and television tag line — "Had enough? Vote Liberal" — fell flat because, apparently, nearly half of Ontarians hadn't had enough of the Tory dynasty. Conversely, the Liberals' ad man, Jerry Goodis, likened the PC campaign to "the good old Normandy technique — assault the beaches of the voters' minds with wave after wave of commercials supported by a pyrotechnic air cover of Davis jingles, until the sensibilities surrender." Even Goodis admitted, "God, even I started to succumb after awhile."

Not only that, but many Liberals must have been scratching their heads at the tax-cut lifeline the federal Liberal Party threw to the Ontario government with just a week to go in the campaign. Davis was probably cruising to victory at that point, anyway, but why Trudeau felt he needed to toss Davis even more manna from heaven is curious to say the least.

Bill Davis watched the election returns at home with some of the charter members of the Big Blue Machine — Hugh Macaulay, Norman Atkins, and Bill Kelly, the party's chief fundraiser. The election night celebration was a family affair for Bill Davis. His wife and kids were with him, celebrating before a few thousand cheering supporters in the Brampton Junior Farmers' Hall. Kathleen Davis's eyes were filled with tears of joy, and the audience clamoured for her to speak.

"She never makes speeches except at home," the victorious premier offered. "And we're not going to change that tonight!"

Davis received a congratulatory telegram from Leslie Frost. It said only, "Glory Hallelujah!" Somewhere in the throng was the rookie mayor of nearby Streetsville, who had only been elected a year ago. Her name was Hazel McCallion.

In Brant County what could Robert Nixon say? He'd given his all in an election in which he was the most experienced leader, but in which, once again, events out of his control conspired to do him in. The federal Liberal tax cut was hardly helpful to his cause. And the Ontario public, which had so embraced Trudeaumania only three years earlier, was now souring on the federal Liberal leader. The provincial Liberal brand wasn't in great shape and the federal one was even worse off. Nixon was only stating the obvious when he acknowledged on election night: "Basically, people have confidence in the conservative traditions of this province. They have shown a great reticence to opt for a change."

While that might have been true, 44 years after that election, Nixon can still work himself into quite a lather about what he says was Bill Davis's exploitation of the Catholic school funding issue for partisan advantage. "What he'd done was take the deliberate decision to turn what had been through our history a divisive, unhealthy battle or difference of opinion into once again a winning political manoeuvre," he says.

Nixon might have believed in his bones that more funding for Catholic schools was the right thing to do, but it's doubtful many of his constituents in Brant County felt the same way. On election night at the Liberal campaign headquarters in Paris, Ontario, Nixon was approached by a group of "old Scotch farmers," as they were called. They were all lifelong Liberals. One looked at the province-wide results and said to Nixon, "Well, it's the Catholic school issue."

Nixon responded, "Well, what about you guys? How come you could support me?"

One farmer retorted, "Oh, Bob, we know you didn't mean it."

Over at NDP campaign headquarters it was a similar scene. For much of the night, Stephen Lewis was trailing the PC candidate in his Scarborough West seat. The leader paced back and forth with a grim look. His father, David, who had just won the federal NDP leadership six months earlier, nervously whistled through his teeth. By the end of the night, the younger Lewis had kept the riding in NDP hands, but only by 475 votes. The older Lewis listened to his son's concession speech with tears in his eyes. "I had too much hope," David Lewis said.

Stephen Lewis acknowledged a post-election bitterness that he described as almost "congenital" among New Democrats. The biggest heartbreak for Lewis: he was so confident he could improve the NDP's seat count, and yet after giving it everything he had, he didn't. While the NDP were fighting Tories and Liberals, they were also fighting among themselves. The "Waffle" movement — a hard left, even more ideological faction within the NDP — made Lewis's campaign a nightmare. He'd say one thing and the Waffle would contradict it. In his book *Unfinished Journey* about the Lewis family history, author Cameron Smith says the press loved reporting on the NDP's internecine struggles. But to come one seat shy of beating the Liberals and becoming the official opposition for the first time ever was infuriating for Lewis, and he blamed the Waffle. It all took its toll.

"We fought the election with and against the Waffle rather than with and against the Tories," Lewis said in *Unfinished Journey*. "You can't imagine those meetings. They were raw hatred on both sides."

"He lasted through the campaign, but he was strung out," Smith wrote of Lewis. "[It] reinforced the idea that he was an aggressive hawkish young guy."

Nevertheless, the younger Lewis had to acknowledge the PC ad team did its job. It successfully created a personality cult around Ontario's premier. Plus, Lewis had to admit, Ontarians knew and liked Bill Davis. The premier "had spoken at every school in the province," Lewis told Cameron Smith. "He was grounded in the soil of Ontario."

Lewis loved telling the following story to illustrate his point. In Scarborough North, the riding right next to his own, Tory cabinet minister Tom Wells was out knocking on doors when a woman answered.

"Hello," he said, "I'm Tom Wells and I'd like to ask for your support in the election."

"I'm voting for Bill Davis," the housewife replied. "Clear out."

Davis did it. He kept the PC dynasty alive. He earned the right to govern Ontario for four more years. The Big Blue Machine enhanced its reputation as the go-to-guys if Tories anywhere in Canada needed to win. After the election, Dalton Camp's advertising agency won the

Ontario government's tourism account. Yes, it was patronage, but the agency also did a bang-up job on one file in particular. It came up with a new slogan for the province that was simple and elegant and has stood the test of time. Ontario became "Yours to Discover." The premier liked the slogan so much that he had it put on the province's licence plates, where it's remained for 45 years.

10

TROUBLE

It's a funny thing about majority governments in our first-past-the-post system. They often give the impression that the winners are far more popular than they really are. Yes, by the standards of a mature three-party parliamentary democracy, Bill Davis's 44.5 percent of the total vote in the 1971 election was an extremely respectable, solid number. Because of the way the votes split, it gave the PCs fully two-thirds of the seats in the legislature. In fact, there were so many Tory MPPs now at Queen's Park that they couldn't fit all the government members on one side of the legislature. They had to put a group of about 20 MPPs on the opposition side. The new kid on the block, Dennis Timbrell, christened that group "The Rump," and since they sat in alphabetical order so as not to show any favouritism, you can guess where Timbrell ended up sitting.

"You really know you're a backbencher when you sit in the back row of The Rump," Timbrell now says, recalling those giddy first days in the legislature.

Having that many seats created an impression that the Davis government was far more popular than it really was. After all, more than half the voters in Ontario did vote *against* the Progressive Conservatives, but because they split their votes so evenly between the Liberals and New Democrats, it gave the Tories a massive victory. Having that many seats also creates high expectations — perhaps unreasonably high expectations. Nevertheless, there is nothing more powerful in any democratic country than a Westminster-style parliamentary majority. You control every ministry, committee, patronage lever, judicial appointment, and decision of any significance. Because of that, some of your people tend to get sloppy and make stupid mistakes. As long as you keep your backbenchers happy, onside, and voting your way, you can essentially do whatever you want for four years. That's both a blessing and a curse. Somehow the electorate, opposition, and media instinctively know all this, which can quickly turn what should be a majority government's time of triumph into quite a miserable experience.

And that's exactly what happened to William Grenville Davis's first majority government.

With the dynasty secured for four more years, 1971 came to an end without much controversy. The public wouldn't have taken notice, but Davis was determined to take control of the levers of the PC Party, which had so botched the leadership convention. The first step in that regard was to ditch Arthur Harnett, the executive director of the party. That position was supposed to be the prerogative of the party president, in this case, Alan Eagleson. But Davis had other ideas. He wanted his own man in the job, and despite technically having no constitutional authority to do so, Davis appointed Ross DeGeer on January 1, 1972, to be the party's new executive director. Eagleson lived with the decision. DeGeer was part of Allan Lawrence's team but had loyally signed on to help what was now Davis's "Big Blue Machine." Hugh Macaulay thought DeGeer's appointment imperative to ensure the party, the premier's office, and the caucus all sang out of the same hymn book.

Davis did a massive shuffle of the cabinet he'd inherited from John Robarts in March 1971. But almost immediately thereafter he started considering a lot more significant government reorganization — not just changing the players in their departments but really thinking through how policy moved up the political food chain and eventually got implemented. To that end, he had some help from his predecessor. Davis had inherited John Robarts's Committee on Government Productivity (COGP), a blue-ribbon panel of some of the province's most influential civil servants and important private sector executives. Robarts wanted government to run more efficiently and wasn't convinced that it was actually set up to do so. So he got two of the heaviest hitters he knew in government and business to chair the COGP and think about reimagining how Queen's

Park could work. His trusted treasurer, Charles MacNaughton, was the point man at the legislature. And from the private sector he tapped John Cronyn, his friend from London and president of Labatt Breweries.

In 1969 James Fleck joined the committee in a most unusual way — he was both the committee's executive director *and* a member of the body, tasked with setting up a process whereby this eminent panel would meet, discuss ideas, issue interim recommendations, then follow up on those recommendations with progress reports, so the public could actually see that something was happening. The last thing Fleck wanted was another report that was going to sit on a shelf and collect dust. Two years younger than Davis, Fleck had been considered a rising star for years. He was educated at University of Toronto Schools where he topped his class in mathematics and science, then became a "gold medallist" at the University of Western Ontario. In 1964 he garnered attention by becoming a Ford Foundation Fellow at Harvard University where he graduated with a doctorate of business administration and finance.

After Robarts left and Davis took over, John Cronyn convinced the new premier that the best way to implement the recommendations of the COGP was to install Fleck as Davis's new chief of staff. For extra good measure, to show the government was going to operate in a more businesslike fashion, Fleck's title was changed to "chief executive officer in the department of the prime minister of Ontario."

What resulted was a complete overhaul of how the cabinet worked. Davis agreed to establish a new "inner cabinet" — a policy and priorities committee — similar to the way the federal government organized its cabinet structure. It would weed out less pressing matters and advise the premier on major policy initiatives. Davis was also reworking the existing "treasury board" of cabinet to review the management of government programs. This new structure also gave Davis another means of calming the post-leadership convention tensions. Allan Lawrence, Darcy McKeough, Robert Welch, and Bert Lawrence were all appointed to the new inner cabinet, along with the premier's own leadership campaign chairman and now former treasurer Charles MacNaughton.

And there was so much more. After unveiling perhaps the largest shuffle in Ontario history only a year earlier, Davis now shook things up again with some even bigger moves. "Before this time there were too many things that were worked out on the back of an envelope," recalls Jim Fleck. So the premier's office created four "super-ministries," thinking this more streamlined system would make government and decision-making more effective. For example, the still only 39-year-old Darcy McKeough was proving to be a minister Davis could count on even more, so he added to McKeough's responsibilities, making him the head of a newly designed super ministry called TEIGA: treasury, economics, and intergovernmental affairs, *and* giving McKeough the municipal affairs portfolio to boot. Allan Lawrence was now the provincial secretary for justice, meaning all issues related to justice (attorney general, corrections, public protection) would flow from various line ministries through him. Robert Welch was provincial secretary for social development, so all issues related to education, health, colleges and universities, and social services would go through him before cabinet took a decision. Bert Lawrence became provincial secretary for resource development with similarly enhanced responsibilities for labour, trade, agriculture, natural resources, environment, transportation, and communications. Davis never liked the term "super minister" (too ostentatious for his Brampton sensibilities). He preferred "policy minister." The thinking was that the line ministers responsible for specific departments (health, education, agriculture, et cetera) could bring policy ideas to the "policy ministers," who could become real experts on a wide range of issues. Those super ministers would then go through the proposals in detail, theoretically weeding out the policy and political problems so that by the time an issue came before the entire cabinet, it could sail through much more quickly and efficiently. Of course, if the item were particularly contentious, the whole cabinet could still have a go at it.

Davis described this reorganization as "the most massive of any government attempted on this continent." Was it really?

All these years later Jim Fleck laughs and asks, "Why not?"

No study was ever done to prove Davis's rare boast, but to be sure, this was a very big deal. And yet, strangely enough, Davis was a no-show for the swearing-in ceremony of his new super ministers. He was on a family vacation in Florida and spoke by telephone to the four new super ministers and their wives before the ceremony. It was the first of many indications over the years that when Bill Davis was away with his family it would occasionally (maybe frequently?) be difficult to drag him back to Ontario's capital to attend to political matters.

On paper this reorganization might have made a lot of sense, but politics isn't practised on paper. When Jim Fleck saw who the new super ministers were, he was concerned. Just like the composition of the government's new inner cabinet, the super ministers were all former party leadership rivals of Davis's. The premier no doubt wanted to give his former rivals these new big jobs to help smooth over the wounds of the convention. But what the rest of the cabinet and caucus saw was further centralizing of government and a formal (rather than informal) pecking order resulting in jealousy and bitterness.

The best organizational flow charts developed by powerful executives and brilliant academics couldn't stand up to good old-fashioned political human emotion. The *Globe and Mail*, in a clever turn of phrase, wondered whether the new ministers were really "super or merely superficial." The provincial secretary system created a ton of bad feelings between the backbench and cabinet, between lower-ranking and higher-ranking cabinet ministers, and between everyone and Jim Fleck. Except for Darcy McKeough who still had his fingers on the levers of all spending, the other super ministers soon found they might have had a lot of cabinet clout but the public didn't know it. During Question Period, the ministers with line responsibilities handled all the issues because they were the ones actually running the departments and cutting the ribbons. The super ministers virtually disappeared. They had a lot of clout when it came to approving policy decisions, but it was all behind the scenes. The lack of exposure rankled and gave way to rumours that Davis's backroom boys devised this scheme to keep the premier's profile high and his rivals' profiles low. One day during Question Period, Stephen Lewis stole the show in a way that only Stephen Lewis could.

"I have a question for the minister of resource development," the NDP leader began. "What do you do?" And then Lewis sat down.

"Oh, his timing was so exquisite," recalls Floyd Laughren, a future finance minister from 1990 to 1995 but in his first term as an MPP at the time. "Bert Lawrence was totally frozen. It was wonderful!"

The system might have worked if the provincial secretaries had all abandoned their hopes of someday replacing Davis. For example, Allan Grossman's time as provincial secretary for resource development was considered more politically successful because Grossman never had any aspirations to succeed Davis. He was already 64 years old when he got the job and didn't mind having more power and less exposure. But that was in 1974. Such was not the case in 1972. If for whatever reason Davis were to leave his post early, certainly Allan Lawrence and Darcy McKeough still had aspirations to replace him, and that meant keeping their profiles high. Ed Stewart, who would go on to become Davis's secretary to the cabinet (in effect, the premier's own deputy minister), said for this structure to work it "required a sense of collegiality that was notably lacking. Holding on to one's turf proved to be a far stronger motivation." It was only the first sign of trouble, and eventually the provincial secretary positions all disappeared with the super ministers moving to take over old-fashioned ministries just as before.

Fortunately for the Tories, the official opposition was having troubles of its own. Having now lost two consecutive general elections, Robert Nixon figured it was time to let someone else lead the Ontario Liberal Party. He announced he would step down pending the selection of a new leader. But he didn't intend to go down with a whimper. In his response to the throne speech on March 6, 1972, he noted that Davis's 1971 list of election promises included free medicare to seniors, extending hospital coverage to nursing homes, and $150 million worth of tax rebates, which he called "the most blatant political bribe that in my memory and experience has ever been offered in this province to assist farmers." Forty-five years before a federal Conservative cabinet minister named Pierre Poilievre was chastised for handing out $3 billion in "universal child benefit" cheques three months before an election while wearing a golf shirt emblazoned with a Conservative Party logo, Bill Davis was sending rebate cheques to farmers in envelopes containing messages from the agriculture and municipal affairs ministers. And Bob Nixon didn't like it one bit: "It made my stomach turn over and my heart turn cold, because that was pretty blatant political bribery," he said at the time. "It was unworthy of him or any other premier."

But Nixon's "last hurrah" speech didn't seem to faze Davis, who took it all in stride. Davis insists to this day he never disliked Nixon despite their fiery public exchanges and lack of warmth in their relationship. In fact, after Nixon announced his intention to depart the leadership, Davis commented to Liberals across the floor of the legislature: "You fellows are going to have to go a long way to find a better leader."

Bill Davis then experienced a kind of George H.W. Bush moment. At the 1988 Republican National Convention Bush famously encouraged

Republicans to read his lips, promising them no new taxes, and Davis vowed the same during the 1971 election campaign. But at the end of March 1972, when treasurer Darcy McKeough unveiled the budget for the 1972–73 fiscal year, there they were: tax increases on beer, liquor, tobacco, gasoline, and real estate sales, plus fee increases for driver's licences, marriage licences, GO Transit, park use, toll bridges, the Ontario Science Centre, and the provincially owned theme park on Toronto's waterfront, Ontario Place. There were also fee increases for attending universities, nursing schools, and teachers' colleges, while grants for post-secondary students were reduced. To be sure, most of the increases weren't huge. For example, driver's licences went from $20 to $23, entry to the Science Centre went from $1 to $1.50 for adults, and the gas tax went from 18 to 19 cents per gallon. But the breadth of items being taxed took many by surprise.

Jim Breithaupt, the Liberal MPP for Kitchener, joked that Davis had kept every election promise except the one not to raise taxes. "Since he made no other promises, the score is 100 percent failure," Breithaupt said.

The NDP's Donald C. MacDonald called the 180-degree turn "a breathtaking measure of self-righteousness and hypocrisy and cynicism."

It's true that McKeough did raise a lot of different taxes when the Tories promised they wouldn't. But that's the way it always happened in Ontario. John Robarts pledged no tax increases before the 1963 and 1967 election campaigns, and in both cases, he immediately did raise taxes in the ensuing budgets. In 1968 Ontarians experienced the largest tax increase in their history.

"I was a piker," McKeough observed at the time about his own tax increases, compared to the 1968 Robarts budget.

Relative to today's numbers, the 1972 Ontario budget seems perfectly quaint. Total government expenditures were only $5 billion for the whole fiscal year. The deficit forecast, because of the tax increases and spending restraints, was declining to $597 million, down from $653 million the year before. And again, by the standards of the time, the Davis government really did put the brakes on spending. In the previous year, spending had increased by 15 percent. Darcy McKeough was holding it to 4.5 percent this year, which was the lowest rate of increase in two decades.

Seen through the lens of today's sensibilities, the budget appeared to be delivered by a government with a political tin ear. But remember: this was four and a half decades ago. The public stampede toward politicians promising tax cuts was still more than two decades away. Three successive "big-deficit" spending budgets aimed at stimulating the economy resulted in a doubling of the provincial debt — the accumulated deficits from Confederation to the present. But as a percentage of Ontario's economy, the debt was only about 10 percent, nowhere near the alarming 40 percent of today. In fact, at more than $300 billion Ontario's debt today is the largest of any sub-national jurisdiction in the world.

The 1972 budget wasn't balanced. In fact, expressed in today's dollars, that 1972 budget deficit clocked in at nearly $3.4 billion — not insignificant but nothing close to the worst deficit incurred by an Ontario government, namely, Liberal Finance Minister Dwight Duncan's $14.1 billion deficit in 2009 during the throes of the Great Recession.

In fact, it might be hard to remember that even in tough economic times Ontario's numbers didn't look so bad. From 1970 to 1971, Ontario's gross provincial product increased at a rate of 9 percent, and McKeough was forecasting nearly 10 percent for 1972. Today the Ontario government is thrilled that the economy is expected to grow by slightly more than 2 percent annually. The unemployment rate was 5.2 percent in 1971 and despite a soft economy was expected to drop to 4.8 percent. As this book goes to press, Ontario's unemployment rate for the past many quarters has been around 6.5 percent. And the provincial retail sales tax in 1971–72 was only 5 percent. Today, it makes up 8 of an overall 13 percent harmonized sales tax. (The HST is a combination of the federal Goods and Services Tax and the province's former retail sales tax.)

Another comparison is the size of the public service. Ontario's population in 1971 was 7.7 million people, and yet there were more than 70,000 people directly employed by the government. Today Ontario's population is approaching 14 million people, and yet the size of the public service is actually smaller — around 60,000. All of the above numbers suggest Bill Davis truly was a progressive conservative. When spending restraint was called for, the government was capable of doing so. For example, spending on health care for 1972–73 was estimated at $1.28 billion. Even expressed in today's dollars, that would be less than $7.5 billion. But today's Ontario government spends north of $50 billion on health care annually. The 1972 budget was also a historic one for the province, insofar as for the first time

ever, health-care spending would surpass spending on elementary and secondary school education. The trend has continued to the point where today
we spend more than *twice as much* on health care as we do on education.

However, make no mistake: unlike other conservatives who campaign professing their hatred for government, Davis believed government
had a greater obligation to its citizenry than simply to get out of the way;
he believed in the power of the government's ability to improve people's
lives. Government was involved, and Davis made no apologies for that.
In fact, based on the treasurer's language, government was downright
sexy. In his budget speech, Darcy McKeough made frequent references to
the budget's "fiscal thrust," its "economic thrust," or its "dynamic thrust."
Stephen Lewis observed: "This is the most astonishingly Freudian budget"
he'd ever seen. Even the Tories hammered their desks in laughter.

One of the things the 1970s brought to the Province of Ontario was a
much nastier press gallery at Queen's Park. The days of Premier Robarts
cavorting around Yorkville jazz clubs with women who weren't his wife —
and the press being quiet about it — were now over. Without anyone formally announcing that politicians' private lives were now fairer game, the
scrutiny of politicians was about to get kicked up a whole lot of notches.
Premier Davis and his provincial secretary for resource development,
Bert Lawrence, were about to find this out in a very unpleasant fashion.
Just one month after Davis enjoyed plenty of complimentary headlines
for the way he had restructured government, the papers were now after
him because he and Lawrence had used government aircraft to fly their
families for Easter vacations. In both cases it would have been cheaper
for the politicians' families to fly commercial. But in both cases it seemed
the expectation was that the taxpayers would foot the bill for their flights.
Davis argued with some justification that whenever he was absent from
the legislature he was still "on duty," needing security and a convenient
way of bringing government papers with him.

"In reality there are no days off and no holidays from the job," he said
to explain why he used a government aircraft to fly his wife and five children to a ski trip in Vermont.

The government's $2 million executive jet purchase was always a gift
for the opposition in Question Period. Before the purchase became official, Liberal MPP Vernon Singer asked Davis to confirm or deny rumours

that he was about to buy a jet. The answer was classic Davis, obfuscating at his best: "The decision-making process has not reached the point where a decision has been made," he said.

In Lawrence's case the minister and his family were apparently invited by the Cuban government to enjoy some skin diving at Veradero, a beach resort about 60 miles from Havana. When the minister for resource development suggested the trip was akin to a trade mission, Stephen Lewis wasn't buying. "That's a queer, contrived excuse for the use of government aircraft that extends far beyond the bounds of the chauffeur-driven limousines the ministers now have." And because he is Stephen Lewis, you knew a clever line wasn't far off: "I don't know what kind of natural resources he hopes to see under the water at Veradero," he added.

But the premier defended his use of government aircraft for personal use, saying it contributed to the "efficient discharge of my official responsibilities." Davis predicted the use of government aircraft would become commonplace in politics "and cease to be a subject of curiosity or concern even among the most partisan critics."

That prediction might have been fine for the future, but it wasn't convincing anybody in the 1970s. In fact, the issue got so under Davis's skin that he uncharacteristically lost his temper during Question Period when interrogated by future Liberal leadership aspirant Donald Deacon, the MPP for York Centre. Deacon wondered whether Davis intended to regard the jet and ski vacation as a taxable benefit at tax time. The Tory backbench hit the roof. They began shouting "Sit down and shut up" at Deacon. Davis repeated his defence about having a 24/7 job but then went for the jugular, adding this would never be a problem Deacon would have to deal with because "he will never have this responsibility." The premier went on to predict Deacon's leadership bid would end in failure (it would) "and he will never have the problem of determining when one's public responsibilities begin and end." The premier was on fire, and Deacon sat in silence.

In fact, the issue turned into such a stinker for the government that by the end of 1973 Davis placed a complete prohibition on the use of government jets for personal use by his ministers and himself. He then reimbursed taxpayers more than $20,000 — half his annual salary — for the personal flights he'd made at public expense. In future, he said, the PC Party would pay for such flights. Interestingly enough, Stephen Lewis expressed concern about Davis's blanket ban, saying the government jets gave Davis "a measure of flexibility he ought to have." It is hard to imagine an opposition leader uttering such an understanding statement today. But it didn't help. The troubles continued.

The year 1972 turned into an *annus horribilis*. Scandal after scandal rocked the Progressive Conservative government. None of it ever touched Davis himself, but the constant drumbeat of negative headlines had to hurt the new premier's lustre. It certainly prevented the government from getting much good news out. For example, it was in 1972 that it emerged that land owned by Dalton Bales, the former attorney general, and two partners was expropriated by the province for three times the price paid for it merely three years earlier. Bales offered to resign from cabinet, but Davis refused. However, it was also in 1972 that the government's most important cabinet minister, Darcy McKeough, did resign. The *Globe and Mail* published a story indicating that when McKeough was municipal affairs minister in the Robarts government he approved the subdivision of land in Chatham, in which it turned out he had a financial interest. McKeough tried to fight to keep his job, insisting he'd done nothing wrong. But he went for a private lunch with his hero and former premier Robarts, the godfather to the McKeoughs second-born son, who advised his protégé he really did need to step down. McKeough did, and it sent the Davis government reeling.

But there was more. The public learned that the Canadian subsidiary of a Swiss-owned company called Fidinam gave the PC Party a $50,000 donation at the same time the cabinet was considering bids to build a new Workmen's Compensation Board headquarters. Fidinam won the bid and the ensuing outrage gave the opposition plenty of fodder for calling Davis the head of a "scandal-a-day" government.

Davis even had a tough time catching a break from the generally liberal *Toronto Star* despite taking a controversial, pro-union stand. In the spring of 1972, the Canadian Wire Service Guild was engaged in a labour dispute with the CBC that had persisted for five weeks. The CBC replaced its unionized camera crew at Queen's Park with a non-unionized freelancer. One April day the premier walked out of the legislature, but before giving an interview to a scrum of journalists waiting for him, he asked whether the non-unionized CBC crew were among the journalists. When told it was, Davis moved away to another location. The guild sent Davis a note thanking him for his "courageous" stand. But the *Star* wrote an editorial headlined: "Davis Was Wrong to Avoid CBC Crew." The supposedly pro-labour *Star* said the premier owed it to the public to be interviewed by all legitimate news media. Opposition leaders Nixon and Lewis also refused to be interviewed by the CBC crew, as did Newfoundland Premier Frank Moores and Nova Scotia Premier Gerald Regan. But the *Star* saved its selective criticism for Davis alone.

As the summer of 1972 came to a close, Bill Davis did something that at least temporarily brought the government some respite from the constant drumbeat of bad news. It all had to do with one of the two women named "Margaret" in his caucus.

Margaret Stewart was originally from Leamington, Ontario. She married a newspaper editor named Guy Birch in 1949, and the couple settled in Scarborough and raised two kids, a son and a daughter. Once both kids were in school, Margaret began to volunteer at the local general hospital. She was evidently quite effective there because before long she became chair of the Scarborough board of health in 1963, then four years later joined the Mental Health Council and the Social Planners Council. In 1970 she was chosen Scarborough's citizen of the year. That brought a call from Health Minister Tom Wells, who asked Margaret whether she'd ever thought of being a candidate for office. Birch was shocked. "Imagine that," she told her family, "they want me to run provincially."

The family discussed it and concluded: "Go for it, Mom!"

Birch had never met Premier Davis but had always admired him. "There was something about him that was reassuring," she says. "He was the epitome of a good politician — honest, and wanting to serve a purpose."

Birch signed up to run in Scarborough East, a riding that featured tough three-way fights over the previous two elections. In fact, in the election in 1967, the Liberals took the riding with 34.2 percent of the votes, while the PC candidate came second with 33.1 percent and the New Democrat third with 32.7 percent. It was anybody's for the taking. But in 1971 it was Margaret Birch who took it for the Tories with 41 percent of the votes — a solid victory.

Premier Davis put Birch in charge of creating new programs for young Ontarians (there was no minister responsible for youth at this point), and working for Birch was a 17-year-old Tory partisan who would eventually spend a lot of time toiling for Tory causes over the years. His name, appropriately enough, was John Tory. Birch remembers Tory "wearing checkered pants and the most outlandish clothes." Together they worked to create summer jobs programs for Ontario youth.

Birch evidently impressed the powers that be, because in September 1972, while travelling with a Queen's Park delegation in England, she got a call from Premier Davis. "Margaret, please come home immediately. You're going to be a cabinet minister." And with that phone call Davis did something none of his 17 predecessors had ever done: he made the decision to appoint a woman to the executive council of the Province of Ontario.

"She was an extremely pleasant lady," Davis told me in 2015, explaining why he appointed Birch. "She was from Scarborough. Everybody liked her. She was intelligent. What more do you want?"

Birch landed at Toronto International Airport, whereupon the police immediately boarded the plane while it was still on the tarmac. As they hustled her onto another plane to fly to Toronto Island Airport, other passengers on the flight were buzzing, wondering what in heaven's name was going on. Why were the police urgently removing this woman from the plane? At the island airport a car was standing by to take her to Queen's Park for the swearing-in ceremony. "I didn't even have time to put any lipstick on," Birch remembers.

On September 28, 1972, Margaret Birch made history, becoming the first-ever female cabinet minister in Ontario history. Birch started at the very bottom of the ladder — minister without portfolio. She had no idea what the job entailed, but she was sure of one thing: this 51-year-old Scarborough mother of two wasn't the slightest bit intimidated at being the only woman in the room.

"I was always used to dealing with a lot of men," she says, referring to her volunteer work.

"Did you ever wonder what it would be like, whether you'd have to deal with sexist behaviour or the like?" I asked her.

"I never heard an off-colour joke ever," Birch insists. "Bill Davis wouldn't have tolerated it."

But breaking the gender barrier in cabinet wasn't Birch's only claim to fame. At this point in its history the downtown Toronto haunt for conservatives for nearly a century, the Albany Club, still only permitted male members. The federal PC leader, Robert Stanfield, was about to make a guest appearance at the club, and Birch wanted to go. But, of course, that wasn't permitted. Birch approached the premier to discuss the issue.

"If I'm good enough to sit in this cabinet with all these men, surely I'm good enough to be a member of the Albany Club," she told the premier.

"You're right," Davis answered. "We'll work on that."

And that's how Margaret Birch also became one of the first three female members of the Albany Club. Her proposer was none other than the 18th premier of Ontario.

Not surprisingly, many observers thought Birch got into cabinet solely because she was a woman and regarded her as a token appointment. She also wore her hair up in a rather old-fashioned, suburban way, which allowed some to typecast her. But those externalities couldn't convey the hardscrabble life that Birch, in fact, had led.

Margaret Birch left school in Leamington at the age of 12 because her father got cancer and her mother had to work to support the family. There were four younger siblings to care for and a baby on the way. Remarkably, her mother was back at work three days after delivering her sixth child at home with the assistance of a midwife. But it was left to Margaret to take care of the family. Somehow Margaret's father survived his cancer and lived to be 78 years old.

"We did what we had to do," says Birch, reflecting that greatest generation's stiff-upper-lip attitude in dealing with life's challenges. At age 16 she worked in the tobacco fields of Southwestern Ontario for $3 a day. Then she toiled at the Heinz plant where her job was to get the labels on the bottles and make sure they were straight. She worked in a five-and-dime store, she babysat — anything to make money and help her family get by.

"I never felt deprived," she says. "And a lack of education never held me back from what I wanted to do."

When she did attend the Albany Club event, Birch got some stares from men who thought she shouldn't be there. But given her background, the notion that Margaret Birch was going to be intimidated by a bunch of old fat-cat Tories was truly fanciful. By the time her political career was over, she had dined with Queen Elizabeth II and the Queen Mother, been on the Royal Yacht *Britannia*, and met Indira Gandhi. In fact, she hit it off so well with Gandhi that the prime minister invited Birch to come visit her in India. But Gandhi was assassinated before the visit could be arranged.

Davis knew Birch was interested in health issues and let her loose as a new cabinet minister to get things done. Birch toured all kinds of health-care facilities and was appalled at the lack of attention and care residents were receiving. She worked with six different ministries to get improvements made. "Some of the people were so lonely they just wanted to hold my hand," she recalls. So Birch arranged to have music and dance parties brought into seniors' homes, nursing residences, and veterans' hospitals. It might seem like a little thing, but she got "happy hour" introduced in the veterans' hospital so former soldiers could enjoy a wee nip at the end of the day. "I went to Bill Davis and got support for that," Birch says. "It gave people something to look forward to."

As chair of Scarborough's Board of Health, Birch could see the needs in her community. As a minister, she could make things happen. She toured mental health facilities (then called asylums) and emerged in tears after seeing people in cages. She told the minister and deputy minister of health that Scarborough needed a new hospital with better mental health services, and worked hard to get both. Opposition members frequently approached her with other ideas to improve things. It was a good and collegial time to be in politics.

She didn't always agree with Davis's decisions. One day in cabinet the premier looked at Birch whose facial expression betrayed her opposition to an announcement. Davis said: "Margaret, I can see that you don't approve. But sometimes we have to do things for the good of all." Davis's approachability made Birch a big fan of her premier.

As 1972 was coming to an end, Davis lost two of the government's more significant pillars. Perhaps recognizing that his future in provincial politics was never going to be what he'd hoped for, Allan Lawrence quit and made the move to national politics. Today Davis insists he and Lawrence by this point had become good friends but that Lawrence "clearly wanted a change. He thought he had a future with the federal party, so I neither encouraged him to stay or to go."

Pierre Trudeau's Liberal government had quickly fallen off the rails, Robert Stanfield's Progressive Conservatives increasingly looked like a solid alternative, and so Lawrence sought and won a seat for the federal Tories in the Central Ontario riding of Northumberland-Durham in the

October 1972 election. Davis actually stumped quite a bit for Stanfield in that campaign, suggesting, "If you like me, you'll like this guy, too." It was Davis, once again, being the loyal Tory. He also attended one rally on behalf of a 21-year-old candidate who had supported him a year earlier at Davis's own leadership convention. That candidate was Hugh Segal, seeking election in Ottawa Centre. Segal didn't win, but he cut the Liberals' margin of victory from almost 8,000 votes in the 1968 election to 1,200 votes in 1972 and says Davis's support was no doubt helpful in his near-victory.

That 1972 contest saw the federal Liberals returned to power, but with a minority government of only 109 seats compared to the Tories' 107. It's true that Lawrence gave up a powerful seat at the provincial cabinet table for one on the opposition benches of the legislature. But given the trend nationally, one had to think he'd be back in the cabinet before long, and, in fact, he was. When Joe Clark won the 1979 election for the Progressive Conservatives, Lawrence was appointed to a double portfolio: solicitor general and minister of consumer and corporate affairs. Of course, it's also true that his seat at that cabinet table didn't last long.

In the midst of Davis's ongoing political difficulties, he got some sad personal news in early 1973, as well. His father and hero, A. Grenville Davis, died on February 16, 1973. The elder Davis had been unwell for too much of his life and it was somewhat of a surprise that he actually managed to live to the age of 80 in spite of poor health. He did manage to see his only son sworn in as the premier of Ontario, which no doubt gave him enormous pride. But his death also left a void in the premier's life at a time when Bill Davis hardly needed more bad news.

Two months later, after nearly 15 years at Queen's Park, Charles MacNaughton retired. The good news was that MacNaughton's Huron riding and Lawrence's St. George riding in downtown Toronto had both been in Tory hands since 1943 and surely would stay there. So even though permitted by law to wait as long as six months before calling the two by-elections, Davis struck quickly, circling March 15, 1973, on the calendar as the date on which he'd have both by-elections. What the premier found out on that date was that his government was in a heap of trouble. The Tories lost *both* contests. Huron went to the Liberals' Jack Riddell, who would become a future agriculture minister in David Peterson's government in 1985. But the St. George results were even more shocking. The Tories had hoped to welcome another young and rising star to the fold in 40-year-old Roy McMurtry, the premier's long-time friend from his University of Toronto days, and whose influence in helping to make peace between the Davis and Lawrence camps after the 1971 leadership convention was significant. But McMurtry and company ran into some strong anti-Tory winds and another force of nature named Margaret Campbell. Campbell had actually been a lifelong conservative but was now a Toronto city councillor allied with the David Crombie–Jane Jacobs reform wing of the council. Campbell defeated McMurtry by nearly 1,400 votes and became the first female MPP the Liberals ever elected to Queen's Park.

The rest of 1973 didn't get any better for the Tories. A good friend of Davis's, Gerhard Moog, won an untendered $44.4 million contract to build a gleaming new headquarters for Ontario Hydro at the corner of College Street and University Avenue in downtown Toronto. Moog had already enjoyed considerable government business. He owned the Canada Square complex at Yonge Street and Eglinton Avenue in midtown Toronto, which became the headquarters for TVO, the new provincial broadcaster. And there were newspaper stories about how he and Davis had travelled through Europe together. The optics weren't great. On April 27, 1973, Davis tabled a letter in the legislature from the Hydro-Electric Power Corporation (HEPCO) that suggested the company actually evaluated four different proposals before landing on Moog's design. However, the next day the *Globe and Mail* had some more damning evidence — that Moog's plan was based on architectural designs paid for by HEPCO itself. Two days later there was another indictment on the process: yes, there were four bidders for the project, but the deck seemed to be stacked for Moog, since the three other proponents actually had to approach HEPCO themselves to be allowed to bid, then received information on how to bid that was virtually useless.

It got worse. One of the would-be bidders was Don Smith, head of the Ellis-Don construction company and a well-known Liberal, who was told by two backroom Tories to "keep your mouth shut or you'll never get another government job." In spite of so much evidence to the contrary, HEPCO continued to insist all four companies were treated equally in their pursuit of the contract to build the new Ontario Hydro building.

To get the story off the front pages, Davis established a legislative committee on May 1 to investigate the Moog–Ontario Hydro situation. The committee reported in October and unanimously found no evidence to substantiate the allegation that Moog got the deal because of his friendship with the premier. But given how long the Tories had been in power and what a formidable patronage machine the party had become, many people assumed the worst. "Like everything else, the negatives appear in bold print," Davis bemoaned at the time. "The results don't always appear in the same priority." Ironically, Moog thought the deal was so good for Ontarians that he later sued the province, saying he was entitled to further compensation. James Fleck called the affair "very distracting."

As 1973 came to a close, Davis moved to recognize what was becoming increasingly apparent about the job of an MPP. In the 1960s being a member of the legislative assembly was definitely a part-time job. In fact, unless you were in cabinet, you were supposed to have another job that kept you in touch with your community and "real life." The legislature didn't sit all that much and the place shut down over the summer. But as the 1960s gave way to the 1970s, the role of a politician was starting to become more than a part-time gig. Davis also insisted the caucus meet at least once a month, including during the summer. Because of the added workload, Davis was prepared to give MPPs a raise as recommended by an independent commission. But given the government's unpopularity at the time, the decision wasn't greeted by the electorate with any enthusiasm.

Sometimes in government it's easier to agree that a certain policy is the right thing to do than it is to actually explain to the public why it's the right thing to do. Such was the case with Davis's efforts to create regional governments. In the 1970s, Ontario was bursting with hundreds and hundreds of small municipalities. It made sense from the point of view of offering local services more efficiently to amalgamate some of those local municipalities. Did small regions of the province really need 15 mayors, 15 fire departments, 15 water departments, and so on to serve 100,000 people? Davis didn't think so. As a result, on January 1, 1974, after considerable consultation but not much local buy-in, the province created new regional governments for Durham, Hamilton-Wentworth, Waterloo, and Haldimand-Norfolk.

On the same date, the province also allowed the town of Mississauga to annex two of the other Peel County communities that had withstood a previous attempt to amalgamate them into a bigger town of Mississauga:

Port Credit and Streetsville. The mayor of Streetsville fought this annexation tooth and nail. Her name was Hazel McCallion, and she demanded the local MPP — Bill Davis — attend a community meeting and explain why he was allowing this appalling annexation to proceed. McCallion went on to suggest that if he didn't want to attend that meeting, he ought to resign, since her faith in him "has been completely shaken." What did Davis do? Of course, he showed up. In June 1973, he entered a community hall of 500 people who lustily booed his every utterance. McCallion was still ticked off with Davis, who again refused to intervene, but she admitted in her memoir *Hurricane Hazel* that everyone in the room respected him for coming. Ironically, four years later, McCallion went on to become mayor of the new, bigger Mississauga and remained the mayor until stepping down in 2014 at the age of 93. Through the years, Davis would tease McCallion that she owed her entire career to his foresight, but in 1974 the obvious benefits of a bigger, amalgamated Mississauga weren't apparent yet.

All of those new regional governments might have made sense on paper, but many people feared the historic communities in which they lived would disappear as the larger bureaucratic entities took hold. It gave people another reason to be angry at the Davis government, and as they did in 1973 in by-elections in Huron and St. George ridings, voters in two other constituencies showed just how upset they were. The government held by-elections in October and November 1974 to replace Fernand Guindon and Bert Lawrence. Guindon, like Allan Lawrence, tried his luck on the federal stage but lost to future Liberal cabinet minister Ed Lumley in Stormont-Dundas. Meanwhile, Bert Lawrence had been dropped from the cabinet earlier in the year and retired from politics. But again the Tories lost both by-elections: in Stormont (to the NDP's George Samis, who would hold it for more than a decade) and in Carleton East (to the Liberals' Paul Frederick Taylor, who would lose the seat within the year). The Tories were now zero for four in the by-election department under Davis's leadership.

"It was just the constant steady stream of things," recalls Jim Fleck. Whenever the governing party thought it had turned the corner on one troublesome problem, another was waiting just around the corner. Fleck remembers with an amusement that can only come more than four decades after the fact how, whenever he and the premier went out of town, they had to wait endlessly for the old telephone-based fax machines to transmit the latest scandalous article from the *Globe and Mail.*

"None of this stuff had anything to do with Davis," Fleck says. "But it did tarnish the government's image."

Jonathan Manthorpe led the *Globe and Mail's* "scandal-a-day" coverage, eventually writing it all up in an influential book called *The Power and the Tories.* One day someone from Davis's press office approached the journalist, telling him the cabinet had just experienced an unusually stormy session, with many ministers screaming at one another. In the midst of it all, the premier leaned over to the official and said: "It's on days like this I wish I was half as Machiavellian as Manthorpe thinks I am."

But the worst was yet to come. In the midst of all of these by-election debacles, Ontario was about to go to war with its 105,000 teachers. And the results would leave plenty of scars on everyone. In 2016 we are all too accustomed to seeing teachers and the government at loggerheads. In the early 1970s, it was unprecedented and brutal.

As Bill Davis well knew, the 1960s were a wonderful time to be the minister of education in Ontario. Revenues were flowing into the treasury as never before, schools were being built, and teachers were being hired. In Nova Scotia a self-described "very junior aide" to a provincial cabinet minister gazed west with admiration and concluded Ontario was a "guiding light" to all the other provinces when it came to educational achievements. That junior aide's name was David Dingwall, who would go on to meet Davis at a future federal-provincial conference and marvel at how the premier of Ontario wanted to shake hands not only with the best-known cabinet ministers but also with the lowest folks on the political totem pole such as Dingwall. He never forgot the premier's kindness. Dingwall would go on to become a cabinet minister in future Jean Chrétien governments in the 1990s.

But the 1970s were very different. The economy was much worse off, and even though the teachers' unions still didn't have the legal right to strike, they were becoming increasingly militant about the state of the education system. From time to time throughout the early 1970s, Ontarians saw mass teacher resignations, work-to-rule campaigns, and one-day strikes the teachers called "study sessions." By the fall of 1973, teachers employed by as many as 17 different school boards threatened to resign en masse by the end of the year.

Education Minister Thomas Wells was on the hottest of hot seats for the government. It was his responsibility to bring peace to the system, but not at any cost. His response was to table Bill 274, which would have rendered the mass walkout illegal and forced teachers back into the classrooms. Those who refused would face fines of $500 a day. But Wells also offered compulsory arbitration to settle contract disputes. The response to Wells's bill was unlike anything Ontario had ever seen before. Those of you reading this thinking, well, it couldn't have been worse than the protests during the Mike Harris years, think again. Those of you who thought that government-teacher relations hit bottom after Premier Dalton McGuinty unilaterally tried to claw back nearly half a billion dollars' worth of salary increases and sick days in 2012 also need to think again. Like McGuinty, Davis fancied himself "the education premier," mostly because he'd had responsibility for the sector for nearly a decade, created the community college system, and had enjoyed such good relationships with the stakeholders for years. But none of that mattered as 1973 came to an end. Bill 274 unified teachers in their opposition to the government as never before.

Two thousand teachers staged a noisy demonstration at Queen's Park on December 11 as their union heads warned that 50,000 teachers would refuse to show up for classes in a week's time if the government proceeded with the bill to curtail their civil rights. During this time, the teachers' main weapon in a salary dispute was to quit altogether. They opposed compulsory arbitration, opposed spending ceilings, and demanded the right to collectively bargain their contracts.

As the teachers protested outside, there was an uncontrollable uproar on the floor of the legislature inside, and not for reasons you might think. On Monday, December 10, the Tories introduced Bill 274 *with the support* of the opposition Liberal Party. But for some reason the Liberals switched sides the next day and joined the New Democrats in opposition to the bill, preferring to see it sent to a committee for further study. Bob Nixon later explained there hadn't been enough time for his caucus to study the bill, thus the change of heart. The ensuing ruckus saw all three parties screaming at one another. Davis blasted the Liberals for "a lack of intestinal fortitude" on tough issues. Nixon accused Davis of bad judgment in pressing ahead when more time to study the bill was a better option. Lewis chided the Liberals for finding themselves in "another Spadina crisis," namely, a split caucus. The minister of public works from the Bahamas was a guest in the speaker's gallery and was observed to say afterward about Canadian democracy: "It's very noisy."

So noisy, in fact, that the speaker of the legislature, Allan Reuter, felt he had no choice but to adjourn proceedings for half an hour — the first such suspension anyone could recall in the history of the legislature. Davis assured everyone that "reasonable alterations" to the bill would be considered. He said he didn't like the bill but felt an obligation to the 175,000 students whose education would otherwise be disrupted midway through the school year.

Things got even tenser outside as the crowd's anger began to boil. Several hundred demonstrators surged through the front doors in an attempt to take over the Parliament Buildings. The group confronted the education minister on the stairs of the legislature chamber and began shouting demands and insults at him. Remarkably, Wells didn't turn turtle and look for a back door to escape. He actually tried to address the crowd. Yes, 40 years ago cabinet ministers saw it as part of their job to be accessible to those with whom they had vigorous disagreements. The mayhem continued as suddenly emergency fire alarms sounded. Firefighters from three trucks entered the premises, looking for a fire from a triggered alarm. They didn't find one, but there was plenty of heat.

"We want our rights!" one teacher shouted at Wells.

"We're standing up for our children's rights," Wells responded, not bombastically but rather in an attempt to lower the temperature. One teacher told him he'd have to build a lot more jails because none of the teachers who intended to resign would be back in the classroom come January. Placards were everywhere, saying things such as JINGLE BELLS, AWAY WITH WELLS. Another teacher sported a clever sign that said: ALL'S WELL THAT ENDS WELLS. At one point the demonstrators appeared poised to rush past the minister and storm the floor of the assembly. It took an intervention by Stephen Lewis, urging the teachers "not to make a martyr" out of Wells and cautioning them not "to press in on him this way" to calm things down. While the Ontario Provincial Police and Queen's Park security looked on with increasing concern, Lewis assured them the opposition would "toughly represent" their views in the ensuing debate. The NDP leader himself called the bill "one of the most objectionable, anti-democratic pieces of legislation in years."

Wells was undaunted, and the bill proceeded through first and second readings. He called his proposed legislation "a responsible bill from a responsible government and responsible men and women in this legislature will support it." He assured teachers that anyone who settled their salary dispute would be exempt from the legislation and personally guaranteed the freedom of any teacher who wanted to offer a legitimate resignation. Furthermore, he said, other provinces had binding arbitration and settlements had been coming in at between 7 and 21 percent. There was adequate room for an equitable settlement, he assured them.

The following day, Wednesday, December 12, the government put a good bit of water in its wine. It offered amendments to the bill, making teacher resignations illegal as of August 31, 1974 — before the beginning of the *next* school year — rather than as of the end of 1973. Compulsory arbitration was still in, but the fines for not showing up for work in January 1974 were reduced to $200 a day and "up to $500 a day."

The teachers' response to that was to stage one of the biggest protests in Ontario history. "Friends, Ontarians, teachers, lend me your ears," said Geoffrey Wilkinson, president of the Ontario Teachers' Federation to 20,000 demonstrators at Maple Leaf Gardens. "I come to bury Davis, not to praise him." Speaking on behalf of more than 100,000 teachers province-wide, Wilkinson ratcheted up the rhetoric even more. "The evil that men do lives long after them, the good is oft interred with their bones. So let it be with Davis and the sooner the better!" At the very least the man knew his Shakespeare.

The Gardens exploded in cheers. The teachers inside (and another 5,000 outside who couldn't get in) staged the one-day walk out, costing them collectively about $1 million in lost salaries. "The bully has never been popular, and we're going to cut the bully down to size," Wilkinson added to more thunderous applause.

Howard Brown was a student at Ryerson Polytechnical Institute near Maple Leaf Gardens in downtown Toronto. He was also part of the Young Liberals on campus. When he heard about the rally, he and his fellow campus Grits decided to attend. "Davis was the enemy," Brown says more than four decades after the event, at which he recalls handing out buttons that said: SAVE US FROM DAVIS.

"He was the guy preventing our happiness, whether it was on student loans, or housing, or getting a liquor licence for our university. Whether it was to show solidarity with the teachers, we thought it was a good idea as Young Liberals to go to that rally."

Robert Nixon also spoke and was warmly received. But the crowd saved its wildest applause for Stephen Lewis, who said the government "has abused, derided, and defiled the teachers while insulting their intelligence and self-respect." With concurrent demonstrations in Ottawa, Windsor, and Sudbury, not to mention thousands more teachers who simply stayed home, the teachers in effect shut down the education system for a day.

Again, Tom Wells addressed his opponents at a Queen's Park rally after the protest at the Gardens. He assured the teachers that their rights as individuals were protected and that the bill was designed to prevent mass resignations. He also held out another carrot — a new bill to be debated in the spring that would allow for many months of free collective bargaining and ample time for discussion. A week later Wells was back on his feet in the legislature making that compromise offer official. Then Bill Davis tossed another peace offering into the mix. He immediately recessed the legislature for its Christmas break without giving third and final readings to the bill at the centre of the fracas. The teacher unions, in turn, postponed their mass resignation deadline until January 31, 1974. It gave both sides the breathing space necessary to find a more permanent, face-saving agreement. Stephen Lewis called the government's backtracking "a stunning victory for the teachers." Davis preferred not to point to winners or losers but saw the compromise as a "reasonable solution."

Interestingly, neither side was pushing for the teachers' right to strike as part of the collective bargaining process. Many teachers themselves saw striking as incompatible with their professional obligations. But as 1974 gave way to 1975, the political earth shifted. Binding arbitration wasn't working. The provincial government hated being on the hook every time a local school board couldn't come to an agreement with its teachers. Then the teachers' unions themselves gradually came to the view that maybe they should be treated as any other trade union would be.

The result was a new, sweeping piece of legislation called Bill 100, which passed in June 1975 and still serves as the template for handling all school strikes more than 40 years later. Teachers would now have the right to strike and school boards would now have the right to lock out teachers. Both sides could locally bargain on salaries and working conditions. An Education Relations Commission (ERC) was created to gauge the temperature of work disputes and determine whether a strike was putting a student's year in jeopardy. If the ERC determined that students could lose their year, it could "declare jeopardy," after which the government could legally legislate the teachers back to work. Given that the principles of Bill 100 are still essentially in place, it turned out to be an acceptable long-range solution to the problem. But it didn't help in the short run. Inflation was rampant in Ontario in the mid-1970s and new federal anti-inflation guidelines, which the province embraced, reopened contracts that had been settled and rolled back wage increases.

It was around this time that one of Davis's most trusted advisers, Hugh Macaulay, came to a sobering and unhappy conclusion. He called long-time Tory stalwart Eddie Goodman and confessed: "I have done everything I can for Davis and it isn't working. We are dropping in the public's confidence like a shot goose." Macaulay asked Goodman to come to Queen's Park, and soon the Toronto lawyer joined the premier's innermost circle of trusted advisers.

No question about it. In less than four years, Bill Davis had gone from golden boy to a whole heap of trouble — never a good thing in the lead-up to a general election.

11

MINORITY (I)

Perhaps one of the most curious things about the lead-up to the 1975 Ontario election was the Liberal Party's choice of its new leader. After suffering his second consecutive loss in the previous 1971 election campaign, Robert Nixon did what leaders are supposed to do — he assumed responsibility for his party's predicament and resigned the leadership. But as the Davis government's problems mounted and Nixon's polling numbers started rising, Nixon had a change of heart. Supporters kept telling him Davis was vulnerable. The familiar refrain was: "C'mon, Bob. Stick around. We'll get him this time."

And so when Liberals gathered at the Royal York Hotel in Toronto on October 27 and 28 to choose their new leader, they selected Robert Nixon to succeed Robert Nixon on the third ballot over Norman Cafik, who was actually a federal Liberal MP. Nixon took a healthy 58 percent of the votes. And if you remember one nasty confrontation in the legislature between Premier Davis and York Centre MPP Don Deacon, in which an offended Davis predicted Deacon would never become Liberal leader, the results of the convention confirmed Davis's prediction. Deacon came third, dropping off after the second ballot after securing only 19 percent of the votes. The results of the convention ensured a Davis-Nixon-Lewis rematch for the next election, the timing of which was still unknown.

Davis and some members of his inner circle watched the Liberal leadership results in a hotel room near the Toronto airport. With his poll numbers looking grim and confirmation that Nixon would be his opponent again, the premier wanted to take the temperature of his senior-most advisers.

"He had too much pride to throw in the towel," recalls Norman Atkins. "But when we went around the table, there clearly was a consensus that we weren't going to throw this guy away. We were just going to roll up our sleeves and get it done. And there were no questions about his leadership from that moment on."

The Davis government certainly took its best shot at changing the channel away from all the mini-scandals that had beset it. In the spring session in 1975, the government brought in a new program to help first-time home buyers and introduced a limited plan for free prescription drugs for seniors. In an appeal to the Tory base and in particular, Ontarians who didn't share big-city sensibilities, Davis struck a Royal Commission into investigating violence in the media. He gave former Liberal MP Judy LaMarsh, just the second female federal cabinet minister in Canadian history (behind Hamilton's Ellen Fairclough) the chairmanship of the commission. During the mid-1970s, Hollywood began producing some of its most memorable, disturbing, and shockingly violent motion pictures ever. *The Godfather Part II*, *Chinatown*, *The Texas Chainsaw Massacre*, and *Death Wish* were all released in 1974. A year later *Dog Day Afternoon*, *Rollerball*, and *Ilsa, She Wolf of the SS* emerged. To many conservatives, these kinds of films were all just too much. It was unclear what a Royal Commission could actually do about these films, but just the idea that Bill Davis shared people's concern about them and gave voice to those concerns seemed to be a popular move.

But lest others think the government was stocked with cultural barbarians, Davis also created a new ministry of culture and recreation in January 1975, and gave the job of running it to one of his most trusted ministers, Robert Welch from the Niagara Peninsula. The Davis-Welch partnership was a rock-solid one. Welch was Davis's point man in the legislature — the government house leader — from 1975 to 1979, whose mission was to get the Tories' bills passed. That was a particularly important assignment once the government's majority disappeared. Welch would go on to become deputy premier from 1977 to the end of Davis's tenure.

At the beginning of 1975 the premier gave Welch an interesting assignment — interesting because Welch seemed to be absolutely the wrong guy for the job. In the 1960s, Canadians were spending a lot of money buying Irish Sweepstakes tickets. It was illegal but no one seemed to care. Canadians enjoyed playing the lottery and the government was essentially powerless to stop it. So, in 1973, Pierre Trudeau's Liberals created the first domestic lottery run by the federal government, the proceeds of which were to go toward paying for the 1976 Summer Olympic Games in Montreal. Over the ensuing three years, the lottery raised more than $200 million for the games. Other provinces took note, and when they saw how lucrative the lottery business could be, considered creating their own provincial counterparts. In Ontario, Davis's cabinet considered the matter in 1974 and most members were strongly in favour. However, there was one cabinet minister who was utterly opposed. He thought if the government got into the lottery business it was akin to endorsing the evils of gambling. He was also the chancellor of the Anglican Diocese in his region of the province and felt in his bones that it was simply wrong for the government to be in the lottery business, and he told Davis so in no uncertain terms.

After hearing his cabinet debate the matter, Premier Davis summarized the discussion and concluded there was a strong consensus for creating Ontario's first provincially run lottery, which would be called Wintario. And which minister would be in charge of getting the lottery up and running? This was Davis's mischievous sense of humour at its best. He gave the job to the minister who was most inalterably opposed to creating the lottery — Bob Welch, minister of culture and recreation. Welch lost that fight, but he won the next one. He was adamant that all profits from the lottery go toward cultural and recreational activities only — building arenas, arts programs, performances, et cetera — and not into the general revenue fund to be spent on whatever the treasurer of the day wanted. And so, in May 1975, the province created the Ontario Lottery Corporation (it would add "Gaming" to its title two decades later once it also gained responsibility for casinos). Welch had hoped in vain that by denying lottery revenues to the consolidated revenue fund he could hold out hope that someday a future government might eliminate the lottery altogether. Of course, it was a hope in vain. Future governments expanded the eligible lottery revenue recipients to include hospitals and then charitable organizations. The lotteries and casinos now deliver more than $2 billion annually to Ontario's bottom line.

In March 1975, the Davis government created a new officer of the legislature to deal with the public's complaints about government: the Ontario
ombudsman. Six other provinces already had ombudsmen, but it was another
indication that the Tories were taking people's complaints with government
seriously. Arthur Maloney, well-known defence attorney, former Progressive
Conservative MP, son of a former Conservative MP, and the principal author
of the 1960 Bill of Rights, became Ontario's first ombudsman.

On the economic front, the government pulled a couple of other arrows
out of its quiver. Treasurer Darcy McKeough, whom Davis returned to cabinet after 10 months in the penalty box, tasked a blue-ribbon panel with
reviewing all future spending by the province. Inflation was out of control
and interest rates were on the way up. The last thing McKeough wanted was
runaway spending by the province and, in fact, his pledge was that whatever
inflation was running at the Ontario government would spend 2 percent
less. He appointed Maxwell Henderson, a former auditor general, to chair
the committee, which included broadcaster and future Liberal senator Betty
Kennedy and Robert Hurlburt, the president of General Foods. McKeough
also temporarily lowered the provincial retail sales tax from 7 to 5 percent.

Davis also found an important job for one of the charter members
of the Big Blue Machine. Dalton Camp was asked to chair a tripartisan
commission on cleaning up Ontario's antiquated and much-criticized
election expenses laws. With the Progressive Conservative Camp as its
chair, and former New Democrat MP Douglas Fisher and former Ontario
Liberal leader Farquhar Oliver as the other commissioners, the "Camp
Commission" recommended tough new rules governing election finances.
Donations would henceforth be capped, campaigns had spending limits,
as well, and it all had to be transparent so the public could see who was
doing what. The recommendations came out in November 1974 and were
enacted in a transformative Election Finances Reform Act in 1975. The
new law became a model for other jurisdictions all over Canada.

Davis led a conservative government, but he never let that get in the
way of doing things that were utterly non-conservative. Take, for example,
his decision to put a 90-day freeze on energy prices. It was a shocking
interference into the market, but as NDP leader Stephen Lewis told Davis
adviser Eddie Goodman: "How can you beat a Tory premier who is prepared to take a crack at the large oil companies?" It was darn good politics.

While those were all considered positive moves for the Tories, they didn't stop the political bleeding. Davis had such a deep understanding of all facets of his government that he came to immerse himself in almost every issue. "Before he knew it, he owned every issue, and you don't want to own them all," says John Tory, then a party volunteer and active in youth politics, who recalls Davis showing up for Question Period on Fridays when most ministers were already back in their ridings, and answering three-quarters of the questions posed by the opposition critics. Davis enjoyed it, but from a political marketing standpoint, he was too connected to too many issues, many of which were unpopular.

The Big Blue Machine discovered it needed all the help it could get, and to that end Ross DeGeer and Hugh Macaulay travelled to the national party's campaign headquarters in Ottawa, hoping to recruit a rising young star of the backrooms. He was director of policy, planning, and communications for the federal PC Party, but Davis's emissaries wanted him to join the provincial party as campaign secretary. They assured him the job would be hard, that he'd be the junior-most person on staff, but that they needed fresh blood to stave off defeat.

The young man being courted thought to himself: *Bill Davis was there for me during my 1972 federal election run, so how can I not be there for him in his hour of need?* And that's how Hugh Segal became the newest member of the Big Blue Machine and a lifelong supporter of Ontario's 18th premier. Segal understood that the Tory core of the province consisted of maybe a quarter of the electorate. So, for any Progressive Conservative leader to win, he had to assure non-Tory voters that he could be trusted with the keys to Queen's Park for a few years. Segal described in his 1996 book *No Surrender* why he felt it so imperative that Davis be re-elected. "Liberalism is a threat," he wrote with his deeply partisan but happy warrior's pen. "This is not a battle between warring elites. This is serious. As citizens, we always pay a huge price for a Liberal period in office, so not letting them be in office is fundamental to everyone's best interests." And so, with that, Segal moved to Toronto two to three days per week, sharing a hotel room with Norman Atkins.

With apologies to Hollywood director John Hughes, his *Breakfast Club* motion picture of 1985 was predated by more than a decade by Bill Davis's own breakfast club. Every Tuesday morning at the Park Plaza

Hotel just north of Queen's Park, Davis had begun to hold meetings of his inner circle of backroom advisers and influential cabinet ministers to go over the most compelling political issues of the day. Attendees included Big Blue Machine members such as campaign manager Norman Atkins, party director Ross DeGeer, policy adviser Tom Kierans, and confidants Eddie Goodman and Hugh Macaulay. Even though these were highly partisan events, Davis's own deputy minister, Ed Stewart, was there playing a huge role. For a while these meetings took place in secret. Participants thought they were an excellent, informal way to discuss political problems and give their best, unvarnished advice directly to the premier. When the existence of the Park Plaza Breakfast Club became public, the media certainly had a field day portraying it as a group of insiders who were trying to subvert the proper policy development process or create another unhelpful layer of bureaucracy between party elites and the grassroots. Some politicians didn't like it because, frankly, they weren't invited (senior cabinet ministers would be added after the 1975 election). Regardless, it was at the Park Plaza that Davis's leadership style truly came into its own. He quickly learned that if he weighed in on an issue at the beginning of the discussion, it tended to stymie the debate that followed. Few would want to get on the wrong side of the premier if they knew his views going in. So Davis made an art of sitting back, chewing on his pipe, and listening carefully to all sides and all contributors before summarizing what he thought was the consensus in the room. Even if you lost the argument, at least you had a thorough hearing. It was one of the ways the premier won the enduring loyalty of so many of his ministers and advisers.

The hierarchy of Davis advisers in the premier's office was also becoming apparent at this time. Clearly, at the top of the food chain was Ed Stewart, whose links to Davis went back to their days in the education ministry. But Stewart and Davis's wife, Kathleen, had both gone to the University of Michigan, so there was that personal connection, as well. In later years the next cohort would include Hugh Segal and John Tory, both of whom hitched themselves to the Davis wagon during their very formative years. Davis loved their insights into what the younger generation was thinking but also relied on their superb competence in running the premier's office. And a third tier comprised Davis's capital *P* political allies: Norman Atkins, Hugh Macaulay, and Eddie Goodman, whose roles increased exponentially around election time. The premier's most complicated relationship might have been with Clare Westcott. The two went back to the Leslie Frost days at Queen's Park, and Davis did come to rely on Westcott as his "Mr. Fixit." But Westcott was never invited to the Tuesday morning breakfast club at the Park Plaza, nor to the ministerial retreats in exurban or rural Ontario, which were great team-building exercises and caused considerable resentments at the time.

"It was a strange love-hate between Bill Davis and Clare Westcott," says Sally Barnes. "They were the closest of friends but disagreed on all kinds of things. Clare used to go off half-cocked on so many things with wild enthusiasm. Mr. Davis let him do his own thing. But Ed Stewart had to keep an eye on him because some of his ideas were crazy. But I don't think Clare had an enemy in the world, which is the ultimate compliment."

Nineteen seventy-five was also the year the premier's office raided the Queen's Park press gallery to add another important member of the team. Sally Barnes, originally from Napanee, Ontario, had been a journalist since her school days when she wrote "the high school column" for one of the local papers. She had grown up in a Liberal household, given that her mother was from French-Catholic stock, and worked her way up the journalism ladder at the *Kingston Whig-Standard*, then the *Toronto Telegram*, before settling in at the *Toronto Star*. She loved politics and was assigned to cover John Turner's campaign in the 1968 federal Liberal leadership contest, won by Pierre Elliott Trudeau on Barnes's birthday, April 6.

Barnes took a decidedly agnostic view of politics — she'd voted for all three major parties — and was even courted by Stephen Lewis's New Democrats to run for them in the 1971 Ontario election in the riding of Davenport. (She said no.) By the time she got to the Queen's Park Press Gallery in the late 1960s, the first big story she covered was the resignation announcement of Premier Robarts. Always looking for the angle no one else had, Barnes counted the number of paces Robarts had to take from his office to the media studio to announce he was quitting, before banging out the lead for her story: "Premier John P. Robarts took the 327 steps to announce he was resigning ..."

For someone who was about to become deeply immersed in Bill Davis's life, Barnes's connection to the next premier of Ontario started slowly. She was assigned to cover Bert Lawrence's leadership bid in 1971, which ended after just one ballot. And even after the convention, when she began to cover the Davis government, she had almost no contact with the new premier.

"I saw him as pleasant but aloof, not an overly friendly person, who dressed in baggy suits and was typically Ontarian," Barnes recalled to George Hutchison in a 1993 interview.

By the summer of 1975 and with Tory fortunes crumbling, Barnes got a call from Davis's Mr. Fixit, Clare Westcott. "We're looking for a token broad to work in the premier's office," he told her in his inimitable fashion. The job came with a big pay increase and the opportunity to see how things really worked inside politics.

Barnes's curiosity got the better of her, so she accepted the job with the assumption she'd work there for six months, then try something else. She knew the press gallery members well, and the PCs obviously hoped to exploit (in the nicest way) her relationship with her former colleagues in the hope of getting some more sympathetic coverage of the troubled Tory government.

But when the premier's deputy minister and secretary to the cabinet, Ed Stewart, found out about the plan to hire Barnes, he hit the roof. "There's no goddamn way we're going to have the premier drive all over the province with a young broad in his car!" Stewart warned.

But Stewart was overruled, and one of Barnes's first assignments was to "drive like a bat out of hell down the 401 to deliver a speech to WGD somewhere around Cobourg," she now recalls. Of course, Davis being Davis, he didn't read a word of it, but the speech and its emissary did arrive in one piece.

William Davis called his second election for September 18, 1975, and unlike his previous campaign, this one would be totally different. He was no longer the new kid on the block, offering a youthful renewal of the Tory dynasty. Much of the electorate now saw him as part of the same tired, old Tory gang, which had suffered through the *drip, drip, drip* of constant bad news and scandal. Davis entered the campaign 14 points behind the Liberals in public opinion. It seemed an insurmountable hill to climb. Then again, the premier did have a great organization behind him — well, most of the time. One night Hugh Segal answered the phone at campaign headquarters.

"Would the campaign chairman be there?" asked the voice on the phone.

"I'm sorry," Segal replied. "Mr. Atkins is in a meeting."

"Do you think he'll be free soon?" the voice inquired.

"Well, I don't know. He's pretty busy. Do you want to leave your name? I'll be glad to have him call you."

"Would you tell him it's the candidate."

"We've got 125 candidates, sir," Segal said. "Which candidate is it?"

"The one in Brampton" came the reply. Yes, it was Premier Davis. Welcome to the campaign, Hugh Segal.

To the extent anyone remembers anything about the 1975 campaign, there were really two significant highlights: the leaders' debate, which was completely different from the 1971 experience, and a policy Davis introduced in mid-campaign, designed to save his sinking ship. You need to remember that in the 1970s Ontario's capital was politically and completely the opposite of what it is today. In the last Ontario election in June 2014, it was the Liberals who captured 20 out of 22 seats in "The 416." But 40 years ago the capital was known as "Tory Toronto" because it was the PCs who dominated with 16 of the city's 25 seats. The New Democrats were actually the second most popular party with six seats, while the Liberals held only three. But the New Democrats had jumped on an issue that was increasingly capturing headlines and giving the party a chance to become the champions of urban Ontario. With inflation roaring at almost 11 percent annually, landlords were jacking up rents to keep up with their costs. But the result was a steady stream of hard-luck stories of tenants unable to afford the rent hikes and being forced to move out. The *Toronto Star* in particular was all over the story. Then, just two weeks before election day, New Democrat canvassers found an elderly woman with a cat who'd had a 75 percent rent increase and was going to have to leave her apartment. As the NDP banged the drum hard for rent controls, landlords, fearful controls were coming, hiked rents even higher than they might otherwise have done. Tenants felt increasingly powerless against economic forces beyond their control. With time running out the Tories were increasingly fearful they were losing the apartment-dweller vote in Scarborough, Mississauga, and downtown Toronto, and if they did, the election truly was over. And so Bill Davis did what for conservatives was the unthinkable: he embraced the NDP proposal for rent controls.

The premier was actually on top of his brief when he outlined what he thought was a simple approach to combatting skyrocketing rent increases from landlords who'd been portrayed as predators by the popular press. The new rules would require landlords to give tenants two months' notice on any future rent increase. If the tenant objected to the size of the increase, he or she had 30 days to file a complaint with a new "rent review board," which the province would establish. If the tenant was satisfied with the review board's determination, end of story. If the tenant wasn't satisfied, the issue could be sent to the courts at no cost to the tenant, and with the rent frozen in place until the courts made their determination. "The tenant will be protected until the decision is made," Davis said at a lengthy news conference in London.

When he was repeatedly pressed by reporters that what he was implementing was a cynical political solution designed to secure tenants' votes, Davis demurred. "Sometimes," he told them, "good government and good politics are synonymous. More often than you think actually."

As a conservative, Davis knew that bringing in rent controls would no doubt have a perverse effect on the housing market and, of course, it did. The building of apartment complexes virtually stopped. Developers turned to condominiums, which were outside the purview of rent reviews. With inflation so high the uncertainty surrounding what landlords could charge for rent seriously dampened any new rental housing construction. But this was no time to worry about the niceties of adversely affecting market economics. The Tories were 12 points behind the Liberals without much time left in the campaign and desperate times called for desperate measures.

Within the PC cabinet there was plenty of opposition to rent review. Dennis Timbrell, the 28-year-old rookie minister without portfolio, argued against bringing in the policy. "I believed then, as I do now, that we could have dealt with the needs of the at-risk population directly without having to impose an expensive, overbearing bureaucracy on the whole rental sector," he said in an interview 40 years after this election. "However, my point of view didn't prevail." Timbrell preferred an approach that would have seen the government kick-start the construction of apartment buildings. But that wouldn't have solved the problem *immediately*, which is what the governing party needed. Ironically, the minister of housing, Donald Irvine, also a rookie MPP from Eastern Ontario's Grenville-Dundas riding, was also opposed to the plan, even though he was responsible for implementing it. Irvine was a good soldier, did his job, then after the election immediately got shuffled out of the housing portfolio. He would serve for two more years, then quit politics.

The Tories must have known that tenants would appreciate the new rent review system. What they didn't know was whether voters would reward the PCs in all the urban seats the party held, or perhaps give credit to the NDP, which had clearly put the issue on the political agenda. In the dying days of the campaign, one journalist asked Davis, "If you lose this election, will you stay on as leader of the opposition?"

For once Davis actually answered a direct question with a remarkably succinct answer: "I haven't contemplated the former and so I'm not considering the latter," he said with uncharacteristic brevity. Also, to show how different this first minister's press conferences were compared to, for example, Prime Minister Stephen Harper's (five questions in total in both official languages and that was it), Davis spent half an hour answering reporters' questions in London about rent review and a host of other issue as well. When the journalist moderating the Q and A told him his time was up, Davis waved him off: "Listen, I've got 100 other answers still to give," he said, then proceeded to do individual scrums with other journalists for another 10 minutes.

Four decades later and looking back on his decision to bring in rent review, Davis admits: "It's not the kind of thing you'd do if you could avoid it. But at the same time, when you do the calculation on the number of seniors who were in that predicament, why wouldn't you do it?" The Tories made a simple calculation: let the market resolve the problem or choose a much less invasive solution and risk losing the election, or swallow hard, embrace an NDP policy, and remain politically competitive. It wasn't a hard call, especially when Davis reminded some of his more conservative backbenchers that if they wanted to remain members of the legislature, they were simply going to have to put a lot of water in their wine. Promising to bring in rent review stabilized the Tory numbers in urban Ontario and seemed to take some of the steam out of a potential NDP juggernaut.

Rent review dealt with the NDP but what about the Liberals? Bob Nixon was still in first place. The Liberals had missed a grand opportunity to finish off the Tories when they declined to embrace rent controls. Private PC polling suggested Nixon could have swept Metropolitan Toronto (as it was then called) had he also agreed to implement rent review. But he didn't. As a result, both Davis and Lewis were seen as the more committed champions of urban Ontario, and it's not hard to see why. The reality was that while Nixon himself was a progressive politician, much of the rest of his caucus simply wasn't. They were from rural Ontario, didn't understand the aspirations of cities, and frankly were more right wing than many of the members on Bill Davis's backbenches. "Our campaign was far too worried about rural votes at the expense of urban votes," admits Howard Brown, who at age 22 was already a deeply committed Liberal activist and soon to become president of the party's youth wing. "We just didn't run a good Toronto campaign."

It was an odd mistake for the Liberals to make because it looked as if Toronto was finally ready to embrace the Grits. The party had an enormous rally at the Toronto-Dominion Centre at King and Bay Streets in the heart of the financial district where between 5,000 and 10,000 citizens showed up to demonstrate their support for, of all people, a 46-year-old farmer from Brant County. The size and enthusiasm of the rally shocked some Tories, who felt they'd finally tamped down the NDP threat in the capital, only to see that the Liberals were now going to be a problem. Young Liberals gave out stickers that said: LICK DAVIS, ELECT BOB NIXON. Christie Blatchford's story in the *Globe and Mail* was headlined with "Nixon Gets Royal Treatment in Downtown Toronto." But try as they might, the Liberals just couldn't convince people that they "got" cities.

There are only so many things a party leader can control during an election campaign, and for the second consecutive election, Robert Nixon discovered one of the things out of his control were the goings-on of his federal cousins. In 1971, just a few days before election day, Pierre Trudeau announced an income tax cut that Bill Davis happily matched. It gave the Tories a lift it turned out they actually didn't need. Again, in 1975, events on the federal scene might have had an impact on the provincial race. Eight days before election day federal Finance Minister John Turner, a golden boy in the Liberal Party for more than a decade, resigned and left public life entirely.

"It put Liberals in a terrible mood," recalls Howard Brown. "It was very depressing when your country's star finance minister resigned. It put a damper on everybody's mood."

Today Bob Nixon disagrees with that assessment, but only to a point. "I was not concerned about the impact," he says. "But others, particularly after the election, were sure it had damaged us." Nixon thought then and thinks today that the Liberal campaign was adversely affected by something else — the stellar performance of the leader of the NDP. "It was just creepy how awfully good Stephen Lewis was," is how Nixon remembers his opponent's performance today.

The liaison in the premier's office responsible for keeping an eye on the 1975 election campaign was John White, the MPP from London South since 1959 and part of John Robarts's London posse. White had seven different cabinet portfolios from 1968 to 1975 and had decided not to stand for re-election. He hired 21-year-old John Tory as executive assistant from April until election day in 1975 and instructed Tory that there was only one thing the young PC needed to know to be successful at his job. As Tory leaned in to hear the wisdom from a veteran minister that might change the course of his political career, White told him: "Every day at 5:00 p.m. you'll hear a buzzer. When you hear that buzzer, go into that room over there and find the key under the Rotary Club flag. Take that key and open that cabinet over there. In that cabinet you'll find a bottle of Scotch. Pour me two glasses of Scotch and bring them to me and we'll be just fine." Yes, Queen's Park was a bit different back then.

For such a young man, Tory was already hip-deep in political responsibilities beyond getting John White his Scotch. He had already managed David Crombie's successful 1972 run for the Toronto mayor's job. In 1974 he won the presidency of the Ontario Young Progressive Conservative association. He found himself getting invited to Davis's ministerial retreats, plus the exclusive Park Plaza Breakfast Club. It was a heady experience, and Tory felt as if he was surrounded by Hollywood superstars who were larger than life.

But for the rest of the Big Blue Machine who didn't quite have those same stars in their eyes, things looked grim. In fact, at one point, the party's chief fundraiser, Bill Kelly, met with Davis and campaign chairman Norm Atkins to tell them the money just wasn't coming in and he intended to cut the campaign's budget by $1 million. Forty years ago that was considered a massive cut, and Atkins threatened to quit if Kelly made good on the threat. Atkins appreciated how hard it was to shake money out of the trees during the 1975 campaign, but he also needed Kelly to know that without adequate funds, pulling off a miracle finish would be impossible. Eventually, Atkins agreed to a much more modest cut and the crisis was averted.

Davis probably never worked harder on any of his election campaigns than he did in 1975. Nowadays, party leaders typically do one or two events during the course of a campaign day. On September 2, Davis started his day at 8:00 a.m. with a press conference for so-called "ethnic media." By 8:30 he was on a bus to Fort Erie to tour a plant. At noon he left for Port Colborne and did an event there. At 2:00 p.m. it was off to Welland to visit the PC candidate's campaign office. At 3:00 p.m. he was on the move again to nearby Thorold to visit the Welland riding's campaign office. Then it was off to St. Catharines before 4:00 p.m. to visit the St. Catharines Market on Church Street and do some mainstreeting. (Yes, in those days, first ministers actually met citizens on the street who didn't have to register for invitation-only party events.) By 5:30 p.m. there was another reception in St. Catharines. The campaign gave him an hour of downtime in Grimsby, but then it was on to the Casablanca Hotel for an 8:00 p.m. reception. By 9:30 p.m., Davis was back on the bus to Toronto but probably not home to Brampton until close to midnight. And virtually every day was like that. At one point the grind of the campaign clearly got to him. Campaigning in the Eastern Ontario riding of Stormont-Dundas and Glengarry, Davis felt the enthusiasm of the crowd for their 69-year-old veteran MPP Osie Villeneuve, who first got elected in 1948.

"I need Osie Villeneuve. You need Osie Villeneuve. Ontario needs Osie Villeneuve, and I want you to make damn sure he's returned!" Davis shouted to the crowd, using language of which his mother clearly wouldn't approve. Davis started to apologize for the "strong words," but the crowd cheered him on, so he continued.

Ten days before election day the Tories had polling that showed them a whopping 10 points behind the Liberals. Norman Atkins put together a high-level Big Blue Machine meeting in Davis's lower-level recreation room at his home in Brampton, at which time he was told he was about to preside over the end of the Tory dynasty.

Unless …

In attendance were Robert Teeter, Brian Armstrong, Alan Eagleson (the party president), Hugh Macaulay, Clare Westcott, and the top party bagman, Bill Kelly. Their mission was simple: convince Davis that unless he mercilessly attacked Bob Nixon at the ensuing leaders' debate with every fibre of his being, Davis's days of being premier were over. He was to attack and never let up. It was imperative that Davis get Nixon to reveal what the Tories thought was a temperament unsuited to the premier's office. The only problem with that advice: the candidate was loath to follow it. Davis knew he had to do it. But he sure didn't like the idea of having to do it.

"I really didn't want to do it because I actually liked him [Nixon]," Davis now says.

The 1975 election featured not one debate but actually three. After the three-way snooze fest of 1971, it was felt a round-robin series of three, one-on-one, half-hour debates would spice things up. Did it ever. The opening round featured Davis and NDP leader Stephen Lewis, and the moderator, Fraser Kelly, had done his homework. He saw in the NDP policy handbook a clause that *obliged* the leader to implement every aspect of party policy as it was laid out in the campaign manifesto. Kelly asked whether Lewis agreed with this obligation. The leader said he did. Every plank in the platform? Lewis confirmed yes. Then Kelly said that meant if the NDP formed the government, it would immediately jack the minimum wage up to $3 an hour, which seems insignificant today, but constituted a huge increase, since the minimum wage was only $2.40 at the time. Lewis felt trapped. He knew the policy was unpopular with a lot of Ontarians who ran small businesses or even big ones for that matter.

"He fudged his answer," recalls Fraser Kelly. "He bobbed and weaved. It became a significant problem for him and slowed him down for the rest of the campaign." After the debate, Lewis was still upset about what he perceived as a trap set for him by the moderator and gave Kelly one hell of a tongue-lashing. However, to his credit, Lewis called Kelly at his home around midnight, acknowledging he'd overdone it, and tried to walk it back. But for the rest of the campaign the NDP leader was constantly on the defensive about his minimum wage policy rather than on the offensive attacking the government.

The second debate was supposed to be between Lewis and Robert Nixon, but it never happened because the NDP leader made an emergency trip to Africa to help with a crisis there. So Nixon was simply interviewed on his own. It didn't matter. Everyone was waiting for the ultimate showdown between the premier and the leader of the official opposition. Five days before election day Eddie Goodman and Dalton Camp helped put Davis through his paces in a private suite at the Park Plaza Hotel.

"We psyched [Davis] up as he'd never been psyched before," recalls Goodman in his book *Life of the Party*.

Broadcaster Fraser Kelly moderated the Davis-Nixon debate and had no idea what he was about to encounter. "I knew very well there was tremendous rancour between the two men," he now says. "Did I anticipate the intensity of the debate? No, I did not."

Kelly could tell before the debate even began that Davis was uncomfortable with his marching orders. The premier walked to the wrong podium, dropped his briefing notes all over the floor, and spilled his water. "He was unusually flustered," Kelly recalls. In the minutes before the debate began, neither candidate would look at the other. The tension was unusually thick. Given the location of the debate, Nixon had every reason to feel uncomfortable. The debate was taking place at CFTO-TV's studios, which were owned in part by John W. Bassett, a well-known conservative and two-time former unsuccessful candidate for the PC Party of Canada. But more than four decades later moderator Fraser Kelly confirms there was no interference from Bassett, and Kelly had free rein to run the debate as he saw fit.

Nixon opened with a throwaway comment about what a good campaign it was, and Davis pounced. He cut his opponent off and contradicted him, saying the campaign was actually nasty and gross and blaming the Liberal leader for it. "When the bell rang, he tore out of his corner like the Manassa Mauler and never stopped throwing punches," wrote Eddie Goodman, evoking the memory of heavyweight boxing champion Jack Dempsey.

Davis continued with his relentless attack, so Nixon counterpunched and came right back at him. The two leaders shocked Ontarians with the ferocity of the debate. It had never happened like this before in the province's history. At one point Nixon had Davis on his heels and the Liberal leader looked straight at Kelly, wondering whether the moderator was going to intervene and bail out the premier. He never did. But he didn't come to Nixon's defence, either, when the tables turned.

"I wanted the people to see them unmasked," Kelly explains. "I got harsh media criticism afterward, but I was happy with it. The people were able to see these two guys unrehearsed and going at it."

At one point Kelly asked *the* crucial question: Did Nixon feel the Davis government had a problem with scandals or was the personal integrity of the premier himself problematic? Nixon answered: it was both. That was an overreach. No scandal had ever actually touched Davis himself, and the public knew it.

"Nixon just totally blew it, lost it," recalls Dennis Timbrell. "I remember watching, saying — 'Gotcha!'"

Davis essentially called Nixon a liar and accused him of running a dishonourable campaign. Nixon responded in kind. The scream fest got so out of hand at times that the premier messed up the moderator's name in entreating him to intervene. "Mr. Fraser! Mr. Fraser!" Davis kept saying.

John Tory was staffing the phones back at PC HQ and was distressed at what he was hearing. "People kept saying the premier was so rude to Mr. Nixon," Tory recalls. "Well, it was so uncharacteristic of him."

Fraser Kelly left the debate stage, thinking: "*Holy shit, have I been through an exchange!*" But on his scorecard he didn't think there was a clear winner, other than the voters, "who got a chance to see the leaders go at it hammer and tong." Kelly's sense was that the public wanted to see Davis respond to the allegations against his personal integrity, and the premier met the challenge. "People did not expect to see that kind of debate from Davis," Kelly says. "He was Bland Billy! To see the premier bare-knuckling it was astonishing. But I really enjoyed it and wouldn't have done it any differently."

Forty years later I remind Nixon that the Tory game plan was to attack him relentlessly in the hope that he'd lose his temper. The now 87-year-old Nixon's reply is: "Well, he certainly did and I certainly did." The former Liberal leader admits he himself was "flummoxed" by Davis's attacks. When he got off the debate set, he was upset with himself, despite his campaign manager's having said the night went quite well. But that debate, plus the famously effective "weathervane" ad, which showed the Liberal leader shifting positions depending on which way the wind was blowing, put the PCs back in the game.

The mood on election night in Brampton was absolutely funereal. However, the good news for Davis was that in the dying days of the campaign he did manage to save the family silverware. His PCs won the largest number of seats, and as such would be called upon by Lieutenant Governor Pauline McGibbon to form the government. But two things happened on election night that hadn't happened for 30 years. First, the Tories' 51 seats represented only a minority of the now 125 seats in an enlarged Ontario legislature. The governing party lost 27 seats compared to its stellar performance in 1971, dropping more than 8 percentage points in the total vote to just 36 percent. In fact, Bill Davis admitted to Jim Fleck, his chief executive officer: "For a moment there I didn't think we were going to make it." It was a rare personal statement for Davis, who had a very businesslike, professional relationship with Fleck and wasn't given to those kinds of confessions.

"The 1975 election loss really humbled him," recalls John Tory. "We thought the PC Party was invincible."

However, the second thing that hadn't happened in three decades was that the social democratic party would form the official opposition. In 1943 it was the Commonwealth Co-operative Federation under Ted Joliffe, and in 1975 it was the New Democratic Party led by Stephen Lewis. But again, just as the first-past-the-post system created an impression that the Davis government was more popular than it really was in 1971, the vote splits in 1975 created some odd impressions, as well. Lewis managed to increase the NDP's percentage of the total vote by less than 2 percentage points to 29 percent, but because of the way the votes were distributed, the NDP *doubled* its seat count to 38 from 19. For the Liberals the distortions were even worse. As it turned out, Robert Nixon actually had a pretty good night in terms of the vote count. The Liberals upped their percentage of the total votes cast by 6.5 percent to 34.3 percent — less than 2 percentage points behind the first-place Tories. But again, because of the splits, the Liberals picked up only 16 additional seats and now stood at 36, compared to 20 from last time. Nixon won many more votes than Lewis on election night, but actually captured three fewer seats. It gave an impression that it was a bad night for the Liberals when, in fact, their numbers were much improved.

Only one man in Brampton seemed downright giddy at the outcome. Hugh Segal had come from the federal scene where Tories had been out of power, with the exception of the Diefenbaker six-year interregnum, since 1935. He told anyone who'd listen that the results offered a fresh start, would lower expectations of the government, and most of all, would force the opposition parties to put up or shut up.

Although Davis lost his majority government, he did get to welcome a few new MPPs who would go on to make significant contributions at Queen's Park. Larry Grossman took over his father Allan's seat in St. Andrew–St. Patrick in downtown Toronto. Grossman was an intensely bright and ambitious member who played politics with his elbows up. He became part of Davis's inner circle and eventually a future party leader. (Darcy McKeough used to joke: "I never really liked Allan Grossman until I met his son Larry.") Roy McMurtry lost the 1973 by-election to Margaret Campbell, so he tried again in the midtown Toronto riding of Eglinton and won this time. McMurtry would spend the next decade as Ontario's attorney general, and run for the leadership after Davis's eventual departure. Keith Norton, who won in Kingston and the Islands, would join the cabinet in less than two years, filling numerous significant portfolios, including health; community and social services; environment; colleges and universities; and education. George McCague won election in Dufferin-Simcoe and would become a future influential chairman of the management board of cabinet; Bud Gregory won in Mississauga East and would join the cabinet in two years as revenue minister.

One MPP who had been elected in 1963 eventually hit prime time in 1975. Lorne Henderson, the MPP for Lambton East, would finally get into cabinet as minister without portfolio. He would eventually become a well-liked chairman of cabinet and agriculture minister, but became best known for the unique way he butchered the English language. Henderson would scratch his ears, then complain to his doctor about "the information" that was causing the discomfort. We think he meant "inflammation."

"When we were out together somewhere in his riding," Davis recalls, "and he had this piece of paper and he'd say, 'Me 'n' the Premier brung you this cheque!' You couldn't help but like him."

What is well known in Ontario political history is that in 1985 the second-place Liberals and third-place New Democrats combined forces to defeat the minority Progressive Conservative government of Frank Miller. They signed an "accord" of agenda items that both parties agreed to pass over a two-year time period. It was a highly unusual play but, of course, totally legal and constitutional. Canadians elect Parliaments; we don't elect governments. Whoever can command the confidence of the majority of the members of the legislature gets the right to form the government, and in 1985 that was Liberal leader David Peterson with NDP leader Bob Rae's backing.

What is barely known in Ontario political history is that Robert Nixon considered a similar scenario 10 years earlier. By 1975 the Tories had been in power for 32 consecutive years, and Nixon thought it was enough. He toyed with the idea of approaching his caucus and debating the notion of combining forces with the NDP to end Bill Davis's time as premier. But he didn't. And to this day he regrets it.

"I should've just gone to Stephen [Lewis], who'd beat me by three members and said, 'Come on, let's throw this government outta here,'" Nixon told me in 2015 in the living room of his then home in St. George. "But we were not really progressive enough. It just couldn't work."

The Liberals in 1975, despite their name, were really a very rural, conservative party, having emerged from the United Farmers of Ontario and "Clear Grits" movements of decades earlier. They were still several years away from becoming the urban, progressive powerhouse, dominating the seat counts in cities all over Ontario. And so Nixon just knew that a discussion with his caucus that ended with the words, "So let's get rid of Bill Davis and make 37-year-old NDP leader Stephen Lewis the premier," was just a non-starter with far too many of his MPPs. And so it never happened.

However, the New Democrats had some intriguing ideas of their own. Shortly after election night, Nixon got a phone call from Stephen Lewis and James Renwick, the NDP member for Riverdale. The call was somewhat mysterious. The two said they wanted to come to Nixon's farm in St. George and "just say hello." Nixon couldn't figure out what the pair was up to, but said okay and invited them for lunch. After the usual small talk, Lewis and Renwick made their pitch: they wanted Liberal leader Robert Nixon, the son of a Liberal premier, to switch parties and join the NDP in the Ontario legislature. For the NDP the outreach made perfect sense. The party had seats and thus a decent beachhead in many of the province's urban areas such as Toronto, Ottawa, Hamilton, Windsor, Peterborough, Welland, Cambridge, Oshawa, and Brantford, as well as good strength across Northern Ontario in Sudbury, Thunder Bay, Algoma, and Cochrane. But the party was getting clobbered in rural Ontario and knew it had no chance of forming a government unless it picked up its game there. Nixon had generations worth of credibility in rural Ontario from which many of his members hailed, but unlike them, was a true progressive, as his father had been. Lewis and Renwick assured Nixon he would have "a prominent place" in a future NDP government, which the pair was convinced could happen with Nixon on the team.

Nixon actually gave the offer serious consideration "briefly." What came to mind was a story his father once told him, when Harry Nixon found himself in the same situation. In 1943 the Tories won a minority government under George Drew, but with only a 38 to 34 edge in seats over the CCF. Harry Nixon held the balance of power as Liberal leader with 15 seats. Harry Nixon once told his son, Robert, that if he'd left the Liberals and joined the CCF at that moment, he believed the CCF would have won the next election. Instead, he stayed with the Liberals, and Drew cleaned up two years later, winning 66 of 90 seats and sending the CCF back into third place. Could Robert Nixon do what his father hadn't done but had considered doing? The answer was no.

"I didn't have the guts," he says, thinking back on that meeting with the New Democrat brain trust from 40 years earlier. "Anyway, it didn't happen."

Meanwhile, Eddie Goodman used another boxing analogy to describe the greatest lesson Davis learned in the 1975 election: "It's like a boxer who takes the worst punch the other guy has in his arsenal, then realizes he's still standing," he wrote in his memoir. In fact, thanks to his near-death experience in 1975, a different Bill Davis began to emerge. He actually started to relax a lot more. Part of it might have been that he was now 46 years old and simply more comfortable in his own skin. His natural sense of humour emerged, and he began to joke a lot more with his audiences. In fact, the premier started to do shtick, a lot like Johnny Carson did in his nightly monologues on *The Tonight Show*. A lot of it was corny, but a lot of it worked.

"We joked about the Johnny Carson warm-up," Norman Atkins recalled. "He always had a few good lines to warm up the audience before he'd deliver the serious message. That's something he didn't do before 1975."

Liberal MPP Sean Conway, who won his first election in 1975 en route to a nearly 30-year career at Queen's Park, says the new Davis style "allowed him to get better connected to people. The change in Davis after the 1975 election was really quite significant."

Davis got so good at the Carson routine that people began to enjoy his endearing and constant references to his hometown and his favourite football team. One night Davis was interviewed live on CFTO-TV's evening newscast by Fraser Kelly. With time on the newscast tight and Davis in the middle of one of his patented long answers, Kelly interjected, "Premier, let me sum it up: Argos, Argos, Argos. Brampton, Brampton, Brampton."

Thus ended the interview. Kelly thought it was a cute way to get out of an interview that was going long. His viewers didn't. They lit up the switchboard, furious that the newscaster was showing such disrespect to the premier. "I thought I was being good-humoured," Kelly recalls. "But the public weren't putting up with it."

It was also around this time that Bill Davis made a subtle change that seemed to capture a lot of attention and meet with significant public favour. The premier traded in his cigar for a pipe. The official explanation was that good cigars were getting too expensive. But the other reason was that Davis looked like a bit of a Tory fat cat with the cigar. And, of course, those were the days when smoking indoors was the norm. "I used to get notes from people watching me at first ministers' meetings with a cigar," Davis now says. "When I switched to a pipe, people thought I'd become a professor or something." The pipe helped transform Davis's image to something more avuncular, and frankly, more acceptable to the public. *Toronto Sun* cartoonist Andy Donato had fun with the switch. He drew Davis smoking the new pipe with the cigar stuck in the pipe's bowl.

Meanwhile, Davis also came to understand that, after such an activist first term, maybe he'd been too much in people's faces. Hugh Segal liked to compare the Ontario government to a cleaning lady — you wanted her to be reliable, do a good job, not cost too much, not get in the way, and for heaven's sake don't break anything. For the premier that meant slowing things down a bit, which was easier to do in a minority legislature, since the consent of one of the other two parties was now necessary to get any new policy through. Davis remembered some other advice he got from Thomas Kennedy: in politics you don't often get in trouble for the laws you don't pass or the speeches you don't give. Davis eventually turned this approach into such a fine art that the running joke became: "Don't put off until tomorrow what you can avoid doing altogether." The premier began to understand that sometimes the best policy was to stay out of the way, do nothing, and let problems resolve themselves.

While Bill Davis is a modest man, he's also today at a point in his life when he can occasionally let his hair down and acknowledge his victories. And yet, while reminiscing about this election 40 years after the fact, Davis remains remarkably even-keeled about the whole thing. It's as if he still knows all these years later that he dodged a political bullet in 1975. The dynasty could have ended then and he'd have been the villain in the history books.

"I think we got the better of Robert in the latter stages because he had been somewhat conflicted on some of the policies," Davis now says.

When you stripped away a lot of the noise of Question Period, Ontario's minority legislature actually worked quite well. Davis was smart enough to realize that he could tack left or move right, depending on the issue, to pick up votes from either of the two opposition parties.

"The attitude of the Davis government was dramatically different from the arrogance of Stephen Harper's minority governments in Ottawa from 2006–2011, with its unconcealed contempt for the institution of Parliament during those years," wrote Roy McMurtry in *Memoirs and Reflections*, his autobiography published in 2013. "The three party house leaders worked effectively together in agreeing on other business in the legislature."

That was an approach promoted at the top by the premier.

"As time went on, I think he became more and more comfortable with saying, 'Yeah, this is what people are prepared to do and this is what they're not prepared to do,'" explains Bob Rae, Ontario's 21st premier. "The whole story of his survival in a minority parliament is the ability to read that."

"I must say, to his credit, Davis let the majority run the government," Bob Nixon now says. "I don't think there was ever a time when the elected members of the legislature actually had their hands on the controls of the province." Davis and Nixon met sometimes, but Davis and Lewis met a lot. "I watched Davis fall in love with Lewis right before my eyes" is how Nixon puts it today. Apparently, the feeling was mutual. Lewis rose in the legislature one day as opposition leader, looked across the floor at the premier, and actually said: "As much as this might embarrass you, I have to tell you, I like you." Try to imagine that happening anywhere in Canada today. You can't. The two leaders would go on to develop a warm friendship that lasts to this day.

Meanwhile, Hugh Segal might have been the youngest member of the Davis crew, but he did have one thing going for him at this time that no one else in the premier's office had: experience from his time in Ottawa in dealing with a minority Parliament (1972–74). Ed Stewart offered him the job of the premier's legislative assistant, a time Segal would describe as the happiest two years of his life. He and Stewart represented opposite sides of the advisory coin. Segal's job was to ask whether a particular policy was consistent with Progressive Conservative principles and the Tory sense of what was in the public interest. Stewart's job was to ask whether a policy was in the public's interest, regardless of what might be in the PC Party's interest. Furthermore, the addition of Segal to the Tuesday morning breakfast club at the Park Plaza Hotel immeasurably livened up those confabs. The premier loved nothing more than to see Segal and Goodman go at it hammer and tongs on policy issues. Segal brought the passion of youth; Goodman, dropping the occasional profanity, brought experience. Both were bombastic, intellectually whip-smart, urbane, and Jewish — all qualities Davis wasn't. It was as if he was living vicariously through their outgoing outrageousness. But beyond just a good show, those debates allowed Davis to hone what would become one of his most important skills — listening to advice, then pushing back on that advice to consider all of the potential consequences from it.

"He could look over the mountain" is how Sally Barnes described it. "He would sit there puffing on his pipe and say, 'Yes, but if we do *this* in six months we'll be right up to our ying-yangs in *that*.'" It forced everybody to up their game.

There are two postscripts to the 1975 election worth mentioning. First, it's hard to tell how much Ontarians embraced Davis's rent review policy. Landlords still moaned that they couldn't afford to maintain their housing stock because the rent review boards wouldn't allow them to earn adequate rental income. Tenants, meanwhile, complained that rents were still allowed to go up too much. Maybe if both sides were equally unhappy, that was as good as a government could expect. Davis does make one important observation about the system, which has only been tinkered with by successive governments in the 40 years since its implementation: "I think some people will say it was wrong still," he allows, "but it's funny that it didn't disappear the moment I left." As with so much of Ontario today, the process governing landlords and tenants is essentially the same one created by the Davis government four decades ago.

And, finally, having now lost three successive elections, Bob Nixon's time as Ontario Liberal leader truly was over. But his contribution to Ontario politics wasn't. Nixon would enjoy a great second act in politics, but that was still 10 years away. For now it was time to see what Stephen Lewis could do as opposition leader and what the third-place party could do to find another leader who could finally break through in urban Ontario. So, of course, in the predictable, dull world of Ontario politics, the Liberals chose a completely predictable figure to take on that job: a 37-year-old Jewish psychiatrist from Montreal who had just won his first election.

Maybe Ontario politics wasn't so predictable, after all.

12

MINORITY (II)

Nineteen seventy-six started with Liberals gathering at the Four Seasons Hotel in Toronto on January 24 and 25 to pick a new leader in what turned out to be a tight three-horse race between two rookie MPPs and a third who had been elected in 1971.

Leading the first ballot with 32 percent support was Dr. Stuart Smith, an exotic choice to be sure for a party whose roots were still overwhelmingly rural and agrarian. Smith won his first election in Hamilton West only four months earlier. He had wanted to run federally in the riding of Mount Royal in the 1965 Canadian election, but the party wanted another guy for that riding: Pierre Elliott Trudeau. So Smith moved to Ontario and gave the future prime minister one of his best future punchlines: "I see Stuart Smith is here. Had things worked out his way, he'd be prime minister of Canada and I'd be an MPP in the Ontario legislature."

Smith was a dramatically different choice from the previous Liberal leader, Bob Nixon, whose roots in the province went back more than a century. Smith's message was one Liberals didn't always want to hear, namely, if the party insisted on being a rural rump with no appeal to voters in cities, it could never hope to govern an increasingly urbanizing and multicultural province.

Placing second on the first ballot with 26 percent was London Centre MPP David Peterson, like Smith, a newly minted MPP. Peterson was even younger than Smith — only 32 years old — but almost from the moment he set foot into Queen's Park there were rumours of his interest in the leadership. His father, Clarence, was a signatory to the CCF's Regina Manifesto. His father-in-law, Don Matthews, was a former president of the federal PC Party.

The potential kingmaker at the convention was 36-year-old Albert Roy from Ottawa East, whose unexpectedly good speech and solid performance at the convention gave him 24 percent support, breathing right down Peterson's neck. The third and final ballot featured Smith versus Peterson, with Roy declining to support either contender. Like Davis, who won a 44-vote squeaker, Smith barely won his convention, as well — by just 45 votes out of nearly 2,000 cast.

The results said something interesting about Ontario, which had a reputation of being a closed shop for white Anglo-Saxon Protestants. Yes, it was 1976 and the province was beginning to welcome different ethnic groups in increasing numbers. But of the 125 members of the Ontario legislature, only 15 — 12 percent — came from non-English or non-French backgrounds. (Today 41 percent of Ontario MPPs come from neither English nor French backgrounds.) By 1976 the NDP and Liberals now both had Jewish leaders. There were six Jewish MPPs in total, including newcomers Larry Grossman, Marvin Shore, and Stuart Smith, and veterans Stephen Lewis, Vernon Singer, and Sidney Handleman. There were four MPPs of Italian background: NDPers Tony Lupusella and Odoardo Di Santo, and Liberals Vince Kerrio and Remo Mancini.

While no one in Toryland was thrilled at being reduced to a minority government (save and except for Hugh Segal, the preternaturally happy warrior), it's also fair to say that if the PCs had to govern in a minority legislature, they were fortunate to have Bill Davis at the helm. Canadian political history is rife with examples of Tory first ministers who badly underperformed in similar circumstances. In 1979 the federal Progressive Conservatives under Joe Clark won a minority government. Clark famously said he would operate as if he had a majority, so confident was he that at the end of the day he held superior cards to the leaderless Liberals. It didn't work out that way, and the PCs were shown the door by Canadians nine months later. Similarly, the Tories under John Diefenbaker won only a minority government in 1962. Less than a year later Dief was out and the Liberals were in power for the next 17 straight years.

But Bill Davis was a different kind of Tory leader. First and foremost he wasn't a hater. He understood that all 125 members of the Ontario legislature got there because they were committed to public service, even if some of them on the opposition benches, as he loved to say, were "philosophically misguided." Of course, when it came time for the grand consultation with the public, otherwise known as elections, Davis was as tough and competitive as it came. But between elections he genuinely wanted to get stuff done and understood that meant co-operating with one of the opposition parties.

While Davis's relationship with Stuart Smith wasn't as friendly as his friendship with Lewis, it was surprisingly okay by today's standards, in which disgust and mistrust among party leaders seem to be the norm. The PC and Liberal leaders had a healthy respect for each other. Given that it was a more civil time in politics, it wasn't unusual to find the two leaders up on the third floor of the legislature, late on a Friday afternoon, having a drink in the press gallery lounge with members of the media after the week's proceedings were done. (Davis's drinks were decidedly more non-alcoholic than those of the reporters present, no doubt.) The two leaders learned how to fight like hell during Question Period, but also get the public's business done in a minority legislature. It was a tone Davis set — he simply didn't see his opponents as enemies to be crushed. Try to imagine Stephen Harper and Thomas Mulcair getting together in the Prime Minister's Office to discuss issues and you have some understanding of how differently Bill Davis saw his political adversaries.

In fact, on several occasions Smith met with Davis in the premier's office to make policy recommendations. "I told the premier I would go to the wall to ensure that my caucus was in support of amendments to the human rights code protecting the rights of gays and lesbians," Smith recalls. Given that both parties had significant factions of social conservatives in their bases, it would have been a hard commitment for both men to achieve. Smith was ready to give it a try, but Davis rejected the idea. (Even when the Liberal government of the late 1980s *did* make those changes, they didn't come without a lot of consternation in some quarters.)

Smith was also ahead of his time when he met with Davis on another occasion and urged the premier to make the province's colleges and universities work together better. Even today this is a hard sell for some in the post-secondary system where turf protection is rampant, where some colleges want to become universities, where many universities still turn up their noses at the colleges, and where some colleges want the right to grant degrees rather than diplomas, unconcerned about whether that devalues the "brand" of a degree. Having said that, it's typical for students today to go to university for a good arts education, then transfer to a community college to get training that more directly leads to a job. Smith tried to get Davis to see increasing linkages between universities and community colleges, but at this point, according to Smith, Davis wasn't buying. Nevertheless, the bigger political story here is that at least the premier's door was open, something of which first ministers in today's Canada might take note.

One significant change in public policy at this time came as a result of a tragedy befalling a member of Davis's inner circle. One of Eddie Goodman's daughters, a student at the University of Western Ontario, was driving home along Highway 401 when she got into an accident and was thrown from her vehicle. An investigation concluded that had she been wearing a seat belt she would have survived the accident. "Davis was so shaken by the tragedy of loss of this young life, he made it known we were going to enact seat-belt legislation," recalls Sally Barnes. The government took a daily hammering over the issue with numerous commentators, particularly Gordon Sinclair on CFRB Radio, decrying the infringement on individual rights. But Goodman's constant championing of mandatory seat-belt legislation, along with the premier's view that too many senseless deaths were happening because people didn't want to wear their seat belts, carried the day. On January 1, 1976, Ontario became the first jurisdiction in Canada to require drivers to wear seat belts. And no one seems too fussed about it today.

Nineteen seventy-six was also an Olympic year for Canada. While Montreal hosted the Summer Games, there were some regattas near Kingston that Davis attended, hosting Queen Elizabeth II and Prince Philip, as well. Another indication of how well Davis treated the people he worked with came one day when RCMP officers were apparently tossing their weight around organizing logistics for the Royal Couple.

"The Feds always had a burr up their asses" is how Nick Lorito, Davis's driver, described the scene.

But the premier had other plans. He huddled with Lorito and told him, despite what the RCMP had planned, that he intended to guide the Royal

Couple toward the premier's own security detail, his driver, and some of his other staff who were in attendance. He told the Ontario Provincial Police photographer to be ready. Sure enough, Davis escorted the Queen and Prince Philip away from the route previously intended by federal security officials and toward his Ontario delegation. Nick Lorito got his picture taken, shaking hands with the Queen. Davis muttered quietly to Lorito, "We're in Ontario now." Lorito still prizes the picture, taken 40 years ago.

Strangely enough, one of the most important events to affect Ontario politics in 1976 was something that happened next door. In November, and for the first time ever, the people of Quebec elected a majority separatist government. René Lévesque's Parti Québécois went from 6 to 71 seats in one election as Quebeckers punished Robert Bourassa's Liberal Party. The rest of the country in general, and Ontario in particular, was gobsmacked. What did this unprecedented verdict mean for the country? Was Canada about to come apart? No one knew what Lévesque's victory portended, but whatever it was it probably wasn't good for the rest of Canada.

Davis's advisers focused considerable attention on how Ontario should respond to the outcome in Quebec. Hugh Segal in particular thought the PQ win created a dynamic the Tories should pounce on. He thought the Ontario government needed a stronger mandate to stand up to Quebec's separatist demands, including a referendum that was sure to come. So the PC government engineered its own defeat in the legislature to precipitate an election just 21 months after the previous one. The Tories put forward a bill changing the percentage by which landlords could increase rents under the new rent review system, but the New Democrats and Liberals combined to defeat the measure. To the opposition's surprise, the Tories decided to treat the bill's defeat as a confidence measure, and so once again, Davis marched off to Lieutenant Governor Pauline McGibbon's suite to request that she draw up the writs for Ontario's 31st general election to be held June 9, 1977, and he did it despite advice from Norman Atkins *not* to do it.

"There are always inherent dangers in an unnecessary election," Atkins told George Hutchison a decade and a half later.

While all of the factors described above no doubt contributed to the early election call, there was another major explanation behind Davis's moves. Bob Teeter's polling suggested the PCs could reclaim their majority government if they acted now. And so they did. Norman Atkins would chair the campaign; Ross DeGeer would manage it.

"I half enjoyed the campaign," Davis now says. "We were well received everywhere."

Davis only *half* enjoyed the campaign because the results were, to be charitable, underwhelming for the Tories. After all that campaigning, effort, and expense, the people of Ontario saw fit to give Davis's PCs just 3.6 percent more votes and only 7 more seats. Bill Kelly, the Tories' chief fundraiser, was furious at having gone to the wall to raise all the money needed for yet another campaign less than two years after the last election. Another casualty was Bob Teeter's reputation. Until now he had been a kind of golden boy in Ontario Tory circles. Now, because the PCs won only another minority government, Teeter was vulnerable to being replaced.

"I wasn't upset with Teeter," Davis says nearly 40 years after that election. "If you relied solely on the numbers, we could have won."

The trouble for the Tories was that several Liberal MPPs were personally more popular in their constituencies than Teeter thought, and thus held on to seats the pollster figured they'd lose. If Teeter erred, Davis says, "it was a mistake in not understanding that we went back to the polls too soon." The premature election call, mixed with the fact that the PC Party was taking an increasing amount of flak for using an American pollster, sealed Teeter's fate. He would soon be replaced by a most un-conservative-looking pollster named Allan Gregg, who preferred leather jackets, jeans, and an earring to the normally staid three-piece suits favoured by the rest of the Big Blue Machine.

Did Davis have any difficulty accepting the iconoclastic Gregg, 23 years his junior, as his new numbers guy?

"I didn't know him at all, but I felt comfortable with him from day one," Davis now says.

And what about the leather jackets and blue jeans?

"I did have children, you know." Davis laughs, suggesting the premier might not have shared Gregg's fashion taste but did understand from his own kids the trends favoured by the younger generation.

Regarding those 1977 election results, it was as if the people of Ontario were saying: You may think you need a majority to deal with Quebec, but actually you're a premier, not the prime minister, and we like things the way they are. The Progressive Conservatives won 58 of 125 seats, based on 39.7 percent of the total vote. It was a better number than either Bob Rae's in 1990 or Kathleen Wynne's in 2014. And yet they both won majority governments with their inferior vote percentages.

In fact, the big news of the election had nothing to do with Davis's Tories but rather with the opposition parties. The NDP under Stephen Lewis appeared to be on a slow but unmistakable upward trajectory: 27.1 percent of the votes in 1971, almost 29 percent of the votes in 1975. Lewis never thought he'd win the 1977 election, but he had hoped to continue to chip away at the Tories' lead and put a real scare into Ontario's natural governing party. Instead, Lewis lost a point in this campaign, dropping 5 seats in the process and falling back into the NDP's more traditional third-place standing in the legislature. But Stuart Smith couldn't gloat about the results, either. True, the Liberals moved back into their traditional second-place spot and reclaimed official opposition status. But the party actually dropped nearly 3 percent of its vote from 1975, losing 2 seats in the process.

There were two particularly noteworthy newcomers to Ontario's 31st Parliament. For the PCs the 1977 election marked the debut of Robert Elgie, MPP for York East, which is actually in the Toronto borough of East York. Elgie, plain and simple, was brilliant. He was a brain surgeon and a lawyer. His father, Goldwin, had been an MPP from 1934 to 1948 (excepting a two-year hiatus from 1943 to 1945). Despite the father's lengthy time in the legislature, he was never a cabinet minister. His son would have more luck. Just 14 months after becoming an MPP, Robert Elgie was appointed minister of labour. He was as red a Red Tory as they came and had excellent relationships with members on the opposite side of the legislature. (In fact, when Davis eventually wanted to shuffle Elgie out of the labour portfolio, the latter begged him not to, saying he wanted to clean up one last item on his ministry's agenda. Davis turned him down with: "Robert, don't you think we've tested the Tory core enough?")

The other rookie elected in 1977 was a teacher and city councillor from St. Catharines named Jim Bradley, who would go on to become one of the most consequential environment ministers in Ontario history when the Liberals assumed power in 1985. Amazingly, at age 71, Bradley is *still* a member of the legislature, having won 11 straight elections and served in the cabinets of David Peterson, Dalton McGuinty, and Kathleen Wynne. He is today the longest-serving member of the current crop of 107 MPPs at Queen's Park.

One thing the Tories were always crafty at was using the spoils of government for partisan advantage. Two results in the 1977 election reflected that. The PCs hoped to be able to improve their seat count in Metro Toronto, but the popularity of individual Liberal MPPs made that tough. So Davis handed patronage appointments to two well-ensconced Toronto Liberal MPPs before election day to open up those seats and give his party a better chance at winning them. The Tories took them both.

Phil Givens, the former mayor of Toronto who had held Armourdale for the Liberals since 1971, was appointed to the Metro Toronto Police Commission. In 1977 Bruce McCaffery took the seat for the PCs and would enjoy a brief stint in cabinet from 1981 to 1983. And in Wilson Heights, Vernon Singer declined to run again for the Liberals after accepting an appointment to the Ontario Municipal Board. Once again, the PCs snapped up the now-vacant seat by a huge 24-point margin. David Rotenberg would hold the seat until 1985 when he was defeated by Monte Kwinter, who at age 85 is *still* the MPP for that part of Toronto and is now the oldest MPP ever to serve at Queen's Park.

Other newcomers included Alan Pope, a well-known candidate from Cochrane South in Northern Ontario, who had lost in 1975 but was successful this time. Pope would serve in the cabinet from 1979 to1985 and run unsuccessfully for the party leadership in November 1985; Brian Charlton took Hamilton Mountain away from the PCs by just 300 votes and would hold three portfolios in Bob Rae's NDP government; Ottawa West's Reuben Baetz would hold five different cabinet jobs between 1978 and 1985; and George Taylor from Simcoe Centre would succeed Roy McMurtry as solicitor general from 1982 to 1985.

One of the first things Davis did on election night was to address the public's concern about his opportunistic election call. The premier committed to working with the opposition parties and pledged not to call an election for four years. Nevertheless, Stuart Smith had something up his sleeve. While sitting in the legislature, he looked over at the NDP caucus and thought for sure there were at least eight members on Lewis's team who were pragmatic, progressive MPPs. The more he contemplated it, the more he thought Liberals and New Democrats should join forces in the hope of better challenging the Tory hegemony. Strategically speaking, one of Davis's great strengths was keeping his opponents off balance. Despite Lewis's occasional forays into ideological far-left territory, Davis made sure to prop up the third-place party every now and then by giving it a political victory. It was crucial to Tory fortunes to keep the opposition as evenly split as possible. As long as the anti-PC vote had two viable options, the Tories could theoretically govern forever. Smith knew this. Lewis knew this. Everyone knew it. But, of course, both the Liberals and New Democrats figured *they'd* eventually become *the* alternative to the Progressive Conservatives, and so Smith's efforts to talk increased co-operation, maybe even a merger, with the New Democrats went nowhere. And Bill Davis was just fine with that.

Having now led the NDP into three consecutive general elections and finding himself once again back in third place, Stephen Lewis determined now was the time to leave provincial politics, and Davis was genuinely saddened to see him go. He and Lewis had developed a friendship that lasts to this day. In January 1978, Lewis invited Davis to appear on the soon-to-be-former NDP leader's radio show *Talk Back*. "It's no secret that I have an affection for him and an admiration for him," Lewis told his listeners. "We square off in the legislature but we're friends."

In May 1978, the premier attended his first-ever NDP meeting — a farewell roast organized by Lewis's Scarborough West riding association. Davis was at his Johnny Carson best, teasing the soon-to-be-former NDP leader that despite always dressing down he secretly always wanted to wear a blue three-piece suit. With that, Davis presented his friend with a doctored portrait of Thomas Gainsborough's *Blue Boy*, with Lewis's head superimposed on it. Lewis collapsed in laughter. Davis then wished Lewis "heartfelt wishes for a brilliant future anywhere on earth but the Ontario legislature." In the summer of 1978, on the last day the legislature would sit — and coincidentally the last day of Stephen Lewis's career as a provincial parliamentarian — MPPs watched as the former NDP leader and the current premier left the chamber together as the last sitting ended.

The 1970s also brought to the province an organized crime scare that deeply concerned authorities. The Commisso Family had created a criminal enterprise on a par with some of the most powerful Mafia families in Italy. They imported and distributed heroin, fenced stolen goods, dealt counterfeit money, and brazenly murdered their enemies. At one point the Ontario Provincial Police became extremely concerned about the Davis family's own safety, eventually moving a security detail into the premier's home in Brampton.

"That was terrifying," Kathleen Davis admitted. "I was very uncomfortable with that, but I loved the men who were helping Billy. They were the best guys in the world. I felt it was okay if they were around." OPP officers Bob Guay and Peter Balog, in effect, became members of the Davis family, given how much time they spent with the Davises over the years.

In fact, for a shy, introverted man, Bill Davis could occasionally be capable of quite unexpected intimate gestures. It was during these minority government years that one member of the Queen's Park press gallery was going through a divorce — a somewhat rare occurrence for the time — and would be left with custody of his two children, an even rarer occurrence. As the journalist was leaving the building one day, Davis and his entourage were entering. The premier took the reporter aside by the arm, away from the earshot of his team, said he'd heard the news about the reporter's marriage, and expressed his concern. He told the reporter to call him at home any time if he needed someone to talk to. The reporter never did make a call but believed Davis's reaching out was sincerely intended. Perhaps Davis saw in this reporter's story an echo of his own — a husband suddenly finding himself alone and responsible for his children.

Meanwhile, a year after winning yet another minority government, and in the lead-up to the PC Party's annual general meeting, mischievous rumours began flying all over Queen's Park that Bill Davis was about to quit politics. The story went something like this: disappointed that he couldn't win a majority against a rookie Liberal leader and a less popular NDP leader, and aware that many of his senior ministers wanted a shot at the leadership, Davis would throw in the towel. NDP MPP Mac Makarchuk of Brantford had already publicly predicted that Davis wouldn't lead the Tories into the next election, whenever that might take place, because he'd failed to recapture the majority he had in 1971. Politics, of course, abhors a vacuum, and even though there wasn't any evidence that Davis was considering leaving, nor a single anonymous quote from any of his advisers, the stories just gathered steam. In August 1978, the *Sault Daily Star* went as far as to criticize all the media and politicians who were engaging in "baseless speculation on the future of Premier William Davis." Davis wasn't giving any outward indication that he was tiring of the job, in fact, quite the contrary. He'd just turned 49 years old at the end of July 1978 and certainly wasn't exhibiting any of the burnout John Robarts was showing near the end of his premiership. But it was summer and perhaps people were bored.

The "story" of Davis's future just wouldn't go away. Queen's Park columnists such as Derek Nelson were writing columns pointing to "a failure in leadership by the Conservatives." Nelson pointed to a declining manufacturing sector (yes, people were noticing almost 40 years ago) and an increasing diversity in Ontario's population, and yet the journalist wrote about what he saw as "something less than inspired leadership" and "a drift and decay in the present government." A headline on one of Nelson's columns referred to "No Firm Guiding Hand," with speculation that as many as 10 cabinet ministers would jump at the chance to run in a leadership race to replace Davis.

The feeding frenzy around Davis's status just wouldn't let up. Eventually, one of the premier's senior advisers was quoted anonymously as saying: "It is critical that Davis say to the party and the faithful what he is doing." Davis had previously said that he wanted to be premier during the Quebec referendum, which was slated for May 20, 1980. But that was only nine months away. What were his intentions after that? Even as Davis considered how he intended to respond to this public relations challenge, two other cabinet ministers made big news, complicating the premier's life. Of all the cabinet ministers Bill Davis worked with during his quarter century at Queen's Park, it's hard to think of one he had more respect for than William Darcy McKeough, "The Duke of Kent," so named for the riding of Kent West then Chatham-Kent represented by him since 1963. McKeough, of course, was the kingmaker at the 1971 leadership convention, who moved to Davis on the fourth ballot and helped the then education minister become party leader and premier. Despite McKeough's being much more conservative and not nearly as progressive as Davis, the two men worked together exceedingly well. Davis knew what a smart and gutsy minister he had in McKeough and consistently put more and more responsibilities on the Duke's plate. He was Davis's treasurer, minister of economics and intergovernmental affairs, as well as municipal affairs, and president of the treasury board of the cabinet, and if you can imagine it, he was for part of the 1970s all of those things at the same time. In the mid-1970s the economy softened and the deficit reached $1.5 billion. Even taking inflation into account, that's a $6.29 billion deficit today — not nearly as big as some of the deficits the government has run over the past several years, but considered stratospheric at the time. But a deeper look at the books showed McKeough actually had a firm hand on the province's financial tiller. Ontario was building new hospitals, schools, colleges, universities, highways, bridges, sewer connections, et cetera, and the annual bill for it all added up to $1.5 billion. McKeough told his cabinet colleagues if he were running a private business,that $1.5 billion would go on the balance sheet as capital investment and he'd depreciate it over time, making the expenditure not seem so big. But Ontario Inc. wasn't a private business, it was the government, and so every dollar spent on infrastructure went on the province's books as a full dollar spent. McKeough calmed his colleagues by reminding them that operationally the province was breaking even. It was only when capital expenditures were added that the deficit appeared. The bond ratings agencies seemed to agree with his logic, since Ontario had a triple A credit rating. The bottom line was that McKeough always had a sharp eye for the bottom line, and as a result, Davis relied on him heavily.

But in spite of all the rumours of Davis's departure, McKeough clearly didn't believe the premier was going anywhere, because on August 16, 1978, the Duke of Kent shocked everyone by retiring from Ontario politics, and unlike federal Finance Minister John Turner who had retired three years earlier only to return nearly a decade later, McKeough never did make a comeback. He went into the private sector, became a much sought after corporate director, and his departure left a huge hole for Davis to fill.

Then, in early September 1978, it emerged that one of Davis's ministers had telephoned an assistant Crown attorney on behalf of a constituent. The appearance of attempting to interfere in the justice system is something that should have occurred to a 15-year veteran of the legislature, as George Kerr was. That it didn't occur to the MPP who was also the solicitor general of the province was truly problematic. Kerr insisted, and Davis believed him, that there was no attempt to obstruct justice, that he was only trying to obtain information about a case. And so for three days the premier tried to withstand calls for Kerr's resignation. But the pressure got to be too much for all concerned, and on September 9, Kerr offered and Davis accepted his solicitor general's resignation. Kerr would stay in politics until 1985, but he would never get back into the cabinet.

Davis's advisers cleverly managed to bury the Kerr resignation story because on that same day the premier finally confirmed to 1,800 delirious delegates at the PC Party's annual general meeting that he wasn't going anywhere. Davis got a prolonged standing ovation when he said he would lead the party into the next general election and that he had no plans to call it until 1981, four years after the last one, as he'd promised in 1977. With that, the summer of speculation finally came to an end.

By the fall of 1980, Davis's political fortunes had really turned around. He had truly become the "Master of the House," utterly comfortable inside Queen's Park and able to overcome his innate shyness when working crowds around the province. The transformation from the sometimes awkward 41-year-old technocratic rookie leader to Ontario's 49-year-old version of Johnny Carson, putting people at ease and exuding comfort wherever he went, was almost complete. The only thing Davis needed to finish the successful transformation was an election that would restore the Tories to a majority government. Polling suggested that could happen whenever the premier made the call. His approval rating was a stratospheric 84 percent.

They say all things are possible in politics but whoever said that wasn't living in Ontario in 1980. For the opposition parties, the sad fact was their prospects appeared absolutely hopeless. One day opposition leader Stuart Smith met with a group of Liberal "wise men" led by Pierre Trudeau's "Rainmaker," Keith Davey, to consider his options. Davey told Smith he had to throw out the typical political rule book and be prepared to entertain some truly controversial ideas if he were to have any hope of competing with Davis in the election that was soon to come. The Rainmaker thought there were three policy changes Smith could champion that would help the cause. First, the Ontario Liberals would have to support construction of a new airport in Pickering, east of Toronto. Second, they would have to force the eviction of the few hundred tenants who lived on the Toronto Islands. And, finally, they would have to favour completing the Spadina Expressway, whose cancellation brought Davis considerable good publicity in the lead-up to the 1971 election.

Smith was in a quandary. Davey might have given him a recipe of, frankly, cynical political moves to make the Liberals more appealing, but the problem was that Smith didn't believe in doing any of them. He saw that the same geniuses who had built Mirabel Airport were champing at the bit to build an airport in Pickering, and as a Montrealer, he knew what a white elephant Mirabel was. He knew the Toronto Islanders were probably all NDP supporters, so attacking them made for good politics. But he also believed it was wrong to kick them out of their homes and thought their presence on the islands probably ensured that criminal elements didn't move in and take over that space. And build Spadina? Not a chance! Smith had spent five years burnishing his environmental credentials and told Davey it would look craven and opportunistic for him suddenly to become the champion of the automobile, especially since Davis had already established his reputation as Mr. Public Transit. Smith got into public life to champion policies that were supported by evidence, not take contrary positions because they might be politically advantageous. By insisting on maintaining his integrity, Smith disappointed Davey, who thought the Liberal leader lacked the political "flexibility" needed to be a successful politician. Today, three and a half decades later, Smith doesn't dispute Davey's conclusion, but simply maintains he wasn't cut out to be a cynical weathervane of a politician who would easily or routinely change positions for political gain.

So things were going well for the Big Blue team. The key was to make sure no controversial issue bubbled to the surface that could disrupt the government's march toward a new majority. So, of course, this being politics, something did.

13

FRENCH

Some controversial issues that appear on a government's radar require a single decision that resolves matters for a generation or more. Other issues are like the New York Yankees playing for the World Series — it seems to happen every few years whether you like it or not.

Such was the case for the Davis government when it came to official bilingualism. As much as the premier always felt he had found the right balance when it came to French-language rights in Ontario, the constant drumbeat from those wanting the province to become officially bilingual almost never went away.

Quebec might have the most bilingual citizens in Canada, but it is not an officially bilingual province. In fact, there is only one officially bilingual province in Canada where French and English are treated absolutely equally — New Brunswick. Ontario was urged throughout the Davis years to join New Brunswick and become officially bilingual, and those demands usually became more pronounced whenever the country was engorging itself on yet another round of constitutional talks. When Davis became premier in 1971, the entire population of New Brunswick was less than 650,000. Because of the province's Acadian history, there was always a significant "French fact" living there. Today, for example, nearly a third of the province's population identifies itself as French. During Davis's time, that number was as high as 43 percent.

But in Ontario the numbers claiming their mother tongue was French were never close to that high. It was always around 5 percent of the population, which really isn't indicative of the facts on the ground, either. In some places such as Sudbury, the French-speaking population is as high as 40 percent. In other places, it's negligible. How to craft a French-language policy province-wide that would find favour with the majority of the public was always one of the most difficult and frustrating issues on the Davis government's plate.

Official bilingualism became the law of the land in Canada in 1969 through the Official Languages Act. It came in response to recommendations from a Royal Commission on Bilingualism and Biculturalism, known as the "B & B Commission." Essentially, it gave French and English equal status in federal institutions (Parliament and the courts) and protected the language rights of the English minority in Quebec and the French minority outside Quebec. Before the Official Languages Act, Ottawa was very much an English-speaking city where French was sort of tolerated. Today it is a truly bilingual capital where French and English are equally used and respected. Part of the thinking behind the act was that by putting French on a legally equal plane with English it would take some of the steam out of the Quebec separatist movement, which was gaining currency by the late 1960s. It was also important symbolism that the two founding peoples of the country ought to feel comfortable accessing national institutions in either official language, regardless of where in the country they lived.

However, once Canada became an officially bilingual country, the next target of those who wanted to expand the practice was the provinces. Quebec weighed in first, but not in the way that proponents of bilingualism wanted. In 1974 Liberal Premier Robert Bourassa enacted his province's version of the Official Languages Act (better known as Bill 22), which made French and *only* French the official language of Quebec. Two years later Bourassa lost power to the Parti Québécois, and in 1977, the new premier, René Lévesque, went a step further. The National Assembly introduced the Charter of the French Language (better known as Bill 101), which initially prohibited signs visible to the public in any language other than French. The government eventually walked that position back a bit, allowing for English on signs but only if the French language was more dominant in appearance.

When Quebec passed Bill 101, the ripples were felt right across Canada, but particularly next door in Ontario. Some pushed the Davis government to enact official bilingualism in Ontario, partly to show Ontario was more magnanimous than Quebec and partly in the hope that by implementing the policy Quebec would appreciate the symbolism and have one less reason to separate. Some also feared Ontario's relatively small French-speaking community might simply disappear without that legal protection, surrounded as it was by a sea of English-speaking communities.

Naturally, many Ontarians reacted exactly the opposite way. They were furious at Quebec's treatment of its anglophones as second-class citizens and couldn't imagine lifting a finger to enhance the role of French in Ontario society. This was, after all, almost three years before the first referendum on separation in Quebec. Still, the Canadian language pot was beginning to boil.

It was with this undercurrent of linguistic tension that Premier Davis took to one of the country's highest-profile podiums — the Canadian Club in Toronto — for a major address on the issue on February 4, 1978. The premier reconfirmed that Ontario would *not* be adopting official bilingualism, but he also resisted taking the bait that many anti-French supporters in the Progressive Conservative Party no doubt wished he had. To those who wanted Ontario to take that next linguistic step as a symbolic gesture of good faith to Quebec, Davis said: "It is support, understanding, and commitments that are being sought, not symbolism." And rather than go for the easy cheap shot against the separatist premier of Quebec, he actually took aim at the Pierre Trudeau government, saying Ontario would leave "self-serving proclamations of bilingualism to our federal friends."

Ontario's French fact at this stage in its history wasn't even 500,000 strong out of a total provincial population of nearly 8.5 million. If you added to the count those who weren't French descendants but could speak French, the number would reach 800,000 — still not even 10 percent of the province's total population. Davis just didn't see how it made any sense to incur the costs, both financial and emotional, of making Ontario officially bilingual.

"Ontario has chosen moderation, careful progress, and practical programming in this area," he told the Canadian Club. "Our approach is diametrically opposed to the ill-fated federal implementation. My government is not about to repeat here the precise errors committed elsewhere, errors this country is still paying for in more ways than one."

The tightrope Davis was walking on the bilingualism issue was tricky indeed. His was still, of course, only a minority government in the Ontario legislature, and the opposition parties — the Liberals under Stuart Smith and the NDP now under their new leader, Michael Cassidy — both favoured official bilingualism for the province. Both opposition leaders were also fluently bilingual, a skill that has eluded Davis his entire life. (He could read and understand French reasonably well, but never felt comfortable speaking it in public.)

Davis feared stirring up anti-French feelings in the Tory heartland, but by the same token he was more than miffed at the federal government's two-faced stand on the issue. The federal Liberals under Pierre Trudeau had twice promised to flow money to all the provinces to expand support for second-language education. When Davis spoke to the Canadian Club audience, none of that money had yet been transferred. For his part, Davis had already championed expanding French-language services "where numbers warranted." As minister of education in the 1960s, he had presided over the creation of what was then the world's largest non-denominational French-language school system outside France. The policy of "where numbers warranted" pertained to the courts and in health care, as well. The *Toronto Sun*, often a critic of Davis's for not being conservative enough, published a February 13, 1978, editorial under the banner headline "Davis Right."

"What possible good would it do to stir up a backlash, fan the flames of division and rancor, and end up with the way Ottawa's grand bilingual experiment did — with hundreds of millions of our tax dollars wasted?" the *Sun* asked.

On the same day, however, the *Oshawa Times-Gazette* offered the opposite advice. "Make the Gesture, Bill" was its headline. The editorial quoted federal cabinet minister Marc Lalonde, who said: "It is true that it would be a symbolic gesture, but it would be the kind of sign of good faith which French-speaking Canadians could see as tangible evidence that English-speaking Canada cares." Lalonde also admonished Davis, saying refusal to make Ontario officially bilingual would be exploited by Lévesque's Parti Québécois in a potential referendum campaign. The editorial concluded: "Make the symbolic gesture, Bill Davis, make the gesture."

But Lalonde wasn't Davis's biggest headache. NDP leader Michael Cassidy upped the ante when he said the premier's refusal to back official bilingualism "is telling Quebec in every headline that we don't give a damn." It was an inflammatory charge, and Davis didn't like it one bit. He blasted (in his calm Bill Davis way) Cassidy for "being irresponsible and he knows it." But Cassidy wouldn't leave it there. "This is an area where leadership is called for and Bill Davis ain't capable of it," he piled on. "As a consequence, he's putting the whole country at risk." The NDP then put added impetus to its leader's words by having Cornwall MPP George Samis introduce a private member's bill, calling on the government to make French an official language in Ontario.

Joe Clark, now the federal Progressive Conservative chief, also weighed in while doing interviews on the second anniversary of his February 1976 PC leadership win. "I can sympathize entirely with the Davis position," he said.

But the Ontario NDP wasn't backing down. In March 1978, the party moved a non-confidence motion against the Davis government. Unlike opposition motions that are routinely introduced and swatted away in a majority legislature, this one could have been problematic for Davis, who only held the largest plurality, but not a majority of the seats in the legislature. But if he feared for his government's survival less than a year after the last general election, he didn't show it.

"I now realize," Davis said of Cassidy, "that we are dealing with an absolute purist who takes comfort in the analyses of both bygone times and bygone ideas. He is, and I say this with both awe and respect, developing a new slot for the political spectrum of the left — a slot for pre-history." Fortunately for the Tories, the Liberals declined to join the NDP in voting "no confidence" and the government survived another mini-crisis.

Interestingly, in a community with a substantial francophone population, the *Sudbury Star* was also urging Davis to hang tough. "It would be political suicide for Premier Davis to get involved in any kind of 'creeping officializing' of French language rights," editorialized the newspaper. "There has been considerable backlash among English-speaking Canadians over the dozen years of having the federal government push bilingualism in its abrasive, awkward way. A move by Ontario in the same direction would serve to exacerbate this."

Naturally, pro-bilingualism groups in Ontario were disappointed. "He has always been apathetic towards the francophone cause," noted Marc

Bissonnette of Association canadienne-française de l'Ontario (ACFO), the province's top French-language rights group.

The temperature on the issue hit the boiling point in, of all places, Exhibition Stadium in Toronto at a Blue Jays baseball game. When the anthem singer switched from English to French, some people in the crowd began booing, and it wasn't just a few malcontents. At the same time some members of the Ontario legislature refused to attend a reception given by Premier Davis for his Quebec counterpart, René Lévesque. However, the MPPs who did attend the reception found a respectful and charming Quebec premier, nothing like the fire-breathing socialist separatist they'd been led to believe Lévesque was. In fact, Floyd Laughren, the NDP member for Nickel Belt, attended the reception and spoke to Lévesque.

"Mr. Laughren is from Northern Ontario," Premier Davis offered by way of an introduction.

"Actually, I'm originally from Shawville, Quebec," Laughren clarified, referring to an English enclave that had a reputation for being virulently anti-French and anti-Catholic.

"I don't blame you for leaving," Lévesque replied to the laughter of everyone within earshot of the conversation.

However, some other MPPs were miffed at Lévesque, not only for Bill 101 but also because Quebec was about to bring in a new regulation making it more difficult for Ontario construction workers to be eligible for jobs in Quebec. While the two premiers met face to face on the issue, a solution wasn't forthcoming. The result was an unfair situation allowing about 15,000 Quebec construction workers to take jobs on Ontario projects, while only a few hundred Ontario workers could do likewise in Quebec because of more stringent requirements in *la belle province*. Davis did a slow boil, then retaliated. "With great regret and reluctance," he asked Ottawa to refer Quebec's discriminatory legislation to the Supreme Court of Canada to determine whether it was, in fact, constitutional. If the courts ruled that it was, then Davis pledged to introduce his own legislation prohibiting Quebec workers from holding construction jobs in Ontario.

"Hot damn!" wrote Claire Hoy in the *Toronto Sun*. "There's a little backbone in old Billy Davis yet."

Sadly for Ontario workers, Davis's drawing a line in the sand in June 1978 ultimately had little effect. To this day Ontario construction workers

are still being discriminated against and no subsequent Ontario government has been able to resolve this intractable problem.

Meanwhile, the Ontario Liberals put forward an idea they thought
could have the same effect as official bilingualism without actually calling
it that. The party's justice critic, Albert Roy, from the riding of Ottawa
East, introduced his own private member's bill designed to "give legal def-
inition to the rights of citizens to have Ontario government services provided in French." The majority of the members of the legislature actually
approved the bill for first and second readings. Two cabinet members —
Resources Development Minister René Brunelle from Cochrane North,
and Tom Wells, the education minister from Scarborough North — both
spoke in favour of the bill. Another Liberal MPP opined that "Never in my
brief time in this House have I participated in a debate that's been more
emotional, and I'm so terribly proud with the tone, moderation, and community feeling. There's been so little heckling." Those sentiments belonged
to someone who had only been an elected politician for less than three
years. His name was David Peterson, the MPP for London Centre.

But then something happened. Premier Davis put on the brakes.
He released a statement saying the "existing unwritten program
already adequately dealt with the provision of services to Ontario's
French-speaking minority," and that was that. The bill was stopped dead
in its tracks as the government had no intention of allowing it to go forward any further. Even though this was a minority legislature, it was still
the responsibility of the government of the day to call bills forward for
the entire assembly's consideration. Turmoil ensued, some of it just predictable theatrics: the *Hamilton Spectator* apparently found some opposition members who also shared the premier's concern about a potential
backlash even to this watered-down bill.

"The premier applied the brakes when the legislature was ready to
rush blindly into legislative proposals that could have resulted in bitterness and acrimony in areas where common sense and reason now prevail," the *Spectator* declared.

But David Peterson wasn't happy: "I'm very disappointed," he said.
"In an afternoon when we were ennobling the whole miserable process,
in a community spirit, wrestling with a difficult problem, the premier
unilaterally does what he does." But Tory MPP Gordon Walker from

the riding right next door to Peterson's thought the bill had the potential to be a bureaucratic nightmare and apparently his view was persuasive in caucus.

ACFO weighed in: "I'm so flabbergasted, I'm telling you I just can't believe it," said Gisèle Richer, the president. "I'm just astounded."

The *Toronto Star* shared ACFO's disgust: "Tricky Billy Davis, the sly silver fox of the Tory government: Because he feared a red-neck reaction among some voters — the kind who booed the singing of *O Canada* in French at the baseball stadium — he turned a fine performance by the Legislature into a hollow mockery of principle."

But the *Toronto Sun*'s Claire Hoy uncharacteristically defended the premier again, writing: "Now that the large delegation of frenetic knee-jerkers in the media, politics, and elsewhere have had to opportunistically set new records for levels of self-righteousness over Bill Davis' reaction to a French services bill, let's hear from the other side." The headline on Hoy's column was: "Davis Was Dead Right to Give French Bill the Axe."

The issue was white-hot. The newspapers were filled with letters every day, praising and chastising the premier. "Thank you, Bill Davis, for having the guts to say 'no' to the big push to make Ontario a bilingual province," wrote E.L. Gilchrist from Thornbury. "Davis has my support and vote for sure."

"When the private member's bill on French was quashed, it gave me a new respect for Premier Bill Davis," wrote Ken Grigg from London. "The other two parties, instead of playing politics, should start thinking of the will of the people."

And R.G. Bell from Toronto wrote: "Premier William Davis was right to stop the French-language bill dead in its tracks. His decision is applauded and will long be remembered by the 95 percent of the population who are grateful Ontario is a product of the English language and culture."

The debate raged on. Bob Cohen, writing for the Southam News chain in June 1978, said Davis was wrong to be so overly concerned about a backlash. "No matter what the practical political realities, somebody — especially an important national leader — has to stand up for what is right. And when the bell tolled for William Grenville Davis, he did not have what it took."

And then Pierre weighed in.

Prime Minister Trudeau also criticized Davis, saying he "doesn't realize how damaging his actions can be to the rest of Canada." While acknowledging Ontario had made "substantial and real progress" on improving the rights of its francophone citizens, Trudeau allowed that French-speaking Ontarians were "genuinely and justifiably disappointed" by Davis's actions.

The death of Albert Roy's private member's bill brought the debate to an end, but only temporarily. The official bilingualism issue was always simmering just below the surface. Less than two years later Quebeckers and the rest of Canada would engage in the first of two heart-stopping referendums on whether Quebec wanted to remain within Canada. While the federalist forces ultimately won the May 20, 1980, referendum by a relatively large nearly 20-point margin, it didn't take long for the language issue to roar back. Later that year, as first ministers began negotiating a possible patriation of the Constitution with an entrenched Charter of Rights and Freedoms, Pierre Trudeau once again went to the wall for official bilingualism in Ontario. This time, he had an unusual ally in the premier of New Brunswick. Richard Hatfield felt he could speak with considerable authority on this issue, given that his was the only officially bilingual province in Canada. He and Trudeau and Davis also made up the only three jurisdictions in Canada that at this point were in favour of patriating the Constitution with an accompanying Charter of Rights and Freedoms. And yet, in October 1980 at a news conference held at the Carnegie Endowment for International Peace in New York City, Hatfield inexplicably attacked Davis with comments guaranteed to bring no peace to the issue at all.

"The anti-French feeling is in Ontario," Hatfield said. "That has to be exposed." Hatfield then portrayed his fellow Progressive Conservative premier as a rejectionist on language rights. Given the bigger constitutional agenda at play, the comments were astonishingly harsh.

"The charges are a bunch of nonsense, and it really offends us," responded Thomas Wells, now Ontario's intergovernmental affairs minister. Some wondered whether Hatfield wasn't pandering to the 43 percent of his constituents who were French.

Regardless, Premier Davis rejected Trudeau and Hatfield just as forcefully. The premier insisted Ontario would continue its practice of quietly extending French-language rights, but "forcing bilingualism on any provincial government by constitutional means would evoke the kind of bad feeling and resentment which will set the cause of French-English relations back many decades," he told Trudeau. These three men — Trudeau, Davis, and Hatfield — who were so instrumental in patriating the Constitution simply never could agree on this issue of provincial official bilingualism.

Three months later four Quebec Liberal MPs and a crush of reporters crashed Davis's return to Toronto International Airport from a Florida vacation. They begged him to entrench in the Constitution the French-language services Ontario was now offering. Once again Davis rejected the appeal.

Although Davis had almost no confidence at all in his own ability to speak French, he once made a significant exception. In the lead-up to the Quebec referendum in the spring of 1980, he travelled to Quebec, accepting an invitation from the Montreal Board of Trade to make the case for a renewed Canadian federation and Quebec's place in it. The premier actually did roll out some of his halting French in his speech. "I could speak French as well as John George Diefenbaker, which is to say not very well at all," Davis today jokes when recalling the speech. When he got back to Queen's Park, the premier received a call from Quebec's René Lévesque. He expected Lévesque to criticize the speech or maybe tell him to mind his own damn business. Instead, Lévesque congratulated him on the effort and urged him to return. "Our poll numbers went up 2 points overnight," Lévesque told him. "Come back anytime."

Through the years, Ontario governments of all stripes have expanded French-language services. Even the Davis government dedicated further resources to making the courts bilingual. In that case the record shows the premier actually had little to do with it. His attorney general, Roy McMurtry, who had known Davis since their University of Toronto days together, simply took advantage of his close relationship with the premier and got it done. His first significant decision as Ontario's new attorney general in 1975 was to make Ontario's courts bilingual where there was a demand for French-language services. And so, without great fanfare, he implemented a policy of having the courts hear cases in French, combined with the laborious process of translating all of the province's laws into French — all without gaining prior approval from the premier's office. Albert Roy, whose private member's bill caused so much fuss a few years earlier, praised McMurtry for his "laudable recklessness. The attorney general's sincerity on this is impeccable."

McMurtry was no doubt influenced by his own sense of what was the right thing to do. Improving French-language services was a hugely important issue to the province's francophone community, regardless of how big or small it was. In his autobiography *Memoirs and Reflections*, McMurtry recalls discussing the issue with his cabinet colleague, René Brunelle, nicknamed "The Man from Moonbeam." (Moonbeam was the actual name of a town in Brunelle's Cochrane North constituency.) One day Brunelle told McMurtry that 95 percent of the legal proceedings in his riding — judges, lawyers, Crown attorneys, police officers, and witnesses — took place in French. But everything had to be translated into English because only English was the officially recognized language of the courts. McMurtry agreed with Brunelle that this was insulting to the Franco-Ontarian community and pledged to do something about it.

Given how toxic an issue this was both at the federal and provincial levels, McMurtry simply decided to move forward with bilingualism in the courts without consulting his premier about it. Eventually, when Davis found out about his attorney general's moves, he wasn't pleased. McMurtry explained he took the approach he did to give Davis the distance from the policy McMurtry thought he might need. There was no sanction, no rapping of McMurtry's knuckles, despite the political pickle the attorney general was thrusting on the premier. In the end, Davis agreed with his attorney general, although he would also telephone him from time to time and ask: "What new government policy have you announced today and would you like to share it with me?"

By the time McMurtry retired from politics in 1985, the right to a bilingual trial existed in most of the province and French was officially proclaimed as an official language in the Ontario Courts of Justice Act. McMurtry got it done, but it's also fair to say Davis let it happen. When things got too hot, he could always have called his attorney general onto the carpet, forced him to reverse course, or even fired him. He did none of those things.

"He did things the Bill Davis way" is how John Tory describes it. "He kept pushing the envelope of providing French-language services, but he would have risked it all if he'd declared Ontario officially bilingual."

There are two ironic postscripts to this debate. First, in 1985, David Peterson became Ontario's 20th premier. Faced with the option of fulfilling his party's long-time position to make the province officially bilingual, or merely improving services where numbers warranted, he chose the latter. In 1986, with the support of the NDP led by Bob Rae, Peterson's minority government passed the French Language Services Act. It guaranteed French services to francophones in 23 designated areas of the province, in other words, *where numbers warranted*. And the French language routinely began to be used in debates and during Question Period in the legislature. However, even doing that stirred up anti-French bigotry in some parts of Ontario. In 1989, when the Liberal government held its caucus meeting in Brockville, a handful of idiots stomped on the Quebec flag in protest. It turned into a major brouhaha and nearly torpedoed the Meech Lake Accord negotiations. And in 1990 the city council in Sault Ste. Marie passed a resolution declaring English as the municipality's only official language when it came to the provision of local services.

In the more than three decades since Bill Davis retired from politics, none of the seven premiers who succeeded him has chosen to make Ontario officially bilingual. The Davis formula of "where numbers warrant" is essentially still the policy of Ontario's government. With French-language services now as ubiquitous as they are, making the province officially bilingual at this point would essentially only require a statement proclaiming it. What would have to happen? Simply requiring the publications of the Ontario legislature to be done in both official languages. Roy McMurtry says he regrets this final step hasn't been taken yet. Watching MPPs regularly go back and forth from English to French during Question Period or legislative debates suggests the province is for all intents and purposes officially bilingual already and has been for a long time. In fact, in 1985, David Peterson, the opposition leader then, rose in the legislature to ask a question in French. The premier, Frank Miller, answered in French. Then, when it was his turn, the leader of the NDP, Bob Rae, posed his question in French and Miller again replied in French. It was the first time that had ever happened in Ontario history, and the sky didn't collapse.

Second, an unusual thing happened in Toronto on November 14, 2001. To celebrate the 20th anniversary of the city's French-services committee, Mayor Mel Lastman signed a proclamation honouring someone who was instrumental in the group's creation and two decades of staying power. Among other things the proclamation says (in French): "Without your participation, the committee would not have progressed to become that which it is now. Your efforts, your perspicacity, and your diplomacy have served the committee for these last 20 years. You are today receiving this honour which underlines your contribution to the history of the francophone community in Toronto."

The name on the proclamation reads: Honourable William G. Davis.

14

CLARK

Conventional wisdom says the most intriguing relationship William Davis had with any federal politician during his time in public life had to be with Pierre Elliott Trudeau. And given the juxtaposition of how brutal some of their public political exchanges were with how splendidly they worked together on the national unity file, that's probably right.

But Davis had another relationship with another prime minister that was almost as interesting. It was a difficult relationship to manage because on the biggest issues of their time as first ministers they had massive disagreements. That's not a problematic state of affairs when two politicians are in different parties. But in this case the two politicians in question were in the same party, and that made things inordinately complicated because above all else when it comes to partisan politics the premier of Ontario always wanted to be seen as a party loyalist through and through.

But it was never easy for William Grenville Davis, the 18th premier of Ontario, and Charles Joseph Clark, the 16th prime minister of Canada.

By all rights, these two men should have gotten along famously, because frankly they had so much in common. Davis was born in a small town outside Ontario's biggest city. Clark was born in a small town outside Alberta's largest city. Both got interested in Progressive Conservative politics at a young age. Both had famous fathers with whom they shared a name: Davis's father was a well-known Crown attorney in Brampton with whom he shared a middle name; Clark's father was a well-known newspaper publisher whose first name was also Charles. Both men won the leadership of their respective parties on the first try, both on the fourth ballot, and both by shockingly close margins: Davis by 44 votes in 1971, Clark by 65 votes in 1976. Although Davis is 10 years older than Clark, they both became leaders of their parties at young ages: Davis at 41, Clark at 36, making him still the youngest major party leader in Canadian history. Both also won their first elections as party leaders, Davis in 1971, Clark in 1979. And to put it delicately, both were somewhat awkward and shy in a business filled with backslappers. With all of that in common, it should have been easy to believe Bill Davis when he praised Joe Clark, and he did praise Clark on innumerable occasions. But two little issues always prevented observers from truly believing all those nice things Davis said about Clark: oil and the Constitution.

On February 22, 1976, Joe Clark was the unexpected compromise candidate, winning the national PC leadership from third place on the first ballot to replace Robert Lorne Stanfield. Almost from the get-go, too many Tories had buyers' remorse, and the undermining of Clark was persistent. There was so much enmity between the top two candidates' campaigns — Claude Wagner and Brian Mulroney, both from Quebec — that neither side could bear the thought of the other winning. That dynamic gave Clark his opening. It seemed from the moment Clark won some Ontario observers were determined to find as much evidence as possible that Davis was at the very least being unhelpful to Clark, and at the most, actively undermining him, as others who wanted Clark's job were surely doing.

After Prime Minister Pierre Trudeau called the 1979 federal election for May 22, Davis initiated his rather typical approach: he started slow, then ramped up his game big-time. On April 26 at the Empire Club, Davis offered up only one line about Clark in his speech: "I am confident Mr. Clark knows what he wants." Behind the scenes, however, Davis's contribution was much more significant. In fact, half of Clark's campaign team were charter members of the Big Blue Machine. The reason Davis could probably get away with such a public lukewarm endorsement is that it suited Clark just as well. Trudeau had tried to insult Clark by calling him nothing more than "a headwaiter to the provinces," so having a little appropriate distance from the biggest province might not be so bad.

Davis might have taken his public circumspection about Clark one step too far when he compared the federal leader to his beloved Toronto Argos. He meant to suggest that, like his loyalty to the Argos, his backing of Clark was unconditional. The media inferred something else. At this point the Boatmen hadn't won a Grey Cup in a quarter century and were thought of much the same way people think about the Maple Leafs today — the constant butt of jokes about their ineptitude. A *Toronto Sun* headline screaming "Joe's Like Argonauts" probably wasn't what either man was looking for.

But as election day approached Davis actually campaigned with Clark, saying, "I have great confidence in Joe Clark as our next prime minister," and calling Clark a man of great intelligence "who believes in co-operation, rather than confrontation to solve the many issues facing the country." Davis actually blamed Trudeau for his own "more aggressive posture than might otherwise be the case," saying the Liberal leader's divisive campaign tactics encouraged him to get more involved. By the time election day rolled around, Davis was fully on board, showing up at five rallies for Clark and giving his federal leader as much, or more, support than any premier in memory. He didn't do it out of any love of Joe Clark. In fact, in his book *No Surrender*, Hugh Segal says "there was never any sense of closeness between the two leaders" and that Davis had "grave reservations" about Clark. The Davis people also felt Clark was going out of his way not to be beholden to the premier and his team. Nevertheless, Davis was ever the loyalist and supported Clark.

The 1979 election was a crazy one. The Liberals got half a million more votes than the Progressive Conservatives, but the PCs got more seats — 136 to 114, including 57 out of 95 in Ontario, a higher percentage of the Ontario seats than Davis himself had — so Clark got to punch his ticket to the Prime Minister's Office with a minority government. Naturally, those advisers who were urging Davis to kick the tires on the federal Tory leadership now had to cool it. The job wasn't open and, in fact, the premier and the new prime minister were getting along so well that Davis was Clark's first invited guest at 24 Sussex Drive for a private dinner.

Of course, the harmony didn't last long. As part of his IOU, Davis wanted Clark to go easy on allowing the price of oil to rise, or if it had to go up dramatically, Davis wanted the windfall to go into a national fund that would help Ontario's industries adjust to the higher cost of energy. As an Albertan, Clark didn't and couldn't see this issue Davis's way — at least, not enough for the premier's liking.

In November 1979, the country's eyes were focused on a federal-provincial "energy summit" that was a crucial event for both leaders. The premier was adamant that the country risked falling into a recession if the prime minister allowed the price of oil to increase more than a dollar a barrel, which was the scheduled rise on January 1, 1980. These were obviously the days when governments had a huge and direct say in the price of oil. There was constant tension between Ontario, which wanted low prices for its manufacturers and motorists, and Alberta, which wanted to move toward a world price for its precious and finite natural resource. If the price per barrel was going to rise more than a dollar, then Davis wanted not only a national adjustment fund, but he also wanted the federal government to keep enough of Petro-Canada, the nationalized oil company that the federal Tories despised from the get-go, so the company could take risks where private companies wouldn't.

Davis made his pitch at the energy summit but found no takers. He told his colleagues a proposed $4 a barrel increase would cost the average Canadian family $700 a year in higher energy prices. He talked about a "Made in Canada" pricing regime. The federal, Alberta, and Saskatchewan governments all wanted to move to world prices and essentially accused Davis of pandering to the home crowd. Clark did offer to create a national "bank" for sharing the wealth. But Davis wanted more details before offering an endorsement. It's interesting that such minor twitches in the price of oil could have prompted such national gnashing of teeth. Even in today's dollars the proposed increase would only take the price to $13 a barrel. But Ontarians were accustomed to very stable prices, and the notion that some day oil would sell for $150 a barrel as it did in 2008 was ludicrous. These were very different times.

With René Lévesque a no-show at the summit, it was left to Quebec's energy minister to say out loud what clearly many at the summit were thinking. "Ontario's problem," said Yves Bérubé, "is that nobody likes you." Orland French, a columnist then with the *Ottawa Citizen* who rarely passed up a chance to take a poke at the premier, called Davis "a lonely, sorry figure." Even Pierre Trudeau, now the opposition leader, piled on, suggesting that Davis was a washed-up clerk in the great Canadian hardware store and that Alberta Premier Peter Lougheed, the manager's favourite staffer, was now working the cash register.

But then, as so often seemed to happen in their topsy-turvy relationship, Trudeau tossed Davis a lifeline. At a speech in Toronto he said the Ontario premier was the only first minister attempting to speak for Canada. "I think Canadians are beginning to be ashamed of the spectacle of a federal-provincial conference where there is a prime minister and 10 premiers when the only one who attempts to speak for Canada is the premier of your province," Trudeau said, partially pandering to the province with the largest number of seats in the country, and partially taking aim at Prime Minister Clark. And Trudeau might simply have been trying to do what so many others had, as well, namely, attempting to create as much separation as possible between the premier and the prime minister.

But the biggest test of Bill Davis's and Joe Clark's relationship was still ahead. In December 1979, it truly became problematic when Clark's finance minister, John Crosbie, introduced a deficit-busting budget that raised the federal tax on gasoline by 18 cents per gallon and allowed the wellhead price per barrel to rise by $4. Davis complained bitterly that the budget would take billions away from consumers and push Ontario's economy into recession. Davis had campaigned hard for Clark back in May and helped the Tory leader win 57 seats in Ontario. No doubt he hoped for more when it came to how the federal budget would treat Ontario motorists. Reporters now asked Davis if he would still support Clark as staunchly in any future election. Davis gave one of his patented non-answer answers: "There is no campaign under way." One unnamed PC MP from Toronto poured gas on the fire by saying the Clark government had to consider the national interest while Davis could afford to be parochial — not a wise thing to say when you could be looking for help from provincial Tories during the next election campaign, whenever it was. And it would be sooner than anyone thought.

While Davis was unhappy, he was still trying not to throw his federal leader under the bus. However, his treasurer wasn't so muted. Frank Miller suggested Ontario Tories should only offer Clark conditional support next time around: "Our support should be, let's say, predicated upon their doing what we believe is right," Miller said in his typically refreshing plain-spoken Muskoka way. Oh, and he also mentioned the budget would cost Ontario 20,000 jobs and "damage the economic fabric of our society." Those were unusually tough words by one Tory treasurer about another Tory treasurer's budget, and Ontarians would come to hear them repeatedly over the next two months. (Reporters loved Miller's honesty. He once called Peter Lougheed a greater threat to Confederation than René Lévesque.)

One thing was certain: the federal finance minister wasn't amused. In his memoir *No Holds Barred*, John Crosbie accused Davis of "waging a deliberate campaign to discredit our federal energy policy in order to protect the popularity of his own provincial party in Ontario." Crosbie wrote that he thought Davis should have prepared his constituents for the reality that the price of energy had to go up rather than frighten them with doomsday scenarios.

It was a pretty fundamental disagreement within the federation: Lougheed wanted one thing, Davis another, while Clark and Crosbie tried to find the compromise, and they were all Progressive Conservatives. Liberals rubbed their hands in glee, and it wouldn't take long to see why.

What transpired next shocked the Canadian political world. On December 13, 1979, Crosbie's budget failed to pass the House of Commons, Clark chose to interpret that as a vote of non-confidence in his government, and so less than seven months into Clark's prime ministership Canadians were going back to the polls for another general election. In searching for material for their campaign ads, the Liberals looked no further than the Tory treasurer of Ontario. They used Frank Miller's picture and voice in their ads, then concluded with the tag line: "If the embarrassing Joe Clark Conservative budget worries him [Miller], what should it do for you? This is the time to vote Liberal."

Bill Davis was asked what he thought of the ads: "It's the first time in history that the Liberal Party has been so bankrupt of ideas that it's had to rely on a Progressive Conservative premier and a Progressive Conservative treasurer to develop their policies for them."

That might have been a witty rejoinder, but the federal PCs were deeply concerned about what all that criticism from their Ontario cousins was doing to their brand. Even Martin Goldfarb, who had done polling and focus group work for Davis almost a decade earlier, said Davis's aggressive criticism of the Crosbie budget gave the Liberals a patina of legitimacy when they did it. "Davis created the fear," Goldfarb said. "The task of the Liberals was to maintain it and feed it."

Somehow, over time, a narrative has become established that the Davis-Clark relationship was so badly harmed because of the energy-pricing disagreement that Davis sat out this election campaign. This has been repeated innumerable times over the decades and was no doubt fostered by Davis's first actions after the writs were drawn up for Canada's 32nd general election — he took his annual winter vacation to one of his favourite places on earth, his condominium in Fort Lauderdale, Florida. But a closer look reveals that in spite of everything Davis continued to play the role of loyal Tory soldier. He told the Big Blue Machine to give Clark anything he needed to succeed in the ensuing election campaign. Pat Kinsella, executive director of the Ontario PC Party, confirmed at the time that he and his five staffers would work full-time on the campaign. Kinsella even committed the 58 Tory MPPs to the task and insisted none was showing any hesitancy about getting involved.

Davis's first comments about Clark's predicament were to call the opposition "highly irresponsible" for bringing down the Progressive Conservative government so early in its mandate. He called it "an unnecessary election" foisted on Canadians during the Christmas season for "self-centred and self-seeking reasons."

And Davis went further. He reiterated that he and other provincial Tories always answered the bell for their party's national leader when support was sought. In fact, it was Peter Lougheed, when asked what he intended to do for Prime Minister Clark, his fellow Albertan, who responded: "No comment. After the election, I'll have a comment." And yet, somehow over the years, it's Davis who's been often criticized for abandoning Clark in the young prime minister's hour of need.

Davis actually put himself in a vulnerable position by backing Clark as strongly as he did. At Queen's Park Stuart Smith, the Liberal opposition leader, blasted the premier for putting his party's support ahead of the province. "As soon as the bell rings, the old warhorse is out there again because the political party is more important than the Province of Ontario," taunted Smith. Those comments were understandable, given that Smith was a partisan in a minority legislature looking for any possible chink in the premier's armour. But the *Oshawa Times* piled on in an editorial that said: "Loyalty to a party is a commendable trait. But when that loyalty overshadows the good of the people, it is misplaced loyalty.... In other words, the Tory party is more important [to Premier Davis] than Ontario." To read those words 37 years later is to question the sanity of whoever was silly enough to write them.

It was preposterous to suggest that Davis cared more about his party than the province he was elected to serve. In fact, one of the most interesting paradoxes about Davis over the years has been his steadfast loyalty to the PC Party, while at the same time telling me privately on numerous occasions that he thinks political parties are really just marketing labels. Conservative parties from time to time do liberal things, liberal parties do conservative things, socialists do conservative things and, of course, Liberals and Tories occasionally take a page out of the socialists' playbook, such as when they purchase oil companies (which Trudeau did, and Davis was still to do). For a loyalist, Davis actually had a rather balanced view on the value of political parties. They were a necessary fact of life in politics, needed to distinguish the "ins" from the "outs," and clearly there was a place for partisanship in politics. But obviously in his heart Davis didn't believe in much of the ultra-partisan viciousness in which parties indulged back then, and certainly not in the over-the-top ideological warfare they routinely engaged in during the Stephen Harper years. Even Hugh Segal says in his 2006 book *The Long Road Back* that "the difference between moderate Conservatives such as Bill Davis or Peter Lougheed and moderate New Democrats such as Bob Rae or Gary Doer have never been very broad."

No, the premier of Ontario wasn't putting his party before his province. He was simply offended at what seemed like unfair play by the opposition. Clark deserved a chance to implement his program, Davis thought, or at least the prime minister deserved more than six months to do so. "In my view, to deny him this right is to play chicken with the economy and the nation," Davis said at the time.

Because the election stumping would take place over the Christmas season, Clark decided on a longish campaign: more than two full months. So even if Davis did go to Florida, there was still plenty of time for him to make a contribution to the national Tory cause when he returned. In addition, Clark did have several cabinet ministers who had raised their profiles over the past year and could also be relied on to do more, such as Michael Wilson (the Bay Street investment executive), David Crombie (the former Toronto mayor), Allan Lawrence (the former Ontario cabinet minister), Lincoln Alexander (the first-ever black cabinet minister), Flora MacDonald (the first female secretary of state for external affairs), and Ron Atkey, the employment and immigration minister who granted asylum to 50,000 "boat people" escaping the carnage of Vietnam and Southeast Asia.

As 1979 gave way to 1980, Davis penned a letter to 3,000 key provincial Tory activists telling them, despite the disagreement over oil pricing, their premier was still putting his heft behind the national party leader. Davis said conservatives couldn't trust a Liberal Party that was both for and against wage and price controls, and for and against moving to a world price for oil. And most significant, Davis said he'd soon be out there on the stump with Clark. There was still a month to go in the campaign when that letter went out.

A week later Clark's bus rolled up to Queen's Park and Davis welcomed the prime minister with open arms. The two men strode across the elegant red carpeting inside the legislature, then Davis brought Clark into the Tory caucus room where he was received with a massive ovation for several minutes. The cameras recorded it all. We shouldn't be so naive as to think there weren't some important private conversations that led to that moment. While Davis had to throw in the towel on oil pricing, he did manage to extract from Clark a commitment that Ontario would have a voice on a new commission the prime minister was creating to figure out how oil revenues would be nationally redistributed in the years ahead. When Clark was asked to characterize the support he was getting from the premier of Ontario, he used the word *unconditional*. That's a pretty strong endorsement of a man who was allegedly keeping his distance from the prime minister.

Near the end of January, 3,000 Progressive Conservative partisans rallied for Joe Clark in Barrie, Ontario, and one of them was the province's premier. Bill Davis let it all hang out for Clark. "He is the kind of human being and the kind of Canadian we desperately need in Ottawa in the months ahead," Davis said of his federal leader. "He has my support and the total support of my government and my party." Davis reminded the crowd about Pierre Trudeau's flip-flop on wage and price controls: "I hope people's memories aren't too short," he said. None of these comments sound like the words of someone who is half-heartedly supporting his federal leader, and yet somehow, that narrative has become conventional wisdom over the years.

A week later Davis praised Clark's handling of the Iran hostage crisis, which helped save the lives of many American diplomats hiding in Canada's embassy in Tehran as the revolution against the shah was taking hold. Despite some shameful baiting by Trudeau during Question Period that could have revealed Ambassador Ken Taylor's plans to save those American lives, Clark demonstrated statesmanship and kept the lid on the plot sealed shut. "I think he showed maturity, responsibility, courage, and a non-partisan instinct," Davis said of Clark.

Let's remember one other significant subplot surrounding the 1980 campaign. There were plenty of people in Ontario, and plenty of people around the premier of Ontario, who thought Bill Davis ought to have Joe Clark's job. Nothing would have made them happier than to see Clark fall flat on his face during this election campaign so that Clark would have to quit the leadership and thereby thrust Davis into a position of being a potential candidate. Davis had already been premier for two months shy of a decade — just a little longer than the nine and a third years enjoyed by John Robarts. Had he chosen to keep his head down and let Clark lose on his own, it's highly unlikely many people would have blamed the federal Tory loss on Bill Davis. After all, Clark was the author of enough of his own misfortune. But by the end Davis had brought his A-game. He was a loyalist to the core. If Clark was defeated, no one could blame the premier of Ontario.

By the time the campaign was over, Davis had done just as many events with and for Clark this time around as he did in the spring of 1979. But this time the results were very different. Pierre Trudeau welcomed everyone to the 1980s by reclaiming his majority government: 147 seats to just 103 for Clark. The Tories lost less than 3.5 percent of the total votes cast compared to 1979. But the swing was big enough to end his time in government after just nine months less a day. Davis seemed genuinely saddened by the results and admitted at the end of the day that Clark was a sitting prime minister campaigning to keep his job but couldn't. "I don't think there's a lot of transference," he said, referring to his own efforts for Clark.

Less than four months after a heartbreaking and infuriating federal election defeat for the Tories, Bill Davis found himself at the podium of the provincial party's annual general meeting about to introduce the now former prime minister. Clark's leadership was increasingly in turmoil because some Tories were furious with him for "blowing" their first chance in government since before 1963. Again, Davis remained the loyal Tory. "As long as Joe Clark wants to lead this party, Bill Davis will both follow and eagerly support that leadership," he said. As Clark took the stage, Davis lingered beside him, once more allowing the cameras to record that moment of solidarity.

There was a big cake for Joe Clark at the event. The Tory leader had just turned 41 years old the day before. Having done his best for his national leader, Davis was now forced to focus much more resolutely on the provincial scene. His minority government was almost three years old now — five years old if you include the previous minority legislature from 1975, much longer than most of these situations last. It was time to consider the next big political decision on his desk: when to call a provincial election in the hope of recapturing what he once had but had since lost — another Progressive Conservative majority government.

15

MAJORITY (II)

As Ontario's 21st premier, Bob Rae, once told me after losing the 1995 Ontario general election to the 22nd premier, Mike Harris: "There are some elections that just aren't winnable." That was certainly the case in 1995 for Rae's New Democrats. Too much had happened over the previous five years, and well before the writs were drawn up, everyone knew the NDP just wasn't going to be a factor in that campaign. The party started in a distant third place, remained there for the entire campaign, and ended up there on election day, June 8, 1995.

The 1981 Ontario general election was similar, insofar as, for both the opposition Liberals and New Democrats, it just simply wasn't winnable. Bill Davis was riding a crest of popularity going into the campaign that the other parties just couldn't touch. A big chunk of Ontarians had simply grown very comfortable having William Davis at the helm of Ontario Inc., now for a decade, and no matter how good Stuart Smith or Michael Cassidy, the new NDP leader, were, nothing was going to invade that zone of comfort. Three and a half decades after the 1981 election Robert Nixon summed it up this way: "Mike Cassidy was impossible and our guy [Smith] was impossible. How could Davis miss?"

Notwithstanding Nixon's after-the-fact analysis, the campaign actually got off to a terrible start for the Tories. After the writs had already been drawn up and the candidates were off on the hustings, Environment Minister Harry Parrott called his staff together to inform them that he'd changed his mind and wasn't going to run, after all. When Davis's staff found out about it, they hauled Parrott in for a chat with the premier. Parrott left the meeting thinking he'd clearly told Davis he'd had enough. Conversely, Davis felt sure he'd convinced Parrott to stick around for another two to three years. It was a classic case of miscommunication, and the newspapers had quite a bit of fun at the Tories' expense.

Meanwhile, if Stuart Smith's problems both inside and outside his party were an issue, Michael Cassidy's troubles were even worse. He was elected a New Democrat MPP during Davis's first election as premier, and over the 10 intervening years at the legislature developed a reputation as a financial wizard. Cassidy attended Trinity College at the University of Toronto and the London School of Economics. He even did a stint as bureau chief of the *Financial Times* in Ottawa. His father, Harry, was a founding member of the NDP's forerunner party, the Co-operative Commonwealth Federation, but Harry switched to the Liberals, ran for the leadership of the provincial party in 1950, and came second to Walter Thomson.

After Stephen Lewis led the NDP to a third-place finish in 1977 and then resigned, Cassidy ran for the job to replace him, defeating fellow MPPs Ian Deans and Mike Breaugh on the second ballot at the Sheraton Centre in Toronto. Deans's support of the federal government's imposition of the War Measures Act proved to be too much for too many delegates to swallow. After his defeat, he left Queen's Park and got elected to the House of Commons. (Actually, in a strange coincidence, all three of those leadership candidates would go on to become MPs after their tenures at Queen's Park ended.)

Almost immediately Cassidy was at odds with much of his party. He had none of Lewis's performance skills, and the difference was plain for everyone to see at campaign time. Graham Murray, a former candidate and researcher with the party, called Cassidy "abrasive, difficult, impetuous, and headstrong. He wasn't liked. He wasn't a 'clubbable' man.'" Former Liberal MPP Sean Conway, who spent nearly three decades at Queen's Park, once referred to Cassidy as "an ice cube with a sheet of sandpaper draped over it." Before long the razor-thin margin between the Liberals and NDP disappeared, and the New Democrats were, as Murray described it, "clearly mired in third place. We expected the worst for the 1981 election."

One of the issues Cassidy had championed during his leadership run was to revise the Ontario Human Rights Code to offer increasing protection to gays and lesbians. Robert Elgie, Davis's own labour minister, championed the idea inside the PC caucus. But the right wingers howled over it, propelled by Claire Hoy's columns in the *Toronto Sun*. In his own heart, Davis was probably in favour of making the change, but the amount of political capital required to get it through would have been huge. He agonized over the issue as he watched the highly respected Bob Elgie repeatedly get beaten up over it.

But Davis received an unexpected lifeline from the NDP leader. Cassidy's office was in such disarray that he made significant changes. Some advisers, including Graham Murray, left only to be replaced by others who wanted Cassidy to soft-pedal his support for gay rights. This was 1981, after all. Homosexuality was still very much a taboo subject for the vast majority of Ontarians. Murray, who had been planning to run for the party in 1981 in the Toronto riding of Eglinton, was so appalled by Cassidy's backing off this campaign pledge that he refused to run.

"Gay rights were a touchstone for other issues," Murray said. "If you'd do it to them, why should other groups believe you'll stick by them?" Murray argued the NDP "would lose votes from the gay community and wouldn't gain any homophobe votes."

But Cassidy had a more basic problem — his name and persona conjured up ... nothing. "Davis was calm," Murray offered. "Nixon was historic. Lewis was passionate. Rae was intelligent and eloquent. What was Cassidy? No one knew."

Along with the electorate's increasing embrace of Davis the man, there was also the platform. Most election platforms are forgettable. Only a select few have staying power. Think of Mike Harris's Common Sense Revolution in 1995. Or Jean Chrétien's Red Book in 1993. For the Ontario Tories in 1981, their platform's name was eerily (and not at all coincidentally) similar to their leader's. It was called the Board of Industrial Leadership and Development — BILD, for short — a $1.5 billion plan to stimulate the economy and create new jobs. Half of its budget was to come from the province with the remaining half from the federal government and private sector. The Tories divided BILD into six general areas of interest: electricity, transportation, resource development, new technology, enhancing people's skills, and community improvements.

In the field of energy, the Tories promised to do everything from small ideas such as creating a heat pump rental program through Ontario Hydro to electrifying the GO Transit system in Toronto. For transportation, BILD promised further upgrading of Ontario's shipyards and harbours. In resource development, there would be incentives for companies to develop new mineral exploration methods. More money would be available for skills development and community counselling centres. The PCs would embrace the future with a new Micro-Electronics Development Centre to be built in Ottawa or Cambridge, plus a Computer-Aided Design/Computer-Aided Manufacturing development and testing facility known as CAD/CAM. A new Innovation Development for Employment Advancement (IDEA) corporation would be created to coordinate research and development into new technologies. And smaller communities would be eligible for provincial funding to improve their water and sewer services.

The Tories presented BILD as an all-encompassing, forward-looking blueprint for building on the province's economic success. And the economy wasn't doing too badly, creating 100,000 new jobs every year for the past five years. There were also other programs already put into place by previous Davis governments such as the Guaranteed Annual Income Support (GAINS) program; $214 million in property tax grants to 400,000 senior citizens; and hospital budgets increased 10 percent year over year as part of the health ministry's $4.7 billion overall budget.

"This is the Davis government working for you," the Tory ads proclaimed. "The way to protect that program is to make sure the Davis government is returned to office."

Those were the print ads. The radio and television ads featured a catchy tune and a bit of chutzpah to boot. Somehow the Tories decided to try to convince Ontarians that it was *they* who owed it to Bill Davis to return him to office rather than Davis's job to earn their vote. The lyrics urged citizens to "help keep the promise." The chorus went: "Come on, people, let's keep the promise, Bill Davis can do it, let's keep the promise, help Premier Davis."

Although BILD was presented to Ontarians with great and solemn fanfare, the opposition had a field day with the acronym, referring to it as "bilge." Similarly, they mocked Davis for urging Ontarians to "help keep the promise" to him but wondered when he intended to fulfill all the

promises he'd made to them over the previous decade. In any other election cycle, those criticisms might have hit their mark more effectively. Not
this time. It didn't matter. Both opposition leaders tried throwing everything at Davis, including the kitchen sink, but nothing stuck. With pollster Allan Gregg's new techniques able to determine the party's popularity
on a riding-by-riding basis, the Big Blue Machine targeted 26 ridings that
were "in play" where they thought the election could be won.

A typical example of Davis's Teflon happened in the picturesque village of Tweed in Hastings County where the issue of tile drainage was a
significant local issue. One of the premier's aides spent hours crafting a
long speech on the issue, which Davis was supposed to give at the local
Elks Lodge. Davis went to the podium, set the speech aside, made some
small talk, then walked over to a dusty piano and played the boogie-woogie
version of "What a Friend I Have in Jesus."

"Everybody in the media threw their pens up in the air," Hugh Segal
recalled.

Then Davis reiterated his deeply held view that: "As long as I am premier of this province, Her Majesty will be our head of state." Who was
suggesting otherwise? No one!

"Neither Stuart Smith nor Michael Cassidy had attacked Her
Majesty once in the campaign," Segal adds. "Neither had suggested Gina
Lollobrigida as head of state. And everyone in the hall loved it."

The one opportunity Smith and Cassidy could have had to strike
a glancing blow against Davis never happened. The premier ducked a
potential leaders' debate, making it two consecutive elections in which
Ontarians wouldn't have a chance to see the three major party leaders
go mano-a-mano on television. The consequences to the Tory campaign
for Davis's refusal were nil. But that would be the last time any Ontario
premier could skip a leaders' debate without consequence. (Frank Miller
took some very bad advice in 1985 and declined to participate in the
debate during that election campaign; he was mercilessly pilloried for
appearing to chicken out, since by this time the public had come to
expect their leaders to do at least one televised debate; the leaders in the
1984 federal election would do several.)

Davis's declining to debate, preferring to sit on his large,
front-runner's lead, prompted plenty of well-deserved insults. "He's out

of steam," blasted Remo Mancini, the Liberal MPP for Essex South. "Just old-style politics and slick hucksterism."

One morning as Davis was shaking hands with vendors at a farmers' market in Windsor a university professor refused. "Do something for Windsor and I'll shake your bloody hand," the man growled, unhappy at the level of education funding.

Given no leaders' debate and therefore no opportunity for Smith and Cassidy to get at Davis directly, it was left to others to attempt to do that. Less than a week before election day a major fracas broke out between protesting hospital workers and Tory party faithful, as many as 800 of whom had gathered in Sudbury. In the middle of his speech, Davis hit the brakes and began debating the former president of a Sudbury local of the Canadian Union of Public Employees who had been fired a month earlier for her part in a strike. Claire Hoy reported in the *Sun* that Kay McNamara, a single mother of three, was knocked down as the premier, surrounded by his aides and assembled media, approached the podium. McNamara screamed at Davis, "I'm a mother! How am I supposed to support my kids?"

As 20 hostile hospital workers chanted, refusing to let Davis speak, the premier shot back: "I'm not going to be intimidated by people who have to understand that the law must be maintained."

The protestors kept shouting, "Out! Out! Out!"

Davis tried another approach: "Let's sit down and relax a little bit."

But it was to no avail. McNamara defended her role in an illegal strike, saying, "I have my principles."

The premier, however, was having none of that. "I have my principles, too," he told her. "I'm standing up for them tonight, and one of my principles is respect for law and order. As long as I'm premier ... the law will be maintained and hospital workers are essential."

In four Sudbury-area hospitals, 650 striking workers were reprimanded, 630 were suspended for one to three days, and two were fired.

What is astonishing about the exchange is how unlikely such an interaction during a campaign would be today. Davis and McNamara wagged their fingers in each other's face, going toe to toe. At one point Davis listened for five straight minutes as McNamara spoke uninterrupted, calling Davis "a pig" in the process. The huge crowd cheered the premier as he maintained his composure, yet forcefully told McNamara: "You left those patients. I didn't leave those patients." At times the crush of the crowd, including Davis's security detail, squished McNamara, but Davis warned his aides not to harm her.

"I've got to tell you, it's a fun time in Sudbury tonight," Davis told his hecklers as the event broke up.

Another campaign day in Northern Ontario wasn't particularly noteworthy at the time, but in hindsight it is. Davis campaigned in North Bay, having just come from Parry Sound, for two rookie PC candidates. The two men knew each other well, having both served at the same time on the Parry Sound PC riding executive for outgoing MPP Lorne Maeck. Their names were Mike Harris and Ernie Eves. They would go on to become the 22nd and 23rd premiers of Ontario, respectively. And they got elected as Bill Davis Tories.

"I wouldn't have run if it wasn't for Bill Davis," says Mike Harris today from his office at the Fasken Martineau DuMoulin law firm in the Bay Adelaide Centre in downtown Toronto. "Davis was the guy. He was the man." Ironically, Harris cast his first-ever vote for Pierre Trudeau in 1968. He admired Trudeau's leadership abilities but came to disagree with him vehemently on issues. So cabinet minister Alan Pope recruited Harris, then a school board trustee in North Bay, to run for the Tories, assuring him that the legislature only sat for five months a year and only required his presence in Toronto a few days a week. "Of course, they lied about that!" Harris now says, laughing. "The other thing he told me is: 'We don't think you can win. We just want a good candidate.'" After all, Nipissing had been a safe Liberal seat for more than two decades. Harris had a hunch that if the contest came down to him versus the Liberal incumbent, he'd lose. So he had signs made up saying DAVIS-HARRIS: WHAT A TEAM! with a big picture of Davis and a little picture of Harris on them. In the Italian areas, the signs said: CHE SQUADRA! In the French areas, it was: QUELLE ÉQUIPE!

At this time in Ontario history, and very much unlike today, the PC Party was very competitive across Northern Ontario. Davis taunted Stuart Smith, dubbing him "Doctor Negative" for having no policy for the North. "He sends his northern policy up by telex from Malton Airport," Davis would say, referring to a mode of communication and an old airport name, neither of which exists anymore. "In this riding you can be your own Liberal control board," playing off the Liquor Control Board of Ontario name.

In Eastern Ontario it was much of the same. Seven protest groups, comprising 400 protestors, gathered in Ottawa a couple of days before election day to slam Davis over the size of university fees, the lack of funding for post-secondary institutions in general, better funding for Catholic schools, French-language schools, and institutionalized bilingualism, while some Marxist-Leninists and striking hospital workers joined in. As the protestors tried to outshout 1,200 Tory faithful, Davis referred to the hecklers as "embarrassing the vast majority of students in this province." He pointed out that the students were only paying about 15 percent of the cost of their tuition while taxes covered the other 85 percent.

"We want justice!" screamed one student.

"You're getting more than your fair share," Davis retorted. "I haven't been intimidated by anybody in this campaign and I won't be intimidated tonight. My responsibility is to run this government, and I'm going to do just that. You can shout all night, but my tonsils are better than yours." Then, with an additional taunt for good measure, Davis said: "There are more New Democrats who come to my rally than go to their own."

Federal PC Leader Joe Clark was also in attendance. After hearing well-worn chants of "Save us from Davis," Clark replied: "It's good to be here tonight to save the Province of Ontario from those fellows."

Ottawa police showed up in large numbers to deal with any unanticipated violence, but it never came to pass. One gay rights activist jumped onto a TV platform and shouted, "I demand equal rights!"

Davis was quick to respond: "You've got your 10 seconds on TV now and you're not going to disrupt this meeting. We all have equal rights in Ontario and you know it."

While Davis might have made Ontarians feel comfortable with his style of leadership, he and his team could be tough as nails behind the scenes when they thought the situation called for it. Two months before election day and having just returned tanned and rested from a Christmas vacation in Florida, Davis met with one of his most influential backroom boys, Eddie Goodman, at the premier's Queen's Park office. Goodman had been trying for seven years to put Toronto's so-called Jewish Home for the Aged, Baycrest, one of the leading centres for geriatric studies in North America, on the government's radar. He wanted an addition built for Baycrest's Bathurst Street location and pointed out to Davis that other

hospitals had successfully applied for additions later than Baycrest, and
that Baycrest no longer limited its services to Jewish citizens exclusively.
Goodman had promised to raise $20 million for the institution and had
secured funding from the North York and Metro Toronto governments but
couldn't get anywhere with the health ministry bureaucrats on this one.

As he always did, Davis listened carefully and patiently without making any commitments, but a few weeks later he told Goodman that he'd
personally looked into the matter, agreed it was something the community needed, and gave Goodman the green light to tell Baycrest's board so
that an announcement could be organized.

Goodman immediately reported the good news to Norm Schipper,
his law partner and Baycrest's president, and told him to keep it under his
hat for now. Two weeks later Davis called the election for March 19, 1981,
and Goodman arranged to have the premier make an early campaign stop
there to announce the Baycrest funding initiative. That's when hardball
politics kicked in. Goodman soon learned that the hospital's management
had agreed to let Liberal candidate Elinor Caplan do a campaign event of
hers with leader Stuart Smith at Baycrest just a day or two before Davis's
planned appearance. Goodman got on the phone to Schipper and warned
his friend that if he didn't cancel the Liberal campaign event, he could kiss
Davis and his money goodbye.

"We're not going to be a follow-up act to Stuart Smith," Goodman
told his partner in a story retold in Goodman's book *Life of the Party*.
"You can't expect Davis to go *after* Smith when I made arrangements
quite some time ago for him to be there." Besides that, rookie Tory MPP
David Rotenberg was in a tough battle with Caplan to hold the seat, and
Goodman wasn't about to give up any advantage he had to secure the
Wilson Heights riding.

Goodman was playing a game of chicken with Baycrest. He admits in
his memoir that he never would have allowed Davis to cancel a previously
agreed-upon commitment to appear. But Schipper didn't know that. So
he cancelled the Smith-Caplan early campaign visit. Baycrest would get
its money, and Rotenberg would win re-election.

The 1981 election was unusual inasmuch as the polls essentially
didn't move. From the middle of February to the middle of March, Davis's
numbers were in the stratosphere. Asked by Gallup who would make the

best premier of Ontario, 53 percent answered the current occupant of the office. Only 12 percent opted for Stuart Smith, and a puny 9 percent liked Mike Cassidy. The numbers were essentially the same everywhere in Ontario. Even 30 percent of Liberals and 24 percent of New Democrats surveyed agreed Davis was the best choice for premier.

Davis was different. Even if you didn't support his party, plenty of Ontarians recognized he was plainly the best man for the job.

Toward the end of the campaign, Torontonians who opened their afternoon *Toronto Daily Star* to the editorial page found an endorsement for the Ontario PC Party. Conversely, if they opened their morning *Globe and Mail,* they saw an endorsement for the Liberals. It was a different world back then.

"It is in the best interests of both this province and the nation as a whole that Davis win a renewed mandate," the *Star* opined. "Davis has shown a pre-eminent ability to address the vital national issues on which Ontario's well-being depends…. Davis has proved himself an effective and statesmanlike spokesman for Ontario's vital role in the continuing task of nation-building."

But the *Globe* disagreed with Davis's positions on energy pricing and constitutional renewal and thus backed Stuart Smith. The *Toronto Sun,* with an unhappy headline reading "Davis the Issue" identified with the *Globe*'s "dismay" and called the *Star* "a sycophantic echo of Mr. [Pierre] Trudeau for the past 18 months." The *Sun* editorialized that Davis "deserves to be reprimanded by the people. He will interpret a majority vote as approval." Then, in the next sentence, the paper went on to acknowledge: "If it weren't for his constitutional and energy opportunism, he'd deserve the majority he will likely get."

When he wasn't getting heckled, protested against, or shouted down, Davis's basic humility came through. "There's only one thing that has ever motivated my political life," he would say. "I've had only one ambition and that is to serve the people of this province and to the extent I can the people of this nation. I'm not in it for myself…. I've never regarded the position of premier of this province as a position of power. I regard it as a position of trust, responsibility, service, leadership."

But Davis could also do the corny stuff well. He never shied away "from talking about my feelings about the family, about morality, and about decency." He would help seniors blow the candles out on their birthday cakes or join an elderly music teacher at the keyboard. And he'd stick up for the Queen with: "She will cease to be [the sovereign] only over my politically deceased body."

Election night was as anti-climactic as the polls indicated. On the strength of 44.4 percent of the total votes cast (up 5 points from 1977), Davis's Tories captured an additional 12 seats for 70 in total in a 125-seat legislature. Davis had won back the majority government he inherited then lost through the mid to late 1970s. It was the Ontario Progressive Conservative Party's 12th consecutive election victory, an astonishing record of success. Strangely enough, the Tories took 8 of their new seats from the NDP. And of Allan Gregg's 26 targeted ridings, the PCs had captured a dozen of them. But none of the new PC seats was outside that group of 26. Gregg's polling was spot on, which allowed the party to husband its resources with supreme efficiency. As Hugh Segal described it in Patrick Boyer's book *The Big Blue Machine*, the 1981 campaign featured "a perfect message, perfect leader, and perfect platform."

Once again the Liberals didn't win, but then again they didn't expect to. And there were some significant victories for them on the night. In the later stages of the campaign, Smith focused less on the negative, trying to shake off Davis's mocking nickname, and introduced a more passionate and positive tone. The result was a somewhat more buoyant 34 percent of the total votes cast — 2 percentage points higher than in 1977 but only good for the exact same 34 seats. The particularly good news, however, was firmly establishing the Liberals as the stronger opposition party and more likely alternative if the Tories ever were to stumble — a scenario that would play out just so in four years time, albeit with an entirely different cast of characters.

For the NDP it was a rough night and hard to find even the New Democrats' traditional moral victory: a loss of 12 seats to just 21 in total; a loss of 7 points in the total votes cast to just 21 percent; and unlike the Liberals whose leader at age 42 could legitimately ask for another chance to lead the party into the next election, there was only a recognition among New Democrats that Michael Cassidy would have to go. Within a year he would be replaced as leader by a much younger (11 years his junior) rising star from Ottawa.

Part of the Tories' plan was to make the electorate believe things were just fine and to keep the total vote low. The approach worked, since only 58 percent of eligible voters showed up to the polls (compared to 65.6 percent in 1977), not surprising given the lack of a burning issue radiating throughout the campaign.

In an op-ed piece in the *Star* the day after the election, Peter Regenstreif, who ran focus groups for Gallup, quoted 26-year-old Bill Devine, a furniture finisher. "He appears very passive," Devine explained about the victorious premier. "But there's so much strength underneath that. He makes you feel comfortable. He's got a lot of experience and he'll do a good job."

For his part, Davis interpreted his majority as a mandate to work with Prime Minister Trudeau on constitutional change and against Alberta's desire for higher energy prices. "I am a Canadian first," Davis said on election night. "The future of this country belongs to those who have the courage to believe in it." Ironically, the first person to disagree with that interpretation was Joe Clark, Davis's federal leader, who said the new majority had more to do with Davis's record governing Ontario than any national or interprovincial issue. Clark might have been more right on the facts (the *Globe* agreed with Clark, calling Davis's interpretation of the mandate "astonishing"). But it's also a fact that winners can interpret a renewed mandate any way they like, and Davis preferred to infer that voters were giving him the green light to bring the Constitution home and fight Alberta's Peter Lougheed on oil prices. The *Hamilton Spectator* urged cautious optimism about the ensuing four years, editorializing: "Ontario voters removed the checks on a government's potential for arrogance and complacency. The onus is on the Davis government to justify the confidence the people have placed in it."

The 1981 election was historic for several reasons. It was the first election in 36 years in which the Ontario public rewarded a premier who previously had a minority government with a majority. George Drew last turned that trick for the Progressive Conservatives in 1945, transforming his two-year-old, 38-seat minority government into a 66-seat majority. Even more impressive, Bill Davis became the first premier in 67 years to win four straight elections. Not since Conservative Premier Sir James Pliny Whitney in 1914 had anyone been able to achieve that remarkable feat. (Liberal Premier Sir Oliver Mowat still has the record of six straight election wins, capturing his first in 1871 and his last in 1894, and like Wayne Gretzky's, his records are destined to live on forever.)

The 1981 election also brought to Queen's Park several new MPPs who would go on to make their marks in significant ways. On the government side of the legislature, there now sat three future Ontario premiers: Frank Miller, first elected in 1971; and two rookies — Mike Harris, who defeated Mike Bolan, the former Liberal sitting member, by almost 5,000 votes ("I got elected in a Liberal riding because of Bill Davis," Harris says three and a half decades later); and Ernie Eves, who would soon be dubbed with the funniest nickname of the "Class of '81." Eves's Liberal opponent was Richard Thomas, a well-known broadcaster and environmentalist who was taking his first run at elective office. Eves inherited a 2,400-vote cushion from the former PC member, Lorne Maeck, and managed to hold the seat by an astonishingly close *six* votes. From then on the future finance minister and premier would be known as "Landslide Ernie." Cabinet minister Margaret Birch, now a 10-year veteran, recalls Harris and Eves entering their first caucus meeting "looking like a couple of rubes." She laughs. "They didn't know anything. We took them both by the hand and showed them the ropes."

Other rookie members in the Class of '81 included Don Cousens, who would serve 14 years at Queen's Park, then serve 12 more years in municipal politics as the mayor of Markham. Susan Fish, a downtown Toronto MPP (when the Tories could still win seats downtown), celebrated her 36th birthday just two days after winning her St. George seat and would become a future, well-regarded culture minister. Phil Gillies was only 26 years old when he took Brantford for the Tories. He had been a research assistant in Davis's office and would serve only five weeks in cabinet as minister of skills development before the Peterson Liberals took over in 1985. Gillies would lose his seat in 1987, eventually come out of the closet, and go public as a gay man, then try to recapture Brantford for Tim Hudak's PCs in 2014. He'd lose a close 6-point race to Dave Levac, the speaker of the legislature. James K. Gordon, the former and future mayor of Sudbury, would serve six years at Queen's Park, which was enough time to leave an important legacy — securing for the Nickel City a cancer treatment centre serving all of Northeastern Ontario. Before that Northern Ontarians had to fly to Toronto for their cancer treatment.

Bob Runciman won his first election in 1981 and would serve nearly two decades in the legislature. Like Mike Harris and Ernie Eves, he didn't score an appointment to Davis's cabinet but would make Frank Miller's short-lived cabinet for five months before spending the next 10 years in opposition. Upon Harris's victory in 1995, Runciman would become a major player as solicitor general, correctional services minister, consumer and commercial relations minister, and economic development and trade minister before returning to the public safety and security ministry. Runciman is also the only member of the Class of '81 who's still in politics. In 2010 Prime Minister Stephen Harper appointed him to the Senate where he's eligible to sit until his 75th birthday in 2017.

On the opposition side of the legislature, new Liberal MPPs included 28-year-old Sheila Copps, who in less than a year would challenge David Peterson for the party leadership and finish in a highly respectable second place with nearly 40 percent of the votes. Copps eventually moved to the federal arena and became deputy prime minister in Jean Chrétien's government. Murray Elston won Huron-Bruce, would serve 14 years, and become a cabinet minister in the Peterson government. He was the health minister who once and for all would ban extra billing by doctors (the practice of charging patients beyond what the Ontario Health Insurance Plan fee schedule provided). Tony Ruprecht would spend the next 20 years at Queen's Park, mostly handing out certificates to ethnic communities, which appeared to be his specialty. He would only sit in cabinet for two years, during David Peterson's minority government, and even then only as minister without portfolio.

The New Democrats didn't elect a single new member in the 1981 election.

"By 1981 he [Davis] was everyone's image of what a premier should look like," recalls Gordon Walker, the Tory MPP for London South. "He was everybody's Mr. Ontario."

On this point Davis and Walker agree. "By 1981 I was smarter," Davis admits in a rare use of the first-person singular after I push him to be introspective and analytical about his progress. "Experience means a great deal. I improved with years. I think my sense of humour improved. I think I had more fun. I had fun in the House. I had fun with some of the opposition."

However, the new government really didn't have much time to enjoy itself. By August 1981, Ontario was spinning into its worst recession since the Great Depression. Economic output fell 4.9 percent over six quarters in 1981 and 1982. (By means of comparison, the economy shrank by 3.3 percent over three quarters during the Great Recession of 2008–09.) Inflation in 1981 was eating away at Ontarians' salaries by a frightening 12 percent a year, and interest rates were a stratospheric 21 percent. Just think about what those numbers did to dissuade home purchasers or businesses from investing. It was also a time when the Japanese were taking over automobile manufacturing and the world of consumer electronics. The Ontario everyone had known for the past many decades — the rich, economic engine of the country — was sputtering badly. That was all the more reason, apparently, to have a steady hand on the wheel as Davis clearly was for millions of Ontarians.

It was at this time that Davis truly solidified his relationship with one adviser he would almost regard as another son. John Tory had only been a lawyer for two years when he was asked to join the 1981 PC election team as the campaign secretary, in effect, the assistant campaign manager, working closely with Norman Atkins. After the PCs won the election, Davis tapped Tory to be his new principal secretary. He was 26 years old. The appointment took many people aback, including Tory's paternal grandmother, Jean, who was shocked at the appointment.

"Why would the premier want Johnny to work with him?" she asked other family members. "What could Johnny possibly do for him?" As it turned out, plenty.

Hugh Segal was about to leave the premier's office, but there was about a month of overlap during which Segal showed Tory the ropes. Tory's job was to keep the machinery of government rolling and connected to the priorities of the premier and the PC Party and, of course, to give Davis the best information and advice he could so the premier could make the best decisions possible. One day Segal took Tory, three and a half years his junior, aside and said, "I'm about to show you the hardest part of the job." Segal explained that if Tory wanted to advise the premier, the mountain had to go to Muhammad. "If you wait for him to call you, you'll be in your office waiting forever." So Segal said, "Follow me and I'll show you how it's done."

The duo went from their third-floor offices in the Legislative Assembly down to the second floor where the premier had his office. A huge, imposing, thick wooden door to Davis's actual inner sanctum awaited them both. "Just knock and walk right in," Segal said. And they did.

After Segal departed and it was left to Tory to make that walk by himself, it was initially much harder than it seemed. Tory put his knuckles up to the door, about to knock, but paused because of all the natural doubts that crept in. Was this issue important enough to disturb the premier? And if it wasn't, what would he think of Tory's political judgment? Eventually, the new principal secretary screwed up his courage to knock, walked right in as Segal showed him, and things went fine. That time.

The second time Tory needed to see Davis he once again did the knock and strode right in. But there was no one at the premier's desk. Tory was momentarily confused. He looked around the office and saw no one. Then he walked in a little farther and saw something that astonished him.

Bill Davis is a massive sports fan. Not only that, he knows his sports, particularly football, extremely well. Aware of this, Tory called Rogers Cable TV (where he would one day be CEO) and informed the company that the premier of Ontario loved his sports but wasn't getting enough on Canadian television. Remember, TSN, Canada's first all-sports channel, was still three years away. ESPN, the American trailblazer in sports programming, had only launched two years earlier in 1979. So Tory arranged to have Rogers put a cable splitter in Davis's office to give the premier access to ESPN. No one else in Canada had it.

As Tory peered behind the huge wooden door, he saw the premier of Ontario watching ESPN in the middle of the day. Davis was completely engrossed in the National Football League draft. "He said, 'Come on in, the Dolphins just drafted so-and-so,'" Tory recalls, laughing at the absurdity of it all.

Another time Tory went into Davis's office, prepared to share some distressing news with the premier. Before the principal secretary could get three words out of his mouth, Davis began smiling.

"He already knew," Tory says. The premier always had his own independent sources of information, often keeping him several steps ahead of his advisers and others.

As solid as Davis appeared with his new majority, he wasn't perfect. One misstep came in 1981 when he bought a $10.6 million Challenger executive jet, providing him with an ease of travelling he thought he needed. The juxtaposition of the premier flying in luxury while Ontarians struggled through an economic downturn was problematic to say the least. The opposition hammered him, saying the cost of the plane could have supplied 18,000 children with hearing aids. Jim Bradley, the Liberal MPP for St. Catharines and now the dean of the legislature, about to celebrate his 40th year at Queen's Park, moved a motion forcing the government to sell the jet. Given the Tories' majority, the motion failed, but it still gave Bradley a chance to point out that, "It does little to help people, such as laid-off auto workers, financially strapped senior citizens, struggling farmers, the desperate single parent, or perhaps the forgotten psychiatric patient."

John Tory eventually told the premier he had no choice but to sell the thing. "I'm hearing about it on the street," he told Davis. "This plane is a disaster." Davis eventually relented and traded it in for two water bombers used to fight forest fires.

Another misfire centred on the Tories' near-perfect use of the spoils of power for patronage purposes. Davis personally was able to appoint upward of 3,000 people to 300 agencies, boards, and commissions — the so-called ABCs of government. That patronage machine almost always worked perfectly with nary a hiccup. But one major miscue became public in September 1982 when Morley Rosenberg, a former Kitchener mayor and a New Democrat, claimed he had been promised a judgeship by Davis if he switched parties and ran for the Tories. When Rosenberg lost, he wrote Davis a letter reminding him to "help keep the promise," echoing the slogan of the Tory campaign. Somehow the letter ended up in the *Toronto Star*, and the story became a major embarrassment for the Davis government for several days, particularly when the PC majority on the legislature's justice committee blocked any attempt by opposition members to investigate the matter. Rosenberg eventually recanted his claim, never did get his judgeship, but was appointed to the Ontario Municipal Board, a quasi-judicial position.

Meanwhile, politically, Queen's Park was abuzz with the news in early 1982 that both opposition parties would be having leadership contests in February to replace the vanquished Stuart Smith and Michael Cassidy. Neither race was much of a contest. Both victors captured their crowns on the first and only ballot. Bob Rae left a promising career on Parliament Hill and took a whopping 65 percent of the votes to win the Ontario NDP leadership. Two weeks later David Peterson, an MPP since 1975, did the same with 55 percent of Liberal delegates' support. It would be the beginning of a complicated, up-and-down, three-decades-long relationship between these two significant figures in Canadian political history, both of whom were now vying to become the heir apparent at Queen's Park. Ironically, both would, but they'd have to wait a while, as the master of the legislature schooled them on provincial politics.

"By the time I had entered the scene, Davis was very much in charge," Rae wrote in his book *From Protest to Power*. "I was the new kid on the block who had to be brought down several pegs." Here are a few indications of how supremely confident Davis was at this stage of his political life. One day during Question Period, a Davis minister, Larry Grossman, watched the premier apparently listening to his interrogators on one of the earphones provided at each MPP's desk. The acoustics on the floor of the legislature can be tricky, so many members use the devices to amplify the fuzzy audio. As Davis rose to answer a question, he handed his earpiece to Grossman, who was sitting beside him, with the following request. "Here," the premier said, "follow this while I answer this question." Grossman didn't quite understand what was happening until he put the piece up to his ear and realized Davis had been listening to a World Series baseball game through a separate earpiece connected to a transistor radio hidden inside his desk. Davis, ever the sports fan, didn't want to miss a single at-bat.

Interestingly enough, as Davis got more and more confident and successful as premier, he didn't become more isolated as so often happens. One of his party presidents, David McFadden, says: "The one thing that was distinctive about him was that when a major decision was coming up he consulted broadly. And it wasn't just a small, core group. A lot of leaders today seem to feel that if they get all the true believers in the room, that's consultation. Davis never had that attitude." McFadden says Davis held policy retreats four times a year, inviting representatives from business, social agencies, and universities, along with cabinet and caucus members. "He was very open to ideas. He welcomed those ideas and was responsive to them."

For all the criticism that Davis wasn't a decisive leader, McFadden insists the opposite was true. "When he made the decision, that was it," he says. "He didn't want to hear any more of it." McFadden recalls several times during those Park Plaza breakfast meetings that participants would try to revisit issues the premier had already thought he'd resolved. "He'd say, 'No more. The decision's made.' And that was it. That was the end of the discussion. Davis had the ability to make a decision and stick with it."

One of his most controversial decisions came in late 1982 and focused on compensation for the civil service. With the economy in extremely tough shape, inflation running out of control, and public sector wage settlements going through the roof to keep up, Davis's government brought in a wage-restraint bill that capped civil service salary increases at 5 percent. Unions and the NDP in particular hit the roof, but both levels of government were trying everything to break the back of rampant inflation.

One of the things that gave Davis the most pride during these majority government years was his cabinet. Many of his front-bench ministers were among the most competent and loyal in Ontario history. Although there was plenty of personal ambition among them, they were never publicly disloyal to Davis, and even privately, liked and respected him very much, no matter how much they might disagree with him. Veteran ministers included Frank Miller from Muskoka (industry and trade, treasury, economics); Larry Grossman from downtown Toronto (treasury, economics, health, industry and tourism); midtown Toronto's Roy McMurtry (attorney general); Robert Elgie from York East (labour, consumer and commercial relations); Dr. Bette Stephenson from York Mills (education, colleges and universities); Dennis Timbrell from Don Mills (health, agriculture); Keith Norton from Kingston (health, environment); Leo Bernier from Kenora (minister of northern affairs); Alan Pope from Cochrane South (natural resources); Andy Brandt from Sarnia (industry and trade, labour, environment); downtown Toronto's Susan Fish (citizenship and culture); Dufferin-Simcoe's George McCague (transportation and communications, chair of management board); and the occasionally controversial Gordon Walker from London South (consumer and commercial relations, industry and trade development).

All these years later when I ask Davis which cabinet ministers in particular gave him the most trouble, he instantly quips: "How many names do you want?" But on further reflection he settles on one — Gordon Walker. Walker was from the party's right wing, a Common Sense Revolutionary before anyone had ever used the term. He had a lot of support from that faction of the party and that, combined with the fact that Davis needed someone from Southwestern Ontario, argued for Walker's inclusion in cabinet. Davis might have got an indication that things with Walker were going to be complicated immediately after he offered the London South MPP a seat at the cabinet table in October 1978. Walker's reply: "Give me some time to think about it." That isn't the answer a premier expects to hear when he offers a backbencher a promotion. But Walker prized his independence and, in fact, had already turned down a parliamentary assistant's job from Davis, figuring he merited a position with more responsibilities. However, the next day Walker assented and became minister for correctional services. "It was a modest role, but it was something I thought I could do something with," Walker now says.

Walker decided to focus on justice for victims and apparently did well because on the same day both the *Globe and Mail* and the *Toronto Star* wrote editorials praising his efforts. Then there was a jail riot and breakout at the Guelph Correctional Institute late one night. Walker was at the jailhouse by six o'clock the next morning and gave an update to the legislature that afternoon at two o'clock. The premier complimented him as the pair left Queen's Park later that afternoon.

Less than a year after taking the corrections portfolio, Walker was given the added responsibilities of provincial secretary for justice. When the premier shuffled the cabinet after the 1981 election win, Walker exchanged corrections for consumer and commercial relations, and a year later, got a huge promotion to industry and trade development. If their relationship got off to a rocky start, Davis was clearly signalling a strong confidence in Walker, given the MPP's career trajectory. It didn't last, though. Walker would be demoted and humiliated two years later, the details of which we'll cover in a future chapter.

I have been told that Bill Davis was a stickler for having members of his cabinet behave appropriately both publicly and privately. His inner circle of advisers knew that and as a result kept a lot of incriminating dirt about his ministers away from the premier's naive ears. When the premier did find out about shenanigans occurring, on his watch, did he call his ministers up on the carpet?

"No, I wouldn't get involved, but I would see that somebody else did," he says today. "I was a chicken. I wasn't often a chicken, but one or two, yes."

When I ask Davis whether he ever fired a minister explicitly for having an extramarital affair, he insists he never did. After I offer him the name of a minister whom I know had been having an affair and was, in fact, eventually dropped from the cabinet, Davis immediately replies that the minister's ouster "was well on its way before that! He just lacked the needed competence for the job."

Nevertheless, Davis's old-fashioned Sunday-school teacher ways never really left him. During his premiership, he learned of one female member of the press gallery who had become pregnant and was in a common law relationship with another press gallery member. He seemed genuinely concerned that the two weren't married and mentioned it to some colleagues. He was quite a contrast from John Robarts who, as former Liberal MPP Sean Conway puts it, "understood that we were all fallen angels."

In one of the oddest coincidences in Canadian political history, *two* premiers actually came out of the same small high school in Brampton, Ontario. Because of the five-year age gap between them, they didn't know each other at the time. But Howard Pawley, premier of Manitoba from 1981 to 1988, attended Brampton High at the same time as Bill Davis did. Both men would go on to attend the same first ministers' conferences as premiers.

And the coincidences continue. Both Davis and Pawley were the 18th premiers of their respective provinces. While A. Grenville Davis was hugely influential in making sure his son, Bill, was a Progressive Conservative, Howard Pawley's father played a similar role in his son's life. Pawley's dad ran for the CCF (the NDP's predecessor) in Peel riding in 1937, losing to one of Davis's political heroes, Thomas L. Kennedy, the future premier. When Pawley was about six years old, his local Conservative MP, Gordon Graydon — yes, the same Gordon Graydon who was Bill Davis's first political hero — came to the Pawley home with two CCF MPs he was hosting. Graydon wanted to introduce his guests to the only CCF farmers he knew in his entire constituency — the Pawleys. Something clicked for young Howard during that visit and a seed was planted that eventually took him to the highest office in Manitoba politics four decades later.

So when Pawley and his cabinet secretary, Michael Decter, came to Queen's Park in the fall of 1982 to visit the premier of Ontario and his chief of staff, Hugh Segal, there was a lot of history in that relationship. The two men delighted in pointing out to each other that they both still bought their clothes from the same old tailor in Brampton. When Segal, who had unsuccessfully run for Parliament twice as a university student, suggested he might want to try again some day, the two premiers apparently burst out laughing at the notion that either Segal or Decter would have the patience for the retail side of politics.

In any event, there were two things that happened on that visit that showed just how on top of his game Bill Davis was. Pawley, who'd been premier of Manitoba for less than a year, began asking Davis questions about how the premier of Ontario ran his cabinet meetings. Davis replied: "Well, we're just about to have one. Did you want to come in and see?"

Both Pawley and Decter were gobsmacked at the notion that a Tory premier would open his inner sanctum to a New Democrat. But Davis didn't think like a hyper-partisan, but rather thought he was extending a professional courtesy, and in they went. And not just for some quick handshakes. The Manitoba duo stayed for a good hour, watching Ontario Inc. at work.

"Mr. Davis was so generous and confident and we were so nervous about being in government," says Decter, still marvelling at Davis's openness three and a half decades later. As another sign of the mutual respect these two premiers had for each other, Pawley asked his Ontario counterpart if he minded, while he was in town, whether Pawley could help do a little campaigning in the by-election to replace former MP Bob Rae in Broadview-Greenwood. Davis, of course, took no umbrage at the request, appreciated Pawley's courtesy, and gave the Manitoba premier his blessing. (The NDP's Lynn McDonald eventually won the by-election in October 1982 by 2,000 votes over the *Toronto Sun*'s founding editor, Peter Worthington, who ran as an independent.)

Davis had another noteworthy encounter with the Pawley government. Perhaps the most amusing took place in connection with Minaki Lodge, a controversial and cursed hotel in Northwestern Ontario between Sioux Lookout and Winnipeg. Minaki's roots go back to a modest hotel built by the Grant Trunk Pacific Railway in 1914. CN Rail then bought it with plans to turn it into a first-class wilderness resort. In 1925 it burned down, but CN rebuilt and reopened it two years later. Over the next several decades, the luxury lodge changed hands three times before the Davis government stepped in and purchased it in 1974. Thanks to the influence of the "Emperor of the North," cabinet minister Leo Bernier, the government closed the lodge for nearly a decade and ploughed $50 million into restoring it. The opposition had a field day with Minaki, saying it was the worst white elephant around. But in 1983 the Davis government staged a grand reopening and persuaded the Radisson hotel chain to operate it. Because of Minaki's proximity to Manitoba, Davis invited some representatives of the Pawley government to attend, and as a result, Manitoba cabinet secretary Michael Decter and Muriel Smith, the province's deputy premier and economic development and tourism minister, did just that.

As Davis beamed with pride at the opening ceremonies, the Manitoba delegation enjoyed the warm welcome with interest and curiosity. Then the other shoe fell. After Davis thanked all those who required thanking, he added: "Ladies and gentlemen, our friends in the opposition at Queen's Park thought this day would never happen. The former NDP leader Stephen Lewis attacked us every day in Question Period. But look who's here. We have the cabinet secretary to the Manitoba NDP government, and the deputy premier of the Manitoba NDP government here to celebrate the triumph of this day. Please call Stephen Lewis and tell him what a splendid investment this place is."

"We got played like a bunch of rubes!" recalls Michael Decter, laughing hysterically at the memory of it. "And Davis had the biggest grin on his face."

Sadly, that would be one of the last great days at Minaki Lodge. While the tens of millions of dollars invested in its renaissance no doubt provided considerable economic development activity in Northwestern Ontario, the lodge just never made any financial sense. After the Liberals took over the government in 1985, they wanted to dispose of a project they never supported to begin with and sold the lodge to the Four Seasons chain for a mere $4 million in 1986. But history repeated. The lodge changed ownership several more times with no one being able to make a go of it. In September 2003 it was closed. A month later it burned down.

There is one more Davis-Pawley story. Again during Pawley's first term, the Manitoba premier learned of Ontario's plans to build a coal-fired electricity generation station in Atikokan, Ontario, almost 120 miles west of Thunder Bay near the Manitoba border. Pawley had an idea. He approached

Davis and suggested the Ontario premier could save millions of dollars if, rather than building his own generating station, Ontario Hydro simply bought electricity from nearby Manitoba, which would be infinitely cheaper.

"I could do that," Davis told Pawley, "but that won't get my guy in Atikokan elected." Ontario Hydro ordered the coal plant built, and it opened in 1985. Nearly three decades later Premier Dalton McGuinty ordered it closed as part of his elimination of all coal plants in Ontario. The new Ontario Power Generation company (the electricity generation wing of the old Ontario Hydro Crown Corporation) spent $200 million converting Atikokan to a plant fuelled by wood pellets, and at more than 200 megawatts of capacity, it's now North America's largest power plant fuelled solely by biomass. And just to show that all politics is still local, when Atikokan's future was in doubt, its local Liberal MPP, Bill Mauro, barely held the Thunder Bay–Atikokan seat, first by only 50 votes in 2007, then by 438 votes in 2011. In 2012 the government announced it would secure the plant's future and its 90 jobs by converting it to biomass. Mauro won the next election in 2014 by more than 7,000 votes.

There is a sad postscript to these Manitoba-Ontario stories — on December 30, 2015, Howard Pawley died. He was 81 years old and one of the loveliest guys you'll ever meet in politics. He spent his life fighting for social justice and was appropriately honoured with both the Order of Manitoba and the Order of Canada.

Meanwhile, throughout its decade in power, the Davis government would make plenty of big-spending, controversial decisions. But the granddaddy of them all was still to come.

16

SUNCOR

It's hard to think of a more complicated relationship between two of Canada's most historically significant premiers than that of William Grenville Davis of Ontario and Edgar Peter Lougheed of Alberta. They actually were friends. But they were also rivals. They had so much in common, but their jobs representing such different parts of the country made their seeing Canada the same way almost impossible. Sometimes they got along quite famously with the prime minister of the day, Pierre Elliott Trudeau. Other times they both engaged in a vicious war of words with him. Through it all Davis and Lougheed made headlines galore.

Peter Lougheed was born on July 26. Bill Davis was born on July 30. Lougheed was a year older. Davis got involved in politics at a young age thanks to the interest of his local MP and MPP. Lougheed got interested in politics at a young age because his grandfather, James, was a cabinet minister and senator from Alberta. Davis played high school and university football. So did Lougheed, although the Alberta premier gets the nod here since he actually played for the Canadian Football League's Edmonton Eskimos from 1949 to 1950. Both became lawyers. Both were Progressive Conservatives. Davis was premier of Ontario for 14 years. Lougheed was premier of Alberta for 14 years. They were also the same 14 years: 1971 to 1985. Davis won four elections. So did Lougheed. Davis's political apparatus was so powerful that it was nicknamed The Big Blue Machine. Lougheed's political prowess was so impressive that not a single

PC sitting member lost his or her seat in the Alberta legislature during his tenure. Bill Davis thought about but ultimately didn't run for the national Progressive Conservative Party leadership in 1983, eventually won by Brian Mulroney. Same for Peter Lougheed.

But for all that they had in common, these two great leaders were destined to spend much of the 1970s and 1980s working reasonably well together behind the scenes but fighting in public a lot because they represented different provinces with very different priorities and very different agendas. On several key issues, they simply couldn't see the country functioning the same way. To do so would have been to commit political suicide and neither of these men ever had any interest in doing that.

The obvious flashpoint of the Davis-Lougheed relationship was oil — Alberta had lots of it, Ontario had almost none of it, but needed lots of it. Alberta saw its precious natural resource as finite and understandably wanted to get as high a price as possible for it, so the revenues could be invested in more and better provincial services. Ontario, as the proverbial engine of the Canadian economy, wanted as low a price for oil as possible to enable it to continue to prosper economically, thereby producing the tax revenues that supported much of the Canadian welfare state. They were two regional politicians with national stature simply doing their jobs at a time when the price of oil was in tremendous flux because several Middle Eastern sheiks started to flex their muscles. As the world price of oil rose, Lougheed wanted in on some of that action for Alberta, and got some. The price rose from $4 a barrel in 1973 to $14 a barrel by the end of the 1970s. But the world price was $24 a barrel. Conversely, Davis thought Alberta's (read: Canada's) oil ought to be a stabilizing influence on the price Ontarians paid. What was the point, he thought, of Canada having such an abundance of oil if that abundance couldn't be used as a buffer against such widespread international uncertainty? It's hard to say Davis was in the right and Lougheed in the wrong, or vice-versa for that matter. But some of their struggles were titanic and certainly ratcheted up the national temperature from time to time.

As a westerner, Lougheed saw a country that for more than a century implemented policies designed to ensure Ontario's prosperity, for example, through high tariffs to protect that province's manufacturing base. Davis saw a lot of the wealth those tariffs created *not* going to his fellow Ontarians, but rather to the American owners of the province's manufacturers or the U.S. owners of those Ontario nickel, uranium, and gold mines. He was also aware that Ontarians from time to time spent more than they had to for western resources, all for the purpose of creating more national harmony. For example, when Alberta started making noises about letting "the eastern bastards freeze in the dark" because Ontarians didn't want to pay a world price for their oil, Ontario responded in kind. This was three and a half decades before Ontario had closed all its coal-fired generating stations. In fact, Ontario Hydro, the province's former electricity generation and transmission Crown Corporation, relied heavily on noxious, polluting coal to keep the lights on. Energy Minister Robert Welch, one of Davis's most trusted and capable cabinet colleagues, suggested that Ontario could get all the cheap coal it needed from sources closer to home, namely, northeastern American states. "We always try to buy Canadian," said George Ashe, Welch's parliamentary assistant. "But there is a limit to doing so." Ashe made those comments at a meeting of coal producers in Banff, Alberta. Nothing like going right into the lion's den to deliver some unwanted news.

As the 1970s came to an end, Bill Davis found himself between a rock and a hard place over energy, ironically, with two fellow Progressive Conservatives. He was at loggerheads with Peter Lougheed over energy prices. But he also found himself increasingly offside with his national leader, Joe Clark, who might have sympathized with Davis on official bilingualism for Ontario but certainly couldn't share Davis's position on what Alberta felt it was entitled to for its oil. Davis was a good soldier for Clark in the days leading up to the May 22, 1979, general election, campaigning for Clark, and perhaps more important, slagging Pierre Trudeau at every turn. But as it became apparent that Prime Minister Clark wasn't going to cut Ontario any deals on oil pricing, despite the province's having elected 57 PC MPs (out of 95 seats in total), Bill Davis's enthusiasm for his national leader waned significantly. That would prove to be crucial when the Clark government unexpectedly fell after only nine months in office.

Here's how Davis saw the problem. Because of their different priorities, Ontario taxpayers forked over 65 percent more in taxes to their provincial treasury than Albertans did to theirs. Conversely, if Ontarians paid taxes at the same rate as Albertans did, they'd realize an instant 36 percent tax cut. And that's not even including sales tax. Alberta, of course, had no sales tax, while Ontarians in the late 1970s paid more than $2.3 billion annually in sales taxes. So Davis was clearly unhappy with the notion that Alberta could raise the price of oil to world levels, then keep 45 percent of the oil revenues for its treasury.

"The prices should be below United States levels and reflect the legitimate needs of the producing-consuming provinces," Davis said in September 1979 in a speech in London, England, at the Canada–United Kingdom Chamber of Commerce, part of a 15-day business tour of several European countries. He called the Clark government's policy of allowing the country's oil prices to rise to world levels "illogical, and not in the best interest of Canada."

Ontario had someone with impeccable credentials doing the math — Douglas Hartle, an economist with the University of Toronto's Institute for Policy Analysis, who was previously a deputy secretary of the treasury board and research director for the Royal Commission on Taxation. Hartle estimated a rise of just $7 in the price per barrel of oil would represent a $300 increase to the home heating and driving costs of the average Ontarian, not to mention the disadvantageous position in which Ontario businesses would find themselves. Inflation would jump 3.2 percentage points; the province's gross domestic product would fall 1.5 percent. That represented a massive wealth transfer from central to western Canada that no Ontario premier could countenance. The economics were terrible, and the politics were worse. Davis found himself, already two years into his second minority government, caught in an intra-Tory Party fight with Lougheed and Clark, all while the province was going through difficult economic times.

In spite of all this, behind the scenes, Davis and Lougheed got along well, liked each other, and from time to time got their provinces into significant business deals together. The first deal of significance was over a company called Syncrude. The Syncrude research consortium was established in 1964 but didn't produce its first barrel of oil from the Athabasca Oil Sands of Alberta until 1978. With five billion barrels of provable and probable reserves, it's one of the most significant energy production projects in the country, with ownership stakes today held by companies and governments around the world. Canada Oil Sands Ltd., Imperial Oil, Suncor, Sinopec, Nexen, Nippon Oil, and Murphy Oil all own chunks of it today. But back in the 1970s Syncrude was having a devil of a time getting off the ground. In fact, it was on the verge of collapsing. Canada's biggest oil exploration companies were too nervous about Syncrude's potential. So Lougheed set up a meeting at a hotel in Winnipeg with Jack Armstrong, Imperial Oil's chairman and CEO, and Bill Davis. What quickly became apparent was that unless Ontario bought into the deal, the deal was dead.

"They both said, 'We can't do this unless Ontario comes in,'" Davis now recalls. "And so we did. And that's what started the oil business the way it is now in Alberta." The year was 1975.

Despite the fact that Alberta needed Ontario in on the deal to make it work, it wasn't always smooth sailing between the two premiers. The federal energy minister, Donald Macdonald (Davis's old Osgoode Hall Law School classmate), was also a party to the negotiations and offered to put in $300 million on the spot. Davis then offered $50 million on behalf of Ontario. According to Macdonald's memoir, Lougheed responded rudely to Davis and dismissively to the offer. "The chips at this table are $100 million, not fifty," Macdonald quotes Lougheed as saying. "Perhaps you should withdraw and see if you can do better."

One can imagine the reaction if someone other than Bill Davis had been at the table. Profanity, flying binders, storming out would all have been possibilities. Macdonald says Davis merely replied: "Mr. Premier, I'll take your advice on that. If you have further things that we should know about, I hope you'll keep in touch with us. Let's see if we can do a deal." And with that Davis and the Ontario delegation left the room to reconsider their position. Macdonald's take on what he'd just seen: "Premier Davis was, as always, a gentleman in the face of discourtesy." Macdonald was further unimpressed with Lougheed, who kept Davis isolated for two hours and continued the discussions in his absence. Macdonald says it was he who finally went and retrieved Davis back into the room, whereupon Davis announced Ontario would indeed be in for $100 million. Davis said he hoped some of the new petrochemical plants would be located in Ontario, but Lougheed gave him no commitments. At the end of the day everyone was glad to sign on the dotted line. But it was a reminder of the occasionally tense relationship these, and any, premiers of Alberta and Ontario tend to have. That tension would bubble up again in the early 1980s, a story we'll return to later.

In any event, Davis liked the Ontario government taking a 5 percent ownership position in Syncrude for two reasons. First, if the company took off, Ontario could make a healthy profit on its investment. But second, Davis didn't mind the optics of Ontario's investment being seen as an exercise in nation building. It was a story that played into the notion of how Canadian federalism ought to work — one province helping another to achieve its economic potential and destiny. Make no mistake: Bill Davis was a politician who got his votes in Ontario. But to anyone who'd listen, he'd always tell people he thought of himself as a Canadian first, and if he could do something that was good for Canada (and Ontario also), well, bring it on.

When "Team Ontario" returned from Winnipeg, the media pounced on the province's new energy minister who'd been on the job for all of a few weeks. Dennis Timbrell was a bit of a boy wonder in the Tory cabinet. He was the youngest rookie MPP elected in the 1971 election — all of 24 years old. Davis clearly had his eye on Timbrell, because two and a half years later the premier appointed him minister without portfolio responsible for youth issues. Once more Timbrell must have impressed, because less than a year and a half later Davis promoted him again, this time to minister of energy in July 1975. Having that job gave the now 28-year-old Timbrell a front-row seat in Winnipeg, watching a handful of people who would become legendary figures in Canadian politics. Besides Davis, Lougheed, and Donald Macdonald, Don Getty was also there. He was Alberta's energy minister, and although no one knew it at the time, he would become Lougheed's successor as premier of Alberta 10 years hence. (Getty died in February 2016 at age 82.)

The media wanted to know what business Ontario had taking an ownership stake in Syncrude. Timbrell surprised them all with his answer. "I'm announcing to you today that we're going to sell it," the energy minister said.

"What?" came the incredulous response in unison.

Timbrell explained. "When the time is right, and when the future of the Great Canadian Oil Sands program is obviously secure, we will sell. We're not long-term investors here. We're here to help to secure this portion of our nation's energy future."

And that's exactly what happened.

All of this backstory becomes important because it serves as a prelude to one of the most controversial decisions Bill Davis ever made during his premiership. It was set against a backdrop of constantly rising oil prices and an awful recession in Ontario that many said was the worst since the Great Depression. Internationally, these were troubling times. U.S. President Ronald Reagan had been shot and nearly killed seven months earlier, and terrorists had just managed to assassinate Egyptian leader Anwar Sadat less than two weeks before Davis was to unveil his momentous decision.

Given all of this lead-up, the premier of Ontario determined that his province needed "a window" on the oil industry. And so he bought a huge chunk of an oil company called Suncor. The cost: $650 million. That's 650 million "1981 dollars," which would be like spending $1.7 billion today. The purchase entitled Ontario to one-quarter of the company's ownership stake, a quarter of the seats on the board, and an option to buy an additional 26 percent over the ensuing five years. Getting to 51 percent Canadian ownership *and control* was hugely important to the company, since it would then qualify Suncor for hundreds of millions of dollars of incentives offered by the federal government in the National Energy Program. The federal energy minister, Marc Lalonde, praised the purchase, and why not? It further Canadianized the oil patch, something the Trudeau government was encouraging through its $1.46 billion purchase of Petrofina and transforming it into Petro-Canada.

But some observers thought Suncor's asking price was hard to justify. The government of Ontario would pay $325 million of the sticker price out of its general revenues, but it would finance the other half by borrowing the money from Suncor itself at a *17 percent rate of interest.* Furthermore, Ontario was already running a billion-dollar deficit. Hospital administrators, doctors, nurses, school board trustees, teachers — the list was endless — all wondered how there was no money available for their priorities, but apparently the government had $325 million available to buy a piece of an oil company.

Davis announced the purchase in the Ontario legislature on October 13, 1981. Yes, these were the days when big announcements actually happened in the legislature.

Who initiated the idea to buy Suncor is still a bit of a mystery. Hugh Segal, one of Premier Davis's most important advisers at the time, says the original germ of the idea came from Peter Lougheed himself. By this time, Ontario had also sold the 5 percent stake of its original Syncrude investment to the private sector. Treasurer Darcy McKeough realized a tidy $35 million profit for his bottom line, and now Davis was asking Lougheed: "Is there anything else you'd recommend we be in?"

"Lougheed suggested that a private player like Suncor would be an excellent company in which to invest," Segal recalls. "It was profitable and in the oil sands, as well. So the seed was actually planted by Lougheed."

Today Bill Davis says it was well known "on the street" that Suncor was open to selling. There's also a story that, having seen the popularity of the federal government's proliferation of Petro-Canada gas stations all over central Canada, Segal imagined hundreds of Sunoco gas stations all around Ontario and Quebec with the provincial flower, the trillium, all over them. As it turned out, that never happened.

Davis had also heard from his sources in Alberta that Lougheed was eager for Ontario to do the deal. Besides Canadianizing the industry, it also helped give the Alberta government some additional "cover" for its expenditures related to developing the oil sands.

"What they were looking for right from the beginning is a justification on their part for what they were spending" is how Davis puts it today. For all his criticism of Ontario, Lougheed knew that having the Davis government on board would give him added legitimacy. Ontario also inquired at this time about buying more of Alberta's coal. But the sulphur content was too high for Ontario Hydro plants, so that deal didn't get done. However, buying a piece of Suncor was another way of nation building for Davis. Alberta would be happy and the deal, if everything went well, would realize $100 million a year in dividends for the Ontario treasury.

Despite the fact that Davis thought he had all the bases covered on why the Suncor purchase was a good idea, the immediate reaction was one of astonishment from many quarters. First and foremost, many conservatives believed that conservatives just didn't do this, that they shouldn't be players in the private economy. That was what *Liberals* did, and besides, they argued, more often than not the government is lousy at picking winners and losers in the private economy.

But the opposition Liberals at Queen's Park didn't like the idea, either. Their finance critic, David Peterson, criticized Davis for not going for control of the company right away, suggesting as a minority shareholder, Ontario would have no influence on Suncor's affairs. "The polls tell Mr. Davis that the public is for Canadianization, so he's fooling them into thinking that's what he's doing," said Peterson, who was four months away from becoming Liberal leader and eventually having a huge say in Suncor's future.

But even Ross Hennigar, Suncor's president, acknowledged in the company's most recent report to shareholders that "profitability is now at seriously low levels." Hardly a vote of confidence in the company's future.

Davis, however, was optimistic. He had Tom Kierans, his friend and long-time economic adviser from McLeod, Young, Weir (who was the lead negotiator for the province), and other consultants from Price Waterhouse review the transaction from stem to stern, and everyone was convinced that Ontario had got itself a good deal.

As would so often be the case during the Davis premiership (much to the chagrin of Progressive Conservatives), some of the highest praise for the deal came from the New Democratic Party. "Premier Davis has finally seen the light," said Michael Cassidy, the NDP's leader. "His government now admits that public ownership has its virtues." In fact, as a *progressive* conservative, Davis always recognized the need for the state to play a significant role in economic development and it never offended his sense of conservatism to remind people of that.

But the U.S. government was concerned. It saw the National Energy Program as an attack on American capitalism. A member of the U.S. House of Representatives, who would run for president in two decades, said: "This shows the [national energy] program is working just as Canada wants it to. Something has to be done." So said Albert Gore, Jr. Canadians were no doubt amused at an American politician crying foul in this way. After all, Americans owned the vast majority of big businesses in Canada at this time.

The Canadian media reaction was harsh. The *Financial Post* was certainly not convinced. It would be neither the first nor the last to make fun of Davis's "window on the industry" comment. "What are the deep secrets in the business that require the much-talked-about 'window' on the industry?" the paper editorialized. The *Globe and Mail* asked if it was such a good deal, why was there no other private sector company lining up to participate? The *Toronto Sun* was tougher: "What in hell is an allegedly conservative government getting into state ownership for? That's for [Pierre] Trudeau, crypto-socialists and Marxist power-grabbers." Gotta love the *Sun*, which predicted because of the

Suncor transaction that the Tories would be thrown out at the next election, and "the *Sun* will do what it can to help get rid of them."

Where were the newspapers complimentary? Ironically, in free enterprise-minded Alberta, of course — the *Calgary Herald* particularly so, where the deal enjoyed considerable praise.

At this time there were three future Progressive Conservative premiers in Davis's Queen's Park caucus. Two would go on to have a transformational impact on Ontario, although not for another 14 years. Another would succeed Davis as premier with the hope of undoing much of the Davis legacy. Two of them weren't fans of the Suncor deal. The third absolutely hated it.

"I would probably be more on the side of, 'Why are we foolin' around with this?'" admits Mike Harris, Ontario's 22nd premier, from his office at Faskin Martineau DuMoulin in Toronto. In October 1981, Harris was a newly minted MPP from Nipissing riding, having just won his first election seven months earlier. He remembers at this point still trying to set up his constituency office, learn the ropes at Queen's Park, and frankly, find out where the bathrooms were. Even though he opposed the Suncor deal, he still describes himself as "a Bill Davis fan," but that as a new member, "You kinda go with the flow for a period of time." Harris recalls the Suncor deal being presented to caucus as a *fait accompli* with no opportunity for PC members to affect the deal had they wanted to.

The second future premier was nicknamed "Landslide Ernie." Like Harris, Ernie Eves won his first election back in March 1981, but by only six votes in his Parry Sound–Muskoka riding, thus the humorous nickname. The future 23rd premier of Ontario agrees with Harris that "I didn't think it was necessarily the right thing to do," but also supports Davis's decision to present the policy to caucus as a done deal. "If that would have been discussed in caucus or even cabinet, it would have been a nightmare," Eves says today about the situation.

The third future premier in caucus felt a lot more strongly about the Suncor deal than either Harris or Eves. His name was Frank Stuart Miller, and he would soon be Ontario's 19th premier.

"Frank was frigging livid!" Eves remembers. "He was vehemently against the public sector being involved in private business."

Frank Miller died in 2000, so I never had a chance to talk to him directly about the Suncor share purchase. But George Hutchison, a former

London Free Press reporter who became Premier David Peterson's press secretary, sat down with Miller in March 1994 and found out some details that heretofore haven't been made public.

Miller told Hutchison there were four senior elected government officials involved in the Suncor negotiations: Bill Davis, the premier; Robert Welch, the deputy premier and minister of energy; Larry Grossman, the industry minister; and Miller himself as treasurer. All except Miller were proponents of the deal, and as a result, Miller felt he should tender his resignation, which he did. Davis and Miller had even agreed on the date when the resignation would be announced: October 16, 1981, three days after unveiling the Suncor deal to the public. But the first attempt at a deal on Suncor fell through. Other Canadian companies such as Noranda kicked the tires on the purchase, but ultimately begged off. Hugh Winsor teased these titans of industry in his *Globe and Mail* column, asking: "Do they need Uncle Billy to hold their hand while they take a dip in case the water is too cold?" Alfred Powis, Noranda's chairman and president, later said his company declined to participate because the asking price was too high, the return on investment was too low, and with the economy tanking, his company was moving into "survival mode." Not only was his participation in the deal off, but he went on to tell the media: "I'm not saying it is a lousy deal. I'm just saying I don't know why they [the Ontario government] are doing it."

With no other private sector partners coming to the table, Frank Miller apparently thought the entire deal was now off (as was his resignation). But Premier Davis called a special cabinet meeting for October 13 and informed his ministers that Ontario would go it alone, even without other private sector partners. That came as news to Miller, who felt blindsided by the decision. "Frank found out the day of or the night before that we were going to own an oil company!" recalls Ernie Eves.

Miller was livid but not given to losing his temper in front of his cabinet colleagues. "Mr. Premier," he began calmly, "you know what I think about this. To the rest of my colleagues here, I know they're going to go out and support this decision. But I think they deserve an explanation as to why you bought it."

There was an edge developing in Miller's voice. He was being borderline insubordinate to his premier, who had only seven months earlier won a smashing majority government. Davis wasn't amused.

"He cut me down for a good 20 minutes," Miller recalled in his conversation with George Hutchison. "Like a micro surgeon. He recited it all. I was so upset I got up, left cabinet, and went for a walk."

Davis's press secretary, Sally Barnes, was pressed into duty. "What are you doing out here?" she asked Miller. "They want you back in there." Miller told Barnes he just had to leave the meeting and cool off.

"Well, what did you hear in there?" she asked him.

"I just heard a fella taken apart better than anyone ever has!" Miller told her of the premier's figurative wielding of the scalpel.

More than a decade later Miller narrated the story with a kind of joviality that only distance can bring. But he never came around to seeing the issue Davis's way.

"He was fed up with me," Miller says of the premier. "I'd been obstreperous that we shouldn't do it. We were trying to be pseudo-Albertans, getting into the big league with a penny-ante investment. A window on the oil patch? BS!" Miller put it down to Ontario-Alberta rivalry. "They've got it, so we've gotta have it. That's my opinion."

Despite the very public tiff between the premier and his finance minister, Miller, in fact, didn't resign. He stayed on as treasurer for almost another two years until Davis shuffled him to the industry portfolio in July 1983. Somehow these colleagues and rivals managed to bury the hatchet and focus on what was really important at that moment, namely, fighting a devastating recession in which Ontario now found itself mired. However, the recession really called into question the timing of the Suncor purchase. The company's shares weren't exactly a hot commodity, investment was way down in the oil patch, and the skeptics of the purchase were marshalling their voices in saying: "I told you so."

Norman Atkins was also against the deal, although because of the secrecy around it, he didn't have a chance to change Davis's mind about it. He told George Hutchison: "It was a high-risk political decision that was philosophically questionable in terms of a leader of a conservative party." Atkins didn't like the fact that he wasn't asked to do any public opinion polling on the issue, and despite his obvious admiration and affection for Davis, he blasted the Suncor purchase as "a careless decision. It just shows there was a bit of vulnerability developing in Billy Davis's mind as to his commitment in the long haul."

For his part, Davis stayed the course and continued to express faith in the purchase. "The base of the party was not upset in my view," he now says, analyzing the story three and a half decades after the fact. "Some of the 'theologians' who were not of the base, but very involved, they were concerned," he adds in what sounds like a clear shot at Miller. Davis adds some long-time Tories at the Albany Club "were not overly enthused." A week and a half after the Suncor announcement 300 Tory supporters met for a policy conference in London where many MPPs privately groused about the secrecy surrounding the deal. They felt they could have better defended it had they been brought inside the tent sooner. Simcoe Centre's George Taylor spoke for many when he told the *Globe*'s Rosemary Speirs that he didn't necessarily oppose the purchase but was having a hard time defending it to constituents who kept asking the same question: "Why would the government buy into an oil company when we don't have money for schools and hospitals?" Hugh Segal tried to impress upon the backbench that Conservative governments "from time immemorial" got the government involved in what were traditionally thought of as private sector businesses — think Canadian National Railway, the Canadian Broadcasting Corporation, or Air Canada. Taylor concluded then and confirms today that there's "not much left of Tory free enterprise thoughts."

But Donald C. MacDonald, the CCF and NDP leader from 1953 to 1970, told the *Globe* why nailing Davis on the deal politically was so tough. "What I find most exasperating is that he will repeat ad nauseam the Tory truisms about free enterprise and then he'll wade into the economy with a Suncor purchase," MacDonald said. "And when he's questioned by the right wing, he'll belabor them and tell them the history of the Ontario economy has always been one of mixed endeavor. He ends up winning support from all camps."

Then, just a few days after the conference, former Liberal leader Robert Nixon (now just an opposition MPP) played the green card, saying Suncor was the ninth worst emitter of sulphur dioxide pollution in the country and the single worst source in Alberta. Davis had to admit the pollution issue didn't come up during the negotiations, but Nixon's point was: "It's our problem now and what are we going to do about it?"

The controversy around Suncor just wouldn't go away. Outgoing Liberal leader Stuart Smith wanted the government to make public the reports prepared by Mcleod, Young, Weir and Price Waterhouse extolling the deal's virtue. The government refused. The opposition filibustered in the legislature. The government brought in closure. The opposition then crunched the numbers some more and estimated the total price tag could ultimately cost taxpayers $2.4 billion over the ensuing decade when the cost of borrowing the money for the purchase was included. That wasn't just the $325 million borrowed at 17 percent interest rates from Suncor, but also the money the government would need to borrow on the open markets to finance the deal. The premier's office arranged to have the two consulting firms and the Ontario Energy Corporation, technically the arm of the government that purchased the shares, offer backbenchers a private briefing of the deal. Philip Andrewes, the PC MPP from Lincoln, confessed after the briefing: "I am no wiser than when I went in." The same could be said for opposition MPPs who weren't permitted to attend. Bill Davis seemed to be saying to his party and the public: "Trust me, this will work."

"He calls this trust," the *Globe* editorialized. "We call it contempt."

Could the controversy get worse? It could and did. In January 1982, Tom Kierans, the investment banker who put the deal together, confirmed to Southam News that Premier Davis was keeping Premier Lougheed in the loop throughout the negotiations. In other words, Alberta government officials knew more about the deal and knew it earlier than all but four Ontario cabinet ministers and the rest of the PC caucus?

"Bill Davis told Peter Lougheed way before almost anybody knew that he was thinking of doing it," Kierans said. "He didn't ask for his [Lougheed's] permission but he certainly asked if there was going to be any adverse reaction. There wasn't."

Not in Alberta. But in Ontario? There surely was.

Seven months after the Suncor announcement the deal was still making headlines. David Peterson, now the Liberal leader having replaced Stuart Smith, moved a motion of non-confidence in the government because the premier refused to allow a public inquiry, Royal Commission, or public hearings into the deal. The latest firestorm was stoked by a *Globe and Mail* story quoting unnamed "business valuators" who studied the deal and concluded the government overpaid by $300 to $345 million. The newspaper wouldn't name the "business valuators," saying to do so would jeopardize their ability to win future government business. Peterson's non-confidence motion was theatrics, to be sure. After all, Davis had a majority government, and as long as everyone showed up and voted to keep the government alive, it was safe. But given the unrest on the Tory backbenches was that vote a sure thing? Would PC backbenchers really cut off their noses to spite Bill Davis's face? Ultimately, they didn't. But probably not before the premier and his advisers had a good sweat about it.

The Suncor postscript looks like this. Davis would last another four years as premier, succeeded by Frank Miller in 1985. As much as Miller opposed the deal, he never sold the government's Suncor shares once he took over. It's possible he wanted to but didn't hold the reins of power long enough to do so. He was only premier for five months before losing to the Liberals' David Peterson, who became Ontario's 20th premier in June 1985. Peterson made it clear that his thinking remained the same from when he was his party's finance critic. The shares were too few in number to give the province any impact and therefore should be disposed of. In the Liberals' view, the Suncor shares represented everything that was ineffective and incompetent about Tory governments. But Peterson didn't sell the shares, either. As he recalls the events of the late 1980s 30 years later, Peterson says, "We probably wanted to, but they were so depressed we couldn't get anything for them." In fact, the Liberal government was advised that it would be financially foolish to part with the shares at that time, so it didn't.

When Bob Rae became the province's 21st premier in 1990, the Suncor shares became his responsibility. "I thought [the Suncor purchase] was a symbolic move, made partly to match the Feds' purchase of PetroCan," Rae today says. "But we realized in government that it provided no real benefits to Ontario and it wasn't a core business."

Rae's NDP government at the time was more focused on de Havilland, the state-of-the-art aircraft manufacturer in northwest Toronto, which was on the verge of going under and taking thousands of high-paying, high-tech jobs down with it. Rae helped convince what was then the very successful Bombardier transportation company (aerospace, airplanes, subways, trains) to save de Havilland and the jobs. By then no one was paying much attention to Suncor anymore.

"The 1990s were a time we had to focus our energies and our attention," Rae recalls of a time when Ontario was facing the worst recession since the Great Depression. "So we got out of it."

The NDP sold the shares and there was no great outcry. They still weren't worth that much, and besides, given the state of the province's books, any additional revenue the NDP could realize without raising taxes or cutting spending even further seemed like a good idea. In any event, the sale brought an end to Ontario's "window" on the oil industry after a little more than a decade.

Hindsight is wonderful. After the NDP government sold the shares, Suncor became a wildly successful company. In his autobiography *Sun Rise: Suncor, the Oil Sands and the Future of Energy*, Rick George, the company's former CEO, says the government made a huge mistake selling its stake of the company. "They bought high and sold low, which is exactly the opposite of what you want to do," George told me in an interview about his book for TVO's *The Agenda*. George said the Davis government bought the shares for a couple of bucks apiece. The stock has since split several times and as of this writing is trading at around $35 a share. Even David Peterson, whose job back then as finance critic was to point out all the flaws in the deal, acknowledged today that if Ontario had held on to the shares, it would have been a great deal for taxpayers. "Absolutely," he admits, although he's still less bullish than others, given the borrowing costs involved.

Tom Kierans still hasn't forgiven the Liberals for their demonizing the sale after taking over the government in 1985 and talking down the value of the shares.

"Bob Nixon made such a fuss," Kierans now says of the then Liberal finance minister. "He's the most partisan politician I've ever known, bar nobody. He got no advice whatsoever on 'The Street.' These are cyclical stocks, and Davis bought right at the bottom of the cycle."

The facts, as of this writing, are thus: Ontario sold its 25 percent interest in Suncor in 1993 for about $300 million. That quarter share of the company today is worth $12.66 billion. Had the government held on to the shares, Hugh Segal says the dividends from those shares would have been so substantial that "Ontario would be deficit-free as we speak," he insists.

Hindsight is a beautiful thing.

17

CONSTITUTION

On Saturday, April 17, 1982, on a rainy day on Parliament Hill, Queen Elizabeth II officially brought to an end nearly 115 years of constitutional stalemate in one of her former colonies. In several now iconic images from the day, Canadians will remember the photos of the Queen surrounded by the prime minister, Pierre Trudeau; the minister of justice, Jean Chrétien; the minister of labour, Gerald Regan; the registrar general, André Ouellet; the secretary to the cabinet for federal-provincial relations, Michael Kirby; and the clerk of the privy council, Michael Pitfield. One picture in particular shows the Queen beaming regally. It was only years later that we found out why. Trudeau had broken the tip of the fountain pen being used to sign the new Constitution Act, leaving no ink left when it became Chrétien's turn to sign.

"*Merde!*" the minister of justice muttered, using the French word for "shit," prompting a big laugh from the Queen, which photographers dutifully recorded.

There can be no doubt that the Canadian politician who was absolutely indispensable to making that day happen was Pierre Elliott Trudeau, and history has recorded that in exhaustive detail. Missing from the official photos of that moment are any snaps of the other politician who was indispensable to achieving that success. His name is William Grenville Davis. History hasn't recorded his contribution in much detail at all. That's an omission that needs to be fixed, and this chapter will attempt to do so. Never mind that Davis was Trudeau's number one ally throughout the course of the fractious negotiations with the other premiers. Plain and simple, there was a key moment in Canada's constitutional drama in which thousands upon thousands of hours of work and negotiations would have all gone for naught had Bill Davis not intervened with a seminal contribution at just the right moment. And yet there he was, sitting in the rain with his confidant, Eddie Goodman, and all the other premiers, far away from the photographers recording the moment for the history books. "That bothered Eddie, not me," Davis now insists. "If you're saying all the premiers should have been more front and centre, all right. If Eddie had been in my place, which I'm sure he felt he was for 14 years, that would have bothered him. It didn't bother me."

Davis has been reluctant to reveal too much about those behind-closed-doors talks in public. Even on that rainy day in April, seated in the crowd beside his close friend, Eddie Goodman, he would only say: "Well, Counsellor, I don't mind admitting that I'm tired." Then, referring to his fellow premiers, he added: "The others weren't always gentlemen."

First, to put that day on Parliament Hill into context, one has to go back 11 years to shortly after Davis became Ontario's 18th premier in 1971. The first ministers had gathered in Victoria, British Columbia, with a very Canadian mission. Canada was one of the very few countries in the world that still needed its mother country to sign off on any changes to its Constitution because, in effect, the nation's written Constitution was simply an act of the British Parliament — the British North America Act of 1867. Perhaps that made sense in the 19th century when Canada was still very much part of the British Empire. But seven decades into the 20th century, it made no sense at all. True, patriating the Canadian Constitution has never been a simple proposition because of the fundamentally different ways the federal government and the 10 provinces see the country. But in 1971 they came very close to getting it done in Victoria.

Ultimately, however, the effort failed.

But every decade or so another generation of Canadian leaders kicks the tires on completing the mission started in 1867. After Pierre Trudeau's return to power in February 1980, it seemed the conditions were ripe for another attempt to "bring the Constitution home." Those better conditions actually started toward the end of Trudeau's third mandate in February

1979 when Bill Davis offered a significant peace offering to the prime minister. After long arguing the opposite, Davis surprised his fellow first ministers at a constitutional conference in Ottawa by signing on to the Trudeau
position for constitutional change. Davis had long argued that patriating
our founding document ought *not* be done without the consent of all the
provinces and without an agreement on how to amend it. But now he was
joining Trudeau in saying it was time *without further debate* "to bring the
Constitution home to Canada." The premier said Canada's inability for decades to agree on terms of patriating the Constitution "does raise doubts in
the minds of some about our competence to govern ourselves." In urging
the federal government to move unilaterally, Davis said, "I don't want to
leave patriation of the constitution up to my grandchildren," the first of
whom incidentally was still more than four years away from being born.

While Pierre Trudeau was pleased with the apparent momentum
Davis's proposal created, some of the Ontario premier's provincial colleagues were less than enthused. "He is the greatest thief of all time," one
unnamed premier muttered to a newspaper reporter, referring to Davis
and shaking his head in frustration at the skillfully executed *volte- face.*

Bill Bennett put his criticisms on the record, saying it was the very
same idea he had pitched at his first federal-provincial conference in 1976.
"Guess who dumped all over it then?" the premier of British Columbia
asked. "Bill Davis."

Quebec's intergovernmental affairs minister, Claude Morin, told a
tableful of his officials over breakfast the next morning at the Château
Laurier Hotel: "William Davis is either a very sly politician or he is dumb
to make a presentation like that."

On Valentine's Day in 1979 in the *Ottawa Journal*, one of the great
veterans of the Queen's Park Press Gallery, Eric Dowd, offered up a distinctly unloving analysis of Davis's change of heart. He suggested the
premier had a "burning ambition" to play a large role in "saving confederation." Dowd alleged the national unity file was one in which Davis had
been overshadowed by his predecessor, John Robarts, and implied Davis
now needed to take an unusually bold step to make his mark on history. It wasn't a particularly gracious interpretation of events, but it might
not have been totally wrong, either. Politicians are notoriously competitive with one another, even (especially?) when they're in the same party,

and even when they're trying their best to ensure a smooth succession from one leader to the next. Robarts's hosting of a dinner for the Quebec Press Gallery in Quebec City and his mounting of the Confederation of Tomorrow Conference at the top of the newly built Toronto-Dominion Centre truly put the national unity issue at the centre of the country's political stage in a way it hadn't been for a century. Davis's first attempt at constitutional renewal in Victoria, alas, ended unsuccessfully. And he also never quite got the plaudits for strengthening national unity that he might have when he helped save French-language school boards in Ontario as education minister, even though they certainly noticed in Quebec.

Nevertheless, for a more generous interpretation of events, we might hearken back to 1971 and that ill-fated conference in Victoria. In a simple yet elegant phrase, Bill Davis summed up for millions of his fellow citizens what his view of the country was all about. "I am a Canadian who lives and works in Ontario," he said. "It is not the other way around. The whole of Canada is always greater than the sum of its parts." With the benefit of nearly a half century of hindsight, it seems beyond debate that this vision of Canada has motivated Davis's approach to the national unity file rather than some quixotic effort to best his predecessor.

In any event, whatever momentum Davis's new position contributed to constitutional matters, they soon came to a crashing halt. Three months after his olive branch to the federal government — on May 22, 1979 — Pierre Trudeau lost the election to 39-year-old Joe Clark, despite garnering nearly half a million more votes than Clark. As described in a previous chapter, Davis stumped hard for Clark in that campaign, but the reality was that the two Tory leaders were on quite different pages on the constitutional file than Davis was with Trudeau. As a result, not much happened.

But on February 18, 1980, Pierre Trudeau returned from political retirement to lead the Liberals back into power, just three months before a referendum on Quebec's place in Canada was to take place. As they so often say in politics, timing is everything. Quebeckers were being asked by René Lévesque, their province's first openly separatist premier, to render a verdict on this question:

> The Government of Quebec has made public its proposal
> to negotiate a new agreement with the rest of Canada,

based on the equality of nations; this agreement would
enable Quebec to acquire the exclusive power to make
its laws, levy its taxes and establish relations abroad —
in other words, sovereignty — and at the same time to
maintain with Canada an economic association including a common currency; any change in political status
resulting from these negotiations will only be implemented with popular approval through another referendum; on these terms, do you give the Government of
Quebec the mandate to negotiate the proposed agreement between Quebec and Canada?

It wasn't a particularly clear or elegantly worded question, but the gist
of it was: Did Quebeckers want to be part of Canada any longer? Two
weeks before the May 20, 1980, referendum voting day Bill Davis took
to a podium before 1,300 delegates at the Canadian Jewish Congress's
triennial assembly and roused the crowd into sustained applause with a
plea for a united Canada. If Quebeckers were under the impression, Davis
said, that Ontarians only care about good business and good government,
well, they were deluding themselves.

"I will never predicate my involvement, my discussions, or my negotiations on any balance sheet," the premier said. "This country was not
founded on a balance sheet; it is not going to survive on a balance sheet."

It was a warmer and more passionate Davis who tried to stir the
crowd, and it worked. It was also quite a contrast with the speech he'd given
to the Montreal Board of Trade the week before in which his tone and
manner were much more dispassionate. Davis took some flack from the
"Yes" side of the referendum debate when he announced he'd be venturing
into Quebec to speak, even though he'd been invited by the board. He was
labelled "an outsider," which seemed to get his patrician blood boiling.

"Let them choose to call the premier of Ontario or any other premier an outsider if that is their will," he said in a speech to the Empire
Club around the same time. "Quebec and her people are a vital part of
my country and its cities, towns, and villages are as much a part of my
heritage, my homeland, and that of my children as they are of Premier
Lévesque's."

In Montreal he clarified he wasn't coming as the premier of one province telling the people of another province what to do, that he wasn't about to "make threats, to rattle sabres, or to try to intimidate." Having said that, he urged Quebeckers not to underestimate the "compelling emotional commitment of the people of Ontario to the survival of Canada and the continuation of what this country stands for." And then he brought down the hammer: "For 113 years Quebeckers and Ontarians have lived in a partnership called Canada. Sovereignty-association as proposed by the Parti Québécois would be the end of that union, of that partnership — the end of Canada. We reject, categorically and without hesitation, the sovereignty-association proposal. It is unworkable, unacceptable. It is not negotiable." Rarely in his political career had Davis ever been so blunt about anything. But this was Canada that was at stake, and Ontario's first minister clearly felt the need to fight the good fight and be crystal clear about that. Davis even spoke more French than he'd ever attempted in public before and was disappointed when the *Globe and Mail* panned the effort.

"My French was better than Diefenbaker's, which doesn't say much," Davis jokes today about the effort at the Montreal Board of Trade.

Despite having fundamentally different views on Canada, the two premiers of Canada's most populous provinces actually got on quite well. After his Quebec speech, Davis called Lévesque to get his counterpart's take on it. He was actually a bit nervous that Lévesque would take umbrage at his shifting the battle to Lévesque's home turf. It turned out not to be the case.

"Come back any time," Lévesque told Davis. "After your speech, we went up 2 points in the polls."

To reporters Lévesque was even cheekier. While again expressing no objection to Davis's coming to Quebec to speak, Lévesque wondered about whether the speech would have a "boomerang" effect. "If some guy is going to come from outside and tell [people] what to do, I don't think it takes very well," he said. "Would you see me going to Ontario as the premier of Quebec and telling them: 'Look, why don't you kick out Bill Davis's government?'"

On referendum day an astonishingly high 86 percent of Quebeckers showed up to the polls and overwhelmingly opted to stick with Canada. The vote was nearly 60 percent for the "No" side to 40 percent for the "Yes" forces.

René Lévesque gave his tearful *à la prochaine* speech at the Paul Sauvé Arena in Montreal, and Canada as currently constituted dodged a bullet. But part of the victorious "No" side's platform was a promise to re-examine the country's constitutional arrangements to see whether changes could be made to satisfy Quebec's increasingly nationalistic and popular separatist government. And so the next day the premier of Quebec's neighbouring province immediately put forward his interpretation of the referendum results. A win for the "No" side "does not mark the end of a problem but rather the beginning of a solution," Bill Davis generously offered. "It is now our turn to demonstrate equal faith in Canada with commitment and goodwill."

Davis called for a federal-provincial conference to be summoned as soon as possible in the hope of negotiating a new constitutional arrangement for the country. Less than three weeks later he and the other first ministers, including René Lévesque, met at the prime minister's residence at 24 Sussex Drive to compare notes. The first meeting ended on an optimistic tone with everyone agreeing on an agenda of up to a dozen items for consideration, and Davis tossing yet another laurel leaf to Trudeau. While preferring unanimity among the first ministers, he said, "At some point in time you have to make decisions." He was essentially leaving the door open to Trudeau's acting unilaterally at some future date, an option that concerned some of his fellow premiers and even more of his fellow PCs.

As talks continued, two key agenda items began to emerge: patriating the Constitution itself and possibly entrenching what was still being referred to as a "bill of rights." Natural resources ownership rights and reforming the Senate were also significant issues. Once back in Toronto, Davis allowed that he was somewhat miffed at Lévesque's apparent aloofness to the entire process. Yes, the Quebec premier was in attendance, but Davis seemed to suggest that Lévesque's approach was along the lines of: "Fellows, let's see what you produce," as opposed to rolling up his sleeves and negotiating as an equal participant. Davis even uncharacteristically went as far as to acknowledge that he personally chastised Lévesque for his disinterest in the process.

The first ministers gathered again in September 1980 to continue the talks, but progress was hard to find. Even the normally upbeat Davis was hard-pressed to think of something positive to say. "It was a better day than it could have been" was all he could muster in the face of his fellow premiers, almost all of whom were lobbying for more provincial power. Davis was a relatively lonely voice at the table, urging his colleagues to remember that the federal government must have enough jurisdiction over issues to redistribute wealth and implement other national programs, sometimes at the expense of regional self-interest. Even reminding the first ministers that "all of us are Canadians first" apparently got the conference off to a rocky start. Claire Hoy, never one to mince words, wrote a *Toronto Sun* column whose headline was: "Davis Fails Miserably." While acknowledging "it's hard to soar with eagles when you're stuck on the ground with turkeys," Hoy blasted Davis for the conference's failure to launch. "I personally feel ashamed, let down, that my representative at this conference sat puffing contentedly on his pipe while premiers from east and west trained their howitzers on Ontario and lobbed real and imagined grievances at us," he wrote. He accused Davis of "sitting on Pierre Trudeau's knee" and suggested anyone with any sense knew the conference would be a flop.

Hoy's columns used to drive Sally Barnes, Davis's press secretary, crazy. In fact, they've had numerous fights over the years about his words that made her laugh and cry, but ultimately, as she told George Hutchison in 1993: "I can't respect it. He is too cruel. He does a disservice to the process. I don't admire his style of journalism. There's a fine line between scrutiny and harassment and he has no compassion for other people. He's treated some people in the most deplorable way." Barnes wouldn't be the first or last person to feel that way, and Claire Hoy being Claire Hoy, he couldn't have cared less, anyway.

Regardless, the heady, optimistic days of post-referendum victory now seemed quite far in the rearview mirror. Prime Minister Trudeau was championing a new "charter of rights" that would be much more than simply another act of Parliament as the current Bill of Rights enacted by John Diefenbaker's government in 1960 was. Trudeau felt what Parliament gave it could take away, so he wanted something that would ensure civil rights for Canadians that had more force than simply another law. His solution was a new charter, enshrined in a renewed Constitution, which parliamentarians couldn't mess with willy-nilly.

And Bill Davis agreed.

However, Manitoba Premier Sterling Lyon led the fight against the proposed charter, calling it a "fundamental invasion" of provincial powers that would undermine the parliamentary system. Lyon was surely right about the first part of his critique. The charter would empower the courts to interpret parliamentary statutes and reject laws that judges saw as unconstitutional. That was, indeed, an unprecedented challenge to the country's legislatures. But the idea of a charter of rights that packed a more powerful civil rights punch was a compelling one for many Canadians, and the idea found considerable favour in public opinion surveys.

Something worth remembering at this stage is that Davis might not have had as much political leeway as some of the other premiers. This was the fall of 1980 and the Ontario Tories still only had a minority government at Queen's Park. If Davis had moved too far away from the political centre of gravity of the provincial legislature in supporting Trudeau's initiatives, it could potentially trigger a non-confidence vote and thrust Ontarians into a snap election. Liberal leader Stuart Smith even suggested that Davis bring the two opposition leaders with him to Ottawa in the hope of presenting a more united front to the country, but Davis declined. While he said Smith and NDP leader Michael Cassidy were welcome to make their own way to the nation's capital and say whatever they wanted, a Robarts-like "Team Ontario" approach wasn't in the cards. (Robarts did welcome the two opposition leaders — Robert Nixon and Donald C. MacDonald — to sit in his delegation at the Confederation of Tomorrow Conference in 1967, something both opposition leaders spoke of as a very gracious thing to do.)

But a bigger bombshell was about to hit these constitutional talks. Just before Trudeau was set to announce his package of reforms, Bill Davis invited Joe Clark into his office at Queen's Park to give his federal leader a heads-up on what was about to happen. Davis knew he and Clark wouldn't agree on everything related to the package, but he figured they would agree on some things (patriation itself and an economic union). "Let's focus on where we agree," Davis was telling him, "and keep our differences more muted. There's no need to start a civil war within the Progressive Conservative Party." After all, Davis knew his minority government, now nearly three and a half years old, would need to seek a new mandate in fairly short order. And Clark himself, still only a 41-year-old ex-prime minister, would no doubt want to lead the federal Tories into another election in the years to come. The meeting ended with Davis having the clear impression that he and Clark were on the same page on that approach.

So you can imagine the premier's shock when he flipped on the television set at his home in Brampton to find Clark attacking the Trudeau package with abandon. Clark urged his fellow citizens to rally to his side and fight against the plan "for the larger interests of Canada."

The speech made Davis uncharacteristically furious. Writing in the *Toronto Star* on October 13, columnist Val Sears quoted an unnamed Davis aide who expressed shock at how "belligerently" Davis was reacting. Similarly, a couple of days later at a dinner for a roomful of business executives, some of the premier's friends were "dumbfounded" at how "wound up" he was getting.

After months of being told he was Trudeau's toady, Bill Davis's resentment had hit the boiling point. He'd had enough. Davis had put up with rude behaviour from Alberta Premier Peter Lougheed, who two months earlier had actually said in public: "Mr. Davis is sitting in Trudeau's lap." The cartoonists had a field day with that one.

Davis had bitten his lip (or maybe his pipe?) and merely responded a month later: "I think that was an unfortunate thing for Peter to say." Again, trying to be the mature statesman of the group and referring to "those who see this process as one of antagonism or stubbornness" (although not mentioning Lougheed by name), Davis had added, "I have a certain sympathy with the prime minister of this country."

But now it was going too far. Davis thought about all the equalization money Ontarians had put into other Canadian provinces to give them a helping hand. "They taxed our muscle and our brains," he would tell friends privately. In other words: "Now they've hit the mother lode with oil and they want to change the rules? Not so fast." One Davis confidant told Sears: "Bill's really got into the Wheaties. This is the tough side showing now — his mother's side."

Less than 24 hours after Clark's clarion call for Canadians to desert the reform package, Premier Davis dramatically parted ways with his federal leader, calling on all MPs and senators to support Prime Minister Trudeau's plans. The federal PC caucus was said to be badly shaken by Davis's surprise rupture with his federal leader. But the Ontario premier, who can be as blindly partisan as they come during election campaigns, reiterated that partisan politics had no place in nation building. Davis said he was supporting Trudeau's resolution because "it respects what Ontario and her people sought from the beginning. It also helps us honour our commitment to Quebec made during the referendum." Catherine Ford of Southam News described Davis as the "clear winner" emerging from the first ministers' talks. While probably not going *that* far, the two other Ontario party leaders evidently thought the premier was on the right track, since both Smith and Cassidy endorsed the Trudeau package, as well. Davis would therefore have a united hand to negotiate on Ontario's behalf without fear of losing the government.

However, there was a price to pay among conservatives for getting so close to Pierre Trudeau. Hugh Segal, Davis's adviser, was accustomed to getting an earful from party loyalists who frequently asked him: "How can you hang with Pierre Trudeau on the Constitution?"

Segal's response was simply: "We disagree on lots of stuff, but on this we agree. We need to bring the Constitution home. And we just didn't view the federal government as a travel agency for the provinces."

In his book *Life of the Party*, Eddie Goodman reveals he got even tougher complaints. He'd get hate mail from fellow Tories, wondering: "How could you allow Bill Davis to be on the same side as that bastard Pierre Trudeau?" Progressive Conservative MPP Ron McNeil from Elgin riding in Southwestern Ontario was asked by a long-time Tory supporter: "When is Bill Davis going to take over the federal Liberals?" Even Gordon Walker, the MPP for London South and minister of correctional affairs in Davis's cabinet, admitted to feeling "uncomfortable" at the notion of Davis and Trudeau on the same side of such a big issue. Middlesex MPP Bob Eaton, also part of the PC caucus, blamed the media for the reaction, saying too many editorial cartoons with Davis and Trudeau in bed together fuelled the antagonism. Letters to the editor in Ontario newspapers featured alienated Progressive Conservatives. One called Davis a "brownie up to Trudeau." Another said "as long as Davis aligns himself with Trudeau, I cannot vote for him."

Joe Martin is about as true-blue conservative as they come. Martin's hands-on political experience came half a century ago when he was executive assistant to Manitoba Premier Duff Roblin. A graduate of the advanced management program at Harvard University, he went on to become a senior executive with Touche Ross & Partners FCP and even now, about to celebrate his 80th birthday in January 2017, he's the director of Canadian business history, an adjunct professor of strategic management, and executive in residence at the University of Toronto's Rotman School of Management. More important for this story, he's the official historian at the Albany Club, the self-described "premier private club for leaders in Canada's business and conservative political spheres" for the past 134 years, and occasionally offers lectures to members on the club's significance in Canadian history.

Martin was with Touche Ross when he penned the following note to Bill Davis in November 1980:

> I have hesitated for a long time before writing this letter. My hesitation stems from the fact that I disagree with one of your key policies and I do not find it easy to disagree with the Party I have always supported. I think the Ontario Government's stand on energy and the Constitution is contributing significantly to the deterioration of a healthy Canada and furthermore will do the Province of Ontario irreparable harm in the long term. Therefore, I think you should reconsider these policies.

Most of the time, Martin is a happy warrior when it comes to politics. But he can also be as tough and as partisan as they come. Despite the fact that his daughter, Meredith, has worked with me as a producer at TVO for 15 years, he has on many occasions sent me blisteringly rough emails when he thinks I'm being unfair to conservatives on *The Agenda*. So it must have been extremely difficult for him to tell Davis that, as someone who moved to Toronto from the West a dozen years earlier, "I don't think you understand the feelings of Westerners." After outlining in considerable detail where he felt Davis had gone astray, Joe Martin ended his note with: "I beg of you to reconsider your position."

Davis's office wrote back nearly three months later (everything happened more slowly in the days before email). While it wasn't exactly a "form letter," it was fairly staid, considering how emotional Martin had been in his note. Davis admitted he shared Martin's concerns about the "strains on Confederation that the National Energy Program has generated." But on that and the Constitution he offered no hint of reconsideration. "I have great faith in the ability of our nation to resolve the grave conflicts with which it is faced today," Davis concluded before thanking Martin for "the frankness of your letter."

The always quotable conservative columnist Claire Hoy shared Joe Martin's concerns, but as befits writing in the *Toronto Sun*, he put it a little differently: "What's happening with Billy Davis?" Hoy wrote. "Does he need a rest? Is he fighting a mid-life death wish? ... All I know is he continues to throw oil on the flames of his own political demise, aggressively upsetting his traditional supporters, embarrassing Ontario by persisting in his unabashed Pierre Trudeau sycophancy."

Given the daily tirade Davis found himself subjected to, you'd never know that he was just four months away from winning a fourth consecutive election and a landslide majority government. But, apparently, columnists just have to be opinionated; they don't have to be right. In an attempt to stare down a pre-election palace revolt of the PC campaign committee at the Albany Club in early 1981, Hugh Segal told the assembled: "Sometimes leaders have to take some risks. If as a premier and party leader he couldn't win an election by having those views, then he'd rather lose the election."

Davis took the blows, in part because he had a pretty thick skin when it came to criticism, but also because he remembered some advice John Robarts once gave him that seems to have served him and Canada well over the years. "The Ontario government can't get too far away from the federal government," Robarts told him. "It's just not good for the country." On an unrelated note, Davis was said to have considerable sympathy for Trudeau because of his tempestuous marriage to Margaret. Much has been written about the dysfunctional nature of that marriage that needn't be repeated here. Suffice to say, Davis no doubt felt bad for Trudeau when he learned that on the eve of the prime minister's going down to defeat in 1979 his much younger and unhappier wife was at Studio 54 in New York City dancing the night away — a picture that ended up on the front pages of many Canadian daily newspapers.

"Mr. Davis felt sorry for him, all alone in 24 Sussex Drive," wrote Hugh Segal. "What Davis probably didn't know is that Pierre Trudeau wasn't all that alone. But [Davis's] Methodist background didn't allow him to consider those possibilities."

The highlight of 1981, so far, came on September 28 when the Supreme Court of Canada announced its historic ruling on how the federal government could proceed in its bid to patriate the Constitution. It was a classically Canadian decision. The court ruled the government was within its *legal* rights to proceed unilaterally with patriation. Score one for Trudeau. But it added that since much of Canada's Constitution was made up of conventions or traditional practices, it was incumbent on the government to secure the support of "a substantial number" of premiers, as well. Score one for the provinces. It was a deliciously fuzzy split decision that, in effect, threw the ball back to the politicians and told them to settle the matter themselves. Trudeau himself later joked that the court was saying his plans to patriate unilaterally were "legal, but not nice." Did anyone know what constituted a "substantial number" of premiers for Trudeau to proceed? The answer was no. Trudeau already had Davis and New Brunswick's Richard Hatfield onside. Would that be enough? Two out of 10 provinces hardly sounded adequate. But when expressed in terms as a percentage of Canada's population, Ontario and New Brunswick constituted almost 40 percent of the country's people. But as long as Trudeau had Davis alongside, he was off to a good start. And Trudeau was adamant about keeping the premier of Ontario onside.

For example, francophone minorities in Ontario were hoping Trudeau would use the constitutional negotiations to urge Davis to make their province officially bilingual once and for all or enhance French-language education rights. But in a speech at York University (which this author attended as an interested University of Toronto student), Trudeau left them disappointed. "This is not the time to take Bill Davis on," he admonished the audience. "I'm prepared *not* to get what I would like and what would be fair to the minorities in Ontario." When one French-speaking student accused the prime minister of sacrificing his rights essentially to curry favour with Ontario's premier, Trudeau didn't dispute that. "You say I'm doing this in order to get Bill Davis's support? Of course, I am."

The first ministers reconvened on Sunday, November 1, 1981, under what seemed like hopeless circumstances. Seven months earlier René Lévesque won an even larger majority government than in his breakthrough victory in 1976. Mind you, three weeks before that Davis won his majority back. And Pierre Trudeau's Liberals already had 74 out of the

75 seats in Quebec, raising an interesting question about who was a more legitimate spokesman for Quebec at the conference: the premier with a renewed majority government and two-thirds of the seats in the Quebec National Assembly, or the Quebec-born prime minister with 99 percent of the Quebec seats in Parliament.

Trudeau began the conference by having the premiers over for dinner, knowing that fully eight of them were still adamantly opposed to his constitutional package. The following day — the first full day of negotiations — the ludicrousness of Ottawa was on full display when Hugh Segal tried to use a bathroom in the corridor outside the main conference room. Wearing his Ontario delegation badge, Segal was informed by a federal security guard that "This is a federal corridor."

Segal responded politely: "I wonder if I could have a provincial whiz in a federal washroom?"

The answer was no. Segal had to go to the provincial delegations' bathroom, a hefty walk from where he currently found himself. He returned to the conference room and passed a note to Premier Davis: "All the provincial delegations are going to be getting antsier and antsier because the only washroom on this floor we don't have access to," Segal wrote.

Davis passed the note to Jean Chrétien, the federal justice minister. "Do the provinces have the right to be in the bathrooms of the nation?" Davis asked, paraphrasing one of Pierre Trudeau's more memorable lines. Even Trudeau chuckled at that one.

Ontario's premier wanted to see whether he could break the logjam, so in his opening remarks Davis offered to forgo his province's historic right to veto any constitutional amending formula it found unacceptable. Noting that all the first ministers were wearing poppies in anticipation of Remembrance Day, Davis said: "You think of the sacrifices that some of the people have made for the preservation of this country, you think of the compromises that some of our predecessors made, and I don't think it was any tougher for them 114 years ago than it is today." Calling for "a greater measure of consensus," Davis made the conference's first big gambit and opened himself up to considerable criticism from the Ontario PC Party's base. How could it be fair for Quebec to have a veto, but Ontario, with 2.5 million more inhabitants, wouldn't? Why should Ontarians have the same clout at the constitutional amending table as Prince Edward Island, whose population was about the same as the borough of East York's? All of those observations might have been true, but they also mattered less to Davis than getting some movement in the talks, and that they did. While Lougheed, Lyon, and Lévesque — the three L's — were still unyielding, the remaining five premiers in British Columbia, Saskatchewan, Nova Scotia, Prince Edward Island, and Newfoundland were suddenly more open to compromise. It was the most flexibility shown among any group of premiers in more than a year.

Both Trudeau and Davis well understood that the chances of a separatist premier of Quebec signing an agreement making Quebec's place in Canada stronger was a long shot. Nevertheless, they both thought substantial progress could be made. So on the day before the final talks the prime minister and the premier met at 24 Sussex Drive with their top advisers on federal-provincial relations: Michael Kirby for Canada and Hugh Segal for Ontario. Well known at this point was Davis's having already given up Ontario's veto on future constitutional changes. What wasn't yet known is that the premier was also prepared to go even further in the hope of nudging Quebec toward signing on the dotted line. Ontario would have supported giving Quebec a further veto on cultural and linguistic rights as well as on education and immigration issues.

"They could have won substantial language and jurisdictional gains for Quebec," Hugh Segal later wrote in *No Surrender*. "But [PQ cabinet ministers] Jacques Parizeau and Claude Morin couldn't look beyond their own ideology." Segal says in their own zeal to ensure the talks failed Lévesque and his advisers "appeared to freeze at the stick" and left lots of cards on the table they actually should have played. "They were busy fashioning the mythology of failure at the table because they had to cover their own ideological shortsightedness," he wrote.

We won't spend a lot of time here retelling the already well-known chronology of events in the dying hours of this drama. Suffice to say, one of the key moments happened when Trudeau suggested the premiers should patriate the Constitution as it was — at least get the thing home from the United Kingdom. Then Canada's political leaders could continue to negotiate for two years. If an agreement proved to be too elusive, then the federal government would put a new amending formula and entrenched charter of rights directly to the people in a referendum. It turned out to be a trap set for Lévesque who promptly stepped right into it by taking Trudeau up on the offer without consulting any of the other "Gang of Eight" premiers. The English-Canadian premiers in the Gang of Eight rued the idea of a referendum. They didn't like the optics of having to campaign against the popular notion of expanding Canadians' civil rights. But with one referendum already under his belt, Lévesque was confident he could beat back the Trudeau proposal in Quebec, so he agreed. It was a major political miscalculation. Trudeau jumped on it, pronouncing a new "Canada-Quebec alliance" and adding gleefully "the cat is among the pigeons."

Nothing is ever simple in Canadian constitutional politics, and the events of November 4, 1981, are surely no exception. Eventually aware of what he'd just done, Lévesque tried to back out of the referendum agreement with Trudeau, claiming it looked as if the rules were "written in Chinese." He then crossed the river to Hull, Quebec, and retired for the night. In Quebec mythology, here is where the story takes a traitorous turn for the worse. November 4, 1981, has gone down in history in two very different fashions in Canada's two solitudes. In Quebec it's known as the "Night of the Long Knives," the evening when the other English-Canadian premiers allegedly conspired behind Lévesque's back to strike a deal with Trudeau without the Quebec premier's knowledge. Never mind that it was Lévesque himself who opened the door to breaking up the Gang of Eight by agreeing to Trudeau's idea of a future referendum on the constitutional package, which the other premiers were dead set against.

But in English Canada it's the night that three influential attorneys general, who appeared to have nothing in common, met in a kitchen at the Government Conference Centre to kick around some ideas, which formed the makings of the eventual accord. Jean Chrétien was a Liberal from rural Quebec, the 18th of 19 children. Roy McMurtry was a Tory from midtown Toronto. And New Democrat Roy Romanow was a first-generation Ukrainian Canadian from Saskatchewan. They became known as the "Kitchen Cabinet." But the most important development that night has so far managed to elude almost every historian who has written about these events.

No longer.

Later that night William Davis made what should go down in history as one of the most important phone calls ever made in Canadian history. He was in his hotel room on the phone with Trudeau for about

20 minutes. When he emerged, Hugh Segal desperately wanted to know where his premier had left things with the prime minister. But he didn't ask, figuring "it was not necessarily our business." Next, Davis met with the inner circle of his Ontario delegation, which included Intergovernmental Affairs Minister Thomas Wells and adviser Eddie Goodman. He wanted to share two potentially important developments. The first was the realization that "the Chinese food is better in Brampton. There's not as much ginger in the sauce." Yes, he really said that.

The second observation was perhaps more pertinent. "Gentlemen, let's look at our watches. It's about 10:40 p.m. I think history may record that this thing started to go a bit better from this moment on." But again, that's all Davis said and no one pushed him for more details.

What happened on that phone call?

Four years ago, on the occasion of the 30th anniversary of the Constitution's patriation, I asked Roy Romanow on TVO whether he knew what had transpired during that phone call. "I'm convinced," Romanow said, "that Premier Davis communicated to Prime Minister Trudeau that unless he accepted the 'notwithstanding clause,' [Davis] had no choice but to pull out his support from the prime minister."

Had Romanow ever directly asked Davis about the call?

"I've tried to raise this with Premier Davis, but he's too discreet," he said.

Jean Chrétien knew even less about the phone call. Again, 30 years after the fact, Chrétien, Romanow, and Davis all went to McMurtry's midtown Toronto home for dinner to celebrate the anniversary of their achievement. They talked about that moment. Chrétien experienced it from the other end. He knew Trudeau had taken a call that night but never knew who was on the other end of the line. All he knew was that after the call Trudeau yielded on the "notwithstanding clause," which opened an avenue for success. When I ask Davis about the dinner, a mischievous grin comes across his face as he recounts how he taunted his Liberal friend.

"I looked him straight in the eye," Davis says of Chrétien. "I said, 'Jean, you *really* don't know who made that phone call?' And then the light went on!"

Nearly three and a half decades after that historic night, I put the question to Bill Davis directly. He had kept secret the contents of that conversation with the prime minister all this time, and Trudeau had certainly never spilled the beans.

"Did you put an ultimatum to Pierre Trudeau on that call that if he didn't compromise and accept the 'notwithstanding clause,' then Ontario was going to stop supporting him?" I asked. Remember: if Trudeau lost Ontario's support, his reform package was as good as dead. The British government of Margaret Thatcher was already extremely uncomfortable about the possibility of being asked to do the Canadian government's bidding with so little provincial support. It wanted a strong signal from a unified Canada, rather than a divided, fractious message. Could Trudeau have asked Thatcher to patriate the Constitution with only New Brunswick onside? Highly doubtful. Davis had a strong rapport with the prime minister, a strong hand to bargain with, and chose this moment to lay his cards on the table.

Even all these years later, Bill Davis still has trouble giving a straight answer to my question. "I don't think *ultimatum* is right," he says, smiling. "It was a point of view."

That's it?

"Well, the tenor of the meeting *was* different the next day," he admits.

Okay, don't call it an ultimatum. Whatever Davis wants to call it, he clearly left Trudeau with the impression that if the prime minister didn't put some 11th hour water in his wine, Ontario would bail. Trudeau had no option but to acquiesce. And so, working from a draft prepared by Premier Brian Peckford's Newfoundland delegation, several groups worked through the night to dot the *i*'s and cross the *t*'s, eventually coming up with the final compromise proposal. The other English-Canadian premiers in the Gang of Eight endorsed the package when they saw it at breakfast the following morning.

However, when the premier of Quebec walked into that premiers' breakfast, he was astonished to learn that a deal had been reached in his absence. He stormed out of the meeting and warned of "incalculable" consequences.

"I felt bad about René Lévesque," Davis acknowledges all these years later. "He showed up the next morning and found out about it. But there were no knives anywhere."

Hugh Segal, a Quebecker by birth, goes further in *No Surrender*: "The notion that there was some 'Night of the Long Knives' is one of the great convenient nationalist fictions for which there is absolutely no substantiation."

Thirty-five years after the fact we now know that what was achieved during that first week of November 1981 has indeed stood the test of time. Canadians welcomed their patriated Constitution with an enshrined Charter of Rights and Freedoms, and numerous public opinion surveys since indicate the charter remains one of our most beloved institutions.

"I think the charter has replaced medicare as the thing that defines Canadian citizenship," says John Tory, now Toronto's 65th mayor. "Mr. Davis had a sense the charter would glue us together."

The charter guarantees freedom of conscience, religion, thought, belief, expression, peaceful assembly, association, and for the media to do their job. In 34 sections it goes on to enumerate Canadians' democratic, legal, mobility, equality, language, and education rights. Unlike in the United States where the Supreme Court constitutes a third branch of government equal to the president and Congress, there is a "safety valve" in Canada's charter — Section 33, that "notwithstanding clause" Trudeau was forced to accept — giving legislatures the option of overriding judicial decisions they don't like. That clause has never been used by the federal Parliament or seven of Canada's 10 provinces — the political consequences of being seen to override civil rights guaranteed by the charter and the courts have presumably been too high. But the clause has been used in Quebec by both separatist and federalist governments to protect that province's unique character, for example, in 1988 with the controversial Bill 178 to prohibit the use of English-only signs for commercial establishments. However, as another check on legislative abuse, the use of the notwithstanding clause requires renewal every five years.

Other aspects of the new deal: Ontario and Quebec gave up their rights to veto any future changes to the constitutional amending formula; by Ottawa conceding on the "notwithstanding clause," provinces now had the right to opt out of future federal-provincial programs; and the English-speaking provinces agreed to protect French-language minority rights and Quebec grudgingly did the same for its anglophone minority. It was a truly Canadian compromise.

The first ministers also agreed to the so-called "Vancouver amending formula," a threshold for constitutional change requiring seven provinces representing 50 percent of the population. Provinces opposed to new amendments (for example, a new federal-provincial program) could opt out of those programs, minus fiscal compensation from the federal government.

In his closing remarks at the conference, a tired but triumphant Bill Davis could take pride in what was achieved, even if it wasn't perfect. To the prime minister he said: "You have demonstrated what is essential in this country: the ability to compromise and to accept the diversity and the views of so many others." In the same speech, Davis reminded Trudeau that he was a partisan politician, and it was very possible that the next day he would cross swords with him on a different issue. In fact, before long and despite their close working relationship on the Constitution, Davis and Trudeau would soon find themselves at loggerheads over transfer payments, with Davis accusing Trudeau of failing to maintain the federal government's financial commitments to health and education. Frank Miller, Davis's treasurer, would go further, saying Trudeau was putting the two levels of government on a "collision course." But for now it was all compliments.

Before the Ontario delegation was preparing to leave Ottawa, its members gathered one last time. The premier of Ontario thanked them all for their tireless efforts. Segal noted it was the first time he'd ever seen Davis emotional in public, with tears in his eyes. "He felt he had been part of something quite important and meaningful and that Ontario had done its job."

Tom Wells said in that gathering: "We would not have this deal today and there would be no compromise and no new Constitution without our premier. He simply never let Canada down!" It was undoubtedly the most emotionally powerful moment in Bill Davis's 22 years in public life. Tears were running down his cheeks. He couldn't even speak. There wasn't a dry eye in the group as the applause persisted for minutes on end. No one wanted to stop.

When he entered the chamber of the Ontario legislature the next day, Tory MPPs offered their chieftain a rousing standing ovation. Even the opposition members thumped their desks in admiration. Opposition leader Stuart Smith, originally a Quebecker, praised "the contribution of our premier" and expressed disappointment that "the government of Quebec saw fit to oppose so vehemently this compromise."

While the agreement was a historic achievement, it was at the same time, imperfect. The absence of a Quebec signature on the accord was troubling, even though the likelihood of securing that signature from a government dedicated to Canada's breakup seemed pretty remote. Nevertheless, Quebec was and is subject to the provisions of the new deal, despite its declining to ratify it. When Lévesque tried to play one more card — announcing three weeks later that he would veto it — both the Quebec Court of Appeal and the Supreme Court of Canada ruled he actually never had such authority.

A one-time federal Progressive Conservative Party leadership hopeful named Brian Mulroney watched the proceedings with fascination. Nearly three and a half decades later Mulroney says he didn't approve of the 1981 constitutional accord because it lacked Quebec's signature. "But I figured as soon as [Quebec Premier Robert] Bourassa came back in, we'd fix it," he told me. "I figured once the federalists came in, we'd complete the job." Mulroney's prognostication was mostly right. The Liberals under Bourassa returned to power in 1985. A year and a half later, Mulroney managed to get all 11 first ministers to agree to the Meech Lake Constitutional Accord. That agreement died three years later when the Manitoba and Newfoundland legislatures declined to ratify it. So to this day the imperfect 1981 agreement remains in place as, for the moment, the last ratified word on Canada's constitutional circumstances.

When Pierre Trudeau died in 2000, I went to Davis's home in Brampton to interview him about the country's loss. As closely as the two first ministers worked together on some of the biggest issues in the nation's history, Davis interestingly said he never felt he and Trudeau were friends. They were friendly. But they weren't confidants. They put aside differences when they had to in the national interest. "He had a great sense of the country," Davis told me. "I'm a Tory, but I respect others who share an interest in this province and country. I have great respect for those with different opinions. They were wrong, perhaps, but I respected them."

Bill Davis has never made a big deal of the fact that the history books don't recognize the significance of that phone call to Pierre Trudeau at *the* crucial moment in the negotiations. Part of it is his own fault. His modesty has prevented him from boasting about his role in the saga. And his respect for Trudeau and the sanctity of their private conversations has also played a part. But as of July 30, 2016, he is now 87 years old. As one looks at the membership around that first ministers' table, one realizes a sad truth about the march of time. Pierre Trudeau is dead. So are Bill Bennett of British Columbia and Peter Lougheed of Alberta. The same for Allan Blakeney of Saskatchewan, Sterling Lyon of Manitoba, René Lévesque of

Quebec, Angus MacLean of Prince Edward Island, and Richard Hatfield of New Brunswick. Only John Buchanan of Nova Scotia, Brian Peckford of Newfoundland and, of course, Bill Davis remain alive.

So maybe it's time to acknowledge the singular contribution of a man who quietly sat in the rain on April 17, 1982, far from the main stage, while many other dignitaries, who had next to nothing to do with the achievement, preened for the cameras.

18

MULRONEY

As 1982 came to a close, Bill Davis got some horrible news. On October 18 his mentor, John Robarts, the man who had overseen and nurtured his political career, committed suicide. Robarts had suffered a stroke on a flight to a board meeting in Houston a year earlier. He had told a very few close friends and family that he wasn't prepared to live his life as a sick old man, and that if his condition didn't improve after a year of rehab … well, the rest was left unsaid. But given that Robarts's son, Timothy, had already taken his own life at age 21, those close to the former premier had an inkling of the path Tim's father might take. It's hard to think of another politician who loved life as much as John Robarts. He loved people, loved to party, loved to stay out late, loved to hit Toronto's jazz clubs, loved to belt back Scotches, loved to hunt, loved his kids, and loved being in love with his second wife, Katherine Sickafuse, an American divorcee who was 28 years his junior. But after the stroke, all that changed. Robarts wasted away, walked with a limp because one side of his body didn't work, couldn't drink or hunt anymore, and perhaps even worse, many of his old friends stopped calling on him because he was no longer the Chairman of the Board. He was a depressed invalid, a condition neither he nor his second wife signed up for.

Consequently, in the early-morning hours of October 18, the former premier took the shotgun that the PC Party had given him as a parting gift for his years of service to Ontario, walked into the shower stall of the second-floor bathroom at his home in Rosedale, and swallowed his gun.

When Darcy McKeough heard the news on the radio that morning, he began to cry. Numerous sources have described October 18, 1982, as the worst day of Bill Davis's premiership. For a man who prides himself on being stoic when the occasion calls for it, Davis had a hard time keeping it together.

Janet Ecker was in the cabinet meeting when the premier broke the news to his colleagues. "He was visibly moved," she recalls. "I remember it really impressed me because I had never seen anybody of his standing react emotionally. Robarts was clearly someone who meant a lot to him."

As deputy press secretary, it was Ecker's responsibility to write a speech for the premier to deliver in the legislature. She remembers being shocked when Davis delivered the speech, fighting back tears, and at one point significantly choked up. "That was one of the things that really registered on me at the time," she says.

John Tory says it was the toughest day he ever saw Davis experience in his 25 years of public life. The premier did hold it together, but just barely. "People appreciated his having a calm, unflappable demeanour," Tory says.

There was plenty of friction surrounding Robarts's funeral. His second wife, Katherine, who had few allies around Queen's Park, wanted things done her way. Robarts's daughter, Robin, had her views. Being a former premier, the Ontario government's protocol office was involved. And because Robarts died by his own hand, the head of the Catholic Church, Cardinal G. Emmett Carter, refused to be associated with any service. Even Anglican Archbishop Lewis Garnsworthy declined to preside over the ceremony unless organizers called it a "memorial service" rather than a "funeral service." The family agreed to that compromise and Garnsworthy ultimately did preside. In fact, despite his earlier conditions, which so irritated Robarts's family and friends, Garnsworthy actually delivered a stirring, meaningful eulogy at St. Paul's Anglican Church on Bloor Street East in Toronto.

"The manner of his passing saddens all of us," Garnsworthy said. "But I am not the judge of that, and you are not the judges. The issues of life and death are in the hands of a loving and forgiving God. And I am content that it should be so."

Perhaps the most unforgettable image on that day didn't even take place in the church. As Robarts's funeral cortège made its way through the streets of Toronto, a group of construction workers took off their hard hats, stood at attention, and observed a moment's silence as the hearse passed them. John P. Robarts had that kind of effect on people.

B y New Year's Day 1983, Bill Davis was about as secure in his job as it is possible to be in politics. He had reclaimed the Tory majority he inherited from John Robarts 12 years earlier. He had vanquished four other PC leadership candidates in 1971 and four opposition leaders over four consecutive election wins since then — the first premier since Sir James P. Whitney 67 years earlier to win four straight elections. The Liberals and New Democrats had rookie leaders — David Peterson and Bob Rae — both of whom were chosen a year earlier and neither of whom anybody thought posed any kind of threat to Davis's future electoral prospects, including the two leaders themselves.

Despite not having been minister of education for more than a decade, it was still plainly clear that Bill Davis cared more about the education file than any of the others on his desk. He always kept a close eye on that "trifecta" of institutions created on his watch — the community college system, TVO, and OISE. He also did something unusual that premiers generally didn't do. He met once a year with all the university presidents and then again annually with the community college presidents. He just wanted to stay in touch with the post-secondary sector to see for himself how things were going.

"He never lost his love and commitment to education," says Charles Pascal, who in the early 1980s attended those annual meetings as president of Sir Sanford Fleming College in Peterborough. "And he always understood that if we got education right, our economy would do better, health-care costs would go down — education was connected to everything."

Davis and Pascal seemed to hit it off right away. They loved talking education policy and politics and soon discovered they had a couple of family connections: both Davis's wife, Kathleen, and Pascal were from the Chicago area. There was also a University of Michigan connection: Kathleen Davis, Ed Stewart (the premier's secretary to the cabinet), and Pascal (who played varsity baseball for the Wolverines) had all been students at Ann Arbor, Michigan.

One Thursday in September 1983 Pascal was sitting in his office at Sir Sanford Fleming College when the phone rang. It was Dr. Stewart, looking for four tickets to the Ohio State Buckeyes–Michigan Wolverines college football game that was only two days away. It didn't seem to occur to Stewart that trying to find that many tickets so soon before one of America's most important football matchups of the year was basically asking the impossible. But Davis had business in Windsor that weekend, and his cabinet secretary thought it would be neat if the premier could go to the game.

However, calling Pascal wasn't actually such a dumb idea, because he *did* have a connection at the university who could score some tickets. Pascal had to listen to his ticket contact swear a blue streak at him for having the gall to ask for four tickets two days before game day. But the ticket man came through, and Pascal passed the good news along to Davis's office.

Fifteen minutes later Bill Davis was on the phone. "Charles," the premier said, "Kathleen and I want you to be our guest on the weekend at the Dearborn Inn in Michigan. Why don't you get yourself a couple of more tickets and join us for dinner and the game?"

Pascal got back on the phone to his contact, listened to another profanity-laced tirade, but got the tickets, made the trip to Michigan, and joined the Davises, Ed Stewart and his wife, and John Tory and his wife, Barbara Hackett, for dinner and the game. During the dinner, with politics, of course, being the main topic of discussion, Pascal saw Kathleen tease her husband, saying: "Come on, Billy, if you were in the U.S., you'd be a liberal Democrat."

How did Davis react? "He bit down on his pipe a little harder," Pascal recalls.

It's at this moment in our story that it's worth remembering this key fact about Bill Davis's life: ever since he was a teenager, his initial attraction to politics was at the federal level. Gordon Graydon, Brampton's representative in Parliament, was Davis's first political hero. In the 1960s, Davis co-chaired the federal PC Party's Thinkers' Conference at Montmorency, Quebec. Mere months after becoming Ontario's premier, Davis was thrust into the national unity spotlight in Victoria, British Columbia, in which he performed well. A decade later he played the indispensable role, finding the common ground between Prime Minister Pierre Trudeau and the Gang of Eight, resulting in the patriation of Canada's Constitution with an entrenched Charter of Rights and Freedoms. And now political developments would set in motion another array of events, thrusting Davis into the national conversation.

The "Will Bill Davis Go Federal" question had followed the premier for years. It actually started a year after he became premier. Claire Hoy claimed in the *Toronto Star* that Davis had "been carefully charting a step-by-step program designed to make him the leading contender in the event [Robert] Stanfield fails to win the next election and decides to step down." Stanfield didn't win that 1972 election, but he did come very close, trailing Pierre Trudeau by only 2 seats and holding the Liberals to a minority government. Two years later Trudeau won his majority back and Stanfield was done, but by this time Davis was enmeshed in his own difficulties, so there wasn't much talk of him contesting the 1976 federal PC leadership convention won by Joe Clark.

In 1981 Davis had his majority government back, the sharks were circling around Clark, and once again the "Will Bill Davis Go Federal" cottage industry was back in business. In June 1981, just three months after winning his election, Davis felt a need to assure everyone: "I am completely engrossed in my duties as premier and am not giving any thought to entering federal politics now or in the future." That might have been somewhat true for the premier himself, but it surely wasn't for those around him, who Davis always said were often more politically ambitious for him than he was. When pushed further, Davis pointed out there was nothing to discuss since Joe Clark had the job of federal opposition leader, his polling numbers were actually improving — the federal PCs had a 15-point lead over the Liberals in English Canada — and there would be no annual general meeting of the federal Progressive Conservative Party until January 1983. But none of that stopped a good chunk of the federal caucus from continuing to try to undermine Clark. John Crosbie even admitted in his memoir that he'd been "clandestinely" organizing a leadership bid for two years. Davis sent the message out through his own people that he wanted nothing to do with any efforts to kneecap Clark, even though some of his closest advisers were already sniffing around a potential Davis bid. In fairness to them, the premier never quite unequivocally shut the door, either. "You know me," he'd say to the inquisitive media. "I don't deal with hypothetical situations." It wasn't hypothetical for several others, who began to set up organizations and get their ducks in line. Even then Davis would merely say much of that activity was happening thanks to overzealous or overenthusiastic staffers. Nevertheless, in December 1982, Davis and his cabinet minister, Gordon Walker, found themselves standing near the speaker's chair in the legislature when Walker shared reams of public opinion polling printouts with Davis that his own pollster had given him. The numbers showed if there was a leadership race in the federal Tory party, Davis was in a very competitive position even before the bell rang. But Davis didn't betray any reaction to Walker.

"His reaction was absolutely inscrutable," Walker recalls. "He maybe bit down on his pipe a little harder, but that was it."

That takes us to Winnipeg in January 1983 when PCs gathered to render a verdict on Joe Clark's leadership. As far as Bill Davis was concerned, Clark had his support and the premier said so publicly. Yes, there were significant disagreements on energy pricing and the Constitution, but Davis believed, given a second chance, Clark could still be an effective prime minister. A Market Opinion Research poll of delegates to that Winnipeg meeting showed 39 percent would vote for Clark on the first ballot. Peter Lougheed polled 21 percent, Bill Davis 18 percent, with 11 percent to Brian Mulroney and 3 percent to Crosbie. Given how the convention turned out, these numbers proved quite irrelevant. Clark was certainly hoping for a solid vote of confidence in his leadership from the membership, but instead he got what he felt was an ambiguous 66.9 percent support. Other leaders would have taken a single vote above 50 percent and said, "Good enough, I'm staying." But Clark wanted much more and announced to astonished delegates that the number wasn't "good enough," prompting Prince Charles, years later, to ask him: "Why exactly was 66.9 percent support not good enough?"

It was a good question. In effect, Clark was saying 66.9 percent support in January was inadequate, but 50 percent plus one support at an ensuing leadership convention in June would suffice. Nevertheless, Clark resigned as leader, called for a new leadership convention, and announced he would be a candidate, fighting for the job he already had. Bill Davis watched the results unfold in a hotel room in Winnipeg, and in classic Davis style offered *almost* no response to Clark's decision among his private entourage, although one observer did catch him muttering under his breath: "Typical." It wasn't meant as a compliment and it would have been one of the rare moments when Davis let the mask slip in front of others.

Now came the bigger question for Team Ontario: Was this finally Bill Davis's moment to go federal? Certainly, many members of Davis's inner circle had already quietly been organizing a run. And it later emerged on a broadcast of *The National* on CBC that one of the reasons Clark didn't do as well as he'd wanted to was because of Ontario's lukewarm support for his leadership. There were 70 Tory MPPs at Queen's Park, and yet Peter Mansbridge reported that only seven were in Winnipeg, according to the party's own registration records.

Unlike with previous speculation on this question, this time Davis took it seriously. He convened a meeting of the Big Blue Machine and wanted everyone's advice on what he ought to do. On one side of the ledger, Davis was an ideal candidate. First and foremost, he was seen by Tories as an unambiguous winner — unlike Joe Clark who blew the party's first chance at government in almost two decades; unlike Robert Stanfield who lost three elections in a row; unlike John Diefenbaker who flamed out far too quickly after winning the biggest majority government in Canadian history; unlike George Drew, John Bracken, and Robert Manion who never won; and unlike R.B. Bennett and Arthur Meighen who had their brief victories but ultimately were bested by William Lyon Mackenzie King. Progressive Conservatives were starved for a guy who had "winner" written all over him, and Davis surely did.

In addition, Davis was from Ontario, which had the biggest number of seats in the country, and there was a reasonable expectation that he could win most of them. Davis had just participated in a provincial election in which he'd won 70 out of 125 seats (56 percent). Federal Tories would be thrilled if he could turn that trick again. With his majority government of 1980, Pierre Trudeau won 50 out of 95 Ontario seats (53 percent), and many Tories thought Davis could do better.

Yes, he was a premier and therefore could potentially be marginalized by his opponents as a "regional candidate." Clark, in fact, called him that, an insult that rankled given all that Davis had done for his federal leader. But this "regional candidate" had participated in two historic constitutional conferences, including the one that patriated the country's Constitution from the United Kingdom with a Charter of Rights and Freedoms. In other words, Davis's bona fides as a national figure were pretty unchallengeable. In his book *Memoirs*, Brian Mulroney said Clark's use of that expression was a "major gaffe," particularly since Ontarians, unlike others in the country, tend to think of themselves as Canadians first and Ontarians second. Eddie Goodman thought the comment made Clark look "foolish," calling it a "serious blunder." When Goodman called Davis, who was vacationing in Florida at the time, the premier said: "One or two more of those remarks could help me make up my mind." Evidently, Clark also came to realize he'd made a faux pas. He asked Senator Finlay MacDonald to travel to Florida to meet with Davis to smooth the waters, which he did.

Davis had a superb organization behind him, surely access to all the money he'd need to make a competitive run, and a reputation as a good and decent man. And there was that last intangible: the prime minister's job intrigued Davis. It always had. He didn't burn for the job the way, for example, Brian Mulroney did. But he was interested.

On the other side of the ledger were the reasons *not* to go federal. Davis had just been re-elected not even two years earlier with a majority government. He was at the height of his political comfort zone. He loved going home to Brampton, being part of that suburban world, and living as close to a "normal life" as any superstar first minister can. As Hugh Segal put it, Davis couldn't get his head around the notion that the prime minister of Canada couldn't live in Brampton. All of that would come to an end with a move to Stornoway at first and maybe if he were fortunate to 24 Sussex Drive after that. Segal tried to convince him that it could be salutary for the country not to have a prime minister who lived exclusively in Ottawa and that bringing a small-town style to federal politics by spending more time away from Ottawa could be a unique selling proposition. It was wishful thinking on everyone's part, and the premier knew it.

And speaking of Stornoway, that was the other downside of the job. Davis wasn't running to become prime minister; he would be leaving arguably the second-best job in Canadian politics for one of the worst jobs in Canadian politics — leader of the opposition. From his first election in 1959 until this moment in 1983, Davis hadn't spent one second in opposition. Would he want that job? Could he even do it? He'd never asked a question from the opposition benches in the legislature in his entire life.

There was also the "Ontario thing." The province's 23rd premier, Ernie Eves, told me: "There was this feeling that the premier of Ontario could never be the prime minister. The hate factor from the rest of the country — he wouldn't be able to do it." In fact, no Ontario premier from any party has ever become prime minister. Premier George Drew became the federal Progressive Conservative leader from 1948 to 1956, but he never became prime minister. Premier Bob Rae was the interim federal Liberal leader from 2011 to 2013 but opted not to go for the permanent leadership, ultimately won by Justin Trudeau.

There was also the age and stage Davis was experiencing in life. He was 53 years old with five children, had never made much money, and was becoming increasingly aware of that fact. His potential post-political prime earning years were just around the corner. Would he risk a career at a blue-chip law firm and sitting on more than a dozen boards to sit on the opposition side of the House of Commons and possibly never get into government? Those damn Liberals always seemed to figure out a way to beat some very fine gentlemen who led the PC Party over the years. As good as he was now, he had to acknowledge it was possible he might just join that list of former Tory leaders who had such high hopes going in, only to see them dashed by a better Grit leader.

But I haven't yet mentioned the biggest problem Bill Davis had when it came to seeking the federal PC leadership: the man didn't speak French. He could understand it and read a bit of it, but he had no confidence at all speaking it in public and almost never did. In years past that wouldn't have been a handicap. Lots of Tory leaders couldn't speak French. But times had changed. The country had changed. No longer would it be acceptable for *any* party leader not to be bilingual. Another PC leadership candidate, John Crosbie, learned this when he admitted he couldn't speak French, or Portuguese, or Chinese, either, for that matter, and torpedoed his campaign as a result. A unilingual anglophone as a federal party leader just wasn't an option anymore. This deficiency became even more acute when Brian Mulroney, during his campaign, asked PCs how they intended to win any future elections while going 1 for 75 in the seat count in Quebec. That's right: the Liberals had won 74 out of 75 seats in *la belle province* in the 1980 election. Even when Clark won the election in 1979, he still only won two seats in Quebec. Could the unilingual Davis expect to do any better? Yes, John Diefenbaker didn't speak French and cleaned up in Quebec in the 1958 election. But that was a quarter century ago, and the dynamics of that election were unique.

Davis's advisers pointed out all this and more to the prospective candidate. None of the advisers said: "You have to do this" or "You can't do that." It didn't work that way when you advised Bill Davis. They added up the pluses and minuses, and some leaned more in one direction than another. And their advice wasn't unanimous. Norman Atkins and Hugh Segal leaned more to the "Yes, let's do it side" mainly because they really wanted to see Bill Davis as prime minister of Canada and this was the only way to make it happen. Atkins also loved campaigns and frankly relished the thought of doing a national one with his premier. Segal wrote in *No Surrender* that he thought Davis "would bring to Confederation the small-town decency and incrementalism of a politician I believed in profoundly."

Conversely, Eddie Goodman barged into the premier's office one February day and asked him point-blank whether he was seriously considering running for the federal job. Davis's immediate answer was no. His next answer was: "It's highly unlikely I'll run."

Goodman's advice was more along the lines of: "What do you need the headache for?"

Today Davis has a good chuckle when he recalls that advice. "I think Eddie felt that I was better off staying where I was and that I should retire and probably come and work for the Goodman law firm!" He laughs. "We were offered a job at the Goodman firm when I retired. But Eddie and I were too close. It never would've worked."

As Davis pondered, two things began to happen. Other candidates started entering the race: Joe Clark, of course, was in from the moment the bell sounded. Brian Mulroney, whom Clark defeated in the 1976 contest, also came in. Mulroney had no elective experience at any level, but he was perfectly bilingual, a brilliant speaker with a background in the corporate world, a beautiful family, had been a Tory since university, seemed to know every single Progressive Conservative in the country, and was only 44 years old.

Mulroney and Davis had known each other since the 1967 convention that picked Robert Stanfield. While they weren't best pals, they were on good terms and were part of a posse that included Roy McMurtry and Arthur Maloney. Mulroney knew of Davis's accomplishments in Robarts's cabinet, telling me in 2015: "He was a superb education minister. He was the Quiet Revolution for Ontario because of what he did for education." Then, in the mid-1970s, Mulroney and Davis would rekindle their friendship through association with John Tory, Paul Godfrey, and Alan Eagleson. By 1983 Mulroney and Segal were close, which provided another entree into Davis's world.

Clark's former finance minister, John Crosbie, had the biggest personality of all the candidates. He loved nothing more than to work a room into a frenzy of laughter with his great sense of humour but that didn't disguise a big brain and solid policy chops that were part of the Crosbie package. However, the Newfoundland MP's two biggest drawbacks were his lack of French and his ignominious place in Tory history as the guy whose budget was defeated in 1979, sending the PCs back into electoral oblivion.

Michael Wilson was still years away from being known as the father of the Goods and Services Tax. At this point, like Crosbie, he was a former minister in Clark's government and had solid gravitas as a former Bay Street banker. David Crombie, another ex-Clark minister, was seen as too Toronto and perhaps too pink for many of the delegates. Mulroney joked after hearing Crombie's broken French that he couldn't wait, after becoming prime minister, to appoint Crombie as his minister responsible for francophone affairs. The line always got a laugh.

A real wild card in the race was Peter Pocklington, the owner of the Edmonton Oilers. His flat-tax message had some currency among more small-c conservative delegates. And, of course, being Wayne Gretzky's boss didn't hurt his profile. There were two other fringe candidates, as well: John Gamble, a far-right-wing MP from York North, and Neil Fraser, a former civil servant who was fired for opposing the country's conversion to the metric system.

That was the large and competitive field many people were asking Bill Davis to jump into.

The other development came at Queen's Park. As Davis flirted with the notion of going federal, some of his Ontario cabinet ministers began to put their own leadership organizations in place on the chance that Davis might leave Ontario politics, creating a vacancy in the premier's office. Most of them did it on the QT, but one didn't, and he would pay for it.

The pressure on Davis to enter the race got increasingly intense. Typical were letters such as this one from Prince Edward–Hastings MP John Raymond Ellis, who eventually served 16 years in the House of Commons:

> I firmly believe that no one, including yourself, has a devine [sic] right to lead our Party and that there may be dozens capable. I am convinced, however, that of those in the contest now and those proposed, you have the best credentials from every viewpoint.... For that reason I encourae [sic] you, as others have, to contest the leadership and announce as soon as possible. Allow me and your many friends to use what talents we have in a concerted manner to assist in securing that goal for you.

Ellis went on to promise the support of his friends, his organization, and himself to the cause: "Bill, I couldn't be more sincere in sending this letter to you," he concluded. "I know that you are seriously considering the situation. You know that a change is needed. Nothing is ever achieved without hard work. The workers are available and the goal is worthwhile. Let's do it." It was signed "Jack."

"Will he or won't he" became a national obsession for Tories. Even Brian Mulroney asked his friend, industrialist Paul Desmarais, to come to Toronto, have dinner with Davis, and suss out the premier's interest in the job.

Just when Davis had pretty much decided he was *not* going to do it, he took a meeting with a group of supporters from the province least likely to be backing his candidacy. The secret rendezvous took place at the Park Plaza Hotel, one of the premier's favourite haunts. The delegation consisted of as many as 30 Montrealers, all of whom were delegates to the upcoming convention. These weren't just talkers. These were people with votes. Surprisingly, this group of francophones strongly urged Davis to get into the race. They weren't dissuaded by his lack of French, saying Davis's record on French-language services and education in Ontario was a strong argument to counter his inability to speak the language.

"I didn't know that had permeated east of us here," Davis now says about his record on francophone affairs. "They were very adamant and I said I'll think about it."

As the rumours of a possible Davis candidacy grew, the story completely overwhelmed anything happening in provincial politics. It surely wasn't true, but it felt as if the business of the province had come to a screeching halt while the premier figured out what he wanted to do. The subject of every scrum after cabinet or Question Period seemed to be: "Are you planning to run for the federal PC leadership?" Davis came up with a stock reply that exemplified his skill for offering the non-denial denial. "I have no plans to run," he would say over and over and over. Technically, it was true. He had no plans to run. But it didn't mean he *might* not have plans to run at some future point. Eventually, the scrums became a joke. Davis would simply say, "I have no plans to run, and I have no plans to have plans to run." The premier's media office even went as far as to put out a press release in perfect Davis circumlocutory language, confirming he had no plans to have plans to make plans. But as much as he denied it, his aides were quietly admitting he was thinking about it.

Then came an added complication. When the premier of Alberta heard his Ontario counterpart was mulling over a bid, he said he might just do the same thing. We have seen that while Peter Lougheed and Bill Davis could do business together, and from time to time were friendly with each other, they were also (although both deny it) significant rivals for the unofficial title of Canada's most important premier. Davis's supporters thought it was him because his province had the biggest economy, the largest population, the second-biggest land mass, and a mature three-party parliamentary system, which Davis skillfully mastered through six years of minority legislatures. Lougheed's base thought it was him because oil was now the most important commodity in the world and Alberta had lots of it. The political centre of gravity was moving west, and Lougheed wanted the rest of the country to respect that. Also, Lougheed was just as much a winner as Davis was — four consecutive election victories (all majorities) and, in fact, no Alberta PC MLA during Peter Lougheed's time ever lost his seat. True, Lougheed's French was no better than Davis's, but he'd be damned if he was going to let his rival from Ontario have an easy ride to the finish line. If Davis was in, Lougheed threatened he would be, too.

Davis took the threat seriously and was concerned about what an East versus West confrontation might do to both the party and the country. Some of Davis's advisers found this petulance of Lougheed's ironic, since before the last PC leadership race in 1976 won by Clark, Davis actually phoned Lougheed and urged him to get into the race. Lougheed didn't, but it was an indication of how highly Davis thought of his western counterpart. No one was sure whether Lougheed really meant it or whether he was just puffing out his chest as much as he could. But Davis wasn't taking any chances. He'd already heard from Saskatchewan's PC premier that Grant Devine was reneging on his support for Davis's candidacy because Lougheed had threatened him. In fact, the Alberta premier thought he was so important to the entire process that he summoned all the prospective leadership candidates to come to Edmonton and submit themselves to a grilling from the Alberta PC caucus. Talk about chutzpah. But most of the candidates did make the trek west. Lougheed had the influence, and few candidates wanted to risk alienating him and the potential support he represented.

As time marched on, Hugh Segal shared some of his thoughts on the issue via a private handwritten letter to Davis. Segal wrote the note on May 1, 1983, and Davis has kept it all these years. Addressed to "Premier and Kathleen" with less than six weeks to go until selection day, Segal laid it all out for his conflicted boss:

> This is obviously our last chance to get our oar in before you put yourself in the lockup to make the following decision — to go or not.
>
> We can't make it easier by guaranteeing victory. The commitment we have may not all hold; enemies we are counting upon may turn into assets. The other sides have begun to spread anti-Davis trivia. It will not be pleasant. Yes, you may lose.
>
> There is no dishonor in that if the effect is honest and the cause is right. While none of us will be as out front as Kathleen and Bill Davis — we will all face the risk of some loss as well.
>
> If you win — you will not be asked to carry any new burden alone. Donna and I, A.R. [Anna Ruth] and Norman [Atkins], Barbara and John [Tory]; even Ed and Vicki [Stewart] will all disrupt our lives no less than winning will ask you both to do.

Eddie's concern is genuine, prudent and in your interests. But Eddie [Goodman] may underestimate the loss involved in not risking loss for the country's sake. Yesterday's debate was a 2-1/2-hour commercial for you.

There are a million reasons not to do something. There are a million reasons to avoid risk. You have taken many — you owe the country none. You may owe yourself one more — whatever the outcome.

Whatever you decide, you know we'll be with you.

Hughie.

Ten years after the fact, Norman Atkins, in conversation with George Hutchison, perfectly summarized how he thought the conversation went inside the Davis home on Main Street in Brampton. "If Kathleen were to express any view, she'd prefer to have Billy Davis home and not a serious participant in politics at any level," Atkins said. "But she's also the type of person who would have supported any ambition he had. That was part of her strength."

According to Atkins, Kathleen's concerns were never far from the Big Blue Machine's calculations. Its members always wanted to make sure she was consulted and onside with their thinking. They knew Davis drew strength from reconnecting with his family on a daily basis.

"He didn't convey the impression that he had a lot of energy, but he was a very energetic politician," Atkins said. "There were days it must have been difficult for him to get out of bed, but he did."

In May, Eddie Goodman convened a meeting of some of the premier's most trusted advisers at Davis's home. Hugh Segal, Norman Atkins, Hugh Macaulay, Bill Kelly, Ed Stewart, John Tory, Goodman himself, and Davis, of course, were all there. Goodman showed up early to get a jump on the others who were much more anxious to see Davis run. Atkins was the most hawkish of them all. Goodman told the premier that he had been to every Tory leadership convention both federally and provincially since 1938, except for 1942 when he was overseas fighting in the Second World War. He said he knew the federal scene extremely well and here were the facts: (1) the federal caucus was a snake pit and far more right wing than Davis's Ontario caucus; (2) you won't enjoy being leader of the opposition;

and (3) Ed Stewart won't go with you to Ottawa and the rapport you would have with your staff won't be anything like it is at Queen's Park. Goodman capped it all off by brandishing the results of a poll showing the premier couldn't win the convention — he'd waited too long to get organized. Even Atkins had to acknowledge that.

"Billy Davis was a very cautious individual," Atkins said. "He never liked to make a decision that he didn't have to make, especially when it came to his own personal future."

When the others arrived, Goodman took Segal and Atkins aside and showed them the poll of convention delegates. The numbers showed Davis in a competitive position, but they were hardly robust. Atkins was ticked off that Goodman had commissioned the poll without his knowledge, since Atkins would have preferred to ask the questions himself, potentially delivering more hopeful results. Goodman said, "I know that you two guys both love the premier. How can you do this to him?" John Tory also had some polling numbers, courtesy of the Mulroney campaign, that suggested Davis's chances weren't good.

As Goodman left the meeting, he said to Stewart: "Ed, he has decided not to run. Don't you let those bastards change his mind."

And so Bill Davis made his excruciating decision. He called his premier's office staff together and announced to everyone that the answer was no. Mike O'Neill, Davis's executive assistant since 1980, was there. "He told us we were a family here in this office," O'Neill recalls the premier saying. "Then he said we were going to continue to go forward together as a family. And he thanked everyone for their support."

Hugh Segal understood the decision. But there's no getting away from the fact that it saddened him. And three decades of hindsight don't appear to have taken the edge off Segal's disappointment — for him, for Davis, and for the country.

"He would have been the finest prime minister since Sir John A.," Segal says today. "What we had when he was premier was outstanding and compelling. What we lost when he demurred was unfathomable."

Norman Atkins was similarly crestfallen. During an interview on CBC-TV with Barbara Frum airing the night Davis announced he was standing down, Atkins looked as if he was close to losing it. Sally Barnes thought it was the right decision. As much as it pained Davis to have to disappoint Segal and Atkins, Barnes was adamant that "anybody from small-town Ontario, who was a unilingual anglophone, was not going to lead a national political party in the 1980s. If he really wanted to do this, he should have worked on his French, which he never did, because he didn't like to do anything he wasn't good at."

According to Segal in his book *The Right Balance*, Brian Mulroney was the most significant beneficiary of Davis's staying out of the race. Much of Davis's support went to Mulroney, in part because Mulroney welcomed Davis's possible candidacy by calling the premier "a national voice for a strong Canada." Conversely, Clark's "regional candidate" insult came back to haunt him, since the former prime minister picked up little of Davis's support base. Segal wrote that Davis's supporters "did not forget where civility had emerged and where condescension had resided."

Mulroney told L. Ian MacDonald for *Mulroney: The Making of the Prime Minister* that he never thought Davis would actually enter the race, but had he done so he'd have entered the race as the front-runner and might have won. "What Bill Davis could not do is run and lose after such a glorious career," Mulroney told me in 2015. "And there was no guarantee he would win."

Sally Barnes agrees, saying: "I loved the man too much to have him be remembered as a loser."

And John Tory adds: "I thought the worst tragedy for him would be for his political career to end with a loss."

Bill Davis attended the convention as a delegate, not as a candidate, and wouldn't publicly say who he was supporting. I remember covering that convention as a 22-year-old cub reporter for CHFI Radio in Toronto. As I saw Premier Davis enter the hall of the Ottawa Civic Centre, I somehow was the only reporter near him and therefore thrust my microphone in his face in the hope of getting a little exclusive. I asked Davis who he was supporting. He gave a classic, Pablum-like answer: "I'm supportive of all the candidates from Ontario." The premier meant Michael Wilson and David Crombie and thought he was cleverly avoiding my question with this non-answer. But I followed up.

There was actually another candidate from Ontario in the race — MP John Gamble from Markham, whom the Davisites saw as a right-wing fringe candidate. "Does that mean you're supporting John Gamble, too?"

I asked. For the first and perhaps only time I've ever seen it, Davis looked like a deer caught in the headlights. He was trying so hard not to make news, but he couldn't possibly say with a straight face that, yes, he was supportive of Gamble, too. So he did the next best thing. He pretended to see someone over my shoulder he wanted to talk to, took a puff from his pipe, and moved away. My exclusive interview was apparently over.

More than three decades later Davis now confesses the candidate he enjoyed most in that contest was John Crosbie, who was endlessly entertaining. But he says he voted for Brian Mulroney partly because his sister, Molly, was working for the boy from Baie Comeau's campaign and partly because Mulroney actively solicited Davis's support in a way the Clark campaign didn't. Mulroney called Davis asking for advice; the Mulroneys and Davises saw each other socially both at party functions in Ontario and while on holidays in Florida. Compared to the slighting some Queen's Parkers felt at the hands of Joe Clark and his team, this was a welcomed change.

"He had to be discreet about his support and he knew that and we knew that," Mulroney says. "He couldn't be seen with a Brian Mulroney button on, that's for sure."

Bill Davis hasn't talked much over the years about his decision not to seek the federal leadership, perhaps because it remains a bit of a sore point. As much as he claims he never thought *that* seriously about running for the federal leader's job, some feel Davis still carries a tinge of regret for that road not taken. Davis doesn't go too far down the road of what ifs except to say, "Listen, this is only speculation: If I'd have been fluent in French, I might've had a different point of view. I *might* have."

Speaking today from his law offices on University Avenue in downtown Toronto, Bob Rae, Ontario's 21st premier, goes a little further: "My sense was he wanted to run for the national leadership but came to the realization that he probably couldn't win, and even if he won, it would probably be very divisive and difficult. I think he was very disappointed that that's what happened." However, Rae says Davis made the right decision not to contest the federal leadership. "Regretfully, in many respects, because I think he had a great many qualities as a political leader and they grew over time."

Ernie Eves says he always wishes Davis had gone for the federal job: "I just think that he was a totally classy, decent individual who would do the right thing for the country, regardless of where he was from."

In the end, Brian Mulroney won a thrilling four-ballot contest over Joe Clark. Clark led on every ballot except the one that mattered. Back at Queen's Park, there was a noticeable change in the air. Hugh Segal had remarked that after the constitutional breakthrough he saw some of the wind come out of Davis's sails. If that was true then, it was even more abundantly clear after the national PC leadership convention. The premier didn't seem to have as much bounce in his step. Even some of his allies noticed that the combination of having a majority government back, constitutional renewal achieved, and having taken a pass on the national PC Party leadership, things felt just a little bit less focused. Davis would later acknowledge that the summer of 1983 was the first time he started thinking about when he should be making his exit from politics.

But before stepping aside, the premier of Ontario still had one more big decision to unveil. And it was a complete shocker.

19

CATHOLICS

The year 1984 started with a bit of a political shocker. After perhaps the most famous walk in the snow in Canada's history, Pierre Trudeau announced on February 29 that he would step down as prime minister — for good this time. At 15 years and 164 days he would retire as Canada's third-longest-serving prime minister and take with him the satisfaction that his dream of a patriated Constitution with a Charter of Rights and Freedoms had come true.

In Quebec there was shock of a different kind as a disturbed former Canadian Forces corporal named Denis Lortie stormed the Quebec National Assembly, then shot and killed three government employees while wounding 13 others.

At Queen's Park things seemed to muddle along. Bill Davis's personal popularity remained high, there were no egregious scandals weighing the government down, and it was very much a steady-as-she-goes time in Ontario politics. Members of the press gallery could be overheard complaining that things were too quiet, too boring. Some years earlier, when asked by *Globe and Mail* columnist Hugh Winsor why he ran such a boring, bland government, Davis memorably answered: "Bland works." He reminded the gallery it wasn't his job to entertain them; it was his duty to run the affairs of the province in the most effective way he knew. And more often than not, that meant "not getting into trouble for the speeches you *don't* give or the decisions you *don't* make," as his mentor Tom Kennedy occasionally reminded him. Some joked — hell, it was his own executive assistant, Clare Westcott, who said it — that Davis had taken procrastination and raised it to both an art form and a governing philosophy. The joke was: "Never put off until tomorrow what you can avoid doing altogether." Westcott even got his boss a desk ruler inscribed with: "Maybe ... and that's final." But it was surely a winning combination at this moment in Ontario history.

There was one minor controversy at Queen's Park that caught people's attention. In May 1983, one month before the federal Tories crowned Brian Mulroney as their new leader, Ontario Industry Minister Gordon Walker published a book entitled *A Conservative Canada*. Many of Davis's people at Queen's Park interpreted the book as a too nakedly ambitious play for the premier's job and wanted Walker cut down to size. In Walker's defence, he worked on the book when it appeared Davis might be moving on to federal politics and was clearly trying to establish himself as a potential successor. But Davis stayed, and now Walker was far more exposed than any of his fellow ministers, many of whom were also considering provincial leadership bids.

"He wasn't thrilled with that," Walker now acknowledges.

So, in July 1983, Davis called Walker up to his home in Brampton and told him he was being shuffled from the high-profile, important industry portfolio back to his provincial secretary for justice job. Davis told Walker: "I'm not doing this for any reason related to the ministry you had been running." The message was pretty obvious. Walker traded in a ministry with hundreds of employees for one with eight.

"My demotion was a message sent across the airwaves to Larry Grossman, Dennis Timbrell, and Frank Miller," Walker says, referring to other would-be leadership contenders. "Napoleon used to shoot the odd general to keep the others in line, and everyone got the message. He had to take charge of the party again."

And take charge he did. Bill Davis then did something completely out of character that shocked the province's political establishment to its core. He made a decision of historic proportions that more than three decades later is still so controversial that we're still debating it and there is still no consensus on whether he got it right.

To understand the significance of this decision, you have to go back to Canada's very founding as a country in 1867. The grand bargain that enabled the Fathers of Confederation to create Canada included not just minority language rights but minority education rights, as well. It meant that the Protestant minority in Lower Canada (Quebec) would have a publicly funded school system for its children, just as the Roman Catholic minority in Upper Canada (Ontario) would have one for its children. Quebec interpreted its constitutional obligations by funding the "Protestant" school system to the end of high school. Ontario, however, did not.

Ontario took a more literal interpretation of its obligation to fund "common schools" and initially only supported its Catholic schools to the end of Grade 8. In 1964 the Robarts government levelled the funding playing field between the public and Catholic systems by bringing in the Foundation Tax Plan. It also added funding for two more years to the end of Grade 10. And there the funding stayed. There was a young high school student in Richmond Hill, Ontario, in the mid-1960s named Kathleen Wynne who recalls all too well the "bizarre, arbitrary situation" in which public funding to the separate system was cut off at Grade 10. It meant when she started Grade 11 in her local public school there was a significant influx of kids from the local Catholic school system into her school because their parents couldn't afford to pay the tuition to keep their children in the separate school system for the rest of high school.

In Windsor, Ontario, a high school student named Eleanor McMahon had a difficult decision to make. She was attending Assumption College Catholic High School, then one of the largest secondary schools in Canada with 3,000 students. She was told in no uncertain terms by her father, Hugh, that if she wanted to continue at the school through to the end of Grade 13, she'd have to come up with the annual tuition herself. Eleanor was one of seven McMahon children whose father worked at Chrysler. The notion that she'd have to pay her own high school tuition had as much to do with money being tight as it had to do with her parents' desire to inculcate in her a sense of ownership and responsibility for her own education. As a result, from age 15 on, Eleanor got a job as a waitress, sometimes working 30-hour weekends to raise the money required to pay for her tuition.

"Kids today don't get it," she says. "But back then there was a different appreciation of the sacrifices we'd have to make to go to school."

Elie Martel was a rookie MPP from the riding of Sudbury East in 1971. One day in September of that year his wife called to tell him that

Premier Davis had just announced the status quo would remain and there would be no additional funding for Catholic schools. Martel's first reaction was that Davis planned to call the election within a week. He was prophetic. Five days later Davis did just that.

"I'm convinced Bill Davis always believed Catholics had the right to a separate school system," Martel said 20 years after fighting that 1971 election. "He knew better. But his aspirations were greater than what he felt he could deliver."

The journalist Claire Hoy puts it less delicately: "Davis caught them with their pants down," he told George Hutchison in those taped interviews in the early 1990s. Hoy said every time Catholics staged a protest on the education funding issue the PC vote went up. He even alleges the Tories organized some of those pro-Catholic education demonstrations themselves, knowing they would firm up the vote in the Tory heartland, while the Liberals and New Democrats split the pro-Catholic vote. And there actually were some Catholics who opposed full funding of their system to the end of high school, fearing they'd lose control of both the curriculum and the right to favour Catholic teachers when hiring. It was tough, brass-knuckles politics, and as we saw, the PCs increased the size of their majority government in 1971 in part because of Davis's stand on that issue. But the way Davis won that election never completely sat well with him. He isn't about to admit it all these years later, but those closest to him believe it to be so.

One of Davis's most intriguing relationships over the years was with a man who never had to get elected, but he was as crafty and wily as any politician out there. G. Emmett Carter eventually became a cardinal, but he started as a simple ordained priest in Montreal in 1937. It was never his intention to become an expert in the field of education, but as he would know better than most, man plans and God laughs. Carter was named an "ecclesiastical inspector" for the Roman Catholic schools in Montreal, which required him to visit schools, survey everything that was happening, and come up with some policies to improve Catholic education in Quebec. He warned his archbishop he had no formal training in education. "Go, my son, you'll learn" was the reply.

And so he did. Carter earned his bachelor of arts at the University of Montreal, eventually working his way up to a Ph.D. in education by 1947. He created an English section of the Jacques Cartier Normal School, hired the teachers, and ran it so well that it eventually became its own school and was absorbed by McGill University as part of its Faculty of Education.

In 1962 Carter was transferred to London, Ontario — the home-town of the premier of Ontario — where he became an auxiliary bishop. He quickly came to realize how dissimilar the Quebec and Ontario situ-ations were for Catholic education. "The minority had everything they wanted in Quebec," he said. "We didn't have nearly as much in Ontario. Ontario wasn't even-handed. It wasn't as generous as Quebec Roman Catholic authorities were to Protestants there." Carter, having been the de facto minister of education in Quebec, delivered that message to the *actual* minister of education in Ontario, Bill Davis. He would remind Davis that in 1945 Premier George Drew struck the Hope Commission to study the issue of Catholic school funding. The commission came back with a recommendation to fund Catholic schools only to the end of grade 6 and close down one French-language school in Ottawa. Leslie Frost, who succeeded Drew, rejected the commission's recommenda-tions. "It didn't go through," Carter recalled, "but the comparison was very invidious. Ontario looked bad in comparison."

Carter befriended Premier Robarts, who then improved the fund-ing for Catholic schools. "He gave us a chance to survive," Carter said. Robarts and Davis recognized there might be political trouble redirecting corporate tax revenue to the Catholic system, since it had exclusively gone to the public system. So they created the Foundation Tax Plan, "which was a clever political ploy," Carter recalls. "It wasn't equality, but it was enough to keep us afloat. It was a life-saving operation." Ironically, some of the harshest criticism of the plan came from the public school boards, which were upset that the Catholic boards' grants were increasing more quickly than theirs were. But that was the whole point. The Catholics were far behind and needed to catch up, and this plan came up with a mechanism for doing that. The Liberals and New Democrats supported it, but Robarts had some difficulty bringing his backbenchers along.

Interestingly enough, the one party in Canada that was perhaps the *least* interested in God and religion was the one party leading the way on fully funding the Catholic school system. Ever since the early 1950s, the NDP (and the CCF, its predecessor) championed the issue, believ-ing in equality of educational opportunity for all, regardless of race or religion. "If you start from that premise that the Constitution guarantees the right to send kids to separate schools, then you have no alternative but to eliminate these differentials," said Donald C. MacDonald, leader of the Ontario CCF and NDP for 17 years.

During the 1971 election, Carter opposed the demonstrations seeking more money for Catholic schools from Davis. "I tried to go against them," he said. "I argued vehemently to the bishops to stay out of it." They didn't, and Davis cruised to a majority. But Carter never gave up. The bishops met with Premier Davis every year thereafter, continuing to make their case for funding the Catholic system to the end of high school. Davis would listen, smile, tease the bishops a bit, but would never make a commitment. Carter reminded Davis that Ontario's demographics were changing and Catholic immigration was skyrocketing. Davis could see it himself as the Portuguese, Italian, and Filipino communities in Brampton began to grow. One day, while he was mowing his lawn at his home on Main Street, a group of separate school elementary students stopped to talk with him. One student asked him, "Premier, why is it if kids graduate from Grade 10 and want to go to Brampton High School for Grade 11, they don't have to pay anything, but if they want to go to Cardinal Leger for Grade 11, they do?" It was a watershed moment for Bill Davis because perhaps for the first time in his life he was stuck for an answer. He could have given a dreary historical recitation of how he saw the Ontario government's rights and responsibilities toward Catholic students. But that explanation felt less and less relevant in the Ontario of 1984.

Throughout his premiership, Davis and Dr. Bette Stephenson, his minister of education for six and a half years, held occasional yet regular meetings individually with the heads of the Catholic, Anglican, and United Churches. Once, they met with all three church leaders together to discuss the advisability of extending further public funding to the separate school system. The meetings would take place in the premier's office or in the cabinet office next door in the main legislative building. Davis, of course, had been on the record since 1971 as opposing further funding for Catholic schools. His education minister's position was even tougher.

"I did not think there should be separate schools *at all*," Dr. Stephenson told me in 2015 at a get-together at her home in Newmarket. "I thought there should be one public system, which met the needs of all kids." When she told that to Cardinal Carter, he pushed back, explaining how the separate school's education system was imbued with a distinctive "Catholicity." Dr. Stephenson, who was 90 years old and in failing health when we met hasn't lost an ounce of the pugnaciousness for which she was so well known during her days in government. *She* laughs about Carter's use of the word *Catholicity*. "He never ever explained that to me. I've been asking Roman Catholics ever since what that means."

Over the years, Carter continued to press his case and Stephenson continued to resist it. He would talk about the grand bargain between Protestants and Catholics in 1867. She would remind him it was now more than a century later and things had changed. Neither side appeared to be making any progress in convincing the other of the rightness of his or her position. But as was so often the case in the Davis government, getting to a hard and fast decision wasn't necessarily always the goal — however, keeping the lines of communication open and civil often was, and certainly was in this case. Despite their clear differences on the need for Catholic schools, Dr. Stephenson and Cardinal Carter actually got on famously. One year she even made him a homemade Christmas pudding. Carter jokingly told the minister that should remain their secret because apparently Dr. Stephenson's Christmas puddings were better than the ones Carter usually got from his own sister.

Because he had previously been the minister of education, Bill Davis had had a long time to think about how to fund the Catholic school system. In fact, when I asked him in 2015 when he started thinking about fully funding that system, he said: "I was thinking about it from 1962 onward. There wasn't a more fundamental issue that had been part of our political history more so than that issue."

That answer suggests Bill Davis didn't outright oppose fully funding Catholic schools, as much as he was preoccupied with the timing — when could he bring in full funding so the public might be more inclined to accept it? Clearly, the answer wasn't before an election campaign in 1971. But as the 1970s gave way to the 1980s and Davis began to think much more seriously about his educational legacy, this one unresolved issue apparently troubled him more and more. He could look with pride at consolidating school boards, implementing the Foundation Tax Plan, funding Catholic schools to the end of Grade 10, creating the community college system and five universities, putting the provincial broadcaster TVOntario on the air, creating OISE, and treating teachers more as professionals. But fully funding separate schools was unfinished business.

While it was surely easier to implement full funding in 1984 than it would have been in 1971, Davis wasn't kidding himself about getting a free ride on it. He knew some members of the Tory base would think he'd taken leave of his senses. Bette Stephenson, his own education minister, opposed the move. So did his secretary to the cabinet, Ed Stewart, whose days with Davis went all the way back to the early 1960s when he was Davis's deputy minister of education. Stewart told the premier: "Our major obligation is to strengthen and improve the public school system. This will weaken it."

But Davis hoped they'd understand that the time had come to complete what previous PC governments had already contributed so much to, namely, putting the Roman Catholic school system on a more equal footing with the public school system. He couldn't abide the notion that almost half the children in Ontario might get an inferior education. This was an intensely hard issue for the premier and his closest confidants. Eddie Goodman says in his memoirs that it was at this point that Davis simply opted not to discuss the issue with him or Ed Stewart any longer. He knew their views, and they weren't going to change his.

In the spring of 1984, Davis met with Harry Fisher, the deputy minister of education, and simply said, "I think I want to do it." Fisher didn't need to ask what "it" was. The deputy began to put the wheels in motion, which would lead to a bill that would publicly fund the Catholic school system. Still left unsaid was the timing of the matter.

Davis met on a few occasions at the Park Plaza Hotel with senior bishops of the Catholic Church and hammered out an agreement that would be the basis for the bill that would eventually be presented to the legislature. He insisted on protection for public schoolteachers who could be rendered redundant if their Catholic students participated in an exodus from the public to the separate school system. He got a commitment from the bishops that the Catholic system would hire those teachers, regardless of their religion. He also secured a commitment to allow non-Catholic students to attend separate schools.

In the first week of June, Davis went to Cardinal Carter's home for lunch, during which time he told the cardinal he was in the process of "cleaning up my house." Left unsaid, but presumably implied, was the notion that the house was being cleaned up before the occupant planned to move out of it. It seems a good bet that Davis knew — or at least had a pretty strong sense — that he wouldn't be running for re-election the following year and therefore this was an important swan song for his career and, of course, for the province.

The premier took a piece of paper out of his jacket pocket and said to Cardinal Carter, "I am going to present this to the House." It was that other issue John Robarts had left him: the Bishop's Brief. Davis revealed he was going to announce perhaps the biggest *volte-face* in Ontario history. He was not only going to go further in funding Catholic schools than any previous government in 117 years of Confederation but he was also going to repudiate his own position on the issue that had helped him win an election 13 years earlier.

"I lived in fear for a week that it was going to leak," Carter confessed. He didn't want any unanticipated developments to delay or force Davis to cancel his plans. However, this was no slam dunk for the cardinal. Davis had a list of "asks" he wanted from Carter such as a commitment to consider non-Catholics for teaching positions and the possible inclusion of non-Catholic students in the system. Carter, as much a politician as Davis, had his own channels to answer to, and he agreed to recommend those wishes to the trustees and bishops on the church's education committee.

The two men then talked optics. Carter asked Davis whether he should be in the legislature when the premier made the announcement. "No," Davis said. "That would be the worst thing possible." Carter was told to stay away. The premier clearly knew what he was about to announce was going to shake up Ontario politics for a long time to come.

It was not only the substance of Davis's announcement that was sure to be historic, but it was also the way he did it that added to the controversy. While the issue of fully funding the separate school system had been a subject of ongoing debate in the Tory caucus for years, there was never any indication that the topic was coming to a head. But on June 12, 1984, come to a head it did.

Coincidentally, June 12 was Bette Stephenson's wedding anniversary. This would be an anniversary she'd never forget. She arrived at Queen's Park in the morning to be told by Harry Fisher, her deputy minister, that the premier was going to make an announcement she might not like. Yes, you read that correctly: the minister of education knew nothing about that day's historic announcement, but her deputy minister did and was sworn to secrecy by the premier's office. That didn't do much for Stephenson's political blood pressure, which often rocketed into the red zone without much provocation.

The education minister had a pretty good idea what her premier was going to announce. Just the week before she and the premier and the cardinal had a considerably more passionate meeting about the matter. Stephenson left the meeting wondering whether Davis feared he wasn't going to get into heaven if he didn't do something about Catholic school funding.

Premier Davis's Day-timer on Tuesday, June 12, 1984 — typed out by his appointments secretary — indicates the day started with an 8:30 a.m. breakfast meeting with cabinet ministers Frank Miller and Dennis Timbrell. That was followed by a caucus meeting at 10:00 a.m. At 11:30 a.m. there is simply a "Hold" notation for half an hour. Then a noon meeting scheduled with Attorney General Roy McMurtry was scratched out in pen and replaced with the handwritten words: "12–2:00 Spec. Cabinet Mtg." It was at that meeting that Davis informed his ministers he would deliver a speech in the legislature at two o'clock in the afternoon, committing the government to providing full public funding for Catholic high schools right to the end of Grade 13.

For a decision of such magnitude, it's remarkable how many members of that cabinet I've spoken to who don't have a firm recollection of how the announcement went down. Dennis Timbrell, the minister of agriculture, simply recalls Davis informing everyone of the change in policy "in his usual calm way" and doesn't remember much else about the morning other than that Davis wasn't inviting a debate on the matter. "Still, he was very polite and respectful," Timbrell recalls.

Bette Stephenson's recollection was that a third of the cabinet was enthusiastically in favour of the change, a third was violently opposed to it, and a final third thought the issue wasn't all that important one way or another. The provincial secretary for justice, Gordon Walker, was a big supporter of the announcement. He was a long-time friend of G. Emmett Carter's and, in fact, went to Rome to see him installed as a cardinal. Thomas Wells, the former education minister from 1972 to 1978, was onside. Larry Grossman apparently loved the idea because he thought it would inevitably lead to public funding for Jewish parochial schools, an issue of importance to many of his constituents. But Transportation Minister Jim Snow growled under his breath, although he didn't say anything. Two ministers named Frank — Miller and Drea — both uttered a clearly audible "Oh, no!" and Drea was Catholic.

Despite the momentous decision, there was almost no discussion in the cabinet at all. In fact, there were only three questions asked by ministers. Norm Sterling, the provincial secretary for resource development, asked the first two. Sterling wondered whether non-Catholic students would have equal access to the separate system now that it was getting full public funding. The answer was no. Then he asked whether non-Catholic teachers would have equal access to teaching jobs in the separate system. Again, the answer was no. Another minister wondered how much the change in policy would cost. Cabinet Secretary Ed Stewart answered: "About an extra $50 million."

"When I heard the word *about* and such a small number following, I knew there hadn't been a sophisticated analysis done of it," recalls Sterling, who told the premier: "I object to this and I want my objection noted in the minutes of this cabinet meeting." What was the reaction in the room to Sterling's opposition? "You could hear a pin drop," he told me in early 2016.

After the cabinet meeting, the premier gathered the entire PC caucus together to bring everyone else into the tent. Ernie Eves, the future premier, was the parliamentary assistant to Bette Stephenson. Like his minister, Eves got no advance heads-up that the separate school funding announcement was in the works. As Eves remembers it, he says probably more than half the caucus supported the decision, including the member for Parry Sound himself. But like Timbrell, Eves doesn't remember the meeting with any particular clarity. There was no caucus revolt. Members took the news in stride. But Eves does recall one thing: "I remember that Bette was very upset. There's no doubt about that," he says. Then he offers a rare criticism of Davis, a man he admires immensely: "I guess I don't blame her in a way. She was the minister of education and you might want to have talked to her about it!"

More than 30 years later it's interesting what Bill Davis remembers about that day: some pride at resolving an issue that had been around for more than a century, and enjoying the irony of being told his government was on cruise control. "So the last big thing that's been part of history from day one in Ontario I dealt with and made the statement in June 1984," he told me in 2015. "So, if the wind went out of my sails in 1983, they went back in again in a hurry, because if you think that was easy, it was not."

The daily events in the Ontario legislature are technically called "routine proceedings," but there was nothing routine about what transpired that afternoon. The premier bumped into Bob Rae, the NDP leader, at some point earlier in the day. He certainly gave no indication it was about to be a historic day but did say to Rae: "Robert I hope you'll be in the House [later], and I don't think you'll be disappointed." Incidentally, Rae heard the thunderous chant of "Premier Bob" on election night in 1990, but for some reason Davis has always called him "Robert" and is the only Canadian out of the millions who know Rae who does.

With the announcement scheduled for 2:00 p.m., Davis instructed John Tory to telephone opposition leaders David Peterson and Bob Rae to ensure they'd be present in the legislature for the announcement, which Tory did at 1:45 p.m., giving no other details. Minutes to go before one of the most significant announcements he'd ever make the premier confessed to his principal secretary: "You know, this is going to be very difficult." While Davis did think he was about to right a historic wrong, he also knew his province intimately and was well aware of what forces he was about to unleash.

Tory disagreed with his leader and told him the safeguards that he personally negotiated with the bishops ought to ensure smoother sailing. But despite growing up in the Toronto of the 1950s and 1960s, Tory somehow managed to avoid any exposure to anti-Catholic bigotry. "I'd never heard anyone say anything negative about Catholics ever," he confesses. But Davis knew the age-old divisions that were about to erupt.

At the appointed time Davis rose in the legislature when ministers of the Crown traditionally make statements indicating a change of government policy. Few members in the assembly knew what was coming. The premier started innocuously enough: "Mr. Speaker, I wish to inform members of the legislature that the government has undertaken a careful and fresh review of the outstanding issues surrounding public support for the Roman Catholic school system, and this afternoon I wish to outline a new course we have decided to pursue."

The premier then took several minutes to go through the history of this most fractious file. Members of the legislature no doubt were wondering where this was headed. Davis teased his audience some more: "While men and women of courage and conviction have been divided on this issue, up to now no Ontario government has felt it was able to discharge its duty according to these fundamental principles while at the same time granting public funds to a complete Roman Catholic secondary school system. I now believe this can be responsibly undertaken and therefore it is our obligation to resolve the issue."

Resolve the issue? What did that mean? Members of the legislature leaned in to try to understand what exactly Davis was saying. Again, after some more details and talk of "serving the spirit of 1867," the premier finally spilled the beans: "It is, therefore, the government's intention to permit the Roman Catholic school boards to establish a full range of elementary and secondary education and, as a part of the public system, to be funded accordingly. This new program will be introduced at the rate of one year of secondary education for each school year, beginning September 1, 1985."

The premier then went into chapter and verse to explain how full funding of the separate system would be accomplished. He intended to strike an implementation commission that would tackle all the thorny issues his decision would surely provoke: how to handle the transfer of some public schools to the Catholic system, how to treat non-Catholic teachers who wanted jobs in the separate system, and so on.

But Davis wasn't done. Given that the Catholic schools would now receive additional funding, the premier also announced he would strike another commission to study whether *independent* schools ought to have access to public funds, as well, and under what conditions. He wanted those recommendations completed within a year and a half.

As he came to the end of perhaps the most unanticipated speech of his political career, Davis channelled the views of Canada's first prime minister: "As Sir John A. Macdonald explained the accommodations of his time to the majority over a century ago: 'We do not want to stand on the extreme limits of our rights. We are ready to give and take. We can afford to be just, we can afford to be generous, because we are strong.'" The premier added he didn't pretend this was the last word on the matter. He hoped his decision would add to the common interest in the province and concluded by saying: "It is time to put behind us any lingering doubts about our regard to one another and to rededicate ourselves to the bright hopes of our future." And with that he sat down as (almost) the entire legislature gave him a strong ovation.

However, what I also distinctly remember from Davis's announcement were the expressions on the faces of his front-bench ministers as he was speaking. Roy McMurtry, Larry Grossman, Tom Wells, Bette Stephenson, and Frank Miller all sat relatively stone-faced as their premier was about to change history. The speech wasn't interrupted by wild applause at an injustice finally being righted, or any table thumping indicating deeply felt approval at the government's action. But no one sat on their hands, either. There was polite applause at various times and that was that. It was surely an underwhelming reaction given the importance of the decision.

The opposition leaders were then given a chance to respond. David Peterson admitted his party was given a heads-up about a major announcement coming down the pipe, but "I must confess we thought it would be about the [Sky]Dome and not about so significant an issue in the history of this province." The Liberal leader then added: "I am proud today to identify myself and my colleagues with the statement of the premier on this major advance in position. I am not one of those who is going to ask why. I am only going to say 'hurrah.' It is long overdue." Peterson couldn't resist a little jab as he congratulated the government "on its Road-to-Damascus conversion." But he quickly added that the Liberals would assist in any way to implement the policy as expeditiously as possible.

Speaking for the NDP, Bob Rae pointed out that congratulations were also in order for the many members of all parties who over the years risked unpopularity by championing this cause. While supporting the decision, he was also prescient in forecasting the road ahead: "It is going to take a great deal of goodwill, it is going to take a great deal of give and take, and it is going to take a great deal of understanding to make this policy work." That would turn out to be more than prophetic. Still, at the risk of being seen to be a downer, Rae added: "The time was right. We are delighted that this move has been made. Equality has made an important advance in Ontario today." He then finished with some words in French about how proud he was that the government had struck a chord for improving minority rights.

After Davis's historic speech and then the opposition's Question Period, Bette Stephenson approached her premier with a stunning question. "Do you want me to resign?" The premier assured her he didn't.

Stephenson thought about resigning, anyway. "But there were so many other things going on besides that, that I felt I'd better stick around and look after some of them," she told me in 2015. So despite the fact that the minister of education was going to be in charge of implementing a policy she deeply opposed, Stephenson stayed. It's also worth noting that in any other government such a confrontation could have lasted a lot longer and become a lot uglier. It didn't between Davis and Stephenson because she had to acknowledge at the end of the day that the decision was the premier's prerogative, that he had been education minister longer than she'd had the portfolio, so he knew the issues cold. And besides all that, she said, "He'd always been so kind to me." The fact was that it was extremely hard to get angry with Premier William Davis.

Norm Sterling also thought about resigning, but like Dr. Stephenson, opted to stay in the cabinet. There were two issues he had been carrying for a couple of years — a new information and privacy law and the implementation of a Niagara Escarpment plan — that he wanted to see through to completion, and he feared if he resigned, all that work would go down the drain. So Sterling stayed on, and Davis never asked for his resignation, although the premier did toss a few taunts Sterling's way during future cabinet meetings.

"I told Norman that if this was a fundamental matter of conscience for him, I'd accept his resignation," Davis remembers today. "I haven't had that letter yet."

While there were several Tories who opposed the way Davis made the full-funding announcement, there were also plenty of people on the opposition benches on that June day who in hindsight quite liked it. Dave Cooke, the MPP for Windsor-Riverside and a future NDP education minister, thought Davis had no choice but to do it the way he did. "The issue was pretty black and white at that point," Cooke told me in 2015. "You either do it or you don't do it. So why not drop the bomb?" Cooke figured the issue was going to be controversial one way or another, so just get it done.

Ernie Eves agrees: "The premier and his people would know that if they'd had an open discussion in caucus, it'd be all over the media and that would be the end of that probably."

Floyd Laughren, the former MPP for Nickel Belt and future NDP finance minister, also agrees: "Right or wrong, it was the smart way to do it," he says.

However, Cooke adds this caveat: "He might've tried to talk to Bette ahead of time!"

In Windsor, after Hugh McMahon heard the news, Eleanor, his daughter, says: "He was overjoyed. My dad was a Liberal, but he was thrilled in his heart that Bill Davis did this." (Hugh McMahon obviously passed down his politics to his daughter. Today Eleanor McMahon is the Liberal MPP for Burlington — the first Liberal member in that riding in more than seven decades — and in the spring of 2016 she was appointed the minister of tourism, culture, and sport.)

In Queen's Park circles a kind of cottage industry has developed over the years to try to understand why Bill Davis changed his mind. In his book on Premier Davis from three decades ago, journalist Claire Hoy posits the following theory. The story goes that after the 1981 election in which Davis recaptured his majority government he told Cardinal Carter that some time during that mandate he would announce full funding for Catholic schools. But as time marched on, Davis allegedly wanted to go back on his commitment. Hoy then says Carter was so irate that he threatened to denounce the government from every pulpit in the province in the ensuing election campaign. Hoy didn't reveal who his source was for that version of history in the book, nor would he tell me 30 years later who it was. One thing we do know: the two men at the centre of that story have both vehemently denied Hoy's version of events. Cardinal Carter says he almost sued Hoy over the matter, so offended was he by the whole thing.

"My approaches with Bill Davis were totally amicable," the cardinal insisted right up to his death in 2003. "At no time would I even think of threatening the premier of Ontario, and I certainly didn't threaten Bill Davis. That's just plain baloney." In fact, if you look at Carter's modus operandi over the years, his approach was always to befriend the people in power. "My philosophy was honey, not vinegar" was how he put it. Actually, Carter's snuggling up to those in power once got him in hot water with the Liberal opposition at Queen's Park.

In December 1979 at a gala dinner for 1,000 Catholics to celebrate his elevation to cardinal, Carter paid tribute to "men like Leslie Frost, John Robarts, and our present premier for their openness to the consideration of our needs." That, plus the placement of only Tories at the head table, sent Liberal politicians at the event into a frenzy.

Bob Nixon, a United Church member, called it "the most uncomfortable evening of my political life." London North MPP Ron Van Horne, a Catholic, was so ticked off that he put his complaints in a letter to the cardinal, then sent it to the newspapers, as well. He expressed his "absolute dismay and concern about your words of praise and commendation for a Conservative government which steadfastly refuses to extend support to Grades 11 to 13 of the separate school system." Renfrew North MPP Sean Conway, another Liberal and a Catholic, suggested "to say what he said in front of people like Bob Nixon, who stuck their heads on the block for Catholic schools, was completely unacceptable and insulting." Even the former bishop of Hamilton, Joseph Ryan, got in on criticizing the new cardinal. He wondered why Catholics are supposed to praise Davis "because he decided before an election for political reasons not to extend aid to our Catholic high schools." The Liberals wondered why Carter always seemed to suck up to the governing party so much when it was the opposition that was promising full funding, not the Tories.

For his part, Carter said he simply wanted to give credit where it was due, that Robarts and Davis did significantly help the separate schools in the 1960s and had kept the channels of communication open throughout the 1970s. Not only that, he said it was "unthinkable" 20 years ago for the premier of Ontario to mount a dinner in honour of the head of the Catholic Church in Canada and he wanted to show his appreciation.

Naturally, the Tory view on this issue was considerably different from the Liberals'. According to the Tory narrative, Premiers Drew, Robarts, and Davis had all helped the Catholic school system over the years, and according to Eddie Goodman, "received little thanks from the Catholic hierarchy and their flock who keep voting Liberal in large numbers."

Meanwhile, Carter's explanation, not surprisingly, mirrors Davis's. "I think he was less influenced by political considerations and more by the statesmanlike thing to do," Carter told George Hutchison 25 years ago. "It was a sense of fairness. I give him full credit for it." Some in the church, Carter confesses, wanted a fight with the government. "I wanted to be friends," he said. "This was a triumph of good fellowship and good citizenship."

As seems to be his nature, Claire Hoy continues to offer a more cynical interpretation to events. He notes one of Davis's favourite pollsters, Allan Gregg, made presentations replete with charts and graphs, indicating the demographic changes afoot in the province. The old PC base was shrinking and the new immigrants were mostly Catholic. Hoy says the move was simple political expediency. "That's the way he approaches life — Mr. Pragmatist," Hoy told George Hutchison. "There were very few things they really believed in. It made him a successful politician, but I'm not sure it makes him a successful human being."

More than three decades later former Liberal leader Robert Nixon isn't prepared to share Cardinal Carter's views about Davis the statesman. The MPP for what was then Brant-Oxford-Norfolk was in the legislature on that June day in 1984 when Davis made his announcement: "I was absolutely gobsmacked when he did it," Nixon now says. He figures Davis did it because of a deal made between the premier and the cardinal during the 1981 election campaign.

"In my mind, he was simply keeping the promise that he made to Cardinal Carter," Nixon says. "You stay off my back in the election, the time is not right, but I assure you it will be done before I leave office."

Frank Miller opposed the decision, and as he analyzed it, couldn't see how it made any sense at all politically. Most of his own personal staff were Catholic and even *they* opposed it. They feared the strings that would come attached to the money would water down the Catholic system. Miller was also convinced it was a vote loser for the Tories. He figured the party would continue to get a miserly share of the Catholic vote as it always had, and it would lose votes among the Tory core who opposed the policy.

Because the Ontario legislature was almost unanimous in its endorsement of Davis's announcement, it gave people the impression that there was an overwhelming consensus in the province to do this. In fact, there *wasn't*, which would become abundantly clear. Before long tens of thousands of Ontarians would demonstrate in the streets against the policy, and one of the most admired and respected premiers in Canadian history would be compared to Adolf Hitler — and by an Anglican archbishop no less.

20

RESIGNATION

The summer of 1984 was one of the most astonishing in Canadian political history. Four days after William Davis's shocking announcement on Catholic school funding, the Liberal Party of Canada crowned John Turner as its new leader, replacing Pierre Elliott Trudeau. Despite being out of politics since 1975 and having to shake off an enormous amount of rust, Turner won the leadership by a vast 464-vote margin over Jean Chrétien on just two ballots. However, many misinterpreted the ease of his victory. Liberal delegates had given their heads to Turner, but their hearts were with Chrétien. Polls were misleading, suggesting Turner had a lot more popularity in the country than he really did. So the new prime minister struck fast, wasting no time in calling an election on American Independence Day for September 4, 1984. Liberals quickly learned their support was a mile wide and an inch deep. Turner's decade out of public life really showed. Conversely, opposition leader Brian Mulroney had spent the past year tangling with Trudeau in the House of Commons, getting the typically fractious Progressive Conservative caucus actually to sing out of the same hymn book, and preparing for the ensuing election. Mulroney was good to go. Actually, he was very good to go.

One thing the Tory leader never had to worry about was whether Bill Davis would be there for him. If Ontario's premier had stumped for Joe Clark in 1979 and 1980 — for a leader Davis didn't have a tremendous amount of confidence in — then he'd be there for Mulroney, whom he'd supported at the 1983 PC leadership convention and personally liked. In his memoir, Mulroney wrote that he wanted Norman Atkins to be the PC national campaign chair "for the simple reason that I wanted Davis personally onside in the election." He was.

At one point in the campaign Davis spent four straight days barnstorming through Ontario with Mulroney in places where a flashy Quebec businessman might not ordinarily be so welcomed. But when Bill Davis got off a bus with his friend, the national PC Party leader, you could see rural Ontario warming up to Mulroney in ways that might otherwise not have happened. It was during this time that Davis let his mask of modesty slip. One day, in Oxford County in Southwestern Ontario, Mulroney and Davis were chatting at the back of the campaign bus, waiting for an event to begin. The two Progressive Conservative leaders began talking about the Ontario Tories' much-vaunted Big Blue Machine and how grateful Mulroney was that Davis was enlisting it in the service of the party's federal leader. Again, in his memoir, Mulroney quotes Davis as saying: "Brian, the 'Big Blue Machine' is the best at getting the buses to meet your plane, taking you to a room overflowing with supporters, arranging the technology for the reporters to file their stories, and then getting everyone back safely on board the plane. But the leadership, strategy, and message for the campaign, that's what I do. The real 'Big Blue Machine' — you're looking at it right now."

Wow! It seemed an uncharacteristically braggadocio sort of thing for the premier to say. So during one of our interviews on TVO in 2009, I asked Davis about it. Of course, he denied saying it.

"I said to Brian, 'The word *machine* is overstated. I am part of an organization. I will help. If I help, the others will help, too,'" Davis *says* he said.

On a phone call in 2015, I told Mulroney about Davis's version of their conversation. He burst out laughing. "We were in Oxford, Ontario, at the back of the bus. He had the pipe going, and when I asked about the Big Blue Machine, he said, 'Brian, you're looking at it.'"

"He denies saying that," I reiterated to the former prime minister.

"He may deny it, but it happened!" Mulroney continued, still laughing.

Mulroney's point is not to embarrass his old friend. Rather, it's to demonstrate that he thought Davis was such a skilled politician, that the 18th premier was, indeed, the embodiment of the Big Blue Machine.

"Bill Davis had a way of connecting with the people of Ontario that was unique," Mulroney says. "He didn't need advisers to tell him how to do the job. Look what happened when he left. The idea of some Big Blue Machine is a myth. The Big Blue Machine was Bill Davis."

The story highlights one of the more interesting character developments in Davis's life. As long as he could remember, his parents drummed into him the need to be modest, moderate, and never boast about his accomplishments. And until he recaptured his majority government in 1981 Davis followed his parents' wishes. But as he has gotten older, enjoyed more political success, and watched other politicians who can't touch his record enjoy accolades to which perhaps they're not entitled, Davis has let more of the competitive side of his personality — well, let's call it what it is: his ego — come out. It's not a bad thing. In fact, one wonders why it took so long.

Of course, that 1984 election was a magical one for Tories all over Canada. Mulroney won 211 seats — the largest number the winning party had ever captured in the House of Commons — including a whopping 67 out of 95 seats in Ontario. When it came time for Brian and Mila Mulroney to host their first black-tie dinner at 24 Sussex Drive, the guests of honour were none other than William G. Davis, his family, and friends. Guests included John Tory, Hugh Segal, Eddie Goodman, Norman Atkins, and their spouses. Davis's secretary, the legendary Helen Anderson, was there. And so were the five Davis kids.

"We toured the residence, we sang Frank Sinatra songs, and it seemed to be as exciting for them to show us around as it was for us to be there," recalls Nancy, Davis's oldest daughter.

Another indication of how much respect Brian Mulroney had for Bill Davis's advice came when the new prime minister wanted to appoint his first Canadian ambassador to the United Nations. "I wanted someone outside the bureaucracy and I didn't want a prominent Conservative in the role," Mulroney told me. He knew former Ontario NDP leader Stephen Lewis from Lewis's high-profile *Kierans, Camp, and Lewis* weekly panel discussion on Peter Gzowski's *Morningside* program on CBC Radio. Mulroney and Lewis were also guest panellists together during a television broadcast of the 1979 election night coverage. He remembered that Davis had once told him that Lewis and the premier had an excellent relationship when they were both at Queen's Park. When Mulroney called Davis to talk about his idea of appointing Lewis to the U.N. post, Davis's immediate reaction was: "Great idea." Mulroney asked Davis to gauge Lewis's interest in the job. The premier brought Mulroney's offer to Lewis, it was accepted, and Lewis spent the next four years of his life in New York as Canada's ambassador extraordinary and plenipotentiary permanent representative to the United Nations.

"Bill Davis taught me Tories are not all evil," Lewis told the *Globe and Mail*. "Just misguided."

When Mulroney sat down with his senior advisers to put together the first cabinet of a national Progressive Conservative majority government in 26 years, he also sought Davis's advice. "I wanted his judgment on my Ontario MPs and just the overall process of cabinet-making," Mulroney recalls.

Before long Mulroney's government found itself in troubled waters. Despite its overwhelming numbers, for a time it seemed to stumble from crisis to crisis. Several supporters convinced Davis to speak to the prime minister and offer some advice, which he did.

"I told him the people who get you into office aren't necessarily the best people to keep you there," Davis says. Apparently, Mulroney agreed. Shortly after that conversation the prime minister replaced his chief of staff with Derek Burney, a widely respected professional who brought much more discipline and order to the Prime Minister's Office.

B ill Davis was always looking for candidates at any place and at any time. Remember, he wasn't just one of the most successful elected officials of all time; he was also the guy who had run Robert Macaulay's leadership campaign against John Robarts in 1961. So at some point, many months before the next Ontario election was to take place, CBC-TV reporter Robert Fisher found himself in Davis's office with just the premier and John Tory, his principal secretary, in attendance. Fisher was early for a photo op, and so the three men engaged in small talk to pass the time. Then Davis said something unexpected to Fisher: "Robert, as you know there will be another Ontario general election sometime in the next 12 months." Fisher was a native of Cornwall in Eastern Ontario, still had plenty of family living there, and often went back to visit. George Samis, the NDP member there since a 1974 by-election, was planning to step down, so the seat would soon be open. Davis thought the Tories had a solid chance of putting the seat back into the blue column, and he thought Fisher might be the candidate to do that.

"Robert, have you ever thought of running?" Davis asked him.

Fisher, well known for his tough, non-partisan coverage of provincial affairs, offered a brief reply: "For which party?"

Not amused, Davis turned to Tory and simply said, "This interview is over." And it was. Fisher never did run and stayed in journalism for another three decades before retiring in 2015. After announcing his intention to step down from CBC Radio where he finished his career after a remarkable 49 years in journalism, the phone rang in the CBC Radio newsroom.

"Robert, it's Bill Davis," said the voice on the phone.

"Mr. Davis!" Robert replied. Then he offered jokingly, "Are you calling to ask me to run?"

"For which party, Robert?" came the reply from the then 85-year-old Davis, who evidently still remembered a brief encounter in his premier's office from more than three decades earlier.

O ne of the knocks on the Davis government at this point in its tenure was that it was becoming increasingly disconnected from its more conservative backbenchers and, of course, the Tory core of supporters in the Ontario heartland. So it might be surprising to learn that included on the premier's annual fishing trip to Northern Ontario was Mike Harris. The premier would take a couple of dozen men (no women) from his cabinet and caucus and the business community up north to get away from the legislature and get to know people in a more casual way.

"We'd talk about fishing, politics, and life," recalls Harris. "I had more input on those occasions than I would've had at Queen's Park where there weren't a lot of opportunities." For a backbencher such as Harris, who clearly wasn't part of the Park Plaza club, these trips to remote fishing camps provided great offline access to Ontario's first minister. "Every evening we'd be together and at breakfast," Harris says. "We'd always discuss issues. It wasn't official. Everybody paid their own way and everything. Those were good opportunities."

It was early October 1984, and William Grenville Davis was sitting about as pretty as any politician in Canada. He had used the security of his majority government to help usher in constitutional renewal for the Canadian federation. He had fought the recession of the early 1980s and emerged as a uniquely trusted figure in Canada's political firmament. He had announced the historic decision to fully fund the Catholic school system. No politician is untouchable, but at this moment in his political career Davis got about as close to untouchable as possible.

For an indication of how everybody assumed Davis would call and win the next provincial election, expected within half a year, consider this. One October morning at the legislative dining room Liberal MPP Sean Conway and his executive assistant, Tim Murphy, got together for breakfast to plan their future. The premise of their plan was this: Davis would destroy both opposition parties in the ensuing election, and David Peterson would certainly have to resign as Liberal chief. That would kick-start a race for a new leader, and Conway and Murphy needed to put together an organization for Conway's leadership bid. Barely 15 minutes into their strategizing, David Peterson strolled into the dining room and spotted his two colleagues. He wandered over and joined them for breakfast, completely unaware of the fact that they were already making plans for a post-Peterson era at Queen's Park.

The Tories' public opinion polling numbers were going through the stratosphere. A CROP survey taken in June 1984 asked voters who they'd support should an election be called today. Fully 50 percent said Davis. The Tories' voter satisfaction numbers were the highest of any government in the country — routinely between 60 and 70 percent favourable support. With numbers such as that, everybody was wondering when Davis would exploit his popularity and renew the Tories' mandate with what would be a certain fifth straight election win, including a second consecutive majority government. But that wasn't where Bill Davis's head was at. In late September 1984, while attending the Royal Visit at Upper Canada Village in Morrisburg, Ontario, John Tory mentioned something to Davis about the next provincial election. Davis, in turn, let slip something that had clearly been preoccupying him for quite a while.

"I've been thinking about the press conference that'll happen," the premier told Tory. "The first question they'll ask me is, 'Are you committing to the entire term?' If I said I wasn't going to, then they'd ask, 'Why are you seeking a new mandate if you're intending to leave early.'" Tory never shared the contents of that moment with anyone, but that would turn out to be *the key question* that would alter the course of Ontario history.

A couple of weeks before Thanksgiving Day in 1984 Davis took Roy McMurtry and Norman Atkins out for lunch at a restaurant on Yonge Street north of Davisville Avenue in midtown Toronto. He told two of his closest friends in politics that it was time. They tried over and over to persuade him that he needed to take the party through one more campaign, but Davis just wasn't buying. He was convinced the party was in good shape — no, he *knew* it was and had Allan Gregg's polling to prove it.

"The polls showed he would have won a bigger majority," says John Tory. "He was the Man."

Davis also felt confident there were several good candidates ready to take his place as leader. He told the pair he was tired and that concerns about his family's financial state were gnawing at him. Atkins warned the premier there were "some inherent dangers in his leaving at this point," that Davis was the only leader who could have the crucial calming effect needed to prevent the separate school funding issue from potentially boiling over. But Davis couldn't be persuaded to change his mind. With Brian Mulroney just having won the biggest majority government in Canadian history, Davis no longer felt the pressure of being the country's prime Progressive Conservative torchbearer. It was an emotional, tearful lunch encounter that lasted three hours. It also couldn't have come as a complete surprise to McMurtry. After the 1981 election victory, Davis told his friend, the attorney general, "I think I've had enough of Thursday nights." It was a typically cryptic Davis comment until one remembered that elections in Ontario at that time were traditionally held on Thursday nights.

Davis's Ontario Provincial Police bodyguards, Bob Guay and Peter Balog, also had a hunch something was up. They'd notice the premier gazing out the window of his car, puffing his pipe, staring into the distance, preoccupied in a way that was unusual for him.

On Thursday, October 4, going into the Thanksgiving holiday weekend, Davis convened a meeting of his cabinet and told them he wanted to retire before the next election. The ministers wouldn't accept it. They literally refused to accept the news. Bob Welch made a heartfelt, eloquent speech begging Davis to stay. So did McMurtry. Larry Grossman tried a different approach, saying Davis had every right to do what he wanted, that his colleagues would accept and respect any decision he made, "but we desperately need you to stay." Some cabinet members started crying. "Nothing has ever, ever come close to the feeling, almost the despair, people felt," said Eddie Goodman. Despite the fact that at least half a dozen ministers in the room wanted Davis's job, they were smart enough to know that the current occupant of the premier's office represented their best hope to continue the Tory dynasty. Not only that, they loved the guy.

As much as John Tory wanted his boss to hang around, he offered different advice. "My view on these things is, you have a right to retire whenever you want," he told Davis. And to those who thought Davis had a duty to the party to fight another election, Tory asked rhetorically: "Well, when does that duty run out? After 14 years as premier? After 25 years in politics? You still owe something to the party after all that time? No."

For the Davises, Thanksgiving meant gathering at the family's cottage compound on Georgian Bay. It was always one of the premier's favourite places to get away from politics and reconnect with his children. But this Thanksgiving weekend would be very different. It would be *all* about politics, since all of the premier's inner circle of top advisers would be joining him for a discussion about his and the party's future.

The group was genuinely conflicted. On the one hand, to a person, they all believed Davis had put a quarter century of his life into politics and at this point was entitled to do whatever he wanted. He was 55 years old, a perfect age in which to enter the private sector, with theoretically 10 or 15 years of good health and high income awaiting him. Yes, the party would be disappointed if he left and no doubt some of his colleagues would feel let down. Tough. The man had earned the right to go at a time of his choosing.

However, there was another option that went something like this: get us through the election, deal with the separate school funding issue, and two years into your mandate, step aside then. Davis thought long and hard about it. Heck, he'd been thinking about it for months, if not years. Three decades later he explains his decision thus: "The ambivalence was there."

Bill Davis just couldn't put his family and himself through an eighth gruelling election campaign and his fifth as leader if he didn't feel all in. And he didn't. Also, in an era in which too many politicians seemed to have no difficulty lying through their teeth when answering reporters' questions, Davis simply couldn't do that.

"They will ask, 'Are you here for the long term?'" Davis explained to me in 2015. "I cannot avoid it. I cannot lie. I will not say, 'Yes, I am going to stay the whole term,' knowing that I'm not going to. I couldn't do it. It was as simple as that."

The decision was made. There would be plenty of shocked, surprised, and saddened people at Queen's Park, but so be it. There would be no election call. There would be a retirement announcement instead. So, on the Sunday morning of that Thanksgiving weekend, the longest-serving premier of Ontario in the 20th century casually mentioned to his family after breakfast that he was stepping down and would tell the world the following day.

"There were a few tears. It was not easy," Davis recalls. The premier's oldest son, Neil, kept things on a light note when he suggested the drivers of Ontario would have to watch out, since Bill Davis would now be driving himself everywhere. Of course, as either a cabinet minister or premier since 1962, Davis hadn't driven himself anywhere in more than two decades, except when he snuck behind the wheel on drives to the cottage near Honey Harbour on Georgian Bay.

Hugh Segal called Norman Atkins, who was at his cottage in New Brunswick, and said two simple words: "We lost."

The logistics required to organize the retirement announcement of any premier are intense. It's not an exaggeration to say military-like precision is required to ensure a small handful of people are brought into the loop, and perhaps more important, to ensure far more people are kept out of the loop. One man's decision can affect tens of thousands of party loyalists, employees, and interested observers. Accomplishing all of this for someone who was as private as Bill Davis was and who'd had the job as long as he did was an even greater challenge.

Davis decided on the list of people who should be informed that an official announcement was coming. Included on the list was G. Emmett Cardinal Carter, so Davis asked Mike O'Neill, his executive assistant, to call Carter and let him know. Ironically, O'Neill himself didn't know what Davis was going to announce. In fact, he was betting on an election call. O'Neill was never able to reach the cardinal, despite repeated telephone attempts, so he drove over to Carter's home and rapped on the door several times. Still no answer. Alas, Carter was away and would fail to get the heads-up on the announcement. "But it underlined the importance Mr. Davis put on that relationship with Cardinal Carter that I spent so much time trying to get the message to him," O'Neill recalls today.

I have never seen Queen's Park buzzing with as much political electricity as it was on Thanksgiving Monday, October 8, 1984. The premier's office released a statement simply saying that William G. Davis had an announcement to make later that day. Everybody thought he would call an election. The Liberals actually had their bus ready to roll into the parking lot to take David Peterson onto the hustings. Bob Rae and his NDP caucus were meeting in the basement of the north wing to finalize their preparations for the certain election call.

Even people in Davis's office had no idea what he was going to do. His deputy press secretary, Janet Ecker, who would go on to become a cabinet minister in Mike Harris's government, says the office had two speeches ready to go: one for retirement, the other for an election call. John Ferguson, a reporter from Southam News, called Ecker in a quasi-panic, saying he was on deadline and needed some clue about which way the premier was leaning. No communications adviser ever wants to admit he or she is out of the loop, but Ecker was — almost *everybody* was — so she confessed: "I have no idea. I really, legitimately, do not know."

And then, utter confusion. Davis walked into the legislature with his wife, Kathleen, and his son, Neil. You could see the quizzical looks on people's faces. Why would the premier bring his wife and son to Queen's Park to call an election? That seemed irregular. The trio strode into the premier's office on the second floor without betraying a hint to the throng of media recording the scene of what was to come. I was a 24-year-old cub reporter for CHFI Radio watching it all unfold. Approaching Kathleen Davis, I pushed my microphone toward her and asked, "Are you ready for an election, Mrs. Davis?" She just smiled and kept walking.

The Davises marched into a room where the cabinet was assembled, made the announcement official, then worked their way to the first floor and the media studio, which was packed not just with media but also with PC Party supporters who wanted to witness history unfold. Davis walked toward the riser, sat behind a nondescript desk, and broke the news to an astonished group of reporters:

I have written today to the President of the Ontario
Progressive Conservative Association, Mr. David
McFadden, and I informed him of my decision, a very
difficult decision, to step down as leader of our party,
effective the next leadership convention, which I have
asked Mr. McFadden to arrange for the earliest appropriate date, hopefully in January of 1985.

Three decades later David McFadden now admits even he didn't
know until the day before this news conference which way Davis would
decide, despite meeting weekly with the premier during his entire tenure
as party president.

Davis seemed genuinely overcome by emotion as he negotiated his way
through the speech. Despite being jammed to the rafters, the room was dead
still. As the premier brought a finger to his cheek to brush away a tear, the
rat-a-tat-tat of still-camera shutters could be heard clicking away, momentarily bringing him out of his emotional state. Davis immediately regained
his composure and proceeded with the rest of his prepared remarks:

There's no more honoured or significant way to spend the
better part of one's life than in the service of one's fellow
citizens. And I feel deeply honoured to have had the
opportunity to serve this province and its people. I have
learned from them over these past 25 years. I've learned
about decency, I've learned about tolerance and understanding. The people of our province are capable of tremendous progress and goodwill as they have repeatedly
demonstrated during the past quarter century.

The speech and ensuing question-and-answer session with reporters
is reproduced in its entirety in Appendix 7.

Davis did all the things you'd expect in such a speech — thanking his
constituents; thanking his caucus and cabinet colleagues and pointing to
the party's deep bench of prospective leadership replacements; and looking forward to spending more time with his wife and grandchild, with a
second grandchild only six weeks away.

Remember, this was 1984. The country's first all-news television channel, then called CBC Newsworld, was still five years away. CP24 was still
14 years away. No one had cellular phones. In other words, the news of
Davis's retirement didn't blast across the province the second it happened.
It leaked out slowly as people heard, then telephoned friends.

When Nickel Belt MPP Floyd Laughren heard the news, he admitted
to being "thunderstruck. I really was. I couldn't get it through my head for
a while. I thought, *What is happening? Davis is leaving?* I mean, he was the
institution, right? I couldn't process it." As it began to sink in, Laughren
then asked himself the next question that no doubt millions of Ontarians
were asking: "Why would you leave?" Had Davis called an election, victory was assuredly his.

Davis addressed that question head-on in his retirement statement:

> I have been deeply touched by the expressions of con-
> fidence and loyalty which have caused me to reflect,
> somewhat longer than I had expected, on my decision.
> But having decided to leave political life, it would be
> less than honourable and certainly less than honest for
> me to seek a mandate unless I was personally commit-
> ted to serving a full term.

As we've already established, Davis has never been particularly
lovey-dovey in public when it comes to complimenting his wife. But that
day was different and the premier acknowledged his and the province's debt:

> Twenty-six years is a long time for any one assignment in
> anyone's life. And if that's true for me, it's certainly more
> than true for Kathleen who has soldiered through the
> many sacrifices with a devotion and a sense of commit-
> ment which has [*sic*] made her as much a servant of the
> people of this province and to the party, as really anyone
> holding elected office.

Three decades later I asked Kathleen Davis whether it was she who
finally convinced her husband to retire. Did she pressure him into finally

calling it quits? She insisted not. "He was such a star," she said. "I couldn't think of him doing anything else."

It's not unknown at moments such as these for a departing politician to take many minutes to list all of his accomplishments worthy of the history books. Interestingly, Davis took about 30 seconds to list only two: the constitutional success of 1981 and the advancement of minority language rights. He was utterly modest to the end.

He ended his prepared remarks thus: "It is because of my confidence in the capacity of the Ontario Progressive Conservative Party to meet those challenges and opportunities and to do so in a humane and competent fashion that I feel confident in passing on the leadership of this dynamic and humane party." The speech might have come to an end, but Davis wasn't done. No doubt looking up and seeing the faces of so many loyal soldiers prompted him to continue. He got caught up in the momentousness of the occasion and began naming many of the people with whom he enjoyed his journey through politics: his son, Neil; his secretary, Helen Anderson, "who I sometimes facetiously, but not always facetiously, say runs the Government of Ontario," who went back to Davis's days in the Department of Education in 1962; and his Mr. Fixit, Clare Westcott, "who has been invaluable for the same length of time …" At this point it seemed as if Davis feared his list of people and reminiscences would never end, so he began listing the names more quickly and without additional comment. "Dr. Ed Stewart, Mr. [John] Tory, Mr. [Michael] Danaher, Laird [Saunderson], and Hughie Segal …" Then Davis must have caught a glimpse of a crying John Tory, his principal secretary, because he began to speculate about Tory's future, which stopped Davis cold.

"I don't know what Mr. Tory is going to do because he is a great young man with a tremendous future, who is a bit of a partisan, but, John, uh —" That's all Davis could say. He was barely keeping it together. Tory didn't even notice that it was the reference to him that ultimately did Davis in. He was too overwhelmed at the end of an era. There were several seconds of silence, observers unsure whether Davis had more to say or that was it. Reporters, who had copies of his speech, knew there were no more prepared remarks to give. But Davis had been vamping for the past few moments, and nobody seemed particularly anxious to see it end. But that was all Davis could muster. Progressive Conservative partisans in the room spontaneously began to clap to fill the silence, bringing the premier's official remarks to an end.

"I don't think people realize how extremely emotional those moments are," Tory told me in the office of the mayor of Toronto overlooking Nathan Phillips Square. He should know. Tory had found himself in the same media studio in 2008 when he stepped down as Ontario PC Party leader after losing a by-election designed to return him to the legislature after losing his seat in the 2007 general election. In that case, Tory had managed to keep it together until I'd asked him whether he'd spoken to Bill Davis, and if so, how the call had gone. Tory hadn't been able to hold back his emotion any longer and confessed the tears that were flowing had more to do with disappointing his mentor than any setback he personally felt. (His phone call from Davis on October 27, 2014, was a lot more fun, as the pair revelled in Tory's improbable victory in the Toronto mayoralty race.)

In any event, at Bill Davis's resignation announcement, questions from journalists came next. The first was from CKCO-TV's Paul Rhodes, who 10 years later would become one of Premier Mike Harris's most important advisers. Rhodes tried to get Davis to rank his accomplishments, but the premier, his United Church modesty kicking in, wasn't having any of that. He started with a joke ("I just hope that some author gives it more than two paragraphs"), mentioned the Constitution again, then added that essentially what he'd offered Ontarians over the past nearly 14 years was good governance provided by a team of decent men and women — hardly the stuff of which headlines are made, but very consistent with Davis's personality.

Also consistent were Davis's non-answers to the next several questions. Bruce Stewart from the *Hamilton Spectator* wondered whether the premier could say exactly when he thought about stepping down. "Well, not really." Then why now? "Well, there's really no good time to go, could have been three years from now, could have been three years ago." Claire Hoy was his typical, abrupt self in following up, pushing Davis to be more specific, then muttering under his breath at his dissatisfaction with the answer when the premier refused to do so. If you read the transcript in Appendix 7 of this book, you might sympathize a bit with Hoy's frustration. Davis was his circumlocutory best, teasing reporters with how little information he was actually divulging.

More questions ensued: When did he tell his cabinet? How did his family react at that Thanksgiving dinner? Will he miss the media? Might his departure affect Toronto's chances of securing a domed stadium? Davis joked his way through all the answers.

The CBC's Robert Fisher asked him whether he'd accept a Senate appointment. Davis dodged the question, then concluded his answer with: "Would you?"

That prompted a reporter at the back to shout at Davis: "What do you say? What do you mean?"

Laughter erupted. Eventually, Davis admitted that if he was now looking for a change in career from politics, going to the Senate didn't exactly constitute change. In fact, Prime Minister Mulroney *did* offer Davis a Senate seat, but Davis turned him down. The notion of living one-third of the year in Ottawa — or more particularly, away from Brampton — was a non-starter for Davis. (Davis went on to tell Mulroney that while *he* wasn't interested in the job, he knew that Brascan CEO Trevor Eyton *was* interested, so the prime minister gave the appointment to Eyton instead. He served in the Senate from 1990 to 2009.)

There was one moment in the news conference when Davis's wishful thinking clearly overwhelmed his powers of prognostication. Someone asked him whether his efforts to extend full public funding to separate schools might be jeopardized by his departure, given all the controversy that was "swirling." The premier picked up on that trigger word — "I'm not sure the fallout is *swirling*," he insisted — while adding it was certainly possible for the media to find *someone* in a province of nine million people to express opposition to the policy.

"But I am very confident that that change will be effective, and it will be done with a minimum amount of difficulty, in spite of the fact that you will find somebody tomorrow morning, six months from now, five years from now who might offer some controversial comment too," Davis predicted. On that one he wasn't even close to being right.

Having said that, it's an indication of the esteem in which even the press gallery now held the premier that some of the questions focused on how the party would survive without him. Catholic school funding was one example. Another journalist's question contained the word *irreplaceable* to describe Davis's hold on Ontario politics.

"No," Davis interrupted, "no one is irreplaceable, indispensable, et cetera." He then made another bet on the future that turned out not to be true. Of his cabinet colleagues, one of whom would presumably be his successor, he said: "They're pretty tremendous people and they'll make it work." As it turned out, they couldn't and didn't.

Orland French covered the press conference for the *Globe and Mail*. He'd been a tough critic of Davis over the years, but on this occasion wrote: "You will find a great deal of honour and class in [Davis's] decision to retire, much more than you will find among those in the Tory hierarchy who urged him to run and then quit and to hell with a commitment to the public."

Today David McFadden knows he may always be remembered as the answer to the following trivia question: To whom did Bill Davis proffer his resignation as PC Party leader? McFadden, the Ontario Tory president, had roots in the party that went back far enough for him to remember that 10 years earlier Davis had almost lost the 1975 election. Many at that time had wondered whether the party had made a mistake four years earlier in picking Davis over Allan Lawrence.

"There was a bit of armchair quarterbacking going on," McFadden admits. "But I've gotta tell you, by 1985 there wasn't a soul who felt that. Davis was so good. What a guy. He was one of the finest people I've ever worked with in politics, if not the finest."

However, as he departed, Davis suggested to McFadden that he hoped to avoid a lot of the messiness the premier saw at the 1983 federal PC Party leadership convention. At that contest the party sustained a lot of negative flak for signing up "Two-Minute Tories" who joined the party only long enough to vote for a candidate's delegates, then disappeared. The most notorious example came when a group of apparently intoxicated men from a homeless shelter were bused to Montreal to vote for Brian Mulroney. Davis didn't approve of these transgressions and therefore tried to ensure that all participants in the 1985 contest to replace him needed to be party members in good standing for a year. Today he says he never *insisted* the party follow his wishes. ("That was a decision of the party. I was in no position to demand anything," he told me in early 2016.) So while those rules did avoid the "Two-Minute Tories" problem, it also prevented any renewal or injection of new blood in a party that was starting to show its wrinkles. And that would prove to be quite problematic when the new leader called an election five months later.

21

SUCCESSOR

It's coincidental that Bill Davis and John Robarts were practically the same age when they decided to give up the premier's office to their successor. Davis was 55 years old and Robarts 54, but the similarities ended there. Davis was at the height of his popularity and easily could have won the next election had he called it and led his party through a campaign. Robarts, by the end of his tenure, was looking old and overweight with a big paunch over his belt. He was still respected, but at the same time no one was begging him to hang around and lead the troops through one more battle as they were with Davis.

There was one other similarity about their departures. It had to do with loyalty. Back in 1970, Bill Davis refused entreaties to set up a leadership organization, so powerful was the loyalty tug to the premier who treated him so well. Now, as Davis's cabinet ministers considered their next moves, the one closest to this premier — Roland Roy McMurtry — was also well behind getting his leadership ducks in order and for the same reason.

McMurtry had a spectacular flame-out in his first attempt to get into politics. He tried as a star candidate to win a downtown Toronto by-election in 1973 when Tory fortunes were going down the tubes. He ended up losing that St. George contest to Margaret Campbell, the first-ever female Liberal MPP elected in Ontario history. But McMurtry tried again two years later, and despite Davis's PCs being held to a minority government, he did win a seat in 1975. Two weeks later he marched right into the cabinet as the new attorney general and might have been the most influential person to hold that post in the province's history. McMurtry had so much going for him: a well-connected family particularly in PC party circles, attendance at all the right schools, and a personal history with Davis starting on the University of Toronto Varsity Blues football field in 1950. However, McMurtry used all those advantages and poured them into public life. The combination of an activist nature and a burning desire to improve the human condition of his fellow citizens gave him both a political agenda and the clout to do something about it. McMurtry's knack of tackling big issues brought him constant media attention, so much so that his nickname became "Roy McHeadline."

In his autobiography *Memoirs and Reflections*, McMurtry says he never really considered replacing his friend as premier. He didn't want his work as the province's top legal authority ever to be seen as conflicting with his political ambitions. So while his cabinet colleagues were out speaking to riding associations across the province, ingratiating themselves to future delegates, and building up their organizations, McMurtry wasn't. There was also a part of him that figured after Davis left, he'd go, too, and the Tory dynasty would go with them both. But increasingly McMurtry found people entreating him to run. He was the pinkest of the red Tories considering joining the race, and a lot of people told him those views needed to be represented in the contest. McMurtry also had high name recognition, having had a hand in so many high-profile and controversial issues over the years, from increasing French-language services in Ontario courtrooms to playing a significant role in the patriation of the Constitution, from implementing a mandatory seat-belt-wearing policy to having National Hockey League players charged with assault when they acted like common thugs on the ice (as the Philadelphia Flyers often did). A prospective McMurtry campaign also got a big boost when one of the charter founding members of the Big Blue Machine, Norman Atkins, volunteered his services as campaign chair.

But a McMurtry candidacy had its problems. As influential as he was at the cabinet table, that proximity to Davis was a dual-edged sword. Some were jealous of the attorney general's close relationship with the premier. They noted that McMurtry got away with stuff nobody else could — for example, his unilateral actions on making the courts bilingual without informing the premier ahead of time, or his predilection for showing up late to cabinet meetings or not at all to caucus sessions. When McMurtry went looking for his colleagues' support for a leadership bid, he found there wasn't much there. In fact, one of his caucus colleagues bluntly told him they'd served together in the same caucus for years and this was the first time the attorney general had ever given him the time of day.

Ironically, two of McMurtry's greatest strengths — almost 10 straight years as attorney general, a record to be proud of, and a reputation for integrity — were painted as drawbacks by others. They pointed out he'd never served in an economic or social services portfolio and that his bringing additional French-language services to the courts was box-office poison in rural Ontario, the Tory heartland, from which McMurtry himself received numerous pieces of hate mail. Some feared he'd take that step Bill Davis always declined to take, making Ontario officially bilingual. In truth, McMurtry wasn't opposed to the idea, but at the same time he wasn't pushing it.

Norman Atkins recognized all these vulnerabilities. He had begged Davis to move McMurtry to a different portfolio during a previous cabinet shuffle, thinking the attorney general needed to be in a different ministry that would give him a chance to become more well rounded as a politician. McMurtry had even expressed an interest in taking Davis's old education portfolio. But the premier always nixed the idea. "As long as I'm premier, Roy McMurtry is going to be my attorney general," Atkins says Davis told him. "He'd made up his mind and there was no point in having him consider that any further," Atkins told George Hutchison.

For his part, McMurtry says he never asked Davis to move him to another portfolio because he always assumed when Davis left politics he'd be right behind him. "I wasn't interested in becoming the leader," McMurtry told me in early 2016.

"Besides," Davis said to Norman Atkins, "this is a tough job and I sleep a little better at night with Roy as my attorney general."

There was one other problem McMurtry had: bad timing. A Toronto jury had just acquitted abortion doctor Henry Morgentaler, essentially after the defendant's lawyer told the jury to ignore the law and just do what felt right. As attorney general, McMurtry believed he had no choice but to uphold the law and therefore launched an appeal of the acquittal. Some of the more progressive members of McMurtry's support base were disappointed with that appeal, and as a result, took a pass on supporting McMurtry's campaign.

In any event, after weighing the pros and the cons, Roy McMurtry decided to give it a try, and on November 2, 1984, he announced his intention to try to replace his friend as PC Party leader and premier.

"All of us have the responsibility to continue to view the human condition with curiosity, compassion, and the conviction that we can and must help make our common lot a little better," he said at his kickoff news conference, appealing to the better angels in the party's membership.

It was at this point that the party made a curious decision. Usually, the occasion of selecting a new leader is an opportunity to grow the party's membership. Candidates fan out across the province, sign up new members, and renew interest in the party. Perhaps no candidate has better exemplified doing that than Patrick Brown, the current Ontario PC Party leader, whose support base overwhelmingly came from new members. But this time the party brass feared seeing newspaper stories of "Two-Minute Tories," people who bought memberships to support candidates but had no interest in supporting the party itself. The 1983 federal PC leadership campaign was rife with such stories of candidates signing up patients at mental hospitals or even dead people, so the provincial organization simply wanted to avoid that situation and ruled that only existing party members would be permitted to participate. The downside of that decision was that the party missed an opportunity to bring new folks on board, the consequences of which would become abundantly apparent in the 1985 provincial election. In any event, the rules were the rules, and McMurtry's team pledged to do the best it could.

If there was one candidate in the race to replace Bill Davis who was the most like Bill Davis, that candidate was Dennis Roy Timbrell. Timbrell won his first election in the riding of Don Mills in 1971, Davis's first election as premier. He was the youngest MPP elected that October night, and it wasn't even his first election victory. Timbrell, who was a teacher, first got elected at age 24 as a municipal councillor in the Toronto borough of North York. Six months into that job he realized he was less interested in potholes and more interested in the province. So, talk about chutzpah, Timbrell made an appointment to see Stanley Randall, the MPP for Don

Mills and minister of trade and development. Timbrell told Randall that if he intended to run again, he, Timbrell, would happily support him, but if he intended to retire, then Timbrell would seek the PC nomination and attempt to move up to provincial politics. Randall appreciated Timbrell's bluntness and, in fact, opted to retire before the 1971 election.

After John Robarts stepped down as Ontario's 17th prime minister, Timbrell found himself at a cocktail party in Don Mills where the special guest was the current minister of education, Bill Davis — the same man who had signed Timbrell's teaching certificate, high school graduation certificate, and Grade 13 history prize book. Apparently, everyone at the party was convinced Davis would win the upcoming leadership contest with ease, which rankled Timbrell a bit. So he ended up supporting Allan Lawrence, not out of any dislike for Davis but rather because he felt the party needed a vigorous, competitive contest which, of course, it was.

Coincidentally, just like the convention that picked Bill Davis, Timbrell's own nomination meeting before 1,600 party members at Toronto's Ontario Science Centre had a first-ballot screw-up, forcing delegates to redo the initial ballot. However, unlike Davis, Timbrell won overwhelmingly on the first ballot. At age 24 he was already a bit of a political veteran, given his municipal experience and his being chairman of the Young Progressive Conservatives of Toronto.

Timbrell's ascent in Ontario politics didn't take long. Premier Davis created a new "junior minister" position — the parliamentary assistant. While Timbrell didn't make the first batch of appointments, he made it the second time, in September 1973, as parliamentary assistant to the minister of colleges and universities. Given that the premier himself once headed that ministry, it was a sign that Davis had his eye on this young fellow from North York.

Sure enough, five months later, Timbrell got a call from Davis's much-beloved secretary, Helen Anderson, asking him to come to the premier's office. "Miss A," as everyone called her, was a legend at Queen's Park, having been a file clerk under Premier Mitchell Hepburn. She had also worked for Davis when he was minister of education.

"I'm going to make a few changes tomorrow," Davis told Timbrell. The next day, February 26, 1974, Timbrell was sworn in as minister without portfolio responsible for the youth secretariat. He'd spend a lot of time on university campuses hearing from students that the government needed to get more serious about the environment if it wanted to have any chance to impress the next generation. Timbrell was 27 years old.

One of the greatest days of Timbell's life was shortly followed by the worst. Three weeks after watching his son take the oath of office to join the Davis cabinet, Dennis Timbrell's father died in his son's arms of a massive heart attack. He was 49 years old.

One of the first things Timbrell learned in the cabinet was that Allan Lawrence was no Bill Davis. "I realized then that I almost made a big mistake!" Timbrell laughs today, recalling his vote at the 1971 PC leadership convention. But the cabinet's youngest member did well, and 16 months later, after winning personal re-election in the 1975 campaign by an even bigger margin than in 1971 despite the government being reduced to a minority, Timbrell was promoted to minister of energy. He was 28 years old and quickly found himself with a front-row seat at the province's Syncrude negotiations (see Chapter 16). And despite being the youngest minister at the table, Timbrell says: "It was great. You could speak your mind. It was one of the things I always appreciated about Bill Davis."

Timbrell did less than two years at energy but again impressed the premier at his ability to solve problems with some creativity. Shortly after that 1975 election, Prime Minister Pierre Trudeau imposed wage and price controls on Canadians. At the same time Ontario Hydro was seeking a 30 percent increase in electricity prices and the Ontario Energy Board approved it. This is what's known as a political problem, particularly in a minority legislature. How could a massive double-digit price increase be justified when wages and prices were supposed to be held to small single-digit increases?

At a meeting with Premier Davis, Timbrell outlined the approach he wanted to take. In a highly unorthodox manner, he would appoint a special committee, chaired by the NDP's energy critic, former leader Donald C. MacDonald, and give the opposition more members on the committee than the government. Davis instantly got what Timbrell was up to and approved it. The chairman and president of Ontario Hydro were less than thrilled, given that they'd have to testify before a legislative committee, something that had never happened in the utility's nearly seven-decade-long history. But Timbrell gave the NDP's MacDonald carte blanche to call any witness and have the utility open its books. What resulted, less than a year later, was a unanimous report saying, yes, the rate increases were consistent with both the power-at-cost mandate of Ontario Hydro and the federal wage- and price-control guidelines. To everyone's dismay, two weeks after the report was released, the Ontario Energy Board approved another 20 percent rate increase. Timbrell asked everyone to re-create the process and they did. It was a truly co-operative procedure and showed Ontarians that a minority legislature could actually work well. It also showed Bill Davis that Dennis Timbrell could take political headaches and make them go away.

In February 1977, Timbrell got another call from Miss Anderson to come and see the premier. As Timbrell entered Davis's office, he saw the premier smoking his pipe and sitting behind his desk, which was covered in files. It felt as if he'd been called to the principal's office for a tongue-lashing. Instead, Davis offered his traditional "I'm going to make a few changes tomorrow" line, flipped over a file in front of Timbrell, and simply said: "Health."

Timbrell's response was "Oh, shit!" Davis laughed. Timbrell then said, "See you tomorrow. I'll bring my Bible." He was trading in a ministry staff of 62 for one of 12,000 and was barely 30 years old. The health portfolio had become a constant source of political trouble for Davis. The current minister, Frank Miller, had a plan to close underutilized hospitals and bring fiscal discipline to a sector that was accustomed to receiving huge budget increases every year. As we'll see in greater detail later in this chapter, Miller's plan ran into opposition at every turn, including at the cabinet table where his colleague, Larry Grossman, was fighting tooth and nail to keep Doctors' Hospital in his riding off the chopping block. Finally, Davis simply shuffled Miller out of the post and brought in Timbrell to lower the temperature. So controversial would this issue become that it would be another 20 years before any government touched the issue of hospital closings again when Premier Mike Harris struck his Health Services Restructuring Commission.

An indication of how much Davis trusted and backed Timbrell came a year later. The new health minister was trying to get passed some amendments to the Mental Health Act that would have taken away significant powers from doctors to keep patients committed. Timbrell shepherded the changes through caucus and a cabinet committee but got pushback from a couple of colleagues who were doctors and from the leader of the opposition, Stuart Smith, who himself was a psychiatrist. There was a lot of going behind Timbrell's back directly to the premier to try to get the health minister to back down. Eventually, Timbrell got a call from Helen Anderson. "The premier would like to see you," she said. This time it wasn't about a cabinet promotion.

"Dennis, it's about these amendments to the Mental Health Act," Davis began.

"I figured as much," the minister replied.

"Is this your bill or is this the ministry staff's?" Davis inquired.

Timbrell assured him it was his doing, that he'd written some of the sections of it himself, and was clearly behind the whole bill.

Davis replied: "Okay, that's fine."

End of meeting. The opposition to the bill went away. As soon as Davis heard with his own ears that one of his most trusted ministers wanted the bill, that was it. The premier told everyone else to back off. The changes went through and made a significant statement for patients' rights.

An indication of how perilous it is to be the minister of health is to look at the tenure of those ministers over the years. Timbrell lasted five years in health, making him the fifth-longest-serving health minister in Ontario history and the longest serving over the previous 45 years. Now that health spending represents more than 40 percent of the budget, crises regularly arise and ministers seem to be shuffled every other year. In all his time as minister of health, Timbrell says he was only overruled once by Davis. The minister was looking into changing the age of consent for surgical procedures. It opened up the possibility that younger teens could have abortions without their parents' knowledge, but Timbrell was prepared to proceed, anyway. As soon as word got out, the premier's office was inundated with messages from the archbishop of the Catholic Church, the primate of the Anglican Church, the moderator of the United Church, the chief rabbi, and so on. Timbrell's phone rang. It was the premier's deputy minister, Ed Stewart, saying, "The premier wonders if you would mind ..."

Stewart didn't even have to finish his sentence. Timbrell said, "I'll back off."

However, the health minister did get support from Davis on a controversial attempt to amend the Public Hospitals Act, allowing the minister to appoint a "supervisor" in the event a hospital went "rogue." Nowadays, supervisors are routinely appointed to clean up a hospital's financial or health service problems. But 35 years ago it was an enormously controversial thing to suggest. Hospitals prized their autonomy, and the government was never considered the good guy when it intervened in hospital affairs. Exacerbating the problem was that one of the hospitals in trouble back in 1981 was Toronto East General in Timbrell's own riding. The minister thought they were refusing to follow protocol in submitting their budget. Timbrell got the amendments through; in a twist of fate, in 2001, the former health minister was sent into Ottawa Hospital as a supervisor by the Mike Harris government.

One of Timbrell's longest-lasting contributions as health minister was to create the Assistive Devices Program along with Margaret Birch, the first-ever female cabinet minister and at the time provincial secretary for social development. Back then there was no public financial assistance for children who required walkers, braces, or wheelchairs to get around. Timbrell and Birch got Davis onside and made it happen. And Timbrell warned all the deficit hawks in cabinet: "I'm telling you right now, we're starting with kids but eventually it's gonna be everybody." And today it is. "That program is Margaret's and mine," Timbrell says with evident pride. "And the premier was very supportive."

What happened next in Timbrell's career caught everyone off guard. He'd been a successful health minister both in terms of implementing new policy and keeping controversies out of the media. The margins of his personal victories in Don Mills kept increasing, from 5,000 votes in 1971, to 5,600 in 1975, to 8,800 in 1977, to more than 12,000 in 1981. So he went to Davis and said, "Next time you're thinking of shuffling the cabinet, I could use a new challenge." The premier asked Timbrell what he fancied. The answer was agriculture.

Davis said, "Leave it with me."

In February 1982 when Davis shuffled his cabinet again, there was Dennis Timbrell, representing a midtown *Toronto* riding, sworn in as minister of agriculture and food. Many in the press gallery at Queen's Park couldn't figure it out. Why would the health minister, one of the highest-profile positions in government, responsible for spending so much money, want an apparent demotion to a portfolio where his budget would be a fraction of the size it once was, and where he'd starve for media attention? It made no sense.

But Davis understood Timbrell's modus operandi immediately, and despite the odd optics around putting a guy from Toronto in that post, supported it. "He didn't bat an eye" was how Timbrell described the request more than three decades later. Davis knew Timbrell had come from a rural background. Timbrells had been farming in Frontenac and Lennox and Addington Counties since the 1780s. And he also understood that Timbrell wanted to build credibility in rural Ontario that could prove very useful at a future leadership convention.

Timbrell spent three years in the agriculture portfolio, getting a farmers' assistance program through cabinet, and developing a red meat strategy with an income stabilization program for producers. He also commissioned the first-ever study of women in rural Ontario — their needs, hopes, and aspirations, separate from the gamut of programs offered by other ministries in government. But being a Toronto member of the legislature, Timbrell was uniquely placed to bring urban and rural together by creating a program that would gather surplus food — fresh poultry, hams, canned goods, dry goods, produce, et cetera — to put together more than 9,000 Christmas food hampers each year for needy families in the Toronto area, as well as $50,000 in food vouchers for distribution to families in remote northern communities. And perhaps strangely for a politician, Timbrell forbade his political aides from publicizing the initiative, perhaps to avoid stigmatizing recipients.

The new minister of agriculture also surprised the Ontario cabinet and the civil service when he insisted on owning up to a mistake he and his bureaucrats had made related to a set of communications put out by the ministry in 1983 dealing with a string of bankruptcies of grain elevator operators. When the Ontario Federation of Agriculture (OFA) expressed its dismay at the foul-up and demanded compensation for some grain growers, Timbrell initially balked. But he then spent some of his Christmas break rereading everything published by the ministry and reviewed everything he'd said in the legislature about the issue. When the OFA and the minister met again in January, Timbrell had to confess his ministry's communications could have been misinterpreted, and as a result, he successfully pushed a compensation plan through the cabinet to which Premier Davis consented.

"I have always believed that a minister of the Crown must mean what he says and say what he means," Timbrell now says of the incident. "It is an understatement to say that they were shocked to hear what I said, and even more so when I told them of the compensation plan." Such moves ensured Timbrell's relationship with an important constituency stayed on the up and up.

On Thanksgiving weekend 1984, Timbrell and his wife were at a friend's cottage near Owen Sound when the phone rang.

"Why aren't you on the way to cabinet?" the voice said.

"Why would I be?" Timbrell replied.

"Because Davis is gonna quit!" came the answer.

"What?" asked a near-speechless Timbrell.

The agriculture minister bundled up his family, scooted back to Toronto, and made it to the cabinet meeting just in time to see Bill and Kathy Davis and their son, Neil, walk in.

Dennis Timbrell had obviously thought about this day for some time, so he was not in any doubt about what ought to happen next. Twenty minutes after the premier shared his news with the cabinet, Timbrell was back in his office on the phone, figuring out when he should announce his intention to be a candidate for the soon-to-be-vacant leadership of the Ontario PC Party.

A s we've heard, Bill Davis had a long-standing friendship with Roy McMurtry and a lot in common with Dennis Timbrell. But besides the fact that they both wanted to be premier of Ontario and their fathers were their personal heroes, Davis had little in common with the third candidate interested in replacing him: Lawrence Sheldon Grossman. Like McMurtry, Grossman failed in his first attempt to get into politics. He ran for a seat on Toronto City Council but came in a weak third behind two future mayoralty candidates: Anne Johnston and David Smith, the latter of whom went on to become a Liberal cabinet minister and senator. However, like McMurtry, Grossman tried again, also in the provincial election of 1975, and won his St. Andrew–St. Patrick riding by a mere 2 percentage points or 447 votes. But Grossman, like McMurtry, had a leg-up on every other new member of the Class of 1975 and some resented him for it. St. Andrew–St. Patrick wasn't quite *his* seat. His father, Allan, was first elected in what was previously called St. Andrew riding in 1955. So Larry inherited a solid downtown Toronto Tory seat, a loyal riding association and organization, and a prominent last name.

Allan Grossman would go down in history as the man who in 1955 defeated J.B. Salsberg, the last communist member of the Ontario legislature. It was an achievement that Allan's son often mentioned when he felt a need to burnish his conservative credentials. Premier Leslie Frost put Allan in the cabinet in 1960, making Grossman the first Jewish Progressive Conservative cabinet minister in Ontario history. In 1934 Premier Mitchell Hepburn appointed Liberal MPP David Croll as the first Jew ever appointed to the cabinet, but the Grossman appointment was seen in the Jewish community as being just as significant, even though it came more than a quarter century later. The Tories were considered more anti-Semitic than the Liberals, so the notion of a Jew cracking that ceiling was seen as truly groundbreaking. Allan Grossman served as an MPP for 20 years and was a minister in the cabinets of three different premiers: Frost, Robarts, and Davis. In 1975 he handed over that entire legacy to his son, Larry.

As already mentioned, Bill Davis and Larry Grossman both worshipped their fathers, but the similarities ended there. Davis was rural/exurban, whereas Grossman was very downtown Toronto. Davis was United Church, whereas Grossman was Jewish — too Jewish for some rural Tories, many of whom still had fairly backward views about Jews. Davis was ambitious but smart enough to keep it well submerged under a modest exterior; Grossman was ambitious and didn't give a damn who knew it. Davis was a listener and seemed to have endless patience; Grossman was a talker and occasionally impatient with people whose views he didn't share. One day at a cabinet meeting a small-*c* conservative member was, in Grossman's view, droning on about something of little interest. Grossman leaned over to the premier and asked, "Do I have to sit here and listen to this or can I leave, get some real work done, and come back later?"

Davis calmly replied, "Larry, stay where you are and you'll learn something."

It was a lesson Grossman didn't easily appreciate — the need for leaders to listen to views they didn't necessarily share, the idea that even their opponents deserved a hearing.

Like Timbrell, Grossman became a parliamentary assistant (to Attorney General Roy McMurtry) before moving into the cabinet. But unlike Timbrell, Grossman didn't get into the cabinet by playing by the rules. As mentioned, he came out against his own government's plans to shut down Doctors' Hospital in his riding and was determined to make Health Minister Frank Miller's life as difficult as possible.

After the 1977 election, Davis put Grossman, age 33, into his cabinet as minister of consumer and commercial relations. Whenever asked, Grossman offered this explanation as to how someone who fought his own government was entitled to such a promotion: "The deal is, I get into cabinet and I put the knives away." It's true that Grossman's elevation to the executive council wasn't quite typical, but then again neither was Larry Grossman, and Davis knew it. For all of his personality flaws, Grossman was whip-smart and capable as hell, and the premier knew talent when he saw it. Davis left him in that junior portfolio for only a year before giving Grossman a major promotion — to minister of industry and tourism, a post very similar to the trade and development portfolio to which Davis had appointed Grossman's father seven years earlier.

Grossman lasted three and a half years in that position before getting shuffled to health, which he took over from Dennis Timbrell. But unlike Timbrell, Grossman only lasted a year and a half at health; Davis soon had bigger plans for him and promoted him to treasurer in July 1983 where his relationship with the premier became closer. At least Grossman thought it had become closer. He learned under very amusing circumstances that his relationship with the premier wasn't as close as he'd figured.

Whether you were an MPP, a cabinet minister, a civil servant, a deputy minister, or a member of the media, one thing you never did was call the premier by his first name. The only people who called the premier "Bill" were his wife and his childhood friends from Brampton. To this day John Tory, the 62-year-old mayor of Toronto who has known Davis since he was a teenager and worked in the premier's office for him while in his twenties, can't call his political hero by his first name. The same goes for former Senator Hugh Segal, another senior Davis adviser who has known the former premier for almost half a century and doesn't call him Bill.

But one evening, not at a cabinet meeting but in a more social setting, Larry Grossman was determined to call the premier by his first name to show how close a relationship they truly had. Davis, Tory, Segal, and Grossman were in conversation about something. Grossman had decided tonight would be the night and strategically waited for the right casual moment to call the premier by his first name. And he did. The conversation came to an instant halt. Davis bit down on his pipe a little harder. Segal and Tory were mute. It was beyond an awkward silence. It was painful. "It's as if the word fell off a table and crashed onto the floor," Grossman told me years later. That was the last time the treasurer ever called the premier "Bill."

One of the annual rituals Ontario's treasurer or minister of finance has is to fly to New York and meet with the credit-rating agencies. In recent years, Ontario's credit rating has bounced around a bit, but by 1984 it had only ever been Triple A, and it was a point of pride among treasurers to keep it that way. Before the ratings houses embarrassed themselves with their ravenous and borderline corrupt practices that helped usher in the Great Recession, it was considered one of the most important signs that the international financial community had confidence in the treasurer and his government if the minister kept the credit rating at Triple A. So, in the spring of 1984, Davis and Grossman travelled to New York to convince the people who were going to loan Ontario a lot of money to cover its deficit that things were actually under control.

For Grossman it was a crucial meeting in two ways. First, he knew there was every possibility that the premier would call an election later that year, and if he didn't keep the credit rating at Triple A, he'd be handing the opposition a gift on a silver platter and denying the Tories their perpetual ace in the hole, namely, prudent stewardship of the economy. The other issue for Grossman was that if Davis stepped down (as seemed unlikely but was still a possibility) the treasurer knew he wanted to be a candidate for the leadership and it was hardly going to help that effort to be the first Tory treasurer to lose the Triple A credit rating. All of which is to say that this meeting in New York was hugely important to Grossman. And yet, for some reason, the treasurer had a devil of a time getting the premier's attention to give him a thorough briefing on the province's finances. It wasn't until the two men were in a limousine in New York City en route to their meeting with the ratings agency that Grossman finally had a moment alone with the premier to brief him. But even that was problematic. As Grossman tried to get the premier to focus on the state of the finances of Ontario Inc., Davis kept perusing the sports pages of one of the local newspapers to see whether the two could catch a baseball game while in town. Grossman tried to remain patient but, in fact, he was doing a slow burn because the premier seemed completely uninterested in his treasurer's briefing.

"Oh, look," Davis told him, "the Phillies are playing the Mets tonight." Grossman was about to have a hemorrhage.

The two arrived for their meeting, and Grossman was convinced it was going to be a disaster because Davis was so ill-prepared. He saw his entire career passing before his eyes. Davis marched into the meeting, puffing his pipe, and thrust out his hand to meet the ratings agency officials. As they gave their names, Davis began asking where they'd gone to university. One of them said Syracuse. The premier instantly began going on about the outstanding freshman centre the Orangemen had playing on that year's basketball team. A second official said he'd attended the University of Michigan. The premier's wife, Kathy, had attended Michigan, so Davis waxed eloquent about the campus and the football team's excellent starting quarterback. And so it went. Grossman watched in awe. Davis had no idea who he'd be meeting and therefore had no opportunity ahead of time to brush up on his U.S. college sports. He just knew this stuff, and more important, he knew the value of making these folks feel that what was important in their lives was important to him, too.

It was a brief meeting. Davis warmed them up, Grossman quickly went through the financial tables, and as they left, Davis thanked them all *by name* of course. Lo and behold, the credit rating remained intact at Triple A.

"That went pretty well," the premier told Grossman after the meeting.

"Piece of cake, Premier," Grossman replied, not betraying a hint of any of the terror he'd felt only an hour earlier.

There's no question that of all the pretenders to Davis's throne Larry Grossman was the most outwardly ambitious for the job. Part of that ambition stemmed from the fact that Grossman had done every job of significance in the cabinet and there was only one other job he hadn't done that he was interested in and that was Davis's. He also thought of his own father and how proud Allan would be to see his son, a Jew, as leader of the Progressive Conservative Party and premier of Ontario. Grossman wanted it for his father as much as, if not more than, for himself. It would be the most remarkable indication that the Ontario PC Party had turned its back on its discriminatory past practices and embraced the increasingly diverse demographic makeup of the province.

Having said that, with the separate school funding announcement still brewing under the surface (and soon ready to explode), and with both opposition parties having rookie leaders, Grossman firmly believed it was imperative for the party's prospects that Davis stay, win the election, get the Catholic funding issue put to bed, and then retire — and he told him so. The two men had a private chat in the premier's office where Grossman made those very arguments. When Davis told him he was really just ready to go, that he'd been at Queen's Park for a quarter of a century and it was simply time, Grossman begged him: "Just get us through the election. You can retire a year later, but we really need you to get us through this next election." Davis understood the arguments. He'd heard them all before. Grossman understood, and as much as he had confidence in his own abilities to win the leadership and the ensuing election, he knew the second of those tasks would be immeasurably more difficult without Bill Davis at the helm.

Right-wing conservatives around the world — as opposed to Red Tories or more pink-hued Progressive Conservatives — were feeling very upbeat around Thanksgiving 1984 when Bill Davis announced his retirement. Ronald Reagan was less than a month away from winning his second consecutive landslide as president of the United States. Reagan had won 44 states in defeating Jimmy Carter in 1980 and was on the verge of winning 49 states in November against Walter Mondale, Carter's vice-president. A little over a year earlier Margaret Thatcher had won a smashing re-election majority over Labour's Michael Foot. And in Canada a little over a month earlier Brian Mulroney, seen as more of a right-wing conservative than he turned out to be, captured an astonishing 50 percent of the total vote en route to 211 seats — the largest number in Canadian history — thrashing John Turner's Liberals and Ed Broadbent's New Democrats. Two years earlier the conservative-leaning Helmut Kohl had become chancellor of West Germany. It was a good time to be a conservative.

To be clear, these conservatives weren't Bill Davis's kind of conservatives. When he met Margaret Thatcher, Davis couldn't help but remember one of the most chilling things she said to him. "Do you know why I love this job so much?" Thatcher asked him. "Because how else could a person like me enjoy so much power!" The word *power* was practically banned at Queen's Park during Davis's time. One never spoke of wielding power, only being of service. It might sound corny, and it's not as if Davis never enjoyed the spoils of power, but to talk about it so brazenly with someone she barely knew — Davis found that astonishing.

There would be one more candidate for the PC leadership who never shied away from admitting his admiration for Margaret Thatcher and Ronald Reagan, even though both the liberal media and the Red Tory faction of the PC Party thought it was a mistake to reveal such a thing. That man was Frank Stuart Miller.

The conventional wisdom around Ontario politics in the mid-1980s was that no leader from Toronto could ever successfully win the premiership — there was simply too much hate for anything related to Toronto in the rest of the province. Davis, of course, was from Brampton; Robarts from London; Frost was born in Orillia; Drew in Guelph; Hepburn in St. Thomas; George Henry in King Township; G. Howard Ferguson in Kemptville in Eastern Ontario; Ernest Drury in Barrie; William Hearst in Bruce County; James Whitney in Dundas County in Eastern Ontario; Oliver Mowat in Kingston; and so on. So it might come as a surprise that the first premier of Ontario ever born in Toronto was, in fact, Frank Miller, who was born on May 14, 1927, and grew up in Toronto — eight years at Regal Road Public School and two more at Oakwood Collegiate. He had four older sisters and was the youngest by far of the five children, born when his mother was 42 years old. He learned first-hand about hard work and the harshness of life. His dad, Percy Frank Miller, worked two jobs most of the time, and his mother, at age 55, got a job as a maid to help the family make ends meet after Percy suffered a stroke when young Frank was only 12. Percy recovered somewhat but felt he needed to get out of his sickbed and earn some money. Those were the days before unemployment insurance, so against doctor's orders he went out and got a job. A year later, Percy Miller dropped dead.

Frank Miller had his first paper route when he was 12 years old and delivered 150 *Toronto Stars* and *Toronto Telegrams* every day. He earned

5.4 cents per customer every week. He learned the profoundly simple but important lesson of showing up and delivering the goods on time because if you didn't there was someone else there who would take your paper route from you. He grew up in the west end of Toronto during the Great Depression, never felt deprived, but did remember the neighbours taking up a food collection to give to the Millers after Percy's death because the family had no food. Frank Miller recalls his father having one overwhelming wish for him — that Frank get as much education as possible and not have to work dirty factory jobs as he did. Eventually, when Frank was 15, the family moved to Muskoka where his mother, Margaret Stuart McKean, was born, commencing a lifelong love affair with that part of Central Ontario. Miller attended a tiny high school in Gravenhurst and really began to shine scholastically. As unlucky as some of Miller's youth was, he was fortunate in one thing: the Second World War ended five days before his 18th birthday. He liked the glory and discipline of wearing a military uniform, which he did from the age of 14 on in the air cadets, but he was very happy not to be shipped overseas to fight and die as a teenager.

In 1945 Miller won a scholarship to attend McGill University in chemical engineering. It was his first time away from home, and he was miserable. He came from a family of Methodist teetotalers and yet was stuck in a dormitory room with 20 kids, most of whom were noisy and drinking all the time. But he stuck it out and spent summers working back home in Muskoka, washing dishes at Sloan's Restaurant in Gravenhurst. As much as he didn't like McGill, one very good thing happened while Miller lived in Quebec. He met his future wife, Ann, who lived in the same village where one of his sisters lived. She was a working-class English immigrant, born in Glasgow, who like Miller, had a hardscrabble upbringing. Ann was working full-time by the time she was 17. The couple married when he was 23 and she was 21 when Miller got a job at Rubberset, the shaving and toilet brush manufacturer, immediately after graduating. He became the second-highest-paid graduate from his McGill Class of 1949, so he sawed the logs himself at a neighbour's sawmill and built a house for $3,200, paying cash. Miller also started doing something that became a lifelong passion: he bought and flipped cars for a tidy profit. Frank Miller was learning all the skills he'd eventually need to be a successful cabinet minister. But that was still years away.

There were still some hard times ahead for Miller. He switched jobs numerous times (his choice) and lost money on some bad deals that required him to bust open his wife's penny piggy bank in 1952 to pay for food. But his 10 years in Quebec during two different periods of his life in three different locations all resulted in mostly happy memories. Miller could never recall being treated poorly by francophones whose language he picked up fairly easily.

Miller did well at engineering but had to admit to himself that it bored him. So the Millers moved back to Muskoka, Bracebridge specifically, and had three children (years later they would adopt another). During that time, Frank became a Grade 12 and 13 chemistry, math, and physics teacher. But a salary dispute with the school ended that, so it was on the road again, first to Brantford as a sales engineer in industrial finishes, then to Quebec again, and finally to Muskoka once more. The Millers got around, but this time something clicked. Miller saw a summer lodge in the newspaper one morning and literally bought it that afternoon — the Patterson Kaye Lodge in Bracebridge — for $72,000. He didn't have enough money but borrowed $15,000, sold both cars, put the last $5,000 he had in the bank toward the lodge, taught school again, sold cars again, sold paint, and ran his new acquisition, all at the same time. Amazingly, his wife supported this craziness.

The next part of the Frank Miller story was downright scary. He'd become very ill on and off since 1958. As it turned out, he'd developed hepatitis B from chemical poisoning at work. Nevertheless, he bought another lodge and a car business. By June 1966, Miller was in a Toronto hospital for a three-month stay, his weight was down to 106 pounds, and he was told: "We're sorry. We're not sure we can do anything for you." Maple Leafs great Harvey "Busher" Jackson was in the bed next to him, and Miller watched him die of liver cancer.

On July 3, Miller woke up from surgery and was promptly told he was unlikely to last a week. He was 39 years old and filled with regret about all the things in life he wouldn't live to see. Miller was determined to get out of his sickbed, though, so he walked to the bathroom for a drink of water, fell, and smashed his head. Every tube came out of his body and his heart stopped. Had he been in Bracebridge rather than in Toronto where his doctor had sent him for treatment, he surely would have died. He had a complete blockage of all his body's bile ducts.

No one quite knows how, but Miller's health started to improve. He'll tell you he *willed* himself better. But his stir-craziness got the better of him and he checked himself out of hospital too quickly. He was soon experiencing immense stabbing pains in his stomach, so it was back to hospital for another eight weeks. Eventually, Miller recaptured his health, but what a journey that was.

Miller described all this in tape-recorded conversations two decades ago with former *London Free Press* reporter George Hutchison. He acknowledged that "you do pray when you're dying" and promised to do something useful with his life, which did improve. Over the next five years, he became financially comfortable but wanted more, which led him to a more active interest in politics. Back in the early 1960s, Miller had run for a seat on the Monck Township council but lost. He discovered losing wasn't so bad and enjoyed making the effort.

As a businessman, he saw governments, in his view, far too often acting irrationally, so he worked on the 1967 provincial campaign for John Robarts's Progressive Conservatives. Then in 1971 just a month before election day, the MPP for Muskoka, Robert Boyer, suddenly quit. Miller assumed a lengthy lineup of candidates would want to contest the safe Tory seat, but five days before the nominating meeting there was only one no-name candidate in the race. Miller was approached by a couple of party types from Huntsville who thought the riding could do better and urged Miller to get in. The problem was that the day Boyer resigned Ann Miller broke both her legs skiing, so the timing wasn't great, to say the least. But Ann Miller told her husband: "If you want to win, you'd better get to work."

The nominating meeting was, propitiously, on Miller's birthday: May 14. The new premier, Bill Davis, was in attendance. Davis made a habit of attending nominating meetings to bring some attention to them, not to endorse any particular candidate. Miller's opponent spoke first, and all Miller could think was: *Gosh, this guy is boring. I've gotta be funnier than that.* So he started his speech with a joke that today would be considered in terribly bad taste, but in 1971 got quite a laugh. "A lot of people in this room don't think I'm serious about running for this job. Well, look in the front row. There's my wife. The story is she broke her legs skiing. In fact, her legs are broken because she said she would vote for the other guy." Miller won by nine votes over Bernard Reynolds from Huntsville, then he won him over. Reynolds became his official agent. And on election day in 1971 Miller kept Muskoka in the Tory column.

Just as Leslie Frost chose rookie Bill Davis to give the government's response to the Speech from the Throne, Bill Davis granted Frank Miller the same honour after the 1971 throne speech. Miller watched Bob Nixon respond for the Liberals and refer to his own father, Ontario's last Liberal premier. Then Stephen Lewis got up for the NDP and talked about his father, the current federal NDP leader. Next, Miller took centre stage and said: "Mr. Speaker, I've listened to the other speakers and how they learned their politics. My problem is, my dad died when I was 13 and I can never remember him talking about politics. So unlike the other two speakers, I was able to choose the right party."

Like Timbrell and Grossman, Miller started as a backbencher, then a parliamentary assistant to the minister of health, but Premier Davis obviously saw something he liked in the Man from Muskoka, because 16 months later, in February 1974, he gave Miller a huge promotion to minister of health. Miller had once met former Premier Robarts who told him Queen's Park was so complicated that he thought no one should go into cabinet until he'd spent eight years on the backbenches. Robarts himself had served seven years there. Miller, however, didn't spend even two and a half years as a backbencher before gaining the government's biggest-spending portfolio. Premier Davis wanted to shuffle the previous minister, Richard Potter, out of health. Dr. Potter told the premier's office that Miller could run the department with one hand tied behind his back, so Davis gave the parliamentary assistant from health the big job. Miller said the premier told him: "Frank, I need someone to cut costs and that's your job. The previous guy could take out an appendix, but I don't need that now." Miller took Davis's instructions seriously. Maybe too seriously.

Miller was in health for six months when he realized what every health minister learns — Ontario doesn't have a health-care system, but rather "a hodgepodge of competing providers all with egos so high they'd rather have you die then go to someone else's care."

The watchword of the day in the mid-1970s was *restraint*. Miller was ordered to cut $50 million out of health, so off he went. Figuring the public would need a chance to ventilate, he ordered province-wide hearings, invited the Ontario Medical Association and the Ontario Hospital

Association to attend, and came up with a most unorthodox plan. Miller told his cabinet colleagues they had to approve his plan to close 15 hospitals — five private and 10 public. When they asked which ones, Miller responded: "I can't tell you. Some of them are in your ridings, and if I tell you, you'll fight me." Miller demanded that the cabinet give him the right in principle to do this and got it — twice. He warned that some of them weren't going to like his choices. But he felt he needed a free hand to implement the treasurer's $50 million spending cut. Cabinet gave it to him. Miller then resolved that no hospital would learn about its fate in the media or by letter. He showed up at each hospital and broke the news personally, trying to be as sensitive as possible under the circumstances. Miller's problem was that closing a single hospital bed would save $25,000 per bed per year, but closing an entire hospital saved $100,000 per bed per year. So the logical choice was to shut hospitals and realize four times as much savings. But as Miller quickly learned, "Logic doesn't prevail in health care."

Miller would find that out in spades on a winter trip to Hanover in Grey County. He and his four-person team flew up in a single-engine turbo Beaver, but no one told them the Hanover airport wasn't used in the winter. The airport was buried in six feet of snow, so Miller's plane landed and sank. It was an omen. They drove 15 minutes to Durham, where it looked as if the entire town was waiting to confront the minister of health. After a three-hour discussion, things got tense. "Some old lady started beating me with a sign on the knees," Miller remembered. The police chief came in and asked the mayor to declare a state of emergency. "He believed the crowd would lynch me," Miller says. The Ontario Provincial Police came in and essentially took over the town. They moved Miller to the boiler room, where the nursing staff actually worried about his safety. Their plan was to place Miller on a stretcher, put a sheet over his head, and take him to an ambulance. It didn't come to that, but the actual plan of attack wasn't much better. When the OPP officers arrived, they put in a flying wedge of big, tall men. As they tried to get the minister to a waiting car, stones and snowballs started flying in his direction. When Miller got into the car, the crowd tried to roll it. "It was amazing how a crowd becomes a mob so quickly," Miller recalled.

Finally, the stress of scenes such as that one, repeated in every community, overwhelmed Miller. He was playing hockey at Maple Leaf Gardens (he was the goalie on the MPPs' team) when he suffered a heart attack. Two women from the Liberal caucus took him to Wellesley Hospital.

Miller went home to recover. When he returned to Queen's Park, Premier Davis asked him if he wanted to go back to health and remarkably he said yes. "I put my name on the line and did these things and believed in it and took the heat for it," Miller told George Hutchison. "No other minister in my time got the heat I got, outside of some scandal."

In January 1977 at a cabinet meeting, Miller hit the wall. "The chamberlains of the cabinet were always there," he said. One of Miller's predecessors in health, Tom Wells, suggested Miller back down. "Tom Wells was the greatest appeaser we ever had," Miller recalled. "A great politician right to his manicured fingertips. I don't know what principles he stood for other than getting re-elected." Miller's view was: "Why back down? We've already suffered the political harm and backing down doesn't get you off the hook."

Four days later Bill Davis got Frank Miller off the hook. On February 3, 1977, the premier shuffled him to natural resources, thereby lowering the temperature in health care. Miller actually enjoyed being minister of natural resources. He got a forest regeneration policy implemented, whereby logging companies were now on the hook for replanting what they cut. But it was politically where Miller had his biggest awakening. His staff told him he ought to think about being a leadership candidate when Bill Davis stepped down. That resignation was still many years away, but Miller agreed to give his staff an hour a day for pure leadership politics — meeting the right folks, staying a little longer after giving a speech to shake hands, et cetera. Even the premier, perhaps remembering how his own leadership ambitions were almost torpedoed by his refusal to set up an organization in advance, encouraged Miller to do so.

In August 1978, Davis must have figured things had cooled down enough, because he gave Miller the most influential job in the cabinet: treasurer, minister of economics, and intergovernmental affairs (TEIGA). Miller loved it.

"Being treasurer is even more powerful than being premier," he said. "I never showed Premier Davis a budget until a week before presenting it." It was another indication of how Davis trusted his ministers to do their jobs and didn't intervene unless things went terribly wrong.

On March 19, 1981, Bill Davis's most fervent political wish came true: his Progressive Conservatives reclaimed the majority government they had lost for six years. Davis was ecstatic, or as ecstatic as bland Brampton Billy could be. One week after the election Davis and Frank Miller had what would turn out to be a historically important telephone conversation. Miller was on vacation at Mont Tremblant in Quebec and told the premier he wanted to remain as treasurer. Davis was happy to do so and even promised not to block as many of the more right-wing initiatives Miller wanted to champion. But the premier also did something that few could imagine him doing. He started giving Miller advice on running for the PC leadership. This seemed passing strange for two reasons: first, the ink was barely dry on the 1981 election results and yet Davis was already considering succession planning; and second, while no one knew exactly who Davis preferred to see replace him, it was a given that the answer wasn't Frank Miller. And yet there they were, the two senior-most figures in the PC government having a very important and very secretive conversation about the post–Bill Davis PC Party.

"You won't want to be in treasury when I retire," Davis told Miller. "It's no place to run for the leadership from. So consider that." Astonishingly, Davis was telling one of his most problematic colleagues that he'd happily shuffle him somewhere else when he wanted it, making Miller a more appealing candidate. It was conventional wisdom in politics that the guy who was responsible for raising taxes and bringing in big deficits in the midst of a recession wasn't going to be the most popular guy around. Davis offered Miller a chance to compete for the leadership from a more felicitous portfolio, and both men kept that information in their back pockets.

Miller, though, remained in the treasury portfolio, and strangely enough, the one thing he might be remembered for during that time had to do with someone not taking out the garbage carefully. In the lead-up to the 1983 budget, reporters from the *Globe and Mail* rifled through the garbage bags outside the Frost Block and found what looked like authentic budget papers. When the *Globe* published the information, some people considered that a budget leak and thought Miller should resign. Miller himself felt strongly that he *should* resign, even though he had nothing to do with the screw-up. He took 10 days to consider all the arguments and consulted constitutional scholars. If he didn't quit, was he undermining the concept of ministerial responsibility? But if he did quit, was he raising the ethical bar to precedent-setting new levels that could make future treasurers vulnerable to any disgruntled civil servant? Eventually, Miller concluded it would be "stupid to do something that no one will learn from and truncate my career." He stayed and presented his budget.

Another thing shocked Miller when he was treasurer. One day he got an off-the-record visit from Robert Macaulay, the superstar cabinet minister from the Robarts years, the brother of one of Davis's Big Blue Machine advisers, and the man whose leadership campaign in 1961 Davis himself ran. Macaulay told Miller: "Some of us want you to run. Bill Davis knows we're having this meeting and he approves." Miller later checked Macaulay's story with Davis himself and the premier confirmed it: he did know about it and encouraged it.

Miller had only planned to spend eight years in public life, but by July 1983, when Premier Davis planned to shuffle the cabinet again, it was now 12 years and counting. Davis knew Miller wanted an easier portfolio, and hearkening back to the commitment he'd made Miller two years earlier, he gave the treasurer his pick. Miller chose industry and trade. He still wasn't sure in his own mind that he intended to be a candidate to replace Davis when the bell rang. But he continued to indulge his staff and dedicate a certain amount of time each week to raising money, holding fundraising dinners, phoning potential supporters, setting up a campaign headquarters, and so on. He thought he was doing it on the QT, so as not to seem disloyal to Davis (even though he had the premier's okay to do it) and not to take the public's eye off the government's overall agenda. He also believed Davis adviser Hugh Segal was "feeding the rumour mill that I was doing things to be ready for leader," Miller said. "I was never sure, but I was suspicious." Miller also had to acknowledge that if Segal were doing that, it was fine. If Miller was lining up his ducks for a run at the leadership, he was fair game and knew it. For his part, Segal today says: "I was focused on both preserving Davis's standing as premier and did worry about Miller and some of his folks working to destabilize or shorten Mr. D's term."

Bill Davis shows Massachusetts Senator Edward Kennedy around Queen's Park in January 1976. *Office of the Premier of Ontario*

Bill Davis met numerous international figures, including Reza Pahlavi, the shah of Iran. *Office of the Premier of Ontario*

Ed Stewart was Bill Davis's deputy minister in the Department of Education. He eventually joined the premier as his secretary to the cabinet and was his most significant adviser. *Office of the Premier of Ontario*

Clare Westcott (right) was one of Davis's longest-serving advisers and political problem solvers. Now in his 90s and fighting vision problems, Westcott still speaks almost daily to his former boss by phone. He's pictured here with the father of the hydrogen bomb, Edward Teller. *Office of the Premier of Ontario*

Davis had a complicated relationship with Alberta Premier Peter Lougheed. They were both PC premiers who served for 14 years and won four elections apiece. But they were famously on opposite sides of the energy pricing and patriation issues, causing enormous friction for a time. *Office of the Premier of Ontario*

Bill Davis at the Constitutional talks in Ottawa in November 1981, flanked by advisers Rendell Dick and Ed Stewart in the background. *Office of the Premier of Ontario*

Bill Davis leads Team Ontario at the Constitutional talks. In the front row (left to right): Intergovernmental Affairs Minister Thomas Wells, Davis, federal Justice Minister Jean Chrétien, and Prime Minister Pierre Trudeau. *Office of the Premier of Ontario*

CONSTITUTION BED

Bill Davis was pilloried by the newspaper cartoonists for supporting Prime Minister Pierre Trudeau's efforts to patriate the Constitution. *Office of the Premier of Ontario*

Talking constitutional renewal with (from left to right): Michael Pitfield, Jean Chrétien, and Pierre Trudeau. *Office of the Premier of Ontario*

Bill Davis, with his omnipresent pipe, engages in discussion at the Constitution talks with (from left to right) Ed Greathead, director of federal-provincial relations in Ontario's Ministry of Intergovernmental Affairs; Intergovernmental Affairs Minister Thomas Wells, and Attorney General Roy McMurtry. *Office of the Premier of Ontario*

Team Ontario at the Constitutional talks in Ottawa. Beside Bill Davis is his attorney general, Roy McMurtry; behind them (from left to right) are Intergovernmental Affairs Minister Thomas Wells (partially obscured), Secretary to the Cabinet Ed Stewart, Treasurer Frank Miller (also partially obscured), with special adviser Hugh Segal in the back at the right. *Office of the Premier of Ontario*

A quiet moment with Pierre Trudeau, Roy McMurtry, and Thomas Wells. *Office of the Premier of Ontario*

In her memoir, future governor general Adrienne Clarkson described Bill Davis as the best boss she ever had. Davis appointed the then journalist to a post in France where she promoted Ontario culture. *Office of the Premier of Ontario*

Bill Davis in conversation with Saskatchewan Premier Allan Blakeney (left) and Prime Minister Pierre Trudeau. *Office of the Premier of Ontario*

A big celebratory cake surrounded by Bill Davis's mother, Vera; sons, Neil and Ian; and wife Kathleen. *Office of the Premier of Ontario*

Bill Davis is flanked by Lieutenant Governor John Black Aird and cabinet ministers Roy McMurtry and Thomas Wells. *Office of the Premier of Ontario*

Bill Davis and British Prime Minister Margaret Thatcher met several times during their political careers. *Office of the Premier of Ontario*

One of the highlights of Davis's premiership was meeting Pope John Paul II, the first pope ever to visit Canada, who came to Toronto and Midland as part of that historic 1984 trip. *Office of the Premier of Ontario*

Brian Mulroney solicited Bill Davis's support when he led the PCs to Canada's largest-ever majority government in 1984. *Office of the Premier of Ontario*

Bill Davis enjoyed campaigning with Brian Mulroney during the federal election campaign in the summer of 1984. *Office of the Premier of Ontario*

One of the many different election campaign buttons featuring Bill Davis's image. *Steve Paikin*

Bill Davis, puffing his ever-present pipe, prepares to tie up the flag at his cottage on Georgian Bay. *Davis Family*

Bill Davis was made a Companion of the Order of Canada in 1985 by Governor General Jeanne Sauvé. *Office of the Premier of Ontario*

Bill Davis with his mother, Vera, at the family cottage on Georgian Bay. *Davis Family*

Despite being in different parties, Bill Davis and Premier Kathleen Wynne have a close relationship. They're seen here at a question-and-answer session at Massey College in 2016. *Steve Paikin*

John Tory is one of many Bill Davis disciples now in politics. The premier's former principal secretary became Toronto's 65th mayor in December 2014. *Steve Paikin*

A big reunion at the Georgian Bay cottage of three generations of the Davis family. *Steve Paikin*

Bill Davis with the author outside the former premier's Fort Lauderdale
condominium. *Steve Paikin*

In mid-September 1984, Miller's ambivalence about running for the leadership really became apparent. He suspected the Ontario Tories were getting close to calling an election and expected not to be a candidate in that election. Miller and Davis had a secret meeting in the premier's den at his home in Brampton where the Man from Muskoka broke the news.

"My riding is having its annual general meeting in two days, and I've told the executive I'm not running again," Miller told Davis. "I want this to be known in advance so they can choose a candidate to replace me."

The next words out of Davis's mouth might be, above all others in his entire political career, the ones he wishes he could take back.

"Can you call that off?" the premier asked.

"Why?"

"Frank, you shouldn't do that."

Again, Miller was perplexed. "Why?"

"I have a list of people who should be running for my job and you're on it," the premier explained.

Miller protested. "Premier, I've already said I'm not on it."

"It doesn't matter," Davis retorted. "You're on mine. Besides, do you think you'll have any influence on choosing my successor if you're retiring? You're the minister of industry and trade, for goodness' sake. I think you'd better call off that meeting." Then came an extraordinary admission: "I haven't even told Kathy this yet, but I'm not going to run again."

Miller had one of the greatest scoops in Ontario political history. Nevertheless, he couldn't bring himself to believe it. Somehow he still figured Bill Davis would lead the PC Party into the next election, then step aside quickly. But just in case, he called his riding association and cancelled the meeting he'd scheduled to announce his retirement. Frank Miller wasn't quite a leadership candidate, but he wasn't quite retiring, either.

Miller was at his cottage at Acton Island on Thanksgiving weekend when he got a call to come to Toronto for an emergency meeting. The premier had an urgent announcement to make. Despite what he'd heard directly from Davis's mouth less than a month earlier, he felt sure Davis was going to call an election and thought, *To heck with it. I don't need to be there for that.* He turned on the radio, and as soon as he heard the first three words of Davis's press conference — "Kathy and I …" — he knew he'd guessed wrong.

"Oh, my God!" Miller said to his wife. "He's retiring."

Four men. Four cabinet colleagues. Four rivals. Four Torontonians, although Miller had completely rebranded himself as Mr. Rural Ontario. Their political careers all had so much in common, and now so did their ultimate ambition: they all wanted to replace William Davis as leader of the Ontario Progressive Conservative Party and become the province's 19th premier.

Dennis Timbrell got out of the gate early. The same weekend Davis announced retirement Timbrell visited Miller and asked for an endorsement for his leadership bid. Miller, who still hadn't told anyone whether he was in or out, gave his good friend Timbrell a cryptic answer: "Dennis, if there's anyone I'd back, it would be you." Timbrell heard an endorsement for his campaign, but Miller certainly didn't intend it that way. He did tell Timbrell: "I don't think I'm going to be running," but he certainly wasn't categorical about it.

The Thursday after Thanksgiving Monday Miller and his wife had their first serious conversation about the leadership. He told her he didn't thirst for the job, but at the same time he didn't see in any of his anticipated competitors the qualities he thought were necessary at that moment in Ontario's history, namely, unwinding government, simplifying matters, eschewing "fancy new policies." Ann Miller asked her husband *the* key question: "Do you want to spend the rest of your life wondering whether you should have tried?" As it turned out, no, he didn't. Frank Miller, the reluctant candidate for so long, became the first candidate to declare his intention to run for the PC leadership. When Dennis Timbrell heard the news, he was crushed. From that point forward he considered Miller a traitor.

Bette Stephenson also had a problem with Miller's announcement. The two of them were ideological soulmates in the cabinet and had made a commitment to each other — if Stephenson ran for leader, Miller wouldn't and vice versa. They were close friends and almost became family, as well, when Miller's son, Norm, and Stephenson's daughter, Mary Kay, were engaged to be married. (The engagement was later broken off.) But when Miller threw his hat into the ring Stephenson's leadership ambitions ended.

"I must say," she told me 30 years after the fact, "I was a little disappointed when he did say he was going to run." Nevertheless, Stephenson publicly endorsed Miller's bid. So did Claude Bennett and Gordon Walker, two of the other more right-wing members of the Davis cabinet, who also kicked the tires on running but ultimately passed. Walker very much wanted to run but realized it would be a mistake to split the party's right-wing vote with Miller, and since Miller was more popular, Walker stood down. In hindsight he says he wishes he'd run for it. "That was the one time in my life I chose the wrong direction," he now says. However, at the time Miller dazzled all observers by lining up the most caucus support: he had 27 of his fellow Tory MPPs onside, far more than Timbrell's 18, Grossman's 10, and McMurtry's 8.

As Davis himself surveyed the field, there was one name missing that he'd like to have seen there: Darcy McKeough. Davis urged his former treasurer, who had quit politics six years earlier, to seek the job, but McKeough declined and Davis was disappointed. Of the four men running, Davis's heart was with McMurtry, but he hesitated getting involved, fearing his actions might alienate others.

"You can't keep these things a secret," Davis recently said. "If you're going to do it, you've got to do it in a way that some people end up knowing about it."

As Miller began to put his team together, he ran into his first crisis. One of the Big Blue Machine's top drivers, Norman Atkins, bailed on him. Atkins had earlier approached Miller, asking if he could serve as his campaign chair, and Miller had agreed. But when McMurtry leaped into the race, Atkins not only jumped ship to the attorney general but also denied ever saying he'd work for Miller. "He didn't say, 'I've changed my mind,'" Miller recalls of the confrontation with Atkins. "He said he never said he would. He came to me for goodness' sake!" Miller was stunned and the two parted company. (Atkins died in 2010 and thus couldn't confirm or deny this story.)

By all rights, Larry Grossman should have had the hardest time gaining any traction in the race. The New Democrats were the first party in Ontario to have a Jewish leader — Stephen Lewis in 1970. Then the Liberals chose Stuart Smith in 1976. But the Progressive Conservative Party, with its Tory bedrock base in rural Ontario? Having a Jewish leader always seemed a bridge too far. The reality was that too many PC Party members thought Grossman was, as the saying went, "too short, too Toronto, and too Jewish."

But Grossman put together a fantastic team that included pollster Allan Gregg, and Grossman himself was an indefatigable candidate. He never quite came out directly and referred to his religion when seeking the support of delegates. But he often hinted at it, referring to himself as "a different kind of candidate" from what the party had been accustomed to, without ever being specific about what that meant. I can remember talking to one of Davis's inner circle advisers, Eddie Goodman, at this time. Privately, I asked Goodman, who is Jewish, "Can you imagine this party choosing a Jew as leader?" He paused for only a second before saying: "Maybe they'll think we need a smart Jew to get us out of the troubles we're in." Neither one of us knew it then, but Grossman's religion would turn out to play a significant role in both the strategy and outcome of the convention.

Thousands of Tories gathered at the Coliseum at Exhibition Place on January 25, 1985, to choose their next leader, and the man upon whom their hopes for continuing the dynasty rested. Backbench MPP Mike Harris was supporting Frank Miller, which was causing him enormous headaches back home in North Bay. When Harris told officials at his Nipissing riding association early in the race that he wanted to endorse Miller, they all tried to dissuade him from doing so. Apparently, the tradition was to wait for the Big Blue Machine's Norman Atkins to tell them whom to support. Harris was having none of that, decided to back Miller early in the process, and then began replacing his riding executive with people who were more loyal to him than PC Party headquarters.

The now 42-year-long Tory dynasty was both a blessing and a curse at this convention. It certainly gave the Progressive Conservatives an aura of invincibility that they lorded over the other two parties. During intense moments in the legislature, Davis often referred to "the realities of March 19," which was code for: "We now have a majority government over here and you don't." But Dennis Timbrell candidly admitted during our conversation in 2015 that a day didn't go by when he didn't wonder the following: "What if I win and what if I am the end of the line that started with George Drew?" Timbrell never asked the man he hoped to replace for advice. He just didn't

want to put Davis in an awkward position. He knew about the premier's close
and long-standing friendship with McMurtry and assumed a similar relationship existed with Grossman, given the premier's connection to Larry's father.

The contest was shaping up as most Progressive Conservative conventions do: a battle between the more pragmatic Red Tories (represented by
Timbrell, Grossman, and McMurtry) and the more ideological right-wing
ones (championed by Miller). This was an old-style delegated convention
rather than the "one member, one vote" points system the party now uses.
The first ballot was close and indicated a tight, competitive fight to the
finish. As expected, Miller led on the first ballot with 591 votes, but that
was good for only 31 percent support. Timbrell came second with 421
votes or 25 percent. But Grossman was nipping at his heels in third place
with 378 votes, good for 22.4 percent support. McMurtry's late entry into
the race clearly hurt, since the attorney general came last with 300 votes,
good for only 18 percent support. One of those 300 votes belonged to Bill
Davis, who voted for his long-time and dear friend. McMurtry was forced
off the ballot and endorsed Grossman.

"We had the province with us," said Norman Atkins, McMurtry's
campaign boss. "We just didn't have the party." Atkins was right. A
pre-convention poll showed McMurtry as the top choice of Ontarians,
but alas, the last choice of Tories at the convention.

The second ballot was a thriller and changed the course of history.
Miller broadened his lead to 659 votes, good for 39 percent support. But
Grossman shocked the hall by moving past Timbrell into second place by
an agonizingly close margin: 514 to 508 votes. In percentage terms it was
30.5 to 30.2. The look on Timbrell's face when the vote was announced was
heartbreaking. In fact, the tally was so close that party officials counted
the ballots a second time. But the result was the same: Timbrell was out.

"To Dennis, it was a lifetime ambition," Miller told George Hutchison
nearly a decade later. "He was hurt but honourable. He was crushed by his
defeat." Like McMurtry, Timbrell moved to Grossman and endorsed him
in advance of the third and final ballot.

In the end, it was pretty close — not as close as Bill Davis's 44 votes
over Allan Lawrence — but close enough. Frank Miller prevailed by 77
votes. It was 869 to 792 in the delegate count — 52.3 percent to 47.7 percent. Tory delegates had narrowly chosen to abandon an approach that

had served them well for more than four decades. Each time, at a key moment, the party had chosen a moderate conservative from the next generation to take the party to its next triumph. This time it turned its back on that formula, selecting an unabashedly right-wing conservative who was actually two years older than the outgoing premier. With his leader about to cede the premiership officially and his candidate defeated, Norman Atkins simply broke down and cried at the convention.

"I couldn't address the fact that the Davis era really was over," he said. "It was such a wonderful experience. Working with Billy Davis even in the worst circumstances was a pleasure. He was a remarkable, decent, wonderful person. He made you really feel good about politics."

The winner's theme song blasted through the Coliseum. "We are Miller's Ontario ..." and one of the first things Miller pledged to do in his new Ontario was to get rid of Atkins and the Big Blue Machine. It was a message that played well among the 52.3 percent who had backed the new premier. But as we shall see, Miller might have cut off his nose to spite his face.

I have always wondered who Bill Davis voted for at that 1985 convention. Naturally, he never told a soul. Years later I asked his oldest son, Neil, who his father voted for.

"I have no idea," he said.

"Have you ever asked him?"

"No, I haven't."

"Why not?"

Neil smiled. "I guess I figured if I did he wouldn't tell me, anyway." No doubt he was correct in that assumption.

Years after that convention I asked Larry Grossman where Davis marked his X.

"He voted for Roy McMurtry on the first ballot and voted for me on the two subsequent ballots," Grossman answered confidently.

"Did he tell you that?" I asked Grossman.

He laughed. "Are you crazy? But trust me, that's what he did."

"How do you know?"

"Because there's no chance he did anything else other than that," Grossman concluded, appearing as certain about something as I'd ever seen him. Still, I wasn't convinced.

In June 2009 I invited Bill Davis to come to TVO to do an interview on the occasion of the 50th anniversary of his first election as an MPP. As the former premier was getting his makeup put on before the interview, I urged him to go against his typically bland persona and say something really provocative, just for fun. He assured me that wasn't likely to happen.

"Well, how about telling me something here in the makeup room that we don't have to talk about on the air," I followed up. "Tell me a secret you've never told anyone else."

To my surprise, Davis didn't shut me down. "Well, what do you want to know?"

"I want to know who you voted for at the convention to replace you as leader in 1985," I said. "I know you voted for your pal, Roy McMurtry, on the first ballot. And Larry insisted you voted for him on the second and third ballots. But, of course, he didn't know that. So tell me now: who did you vote for?"

Davis paused, got very quiet, and simply said, "Dennis."

"I knew it!" I shot back.

I had always assumed that Davis marked his ballot for the MPP for Don Mills because in Timbrell he saw someone much like himself: a next-generation, moderate Tory, bland but very competent, who could keep the dynasty going. And despite all the leadership advice Davis had given Miller, I knew it was impossible that Davis could actually have voted for him. Even when Timbrell was knocked off the ballot, Davis couldn't bring himself to vote for either of the two remaining contenders. He stood in line, pretended to vote but, in fact, dropped an empty, unmarked ballot into the box.

A fuller explanation for his vote was offered by Davis in 2015: "I was very sympathetic to Larry. Listen, if there was a loyalist around, he was one of them. He really was. The only reason I didn't support him was because I didn't think he could win. I think he could've won in Metro [Toronto,] but I'm not sure he could've won in other parts of the province. Dennis could've."

In 2015, when I told Timbrell the story of who Davis had voted for, he seemed quite emotional at hearing the news. "Did he really?" was all he said at first. After a long pause, Timbrell went on to tell a story about the 90th birthday party in 2011 some friends had for Margaret Birch, his former cabinet colleague. Bill and Kathy Davis were there, and as they were about to make their exit, Davis turned to Timbrell and in front of a roomful of people said, "You know, if you'd won in 1985, we'd still be in power."

The reason why Dennis Timbrell didn't triumph in a convention he was poised to win has never been told in much detail. There have been rumours about it over the years, but it's never quite been nailed down — until now. How was it that Grossman passed Timbrell on that second ballot? Miller himself suggested: "It was a tribute to Larry and his organization that he did as well as he did." Yes, partly. But there was so much more to the story.

After Timbrell's defeat, he ran for and won re-election in 1985 but retired in 1987 rather than compete in what turned out to be the worst election for the Progressive Conservative Party in Ontario history. A couple of months after his departure he got a call from a long-time Tory activist in Eastern Ontario. The man was calling to offer an apology. Timbrell wondered for what? The fellow then went on to reveal what was a top-secret strategy in the Miller campaign. The strategy worked, but it also didn't reflect well on the people who executed it and reminds us that the PC Party three decades ago still had a long way to go to accept some ethnicities into their midst.

Miller's campaign team suspected the Man from Muskoka would have a hard team defeating Timbrell on a final ballot and that the "Anybody but Miller" forces would ultimately be too strong to overcome. However, they also suspected that should Miller find himself on the final ballot with Grossman, Miller's chances of winning would improve exponentially because there were still plenty of Tories who just weren't going to pick a Jew to lead their party.

The activist confessed to Timbrell that he was the delegate on the Miller campaign who was responsible for "loaning" as many as 40 Miller delegates to Grossman for the second ballot only. The strategy worked but just barely, since Grossman *did* edge Timbrell, forcing Miller's gravest threat off the ballot. Then, of course, those 40 delegates went back to Miller for the final ballot and ensured his victory.

Timbrell had heard rumours over the years of some kind of plot like that but was mortified to hear how precisely organized the effort was. He ended the conversation abruptly, saying, "Well, I hope you're very proud of what you've done to the party and to Ontario. Goodbye."

I am one of those who believe that had that Miller campaign

strategy failed, that had four delegates changed their minds and voted with Timbrell, the entire course of Ontario history would have been different. Miller was sworn in as Ontario's 19th premier on February 8, 1985, governed briefly, then called an election for May 2. During his premiership, he did consult Bill Davis on who should run the Tory election campaign, and not surprisingly, Davis suggested Norman Atkins and the Big Blue Machine. Miller listened but turned down the advice. Perhaps his unfortunate confrontation with Atkins during the leadership campaign played a part in his decision. Perhaps choosing Atkins was a non-starter, given how much antipathy there was between Miller's wing of the party and the Davis backroom machine. Regardless, Miller went in another direction, entirely shutting out the Big Blue Machine from his campaign operation and appointing Patrick Kinsella as his campaign manager.

For his part, Atkins insisted he held no ill will at Miller's decision, that if a leader doesn't have complete confidence in his campaign chief and doesn't give him the requisite authority to make decisions, it simply won't work. Atkins told Miller he respected his decision and wished him well, but it was a curious decision by Miller, given Atkins's successful track record in Ontario, and at the federal level, where he'd just helped Brian Mulroney win the biggest majority of all time. But there was too much bad blood in the water. In fact, Atkins once described Michael Perik, Miller's principal secretary and the person who ran Miller's leadership campaign, as "the most mean-spirited man I've ever met in my life."

Three decades later Davis referred to Miller's decision to shut out the Big Blue Machine as "unwise," which is about as critical an adjective as he's prepared to use when he's on the record.

Almost nothing in that 1985 election campaign went well. Miller changed. His campaign team told him he couldn't be himself anymore — open, accessible, funny, shooting from the lip. They turned him into a cautious candidate who began to doubt himself. At one point Miller walked to the back of the media bus and confessed: "They won't let me talk to you guys anymore."

When it came time to discuss a leaders' debate, Miller demurred. Just like Davis before him in 1977 and 1981, he declined to participate, except that it wasn't 1981 anymore and both the media and public now *expected* their leaders to debate. In the federal election eight months earlier, not only did the leaders debate several times but they also provided Canadians with the most memorable exchange ever — Brian Mulroney's "You had an option, sir" confrontation with John Turner. Even more, Ronald Reagan, an incumbent president, debated Walter Mondale. If those candidates could debate, why couldn't Miller? The new premier got creamed for ducking what the electorate now saw as its right.

The Tory campaign was off from the get-go. The crowds were small and unenthusiastic. Miller wanted to run on his "Enterprise Ontario" platform of lower taxes and breaks for business, but it just didn't grab any traction. Timbrell, who was now the women's issues minister, had tried to get some references to equal pay for work of equal value and child care into the platform, but Miller's advisers rejected that, saying: "Those aren't our issues." Sure enough, one day on the hustings, equal pay became the issue of the moment and Miller didn't have much to say about it. Now his advisers were scrambling to get Timbrell to a phone, so he could brief the premier on the issue. Timbrell's advice was simple: "Tell those stupid bastards that are advising you to remember what I said to them in March."

Meanwhile, Miller's two opponents, David Peterson and Bob Rae, both more than a decade his junior, were looking not bad at all for a couple of rookies. And they certainly had more facility than Miller in discussing the details around equal pay and child care. But the worst was yet to come.

Larry Grossman's prediction to Bill Davis that the premier was the only one who could manage the Catholic school issue and win the next election now appeared prescient. The full-funding issue had been simmering below the surface ever since Davis announced it the previous June. But now it was about to explode. At a news conference called by opponents of the Catholic funding decision I asked the archbishop of the Anglican Church, Reverend Lewis Garnsworthy, why he objected so much to the government's new policy. Garnsworthy's response was frightening.

"This is how Hitler changed education policy in Germany — by decree!" he said to an astonished press corps. "And I won't take that back!" There were hundreds of candidates running for office in the 1985 election, but it was left to a clergyman to articulate the unhappiness so many Ontarians felt about Davis's decision. Having said that, people were mortified that a man of God would actually compare anything Bill Davis had done to Adolf Hitler. It was an obscene comparison. Miller called it "odious and totally unfounded." Later that day Garnsworthy had lunch with Canon Derwyn Shea, who would become a Tory MPP in 1995. Garnsworthy simply asked Shea, "What have I done?"

Thirty years after the fact Bob Rae says he think Davis was utterly gobsmacked by the vitriolic reaction from both Garnsworthy and the secondary schoolteachers' union, which mounted huge and vicious protests. "I think he was taken aback by the kind of harshness of their criticism and the harshness of their position," Rae says.

John Tory thinks the former premier's absence from the scene "gave critics the freedom to say things they never would have said to Bill Davis."

Even though all three parties supported the full-funding decision, it was Miller's Tories who were now taking the heat for it, probably because the electorate sensed Miller wasn't really behind the policy because, of course, he wasn't. Behind the scenes, Davis urged Miller to restate his support for full funding, hoping that might stop the bleeding and bring the Catholics back onside. But Miller wouldn't.

"I never intended to make life difficult for Frank," Davis says, "although I did level with him, encourage him, to do something about the Catholic issue. Probably too late."

But Garnsworthy's inexcusable comments weren't the only problem for the Miller campaign. Ironically, another problem came from the PC candidate in Brampton, Jeff Rice, who was replacing Bill Davis on the ballot. When asked whether the PCs were open to rethinking their commitment to full funding for separate schools, Rice answered, "Sure, I'll reassess it." That immediately got the bishops, and by extension, much of the Catholic community concerned that the government was considering reneging on Davis's promise. If there were any Catholics in Ontario considering voting Tory because of the Davis commitment, it's a good bet many of them now had second thoughts after hearing about that.

Election night told Ontarians everything they needed to know about their affection for the Progressive Conservative Party. Frank Miller ran one of the worst campaigns imaginable, yet still won the highest number of seats. It was an indication of how deep the Tory roots really were. Miller took 52 seats compared to 48 for the Liberals and 25 for the NDP. So to come full circle, had four delegates on the second ballot of the 1985 leadership convention voted for Timbrell or Miller instead of Grossman, there's every possibility the Tories would have prevailed. Not to be cruel, but it's hard to imagine Timbrell would have run a worse campaign than Miller. The dynasty probably would have been preserved.

A decade after the events of 1985 Miller talked with a mixture of some bitterness but mostly satisfaction at what had transpired. The original Common Sense Revolutionary took pride in the fact that a kid from the wrong side of the tracks in Toronto thumbed his nose at the establishment and won a leadership convention. But he also blamed Davis for retiring "too late," not giving him enough time, in Miller's view, to establish his own leadership of the party. "I'll take the blame for other things," Miller said, adding he believes Catholic school funding and staying around too long ultimately torpedoed the Miller premiership.

Miller's minority government, of course, didn't last. And unlike in 1975 when Robert Nixon and Stephen Lewis couldn't get to first base on an agreement to defeat the Tories, David Peterson and Bob Rae did defeat the Miller government on a non-confidence vote after signing an "accord" of policy items they agreed to pass through the minority legislature. Miller marched to the lieutenant governor's office, informed John Black Aird he could no longer command the confidence of the assembly, and urged Aird to call on Peterson to form a government.

On June 26, 1985, David Robert Peterson was sworn in as Ontario's 20th premier, officially bringing the 42-year-long Tory dynasty to an end.

As an indication of what a classy guy Miller was, after losing power, he took Norman Atkins out for lunch at the Albany Club and confessed, "I made a mistake. It was the wrong decision," not to task Atkins with running that 1985 campaign.

A decent-sized chunk of the Tory faithful thinks Bill Davis has to share a portion of Miller's defeat. Yes, Miller made too many bad decisions and in the end was obviously the wrong man for the times. But Miller's fans would say Davis contributed to the defeat by running too insular an operation, by initiating huge policy changes such as the purchase of Suncor and full funding for separate schools without adequate support from the Tory base, and not leaving Miller enough time to put his own stamp on the government. But Atkins, in his 1993 interview with George Hutchison, was having none of that.

"I don't think Billy Davis stands up as a hero in the PC Party as he should, like Frost and Robarts, because both *their* successors won," he said. "Davis's didn't. He gets blamed for it, but it's unfair and unreasonable. And when history examines the years of Billy Davis, he'll have to be considered as one of Ontario's greatest premiers."

I've discussed this issue with several first ministers over the years, including Brian Mulroney, who rightly points out that *it is the job* of the successor to wipe off whatever tarnish he or she inherited from the previous leader and win. Frost, Robarts, and Davis all did that. So did Kathleen Wynne after taking over a troubled Liberal operation from Dalton McGuinty in 2013. As McGuinty once told me, "I did my job. I won my three [elections]. I removed myself from politics. I gave my successor a great chance and she seized that and I give her all the credit." Regardless of the hand he was dealt, Frank Miller, as the new premier, had to champion the successes and change the channel on the failures of the Davis years. The record will show that he didn't.

Ironically, of the four contestants at that January 1985 PC leadership convention, the man who would go on to have the greatest impact in public life was the guy who came last. A few days after the convention Prime Minister Brian Mulroney appointed Roy McMurtry to be Canada's high commissioner in London. "Roy couldn't take it quick enough," Norman Atkins recalls. "He wanted an opportunity to find an honourable way out."

McMurtry followed that up with a stint as the Canadian Football League's chairman and CEO. But his crowning achievement was becoming chief justice of the Superior Court of Ontario where he ruled same sex marriage legal, earning him and his fellow judges the *Globe and Mail*'s "Nation Builders of 2003" recognition. He became chancellor of York University from 2008 to 2014. The headquarters of the ministry of the attorney general in downtown Toronto bears his name as well as that of Ian Scott, his Liberal successor. McMurtry, now 84, is still a force in public life.

Dennis Timbrell turned 70 years old in 2016. After leaving politics in 1987, he became president of the Ontario Hospital Association, served on various boards of directors, and became chairman of the Toronto School of Theology at the University of Toronto. He never did quite get politics out of his blood. In 1997 and 2000, he moved to the federal arena, seeking to become the Progressive Conservative MP for Prince Edward–Hastings.

He was unsuccessful both times. Even with both the PC Party and the Reform Party splitting the centre-right vote, the Liberals' Lyle Vanclief won more than 50 percent of the votes both times. In 2006 the City of Toronto named a community centre in Don Mills the Dennis R. Timbrell Resource Centre in Flemingdon Park.

Frank Miller, too, couldn't get politics out of his blood. After retiring from provincial politics, he returned to Central Ontario where he became chairman of the District of Muskoka. He took pride in the notion that he might have been a man slightly ahead of his time. During his brief tenure as premier, he appointed Mike Harris, the MPP for Nipissing, as his natural resources minister. Ten years after Miller's fall Harris won two majority governments running on platforms Miller would have been proud to call his own. Ironically, his family thought his loss of the premiership might have been the best thing for him, since it kept him alive a lot longer. Given his damaged heart, they're convinced the stress of the job would have killed him. Instead, Miller died in 2000 at the age of 73. His son, Norm, has been the MPP for Parry Sound–Muskoka since 2001.

Without question the saddest post-convention story of Bill Davis's disciples belongs to Larry Grossman. After Miller resigned as premier and party leader in the summer of 1985, the Tories held another leadership convention in November of the same year. This one was even closer than Bill Davis's: Larry Grossman defeated Dennis Timbrell by a delegate count of 848 to 829 — 19 votes' difference. But Grossman's timing was bad. The Tories were a spent force, the Liberals under David Peterson were wildly popular, and Grossman led the Tories to their worst showing ever. The Liberals took 95 seats in the ensuing 1987 election. Grossman's PCs came *third* with just 16 seats, and Grossman lost his own St. Andrew–St. Patrick seat to boot. He knew the better thing to do politically was to sit out the second 1985 leadership convention and wait until Tory fortunes could improve. But he feared his father might not live that long and was desperate for his father to see him as leader of the Ontario PC Party. Allan Grossman did live to see his son lead the party and died six years later at age 80.

Larry Grossman loved baseball. He owned season's tickets to the Blue Jays and literally went to every single home game — all 81 — every season in his post-political career. He played baseball, as well, and one day he was patrolling the outfield when a fly ball came his way. However, something was wrong. He was seeing double. After undergoing tests, it was discovered that he had brain cancer. His health deteriorated rapidly. Despite looking haggard and near death, Grossman demonstrated immense class and grace by inviting TVO's cameras to come to his home to record a message for the station's membership campaign. Grossman was a frequent guest on the station's new weekly Queen's Park program called *Fourth Reading* and wanted to show his gratitude. The membership message would be his last public appearance. Shortly thereafter, in 1997, he died at the age of 53. In tribute the city renamed the arena near where he lived the Larry Grossman Forest Hill Memorial Arena.

III

LIFE AFTER POLITICS

22

POST-POLITICS

By the time Bill Davis officially stepped down after a quarter of a century in politics, it wouldn't be accurate to say he knew absolutely everybody in the Canadian political and business worlds. But it was almost true. And despite technically not having responsibilities for international affairs as part of his job, he did know people all over the world. "As you step down as Premier of Ontario, I would like to send you my personal good wishes. I recall with great pleasure my visit to Ontario in the Autumn of 1983 and our subsequent meeting in London. Every good wish for the future." That was from Margaret Thatcher, Britain's prime minister from 1979 to 1990.

Two years later Davis wrote to Thatcher, congratulating her on a third consecutive election victory: "I know how great the feeling of relief is after the campaign ends and in particular after such a successful one. I know that you have many new policies and initiatives to pursue in the years ahead and I write simply to wish you well with these endeavours." Nothing terribly personal, but at least the Iron Lady knew the former premier of Ontario was watching her from afar with interest.

Davis was an inveterate letter writer — not by hand but always typed by a secretary — and he kept copies of all letters sent and received. In mid-1985 after René Lévesque stepped aside as premier of Quebec, Davis wrote his former constitutional foe this letter: "You have always carried out your responsibilities in a determined and dedicated manner, and while we had our differences, as you well know, I always found working with you to be a most enjoyable and stimulating experience." Davis then welcomed Lévesque to the "retired Premiers" club.

Lévesque's office wrote a rather terse "form letter" back to Davis, which Lévesque clearly found unsatisfactory. So, in his own hand, he added at the bottom of the typed note: "Needless to say, this was written by the "machine" which, as you can see, is as fluent in English as your Big Blue one was (and is) in French! Well, the feeling is there, even though a bit awkwardly — and that's what counts. So moreover, with Peter [Lougheed], that'll be a trio of beginners. Salut! René L."

Lougheed stepped aside as premier of Alberta later the same year that Davis gave up the reins of Ontario. And, of course, Davis wrote him, too:

> While we occasionally had differing views on issues of public policy, I always felt those instances arose naturally out of the different responsibilities we had as Premiers, and probably meant, in the final analysis, that we were both doing our respective jobs! … Once again, my congratulations on your many accomplishments, my best wishes for your next career, and my kindest personal regards as always.

In late 1985, after the Quebec Liberals won a massive majority and took back the government from the Parti Québécois, Davis wrote the returning premier, Robert Bourassa, who had so disappointed him a decade and a half earlier at the Victoria constitutional talks. Notwithstanding that, Davis was nothing but magnanimous on this occasion. "You have the faith and trust of the people of Quebec and a clear mandate. I am confident that you will serve them well and with distinction," he wrote.

Bourassa responded: "I was greatly touched by your good wishes on the occasion of my being given a new mandate. May the new year see your fondest dreams come true and may it be filled with peace, happiness, and prosperity." Bourassa's second go-around as premier lasted until 1994. Two years later he would be dead at age 63 of malignant melanoma.

Davis and Robert Nixon never got along that well when they opposed each other in two general elections. But that didn't stop Davis from writing Nixon, now the treasurer of Ontario, to congratulate him on bringing in the first Liberal budget in more than four decades. Nixon responded: "While it isn't something I'd want to do every day, I must say that I enjoyed the process."

To Raymond Bachand, the economic development minister in Jean Charest's Quebec government, Davis wrote: "It was a pleasure meeting you at the dinner the other evening and I feel much better about your government's chances of re-election now that you are a part of it. I would offer to be of some help, but the reality is that it might do more harm than good."

Upon his retirement from politics in 2004, federal Liberal cabinet minister David Collenette wrote to Davis. "I could never have succeeded without the support of people like you," the former defence, transport, and veterans' affairs minister wrote. "You have demonstrated faith in the democratic process."

One of his favourite pen pals appears to have been Bob Graham, the former governor and senator from Florida, where Davis family members love to spend their winter vacations. "Congratulations on your recent success at the polls!" he wrote to Graham, who had just won a U.S. Senate seat, in 1986. "Your Canadian friends knew that this success was never in doubt!" And then, in his last line, a little politics: "I sense you will be pro-Canadian and as I've said to many friends, opposed to acid rain."

Graham responded: "I look forward to getting the benefit of your wisdom on this matter and to contributing to a resolution which will enhance the Canadian–United States friendship."

Back in 1971, at the recommendation of several friends, the Davis family purchased a modest condominium where the Stranahan River empties into the Atlantic Ocean in Fort Lauderdale. The balcony affords a magnificent view of the massive passenger liners and container ships that pass by. Coincidentally, Bill and Kathy Davis honeymooned at the Pier Sixty-Six, now a Hyatt Regency hotel, just a stone's throw from their condo.

In 1988 Davis wrote to Gary Filmon, the incoming premier of Manitoba, to congratulate him on his minority government victory. "I will look forward to watching your government consolidate its support and move on to majority status after the next election!" he wrote his fellow PCs. But interestingly enough, Davis also wrote to Sharon Carstairs, the Liberal leader, who took her party from 1 seat to 20 and official opposition status in that 1988 election. "There will be many interesting days ahead for you and I wish you well in the carrying out of your challenging new responsibilities," he wrote.

When Ed Broadbent stepped down as the federal NDP leader, Davis was there on paper, as well, assuring Broadbent that there is "life after politics," and while the corporate world "doesn't always cause the adrenaline to flow as much as a session in the House of Commons or the Legislature," Davis assured him there would be "an active and meaningful life ahead."

Davis was inundated with congratulatory letters from friends and acquaintances as he considered the next chapter of his life in 1985. Donald Houck, a long-time friend from Brampton, praised Davis's "sense of timing and sensitivity to issues in the best political sense to bring about progress with a minimum of acrimony. I have great personal respect for your key, and probably crucial role, as conciliator in the Constitution talks between the Provinces and the Federal Government."

William J. Mooney, a member of the Canadian Petroleum Hall of Fame who organized the Syncrude meeting in Winnipeg in 1975, praised Davis's "suggestion at that most critical time that we recess and that the public participants should caucus in a separate room to discuss Alberta and the federal government's differences saved the day and allowed the capital required to be pledged that day. It was a Syncrude saving suggestion, Mr. Premier."

Arthur Wishart wrote a congratulatory note from his home in Sault Ste. Marie that began rather formally: "Dear Premier Davis" — despite the fact that Wishart was attorney general in Robarts's cabinet, was also in Davis's cabinet, and was more than a quarter century older than Davis. Wishart continued: "I was inclined to use the salutation 'Dear Bill,' but you are still my Premier and the old bond still holds."

Not surprisingly, the most memorable letter came from his friend, Stephen Lewis, which was so good that it bears reprinting in its entirety:

> Dear Mr. Premier: I send this note from the deepest reaches of the Democratic Republic of the Congo. Mind you, it wasn't so difficult to get here. I simply took the shuttle from Brampton to Nairobi and it was a short hop thereafter. I want to join your legions of friends and hordes of Red Tories in wishing you fondest congratulations on this vivid occasion. And because the internet works only

sporadically, let me quickly and all too briefly say, pulsating with nostalgia, that serving with you in the Provincial Legislature over the years when you were Premier, was truly memorable. I shall never forget it. I shall always value it. You made of politics an art that was at once humane, generous, respectful, and urgent. We often disagreed (my political colleagues have told me not often enough), but there always remained a quality of shared regard and friendship. How astonishingly different from the politics of today. That friendship continues, how I cherish it. Many in this crowd will not know of the remarkable support you have given my Foundation, and how you put yourself out at every turn. For that, too, you have my profound appreciation. It's odd in life how the political wheels turn. Here you are, one of the great Conservatives of your generation; here am I an unrepentant socialist ideologue, but I think of you today from this distant place, with such deep affection and admiration for what you've done, and who you are, and what yet lies ahead. We are all in your debt, Mr. Premier. My warmest wishes, Stephen Lewis.

He might have been *out* of politics but that didn't mean Davis was *free* from politics. When you know thousands and thousands of people, it's inevitable that assistance would continue to be sought, and it was. "I would like to impose on our friendship by asking a favour," wrote former cabinet minister George Kerr, who wanted his old boss to put in a good word on his behalf with Prime Minister Mulroney for an appointment to the International Joint Commission. "A word from you would be a big help and very much appreciated. I think you know I would do a good job," Kerr wrote. Davis did write to "my dear Prime Minister" and put in a good word, but alas for Kerr, he didn't get the job. He died in 2007.

Based on the letters he kept in his personal archives, it looks as if Davis went to bat for almost everyone who asked. George Taylor, Davis's former solicitor general from 1982 to 1985, says: "The premier was always interested in his members. He knew what sports teams we supported. We were all family and were to remain so."

While Davis was influential, particularly now that the Progressive Conservative government of Brian Mulroney was in power in Ottawa, his recommendation obviously wasn't always enough for the would-be recipient. For example, George Taylor put a solid legal career on hold when he became the MPP for Simcoe Centre from 1977 to 1985. When Frank Miller assumed the premiership in February 1985, he declined to put Taylor in the cabinet despite Davis's advice to do so. So Taylor decided not to seek re-election. When he inquired about a possible judicial appointment, he was told the new Mulroney government, on the advice of the Canadian Bar Association, wouldn't be appointing any ex-cabinet ministers for two years. In 1987, when that two-year window expired, Taylor wrote to Davis asking the former premier to get behind Taylor's renewed request for a judgeship, which Davis did. What's interesting about Taylor's subsequent letter to Davis is how much he opens his heart to his former leader in expressing his disappointment with the federal Tories, who offered Taylor only a ceremonial citizenship court judgeship: "I am bitterly disappointed by our federal friends in their final offer. Their optimistic encouragement up until the final offer has caused me a financial nightmare, however, I shall recover with the worldly experience that I should have known better than to have so foolishly relied on their good words."

Taylor found himself approaching age 50, having lost all his former clients to go into politics and now starting from scratch to rebuild his practice. A judicial appointment never did come through, although in 2001 the Mike Harris government appointed him to the Ontario Rental Housing Tribunal.

But it wasn't just Progressive Conservatives for whom Davis went to bat. Blenus Wright was a public servant in the ministry of the attorney general. "It has come to my attention that Mr. Blenus Wright would consider the possibility of a judicial appointment should one become available," Davis wrote to federal Justice Minister Ramon Hnatyshyn, adding such an appointment would enjoy Davis's "strong support." Wright was appointed a judge and served until his 75th birthday in 2009. However, Michael I. Jeffery, chair of the Ontario Environmental Assessment Board, also asked Davis to put in a good word for him with Hnatyshyn. Davis did, but no appointment was in the offing. Jeffery eventually moved to Australia where he taught environmental law. He died in 2013.

As strange as it sounds, Bill Davis insists he didn't give a great deal of thought to what he'd be doing after his political career was over. He needn't have worried. Literally, the day after he announced his retirement from politics, the offers started flooding in. John Tory fielded the calls and kept the offers away from Davis, lest anyone allege undue influence at play in the waning days of his premiership. But Davis had the security of knowing that a couple of his closest advisers would no doubt want him to join their law firms. He also met with Leo Kolber and Eddie Goodman at the latter's home in Palm Beach, Florida, to get some advice. Davis and Kolber knew each other well through the Liberal senator's business activities with the Cadillac-Fairview real estate company. "He opened many malls for me," Kolber recalls today. It was yet another indication of Davis's good relationships in all parts of the political spectrum. Kolber had raised millions of dollars for the Liberal Party of Canada over the years and had been appointed to the Senate a year and a half earlier. But that didn't stop Davis from seeking or Kolber from offering good advice from one of the country's best connected businessmen.

"You're going to be in big demand," Kolber told Davis, "so first of all don't sell yourself short. Pick your spots, don't take small companies, and take your time. Don't be in a rush." Kolber got Davis appointed to the board of the alcoholic beverages company Seagram, which given Davis's teetotalling ways and his mother's steadfast opposition to "antibiotics" was surely an ironic choice. Paul Desmarais offered Davis a seat on the Power Corporation board where Davis was invaluable helping Desmarais deal with issues around leadership succession. The company's CEO, John Rae (older brother of Bob Rae), says perhaps Davis's best quality was being such a good listener.

In fact, it wasn't long after Davis announced his retirement that the job offers started coming in fast and furious. James Bradshaw invited Davis to join the law firm Campbell, Godfrey & Lewtas, despite the fact that the invitation was coming from a self-described "old Grit like me." Fraser & Beatty wrote that they regretted Davis's decision to retire as premier, but as a result, the senior partners were doing "a little dreaming." Smith, Lyons, Torrance, Stevenson & Mayer also made an offer.

And then came more offers from more boards. The Canadian Imperial Bank of Commerce added Davis to its board. Ted Rogers wrote by hand an invitation for the premier to join Rogers Cablesystems Inc.: "It is a family company which has stood its own in international competition. With your help and those of the other directors, it should be fun and yet a grand credit to Canada." Robert Gimlin, the chairman and CEO of Abitibi-Price, wrote: "Bill, due to your capabilities, I know many companies will be seeking an association with you, but I can assure you that none is any more sincere in wanting your participation than Abitibi-Price." J.D. Chaplin wanted the premier for his board at Canadian General–Tower in Cambridge, Ontario. In a strangely worded pitch, Chaplin wrote: "I can see a variety of circumstances where this suggestion would have no particular merit, however, if you were going to take on a group of directorships, I think I could layout an interest case [*sic*]."

The non-profit sector came calling, too. Davis's long-time friend, Edmund Bovey, a member of the Canadian Business Hall of Fame, a trustee with the Art Gallery of Ontario, and a board member of the Toronto Symphony Orchestra, urged the premier to join him on the board of Toronto's Wellesley Hospital where he'd find "an extremely fine and hard-working group of people."

Within a year Davis was on an astonishing 16 boards of directors. As premier, he was accustomed to juggling a thousand things at once, so he apparently never felt overwhelmed by the load. In addition, perhaps part of the explanation for taking on so much was Davis's legitimate concern that he still had five children to pay for.

"I don't think I felt any pressure," Davis now says about the need to earn more money for his family. "But I was worried."

Other friends say Davis now downplays the pressure he felt to provide for his children and future grandchildren. After all, he had virtually no money in the bank, a home in Brampton, and a cottage on Georgian Bay. The house and cottage were his birthright, and selling either of them was unimaginable. There was also the condo in Florida, but that was it. Even 25 years into the future at age 80, Davis would still be sitting on corporate boards that required him to fly all over North America, which appalled John Tory. "When I heard he was taking the red eye home from some board meeting on the West Coast, I told him, 'You don't need to be doing this. It's too much wear and tear on you.' But he has always felt a responsibility to provide for his children and grandchildren. I keep telling him they'll be fine, but he persists," Tory says.

Clearly, Davis's toughest decision was figuring out which law firm to join. Eddie Goodman's eponymously named firm, whose roots went back to 1917, was an option. So was the firm started in 1941 by Davis adviser John Tory's grandfather. It was a tough call because it would mean disappointing either one of his best friends in Goodman or someone he'd come to regard as a son — the current mayor of Toronto, John Tory, who would be joining the family firm.

"I took six or eight months of not sorting it out because I was tempted — because I was very fond of Eddie — but I knew we'd be so close and I wasn't sure what I would contribute," Davis recalls today. And so he joined Tory, Tory, DesLauriers & Binnington, along with John Tory, who would be alongside to help with the transition. What followed was one of the more amusing aspects of life at the law firm. Davis insisted everyone call him "Bill," and everyone did, from the senior-most partner to the junior-most articling student. Everyone, that is, except John Tory, who to this day still can't call his old boss by his first name and never will. In fact, the stories of Davis's political colleagues trying on "Bill" for size are legion. After the 1977 election, Davis took a break to recharge his batteries at his condominium in Florida and invited Hugh Segal to come along. Having just improved the Tories' standing in the legislature and being off in sunnier climes, Segal thought the mood was right for him to try calling the premier by his first name. "Bill, could you please pass the salt?" he asked at breakfast one morning. There was a deafening silence.

John Tory laughs. "Had he not repeated himself, saying, 'Premier, could you please pass the salt,' he'd still be waiting for it."

After making the decision to join the firm that would eventually become known as Torys, Davis heard from his old friend, Peter Lougheed, who had also retired from public life and joined the law firm Bennett Jones.

"I am thoroughly enjoying the experience here and hope we can get together for some exchanges on our adjustments to private life," wrote Lougheed. "I have to acknowledge that it is hard to imagine you joining a firm in Toronto other than the one that starts with 'Tory Tory!'" he added, repeating a joke Davis would no doubt go on to hear hundreds of times during his tenure at that law firm.

For 14 years Bill Davis was the second most important politician in Canada. He once told me he never made a decision he truly didn't want to make — in other words, something that went against his core values, just for political purposes. If that's true, Bill Davis was leaving a world where he was respected, revered, even loved, for a world where he was no longer the top dog, and frankly, would only remain on lucrative boards as long as he demonstrated his value to those companies' chairmen and chief executives. That was different, but Davis insists not as tough a transition as it might seem.

"I appreciated the responsibility in public life, and I took it seriously," he says. "But I didn't live for it. I didn't go into it to satisfy my ego. My ego, contrary to what some people may think, was never part of my makeup and isn't today. So that part [of the transition] didn't bother me. It really didn't."

As it turned out, Davis's gravitas and political skill were marvellous assets for the boards he joined. On the board of the Magna auto parts manufacturer, he was reunited with Ed Lumley, the industry minister during Pierre Trudeau's last term. Despite being in different parties, Lumley and Davis had a great relationship from their days in politics. In 1982 Lumley was trying to ensure the American Motors Corporation (AMC) invested more than a billion dollars in a new plant in Canada. Davis wanted the plant in his Brampton riding, but AMC's corporate policy prevented the company from negotiating with premiers. Talks were only to take place with national politicians. Jose Dedeurwaerder, AMC's president, was a Frenchman who'd come over to the company from Renault and was getting lots of pressure from both the Élysée Palace in Paris and Premier René Lévesque to locate in Quebec. Lumley jokingly told Dedeurwaerder he thought AMC should set up in Cornwall, the minister's hometown. But at the end of the day he suggested Brampton where AMC already had a plant.

"You're close to your suppliers," Lumley told Dedeurwaerder. "If you want to go to Cape Breton, I'll make it worth your while. But I'd go where it's most profitable." It's hard to know what impact the local MPP's constant lobbying of Lumley had in AMC's decision to build in Brampton. But Lumley did tell Davis: "You're worse than any MP I've dealt with!"

Davis and Lumley were a good one-two punch at Magna, which was led by the brilliant but mercurial Frank Stronach. The three men would often meet at Stronach's house, which suited Davis's laid-back, non-confrontational style as a director. "We got a lot done," Lumley recalls. "Opened a lot of plants."

Lumley says he and Davis were instrumental in convincing Stronach to diversify Magna, for example, into horse racing at Santa Anita, a move that proved prescient. "Getting into real estate saved us when we got into financial trouble in 1988," Lumley says. "Davis had a lot of credibility with the banks during our restructuring. It bought us time. He was a superb director, an excellent adviser."

It's part of the job description for every Ontario premier to know a good deal about the auto industry. But beyond that, Davis knew people and what made them tick. "He didn't just support things because the chairman wanted it," Lumley recalls. "He spoke out. He had a lot of influence with Frank. And Frank trusted him because he gave good advice. He was not a yes man." Davis was also smart enough to know not to aggressively challenge Stronach at board meetings if he thought Magna's founder was off base. He would pull Stronach aside afterward and impart his advice quietly.

On one occasion, Stronach rejected both Davis's and Lumley's advice and that turned out to be a mistake. Stronach decided to run for the Liberals in the 1988 "Free Trade Election." Davis suggested he run for the Tories; Lumley urged him not to run at all. Stronach did run and got creamed, losing by almost 7,000 votes to no-name one-term Tory candidate John Cole. "I was happy when he lost because it was good for Magna!" Lumley tells me, laughing.

Davis's relationship with Magna paid off for the Ontario Institute for Studies in Education in a big way. Given his background as a former college president and Ontario deputy minister of education, Charles Pascal had been asked by OISE to do a study on college leadership development. Now Pascal wanted to create a university chair in academic community college leadership in Davis's name, so he called together some members of Davis's posse to seek advice on how to approach the former premier and raise the money. Pascal estimated OISE would need $1 million to endow the chair and wanted the names of 10 people from John Tory and Hugh Segal, each of whom could give $100,000. Almost in unison, Tory and Segal said: "Ask Frank Stronach. He'll give you the $1 million himself."

The next step was to convene the heavy hitters from the University of Toronto with which OISE is affiliated. At the table were Rob Prichard, the University of Toronto's president; the university's chief advancement officer, Jon Dellandrea; Roy McMurtry; and Davis and Pascal. From the start, Davis was uncomfortable having the chair established in his name. "Others are more worthy," he insisted.

Pascal shut him down. "You introduced the community colleges act on May 21, 1965," he told Davis. "The rest is history. There's only one person we can name this after." But Davis's modesty persisted.

He was being difficult until his best friend from his years in politics, McMurtry, chimed in. "Bill, you've got this all wrong," he said. "It's not about you. So get over yourself." McMurtry said it with charm and sweetness, yet firmly at the same time.

Davis finally relented with the proviso that his name be used "conceptually" when approaching Stronach. Oh, and there was one more condition to let his name stand. Davis insisted: "I'm not asking Frank for the money!" Someone else made the "ask" and today OISE's Department of Leadership, Higher & Adult Education features four research chairs, including the William G. Davis Chair in Community College Leadership.

In 2000 businessman Paul Reichmann contacted London doctor, researcher, and entrepreneur Calvin Stiller with a view to creating a REIT — a real estate investment trust — for retirement facilities and nursing homes. What resulted was a multi-billion corporation initially called Residence Retirement REIT, now Revera, which is the second-largest provider of long-term care and seniors' housing retirement residences in Canada, the United States, and the United Kingdom. For nearly two decades, Davis was chairman of the board of the company, based in Mississauga.

"Our only misstep was that the headquarters wasn't in Brampton," Dr. Stiller now jokes.

Stiller first met Davis at the opening of the John P. Robarts Research Institute in London. When he was still premier, Davis was persuaded by Stiller and others to provide $10 million of provincial funding to the institute, which would also serve to honour Davis's predecessor. By the time the facility was ready in 1986, Davis was no longer premier, but went to the grand opening. "He didn't fly in by helicopter," Stiller recalls. "He walked up the sidewalk, puffing on his pipe, and we just clicked." The two men would go on to serve on the Revera board together, and Stiller marvelled at how Davis managed to get issues resolved.

"The way he managed his cabinet was legendary," Stiller says. "He never lost a vote at cabinet because he never took one. And I watched that work with us. If there was a lack of complete consensus, he'd take the matter under advisement. Then he'd call behind the scenes and massage the parties involved so our votes were invariably unanimous."

If the Ontario government intended to pass legislation that could affect Revera, Davis would pick up the phone and skillfully ensure that the government official in question hear Revera's case. "You need to hear this view before you proceed," he'd say. Davis apparently never forced his opinions on his fellow board members or forced others to back down when disagreements took place. His skills as premier — finding the intersections of competing positions — were ideal in finding the sweet spot among strong-willed board members.

On one occasion, there was a particularly sensitive matter the board needed to deal with, and Davis knew Stiller would be the best candidate to handle the matter. Without giving Stiller any advance notice, Davis simply said at a board meeting: "The chair of the special committee that will handle this assignment will be the good doctor." Stiller had been tapped and that was that.

"He didn't interfere with management," Stiller recalls with clear admiration in his voice. "But he had a way of calling up people, asking how things were going, and following up on issues."

Davis also sat on the board of the Home Capital Group, which through its subsidiary Home Trust Company provides Canadians with mortgages, credit cards, and deposit services. Also on the board at the same time was Janet Ecker, his former deputy press secretary. She says when the chips were down, Bill Davis on your board was a huge asset. Just before the onset of the Great Recession in 2008, one of Home Capital Group's subsidiaries was the subject of increased attention from the Office of the Superintendent of Financial Institutions (OSFI), which was concerned about the subsidiary's exposure in the sub-prime mortgage market. Two senior officials from OSFI wanted to meet with members of the board of directors to ensure they were taking their responsibilities seriously. As it turned out, the top OSFI official was a former high-ranking civil servant in the Ontario Public Service when Bill Davis was premier. And, of course, Davis remembered him and launched a charm offensive the OSFI official never even saw coming.

"Davis basically gave the guy shit and the guy never knew it" is how Janet Ecker remembers it. "It was just such a wonderful takedown! But it was done so smoothly and so nicely and it was very effective." Even the chair of the board just sat back, yielded to Davis, and watched the master work.

The former premier wasn't trying to prevent the official from doing his job. But he was attempting to impress upon the official that the company understood there were concerns, was happy to work with OSFI, but wouldn't it be better to work together to resolve whatever issues there were rather than make a federal stink about things?

"I just remember sitting there thinking: *How does he do that?*" marvels Ecker in hindsight. But put yourself in the official's shoes. When a 79-year-old legendary former premier of Ontario urges you to work with him rather than against him, what would you do?

There are files upon files of letters Davis has received and sent, all stored at the Archives of Ontario at York University, and while they don't quite tell the story of his life, they do give insights into his values, personality, and impish sense of humour. For example, when Davis turned 80 years old in 2009, Premier Dalton McGuinty wrote him a congratulatory note. Davis responded by expressing his appreciation, adding: "I hope to be able to join you on your 80th. That is statistically highly unlikely but it is a very pleasant thought." Davis goes on to offer good wishes to McGuinty's mother, who has "demonstrated in the past a possible affinity for at least one person in the Progressive Conservative Party."

In response to birthday wishes from Jim Bradley, first elected in 1977 and now the undisputed dean of the legislature in his 40th year at Queen's Park, Davis teased: "The only thing I am always inclined to remind you of when I hear from you, is to ask the question: would you now wish you had allowed us to purchase the jet?" It was an obscure reference to Bradley's opposition to the Davis government's purchase of an executive jet for the premier, something the Liberals probably secretly wish they hadn't done once the Tories were out and David Peterson, then Dalton McGuinty became premier.

In offering congratulations to Bob Rae's former campaign manager, David Agnew, upon his becoming the president of Seneca College, Davis wrote: "I know that your somewhat questionable political philosophies will not stand in the way of the excellent leadership that you will provide."

When Ian Scott, the former attorney general, invited Davis to a Liberal fundraiser, the former premier declined to attend but sent a note, then referring to the renamed attorney general headquarters, said: "I had really held out some hope, Ian, that with your association with Chief Justice McMurtry and one or two others, including myself, of a somewhat different political persuasion, you might have by this time seen the error of your philosophical ways and become yourself a member of the right party."

As much as he enjoys corny partisan humour, Davis could also be sensitive. When he learned of the death of one of his former deputy ministers of education, he wrote to the man's daughter: "I was very sorry to learn of your father's passing. Jack McCarthy was a great Deputy Minister. Your father made a great contribution to Education in the Province of Ontario."

When Davis's daughter, Nancy Bennett, invited her father to speak at her own kids' Grade 5 social science class at King City Public School, some of the thank-you letters the former premier got in return were quite cute. "It blew my socks off that you knew Pierre Elliot Trudeau and Stock well Day [sic]," wrote Jessey M. Antonacci. "I used to think politics was boring but you made it interesting and exciting," wrote William Hewson. "After listening to your speech you made me want to be a Premier when I grow up."

There was a copy of one letter Davis sent in 2009 that caught me by surprise. He was writing to thank the emcee of an event at Massey College at which Davis received the Egerton Ryerson Award for his contribution to public education. "You did it extremely well, as usual, and I deeply appreciate it," Davis wrote. "If only you would realize that some day you should enter public life yourself, I would then be quite content." The letter was to me. And sorry to disappoint you, Mr. Davis, but that's never going to happen.

Almost a year after turning the Ontario government over to his successor, Davis completed a mission given to him by Prime Minister Mulroney. One of the most annoying irritants between the American and

Canadian governments of the day was acid rain. The prevailing winds carried American pollution, much of it from toxin-spewing coal plants, over the border into Canada. When those toxins returned to the ground in the form of acid rain, it literally began killing Canada's lakes. Ironically, the lakes never looked more pristine, but that was because all life inside them was dying. Beyond an ecological disaster in the making, acid rain was also killing Canadian tourism.

Americans were as uninterested in the acid rain crisis as Canadians were exercised by it. Many U.S. politicians considered Canada's efforts to get them to order better pollution control devices on their factories as a plot to make their businesses less competitive. It seemed impossible to get the U.S. administration to take Canada's concerns seriously. Eventually, Mulroney convinced President Ronald Reagan that Canadian-American relations were facing a crisis because of America's inaction. Because he had a good relationship with Reagan, Mulroney managed to get the U.S. president to join him in appointing two highly trusted associates to find a solution to this problem. Reagan appointed Drew Lewis, his former transportation secretary, while Mulroney tasked Bill Davis with being Canada's acid rain envoy. No one had to tell Davis how serious acid rain was. He could see the evidence at his Georgian Bay cottage and got an earful from tourism operators that they were losing their livelihoods.

The acid rain envoys issued their recommendations in January 1986. Yes, there were people who thought the recommendations didn't go far enough. Davis faced those critics head-on: "I don't think you have to be totally knowledgeable in this subject area to sense that if Mr. Lewis had come in with a report that said we will have a 50% reduction across the board in the United States by 1994 no matter what the cost, that the administration might have found that less than acceptable." As always, Davis's aim was to achieve the possible rather than hold out for the ideal and potentially get nothing. Americans would spend $5 billion (government and industry) to create new technologies to reduce acid rain emissions. The bottom line was that we didn't hear about acid rain anymore. "I needed someone of Davis's strength and reputation to move this along," recalls Brian Mulroney. "I told President Reagan, he's our most outstanding premier."

Bill Davis was paid $1 by the Canadian government for his work on the acid rain treaty. He considered that work to be of such value that he framed the dollar bill, which hangs on the wall of his Georgian Bay cottage.

The Mulroney-Davis relationship was a curious one. Yes, they were both Progressive Conservative first ministers, and coincidentally enough, Mulroney was Canada's 18th prime minister while Davis was Ontario's 18th premier. But after that, they appeared to have little in common. Mulroney was the son of an electrician and grew up in hardscrabble circumstances in rural Quebec. Davis was the son of a prominent Crown attorney and grew up if not in affluent circumstances, then certainly in comfort. At one point in his life Mulroney was a notorious party animal who admittedly drank far too much. Davis constantly avoided the fast lane and has never been drunk in his life. But for some reason these two politicians hit it off, became friends, socialized a bit at their winter places in Florida, and occasionally found themselves invited to the same parties at Miami Dolphins football games in owner Joe Robbie's private box. Psychologists could no doubt have a field day analyzing the contrasts. Maybe Davis secretly craved dipping his toe into the fast lifestyle Mulroney enjoyed. And perhaps Mulroney secretly yearned to be as admired as Davis. Regardless, the two men got on well and there were numerous instances of how much Mulroney cared about Davis's opinion, even after Davis retired from public life.

One such instance took place in the aftermath of the first Ontario PC leadership convention in 1985 won by Frank Miller. Mulroney and Roy McMurtry had been friends for years, and when the prime minister saw McMurtry's first-ballot exit at that convention, he resolved to appoint McMurtry as Canada's high commissioner to the United Kingdom in exchange for a pledge from McMurtry to be a candidate for Mulroney in the 1988 federal election. But when McMurtry's term in Britain expired, the former attorney general came home and instead of running in that 1988 election returned to practising law. In his memoir, McMurtry insists he never gave Mulroney an undertaking to run in that election, but Mulroney's recollection is quite different, and after seeing

McMurtry's memoir, the former prime minister wrote John Tory a letter, restating the facts as he remembered them. In 1991 the position of associate chief justice of Ontario opened up and McMurtry's name ended up on the short list. When that list went to the PC cabinet in Ottawa, there was considerable opposition to McMurtry's potential appointment. Comments such as "he left us in the lurch in 1988" were heard at the table. Knowing how close Davis and McMurtry were, Mulroney thought he'd check with Davis's adviser, John Tory, before making the appointment. Tory checked with his former boss, then relayed the news to his current boss: "He likes Roy."

Apparently, that was all the prime minister needed to hear. "That ended the discussion," Mulroney now says. "I appointed McMurtry to the dismay of many." McMurtry went on to have a judicial career of major consequence. But the story is retold here as an indication of how seriously Mulroney valued Bill Davis's advice, even after the former premier retired from politics.

W hile Davis was trying to put together his post-political career in 1985, the politicians he'd left behind at Queen's Park were attempting to implement one of the most historic decisions he'd ever made. The new informal alliance between the Liberals and New Democrats was holding public hearings on how to implement full funding for Catholic schools that Davis had promised before retiring. Most of the legislative committee's work was taken up debating the finer points of how to structure the bill. For how many years would the separate system be allowed to favour hiring Catholic teachers before it had to open its hiring practices to non-Catholics, as well? Under what conditions would non-Catholic students be permitted to attend separate schools? How would the province handle the sensitive situation where the Catholic system would need to take over schools previously run by the public system? Each of these items and many more like them were potential bales of hay that awaited some arsonist who might be willing to toss a match on them for political gain. So the Liberal and New Democrat MPPs on the committee had to proceed with extreme caution. As is typically the case with legislative committees, much of the work was done away from the cameras, not out of a desire for secrecy but simply because none of the committee's deliberations made for great television.

One witness's appearance changed all that.

Fifteen months after he rose in the Ontario legislature to announce his government's intention to extend full public funding to the Catholic school system, William Davis returned to Queen's Park to answer MPPs' questions and face a barrage of cameras. It's safe to say the social development committee of the legislature had never experienced a day like this. The room was packed as Davis spent an hour and a half taking committee members through his thinking. At times he was serious, at other times hilarious. He was thoughtful one moment, then playful the next with the MPPs, who might have had a mind to grill him harder on what he was thinking but simply couldn't. Davis was clearly in command. This was Queen's Park, his turf for a quarter of a century. Liberals and New Democrats supported his change of heart and therefore had no interest in embarrassing him. Tories who were still technically in favour of full funding but actually provided most of the opposition in the committee just couldn't bring themselves to challenge their former leader's assertions. Even if they'd tried, Davis would have made mincemeat out of them, so comfortable was he in those familiar surroundings.

Actually, before the hearings began, the Liberals wanted to meet with Davis to ensure the father of what was now *their* policy was onside with the new government's intentions. It was left to the executive assistant to Education Minister Sean Conway to meet with Davis and provide a full briefing on the new government's plans. Tim Murphy would go on to become an MPP, Ontario Liberal Party president, and chief of staff to Prime Minister Paul Martin. But at this moment he was a nervous ministerial aide and wasn't quite sure how to deal with, as he put it, "the colossus astride Ontario politics."

Davis and Murphy met before the hearings at a secret location where the current minister's assistant put aside an hour to brief the former premier. Murphy came armed with binders full of statistics and charts, ready to sit down with Davis, and begin the briefing. He needn't have bothered. Davis walked in, asked Murphy what the total education ministry budget was, what the additional commitment for full funding would require (Ed Stewart's "about $50 million annually" was still the operative number), and how many additional students that would serve. Murphy answered, Davis thanked him, and that was that. Briefing over.

It's hard to know what observers at the committee might have been hoping for from Davis. To be sure, he went through a lengthy recitation of his reasons for announcing the policy change: that it would complete the agreement made to Catholics in 1867 at the time of Confederation, that it would end an "arbitrary and inequitable" situation, that times had changed and this was the right thing to do, that a little competition wouldn't damage the public school system, that there was plenty of excess school capacity in the system already to accommodate this change, and so on. The former premier quoted perhaps the greatest Conservative of them all, Sir John A. Macdonald, as he did when he announced the policy change in the legislature: "We can afford to be just [to separate school supporters], we can afford to be generous, because we are strong."

Davis never went as far as to acknowledge any guilt over his 1971 election victory. He never has. But he did allow that his 1971 decision *not* to provide additional funds to the Catholic system "was probably the most difficult one ever made in my political life. I believed in what I was saying at the time, but I have to say I was never totally comfortable with the position I had taken."

In effect, Davis was publicly confirming what some of his closest advisers would more forcefully confirm to me years later. Hugh Segal suggested: "I think he always felt a little guilty over the 1971 election victory being on the backs of the separate school issue."

And Norman Atkins, one of the architects of that 1971 landslide, offered: "There was something about his success in that campaign that bothered him, something he wanted to correct."

Perhaps the combination of the emotion of being back at Queen's Park plus the hero's welcome he received from the committee put Davis in a confessional, expansive mood. How else to explain this additional bit of insight into the internal debate he had no doubt been experiencing for a decade and a half: "Mr. Chairman, if somebody wants to say I changed my mind, he is right. I am not here to apologize for that. I am not here to explain it, except to say very simply that I was the head of government. I had responsibility for close to nine million people, many of them young people, with systems that had their roots in history and tradition. As the head of government, I felt the time had come to make a move in this difficult and sensitive area." Davis wasn't backing away from what he said in 1971. He still thought it was desirable for all of Ontario's children to be educated in one secondary school system. But the facts on the ground had changed. More and more Catholics were coming to Ontario, they were staying through to the end of high school in the Catholic system, and that meant too many of them wouldn't receive the education they ought to have because of the fiscal inequity. Furthermore, since Ontario was being urged to get rid of Grade 13, anyway, the cost of implementing the policy ought not to be as expensive as some feared.

Committee members questioned Davis's approach to his about-face — no province-wide public hearings, no blue-ribbon panel to study the issue, no indication to his cabinet, caucus, or even education minister that he was about to announce a significant new government policy. Davis shut them all down. "The result of that would be totally predictable," he said. "Some of the rhetoric would have been regrettable, and the confusion it potentially could have created would not have been appropriate."

Davis finished with the committee, then participated in the mother of all scrums with the media. One thing became abundantly clear. The former premier was enjoying himself immensely. He missed the cut and thrust of a good scrum, took every question, and even then appeared to be in no rush to leave. As performances by ex-politicians go, this one was right up there with Jean Chrétien's "golf balls" seminar at the Gomery Inquiry in 2005. It was simply an old master showing the kids how it's done.

While it was Davis who announced the plan to extend full funding to the Catholic system, history will record that it was actually the Liberal government of David Peterson with the backing of then NDP leader Bob Rae that brought the Davis promise to fruition. The Liberal-NDP alliance *did* hold public hearings across the province to get advice on how to implement the policy, and from time to time, Davis's concerns about stirring up anti-Catholic feelings came brewing to the surface. There were huge demonstrations organized by the public schoolteacher unions opposing the policy. It speaks well of Ontarians that there was actually very little overt religious bigotry on display at these demonstrations. Critics talked about their fears of a weakened public education system and weren't buying the promises of teacher protection to which the government had committed. However, every now and then, the anti-Catholic mask slipped. At hearings in Windsor the chairman of the Essex Public School Board insisted the policy would undermine the strength and character of the "Protestant" school system.

There were also plenty of odd moments of historical irony. As the politicians worked their way through the political process, others started a legal avenue, as well. The Liberal government referred the full-funding bill (Bill 30) to the Ontario Court of Appeal to get its advice on the legality of what the province was attempting. Attorney General Ian Scott, one of the country's great legal minds, thought this strategy was extremely dubious and feared the courts would rule the bill unconstitutional, since it contravened the charter. But Education Minister Sean Conway, *not* one of the nation's great legal minds, disagreed, insisting the judges would understand the historic compromises that went into creating Canada and wouldn't overturn a policy that honoured that compromise. When the court ruled in 1986 that Bill 30 was indeed constitutional, Conway enjoyed a moment of triumph over his cabinet colleague. Opponents appealed the Ontario court's decision to the Supreme Court of Canada, which in June 1987 also ruled the new law constitutional.

But there was more. A coalition of groups sought an injunction to stop the initial extension of funds to Grade 11. Most saw it for what it was — a last-ditch legal Hail Mary pass that had no chance of success. The government was particularly heartened when the case came before Judge Joe Potts, a lifelong Liberal who had run and lost twice to the Tories in 1963 and 1967. But Potts granted the injunction, temporarily sending everyone into a tizzy. The divisional court later overruled Potts's decision.

On one lovely evening near Peterborough, Charles Pascal hoped to get a deeper understanding from Davis beyond what the former premier had told the committee. Pascal, as president of Sir Sanford Fleming College, arranged to have Davis awarded an honorary diploma — the first of its kind given out by Fleming — in recognition of Davis's creation of the community college system. During one moment at a luncheon before the convocation ceremony, Pascal had Davis's undivided attention and figured this was a good moment to see how far he could push the father of full funding.

"Mr. Davis," Pascal began, "I'm going to give you five scenarios of why you decided to give full funding to the Catholic schools." The college president then laid them out: (A) Attorney General Roy McMurtry advised Davis to do it, seeing storm clouds brewing in advance of the next election; (B) Davis and his principal secretary, John Tory, were riding in the premier's limousine in the Dufferin and St. Clair area of Toronto and suddenly noticed the burgeoning Catholic population in Ontario's capital; (C) Davis was on the 18th tee, golfing with Cardinal Carter, who grabbed the premier's club on the backswing and said, "Premier, now!"; (D) all of the above; or (E) none of the above.

"Which was it, Premier?" Pascal asked.

Davis paused. Then he leaned forward as if to share some insight he'd held back from his cabinet colleagues, from the cardinal, from the media, and from the legislative committee, and asked Pascal: "Can you please pass the salt, Charles?"

When it actually came time for Queen's Park to vote on Bill 30 — the proposal that would give legislative authority to the separate school funding changes — the bill passed almost unanimously. Only one MPP voted against it: Progressive Conservative Norm Sterling, now an opposition MPP. The PCs had a caucus meeting for their 52 MPPs to determine how they were going to vote. Frank Miller, now the opposition leader, decided the Tories should continue to support their original position and vote for Bill 30. When Sterling told him he was still opposed to the policy and intended to vote against, Miller came down on him hard in front of his caucus colleagues.

Nevertheless, Sterling was adamant and resolved to resign from the PC caucus and sit as an independent. He went to the clerk of the legislature, Roderick Lewis, and informed him of his plans to do so, even agreeing on where his new seat would be in the back corner of the back row. But at the last minute, just before the vote, Larry Grossman came running to Sterling to inform him he would be permitted to vote against the bill and remain in caucus. To this day Sterling has no regrets about being the sole holdout on that day and, in fact, believes his "No" vote saved his job. In the ensuing 1987 election, he was one of 16 PC MPPs who survived the Liberal landslide, holding his Carleton riding by just 467 votes, thanks in no small measure to public schoolteachers who voted for him. "That was one of my proudest moments of standing up for what I believed in," he now says. Ironically, however, seven of Sterling's eight grandchildren are now being educated in the separate school system. Sterling, now 74, remained an MPP until 2011, retiring from politics after losing his riding's nomination battle to fellow PC candidate Jack MacLaren. After 34 years, he left the legislature as the longest-serving member of the PC caucus at the time.

As a postscript, there have been other attempts since Davis's departure to deal with the potentially toxic mix of education, religion, and politics. Many Ontarians still don't understand why Catholics have their choice of a fully funded secular *and* a fully funded religious school system to which to send their children — a right no other religion has. In 1999 that view received even more legitimacy when the United Nations human rights committee declared Ontario's practice of funding one religion to the exclusion of all others to be discriminatory. The Mike Harris government attempted to address this issue when it introduced the Equity in Education Tax Credit, which gave some tax relief to parents who wanted to send their children to religious or private schools. But the Dalton McGuinty government eliminated the tax credit when it assumed power in 2003, arguing every dollar possible needed to go to public, not private education.

In 2007 PC leader John Tory, Davis's former principal secretary, tried to address the religious inequity issue by offering some public funding to other faith-based schools. Once again Bill Davis's and Charles Pascal's paths crossed over the issue. Tory thought the public would be more likely to embrace his idea if he had a former popular premier as part of his implementation strategy. So Tory had Davis sign on to be chairman of a commission that would oversee what was hoped would be a smooth implementation of the policy. And Davis wanted Pascal involved, as well. So he phoned Pascal, who was now executive director of the Atkinson Foundation.

"Charles," he began, "I hear you've been on sabbatical. How would anybody know?" Obligatory jokes aside, Davis then moved in for the "ask." "You may have heard that the next premier of Ontario has a plank in his platform for independent religious schools. I want you to be one of my co-commissioners on the task force."

Pascal, who had been travelling the world on sabbatical, had just returned, and hadn't heard details of the idea, was silent. Then he asked incredulously, "He's going to do what? You're joking, right?"

Davis then spent the next 20 minutes trying to convince Pascal that "it was a matter of equity," that since tax dollars had already been extended to Catholics, it now needed to be extended to other faiths, as well. Davis almost implemented the same idea decades earlier for Jewish schools, but Pascal was having none of it.

"Two wrongs don't make a right," he told Davis. "I think John [Tory] can win the election, but this is a huge policy mistake. I can't do it."

It was an uncomfortable moment for both men, both of whom had spent so much of their adult lives utterly devoted to improving Ontario's education system: Davis as education minister and premier; Pascal as a community college president, professor at OISE, head of the Council of Regents, deputy minister of education during the early 1990s, and as Dalton McGuinty's early childhood education czar.

But Pascal went further. He not only told Davis he couldn't help the man he respected perhaps more than any other in Ontario political history but added he would spend a considerable amount of time coordinating a public communications strategy opposing the scheme. Pascal ended the call almost begging Davis to tell Tory: "Please don't have him do this."

Tory himself called Pascal later that night. They spoke for more than an hour. Pascal warned the PC leader that his policy would stir up all the old anti-Catholic school funding crusaders. He urged him to add a comparative religion class to the province's curriculum if he wanted other faiths to feel more comfortable in the public education system. Tory said that wasn't satisfactory, that he'd made a commitment when he won the leadership of the PC Party in 2004 to deal with the inequity in religious education funding, and this was his solution. The call ended civilly with both men "agreeing to disagree."

Tory did introduce his faith-based funding plan, and from that moment on, PC fortunes faded and the Liberals' soared. In June 2007, both parties were tied in the polls — it was a dead heat. On election day, October 10, Dalton McGuinty's Liberals captured 42 percent of the total votes cast; John Tory's PCs, only 32 percent. Analysts were unanimous in pointing to the faith-based school funding plan as the single most important reason for the Tories' loss.

But one of the other morals of the story was how a small group of friends passionately disagreed on this policy plank, yet somehow remained friends. "To their credit," Pascal says in admiration, "there were no hard feelings." As another indication of how loyal Bill Davis's friends are to him, Pascal asked both Bette Stephenson and Roy McMurtry — two of

Davis's former cabinet colleagues — to sign on to his campaign opposing Tory's plan. Even though both agreed with Pascal and disagreed with their former party's strategy, neither would join Pascal's crusade to torpedo the policy. "Their friendship and loyalty to Mr. Davis was too strong," Pascal recalls. "And that's the way it should be."

Increasing numbers of Ontarians seemed to be saying that the solution to this problem wasn't to fund other religions; it was to de-fund the Catholic system. In fact, the Green Party of Ontario included that plank in its platform and doubled its traditional vote to 8 percent. But no mainline party has considered it, and so Ontario continues to have multiple, publicly funded school systems: a Catholic one and a secular one, in both French and English. Everyone seems to acknowledge that if you wanted to build a school system from scratch, you wouldn't create what Ontario now has. But given the tumult over Bill 30 and Tory's effort to extend public funding to all religious schools, no politician seems prepared to touch the "third rail" of Ontario politics. For better or for worse, 30 years after he left public life, Ontario's education system today is Bill Davis's education system.

There are several unusual postscripts to the religious education story in Ontario. Remember how mortified Robert Nixon was when Davis won the 1971 election, essentially by declining to offer more public funding to the Catholic school system? Nixon always thought fairness dictated fully funding the Catholic system. And yet, in 2015, he told me if you drive around Brant County now, you'll see they just opened two brand-new schools. "They're basically identical, one public and one Catholic, and I'm not sure what my feeling is about it." It sure sounded as if Nixon was having second thoughts about the advisability of spending billions on two parallel systems.

The second postscript comes from another former Ontario party leader who always supported full funding for the separate school system. Bob Rae now says Ontario needs "one publicly funded system that would be far more integrated than the current one is." He stresses he's not talking about cutting off funding for the Catholic system. But he does acknowledge two fully funded school systems have resulted in more administration, more overhead, and more duplication than is necessary.

Davis, of course, came out with his change of heart on this issue in 1984 and hasn't changed his mind at all about his *volte-face*. In fact, if you visit Cardinal Leger Secondary School in Brampton, you'll now see something rather unexpected. In the summer of 2015, political and educational dignitaries, including Education Minister Liz Sandals, gathered at the school to dedicate, bless, and officially rename the school's new athletic field. It is now called the William G. Davis Field. Yes, this Catholic school's field is named after the premier who won an election in large measure by denying schools such as this one the access to equitable funding to which they felt entitled. It's the icing on the cake that was baked more than 30 years ago when a group of Cardinal Leger students interrupted the premier of the day on his front lawn as he was cutting his grass to ask why Catholic schools weren't fully funded as their public counterparts were.

Only in Ontario.

There are very few responsibilities that former premiers of Ontario are obliged to take on. But the one thing on every premier's must-do list is choosing an artist to paint his or her portrait that will then hang forever on the second floor of the legislature building, just outside the office of the premier of Ontario. Davis approached this obligation in the same way he grappled with many issues when he was premier. He delayed it for about as long as he possibly could. In fact, Frank Miller who succeeded Davis as premier had already had his portrait commissioned and hanging for three years before his predecessor got around to doing likewise. So when many of his former Tory colleagues gathered at Queen's Park on October 19, 1989, to see Davis's portrait finally unveiled, it was an event that was long overdue.

The then premier David Peterson kicked off the proceedings with a well-worn line: "One of the great joys of the premier of the province and one of the great traditions is to preside over the hanging of your predecessor," Peterson joked.

Davis procrastinated for so long in part because that's his way and in part because he really did want to sort of disappear after leaving politics. For more than a quarter of a century, he had led so much of his life in public that he simply wanted to lie low for a good while. At this point in Ontario history it was a rarity for a former premier to write his memoirs. The last to do so was E.C. Drury, and that was more than six decades earlier. So there was no organized effort to marshal Davis's personal papers or even write op-eds for the newspapers. The procrastinating got so ridiculous that it prompted Rosemary Speirs to write a column in the *Toronto Star* headlined: "Bill Davis, Please Sit Still for Your Official Portrait." She surmised the former premier likened having his portrait done to going to the dentist.

But eventually Davis had to succumb to this unavoidable obligation. More than three years after leaving the premier's office he finally selected Hungarian artist Istvan Nyikos to paint his portrait. Many of Davis's former colleagues showed up to enjoy the ceremonial hanging, including Frank Miller, Bob Welch, Lorne Henderson, Larry Grossman, and Norman Atkins (all of whom, incidentally, Davis has outlived). Hugh Segal and Sally Barnes were there, too, as was Lieutenant Governor Lincoln Alexander, a one-time fellow Tory.

The reaction of the audience when the portrait was finally revealed was splendid. It was as if everyone collectively said: "That captures him, bang on." Davis is dressed in a conservative suit and tie, seated in a wooden chair, and surrounded by bland wood-panelled walls and white drapes on the windows. He has his right leg crossed over his left, while holding his signature pipe in his right hand. In classic Davis form, his face couldn't be more sphinx-like. He is neither smiling nor frowning. He doesn't appear to be happy or sad.

Bland still works.

T he 1993 federal election was a shock to the system for red Tories such as Bill Davis. The Progressive Conservative Party of Canada basically exploded after Brian Mulroney's departure. The Quebec nationalists in Mulroney's caucus left to form the Bloc Québécois. The western populists left to create the Reform Party. What was left were the Red Tories in a mostly abandoned Progressive Conservative Party of Canada. Now under Kim Campbell's leadership, the PC Party still managed more than two million votes. But they were spread so widely across the country that the party won just 2 seats. The Bloc and Reform, both with support concentrated in only one region, won 54 and 52 seats respectively. The Liberals with 41 percent of the total vote won a majority government under Jean Chrétien. Without going into chapter and verse of the enmity between the PCs and Reform, the fact was that the split in the centre-right vote allowed the Liberals to cruise to two more majority governments in 1997 and 2000, despite winning only 38.5 percent of the votes in that 1997 campaign. Reform tried several outreaches to their Tory cousins: a "Winds of Change" conference leading to a United Alternative, then the Reform–Conservative Alliance. A breakaway group of disgruntled Alliance MPs then sat with the PCs for a time and it looked as if the two conservative parties would never get their act together and the Liberals would just keep on winning. Even in the 2000 election with the PCs on life support under Joe Clark's leadership once again, the party still managed more than 1.5 million votes (good for 12 seats), thereby depriving the Canadian Alliance under leader Stockwell Day with more than twice as many votes of making any real progress.

Enter Stephen Harper. The former Reform MP returned to public life, winning the Alliance leadership in March 2002. A little over a year later there was a by-election in the Southwestern Ontario riding of Perth-Middlesex. By-elections rarely have significance beyond the candidates contesting them. But this would turn out to be one of the most consequential in Canadian history. The Progressive Conservative candidate, Gary Schellenberger, staged an upset victory, defeating the Liberal candidate by 1,000 votes. The Alliance candidate was 5,000 votes behind Schellenberger, a remarkably poor showing in what should have been the kind of riding the Alliance ought to have won if the party had anything going for it.

Two important things happened in the aftermath of the by-election. Ten days later, on May 31, 2003, Peter MacKay won the leadership of the PC Party. And Stephen Harper decided he'd had enough of losing. Even though the Alliance was in the black, fundraising was becoming tougher. Donors were tired of giving to what seemed like perpetual losing causes. So, in June, when MacKay walked over to Harper in the lobby of the House of Commons and said, "You and I have to talk," Harper was more than open to the conversation. Despite the fact that MacKay won the PC leadership in part because he signed a piece of paper promising to build (rather than merge) the party, he told Harper he was "open and interested" in pursuing the possibilities. Both leaders appointed three-man teams of emissaries, and when the PC delegation indicated it was willing to discuss full-blown merger talks, it was game on. The PC team included former deputy prime minister Don Mazankowski, former house leader Loyola

Hearn, and a guy named William G. Davis. Brian Mulroney said Davis's contribution was essential to getting the parties back together. How did the former premier contribute? "By walking into a room and sitting down and saying: 'We need this for the party and for Canada,'" he said.

According to John Ibbitson's fine biography of Stephen Harper, the new Alliance leader gave simple instructions to his negotiating team of former Alberta cabinet minister and Reform MP Ray Speaker, Gerry St. Germain, and Ontario MP Scott Reid: give up almost anything, but get a deal. The emissaries had several meetings, and the negotiations didn't go particularly smoothly. The PCs did win some early concessions: the equality of English and French in all institutions of Parliament; the dropping of any citizen initiatives or referendums and the Triple-E Senate; and the assumption by the Alliance of the PC Party's debts. But there were huge stumbling blocks, as well. The Alliance wanted "one member, one vote" rules for picking future leaders. That was a non-starter for the PCs who feared being over-whelmed under that scenario. The Tories wanted each riding, regardless of how many members it had, to be worth 100 points. The points would be divided according to the percentage of the vote each candidate got. Dropping the "one member, one vote" principal was anathema to Harper.

Here's where Bill Davis came in. Davis was en route to his cottage on Georgian Bay when he got word via fax at the local marina in Honey Harbour that the emissaries wanted a conference call. And so, in the second-floor office of what's now called the Nautilus Marina, Davis hopped on the call and gave the second most important ultimatum to the folks on the other end of the line. Two decades earlier he'd told Pierre Trudeau by telephone that if he didn't put some water in his wine, there would be no constitutional agreement. Trudeau did. This time he told the Alliance negotiators that unless they caved on their "one member, one vote" rules for leadership races, the merger was off. Davis hung up, then waited 15 minutes for the return phone call. When it came, the voice on the other end simply said, "We have a deal."

On consecutive days in December, 96 percent of Alliance members and 90 percent of PC members voted yes to creating the new Conservative Party of Canada. Three months later Harper won the party's first-ever leadership convention over Belinda Stronach and Tony Clement, then improved the party's fortunes in the June 2004 federal election, picking up 27 seats and holding Paul Martin's Liberals to a minority government.

In the lead-up to the January 2006 general election, Bill Davis did something that made a lot of Ontario Tories take notice — he did a very high-profile campaign event for the new Conservative Party leader. At a brewery at the corner of Mount Pleasant and Eglinton Avenues in midtown Toronto, Bill Davis said that despite Stephen Harper's Reform and Alliance past he felt very comfortable campaigning for and endorsing the first-ever leader of the new Conservative Party of Canada. "Stephen Harper is a member of parliament from Alberta," Davis began, "but like all good things in this world, he started right here in Ontario." The former premier went on to praise Harper "for his decency, his integrity, his leadership, and his values; for his respect for the views of others and sensitivity to the legitimate role of provinces…. I am not only comfortable with Stephen Harper, but I am enthusiastic about what a new Harper Conservative administration will achieve." Despite using words I suspect many of which he would choose to take back today, Davis's fulsome introduction of Harper sent an important signal to Red Tories in Ontario that the new leader was A-okay. Sure enough, Harper's performance in Ontario was significantly better en route later that month to his first of three consecutive election wins.

Why would Davis help a man he knew didn't share his brand of conservatism? Maybe, given Harper's role in merging the two conservative parties, he felt he owed it to the man to give him a chance. Maybe he hoped to have the new leader's ear going forward. Unquestionably, his loyalty to Conservatives and this new entity was a factor. Regardless, Harper certainly didn't reciprocate. None of Davis's allies, such as then Senators Hugh Segal or Norman Atkins, or John Tory, ever penetrated the new leader's inner circle.

Bill Davis remains to this day a loyal Tory. His friend, Roy McMurtry, has found it increasingly difficult to be that. In his own memoir, McMurtry openly criticized Stephen Harper's and Mike Harris's styles of politics. He accused Harper of "an intense lack of compassion" and doing "a great deal to undermine the accountability of Parliament as well as fuelling a poisonous partisan atmosphere." He blasted Harris for "demonizing people on welfare." McMurtry now openly proclaims his affections for non-conservative political options. He has admitted voting for Green Party candidate Peter Elgie, no doubt in part but not totally because Peter is the son of McMurtry's former cabinet colleague, Robert

Elgie. McMurtry also endorsed Ontario *Liberal* leadership candidate Eric Hoskins during the 2013 contest won by Kathleen Wynne.

Bill Davis shares his former attorney general's feelings on Stephen Harper's brand of small-*c* conservatism, although he would never say it publicly. He remains a loyal Tory. When I recently asked Davis whether he had ever voted for any party other than the federal Conservatives or Ontario Progressive Conservatives, he immediately shook his head. He did add, however, that on rare occasions he didn't vote. That is about as significant an act of conservative civil disobedience as Davis is capable of.

Since Davis retired from politics, there have been nine federal elections and eight Ontario elections. There have also been four federal PC leadership contests (the winners were Kim Campbell, Jean Charest, Joe Clark, and Peter MacKay), one Conservative Party leadership contest (won by Stephen Harper), and seven Ontario PC leadership contests (won by Frank Miller, Larry Grossman, Mike Harris, Ernie Eves, John Tory, Tim Hudak, and Patrick Brown). At this point in his life Davis has never felt an obligation either to publicly campaign for his party or to publicly support any leadership candidate, in fact, quite the contrary — he has usually stayed on the sidelines. However, occasionally he has entered the fray. As mentioned earlier, he regards John Tory as a son and publicly backed his former adviser when Tory successfully contested the Ontario PC leadership in 2004. The same goes for Hugh Segal when he sought the federal PC leadership in 1998. Davis endorsed Segal, was present in Segal's campaign literature, attended Segal's speeches at the Empire and Canadian Clubs, sat in the "Segal Box" as the speeches were delivered on convention day in Toronto, and was at Segal's campaign headquarters in Kingston the night the ballots were counted. Joe Clark romped to an easy two-ballot victory, and Segal's immediate memory of the contest more than a decade and a half later was how awful he felt letting his former boss down.

Those endorsements were perfectly understandable. Davis's endorsement in the first-ever Conservative Party of Canada leadership race in 2004 was more problematic because the former premier found himself between a rock and a hard place.

Tony Clement first saw Bill Davis at a 1975 Ontario election rally. Davis was fighting for his political life, and Clement was a Grade 10 student and member of the Young Progressive Conservatives trying to help his single mother keep her job. Clement's mother worked in York North MPP William Hodgson's office, so young Tony was told to help the Tory cause. He caught the political bug and has been in the game almost non-stop ever since.

In fact, Clement's last name wasn't Clement yet. He was Tony Panayi, born in Manchester, England, to a Cypriot father who wasn't much part of Tony's childhood. His mother would eventually marry Bill Davis's attorney general, John Clement, the PC MPP from Niagara Falls, and Tony took his stepfather's last name. By the time Davis recaptured his majority government in 1981, Tony Clement was on the YPC executive, frequently rubbing shoulders with the premier and advising him on youth-friendly policies. After Davis retired, Clement twice backed Larry Grossman for leader, then Mike Harris for whom he served as party president, then as assistant principal secretary. Clement's next move in the fall of 1994 was, by his own admission, ill-advised. He decided to run for the High Park–Swansea seat on Toronto City Council being vacated by Derwyn Shea, who was going to run provincially for Harris. Inexplicably, three conservatives contested the seat against a single New Democrat. Not surprisingly, the three conservatives split the right-wing vote and the NDPer won. His name was David Miller, who would become Toronto's 63rd mayor nine years later. Clement, meanwhile, put his tail between his legs and thought about going back to Queen's Park to beg for his old job back.

Then Bill Davis called.

Here's how Davis's mind works. Davis knew Clement was married to Lynne Golding, whose family was from Brampton. Golding's grandfather, Jim, was on the Brampton School Board in 1946 with Davis's father, Grenville. Davis himself had a history teacher named Hannah Golding who was Lynne's great-aunt. So even though Tony and Lynne now lived in High Park in Toronto, Davis saw possibilities.

"You're an articulate fellow, Tony," the former premier told him. "You'll run hard and I think you have a really good chance of winning. So please consider running in Brampton South." That was Davis's own riding.

Clement asked his wife what she thought of him running for the PCs in the upcoming 1995 election. The Mike Harris Tories were trailing the Liberals by 20 points. She thought it was nuts but said, "Do whatever you damn well please." Clement took that as a yes. Despite the Tories' low standing, there would be a contested nomination for the PCs in Brampton South, but the former premier put his thumb on the scale for Clement.

"Mr. Davis would always come to any fundraisers I would have," Clement recalls. "He would suggest people I should talk to, to get more support in the riding, all those things. He was a great mentor to me."

The 1995 Ontario election was one for the history books. For the first time in more than 70 years, the third-place party in the legislature went from worst to first in one election. Harris won a stunning majority government with 44.8 percent of the total votes cast, a number incidentally that Bill Davis never reached in any of his four elections. And Tony Clement captured Brampton South by more than 6,000 votes. Given his roots in the party and personal connections to the incoming premier, Clement dared to hope he'd get a call from Harris to join the cabinet. Instead, he got a call from another Progressive Conservative premier — Bill Davis.

"There's gonna be a new cabinet tomorrow and you're not in it," Davis said.

Clement was crestfallen. "I thought I had a shot," he told Davis.

"No, you don't have a shot right now," the former premier said. "Just keep calm, keep patient, and your time will come."

Clement still doesn't know how Davis knew. Despite being out of government for a decade, the former premier clearly still had good sources at Queen's Park.

Two years later Clement was parliamentary assistant to Premier Harris. Again Davis called. "There's gonna be a cabinet shuffle tomorrow and you're going to be in" was the word. Again, Clement had no inkling that a cabinet shuffle was pending and that he was going to become minister of transportation.

"He was kind of like my guardian angel, kind of looking out for me and encouraging me," Clement now says. For the eight and a half years Clement was Davis's MPP, he would drop in to the former premier's home around Christmas and get some advice. "I treated him with respect, as he deserved, as he had earned," Clement says. "And, of course, he had a political mind like a steel trap, so why wouldn't I listen to some of his suggestions and insights?"

Interestingly, Clement says Davis never wanted anything from him. Typically, Davis would warn Clement that the government might be acting too harshly on this, or "couldn't you smooth out some of the rough edges on that? I felt like I was at least one of the surrogate sons that he had an eye out for."

But the surrogate father-son relationship only went so far. Clement soon ran twice for the leadership of two conservative parties: in 2002 for the Ontario PC Party in the contest to replace Mike Harris, then in 2004 in the first-ever leadership contest for the new Conservative Party of Canada. And in neither contest did Bill Davis support Tony Clement for leader. Davis mostly stayed on the sidelines in the 2002 contest won by Ernie Eves. But he very publicly backed Belinda Stronach in the Conservative Party race. Davis was on the board of Magna, the company run by Stronach's father, Frank. It was a no-win situation for Davis.

"That one seriously affected our relationship for a time," Clement now says. No one is ever entitled to anything in politics, but Clement had reason to believe some of the people he knew and served well would be with him. Former premier Mike Harris endorsed Stronach. So did Janet Ecker, Clement's former cabinet colleague. It was hard. But none of the missed endorsements hurt Clement as much as Bill Davis taking a pass. What bothered him so much was that, in so many people's minds, Stronach plainly wasn't ready for the job. "If she were an amazing, brilliant person with amazing ideas about the future of the country, then okay, I can accept that more," Clement says. "But she was 100 percent content-free."

Years later Davis called Clement, who was now the MP for Parry Sound–Muskoka. (Ironically, Clement was now Davis's summertime MP, since the Davis family cottages were all in Clement's new riding.) When he makes a mistake, Bill Davis never quite apologizes outright. But he got close.

"The essence of the conversation was basically that he'd made a mistake in supporting her [Stronach] and that perhaps as future events would show I was worthy of support," says Clement, who would go on to have a significant career in the federal cabinet as minister of health, minister of industry, and president of the treasury board. He is still Davis's summertime MP, although since October 2015, now as an opposition MP. The two men have patched up their past differences and now Davis even feels comfortable enough calling Clement to complain about boats being too noisy or water levels being too low.

In October 2009, to celebrate Davis's 80th birthday, lawyer Sean Adams invited the former premier to come to Cornwall to be gently roasted by his colleagues and raise some money for the highly regarded Children's Treatment Centre. Ed Lumley, the former mayor of Cornwall and federal cabinet minister, emceed the event whose guest speakers included Davis's former adviser, Hugh Segal; Senator Sharon Carstairs; Senator Mike Duffy; and journalist Robert Fisher, himself a Cornwall native.

Lumley warned Davis right off the top: "You may regret coming tonight."

Davis heckled: "I regret it already."

The tone was set. The spirit in the room was strong, but the jokes were lame. Lumley said, "People ask me, 'Ed, why did you leave politics?' The answer is: illness and fatigue. The voters were sick and tired of me."

Senator Duffy said Davis had been around so long that "he knew Absorbine Senior."

Segal said, "I'm not a member of any organized political party. I'm a Conservative." Or: "I'm on a first-name basis with the guest of honour. He calls me Hugh and I call him Premier." Or: "Some of the rules of public life that Mr. Davis taught me, critical to our entire administration: "Never put off 'til tomorrow what you can avoid doing altogether." It was that kind of night. Segal reminded the audience that Davis visited Iran in 1979, four days before the fall of the shah. "The CIA now wants him to do another tour," Segal quipped, adding that the Iranian ambassador in Canada had a message from the shah. "He didn't understand all the references to Brampton."

Sharon Carstairs added this admonition to Davis: "You can't go to Masada and tell them it reminds you of the Caledon Hills," she said. "That's pushing parochialism too far."

By the time Davis got to the microphone, he was ready to return a few punches. To Hugh Riopelle, the Ottawa-area businessman and former member of the Montreal Canadiens, Davis said: "It's always nice to find someone my age who's more senile than I am. I can say that because I know he's not getting back to the microphone."

To Mike Duffy he observed: "I saw all these people coming in and being respectful to you because they knew they were on television. I don't know if they really liked you or not."

Davis shared with the audience the fact that his father was a pretty fine lacrosse player, adding: "The first lacrosse sticks I used were made in

Cornwall, which is irrelevant to this gathering. But then again, most of what I've heard here tonight is irrelevant."

It was a fun night, concluded by Ed Lumley who offered a "senility prayer" for the former premier: "God, grant Bill Davis the senility to forget the people he never liked, the good fortune to run into the ones he does like, and the eyesight to tell the difference."

Technically, Bill Davis has been out of politics for more than three decades. I say "technically" because in some respects he's never left. Davis still loves the game, still loves being even peripherally involved, and still loves the fact that he can get his calls returned because, in a very real sense, he's still a player.

For example, in May 2005, fully 30 years after leaving public life, Bill Davis went to bat for one of the best-known Canadians ever to stand for public office. Peter Kent is a member of the Canadian Broadcast Hall of Fame, having once anchored *The National* on CBC-TV News and been one of this country's most important foreign correspondents. He was there in Southeast Asia in the mid-1970s to chronicle the fall of South Vietnam and the rise of the Khmer Rouge in Cambodia. In fact, the CBC's commercials promoting Kent's work always ended with the tag line: "When the bombs fell in [supply the place name], Peter Kent was there." He worked for NBC News in the 1980s, reporting from the network's Miami, Washington, and New York City bureaus, then became NBC's senior correspondent in Europe. In the 1990s he returned to Canada and anchored Global Television's *First National* flagship newscast.

Peter Kent spent four decades covering the news. So when he decided to pack it in and run for the Conservative Party of Canada in advance of the 2006 federal election, it was a big deal. Party leader Stephen Harper (he wasn't the prime minister yet) did an event with several Conservative notables from past and present to show off the party's new prize catch for the riding of St. Paul's in midtown Toronto. And this time Bill Davis was there. He wanted to endorse Kent, but with one significant proviso.

"What set Bill's endorsement apart was the fact that he said it was entirely conditional on one thing," Kent recalls. "I must, he said with the sort of quiet ferocity that he employed so effectively championing Ontario's big issues, pledge my permanent opposition to an NFL football franchise in Toronto!"

Davis's Canadian Football League bona fides have never been in question. It's a bit ironic, since there's probably never been a Canadian politician who has attended as many American professional and college football games as Davis. But for him the U.S.-Canadian border was important particularly when it came to football. Davis loved nothing more than to watch an NFL game in Miami Dolphins owner Joe Robbie's private box. But he was adamant that the NFL stay in the States and the CFL have Canada to itself.

"It was a serious matter of Canadian identity," Kent says.

Candidate Kent, of course, pledged to the former premier that should fortune favour him as an MP he'd never do anything to endanger the CFL's standing in Canada. "We've shared public moments a dozen or so times since then," Kent says. "When he takes the microphone, I brace myself because I know that if he sees an opening, he will make a point of mentioning his original condition to our audience and demand a renewal of my vow. Of course, I always do."

Kent lost that election in 2006 to the Liberals' Dr. Carolyn Bennett. But in the subsequent 2008 federal election he tried again north of the city in Thornhill where he was successful, eventually becoming minister of the environment from 2011 to 2013. At age 73 he remains the MP for that riding.

It isn't unusual for premiers, cabinet ministers, and journalists, out of the blue, to get a call from Ontario's 18th premier. But others do, too. For example, Alex Barron is one of the most respected and humble doctors I've ever met. He's in the Department of Paediatrics at Toronto's Hospital for Sick Children and goes to work every day trying to make kids' lives better. Dr. Barron is a very soft-spoken guy, so a few years ago when he told me he was ticked off about something, it caught my attention. A loyal Conservative activist, he wanted something and the Harper government wouldn't give it to him. What he wanted was the right to volunteer his services in Afghanistan — to treat Afghan kids who otherwise certainly wouldn't have access to a top-flight doctor — but the military and the government were saying no. They worried about his safety. He told them he didn't care about his safety, that he'd sign whatever waiver they wanted, and just wanted to get over there and help kids. That's Alex. He's the kind of guy who will start telling a story about a child he tried to help and then suddenly have to stop because he's on the verge of tears. He's a mensch.

One day, in 2011, Alex was driving south on Allen Road in Toronto when his cellphone rang.

"Alex, it's Bill Davis," the voice said. Alex, being a staunch Conservative, certainly knew all about Bill Davis but had never spoken to him before in his life.

"What a surprise, Mr. Davis," Alex said. "What can I do for you?"

"Alex, would you consider running as a candidate for the party in the upcoming provincial election in Eglinton-Lawrence?" Davis asked. Before Alex could answer, Davis added, "And how are Helen and Dennis doing?"

"Mr. Davis, you know my parents?" Alex asked incredulously.

"Of course, I do," the former premier answered. "They've been great supporters of mine for years. Now, Alex, if you did run, I'd give you my full support."

Alex Barron didn't run in Eglinton-Lawrence in that election. Rocco Rossi did. Rossi was nominated by Alex Barron, who still shakes his head with delight at the memory of an out-of-the-blue phone call from his former premier.

Bill Davis has never really stopped recruiting for his beloved Ontario PC Party. In late 1975, having just won a minority government, Davis called a meeting at the Macdonald Block at Queen's Park of all the student council presidents from schools in the Greater Toronto Area. The idea was to reinforce how important student governance was and the relevant contribution these 200 or so young people were making to the province. One of the representatives in that crowd was a young man named David Lindsay from Ajax High School, a self-described "kid from the suburbs" who'd never seen the Ontario legislature before. So after the meeting with the premier was over, Lindsay headed for the exit, hoping to see the legislature buildings. Who should he bump into, of course, but Bill Davis, who wondered where he was off to now. When Lindsay told him, the premier said, "Follow me. I'll show you a shortcut through the tunnel."

As they walked to the legislature, Davis made small talk with Lindsay, asking him what school and riding he was from. All Lindsay could think was: *I'm talking politics with the premier of Ontario!*

At one point Davis asked him: "Have you ever thought of running for office?" In fact, five years later, Lindsay was a summer student at PC Party headquarters. And in 1987 he was the PC candidate in Don Mills, losing by fewer than 2,000 votes to financial broadcast journalist Ali Velshi's father, Murad. But Lindsay's best days in politics lay ahead. He eventually became Premier Mike Harris's chief of staff.

Fast forward to 2005 and Lindsay is president of the association that represents all of Ontario's community colleges. He is at a ceremony with former premier Bill Davis, giving out an award to Tyler Charlebois, a Cambrian College student council president being honoured for his excellence in student leadership. As Davis presents Charlebois with his award, Lindsay overhears the former premier asking, "Tyler, have you ever thought of running for office?"

Lindsay laughs. "I'm hearing the same conversation again 30 years later. Mr. Davis is *still* recruiting for the PC Party." While Lindsay did run for the PCs, Charlebois was last seen working in Premier Dalton McGuinty's office. Apparently, that was one fish that got away from Ontario's 18th premier.

On October 2, 2003, provincial election night in Ontario, Linda Jeffrey found herself chosen as the people's representative for Brampton Centre, having eked out a narrow 1,000-vote margin of victory over the former PC sitting member. The phone rang at Jeffrey's home. Without even saying who he was, Bill Davis just started speaking. Of course, anyone involved in politics in Brampton knows that voice. Jeffrey had been on Brampton City Council for a dozen years and had seen Davis at local events, but to say they knew each other would be stretching.

"Oh, my God, this is Bill Davis!" she said, gesturing to her family while still listening to the former premier's words of congratulations.

"If you ever need anything, just call me," Davis told her.

And so began one of the most wonderful, delightful, trying, problematic, and heartbreaking relationships any former and current politician have ever had.

Over the next decade, while Jeffrey was making her way up the ladder of provincial politics, Davis would occasionally call and share his two cents about the issues of the day. When the McGuinty government announced it was allowing mixed martial arts (MMA) spectacles in the octagon in Ontario, the former member for Brampton called the current member for Brampton Centre to complain. The government wanted the revenue, but Davis thought MMA was too brutal and inconsistent with Ontario values. His opposition notwithstanding, MMA did come to Ontario.

Jeffrey had a solid decade-long run in provincial politics, earning three different cabinet jobs before finishing as minister of municipal affairs and housing and chair of cabinet in Premier Kathleen Wynne's government. And then the phone rang again. It was Davis, urging the minister to quit provincial politics and "come home" because her city needed her.

Brampton, Jeffrey believed, had become almost as much of an embarrassment under Mayor Susan Fennell as Toronto had under Rob Ford. The Brampton mayor was constantly in the newspapers for all the wrong reasons: spending scandals, a lack of transparency and accountability with tax dollars, and a salary that was higher than any other mayor's in Canada. An increasing number of Bramptonians were urging Jeffrey to challenge Fennell, including Davis.

"When somebody like Bill Davis suggests you do it, it carries more weight," Jeffrey says.

It took more than one phone call to get Jeffrey to sign on. In fact, Jeffrey recalls on one occasion hearing what she thought was a hospital paging system in the background of one of her calls with Davis.

"Mr. Davis," she said, "please don't tell me you're calling me from your hospital bed."

"Gotta go," Davis said, "Talk to ya later. Bye-bye." Click.

Eventually, Jeffrey got into a field of a dozen candidates vying for mayor, but it was her campaign sign that found itself on to Bill Davis's front lawn. Oddly enough, the Davis family, which usually speaks with one voice on these matters, was split. Neil Davis, the premier's oldest offspring, was backing city councillor John Sanderson. But on election night, October 30, 2014, it wasn't close. Jeffrey captured more than 49 percent of the vote. Sanderson was second with 22 percent, while outgoing Mayor Fennell could manage only 13 percent. It was a spectacular win and led to even more collaboration between the new mayor and the old premier, who would meet frequently at Davis's home to compare notes.

Davis agreed to be on Jeffrey's transition team. In fact, at one point she had to send him home because he was such a distraction to her volunteers. "He knew everybody's mother or their sister or their aunt and he knew that they were good Conservatives and what were they doing with this Liberal," the mayor says. "He was heckling all of my volunteers and they loved it. He's surrounded by all these people listening to these great stories. And he has wonderful stories."

Davis has never hesitated to call politicians of all stripes to offer advice, whether it's wanted or not, and Jeffrey was no exception. He urged the new mayor not to be too impatient, not to try to get everything done in the first few months. Within a few months, Mayor Jeffrey tasked Davis with leading Brampton's effort to secure a new university for the city. Brampton is Canada's largest city without a university, and given Davis's knowledge of the post-secondary world and his connections to decision-makers, both he and the mayor felt his appointment would give Brampton a leg-up on other nearby municipalities that were also competing for a new university. Jeffrey says Davis gave him great advice on who else should be on the university committee, how to manage egos, and whom to enlist in the cause.

"A university is something that he really wants to be part of," she says. "He's been working on that for a long time. So I kinda owe him. I have a lot of time for Bill Davis."

That conversation took place in the summer of 2015 when the new alliance between Davis and Jeffrey was working well. But then it began to come off the rails over the issue of building a new light rail transit line in Brampton. Metrolinx (the Greater Toronto Area's regional transportation planning body), the Ontario Ministry of Transportation, and Mayor Jeffrey all believed the new LRT ought to start in Mississauga, go north up Hurontario Street, cross Steeles Avenue into Brampton, then proceed straight up Main Street to the GO Station, which was also a possible home for the city's new university. But Bill and Neil Davis had different ideas. The Davises urged the mayor to stop connecting the LRT and the university as one, contiguous project. They preferred a different route for the LRT, one that would turn right and go east along Queen Street where they believe an LRT would kick-start more development sooner.

Somehow what might have been a private disagreement turned into a very public spat. During one of their regular meetings at Davis's home, the mayor told him, "Well, if you feel that strongly, I'm prepared to take your resignation. I'm not going to be bullied." Davis demurred and tried to lower the temperature.

Mayor Jeffrey has a complicated relationship with Neil Davis. On the one hand, she feels genuine sympathy for the appalling circumstances of his childhood — losing his mother at such a young age and then having his father not be around much because he was running Ontario Inc. "How abandoned he must've felt," Jeffrey tells me. "I don't think most people knew the sacrifice. He must've been grieving and it was so difficult."

However, the mayor is also extremely ticked off at Neil at what she sees as his use of his father's good name to oppose her on the LRT project. It's ironic that these three have seen their relationship fall apart over the issue that helped make Davis a political star 45 years ago: public transit. In the 1970s, shortly after killing the Spadina Expressway and saving thousands of jobs at the Urban Transportation Development Corporation (UTDC), which designed several high-profile monorails, Davis was chosen the North American Transit Man of the Year. Yet here he was fighting his mayor's $1.6 billion LRT plan, which the province was offering to pay for entirely.

Jeffrey insisted her route for the LRT was essential to help secure a future university. The chair of that blue-ribbon task force designed to find that university then released a statement contradicting the mayor.

"By portending that a particular transit option and route is a precondition to our ability to be successful is not only unfounded but unhelpful as it suggests that this community is not committed to greater transit accessibility which is patently untrue," Davis said.

Jeffrey responded in kind: "I am truly disappointed that the Chair [Davis] chose to insert himself … into a political debate." She went on to accuse Davis of overstepping his mandate and raising questions about the "ethics and relevance of the Panel in participating in issues outside its intended mandate," namely, the route of the LRT.

A whisper campaign began suggesting that Davis opposed Jeffrey's (and Metrolinx's and the province's) route because he didn't want the front of his home on Main Street dug up. Such insinuations frustrated Davis, who told me: "Do you know when the shovels will go into the ground for that? Years from now. I'll be long dead and buried."

But Jeffrey maintained the Davis panel's job was to get a university for Brampton, not weigh in on transit policy. "The Chair has failed to grasp the gravity of the situation," she wrote in her press release. "I am truly disappointed that the Chair has made these comments."

Meanwhile, Metrolinx weighed in from the sidelines. It said unless Brampton City Council approved *its* preferred route, it would cancel the Brampton leg of the project altogether and stop the LRT at Steeles Avenue.

Finally, in October 2015, the two sides had to move their showdown from the City Council chambers to the Rose Theatre, thanks to intense public interest. City councillors heard deputations from 50 interested citizens until almost 1:00 a.m. Forty spoke in favour of the mayor's plan. But when the votes were counted, the old premier prevailed over the new mayor.

The next day I got an email from Davis sent by Sheila Donohue, his trusted executive assistant. It said simply: "Old works" — a clever takeoff on Davis's most famous quote: "Bland works."

Steven Del Duca, the provincial transportation minister, immediately responded by pulling the $300 million meant for the Brampton leg of the LRT project. He said that money would now go elsewhere. Jeffrey, meanwhile, is trying to explore whether anything can be resurrected, including her relationship with Davis.

One thing the brouhaha over the LRT has demonstrated is that Bill Davis still has considerable schlep among a significant faction of Brampton's population. Mayor Jeffrey refers to it as "old Brampton. But I've got one of the youngest populations anywhere in Ontario," she adds. "Very well educated, very diverse, and they don't know who Bill Davis is. In fact, some people didn't know he was alive."

The mayor, however, still professes to love Bill Davis. "I have a lot of time for him, even though he's philosophically misguided," she says, stealing the line Davis always uses to describe those who haven't been blessed enough to become Progressive Conservatives.

Sean Conway was first elected in 1975 in the riding of Renfrew North at the tender age of 24 and stayed at Queen's Park for nearly three decades. In 1986 he was the Liberal education minister who actually had the responsibility to enact Davis's promise of full funding for Catholic schools after the government changed hands. He sat across the floor from Davis in the legislature for a full decade, and yet interestingly, his most memorable "Bill Davis moment" didn't take place at Queen's Park, or for that matter, even while Davis was premier.

On March 1, 2012 — coincidentally the 41st anniversary of his swearing-in as premier — Bill Davis was the guest speaker at an event organized by the Ontario Heritage Trust. The trust runs a premiers' gravesite program in which special plaques and a Canadian flag are mounted beside the final resting place of Ontario's deceased first ministers. On this occasion, friends and colleagues of Davis's predecessor gathered at the Cathedral Church of St. James in downtown Toronto to remember John P. Robarts and unveil a plaque honouring him.

"I've watched Mr. Davis for 40 years," Conway told me in early 2016. "I'm not sure he was ever better than at St. James Cathedral."

Conway and Davis have had a good relationship for two people who spent 10 years tossing barbs across the floor of the legislature at each other. In January 1980, Conway recalls having his wisdom teeth taken out and "looking like George Chuvalo after his fight with Muhammad Ali." While he was recovering at home, there was a knock on the door and a postman presented him with a letter via special delivery. Conway glanced at the letter, which had the "Office of the Premier of Ontario" logo emblazoned on it. He opened the letter to see the following message revealed: "I wish I could be there with you to see the big mouth of the legislature shut down for just one day." Yes, Bill Davis was having some fun at Conway's expense.

But on that day in 2012, surrounded by friends and honouring his mentor, the intensely private Davis was in an expansive mood. He began expressing feelings in public he'd never shared before. "It was the one and only time I saw the guard drop just a bit," Conway recalls.

Davis talked publicly about how Premier Robarts counselled him through the tragedy of his first wife's death. People in the church began looking at each other in astonishment as the former premier, perhaps for the first time ever in a public speech, referenced that awful part of his past. Davis reminded the audience he had a different relationship with Robarts. Being the modest man he is he wouldn't call it a special relationship, even though it surely was. But Davis wasn't like some of Robarts's other political buddies who used to gather at the Westbury Hotel drinking into the wee hours of the morning. Davis was too much the former Sunday schoolteacher to have done that. But Ontario's 18th premier talked about how kind Robarts was to keep the education port-folio for himself when Davis thought he might have to quit politics because of his wife's death.

"It was apparent how much Mr. Davis admired Mr. Robarts, even though he knew he couldn't be like him," Conway says.

After the ceremony, Davis and three of his closest colleagues from his Queen's Park years — Stephen Lewis, Darcy McKeough, and Ian Macdonald — gathered in front of the church to reminisce about some of the best and worst moments of their lives, which they shared with one another.

"It was clear to me on that day that the tragedy of John Robarts haunted them all," Conway says, referring to Robarts's suicide in 1982. "That's a memory of Davis I shall never forget."

On the surface, it would seem that Ontario's 18th premier and the province's 25th premier had very little in common. He's a Tory, she's a Liberal. He got into provincial politics at age 29, and almost immedi-ately, people speculated he could be a future premier. She didn't win her first provincial election until age 49 and was cruising in on 60 years of age before many of her fellow Liberals began talking about her and the party leadership in the same sentence.

But a closer look reveals that William Grenville Davis and Kathleen O'Day Wynne have a lot more in common than meets the eye. Despite both having a lot of popularity in the province's capital, neither is actually from Toronto. Davis, of course, is from Brampton, while Wynne was born, raised, and educated in Richmond Hill, a town of fewer than 10,000 people when she was growing up there. Both made their early political marks in education: Davis in his early thirties as the minister, and Wynne first as a Toronto School Board trustee (prompted to run because of her anger over Mike Harris's education policies), then also as the minister of education from 2006 to 2010. Wynne started elementary school in 1958, the year before Davis's entry into politics, and was a direct beneficiary of Davis's and John Robarts's massive education-system building and reforms. Davis was the education minister throughout Wynne's high school years in Richmond Hill and signed her Grade 13 graduation certificate. (Wynne actually skipped Grade 5 and graduated at age 17.)

One thing that emerges when talking to Kathleen Wynne about education policy in Bill Davis's time is how jealous she is of him. While the 21st-century Liberals, even during relatively buoyant times, were only able to see annual education budget increases of 2 to 3 percent, Davis routinely enjoyed double-digit increases of 30 to 40 percent, much of that contributed by the federal Liberal government of Lester Pearson, which was anxious to kick-start a school-building spree for the new generation of baby boomers. Conversely, the Ontario Liberals under Wynne and Dalton McGuinty dealt with Stephen Harper's Conservatives and spent a decade in mortal political combat, rarely agreeing on anything. Wynne, who had a very successful run as education minister, can only dream about what other things she might have been able to accomplish with the kinds of annual spending increases Bill Davis enjoyed, starting with restoring physical education and outdoor education programs, building more sports facilities for schools, and improving the accessibility and energy efficiency of schools and the like.

"Those were the things that we were dying to do and didn't have the money to do," she tells me in an interview in the premier's office in the main legislative building.

Given Wynne's respect for Davis the man and the minister, I try to imagine what *her* first day as education minister was like, walking into the Mowat Block at Queen's Park and seeing all those pictures of former education ministers such as Arthur Hardy, George Ross, G. Howard Ferguson, George Henry, George Drew, John Robarts, and Bill Davis, all of whom went on to become premier of Ontario. But funnily enough, that moment never happened. When Wynne arrived as education minister, for some reason, the pictures of all of her predecessors had been taken down. One of the first things she did was get them put back up.

The other thing you come to realize when talking to Wynne about Davis and Davis about Wynne is that they both like each other immensely. In the nearly 13 years that Wynne has been in provincial politics, she and Davis have found themselves on numerous occasions at the same public events where more often than not the 25th premier's job was to make a speech honouring the 18th premier. It has almost gotten to the point where the two seem to perform an Abbott and Costello routine. Davis expresses his affection for Wynne but calls her "philosophically mis-guided." He is happy to say nice things about her until 2018 when he will once again vote to oust her government. Wynne expresses her admiration for Davis, knows in her heart that the other Kathleen in Davis's life (his wife) definitely *does* vote for her, and calls Davis the kind of Conservative she likes. The two of them also no doubt agree that Mike Harris and Tim Hudak were not "their kind of Conservatives." I've asked Davis directly whether his respect and affection for Kathleen Wynne means he actually secretly votes for her, even though he always puts a Tory campaign sign on his front lawn. He just sheepishly shakes his head, and Wynne under-stands that. "He is *such* a loyal man, such a loyal human being," she says. "He believes in and has believed in his party his whole life."

When Wynne was the education minister, the phone would occasion-ally ring and Davis's trusted executive assistant, Sheila Donohue, would be on the other end, saying: "Oh, hello, it's Mr. Davis calling for you." The subject matter of the calls was always the same — quite a bit of polit-ical gossip to start with, followed by a few minutes on the topic he really called to discuss. Davis has these exchanges with numerous politicians in all three levels of government and the pattern seems to work for everyone. Davis enjoys still being a player, offering advice and having it solicited by political leaders. And those politicians must enjoy it, as well, since they continue to take his calls, listen to what he has to say, and schmooze with one of the few legends of Canadian politics still around.

For example, when Wynne was education minister, Davis would call with advice on how to balance the interests of the teacher unions and the public. Both parties acknowledge times are significantly different now — remember, teachers couldn't strike when Davis was education minister — and there's simply a great deal more friction built into the relationship between the government and the unions today.

"What he has done for me is, he's helped me put things in perspective," Wynne says. "Whether they had the right to strike or not, he would've fought very hard to keep those relationships strong. And that's what we've always talked about, the need to have an open door and the need to know people and understand their needs."

Wouldn't the premier have known that already?

"Yeah," she admits, "but to have it reinforced by someone who was so successful and who has retained those relationships over time — I mean, people in this province have a deep respect for Bill Davis."

For people of a certain age, namely, baby boomers such as Wynne, the Davis years were good years and the former premier is a living embodiment of those times. "But I also think that he has a great sense of humour," she adds. "He is humble, and in his telling of his history, he's not mean and vicious."

As the father of the community college system, Davis has also advised Wynne to resist a growing trend in that sector. It's one thing for the colleges to want to partner with universities, since each wing of the post-secondary sector performs a distinctive mission. But Davis has urged Wynne to resist the call from an increasing number of colleges to become universities, a view about which she is similarly wary.

"We're of one mind that community colleges serve a vital purpose that universities don't serve and can't serve," she says. "We've got to be careful about that."

Now that she's premier, Wynne also gets unsolicited advice from Davis on other issues — people he thinks she should talk to, either in business or politics, for another perspective on an issue she might not have considered. Interestingly, despite their clearly special relationship, Wynne says Davis has never called her to complain about a decision he didn't like or tell her she got something wrong. It's just not his way.

Because he still cares so much about Ontario's education system, it's not surprising that's the subject Davis will return to frequently with Wynne. "He's such an informed eye, he's such an informed watcher," she says. "I know he knows what's going on." When the Liberals attempted to update the sex education curriculum for the second time (Dalton McGuinty tried but then backed down), there was yet another firestorm of reaction, particularly from social conservative groups. Some of the criticism got ugly and referred either directly or indirectly to Premier Wynne's sexual orientation (she is the first openly gay first minister in Canadian history). Davis called with advice.

"Don't pay too much attention," Wynne says he told her. "He knows the source of the hostility, he knows how much weight there is behind it, and therefore he knows how much attention I should pay to them. So it's not just like it's a pat on the back. It's a pat from a very informed observer."

It isn't completely unheard of for current first ministers to seek advice from former first ministers, even for it to happen across party lines. Mike Harris became premier of Ontario in June 1995, just four months before the second Quebec referendum. Harris once told me he was a novice at constitutional matters and so, before giving a significant speech on the issue, he sought the advice of his predecessor, Bob Rae, who was happy to give it.

But that is rare. Why does Wynne think she has this unusual regular back channel to Davis?

"I have thought about that and I think we're both very practical people," she says. "I don't think we're ideological, either of us, and I think that leads to a sort of view of the world that says, 'Okay, what are the problems that need to be solved?' That's not to say that he's not a Tory and I'm not a Liberal, because we are. But we are on the practical/pragmatic ends of both of those parties."

Wynne and Davis share another accident of history: they were both premiers presiding over minority legislatures — Davis for six years, Wynne for a year and a half, after which they both won majority governments. As Davis did with Stephen Lewis, Wynne says she tried to create a constructive working relationship with NDP leader Andrea Horwath. But it never developed professionally or personally into something similar.

"I failed in terms of trying to create a constructive, collaborative dialogue," Wynne says of that effort. "I wasn't able to make that happen.... We never fostered a strong working relationship."

Part of that might have been because Wynne and Horwath are both competing so aggressively to be the champion of the centre-left vote in Ontario. Unlike with Bill Davis, who wanted to keep Lewis's NDP strong, thereby denying votes to the Liberals, this truly is a zero sum game — Wynne's success comes directly at Horwath's expense and vice versa.

Another explanation is the times in which we live. Davis and Lewis were able to meet informally without the media constantly lying in wait for a comment, followed by the 24/7 *rat-a-tat-tat* of social media ready to pounce. Wynne says at least a third of her conversations with opposition leaders focused on what each of them intended to say to the media after their meetings were over and ensuring that everyone stuck to the script. Time spent on communication was time not spent on substance.

On October 22, 2014, the same day a deranged gunman shot and killed Corporal Nathan Cirillo at the cenotaph in Ottawa, then stormed Parliament Hill in a hail of bullets, 500 very unsettled people gathered at Brampton's Rose Theatre. With the tragedy of those events in the nation's capital hanging in the air, Premier Wynne came to Brampton to congratulate not only her predecessor but also his entire extended family for a half century of service. Catholic Family Services of Peel-Dufferin was doing something unusual. They were honouring three generations — 24 Davises in all — for their service to the region. Wynne spoke with eloquent sincerity when she said: "When I think of who I want to model myself after as premier, Bill Davis is part of that group I look to for inspiration. I'm grateful to have him as a predecessor and mentor."

Davis couldn't resist teasing his successor: "For the next three years, I'll be happy to do anything I can for you," he began. "In the fourth year ..." The audience began to laugh when Davis left out the suggestion he'd have to return to his partisan home and back whoever was trying to dethrone Wynne. Given the closeness of their personal relationship, you almost get the sense that Davis wishes he didn't have to pay lip service to defeating Wynne in the 2018 election. Davis went on to say that he and the current premier don't always agree, "but I can't think of when I have disagreed with her." And in case his being simpatico with the current premier's office holder wasn't yet clear, Davis added: "I have to say to the premier, you're doing extremely well, you're a very decent person, and I think we're very fortunate to have you with us for the next three and a half years as our premier." And there was more. "If someone wants to write that I'm trying to limit her time in office to three and a half years, you're totally wrong." Whoever's running for the Liberals in Brampton in the next provincial election might want to save that quote for his or her campaign literature.

For a man who never fails to remind everyone of what a true-blue Tory he is, William Davis can on occasion say some of the darndest things. The hard-right turn taken by both his federal and provincial party over the past two decades by the 3 H's — Harper, Harris, and Hudak — has on occasion left him feeling adrift in the party to which he's devoted nearly seven decades of his life. At a gala mounted by TVO in November 2013 to thank Davis for creating the provincial broadcaster and his service to the country, the former premier gazed out from the podium and saw the man who replaced John Tory as Ontario PC Party leader. And he couldn't resist. In a roomful of people, Bill Davis gave Tim Hudak a piece of his mind — gently, mind you, but unmistakable just the same.

"Tim, I would say to you, you need some people around you who are middle-of-the-road," Davis said quite firmly. As the people in the room began to squirm awkwardly, Davis added, "I'm teasing now a bit." But, of course, he wasn't.

Wynne was also in the room. "I felt badly for Tim," the premier told me two years after the fact. "But not too badly."

The fact is that Davis simply doesn't like the harder-edged brand of conservatism practised by the 3 H's any more than Wynne does. "I think he's genuinely upset by what's happened to the Progressive Conservative Party and I think it hurts him deeply," says Wynne, who at the time of our interview was embroiled in yet another fight with Prime Minister Harper over his unwillingness to assist Ontario in the creation of the financial architecture necessary for the province to create its own new pension plan. Wynne says the more radical right wing of the conservative movement "despise[s] people who want to collaborate and solve problems. They don't really believe in government." She feels she and Davis are kindred spirits in opposing that approach, which she believes genuinely angers Davis. "And he's not an angry man, so he wasn't gonna lash out, but he felt he had to say something."

At the TVO gala Davis continued, looking directly at both Wynne and Hudak and adding: "At the same time, I say to both of you, it's important that you treat one another with respect. People can have different points of view but be civilized with one another without being critical in any sort of way. That's what I'd like to see at Queen's Park."

It was an old-fashioned dressing-down and had no impact whatsoever. Six months later Premier Wynne launched a $2 million lawsuit against

Hudak for comments he made about her related to the Liberals' gas plant cancellation scandal. Hudak, clearly overreaching in making wild accusations about Wynne, refused to take them back, and as a result got himself sued. Three months later Wynne dropped the suit after besting Hudak in the 2014 election, which ultimately forced the PC leader to step down. No apologies were offered, the lawyers found the right weasel words to make the whole thing go away, but it served as yet another reminder that we're no longer living with the Marquis of Queensbury rules under which Bill Davis and his opponents sparred.

The Wynne-Davis road show had another appearance in June 2015 when the Liberal government announced it would do the opposite of the 1970 Joni Mitchell song "Big Yellow Taxi." Instead of paving paradise to put up a parking lot, the province planned to remove a parking lot and create a park out of it at Ontario Place, which Davis as premier had opened in 1971. To mark the occasion, the government would name a new waterfront trail in the park after Davis. Surprisingly (or perhaps not because of who the honoree was), Wynne told me she didn't run into a single complaint from a single Liberal that the government was honouring a former Tory. "Not a one," she said. "That's what I mean. The respect for Bill Davis crosses party lines."

"You're a very good premier, I can say that for another four years," Number 18 said to Number 25 at the Ontario Place event.

Wynne quickly corrected her predecessor, saying, "You mean *three*," referring to the 2018 fixed election day just three years into the future. Then Wynne joked, "But I'm good with four."

Davis returned the serve. "Listen, I was good for a lot more than that," he said, laughing and referring to his 14 years in the premier's office.

Charles Pascal, the former head of the Atkinson Foundation and Dalton McGuinty's early childhood education czar, loves to ask people who have been around Ontario politics for a while who the first socialist premier of Ontario was. Everybody's first guess is Bob Rae, the first and so far only NDP premier in the province's history. Then Pascal delights in correcting the guesser. "Nope," he says. "Bill Davis." The line always gets a laugh because, after all, Davis did buy an oil company, did bring in rent review, and did from time to time believe in very interventionist government.

But don't try getting Bob Rae to believe that. "It's a joke," the 21st premier of Ontario says. "I don't believe he was a socialist."

Bill Davis and Bob Rae go way back to the days when Davis was Ontario education minister and Rae was a student activist at the University of Toronto. The two also saw each other from time to time in New York City where Rae's father, Saul, was Canada's ambassador to the United Nations from 1972 to1976, overlapping the early tenure of Davis's premiership. In 1978, when Rae won a by-election in Broadview-Greenwood to become an MP, Davis telephoned him, reminding him that he was now officially representing Ontario.

"No, I'm not," Rae teased him back. "I'm representing my riding, but I'm happy to represent Ontario." Rae's words proved to be prophetic; 12 years later he became premier and *did* represent Ontario.

When Rae became Ontario NDP leader in February 1982, it took another nine months for him to find a seat in the legislature. Eventually, he won a by-election when former party leader Donald C. MacDonald retired, opening up the York South seat. The quips between Davis and Rae continued when the premier missed Rae's first day in the legislature as a newly minted MPP. He had a dental appointment.

Rae laughs. "So I wrote him a note saying, 'Sorry you couldn't be there because you were getting your teeth sharpened.'"

It's hard to think of another figure in Canadian political history who has had the mix of assignments Bob Rae has enjoyed (and suffered through) over the past nearly four decades:

1. The boy genius MP and NDP finance critic who moved the motion that defeated Joe Clark's nascent government in 1979.
2. Ontario NDP leader in 1982.
3. Holder of the balance of power in the Ontario legislature after the 1985 election returned a minority legislature.
4. Moved the motion to defeat a second Progressive Conservative government, Frank Miller's, in 1985.

5. Leader of Her Majesty's loyal opposition at Queen's Park in 1987.

6. Premier of Ontario in 1990.

7. Retired from politics in 1996.

8. Appointed to the Security Intelligence Review Committee in 1998.

9. Appointed to the Order of Canada in 2000 and the Order of Ontario in 2004.

10. A very public break with the NDP in 2002.

11. Chair of the Forum of Federations in 2002 and 2003.

12. Chancellor at Wilfrid Laurier University in 2003.

13. Partner at Goodmans law firm, which bears the name of Bill Davis's great friend.

14. Chair of an advisory task force for Premier McGuinty on post-secondary education in 2005.

15. Appointed to chair an inquiry into the Air India disaster in 2005, which cost him his chance to run for the federal Liberals in the 2006 election; his not having a seat after that election undoubtedly adversely affected his ability to win the party's leadership, which he contested in December 2006 but lost to Stéphane Dion.

16. A return to Parliament as a Liberal MP in 2008.

17. Served as interim national Liberal leader for two years, starting in May 2011, after the party's worst showing in history.

18. Held the Liberal ship of state together long enough and well enough that when Justin Trudeau became the new permanent leader in 2013, it was a solid operation he was taking over rather than a picked-over carcass.

Through all those different experiences, the relationship between Rae and Davis metamorphosed. From 1982 to 1985, they were direct political opponents. Five years after Davis's retirement Rae became one of his successors, and the relationship became more personal. By the time Rae contested the federal Liberal leadership, Davis actually showed up at the kickoff news conference to support Rae.

"I'm coming because I like you," Davis told him, "I'm not joining your party."

"Whatever it is that gets you there and makes you feel comfortable being there is fine with me," Rae answered back.

Of course, being Bill Davis, he had to add that he hoped Rae would win the Liberal leadership, then become the best leader of the opposition Canada would ever have.

Rae never bought it. "He didn't hope that," he insists. "He wanted me to win. I think that if I had been the leader of the party in 2006, do I think he would've endorsed Harper? I think he would've had a harder time doing it."

Davis today confirms that's exactly right. "I'm a loyalist and I wouldn't desert my party, but I'd at least have been concerned about this," he says. "It's wrong to say I wouldn't have supported Harper. But don't underestimate my affection and how impressed I am with Bob Rae."

Bill Davis sat on the board of Power Corporation with Rae's brother, John, who was the company CEO. "To have stuck his neck out for my brother speaks volumes about him," John Rae says of Davis.

There was likely no better indication of the trust these two men had in each other, even while political opponents, than in late 1982 when an unprecedented trust company scandal broke. It was, at the time, the biggest white-collar crime in Canadian history, involving fraudulent real estate deals, pyramiding, and shell games, in which the next deal was needed to pay for the previous one. The scheme finally hit the newspaper headlines when the perpetrators flipped nearly 11,000 apartment units in Toronto not once but twice in a matter of days, eventually to an unknown group in Saudi Arabia for $500 million — nearly double the original sale price. The Ontario government intervened and seized the assets of the three trust companies involved — Crown, Seaway, and Greymac Trust. The Canada Deposit Insurance Corporation had to step in to bail out defrauded depositors to the tune of almost $400 million. By the time the case came to court, the associate chief justice of Ontario, Frank Callaghan, said: "The size of the fraud is staggering. There are no other cases that approach this one in their enormity."

The trust companies were provincially regulated, so the entire mess ended up in Bill Davis's lap. There was palpable fear among the tenants and the trust company depositors about the whole crisis. The story was also incredibly complicated as the newspaper headlines got increasingly shrill by the day.

One Sunday in the midst of all of this, Davis's consumer affairs minister, Robert Elgie, phoned Bob Rae at home and said the premier urgently needed to see him in his office the following morning. Elgie shared no details, other than that it was of paramount importance. Rae agreed, and the next day Davis told him the province needed to take over ownership of the trust companies from the three fraudsters. The takeover would require a new law, and Davis, even though he had a majority government, wanted Rae's undertaking that the NDP leader wouldn't delay the new law's passage.

"Well, Premier," Rae responded, "if you think it's got to be done, and Elgie tells me it's gotta be done, and you don't have the legal means to stop it, I'm not going to hold it up."

The same kind of meeting was held with opposition leader David Peterson, and as a result, the government got swift passage of its new law, potentially averting a financial disaster. It's hard to imagine that kind of thing happening today, because the trust required among leaders to make it happen simply doesn't exist.

As trusting a relationship as Davis and Rae had, that didn't mean Rae agreed with everything the Davis government did. By the time Rae got to Queen's Park, Davis's triumph at the constitutional renewal talks in Ottawa had already happened and even Hugh Segal observed that some of the wind seemed to leave Davis's sails after that. Rae put it a little more bluntly in our conversation at his law offices of Olthuis Kleer Townshend LLP on University Avenue in downtown Toronto. He talked about a complacency setting in, both with the provincial Tories and the federal Liberals, both of whom had been in power a very long time.

However, Rae gives Davis full marks for being a very skillful politician. During Question Period, "you were up against the very best," Rae says. "He was always very elusive and effective. I don't think any question fazed him."

Rae also had to marvel at what he calls Davis's "understanding the wind" — knowing when to tack left and right depending on where the premier perceived public opinion to be, plus having good lines of communication open to business, labour, school boards, and so many other interest groups. "He really understood the fabric of the province and all the groups that have to be reconciled," he says.

The NDP has always prided itself on being the voice of labour in the Ontario legislature. But Rae found out in a most unusual way that's not always the case. When the government was preparing to bring in legislation to prevent Toronto's transit workers from going on strike at the same time Pope John Paul II was about to make his first-ever visit to Canada, Rae, as NDP leader, was expected to fight the good fight to at least give collective bargaining a chance. As he was preparing to filibuster the bill's passage, Rae got a call from the premier.

"I know you don't want to support this and I know you want to filibuster," Davis told him. Then he added the words Rae would come to hear numerous times over the years: "But my advice to you, Robert, would be to give the union a call, because I'm not sure that they are quite as opposed to this as you think they are."

As the voice of labour, Rae was happy to tell the premier he *had* been talking to the union and could assure the premier they were both opposed to the government's plans.

"Yes, I know that's what they're telling *you*," Davis replied, "but that's not what they're telling *me*, so you might want to talk to them some more about how far you want to carry your opposition to this."

Sure enough, what the union leadership was telling Rae for public consumption and what it was telling Davis behind closed doors were quite different. The premier was right and Rae moderated his party's opposition.

"There were lots of times when his network of information and his connectedness to all those folks was so good," Rae says. "It was something that I had to watch all the time. He did not govern in splendid isolation. He really didn't."

Again, Rae can admire Davis's record without signing on to all of it. By 1985 both opposition parties managed to convince the public that too many things needed action, which Davis (and then Frank Miller) had let slide, items such as equal pay or affordable housing. Davis might also have been the last premier of Ontario to enjoy a special relationship with his counterpart in Ottawa. After him, Brian Mulroney and David Peterson broke company quite dramatically on free trade, and then both Mulroney and Jean Chrétien "broke faith with us," as Rae puts it, when it came to transfer payments to Ontario. "At that point we were cut adrift," he says.

By the time Davis retired, Rae says, "He was at the top of his game. He was the best there was."

It was after Rae became premier that his relationship with Davis truly flourished. The two premiers and their wives would get together socially, and the four got to know one another in a way that being competitors in politics didn't permit. As he has done for all of his successors, Davis took and made calls to Rae offering advice on a wide range of subjects: any changes to the community college system, the health of the auto industry, Rae's efforts to save the de Havilland manufacturing plant in Downsview, the Constitution, even how to improve his relationship with Prime Minister Brian Mulroney. Davis frequently called to talk about institutions he felt a strong connection to or responsibility for. For example?

"Your employer," Rae says.

"He called you about TVO?" I ask. "What for?"

Davis had some thoughts about who the next chair and CEO of TVO ought to be, taking over from the controversial Bernard Ostry, and whether the provincial broadcaster should try to acquire a new headquarters.

The Ontario Institute for Studies in Education (OISE) was another organization to which Davis felt very attached and weighed in with Rae. Some wanted OISE deeply integrated, even merged, into the University of Toronto. Others, including Davis, worried its mission would be muddied if that merger happened.

"Bill felt a tremendous sense of paternity about OISE," says Rae, who adds when the previous Liberal government was in power, neither institution enjoyed much support from Finance Minister Robert Nixon. "Bob Nixon had his eye on both TVO and on OISE," Rae says. "He did not like either institution and he was ready to toss them over the end of the boat. I think Bill had a very strong reaction against those things, and when I came, I think he felt relieved that that's not going to happen."

Nixon admitted after the fact: "I got hammered on OISE. I had no idea its constituency was so wide."

Ironically, TVO's most vulnerable moments would come under a Progressive Conservative government. As part of the Common Sense Revolution, Mike Harris promised to consider selling some publicly held assets and listed the Liquor Control Board of Ontario and TVO as examples. In 1998 the government appointed Sheldon Levy, who would go on to transform Ryerson University as its president, to travel the province and get public feedback on TVO's future. As soon as Davis learned of Levy's appointment, he suggested the two meet at his home in Brampton "and we can write the report." Levy reminded Davis that his job was actually to crisscross the province and get input from the public.

"But why are you going to do that?" Davis asked him. "You know the results already." Levy learned what he probably already knew — that Davis is like the king of the jungle when someone messes with one of his lion cubs.

In any event, Levy did hold public hearings all over Ontario, heard from 700 people, and compiled 1,000 pages of documentation. Every time he returned to Toronto, he'd get a call from Davis asking him if he was ready to write the report. "Well, just let me look at it," Davis reminded him, "because I want to edit it."

Davis needn't have worried so much. TVO's fans bombarded the hearings. Levy heard comments such as: "In a medium where senseless violence is the order of the day, TVO gives us an oasis of thoughtful, entertaining, educational fare." Or this one: "Public television serves people as citizens, not as consumers." Levy concluded in his report that TVO was "unique … commercial-free, accessible … high quality, educational, and entertaining, offers objective and intelligent programming, and bound up with a sense of provincial identity and community." Bill Davis couldn't have said it any better. The report proved to be a turning point in the provincial broadcaster's history. Whatever momentum there might have been to privatize the station came to a halt after Levy's report. And despite Davis's desire to influence the final report, he now acknowledges all these years later that despite his not-so-gentle nudges, Levy actually didn't show it to him ahead of time, although the father of TVO was certainly happy with the way it all turned out.

Both TVO and OISE are still firmly in business today, and while one hears a lot of rumours at Queen's Park about their futures, one also hears that no government of any stripe will attempt to do anything adverse to either organization as long as Bill Davis is still alive.

Bob Rae's first budget in the spring of 1991 shocked the political and business establishments because for the first time ever the deficit nearly hit $10 billion. All jokes about Davis being the first socialist premier aside, the former premier did call Rae and expressed the business community's deeply held fear that the province's finances were out of control. Rae actually pushed back, pointing out his recession of the 1990s was harsher on the economy than Davis's of the 1980s, that the federal government was providing much less support, and that if you took inflation into account, his deficit wasn't that much uglier than Davis's were. Two years later the two men were on the phone again. This time Davis praised Rae's "Social Contract" approach to reining in spending on public sector salaries by unilaterally abrogating collectively bargained agreements through forced unpaid days off, or as they became better known, "Rae Days."

"You've done more to restructure that aspect of provincial spending than anybody, including me," Rae says Davis told him. Of course, the unions raised hell, withdrew all support of Rae's government, and ended up getting Mike Harris elected, which was as dumb an example of cutting off your nose to spite your face as Ontario politics has ever seen. Rae and Davis had plenty of conversations about Harris. ("Yes," Rae says, "of course, we talked about him, and often.") Rae won't share details of those private chats, but it doesn't take a soothsayer to divine what both men thought of the Harris government. At one point in Harris's tenure Davis even took the extraordinary (for him) step of giving a public speech defending teachers and their unions. Being a Tory loyalist, he didn't come out and explicitly criticize the Harris approach to education reform too vigorously, but it was a clear shot across Harris's bow. As a result, dozens of staffers at Cardinal Leger Secondary School in Brampton signed a thank-you note to Davis, saying: "In recent years as teachers, we have often felt alone and forgotten. You changed that by your recent words in support of the work we do. Thanks for being a positive voice for us."

The staff at Brampton's Notre Dame Secondary School did the same. "Thank you for your continued visible support for teachers and our work in Ontario," their letter said.

Another letter came from a woman named Susan Lyndon, who was on the same PC Youth Association executive as Tony Clement and John Baird, and who voted for Harris. She eventually went into teaching "18 mentally handicapped kids in a leaky portable outside a crumbling school. I finally knew they were wrong. Thank you again for speaking out."

Tom Boone wrote that he "was delighted to see you speak out now at this critical time in education. You may have forgotten this 93-year-old, but I haven't forgotten you, and I extend to you my deep appreciation and regards."

"I read your speech in support of public education," wrote the Honourable Mr. Justice E. Loukidelis from the Superior Court of Justice in North Bay — Mike Harris's hometown. "Bravo!"

Even after Harris's departure and Ernie Eves's becoming Ontario's 23rd premier, Davis continued to raise eyebrows in Tory circles for his occasional public utterances on behalf of teachers. In 2003 he spoke to the Toronto City Summit conference, after which Eves's chief of staff, Steve Pengelly (coincidentally, the son of former Davis cabinet minister Bette Stephenson), wrote to him. "The Premier asked me to send along some factual information about his financial commitment to public education — to ensure that you knew he was very committed to the public system," Pengelly wrote. "He also wondered if you might be considering writing a letter to the *Star* to correct any errors in the reporting of your remarks." It was a not-so-subtle hint that some of the more right-wing Tories were concerned about Davis being seen to be taking them on. What did Davis say that was so controversial?

> I take exception to the view of some people that the public education system in this province is not of quality, because it is. I am prepared to say and go on record as saying that the teaching profession deserves our support. They are competent. They are not underworked and overpaid. They are in many respects the most relevant profession we have in the province of Ontario…. I can tell you that the economic success of this province and of this country will be determined by the priority, the resources, and the encouragement we give to the public education system across Canada.

Davis's words hit the right spot for a profession that felt increasingly vilified after eight straight years of seemingly constant battles with the PC government of the day. (For the record, Harris and Eves insisted they were both big public education supporters; it was the heads of the teacher unions with whom they had huge disputes.)

Of course, Davis's direct personal interest in educational matters goes back more than half a century to his days as the province's education minister, but his family's interest dates back even farther. Davis's father, Grenville, was on the Brampton Board of Education from 1943 through to the end of the decade, becoming chair in 1947. And there might be something educational in the Davis DNA, because so many family members beyond Grenville and William have also chosen to make their marks in that sector.

Davis's wife, Kathleen, has a master's degree in education from the University of California, Berkeley, and taught in San Francisco before marrying the future premier. His daughter-in-law, Ruth, who's married to his oldest son, Neil, taught kindergarten for 25 years and retired in 2015. Davis's oldest daughter, Nancy Bennett, has worked with students with intellectual disabilities for almost the past two decades with the York Region District School Board. She's also on the board of the Access to Better Living and Employment (ABLE) Network, helping special-needs students find work, then easing the transition from school to the workplace. Another Davis daughter-in-law, Rose, who's married to his son, Ian, has taught in the separate school system for 25 years. Ian and Rose's oldest son, Spencer, is at OISE (which his grandfather helped create in its current incarnation in 1973) and just finished his master's degree in education there. Neil and Ruth Davis's daughter, Christine, worked with the Toronto District School Board to provide a therapeutic equine program for Aboriginal students and is expanding that to work with youth suffering from mental health issues. In the post-secondary world, the Davises' other daughter, Kathleen Jr., has taught international law at Osgoode Hall Law School, while Davis's son-in-law, Abraham Drassinower, married to his daughter, Catherine, is a law professor at the University of Toronto Faculty of Law.

Still, the education story reflected deep divisions between Davis's Red Tory brand of conservatism and the Common Sense Revolutionaries who now controlled the party. In fact, throughout his political career, and even after, some of Davis's harshest critics have come from within, not outside, the conservative movement. One can only imagine how those critics reacted in 2000 when Davis was honoured as a "Fellow" of the Ontario Teachers' Federation.

Until the defeat of the Harper government in 2015, the Harold Macmillan–Nelson Rockefeller–Brian Mulroney–Bill Davis more moderate approach to conservatism had been overwhelmed by the Margaret Thatcher–Ronald Reagan–Stephen Harper–Mike Harris brand. The fact that Davis still has such a following in the province and country is a threat to that more ideological conservatism, which in part explains the antipathy many small-*c* conservatives have toward Davis. Having said that, with John Tory's mayoral victory in Toronto in 2014, Tim Hudak's election loss in 2014, Stephen Harper's defeat in 2015, and new Ontario PC leader Patrick Brown's pledge to be a more pragmatic conservative, it seems there is plenty of evidence to suggest that Davis's brand of progressive conservatism might be on the rise again.

"I think Bill himself has an incredible sense of balance and a sense of perspective that not many other people I've met in public life have, and an understanding of the institutional mix, the personalities, the texture of the province, and a surer kind of hand than just about anybody I've encountered in public life," says Bob Rae, who having defeated three Conservative governments on Parliament Hill and Queen's Park isn't inclined to complimenting Tory leaders. "I love the guy. He's a wonderful fellow."

23

FAMILY

Bill Davis was never particularly interested in the weather except when he was at his family's cottage on Georgian Bay, named nearly 200 years ago after King George IV. For some reason on many occasions, Davis's meteorological skills came to the fore either on Sunday night or Monday morning. He would get on the phone to the Office of the Premier of Ontario or to the Ontario Provincial Police and report that a thick, soupy fog was moving into the Honey Harbour area, making any departure from his cottage too risky. The Davis family compound was on an island about a half hour's boat ride from the mainland. Surely, no one would want to risk the premier's safety, having him transported through such dense fog, perhaps causing a collision of some kind.

The funny thing was: inclement weather always seemed to roll in after Davis enjoyed a delightful weekend with his family. It took a while before political and security officials realized the premier was playing his own version of hooky. Given the intensity of his job and the hours he worked, Georgian Bay was the place where he could mostly disconnect from politics and give his children the attention he and they wanted. And so the "Monday Morning Fog" became a standing joke between the premier and his security contingent. Everyone kept secret that fact that the weather was just fine — the first minister simply looked at his Day-timer, saw nothing that was so urgent that would require his immediate return to Queen's Park, and decided to spend another day with his family.

If you've ever seen the part of Georgian Bay where four generations of Davises have gathered for three seasons of the year, you would understand why the premier never wanted to leave. To visit the Davis compound is to step into a Group of Seven painting. The water lapping the shores, the massive granite rock formations of the Canadian Shield, the trees leaning from hundreds of years of being buffeted by winds, the brilliant blue skies that transform into dense cloud — it's all simply too gorgeous. President Franklin D. Roosevelt visited here. Orville Wright, half of the famous Wright Brothers who invented their flying machine more than a century ago, had a place here.

Back in A. Grenville Davis's time, you could buy an island on Georgian Bay for $100, then build a modest cottage on it. That practice of buying a small island and building on it is now illegal, and because of that, as the area has gained popularity, "monster" cottages are now a more common sight on the mainland. The well-known Giants Tomb Island is a stone's throw from the Davis compound, along with Christian, Hope, and Beckwith Islands. Because of the area's accessibility by water, some of the original cottages were built by Americans whose money came from Pittsburgh steel interests or the Singer sewing machine family. In 2015 the locals celebrated the 400th anniversary of Samuel de Champlain's exploration journey through Georgian Bay.

There were other Bill Davis family connections to this place, as well. The grandfather of Davis's wife, Kathleen, was a Scottish immigrant and Methodist preacher living in Atlanta, Georgia. He was asked by the church to go to Toronto, and thus preached at the Bond Street Methodist Church there. That's why Kathleen's father, Roland, spent four years at the University of Toronto's medical school. The family during that time discovered Georgian Bay and built a cottage right near the Davises'. "You could put up any shack on a rock for $25," explains Kathleen Davis. The Mackays evidently loved the place so much that even when Kathleen's father moved the family to Illinois, they kept the place on Georgian Bay despite its being an eight-hour drive away. That cottage is now owned by Kathleen's brother. Bill Davis's maternal grandparents, the Hewetsons, also had a place near here.

There are an estimated 30,000 islands in the Georgian Bay region, a statistic that was fodder for plenty of banter between the premier and his former top adviser, Hugh Segal, who was from Kingston. "Segal used to always boast about the Thousand Islands near Kingston," Davis says. "But we've got 29,000 more."

The next thing you learn about Bill Davis when you see him in this environment is something that only his family knows, and that's his nickname. Apparently, Davis's father, Grenville, was nicknamed "Dutch" and somehow the name got passed down to his only son. So while the five Davis children might call their father "Dad," he is never "Grandpa" to the 12 Davis grandchildren. He is always Dutch to them. I have checked with dozens of Davis's Queen's Park colleagues and not a single one knew about this nickname. It's another indication of how special and separate from his political life Davis's Georgian Bay hideaway truly is. Kathleen Davis has also escaped the more common "Grandma." Again, she is "Mom" to the five Davis children but always "Kai" (pronounced *Kye*) to the grandchildren. The nickname is a shortened version of Mrs. Davis's maiden name, Mackay, but with a particularly Scottish pronunciation.

Because Bill Davis loves this part of Ontario so much, he has participated in a political effort to protect the properties along the shoreline. That's led to one of the most ironic decisions the Ontario government has ever made. In 1991 a non-profit registered charity called the Georgian Bay Land Trust was established to secure and protect more than 1,000 acres of land in the area. The owners of the lands pay property taxes on them, even though there are no services provided and no building permitted. Davis and others wanted the province to exempt conservation lands from property tax obligations. So he went to Ernie Eves, then the finance minister in the Mike Harris government. Eves was apparently sympathetic but ran into pushback from officials in the Ministries of Finance and Municipal Affairs, so the file languished.

By the time Davis circled back for a second attempt, the Tories had lost power and the Liberals under Dalton McGuinty held the reins of government. Less than a year into the new Liberal administration, Davis showed up to the Frost Block at Queen's Park for a face-to-face meeting with Greg Sorbara, the new finance minister. "He strolled through the seventh floor of Frost shaking hands like voting day was only two days away," Sorbara remembers. "All my staff were thrilled to say hello."

Sorbara first got elected in 1985, stayed for 10 years, then opted to walk away from politics as the Mike Harris Common Sense Revolution took Ontario by storm in 1995. But five years later, Sorbara came back to politics at the urging of Dalton McGuinty, who was hoping to return the Liberals to power. During that five-year interregnum, he bought a minor league professional baseball team, the St. Catharines Stompers. When the Stompers drew flies in the Garden City, Sorbara and his partners made plans to bring the team to Brampton, which naturally drew some interest from Brampton's most famous citizen. But the team couldn't get any financial support from the city, so when Brooklyn came calling, hoping to return minor pro ball to that borough of New York, Sorbara and his partners sold the club, which is now called the Brooklyn Cyclones.

I include all this background because as soon as Davis began his meeting with Sorbara, the former premier immediately reminded the new finance minister "of his great disappointment that I had reneged on my mission to bring the Stompers to Brampton," Sorbara recalls. "So immediately I'm on the defensive."

Davis put his case forward regarding the land trust tax issue. Sorbara indicated he might be able to help and talked to his officials about it. "He makes a good case," the minister said to his minions, "and besides, how do you say no to 'Mr. Ontario?'"

The McGuinty government soon passed a regulation exempting the Georgian Bay Land Trust lands from property tax. What's the moral of the story? "Liberals are more effective than Tories," says Kathleen Davis, whose politics have never been as conservative as her husband's party.

When Sorbara eventually retired from politics in 2012, he invited Davis to a farewell party/Liberal fundraiser in York Region. Davis declined to attend but sent this memorable note:

> I am sorry I can't participate in the well-deserved cele-
> bration of your remarkable contributions to public life
> in Ontario. While you have so much left to give in this
> regard, the notion of me spending a nickel for a fund-
> raiser for a lesser political party is something for which I
> am constitutionally unprepared. As well, I am still getting
> over the fact that you failed to locate the Stompers base-
> ball team to Brampton.... For this, you ... and the other
> owners have shown a remarkable lack of vision, given
> that Brampton remains at the centre of the universe. In
> spite of your being philosophically misguided, you have

accomplished much in your public service life and I extend my best wishes and hopes that this will continue, but not necessarily on the Government side of the House.

In the summer of 2015, Bill Davis told me I really should visit his Georgian Bay retreat to get a better sense of why the place has had so much meaning in his life. And so, toward the end of August, we arranged a visit that included his wife, Kathleen, all five of his children, and almost all of his 12 grandchildren. It was a feat of herculean logistics to make happen, but happen it did.

It's an easy 90-minute drive from midtown Toronto to Honey Harbour, the launching point to Georgian Bay's 30,000 islands. The town was founded by Harvey Hewitt from Pasadena, California, with the alliterative double *H*'s being a play off his name. Honey Harbour is a tiny, picturesque town with a small grocery store, a post office, a liquor store, a church, a school, several craft stores, and marinas. Another reason Davis has been so attracted to this place is that while he was in politics this was the only place on earth where he could actually get away with driving his own car and boat. For security reasons, the OPP prohibits any premier from driving his or her own car. But Davis took advantage of the remoteness of this part of rural Ontario to get behind the wheel of the family's station wagon whenever he could. Davis became quite a proficient motorboat captain during his youth, and the joys of driving the vessel from the Nautilus Marina to his cottage have never left him. Even in the summer of 2015, at the age of 86, he still loved to get behind the wheel of his boat and make the challenging trip to the cottage. I say challenging because, as his oldest son, Neil, points out, there aren't many signs around indicating where the water gets shallow or rocky, and boaters need "good local knowledge of the channels around here."

On this cloudy, windy August day, I'm welcomed at the Nautilus Marina dock by Neil, 59, and Neil's younger daughter, Kathleen, who would turn 30 in early 2016. Just as Davis's own children recycle many important names from the family's history, such is the case with the grandchildren, as well. On the half-hour boat ride to the compound, the first things we go over are the names of the next two generations of Davis clan members.

Besides Kathleen Davis, Jr., Neil and Ruth have another daughter, Christine, who at age 32 has just married Nariman Haghighi. Christine is the first Davis grandchild to marry. The wedding took place on the rocky shores of Georgian Bay.

After Neil is Nancy, 58, and she's married to Michael Bennett. They have twin 25-year-olds born six minutes apart: Meg and Michael. Catherine, 56, is the third Davis offspring and is married to Abraham Drassinower. They have two children: Noah, 20, and Emmett, 14. Ian, 53, is fourth in line, married to Rose Hewitt, and they have four children: Spencer, 25, William, 23 (that's right, Bill Davis isn't the only Bill Davis in the family), Robert, 22, and Kerr, 19.

The fifth of Bill Davis's kids and the only one he had with Kathleen Mackay is Meg, 51, whose real name is Sarah Margaret. She's married to Paul Giroux, and they also have twins: 17-year-olds Molly (who's 19 minutes older) and Jack. Because Meg is the youngest of the five, she is the only one of the Davis offspring never to have voted for her father. She was seven months shy of her 18th birthday when her father ran for the last time and successfully re-established the Tory majority in 1981.

The Davises are a "blended" family, but you'd never know it. No one ever makes the distinction between the four children from the first marriage and the one child from the second. Even beyond that, there are several pictures of Davis's first wife, Helen, scattered all over the cottage. This isn't a family that seems to have even an ounce of awkwardness dealing with potential issues of loyalty to either mother. Helen's place in the Davis family history is secure and there for all to see. And the love the children and grandchildren have for "Kai" is abundant and evident.

It would be wrong to come to grand conclusions on the basis of spending a single day with the family. But I've known this clan a little bit for more than three decades. Kathleen Davis seems to display a modest but powerful confidence in her role and position in this family. She is certainly the only grandmother the dozen Davis grandchildren have ever known. But for more than half a century now, she is also the only mother the five Davis children have ever known. She is so modest and unassuming and yet obviously has enough confidence about her place in this world not to be threatened by Helen's presence, which is very much here.

The Davises have now done what many families do as the years march on — they have switched cottages. The main cottage that Bill and Kathy Davis stayed in during his years in politics has now been taken over by Ian and Rose. Meanwhile, the Davis grandparents have moved to another nearby cottage, which was spectacularly redesigned by famed architect Eberhard Zeidler. That cottage retains a kind of Davis modesty, consistent with the look of other nearby places, but the glass addition gives it a unique beauty and consistency with the landscape, as well.

Our first stop of the day is Artist's Island, where we'll have lunch at Bill and Kathy Davis's new cottage. Over lunch with two Davis children and one grandchild, my plan is to toss some subjects out there, then shut up and listen to the stories that emerge. I mention that after the death of MPP Dalton McGuinty, Sr., in 1990, there was an expectation that one of the 10 McGuinty children would run in Ottawa South to continue the family's contribution to public service. But five years before that, when Bill Davis retired from politics, I ask Neil whether he felt, as Dalton, Jr., did, any desire to succeed his father as the MPP for Brampton.

"It was obvious to some that I should do it," he begins, "but not to me." Coincidentally at the time, Neil was 29 years old, the same age his father was when he first stood for the provincial legislature. But Neil felt he needed some more life experience and financial independence and so took a pass in that 1985 election. The local Tories instead nominated Jeff Rice, who lost by 4,000 votes to Bob Callahan, whom Bill Davis had twice defeated in 1977 and 1981.

In 2007 when John Tory led the Ontario PC Party, Neil seriously thought again about running but came to the same conclusion. "Neil does take after my dad in some ways," sister Nancy chimes in. "He needs time to make decisions."

In any event, it likely wouldn't have mattered what decision Neil made. The Liberals under McGuinty won their second consecutive majority government in 2007 and swept every seat in Brampton and neighbouring Mississauga and Oakville.

"Is that to say it's a done issue for you, that you'll never run?" I ask Neil.

"No!" Bill Davis interrupts, and everyone laughs. It's a joke, but one gets the sense that the former premier also sort of means it. He's shared so many of his political experiences over the years with Neil, and you know somewhere deep inside he wishes Neil had followed in his footsteps and taken the plunge into public life. None of the five Davis children has ever run for office and it seems increasingly unlikely that any of them ever will.

"I've never thought about doing it," says Nancy. "But I do have a hard time *not* voting Tory. Just in case he's looking over my shoulder," she adds, pointing to her father. "And I want to stay in the will."

"There's nothing there!" her father interjects. Already the pattern of the day is being established. The children and grandchildren will share their sincere thoughts about a variety of issues, and Dutch will play the role of comedian Henny Youngman. I do discover that Neil has only ever voted Tory. However, Nancy spoiled her ballot in 1999. Apparently, she couldn't bring herself to re-elect the Mike Harris government.

The Davises serve white wine with our lunch, which prompts a question about whether Bill Davis is really the teetotaller he'd have us all believe. "He likes a Bloody Mary," says Kathleen, his wife. "He will drink white wine, but he leaves the glass half full. Now he really doesn't drink very much at all."

But Nancy remembers a story from one of those election campaigns in the mid-1970s. It was at Oktoberfest and her dad found himself at the front of a beer hall with a stein full of suds. The cameras were rolling, so the premier drank the entire stein. "He was as green as I've ever seen him," Nancy recalls. "I couldn't believe he downed the whole thing."

"I pretended to drink it," Vera Davis's son insists, perhaps still in the habit of paying lip service to his mother's prohibitionist ways.

Neil and Ruth's daughter, Kathleen, Jr., is already showing signs of interest in politics. Currently teaching a course in international criminal law at Osgoode Hall Law School (her grandfather's alma mater) and a member of the advisory board at the Canadian Centre for the Responsibility to Protect, Kathleen clearly has a passion for justice. She provided research and legal assistance to the prosecution teams at the International Criminal Court, the International Criminal Tribunal for the Former Yugoslavia, and the Special Tribunal for Lebanon in The Hague. And she completed her LL.M. in international legal studies at New York University where she interned at the Center for Human Rights and Global

Justice and in the Peace and Security Division of U.N. Women. While politics interests her, a run isn't imminent. I also learn her choice of partisan label is less clear than her father's or grandfather's.

"What party would you run for?" I ask.

"Who knows?" she answers. "Time will tell."

Kathleen Davis, Jr., wasn't even born when her grandfather, Dutch, was premier of Ontario. As a result, the Conservative Parties she knows both provincially and federally have been far more right wing than she is.

After lunch we hop in the boat again and head for the main cottage where Bill Davis spent so much of his early life — the one that used to be where the family gathered when Davis was in politics. All five Davis children are now waiting to share their stories.

"This is the place where he had more time," Nancy says. "It was a respite, a getaway." It was here that Davis could play cribbage, gin rummy, or bridge with his kids. Other family friends such as the Dobbses and the Webbs had cottages nearby, as well. Davis and his best friend, Joe Dobbs, would chase each other around the cottage and end up on the ground wrestling. Dobbs was from Cooksville (now part of Mississauga) and helped Davis win his first campaign in 1959. They'd often go fishing at night with large smelting nets, then return at one o'clock in the morning to find Kathleen waiting with a frying pan and butter. "It was loud and it was fun," adds Nancy, who admits the alcohol did flow.

"Bill Davis drank?" I ask.

"He watched," his son, Ian, clarifies.

It was a common occurrence for Davis's political life to merge into his home life in Brampton. Federal and provincial politicians and advisers were a frequent sight on Main Street in the Flower City, but not at the cottage on Georgian Bay.

"He was fastidious about keeping this place separate," Neil says.

As we've already established, Davis loves the water but apparently was hardly ever seen swimming. "He loves to be on top of it," Nancy's husband, Michael Bennett, says. "Not in it."

Neil has fond memories of driving the boat by himself 50 years ago to pick up his father at the marina. He'd be up on his knees to see over the wheel and there were no laws against it back then. Ian recalls that for him best part of the cottage experience was getting there.

The Davis kids occasionally flew up in a de Havilland Canada DHC-2 Beaver, owned by the Ministry of Natural Resources, or even one of the Ontario Provincial Police's helicopters. When the approach was by car, it was the premier who would "bomb down Honey Harbour Road," Ian says. "There were no seat belts and the car would be bouncing so much we'd hit our heads on the ceiling."

The expression that frequently emerges as the stories continue to flow is "blessedly normal." Despite having a father who was the second-most powerful politician in the country, the Davis kids seem to have enjoyed as normal an upbringing as was possible, given the circumstances. They never expected their father to be at school concerts, recitals, or athletic events, but then again, 40 and 50 years ago, very few fathers would have attended these things, anyway. And you could be sure that Kathleen Davis, with her educational background, found the right blend of discipline and love as the parent who did most of the parenting.

Interestingly enough, Bill Davis was a very long-leash parent when his children were young, no doubt because Kathleen was ever-present in the children's lives. But now that he's an octogenarian he's much more hands-on with his adult children.

"He calls all the time worrying about whether I'm going to get to the cottage okay," says Catherine. "He doesn't have the same confidence in my boat driving that he does with the others. He is so much more a helicopter parent to me now than he was then." Back when they were kids, Catherine and Nancy shared a paper route, and they say their father never thought twice about their safety. "He used to let us go swimming at the cottage alone when we were 10 years old," Catherine says. "We used to hitchhike to town alone when we were 10 and 12 years old. Now he worries about 14-year-old grandchildren swimming alone."

As much as the Davis parents tried to shield their five children from the occasional brutal realities of being the offspring of the premier, they weren't always successful. Nancy recalls during her school days feeling judged before people ever met her. "People just assumed you were a snob," she says. Catherine, who would have been 12 years old during Davis's first election as leader, often had to fight against hurt feelings. "I was on the campaign trail and I heard things," she says. "I wanted to cry all the time. I remember thinking, *That's not my dad!*"

All of the Davis children went to public school in Brampton, but there was one temporary exception. On May 28, 1975, a 16-year-old student named Michael Peter Slobodian walked into Brampton Centennial Secondary School with two rifles in a black guitar case and started shooting. Slobodian killed two people and wounded 13 more before turning the gun on himself. There was no explanation for the shooting. In Slobodian's suicide note, he revealed he was "fed up with life." But he also pointed out he loved his parents and family and knew they loved him. Scott Thompson from *Kids in the Hall* fame was one of the students there on that day.

Another was Catherine Davis, who saw it all.

There was no such thing as grief counselling in those days. Many students no doubt suffered from post-traumatic stress disorder. This was still nearly a quarter of a century before the Columbine Massacre near Littleton, Colorado, and no one knew how to handle these kinds of tragedies. It was just utterly unprecedented. Catherine acknowledges, "I started to struggle after that."

The Davises took Catherine out of Brampton Centennial and sent her to an independent school. When someone in the media found that out, it made the newspapers. Bill Davis's children have rarely seen him white-hot with anger, but he was then. He was simply outraged that a newspaper would invade the family's privacy by printing a story about the premier taking one of his children out of the public education system.

"He was fiercely protective of us," Meg says.

Like all parents, there was nothing Bill Davis could do on that day to protect his child from tragedy. But unlike all other parents, he could change public policy in the hope of reducing the odds of having similar incidents occur. And that's what he did. With George Kerr, his solicitor general, Davis immediately got Queen's Park to pass tougher, more restrictive gun possession laws. "That was the first step that was taken anywhere in Canada vis-à-vis handguns," Davis says.

Interestingly enough, for Catherine, horses became a deeply important part of her healing. After her mother died, Helen's father used to take her to see horses during the kids' visits to Windsor. It had a calming and curative effect on Catherine. Eventually, she got her own horse named Cornflakes. After the Brampton school shooting, Catherine spent hours at the barn with her horse and experienced the healing powers of connecting to that gentle, yet powerful animal. Catherine stopped riding in her late twenties and returned to school to earn her master's in social work at the University of Toronto. She worked with street people with mental illnesses but always remembered the positive feelings that came from being with her horse. As a result, Catherine has set up a fund at Tides Canada called the Animal Spirit Fund, which will assist children who have been traumatized by life's events just as Catherine herself was by her mother's death and that inexplicable school shooting.

If Bill Davis didn't want the papers writing about his kids, his children also got the message that they ought not to do things that might get them the kind of attention that could embarrass their father, either personally or politically. "We didn't push the limits too much because we were afraid of getting something in the paper," Meg says. Neil insists when other underage kids might have tried to sneak into bars at the time, the Davis kids didn't. Lest you get the impression that the kids were all a bunch of goody two-shoes, Neil adds it's not quite the case. "We had some parties in the house when they were away," he admits. "But we didn't break anything."

Clearly, the most traumatic event in the life of Davis's oldest four children was the death of their mother, Helen, in 1962 at the age of 31. In terms of what to do with the children, how the Davises handled matters back then is probably not how things would be handled today. Neil went to live with his paternal grandparents. Nancy and Catherine stayed with their Aunt Peggy in New Jersey for several months. Ian, the baby, lived with Helen's parents in Windsor for nearly a year. But then Kathleen Mackay came into their lives in a major way.

"We were very, very lucky when Dad married Mom," says Nancy, who was only four and a half years old when Helen died. "When Mom came, there was order." It's also interesting to note that none of the four older Davis children ever refers to their stepmother in that way. I have only ever heard Kathleen Davis referred to as "Mom," although it didn't start that way.

"She was actually *Aunt* Kathy for a while, even after she and Dad married," recalls Neil, "until one day she took me aside and said, 'Call me Mom.' We've never used the word *step* to describe her."

Kathy had the fifth Davis child in relatively short order after her marriage, thus there are only two years' difference between Ian and Meg, the fourth and fifth Davis children. Perhaps because the four original children were so young and the age gap among them is so small, the kids seem to have embraced the fifth child without much drama. However, Meg, being the youngest, occasionally had to suffer the slings and arrows of outrageous fortune common to many who are the baby of the family. One day Ian and Catherine played tug-of-war with Meg's arms and dislocated her shoulder. Ian remembers it this way: "She was being a suck and Dad ended up spanking me." Meg got her revenge, at one point accidentally breaking Ian's toe.

Regarding the four kids with Helen and the one with Kathleen, Meg says, "Dad never allowed a difference. He didn't like discord." And so the children responded accordingly.

Bill Davis has never been an outwardly emotional person. He was raised in an era when fathers shook their sons' hands and everyone kept a pretty stiff upper lip about things. So he is who he is. For example, in 2013, the Davises invited several dozen close friends to the Brampton Golf Club for a joint celebration: Kathleen's 80th birthday and the couple's 50th wedding anniversary. When it came time for Davis to take the microphone, he offered a wide smile followed by "Happy birthday, and you've been a pretty good wife, too."

"He's a terrible tease," Kathleen Davis says, recalling the event.

"Did you hope he'd say something like 'Darling, happy birthday, I love you.'?" I ask.

"No," Kathy says, "that's not the way he is. We all like dreaming of things being different than they are and I do, too, but they're dreams." However, Mrs. Davis adds: "He's thoughtful and kind and all that stuff."

If there was friction in the house, Catherine says, "he got over things easily. But when his kids walked into a room, his eyes really lit up." Kathleen Davis confirms her husband wasn't a touchy-feely-kissy kind of father, "but if one of the kids jumped into his arms, he'd be delighted."

Despite his public responsibilities, Bill Davis made it a point to get to all of his kids' university convocations. Even more remarkable, he's managed to get to all of the grandkids' convocations, as well.

Because Bill Davis was in public life for so long, it was perhaps inevitable that his children would both take an interest in politics and be adversely affected by it. When Davis forced Pierre Trudeau to accept the notwithstanding clause as the compromise to get a constitutional agreement, he not only took flak from the prime minister about it but then he came home and got another earful from his oldest son. "I gave him a hard time on the notwithstanding clause," Neil remembers.

When Davis became premier, his oldest daughter, Nancy, was just starting high school. She recalls questioning her father on the logic of Catholics having a fully funded school system to the end of Grade 10, but then forcing Catholic families to pay tuition for Grades 11, 12, and 13. Meg Davis's husband, Paul Giroux, was one of those Catholics who had to pay to stay in the separate system through high school. Ian Davis's wife, Rose Hewitt, switched from the Catholic to the public system for high school because of the tuition fees.

Bill Davis was nothing if not a loyalist to his party and his riding. So in 1989 when Meg bought a Honda Civic, her father wasn't amused. "He was disappointed I didn't buy a Chrysler," which, of course, is made in Brampton.

In spite of these occasional political disagreements, Meg says the children were raised "to be like him. We're all Progressive Conservatives." When the Ontario PC Party took a harder turn to the right under Mike Harris and Tim Hudak, Meg says the Davis children all heard at various times, "God, can't your dad come back?"

Having said that, there were numerous occasions when being Bill Davis's offspring was a concern, particularly at school. Neil recalls a time when one of his teachers returned to the classroom from a "Save Us from Davis" protest rally, "which is kind of uncomfortable when you're waiting for your marks from that teacher." Nancy remembers one teacher at Brampton Centennial showing her a picture of Bill Davis in the latest edition of the Ontario Teachers' Federation magazine, followed by a sneering question: "Is this a relative of yours?"

There were moments, of course, when having the premier as your dad could be a bit of an advantage. Neil wasn't a particularly proficient typist. Sometimes, when he was in university, he'd have Nancy type his essays. Other times the premier's personal secretary, Miss Anderson, was drafted to the cause. Neil would accompany his dad to the office, and while Bill Davis was running the province, Neil would be in his father's boardroom writing his essays. Every time he finished a page, off to Miss Anderson it would go. "I'd write, she'd type," Neil says, laughing. Fortunately for father and son, no one was the wiser about the scheme because if word had leaked out no doubt the Davis government would have been shaken to its very foundations. Once, while he wrote, Neil accidentally pressed a button on the floor with his foot, triggering the security alarm. The OPP detail dashed in, expecting to have to save the premier's life, only to find the premier's embarrassed-looking oldest son wondering whether the police were going to bust him for using his father's secretary as his typist.

Neil also remembers when he was a student at the University of Western Ontario he once stopped for gas on Highway 401. Unbeknownst to him, the gas station attendant called the police to inform them that a certain car was driving with an expired licence plate. Sure enough, the OPP soon pulled Neil over and asked him why he didn't have his licence renewal sticker. As one officer read Neil's driver's licence, he saw the last name "Davis" and the home address in "Brampton," put two and two together, then said to his partner, "I don't want to end up in Moosonee. You write this one up."

The former premier himself has caught a few breaks from the police over the years. After retiring from politics in 1985, the province's police force gave him a special identification badge saying "Ontario Provincial Police Commissioner" on one side, and "Honorary" on the other. Once, Davis was pulled over for speeding by a younger cop who had no idea who he was. But apparently the badge scored Davis some sympathy as the cop let him go without ticketing him. Another time Davis was wearing his OPP baseball cap, again while speeding. This time the officer did know him and said, "If I'd known it was you, I wouldn't have pulled you over." The former premier got a lecture but no speeding ticket.

When you ask Bill Davis how many children he has, he'll sometimes say 10 — the five originals and the "add-ons," as the spouses are occasionally called. Ian's wife, Rose, acknowledges she was "intimidated at first" to have Bill Davis as her father-in-law. "But he's become softer over the years." Nancy's husband, Michael Bennett, still calls his father-in-law "Mr. Davis" or "Dutch" — never "Dad." When Catherine's common-law husband, Abraham Drassinower, first met his future father-in-law, he confessed he was a supporter of the New Democratic Party. "He asked me if I liked the landscape here on Georgian Bay," Drassinower recalls. When Drassinower acknowledged that he did, Davis referred to the federal NDP leader of the day and retorted, "Are you aware that Ed Broadbent would nationalize this island?" The premier was joking. Probably.

The evolution of the Davis family is very much like the evolution of Ontario itself. Whereas Davis himself grew up in a Brampton that was almost entirely white, Anglo-Saxon, and Protestant, both his family and his province are now more multicultural. Abraham Drassinower is a Hispanic Jew from Peru who technically has never married Catherine. (Catherine did have an earlier brief marriage that ended in divorce.) Meg's husband, Paul Giroux, is Catholic. Neil and Ruth's older daughter, Christine, just married a young man from an Iranian family. Through the Drassinowers and Girouxs, Bill Davis has Jewish and Catholic grandchildren and clearly loves embracing both the province's and his own multiculturalism. Apparently, the only prerequisite to being accepted by the dean of this family is the obligation to love coming to the cottage on Georgian Bay.

"Our ethnicity has never been a problem," Drassinower says. "The only requirement with him is to like the cottage. When he was 72 years old, he went in for a heart bypass operation. On the way in he turns to Catherine and says, 'If he doesn't like the cottage, divorce him, take the kids, and I'll pay for it.'"

After the operation, when Davis came out of the anesthetic, he said to Catherine, "He's a nice man. You should marry him."

Has the absence of a marriage certificate ever bothered Davis? "He is a tolerant, wise man," says Drassinower. "He's a *Progressive* Conservative. He's not going to go at that."

Having spent a good chunk of time with the 10 Davis children, it was now time to get the rest of the story. So the parents left the family room at the Davis cottage and in came 11 of the 12 grandchildren to share their stories of Dutch. The first thing one learns about the next generation is that they know precious little about their grandfather's premiership. Only the oldest, Christine, was even born while Davis was still premier, and she was only a year and a half old when he retired. As far as this group is concerned, their grandfather is far more interested in their exploits than they are in his. For them he's just Dutch.

One also learns that Davis's second-born grandchild, Kathleen, Jr., born a year after Davis retired from politics, has her grandfather's sense of humour. Like her grandfather, she won a public-speaking competition while in elementary school. When she was victorious in the Grade 5 contest at McHugh Public School in Brampton, Kathleen was asked whether any-one else in her family had had this kind of talent for public speaking.

"No" was her answer.

A couple of years ago when Bill Davis, a former Sunday schoolteacher, made one of his now increasingly rare appearances in church, he told one of the grandkids he was "cramming for the finals."

Kerr, the youngest offspring of Ian and Rose, first learned about Bill Davis's contribution to patriating the Constitution and the Charter of Rights and Freedoms not through discussion at the family dinner table but rather from doing a school project. When the younger of Nancy and Michael Bennett's twins had a Grade 5 project on Canadian politics to do at King City Public School, he pulled an ace out of his deck. "I brought him to our school to speak," says the younger Michael Bennett. "He's spoken to all of our schools." Given Michael's last name, there's nothing that indi-cates he's the grandchild of a political legend. So at King City Secondary School, Michael asked his teacher if he could bring a guest to speak at the introductory law class. "My grandpa used to work in politics" was all he said. It was therefore quite the shock when Ontario's 18th premier showed up to give the guest lecture.

When Kathleen, Jr., was an undergraduate at UWO in London, Ontario, she had to do a project on political leadership. Her assignment was Pierre Elliott Trudeau. Another student was assigned William Grenville Davis. Kathleen wasn't amused when the other student incorrectly introduced his presentation on "William Lyon Davis," plucked a bunch of factoids off a Wikipedia page, and portrayed her grandfather as a fat-cat politician.

This next generation of Davis grandchildren appears to have caught their grandfather's well-known modesty, as well. When Kathleen was at graduate school at Queen's University in Kingston, she invited her grandfather to the convocation. Hardly anyone knew that Bill Davis was Kathleen Davis, Jr.'s grandfather, and she overheard a close friend ask: "Why is Bill Davis here?" This is apparently something the grandchildren have learned not to boast about.

As the grandchildren introduce themselves to me, I inevitably stop the introductions after hearing Ian and Rose's 23-year-old say his name: William Gordon Davis. As mentioned earlier, yes, there is a second William G. Davis in the family. When I ask whether having that name isn't a bit of a burden to live up to, the younger William acknowledges, yes, it is a bit daunting, but mostly it means getting mail intended for his grandfather. Then I realize that Bill Davis has been out of public life for more than three decades and probably few people in the younger William's generation have ever heard of him.

It's perhaps not at all surprising, given their grandfather's lifelong commitment to education, that the Davis grandchildren are all making their way through the secondary and post-secondary school systems quite nicely. Neil and Ruth's older daughter, Christine, is a naturopathic doctor. Their younger daughter, Kathleen, Jr., is working toward her Ph.D. in law from the University of Toronto, teaches law at Osgoode Hall Law School, and is now ensconced at Massey College at the University of Toronto. Nancy and Michael Bennett's Meg did her undergraduate work at Western University and has now finished her first year at the University of Ottawa's law school. Her twin brother, Michael, graduated from McMaster University in Hamilton and is a financial adviser in Toronto, working at Freedom 55. Catherine and Abraham's older son, Noah, is in his second year at McGill University doing general arts. And their younger son, Emmett, is in his first year of high school at Oakwood Collegiate Institute in Toronto. Ian and Rose's oldest of four, Spencer, has his undergraduate degree and master's degree in journalism from Western. He's now pursuing his teacher's degree and a master's in education at OISE. The younger William G. Davis got a bachelor's degree at Wilfrid Laurier University in environmental studies. As many students across Ontario now do, he's following that up in the college system his grandfather created with a two-year stint at Humber College in nutrition and healthy lifestyle promotion. Robert is in his fourth year at Wilfrid Laurier University doing a bachelor's degree in geography. The youngest, Kerr, is in second year at Western University doing general arts. And as for Meg and Paul's twins, Molly is a Grade 12 student at Lawrence Park Collegiate Institute in Toronto and Jack is a Grade 12 student at Northern Secondary School in Toronto. And five days before Bill Davis celebrated his 87th birthday, in late July, he and Kathy became great-grandparents for the first time, courtesy of their oldest grandchild, Christine. The baby's name is Soraya, a traditional Iranian name.

Another indication of how this family respects its history — both happy and tragic — is with a closer look at the grandchildren's names. Kathleen, now 30, and Meg, now 25, more commonly use their middle names which, of course, come from Bill Davis's second wife and fifth child. But on their birth certificates they both share a different first name, Helen, after Neil and Nancy's birth mother. Christine is actually Alma Christine, named after her maternal grandmother and continuing a tradition started by Bill Davis's father, A. Grenville Davis, to be called by their middle name. Meg's twin daughter, Molly, now 18, takes that nickname from Bill Davis's baby sister of the same name. But one of Molly's names also comes from Peggy, Davis's older sister. Molly's full name is actually Mary Margaret Kathleen Davis. The other twin's full name is John Robert William Davis, though he's referred to as Jack. Robert Ian Davis has his father's first name as his middle name. And Spencer has his grandfather's and great-grandfather's middle name, Grenville, as his own. Nancy's male twin son is named after both his father and his uncle: George Michael Neil Davis. Yes, this is all very confusing, but lovely, too.

At the end of the day, and just before taking the boat back to the marina in Honey Harbour, I manage to find myself in a room full of nearly 25 talking, laughing, and shouting Davis family members. Somehow in the midst of this delightful chaos I manage a quiet moment with the oldest man in the room. He is seated in his comfy chair, surveying his family, and smiling.

"I really thought it was important to get you up here to see why this place is so important to me," Bill Davis says.

As we both look out at three generations of Davises, the picture really crystallizes. This has always been the one place where Bill Davis could really connect with his family. Politics never really takes a break when you're the premier, but this was the single place on earth where it came close. In Brampton, Bill Davis just wasn't around much — the obligations of the job were simply too great. But if Georgian Bay was two and a half hours away from the Ontario legislature, it might as well have been two and a half light years away. It was a different universe. And for decade after decade it's been the one spot where the entire Davis clan can get away from it all and just be themselves. The physical beauty of the landscape contributes to that. The fact that they all appear to enjoy one another's company so much is clearly an added bonus. The importance of this place seems to take on even more meaning as the two Davis grandparents try to deal with the health challenges that are inevitable for two people now in their eighties.

On this August day in 2015, Bill Davis is a frail-looking 86 years old but is still sharp as a tack upstairs. He continues to drive his boat and is actually physically quite a bit better off than he has been. Neil has apparently successfully pestered him to get on his treadmill to do his exercises, and that's having a positive impact. Kathleen is in reasonably good shape these days; however, more than a decade ago, she had a mastectomy, which she openly and courageously discusses. "It was scary," she admits. "I can remember the kids coming to the hospital and were very reassuring because I was scared. They were very loving and sweet to me so I could go get operated on and not be panic-stricken." Thankfully, the operation was a success.

As I come to the end of my visit and prepare to leave, I thank and shake hands with my host and leave three words with him. "You are blessed."

Bill Davis smiles. He knows it, as well.

24

LEGACY

It is a testament to her talent, drive, and wisdom that a woman who was born to survivors of the Holocaust in a displaced persons camp in Germany less than a year after the end of the Second World War could grow up to become a judge on the Supreme Court of Canada. That says a lot about Rosalie Silberman Abella, the first Jewish woman ever appointed to the high court. It also says something about life's possibilities if you're lucky enough to grow up in Ontario, which Madame Justice Abella was able to do once her family moved here in 1950. So it is no small praise when someone, who always says "call me Rosie," offers the following observation: "Bill Davis and John Robarts defined the Ontario I became an adult in." That's a pretty good testimonial.

Davis was premier in 1976 when Abella at the tender age of 29 was appointed a family court judge. She was the youngest and the first pregnant judge appointed in Ontario history. Abella met Davis a few times when she was on the Premier's Advisory Committee on Confederation from 1976 to 1981. "He was dazzling," Abella recalls. "Always the smartest, savviest, and most charming person in the room."

Former Governor General Adrienne Clarkson was hired by Bill Davis during the early 1980s to serve as Ontario's agent general in France. At the time Clarkson was a high-profile journalist with the CBC current affairs program *The Fifth Estate*. In her book *Heart Matters*, she describes Davis as "the best boss I ever had."

Unlike so many first ministers whose tempers are legendary, I have yet to find anyone who could tell me a story of when Bill Davis lost his temper, even when his staff, MPPs, civil service, or corporate management let him down. "His demeanour and disposition," marvels John Rae, CEO of Power Corporation, "I just don't ever recall him being intemperate at any time."

Ontario's first-ever female cabinet minister, Margaret Birch, describes her former boss as "always willing to listen. He never shot down an idea. If he disagreed with you, he'd tell you without shooting you down. He never left you feeling put down." Davis has sent Birch a Christmas card ever year and she's kept them all. There is a roomful of pictures of Birch and Davis in her home in Pickering. Davis was a guest at her 90th birthday party five years ago. "We haven't had anyone in the premier's office since then who was better than Bill Davis," she says. "He's a shining example of what politicians should be like."

"He just never barked back," says John Tory, who worked with Davis almost every day for 13 straight years at Queen's Park, on the Acid Rain Commission, and at the law firm. "He was the best boss I ever worked for. He was so even and balanced."

In the seven years Sally Barnes was Davis's press secretary, much of it through the tense times of a minority legislature, "he never raised his voice," she says. "Now there were times when he wouldn't speak to me! He freezes you out. You knew by isolation that he was upset."

Of the hundreds of people I've spoken to over the years about Bill Davis, only one has ever claimed to have heard him swear. In 1984, when Paul Godfrey called the premier to inform him that he was stepping down as Metro Toronto chairman after more than a decade to take over as publisher and CEO of the *Toronto Sun*, Godfrey says there was a momentary astonished silence on the other end of the phone followed by Davis saying, "No shit." I challenged Godfrey three times on his story, insisting it can't be true, that *no one* has ever heard Bill Davis swear. Godfrey swears the swearing story is true. Davis, of course, denies it, but not too strenuously.

When John Tory ran for mayor of Toronto in 2014, entering the race 25 points behind former NDP MP Olivia Chow and having lost the last several elections he'd contested, Davis was worried. He has become fiercely protective of Tory because of all those losses. While he didn't necessarily share those feelings with Tory himself, the former premier did call Tory's wife, Barbara Hackett, urging caution before Tory threw his hat in the ring. "I just don't want to see him get hurt," Davis told Hackett, although he never explicitly opined that Tory shouldn't enter the race. Davis and Hackett had a great relationship, no doubt contributed to the first time he called his principal secretary at home.

"Is the lord of the manor there?" the premier asked Hackett.

"You're speaking to her," Hackett answered without missing a beat.

During the mayoralty campaign, Tory often sought Davis's advice on how to handle the Ford brothers — first Rob, then Doug, after the mayor's ill health forced his exit from the race. "No one is perfect, but his advice was always wise," Tory recalls. When the Fords attacked, Tory would try to lower the temperature, expressing his "disappointment" in the Fords' tactics, rather than rising to take the bait. "Used to drive Doug crazy!" Tory now says.

Davis's sense of where the broadest swath of the Ontario public was on any issue has been widely regarded as one of his greatest strengths. "He had an instinctive understanding of Ontario" is how Kathy L. Brock, professor in the School of Policy Studies and Department of Political Studies at Queen's University, describes Davis's talent. "He could bring together people from every background, he could speak to them in a very real way. Ontario has not lived up to that standard since." Brock says Ontario might have been a less polarized place back in Davis's time because he purposefully set that tone. "I think a political leader can really do that," she says. "He's part of the reason why Ontario is a tolerant society, the good society that it is today. His legacy carries on. I honestly believe that."

Hugh Segal saw and continues to see Davis in so many different ways. "I saw him confront bigotry, small-mindedness, and stupidity in society, government, and party, and build understanding, generosity, and decency in the most remarkable of ways."

Eddie Goodman, who died 10 years ago, actively participated in 25 federal and provincial election campaigns during his years in politics. "I have never seen greater camaraderie than existed in the 'Big Blue Machine,'" he wrote in *Life of the Party*. And we know who deserves the lion's share of the credit for that.

"There is no more decent man I've ever encountered in politics," Brian Mulroney told me in 2015. "He's an Ontario gentleman with a wonderful, old Protestant work ethic. That's why he was so effective." In 1988, three years after Davis left politics, Mulroney's re-election campaign bus stopped outside the Davis residence on Main Street in Brampton en route to an event. There was Davis out mowing his lawn — just another example of how the former premier never lost touch with who he was and where he came from.

Bob Nixon clashed with Davis perhaps more personally and with more vitriol than any other politician, yet still acknowledges that "people liked him. He was intelligent, took good advice. He was unthreatening, not self-centred in any way." But what about the Ontario Hydro building scandal that Nixon's party made such hay about back in the 1970s? "Turned out it's quite a good building," says Nixon, the former chairman of Atomic Energy of Canada Ltd. "Still is."

Frank Miller's brand of conservatism was rarely the same as Bill Davis's, and yet the man who succeeded Davis as Ontario premier always said he had an excellent personal relationship with Davis. However, Miller added: "He was a very private man. Anyone who said they were his confidant was fooling themselves. He was detached from all of us and didn't let his personal side show at all."

One of the difficulties of celebrating his 87th birthday, as Davis did in July 2016, is that he continues to outlive so many of his friends and colleagues. Fourteen years ago, in the summer of 2002, Davis himself had heart bypass surgery but did recover. He is still intellectually very sharp, physically quite frail, although he has actually seen an improvement in his health over the past year. Nevertheless, he's had the misfortune of burying too many of his former ministers. Just from the Class of 1981 alone, the premier's last in the legislature, the following ministers have died: Reuben Baetz (1996, age 73), Larry Grossman (1997, age 53), Frank Miller (2000, age 73), Robert Welch (2000, age 72), Thomas Wells (2000, age 70), Lorne Henderson (2002, age 81), Bruce McCaffery (2002, age 63), Frank Drea (2003, age 69), George Kerr (2007, age 83), James Snow (2008, age 79), Robert G. Eaton (2009, age 71), Leo Bernier (2010, age 81), Keith Norton (2010, age 69), René Piché (2011, age 79), Robert Elgie (2013, age 84), George McCague (2014, age 84), George Ashe (2014, age 81), and Milton "Bud" Gregory (2016, age 90). And these are just the cabinet ministers, not the backbenchers or opposition members.

But by far the loss that hurt Davis the most came on September 25, 2004, when the man who was his closest adviser and colleague, Ed Stewart, succumbed to a stroke at age 74. The obituary in Stewart's hometown *Windsor Star* said in accordance with his wishes there would be "no list of academic achievements, no record of career positions held, no honours given him. An unusual notice to many, perhaps. But to those who truly know the measure of the man, not at all. He was a man of stature and of true humility." Stewart was cremated in a private ceremony. The obituary went on to quote Eddie Goodman, who said: "If he thought that something was wrong, either because it was improper or because it was not in the best interests of the government or the people of Ontario, you could stand on your head and do cartwheels and he would not budge an inch. This is not to suggest that he wasn't open to persuasion, he just was not open to the slightest impropriety. During the almost eleven years that I viewed his service to Davis from a close vantage point, he never once forgot who was the premier and who was the deputy, nor did he hesitate to speak his mind even when he knew the advice was not going to be welcomed by the premier."

Claire Hoy described Stewart as the "king of all Davis doesn't survey (and much of what he does)."

Davis's former press secretary, Sally Barnes, who spoke at a later memorial service for Stewart, says the Windsorite engendered such loyalty among those who knew him that Hugh Segal said at the same memorial service he'd take a bullet for Stewart. "And I believed him!" Barnes says. "Any enemies Ed may have had along the way resulted from his personal and professional frugality. He was a Scot, after all. He ate regularly at McDonald's and lived in a small bungalow in Etobicoke."

During their years running Ontario Inc., Davis loved the fact that Stewart shared his sense of modesty. "His interests were more for me than him," Davis told me in 2015. "His interests were more for the government than him. He was not the kind of person who was looking to do something to enhance his reputation. He was there to do what was right."

Davis and Stewart had a final get-together at the Trillium Health Centre where Stewart eventually passed away. It was incredibly difficult for Davis to see his old friend looking so sick.

As we've seen numerous times over the years in his relationship with successive premiers, cabinet ministers, or mayors, Bill Davis still wants to be a player. Why?

"Because he can," says one of his former ministers, Dennis Timbrell, who will turn 70 in November 2016. "He knows people will take his calls and he knows people will listen to him. He's respected by people in all parties."

Other politicians have been described as "Tim Hortons Conservatives," most particularly Stephen Harper and Mike Harris. But Davis was, too, a quarter century before either of them was. Part of Davis's talent, however, was that he felt just as at home in the Toronto Club as he did at the Kiwanis Club. Hugh Segal says Davis mentioned his hometown at least three times in every speech partly because it was good shtick and partly because it was important to remind Ontarians he wasn't a city slicker, even though he felt comfortable among the elite. His values were "synonymous with the values of parsimony, generosity among people, community life that meant something, volunteerism, and a family structure that was the centre of life," Hugh Segal says.

Eddie Goodman concurred with the view of Davis as "a simple Christian with all the small-town virtues, yet who possesses more sophistication, intellect, and political acumen than he has ever revealed."

Canada's former ambassador to the United States, Allan Gotlieb, and his wife, Sondra, threw some of the best dinner parties Washington, D.C., has ever seen. In his memoir *The Washington Diaries*, Gotlieb confessed: "Of all the big shots in attendance, I enjoy Davis' company the most and he's the least pretentious person in the room."

Every Wednesday morning Hugh Segal and Ed Stewart would travel to the premier's home in Brampton to pick him up. The scene was always so unusual. Davis had a little office in his home with everyday people from Brampton visiting in the hope of getting their everyday problems solved. Kathy would be getting the kids' breakfast and out the door for school. No paid staff attended to these matters. "Bill Davis slept in fewer hotel rooms than any first minister in any jurisdiction," Segal concluded.

One time in the riding of Quinte during his premiership Davis attended the opening of a new provincially funded facility, perhaps a hospital or a school. The premier cut the ribbon, then began to give a speech: "This is such a great event that even the local Liberal MPP Hugh O'Neil is here," he joked.

The next day at Queen's Park O'Neil received a note from Davis. "Hughie," it began, "I hope you weren't offended by my remarks yesterday.

But my handlers don't like me talking about the opposition and that was the only way I could acknowledge your presence."

On another occasion, during Question Period, the proceedings were interrupted by a woman in the front row of the public gallery, facing the government benches, who was clearly in distress. She started yelling, "Billy, Billy, help me out! Please, Billy, you have to help me!"

"Davis looked absolutely stricken," recalls Graham White, the long-time political science professor at the University of Toronto who was in the legislature to witness the moment. It became apparent that Davis wasn't embarrassed by the outburst, but rather he wanted to do something to help the woman in distress. He turned around to cabinet minister Margaret Birch, who immediately left the chamber and went up to attend to the woman in question. "It was obvious to me that Davis said to her, 'Go up there. See what you can do,'" White says. "She did and that solved it." White adds he's under no illusions about how tough a politician Davis could be when he had to be. "But I just think he was a wonderful human being as premier."

Despite Davis's well-known introversion and extreme discomfort at sharing intimacy, he did on occasion, as Sean Conway said, let the mask slip. When *Globe and Mail* reporter Jonathan Manthorpe was going through a divorce, Davis took him aside, consoled him, and said how bad he felt about the development. "It was a truly poignant moment," recalls Sally Barnes. "He found it so hard to be emotional and talk about personal things. But on occasion he just did."

Barnes also recalls Davis's generosity to another reporter who used to give him fits — Claire Hoy. "He called me in one day because he wanted to visit Hoy's wife who was very ill with cancer," Barnes says. "He wanted me to go to Princess Margaret Hospital with him and visit her."

Davis was also kind to one of his cabinet ministers who also caused him no end of headaches. Frank Drea, the MPP for Scarborough Centre, loved to shoot from the lip. He also had a problem with the bottle. One time, at a PC convention, Drea was supposed to introduce a woman running for president of the party, but probably somewhat hung over, simply forgot her name. As he stumbled his way through the embarrassing moment at the podium, someone shouted the name from the wings and saved the moment from being even worse. "He [Drea] was much loved and the media and opposition cut him a lot of slack," recalls Sally Barnes. "Those were kinder, gentler days."

After the convention, Drea hauled Barnes into his office, whereupon she asked him how things were going.

"Not well at all," Drea answered.

"Why not?" asked Barnes, who had been on vacation at the time and missed the convention.

"I think I made a speech to little old ladies and it didn't go over too well," Drea confessed. "I'm in shit up to my ears with the guy upstairs."

But the guy upstairs had a big heart when it came to Frank Drea, who served from 1971 to 1985 — all of Davis's years as premier. Drea made cabinet in 1978, and despite his occasional lapses, remained on the executive council until Davis's departure in 1985. An indication of how much people liked Drea despite his problems: two other premiers gave him government appointments after his political career ended. Frank Miller put him on the Ontario Municipal Board in May 1985, but even when the Miller government fell the following month, the new premier, David Peterson, appointed Drea to the Ontario Racing Commission where he served almost a decade. Frank Drea died of pneumonia in 2003 at age 69.

One thing you never doubted when Bill Davis was premier: his love for his job. He is perhaps best known for one of the pithiest and shortest quotes in Canadian political history: "Bland works." But I always preferred another quote of his, which came quite accidentally to me after one of our many interviews.

The year was 1986, and I was a general assignment reporter at CBLT, the CBC Television local affiliate in Toronto. I successfully managed to pitch our executive producer, Howard Bernstein, on sending me to Bill Davis's law office to do an interview with the former premier on what life was like for him a year after retiring from politics. Davis agreed to the interview and off we went. Frankly, the interview was rather forgettable. Davis gave some of his standard long, rambling answers to what were probably not terribly original questions. I thought I had "okay stuff" but nothing that was going to lead the evening newscast. After about half an hour, we ended the formal on-camera part of the interview and began to pack up our equipment.

As we were doing so, I mentioned to Davis that it sure seemed to me as if he had life by the tail. I pointed out he worked in a beautiful skyscraper with a superb view of the city; he was undoubtedly making at least five times more money as a corporate lawyer than he did as premier; he was seeing more of his two grandchildren than he saw of his own kids when he was premier; there was a sanity about his current job — no gaggle of reporters sticking microphones in his face every day, pestering him with obnoxious questions, no opposition MPPs trying to cut him down to size; and the hours were surely easier on him. I concluded by saying, "This must be the best job you've ever had."

Davis demonstrated that sphinx-like smile for which he's become so famous and uttered an answer that has stayed with me for 30 years: "Steven, this job on its most fascinating day can't touch being premier of Ontario on its dullest." More than anything else I've ever heard from any other politician that quote forced me to re-evaluate what I had previously thought about the lure of public life and why Ontario's 18th premier enjoyed it so much. That one quote, so unexpected and yet so profound, prompted me to write *The Life: The Seductive Call of Politics*, which begat four more books on politics (this is my fifth on politics and seventh altogether).

It's difficult to compare different eras, but it seems irrefutably true that politics was a lot more fun in Davis's time. The people on the other side of the floor weren't your enemies; they were your opponents. The viciousness often on display by the Liberal Party's "Rat Pack" in Ottawa in the mid-1980s, or the politics of personal destruction often practised by Stephen Harper's Conservative Party in the 2000s, just didn't manifest itself in the same way in the 1970s and early 1980s. The cliché was true: you could beat each other up during Question Period, then go have a beer after it was all over. And there was never an orgy of bilious hatred on social media or 24/7 cable news pontification waiting for you at every turn.

The people around Davis also did politics differently. Admittedly, some of their practices might not have stood up to the hyper-scrutiny of today's uber-watchdogs. But I wonder whether we're any better off for all the added scrutiny. For example, back in the day, Clare Westcott would think nothing of calling up a company executive who did business with the Ontario government and suggest there was a group of kids at an orphanage or church school in Northern Ontario who'd never been to a Maple Leafs hockey game before. Without even talking to Davis, Westcott would say: "The premier thinks it would be really nice if these kids could get to a game." Next thing you knew, the executive would be on the phone to a bus company, tickets would be found, and a bunch of kids from the wrong side of the tracks would get the thrill of a lifetime. That practice would probably violate several sections of the Integrity Act or some other statute today. Are we better off with today's added vigilance? I'm not sure we are.

Davis showed over and over how much he loved being premier, particularly during Question Period, or when sparring with opponents on the other side of the legislature. Once, he was going mano-a-mano with NDP leader Stephen Lewis, who referred to "the premier and his sycophants."

"I had to go to the dictionary on that one," Davis joked years later. "Apparently, I wasn't the only one who didn't quite get it because when I checked Hansard the next day, it said: 'The Premier and his psychopaths.'"

In 1978, to commemorate Canada's 111th birthday, Davis rose in the Ontario legislature to speak. Hansard recorded the exchanges and heckles with a future opposition leader for us to enjoy nearly four decades later:

> **Honourable Mr. Davis:** I'd like to share with members of the House the plans for the Ontario government's participation in helping to celebrate our 111th birthday.
>
> **Mr. David Peterson:** Are you that old?
>
> **Honourable Mr. Davis:** Canada's 111th birthday.
>
> **Mr. Peterson:** I thought it was the number of years you had been in office.

On another occasion, Davis answered a question from one of his own backbenchers, Paul Yakabuski (whose son, John, is currently a PC MPP), about why the government didn't bulk-purchase more often, thereby getting a better discount:

> **Honourable Mr. Davis:** I have to confess to the honourable member that when it comes to purchasing services or goods from the stores, by and large, those purchases are made by somebody other than myself, namely, my wife, and unfortunately on several occasions my children. I will consult with them this evening to see whether they have found this reflected in their purchasing.

Mr. Jim Bradley: Did you get a discount on your condominium?

Honourable Mr. Davis: Like you, I couldn't afford two.

My favourite exchange took place early in Davis's career. MPP Donald C. MacDonald rose before the orders of the day and tore into Davis with gusto. How embarrassing was it that the Progressive Conservative Party of Ontario was sending fundraising appeals to *him*, the former leader of the Ontario New Democratic Party? Is the premier's fundraising team really that disorganized?

Davis had no heads-up that the question was coming. He had to think fast. And this is what he came up with: "Mr. Speaker, I apologize to the honourable member. But you see, our party very recently acquired the subscription list of *Playboy* magazine, which is no doubt where we got the honourable member's name." With that, he sat down and the legislature collapsed in laughter. And so did MacDonald.

Sadly, those kinds of exchanges never seem to happen anymore. Politics has become too extreme, too angry, and too brutal. "I just don't understand the degree of confrontation that takes place nowadays," Davis now says wistfully.

Looking as if you enjoyed the job was something Davis urged on one of his successors. In his memoir *Making a Difference*, Dalton McGuinty wrote that Ontario's 18th premier occasionally called the province's 24th premier and told him to keep smiling.

"I came to treasure the occasional pearls of wisdom offered to me by Premier Davis, even as I served as premier," McGuinty wrote. "His advice to keep smiling seems trite. But it is profoundly important to show voters that you are enjoying every minute of the job and that nothing gets you down. Who wants to be led by a leader who doesn't enjoy the job? How can anyone believe all those bad things your opposition is saying if your reaction is a smile?" McGuinty concluded.

McGuinty also came to experience what every premier after 1985 has encountered. It rarely matters where you are or what event you're attending. If Bill Davis is there, and even if you're the premier, chances are, you're taking second billing. "I would see him at events where he would inevitably receive more applause than me," McGuinty wrote.

From time to time, I talk with McGuinty's early childhood education czar, Charles Pascal, whose influence was paramount in getting the Liberal government, after a staged rollout, to implement full-day kindergarten across the province by September 2014. Pascal and I love to talk baseball and politics, and when he tells a story referring to "The Premier," neither of us is ever under any misconception as to whom he's referring to.

Several years ago during McGuinty's tenure, I was having one of my occasional lunches with Lisa de Wilde, TVO's chief executive officer. I mentioned to her in passing that several things at TVO had been named after people who had played a significant role in the creation and development of Ontario's educational broadcaster. "But ironically," I told her, "there's nothing named after Bill Davis, the guy who created us in the first place. Shouldn't we do something about that? A room. A wing. Maybe the studio where I host *The Agenda*? We should name something after him."

Lisa loved the idea, and to her great credit, championed it and got the board to approve renaming our ground-floor studio where we shoot *The Agenda* the William G. Davis Studio. TVO had a lovely renaming ceremony, attended by the former premier, the current premier (McGuinty), and a future premier (Kathleen Wynne), who was there in her capacity as minister of education. We unveiled a plaque before a packed studio of guests and, of course, Davis stole the show with his Johnny Carson–like monologue, teasing all the Liberals in the room for being "philosophically misguided" except Liberal MPP Monte Kwinter, who Davis said was actually more conservative than half the members of his caucus when he was in government. McGuinty acknowledged in his speech to great laughter, "Everybody loves Bill Davis. Even when I'm talking with my mother and she refers to 'The Premier,' she's talking about him, not me."

In 1973, while Davis was in his first term as premier, he helped create one of the continent's foremost educational, teaching, and research institutions — the Ontario Institute for Studies in Education (OISE). In 2012 OISE renamed its 12th-floor community lounge after Davis and had a ceremony to mark the occasion. University of Toronto President David Naylor spoke of how Ontario was a better place during Davis's days, that there was much more social cohesion in the province. It wasn't a knock on any of Davis's successors, just a statement of fact that the province was a much less polarized place under Davis's leadership.

After the ceremony, I glanced out the window at a southern vista of downtown Toronto. It was hard to find any building of any significance in which Davis didn't somehow have a hand. Today, thinking about that vista, here's what I see. Dominating the view, just two subway stops south is, of course, Queen's Park, the headquarters where Davis became the second-longest-serving Ontario premier of all time. Right across Bloor Street from OISE, there is Varsity Arena where Davis served as Bob Macaulay's campaign manager at that thrilling six-ballot PC leadership convention that selected John Robarts in 1961. And beside the arena is Varsity Stadium where Davis played football for the University of Toronto Varsity Blues and saw the Toronto Argonauts, his favourite Canadian Football League team, play innumerable times. There is the Royal Ontario Museum, which his government funded and on whose board his long-time friend and adviser, Eddie Goodman, once served. There is the Museum subway station, part of the Toronto Transit Commission's University-Spadina subway line that his government helped bankroll. There is the old Park Plaza Hotel (now renamed the Park Hyatt) just a stone's throw from OISE, east along Bloor Street, where Davis and his colleagues held their rather exclusive Tuesday morning breakfast meetings. Farther east along Bloor is St. Paul's Bloor Street Anglican Church where John Robarts's funeral service took place. And a little farther east at Bloor and Parliament Streets is St. James Cemetery, the site of Robarts's final resting place.

Looking back south, there is the John P. Robarts Research Library, which Davis successfully urged the University of Toronto to name after his predecessor. There are all those hospitals along University Avenue — Mount Sinai, Toronto General, Sick Children's, Queen Elizabeth, Women's College, and the Toronto Western over on Bathurst Street — all of which the Davis government funded and which the premier no doubt visited countless times for announcements. There is University College at the University of Toronto where he was an undergraduate student and where he met his first wife, Helen. There is Simcoe Hall across the Back Campus field from University College where Davis was a member of the U of T's governing council.

Farther south, there is Osgoode Hall at the corner of Queen Street West and University Avenue where Davis ultimately became one of eight Canadian premiers and two prime ministers who learned to become lawyers at the law school there. Across the road is the Four Seasons Centre for the Performing Arts, the home of the National Ballet of Canada and the Canadian Opera Company on whose board Kathleen Davis once sat and whose performances she still regularly enjoys (although Davis himself doesn't; she always has to take a friend when she goes).

To the east at Bay Street is the "new" Toronto City Hall where Davis's fellow Progressive Conservative politicians ruled the roost: the first Metropolitan Toronto chairman, Fred Gardiner, whose name graces the expressway along the city's waterfront; the mayor of the old city, Nathan Phillips, whose name is synonymous with the square outside one of the most iconic city halls in the world; Paul Godfrey, at 11 years the longest-serving Metro chairman ever; and, of course, the current mayor of Toronto, John Tory, who's almost like a sixth child to Davis.

Farther east again along Yonge Street is the Elgin and Winter Garden Theatre Centre, which the Ontario Heritage Trust (a non-profit agency within the Ministry of Tourism and Culture) purchased in 1981 and brought back to life. South and east of there is the Albany Club, Toronto's Tory hangout since Sir John A. Macdonald's time and a place where Davis has given countless speeches and had numerous political meetings. Just north of the club is one campus of George Brown College, one of many community colleges Davis helped establish in the 1960s when he was a minister in Robarts's government.

Back farther west on Bay Street north of King is the National Club where Davis's and Allan Lawrence's leadership teams met after the 1971 convention to bring the PC Party back together so successfully. And farther west again in the Financial District is Torys, once named Tory, Tory, DesLauriers & Binnington, where Davis put out his legal shingle after retiring from politics in 1985.

On Front Street is the Royal York Hotel where the former premier gave several addresses to the Empire and Canadian Clubs, and which hosted several policy and hospitality events in advance of his 1971 leadership convention victory. Farther west takes you to the grounds of the Canadian National Exhibition in whose football stadium Davis and Metro Chairman Paul Godfrey sat in the bone-chilling, pouring rain for the 1982 Grey Cup, listening to more than 54,000 fans chant, "We want a Dome! We want a Dome!" and which began the journey in earnest to get a domed stadium built in the Greater Toronto Area. (As if the weather hadn't been bad enough, Davis's beloved Argonauts lost 32–16 to the Edmonton Eskimos, thoroughly ruining his day.)

Davis might be Mr. Brampton, but he is also intimately connected to so much of the province's capital, as well.

The first musings about potentially building a domed stadium in or around Toronto actually go back to just after 1965 when Houston opened what it immodestly referred to as the eighth wonder of the world, the Houston Astrodome, home to its Major League Baseball Astros. By 1972 Davis was offering to join Metro Toronto in paying for a study to determine whether Toronto needed such a domed stadium, where it might go, and what it might look like. The Metro chairman, Paul Godfrey, continued to champion a dome for Toronto but really didn't make much progress. "I've stuck my neck out on this," he told the *Toronto Star* in 1982, "but someone's got to start the ball rolling." Godfrey and his friend, Pat Gillick, the Blue Jays' vice-president of baseball operations, also thought building a dome would nicely help kick-start the province's economic recovery, which was still a couple of years away.

But none of that was as influential as a single torrential rainstorm during a Grey Cup football game, watched by nearly eight million people on television. "If you ever needed proof of the need for a domed stadium, this is your day," Godfrey told the *Star*. The day after the game thousands attended a rally at Nathan Phillips Square and continued the "We want a Dome" chant. It was time.

In June 1983, Davis created a special task force whose job was to look into the feasibility of building a domed stadium in the GTA. Its chair was Hugh Macaulay, Davis's long-time trusted adviser who was chairing the Ontario Hydro board at the time. Metro Chairman Paul Godfrey was also on the committee, as was perhaps Davis's most influential Toronto-based cabinet minister, Larry Grossman. The panel received more than 100 different stadium design and location proposals, and some were truly either wacky or creative. One design would have seen the stadium built on Lake Ontario — not on the mainland beside Lake Ontario but floating hundreds of yards offshore *on the lake*. Many other private sector bids suggested outside the city was the best idea, perhaps creating a New Jersey Meadowlands–like complex in Richmond Hill, or east of the city in Bowmanville, or beside the Woodbine Racetrack in Etobicoke.

By early 1984, the blue-ribbon panel had considered all the options and made its recommendations to the premier: land near the Canadian Forces Base Downsview in North York topped the list as the best location for a new domed stadium. The committee liked the fact that its location in the northwest part of Metro Toronto made it more easily accessible to people all over the Golden Horseshoe, or what's now called the Greater Toronto and Hamilton Area. It would have been a catalyst for developing a part of the city that wasn't close to meeting its potential (North York, Etobicoke, and the southern part of York Region).

"It could have led to Downsview becoming a world-class hub for most major sports, state-of-the-art training for girls and boys of all ages and backgrounds in every conceivable sport activity at all levels of development," says former cabinet minister Dennis Timbrell, who loved the fact that Downsview was selected number one. If that site wasn't able to be acquired (it was owned by three different entities), the Ontario Jockey Club lands at the Woodbine Racetrack were the first backup option, with the Canadian National Exhibition grounds placing third.

Mel Lastman, North York's bull-in-a-china-shop-mayor, was ecstatic and immediately started posting signs around his city saying: NORTH YORK: HOME OF THE DOME. However, buried deep in the fine print of the report was the added proviso that *it would be preferable to have a downtown Toronto location* for the new stadium, but alas, there wasn't one.

Communications consultant Allan Bonner was Mayor Lastman's executive assistant at the time. He has talked to all of the players about the domed stadium decision, and to this day he's still not certain how the dome ended up being moved from Downsview — the Macaulay Committee's prime choice — to just west of the CN Tower at the foot of John Street. Even Bill Davis doesn't recall what happened.

"You have to remember," Bonner now says, "the Macaulay Committee report was sought by Bill Davis, for Bill Davis, to be done with as Bill Davis wanted." In other words, Mel Lastman might have thought that report was the last word on where the dome would go. But it clearly wasn't, because Davis came to have other ideas.

Paul Godfrey certainly didn't care where the dome went. He just wanted it for the millions of fans for whom baseball, football, tractor pulls, and rock concerts were prime cultural activities. Tax dollars had gone into theatre auditoriums and concert halls, Godfrey said, so why not a multi-purpose sports facility? When asked how much the new domed stadium would cost, Godfrey didn't have a clue but pulled $150 million out of thin air. That would prove to be off by several hundred million dollars.

In April 1984, Peter Picherack of Canadian National Railway came forward, proposing to donate seven acres of its land near the CN Tower for the dome. That changed everything. Concerns about Downsview mounted as local groups expressed concerns about tens of thousands of cars coming into their neighbourhoods on a regular basis. Furthermore, the ownership in Downsview was complicated: the Government of Canada, Canada Mortgage and Housing, and Bombardier all had a piece of the action. Conversely, Metro Toronto controlled 90 percent of the land near the foot of the CN Tower through its John Street Pumping Station. CN owned a sliver of it and for future considerations was prepared to deal. The momentum built for the downtown site. The IBI Group, a global architecture, planning, engineering, and technology firm, and architects Crang & Boake Inc. both looked into whether an enormous domed stadium could be shoehorned into the downtown space. They determined it was feasible and began lobbying for the foot of John Street as the best site.

Davis now had a problem. There was increasing evidence and momentum for him to build the dome downtown. But Mel Lastman and other suburban members of Metro Council agreed to pony up tens of millions of property tax dollars on the understanding that the dome would be built in North York. So Davis had to get crafty. According to Trevor Eyton, who was at the time the chief executive officer of Brascan (now Brookfield Asset Management), the premier called him with a very unusual request. Brascan was leading the private sector consortium that was ponying up $50 million toward the dome.

"Trevor," Eyton says Davis told him, "I have to tell my cabinet colleagues that your support for the stadium is contingent on the stadium being downtown."

Eyton was confused. "Premier, my partners and I don't care where the stadium goes."

Davis tried again. "Trevor, you aren't understanding me. I need you to say that your support for the dome is contingent on it being built downtown."

There was a long pause. Then Eyton said, "Premier, our support for the dome is contingent on it being built downtown."

"Thank you," Davis replied, and hung up.

Allan Bonner talked to Eyton about that phone call a couple of years ago. The former Brascan CEO now jokes that "Bill Davis called me to tell me I was twisting his arm."

When I asked Davis about that phone call in early 2016, he had no recollection of it, other than to say, "That sounds like something Trevor would say!"

Ironically, the whole Eyton-arm-twisting story never mattered, since the premier never brought the matter before the cabinet for a final decision, anyway. Dennis Timbrell recalls one meeting at which the premier asked for his ministers' views on where the stadium should go. "But there was no conclusion to the discussion as there wasn't a specific proposal in front of us," he now says.

"Bringing the matter before cabinet for a final decision may have been more of a state of mind thing than an actual occurrence" is how Bonner puts it.

None of this is meant to suggest anything nefarious went on, and with the benefit of more than a quarter century of hindsight, it's apparent that moving the dome downtown was a very smart decision. A quarter century ago Davis was more modest about his role in the SkyDome's success. Today, after some pushing, he's prepared to acknowledge the part he played. "I'll take some credit for that," he now says. "I never look for it [credit], but if anyone deserves credit for the SkyDome, it's yours truly!"

Despite numerous announcements by both Liberal and Conservative federal governments, Downsview continues to be a study in failed potential. Conversely, building what became the SkyDome kick-started massive amounts of development downtown, including: Air Canada Centre (the home of the Maple Leafs, Raptors, and Rock) eight years later, thousands of units of condominium development, shops, restaurants, the CBC Broadcast Centre, the Ripley's Aquarium, a south building extension of the Toronto Convention Centre, the Hockey Hall of Fame, BMO Field at Exhibition Place, and more. It's unknowable how much of that might inevitably have happened. Suffice to say, many American downtowns at this time were failing because so many sports and cultural activities were moving to the suburbs. That's something that Ontario's capital thankfully never experienced, in large measure because Davis had the foresight to finagle his way out of what looked like a done deal in Downsview.

"He was an early proponent into the urban core," Bonner says. "I'd give him that credit." During the early 1990s when the Blue Jays were winning World Series and were at the height of their popularity, the SkyDome somehow managed to get 50,000 people in and out of the core of the city night after night, despite adding only 500 new parking spots to the existing mix. "It's a great use of existing infrastructure," Bonner says. "It does wonders for the downtown. Look how ridiculous the Ottawa situation is," he adds, referring to the NHL Senators' home arena, the Canadian Tire Centre, in suburban Kanata — one of the most illogical arena-placement decisions ever. The place is hard to get to, and hard to leave, and represents a massive missed opportunity to improve the core of Canada's capital.

Davis's choice of the John Street site also had the added benefit of avoiding several ugly turf wars that surely would have ensued had he stuck with Downsview. Lastman was surprisingly muted in his criticism. (Perhaps it's because he was soon able to get a $25 million subway station near Mel Lastman Square at Yonge Street and Park Home Avenue.) One of Davis's own cabinet ministers, James Snow, somehow got himself into the position of backing an Oakville bid "as a private citizen." Dennis Timbrell went to bat hard for the Downsview site. There was also Mississauga developer Harold Shipp's bid to build the dome near the intersection of Highways 401 and 10, not far from Davis's own beloved Brampton. Shipp had money, political influence, and vision. But in some respects, because the John Street location wasn't part of the original Macaulay Committee process, it enabled Davis to disappoint all the other bidders while maintaining the process was still sound and had integrity.

"So we ended up with a location in the end that no one proposed with a design for a stadium meant for a different location," Bonner says, smiling.

The SkyDome opened in June 1989 as the world's first retractable roof, multi-purpose stadium, and what a marvel it was. Architect Rod Robbie's design was breathtaking in its beauty and simplicity. Unlike the dome at BC Place Stadium in Vancouver, this roof opened on beautiful days to let the sun shine in but closed when the weather was miserable. It was the best of both worlds. The first Grey Cup game played there in 1989, unlike the 1982 match in the rain at Exhibition Stadium, might have been the most exciting one ever, as Saskatchewan outlasted Hamilton 43–40 in an offensive shootout. Joe Carter hit one of the most iconic home runs ever, winning the 1993 World Series under the dome. In 1998 Nelson Mandela was welcomed there. Through the years the SkyDome has welcomed rock celebrities, wrestling stars, mixed martial arts champions, and American football, too, which no doubt did *not* thrill Ontario's former premier.

Well after Davis left politics, problems began to arise, although location was never one of them. The design of the stadium constantly changed (adding a hotel and an athletic club), and it quickly became apparent that Godfrey's $150 million price tag wasn't even close. Ultimately, the stadium cost nearly $600 million, and as aesthetically and financially successful as the building was, activities there couldn't cover the massive debt payments. Eventually, bankruptcy was filed for in 1998, and Rogers Communications bought the stadium for a song in 2005, renaming it the bland Rogers Centre, while Ontario taxpayers got stuck paying off the building's massive debt. It led Bob Rae to joke: "Bill Davis thought of it, David Peterson built it, and I paid for it."

Given the central role Davis played in making the dome happen, there was a bit of momentum behind naming the new stadium after him. But the former premier immediately put the kibosh on those efforts. "I think it should be called the Ontario Community Centre," he joked, offering up a suggestion almost as bland as the name currently on the building. However, his comment is yet another example of how modest and self-effacing Davis truly is.

Naming a new domed stadium after an important politician wasn't a completely ridiculous idea. Paul Sauvé Arena in Montreal, where René Lévesque gave his memorable concession speech after the first referendum, is named for a former Quebec premier. In 1982 in Minneapolis, Minnesota, authorities named the new domed stadium there the Hubert H. Humphrey Metrodome after that state's favourite political son, who almost defeated Richard Nixon for the presidency in 1968. And the former home of the National Football League Redskins and Major League Baseball Senators and Nationals in Washington, D.C., is named Robert F. Kennedy Memorial Stadium after the slain 1968 presidential candidate.

To this day there is no one in politics who can give the impression of saying a lot while saying nothing at all the way Bill Davis did. He was the master of obfuscation and circumlocution while at the same time seeming to convey great wisdom in what he was saying. Hugh Segal writes of a time in 1991 when Brian Mulroney was considering asking him to be a senior policy adviser in the prime minister's office on the constitutional file, dealing with the lead-up to the Charlottetown Accord. Davis met with Segal to give him his advice on whether to accept the offer if it came. What follows is long, but I've reproduced it in its entirety because it's vintage Davis:

> You know, Hughie, I don't want to be too blunt about this sort of thing and I'm not suggesting the two issues are related, but you remember when you had that admission to the Kennedy School of Government and I prevailed upon you, while I didn't want to, but felt I had to, back in 1981, to help with the constitution for that one year more and we agreed then that you would do that for Ontario and its belief in Canada? I can't be certain, and perhaps wouldn't be if I could, but you and Donna should not be surprised if, and one never knows how this sort of thing may develop, but in the event you are asked to give perhaps a bit of a helping hand up there on the bridge because the ship of state, well, with the referendum scheduled for the fall, you know he may not be perfect, but as a prime minister, I think Brian [Mulroney] has genuinely tried to do the right thing, especially on free trade and the constitution, which is not to say that mistakes were not made, but you and I know that if they don't restart the constitutional process or if the caucus comes apart, then the country will come apart, and frankly, I don't want to put

too much of a burden on you but, well, if you do not help, that is if you are asked, you may always feel badly because there is only one Canada and, now that I may sound a tad like a former Ontario premier speaking, but it is a great country and one worth preserving for, I guess, your children and my grand children — and, you know, you really should have more than one, I had five, I did my part — but it would be a lot less constructive in terms of their future if that 1992 matter were not in some way sorted out and frankly, there is no one who has a better chance of keeping it together than Brian and so, you know, if you could see your way clear, it would be good for the prime minister and the party although probably disruptive to your own life, even though it's not as if you're 50, you're just 40, so there would be time to make up any economic loss, although I know that would not be your first concern, but Kathleen and I were talking and we can understand how that might trouble a young man with a young family, but in the end the best thing for them is a strong Canada and I think you will be asked to help and I hope you would not rule it out right away without thinking about it and you know, I would not want to impose any pressure, but I can't think of anyone who might be able to help more directly in that regard especially in terms of the dynamics and the politics, than, well, I don't want to be flattering, but I think you know where I'm headed.

Incredible.

Now that he's well into his eighties, Bill Davis has been getting more wistful about life. He enjoys the fact that he's still engaged in the political process, having participated in some way in every federal and provincial election (and a few leadership contests, too) since his departure from politics three decades ago. How much longer he'll continue to do that, he admits, "is not totally up to me." In November 2013, he seemed genuinely emotional when TVO — on the occasion of its 40th anniversary — honoured his contribution to it, to the province, and to the country with a gala dinner at the Distillery District in Toronto. He looked out into the audience and saw John Tory, whose recent political career included a general election loss in 2007, a personal loss to Kathleen Wynne in the riding of Don Valley West, and an ensuing by-election loss in Haliburton–Kawartha Lakes–Brock, which was an attempt to get Tory back into the provincial legislature. And yet Davis told the audience he was sure Tory's best political days were ahead of him. Was he just trying to buck up Tory's spirits?

"I didn't have to do that," Davis says. "I meant it and John knew I meant it."

"He knew I didn't have the bug out of my system yet," Tory says. Sure enough, a year later John Tory became the 65th mayor of Toronto.

The most emotional moment of the evening came when Davis peered into the crowd to find Clare Westcott, his then almost 90-year-old former adviser and friend. "I don't want to embarrass you," Davis said, visibly moved, "but some of the things discussed tonight might not have happened without your presence, your assistance, and on most days, you're lots of fun." The audience then gave Westcott a prolonged standing ovation as the former premier wiped away a tear. Davis and Westcott still speak by phone almost every day. It is a partnership that has endured for more than half a century.

For years Davis has always insisted to me that he never worries about what historians will say about his time in public life. I mostly believe him. Actually, the support of his friends and family has always been more important to him. Nevertheless, he did have the staff in his premier's office keep extensive newspaper clippings of his time at Queen's Park. So I know he cares a little bit more than he lets on. In 2012 when the Montreal-based Institute for Research in Public Policy released its study of the best Canadian premiers of the past 40 years, it listed Peter Lougheed of Alberta in the top spot and Davis as second. When I told Davis about the study, he made several jokes about it and tried to pretend that it didn't bother him. But I could tell it did. Eventually, he let slip that running Ontario, with its mature three-party system, six years of minority government and two recessions, a party that had already been in power for almost three decades, and no oil, was a little trickier than running the one-party autocracy that was Alberta during Lougheed's time.

"I mean, my goodness, being premier of Alberta was like being the mayor of London, Ontario, for goodness' sake!" he told me, laughing, but I suspect not completely joking.

Brian Mulroney put it better. "Back then the premier of Alberta woke up every morning, and the first thing he did is cash a cheque," he told me. "In Ontario you're managing 40 percent of the country's GDP."

Arguably, Davis's most lasting legacy to the country was his role in securing a successful conclusion to the constitutional talks in 1981. But he didn't lose interest in the file after retiring from public life. Both with the Meech Lake Accord in 1990 and the Charlottetown Accord in 1992, Davis weighed in. In a speech in Ottawa in September 1992, Davis admitted Quebec's absence from the 1981 agreement "troubled me then and it troubles me now." He went on to acknowledge the imperfections in the agreement he negotiated, and the imperfections in the Charlottetown process. "But I say to you, as clearly and precisely as I can, that all of these imperfections pale into inconsequence in comparison with the massive imperfection every Canadian would experience in their own life if we fail to sustain the side of 'Yes,' if we fail to sustain the case for Canada."

Davis praised Bob Rae's role in the Charlottetown Accord, saying he was "prepared to go the extra mile for Canada." And he equated a "No" vote as "at best a leap into the dark and at worst it may be a context that makes a leap into the dark look pretty good by comparison." He concluded his speech by saying: "This old has-been will go anywhere, talk to anyone to make the case, that it is time for all Canadians to take "Yes" for an answer, to say "Yes" to Canada.

Who knows how influential Davis's entreaties ultimately were in the final Charlottetown vote? The record simply shows that six provinces and one territory rejected the accord, while only four provinces and one territory endorsed it. Ontario voted "Yes" but just barely: 50.1 percent to 49.9 percent. Constitutional unanimity still eludes Canada.

"What distinguishes the subject of your book from the herd is his uncommon love for people," says Greg Sorbara, Ontario's former finance minister. It's an interesting observation given Davis's well-known introversion. "He relished and still relishes the special heartbeat that comes from human interaction. He did not so much *consult* with folks as he did *engage* them, as a playwright, in a drama that required a very large cast." Sorbara sat in the cabinet of two Liberal premiers — David Peterson and Dalton McGuinty — but he clearly holds a special place in his heart for this Tory loyalist, who agrees with Sorbara's observation.

"If I had any strength, it was that I liked people," Davis says. "I had no trouble with that part of it."

David Peterson, the 20th premier of Ontario, describes Davis as "a real head-scratcher, a real unique guy." Peterson and Davis have never had a particularly close relationship for a couple of reasons. First, Davis was premier when Peterson took on the Ontario Liberal leadership in 1982, and he might have heard one too many lines about "fat-cat Tories hanging out at the Albany Club" or Davis "lying down on his towel on the beach" while Rome was burning back home. Actually, the premier from Brampton and the premier from London were in the legislature for a full decade together. Second, Davis's closest relationship with any ex-Ontario premier is with Bob Rae, and the bad blood between Peterson and Rae has made it hard for Davis to show much affection for Peterson. However, Peterson does like and respect Davis, has a soft spot for him, and made this very prescient observation when we spoke: "He's an extraordinary guy, cloaked in ordinariness." If a better, more concise description of Ontario's 18th premier was ever uttered, I haven't heard it.

Charles Pascal says the secret to Davis's success was his ability "to live in the grey domain. He was comfortable living in the world of grey rather than black and white. That allows for conversations to be reciprocal. It's the art of the possible. He's fiercely partisan, but it's a joyful partisanship that would allow him to converse across the aisle."

Gordon Walker, the sometime burr under Davis's saddle, admits some of the tension between the two resulted from Walker's "more orthodox, small-c, right-wing conservatism," and the premier's "moving according to where he felt it was necessary to move. He was more fluid." Davis loved nothing more than to tease Walker whenever his minister on the odd occasion showed a similar flexibility in his views. "He'd have great fun at my expense pointing that out," Walker says. Still, more than three decades after Davis's departure from office, Walker acknowledges Davis's conservatism "is a more successful offering. It works better than a more orthodox or rigid approach. It was more successful to bob and weave."

John Tory points to Davis's "immense patience, and a profound belief that moderation in all things would get you further. He also had an innate sense of how much bold change Ontarians could accept."

A s I write this in the spring of 2016, Bill Davis is almost 87 years old. He has buried too many of his cabinet colleagues, not to mention his fellow premiers and, of course, Prime Minister Pierre Trudeau, too. Sitting in the office of the mayor of Toronto, gazing out over a beautifully lit Nathan Phillips Square, I ask John Tory about the inevitable day when his political hero will no longer be with us.

Tory pauses for a long time. His eyes get red. "I think about it all the time," he confesses. "I was thinking about the time when I once took a walk with my father who died at 81 and seemingly in great shape. He once said to me, 'When I'm not here ...' and I didn't want to hear it. We think these men are going to live forever. And I ask myself, how will I feel if Mr. Davis dies and I haven't spoken to him in a while? So I pick up the phone. But I can't talk about this because I'm just going to assume he's going to live forever."

My meeting with Mayor Tory was supposed to last 45 minutes. We're now at the 75-minute mark. This mayor enjoys talking about Bill Davis. When he was sworn in as Toronto's 65th mayor, Davis was standing right beside him on the floor of City Council, beaming as the chain of office was placed around his protégé's neck. Their relationship has lasted almost half a century. As the mayor walks me to the door, he reminds me that if I need clarification of anything not to hesitate to get in touch. It's clear John Tory wants the record of Bill Davis's life to be as accurate as possible. As we shake hands goodbye, an emotional Tory says: "He's my mentor. He's my ..."

Another long pause.

"Everything."

William Grenville Davis is now at the point in his life where he seems quite comfortable with the verdict on his time: "Historians will do what they want to do. I don't worry about what they'll say." Having been around for a very long time now, Davis has heard it all: he was too interventionist, he abandoned conservative principles too often, he governed according to whatever way the public opinion polls told him to, and he indulged in partisan patronage too much.

"I did my best, made the judgments I thought were right," he says. "I'm being very modest, but I'm not uncomfortable with the record of achievements." That almost sounds like a boast. The next line certainly sounds like one. "On occasion I may have made a mistake, but I can't think of any at the moment!" says the man they once called bland, laughing his way toward immortality.

APPENDIX 1:

CABINETS

Final John Robarts Ministry on February 28, 1971
Lieutenant Governor W. Ross Macdonald

Premier and President of the Council	John Robarts
Treasurer and Minister of Economics	Charles MacNaughton
Minister of Agriculture	William Stewart
Minister of Correctional Services	Allan Grossman
Minister of Education and University Affairs	William G. Davis
Minister of Energy	George Kerr
Minister of Financial and Commercial Affairs	Bert Lawrence
Minister of Health	Thomas Wells
Minister of Highways	George Gomme
Minister of Justice and Attorney General	Arthur Wishart
Minister of Labour	Dalton Bales
Minister of Lands and Forests	René Brunelle
Minister of Mines and Northern Affairs	Allan Lawrence
Minister of Municipal Affairs	Darcy McKeough
Minister of Public Works	Jack Simonett
Minister of Revenue	John White
Minister of Social and Family Services	John Yaremko
Minister of Tourism and Information	James Auld

Minister of Trade and Development	Stanley Randall
Minister of Transport	Irwin Haskett
Minister Without Portfolio	Fernand Guindon
Secretary to the Cabinet	J. Keith Reynolds

First Bill Davis Ministry as of March 1, 1971
Lieutenant Governor W. Ross Macdonald

Premier and President of the Council	William G. Davis
Minister of Justice and Attorney General	Allan Lawrence
Treasurer, Minister of Economics, Chairman Treasury Board	Darcy McKeough
Minister of Education	Robert Welch
Minister of Health	Bert Lawrence
Provincial Secretary and Minister of Citizenship	John Yaremko
Minister of Trade and Development	Allan Grossman
Minister of Agriculture	William Stewart
Minister of Highways and Transport	Charles MacNaughton
Minister of Public Works	James Auld
Minister of Financial and Commercial Affairs	Arthur Wishart
Minister of Lands and Forests	René Brunelle
Minister of Municipal Affairs	Dalton Bales
Minister of Social and Family Services	Thomas Wells
Minister of Tourism and Information	Fernand Guindon
Minister of University Affairs	John White
Minister of Energy and Resources Management	George Kerr
Minister of Correctional Services	Syl Apps
Minister of Labour	Gordon Carton
Minister of Mines and Northern Affairs	Leo Bernier
Minister of Revenue	Eric Winkler
Minister Without Portfolio	James Snow
Minister Without Portfolio	Richard Potter
Minister Without Portfolio	Edward Dunlop
Secretary to the Cabinet	J. Keith Reynolds

Second Davis Ministry, February 2, 1972
Lieutenant Governor W. Ross Macdonald

Premier and President of the Council	William G. Davis
Provincial Secretary for Justice	Allan Lawrence
Treasurer, Minister of Finance and Intergovernmental Affairs, Minister of Municipal Affairs	Darcy McKeough
Provincial Secretary for Social Development	Robert Welch
Provincial Secretary for Resource Development	Bert Lawrence
Provincial Secretary, Minister of Citizenship, Solicitor General	John Yaremko
Minister of Revenue, with Responsibility for the Ontario Housing Corporation	Allan Grossman
Minister of Agriculture and Food	William Stewart
Chairman of the Management Board of Cabinet	Charles MacNaughton
Minister of the Environment	James Auld
Minister of Social and Family Services	Rene Brunelle
Attorney General	Dalton Bales
Minister of Education	Thomas Wells
Minister of Labour	Fernand Guindon
Minister of Trade and Development, Minister of Tourism and Information	John White
Minister of Colleges and Universities	George Kerr
Minister of Correctional Services	Syl Apps
Minister of Transportation and Communications	Gordon Carton
Minister of Mines and Northern Affairs, Minister of Lands and Forests, Minister of Natural Resources	Leo Bernier
Minister of Financial and Commercial Affairs, Minister of Public Protection	Eric Winkler
Minister of Public Works, Minister of Government Services	James Snow
Minister of Health	Richard Potter
Deputy Minister, Cabinet Office	Carl Elroy Brannan

APPENDIX 2:

STOPPING SPADINA (1971)

Statement by the Honourable William Davis, Prime Minister of Ontario, on the Future of the Spadina Expressway in the Legislature, Thursday, June 3, 1971

I should like to inform the House of the Government's decision in the matter of the William R. Allen (Spadina) Expressway.

As all of us know, this has been an issue of anxious interest to the people of Metropolitan Toronto and, since Toronto is their capital city, to the people of Ontario. The subject has been exhaustively debated, the project itself has been examined and re-examined, substantial sums of money have already been invested in planning, preparation, and in construction. Literally years of time have been expended by various public bodies, professional groups, citizen organizations, and private individuals in vigorous discussion and debate on the merits, or otherwise, of this project.

Together with my colleagues, and in consultation with our experts, I have studied the project again so as to reach a final determination in the matter. As a new Government, and without prejudice to the past, it is our responsibility to do so. We are fully aware that our decision will represent not a judgment upon the past, but a decision upon which policies for the future will be built.

Mr. Speaker, I do not propose on this occasion to re-argue the case for or against the Spadina Expressway. The arguments are so familiar to so many that a reiteration of them would be an imposition. I will say, however, that the decision has been difficult, one which will be difficult for many to accept, and as disappointing to some as it will be pleasing to others. The issue of the Spadina

Expressway is not only a substantive one, but it has become a symbolic one among the population at large, whose legitimate concerns for the planning and development of the capital city, or their province, their communities, and their transportation facilities are all keenly felt, and whose interest in conserving their urban amenities and environment has become one of the highest priority.

Mr. Speaker, the Government of Ontario does not propose to proceed in support of the plan for the Spadina Expressway.

We do propose to co-operate with the appropriate municipal authorities in the development of alternative transportation facilities in which we shall offer appreciably greater provincial financial assistance for rapid transit services, including land acquisition and parking, in connection with these services.

It is our conclusion that if we are to serve adequately and sensibly the transportation needs of the Toronto area, both in the suburbs and downtown, we must place our reliance on means and methods other than those which will encourage and proliferate the use of the passenger car as the basic means of transportation.

In the final analysis, Mr. Speaker, in determining how best to serve the future needs of Metropolitan Toronto, we must make a decision as to whether we are trying to build a transportation system to serve the automobile, or one which will best serve people. If we are building a transportation system to serve the automobile, the Spadina Expressway would be a good place to start. But if we are building a transportation system to serve people, the Spadina Expressway is a good place to stop. It is our determination to opt for the latter.

In taking this position, I am well aware — and sensitive to the fact — that we are reversing a decision which was taken by the majority of the elected representatives of Metropolitan Toronto. I have no doubts as to the strength of their convictions in this matter, nor do I question the matter of their right to determine their interest, as they see it, and as they saw it in 1963, when the Ontario Municipal Board first gave approval to the application of Metropolitan Toronto to construct this Expressway. But the Government and Legislature of Ontario have their responsibilities as well, and their interests. We can do no less than discharge them in the light of present-day circumstances. So say, Mr. Speaker, I would hope the judgment of the Legislature will be consistent with that of the Government.

There have been profound and significant changes in regard to the evaluation of this project since its original conception. Not the least of these has been the cost of it. Seven years after the Ontario Municipal Board's approval was given, the estimated cost had more than doubled. But more important, in my judgment, has been the growing evidence and accumulative experience gathered elsewhere on this continent which demonstrates the ultimate futility of giving priority to the passenger car as a means of transportation into and out of the cities. In some instances, the decision may have been late in coming, but for Ontario, so far as Toronto is concerned, we believe the time to act is now.

Further, Mr. Speaker, this Government cannot help but heed the rising public anxiety and concern in questions relating to pollution and environmental control. I trust that our decision will give further assurance of our determination to respond to those concerns.

I have no doubt that while the estimated cost of this Expressway has doubled over the past seven years, the numbers of the general public opposed to the undertaking have multiplied many times over. Whether such would constitute a majority or not I cannot say, but it is at least a substantial and significant minority, including, I might add, vast numbers of those who will inherit the cities and the environment we are now creating, I am confident that if the people of the Toronto of tomorrow were consulted, they would give overwhelming approval to the decision their Government has taken today.

Mr. Speaker, Honourable Members of this House, whatever their constituency, share with me, I am sure, an admiration and affection for our provincial capital. We are proud of its growth. We are the beneficiaries of its commerce and industry and its cultural developments. As a capital city, there are few, if any in North America more generously endowed with natural beauty and attractions.

Toronto has downtown residential areas, historic landmarks, parklands, and recreational facilities which are almost unique to urban life today and which will be beyond value or price to the urban life of tomorrow.

It would seem to me imperative that those of us who have responsibility and, I might add, final authority, must do all we can to maintain the quality of our urban life, preserve our ravines and parks, conserve our residential communities, private homes, and historic landmarks, and enhance and repair our waterfront.

Anyone who has this week visited the newly created Yonge Street Mall will be visibly struck by the realization of how much the people of this city enjoy and value its attractions when given the opportunity to do so freely. One might borrow some of the popular rhetoric and say, looking at the thousands of cheerful Torontonians and their neighbours making use of the Mall, that the streets belong to the people.

In any event, Mr. Speaker, the city does not belong to the automobile. We have taken this decision in the clear understanding that those who live in the suburbs for whom Toronto is their place of work, or the scene for their pleasure, that alternative, efficient, and economic means can and will be provided for their transportation requirements.

As for those who will continue to live in the city, we recognize their need for a transportation system that provides maximum facility and convenience but which will neither depreciate nor destroy their community life.

Mr. Speaker, I would express the hope that our conclusion will lead us directly into intensive discussion which will apply to the future and that we will not find ourselves re-arguing the past. To do so may provide some satisfaction to our critics but, in terms of the public's transportation needs, it will not get anyone anywhere. The spirit which has motivated our decision is both positive and progressive.

We shall be prepared very shortly to discuss with the appropriate municipal authorities new proposals for financial and other assistance in meeting their needs. We shall do so with the greatest goodwill, and in the understanding that both they and we seek the same achievement, which is to maintain a city and a life for its people that are an inspiration and example for all and a source of pride and satisfaction to the people of Ontario.

APPENDIX 3:

NO TO SEPARATE SCHOOL FUNDING (1971)

Statement by the Honourable William Davis, Prime Minister of Ontario, Re the Question of Extended Public Assistance to the Separate School System, Queen's Park, Tuesday, August 31, 1971

I had indicated on an earlier occasion that the government would make a statement of policy on the question of extended public assistance to the separate school system.

My colleagues and I have considered this matter exhaustively, realizing its importance to the people of Ontario, and with profound respect for the views of various interested parties, all of whom, however disparate their opinions may be, hold them with equal conviction and sincerity.

There are few issues in the realm of public policy where the reconciliation of differing views and the possibility of compromise are so difficult to achieve, and few issues which have the potential of creating misunderstanding, stirring prejudice, and inviting recrimination. But the issue cannot be resolved by avoiding it, nor would any party to its consideration be satisfied with an attempt to resolve it by ambiguity, nor by resorting to some temporary expedient.

There can be no doubt that Ontario's present separate school system at the elementary grades level exists as a matter of right, deeply rooted in historic precedent, representing the position of past generations of political leaders and private citizens, and that this right is firmly entrenched in the Constitution. The separate school system was established in the interest of those of the Roman Catholic faith, and the administrative responsibility is primarily and principally that of the Roman Catholic Separate School Trustees. The academic curriculum is fully compatible with that of the public school system. While Ontario's separate schools in the elementary grades do not limit their enrolment exclusively to Roman Catholic students, they attract few children of other denominations or religions, if for no other reason than the natural limitations of space and facilities.

As for the public elementary schools, these are open and accessible to all, without limitation or distinction. Children of every denomination, and of all faiths are represented, and it is the right of the Roman Catholic parent and child, where both systems are available, to choose freely between them.

The Government of Ontario has come to consider each of these in the elementary system — public and separate — as part of the whole, subject to the same general requirements as to standards and curriculum, and each entitled to an equal measure of public support and assistance.

It is clearly understood that there is not, nor could there be, any attempt by government to diminish the right of Roman Catholics to have free access to their own separate elementary schools, nor could there be any government policy which would have the effect of inhibiting the right of choice of parent and child to attend the public schools, if such is preferred.

Whatever the wisdom and foresight of its architects, none could foresee a century ago the educational system the people of Ontario enjoy today, the many changes it has undergone, the expansion of its services and facilities, the broadening of its curriculum and the significance of both its value and its cost to the community.

From the outset, as the secondary schools grew to become an integral part of the public school system, they have been determinedly and deliberately non-denominational and nonsectarian. Such has been a fundamental characteristic of government policy, from the time of Ontario's first prime minister, the Honourable John Sandfield Macdonald, and this policy has been supported by every party while in power since that time.

It will be recalled that one of Macdonald's first initiatives in the field of education was to terminate grants paid over the preceding three decades to church-related colleges and universities. Flowing from that decision, in the long course of events, Ontario has today a widely accepted, well-established system of non-denominational publicly supported universities.

At the same time, over the years there have been continued changes in the financial arrangements with regard to the separate schools at the elementary level, all of them salutary. I have little doubt that further changes can and will be made. In any such system anomalies and inequities are inherent and only patience and goodwill can resolve and remedy them.

Without question, the separate school system today represents a much broader program and a far more substantial commitment than could have been envisioned at the time of Confederation. It serves its purpose well and remains a source of satisfaction to its supporters, just as it has been a contributing factor to the stability and steady progress that has characterized the development of our province and its people.

At the turn of the century, when secondary education was unavailable to many young people, the suggestion was made, and agreed upon, that public school trustees be granted the power to operate classes in elementary schools through to what is now the Grade 10 level. Soon after, the same privilege was extended to separate school trustees. None the less, while the decision offered a practical and sensible solution for many who would have been otherwise disadvantaged, it was never intended as an encroachment upon the principle of a free, nondenominational and nonsectarian secondary school system, accessible to all and supported by all.

The Government of Ontario believes it has an essential responsibility to maintain this principle and is sustained in this belief by the judgements and policies of its predecessors, and, in the last analysis, by a consideration for the broad general interest of the people of Ontario. The Government has therefore concluded that it cannot support the proposals of the Ontario Separate School Trustees Association.

In the question as to whether or not the Government of Ontario should extend tax support to secondary separate schools beyond Grade 10, we do not believe the refusal to do so rescinds any constitutional right, nor does it offer any future limitation or condition to the voluntary decision of any parent or child to choose between a secondary education in the public school system or in the private school of their choice.

If, on the other hand, the Government of Ontario were arbitrarily to decide to establish and maintain, out of public funds, a complete educational system determined by denominational and religious considerations, such a decision would fragment the present system beyond recognition and repair, and do so to the disadvantage of all those who have come to want for their children a public school system free of a denominational or sectarian character.

To embark upon such a policy could not be, in reason or justice, limited to some faiths and denied to others. Nor could it, in logic, be limited to the elementary and academic secondary school systems alone. We would inevitably be obliged to proceed throughout all our educational institutions to fragment and divide both our young people and our resources from kindergarten through post-graduate university studies.

We have spent considerable time examining the contention set out in the brief of the Separate School Trustees that the new emphasis on continuous education and greater flexibility of curriculum offerings makes it mandatory that the separate schools be allowed to extend their program beyond the Grade 10 level.

It should be stressed, however, in response to that contention, that there can be no valid educational program that does not take into account the interests, intellectual abilities and the psychological growth of children at various stages in their development. As a result, effective integration of elementary and secondary education must be carried out through the curriculum design, through varied learning methods and through a whole variety of organizational arrangements. There will be no real break in continuity of learning, whatever the authorities involved. If the receiving school is organized to deal with students on an individual basis.

In the public school sector, children move from one school to another at various stages of their development and the traditional advance from an elementary to a secondary environment now takes place at all levels from Grades 7 to 10. Indeed, it is thought advantageous if the children do move from one environment to another during various stages of their learning program. Thus, there seems no reason why young people who may originally enrol in separate schools cannot move to more advanced stages of their work within a public secondary setting at either the Grade 8 level, which the majority now do, or at Grade 10, without adverse effect on their educational progress, if appropriate planning for such change is carried out.

Argument is frequently made as to the financial implications inherent in an extension of public support for private schools. There can be no doubt of the substantial costs and, implicit in such an assessment, there must be the realization that the standards and quality of education would inevitably suffer, with their subsequent social implications, as the resources of our taxpayers came to be increasingly strained.

Nevertheless, no such principle ought to be upheld solely for the material reason that to abandon it would be costly. However much the question is argued, the conclusion is inevitably based on the general merit and value of a single, universally accessible, publicly supported secondary school system. And it is this fundamental conclusion that the government finds itself compelled to restate and reaffirm.

The people of Ontario, whatever their opinion or interest in this issue, are entitled to know the position of their government. In recent months, I have been reminded of the possible political effects of taking one decision or another. As to this, I can only say, on behalf of my colleagues, that our decision has been made, as much as is humanly possible, without regard to any political consideration, advantage or disadvantage.

Whatever the decision, it would almost certainly provoke vigorous dissent, since, as I have said, none of us has any doubt as to the strength of conviction and the sincerity of those opinions held by others which are contrary to our own. Despite disagreement, I can only express the government's respect for the opinion of those who may be disappointed with this decision.

The question of extended or expanded public assistance to the separate school system has at various times in the history of this province been a matter of intense and vexacious [sic] public controversy. There is nothing to suggest in this experience that such times have been productive or rewarding to any party to the controversy.

At the same time, we cannot ignore or overlook the presence of a basic disagreement as to educational policy. The spokesmen who are in support of extended public assistance to the separate schools are convinced that the education of children involves a close relationship between a particular religion and general knowledge and that this relationship must be a foremost consideration in the educational process.

To accept such a philosophy, and to foster it, the government would be obliged to create an entire educational system which would be, at the very least, a dual one, comprising a system for Roman Catholic students and another for all other students, or the government would be obliged to provide a system for Roman Catholic students, and a further system for Protestant students, another for Jewish students, and possibly still others representing the various denominations of Protestant and other faiths.

Any one of these, as I have said, would be tantamount to the abandonment of the secondary and post-secondary educational system as it exists today, in which the education of the student, while it reflects the ethical and spiritual values of the community, and while teaching respect and tolerance for all religions and creeds, remains, none the less, nondenominational and nonsectarian in character.

While the government believes its position should be stated unequivocally in regard to the basic issue, this by no means precludes the consideration of further measures which might well be undertaken to ensure that our responsibilities to the school system, including those to the separate schools, are discharged in an equitable manner.

We believe, for example, there are opportunities within the existing system for all children of Ontario taxpayers to share in the benefits of programs, facilities, and services provided by public elementary and secondary schools on a part-time basis, if so desired.

In addition, we are ready at all times to consider ways of making our school system more responsive to the valid needs and expectations of our society. In this connection, one reason which has been given by a number of groups seeking tax support for religious-oriented schools is that the public system does not include sufficient emphasis on moral and ethical values. This is a matter which we are considering very carefully.

While our society has rightfully rejected any dissemination of particular sectarian beliefs in the public schools, nevertheless our system has always included the objective of imparting those basic moral and ethical values upon which our very society is based.

It may be that through an earnest effort to avoid sectarian influences our system has not sufficiently stressed this valid objective. Certainly at this time in our history we are becoming increasingly aware that intellectual and material achievements in themselves are insufficient unless they are directed in the service of mankind in accordance with the highest principles.

There is, I hope and believe, a mutual recognition of the potential for further improvement in our present system, as there is scope for innovation and change. There is, as well, a profound willingness on the government's behalf, to maintain a spirit of goodwill and understanding, regardless of the differences that are obviously profound. We recognize that the ultimate concern of each and all of us is that the youth of Ontario must, in all events, continue to enjoy the benefits of an educational system as excellent as human resourcefulness can provide.

APPENDIX 4:

ELECTION CALL (1971)

Statement by the Honourable William Davis, Prime Minister of Ontario, Announcing the Dissolution of the 28th Parliament of the Province of Ontario, Parliament Buildings, Queen's Park, Toronto, Monday, September 13, 1971

As all of you know, the power of dissolution is one of the very few personal prerogatives enjoyed uniquely and exclusively by the head of government in our parliamentary system. I have, for the first time, exercised that personal prerogative today. I have asked His Honour, the Lieutenant Governor, to dissolve the Legislature and writs will be issued for a provincial general election to be held on Thursday, October 21.

On becoming Prime Minister of Ontario on the first of March, I was aware, as you would be, of the fact that I was holding office without any personal public mandate. It is natural, in such circumstances, that a head of government would be anxious to confirm his leadership at some early date.

Nevertheless, on taking office, I believed it essential to make a number of decisions of pressing public interest and concern. Some of these represented new directions in government policies, some confirmed existing ones, while others provided changes and alterations. New legislation was provided in response to the urgent requirement for government action in a number of policy areas.

Since March 1, the record will show that more than 150 individual items of legislation have been passed or initiated and, as was indicated at our conference this morning, there is always more to be done.

Furthermore, it seemed only reasonable that I would want to give the people of Ontario an opportunity to make some judgment of their new Prime Minister, as to the kind of leadership he would provide them in that office. I hope the past six months have been sufficient in that regard and, of course, I would hope their impression would be favourable.

Now I believe it appropriate, and in the general interest of all concerned, that I seek a mandate of my own.

We are, as all of us recognize, undergoing a difficult period in Canada's history. National problems not of our making, and external decisions not of our choosing, all combine to present difficulties and challenges to our provincial economy. Despite our wealth of talent and resources, Ontario is not immune to conditions elsewhere.

This is, I believe, a time when the quality and calibre of government are of vital importance to every citizen in Ontario. It is especially a time when the people of Ontario require leadership in the management of their affairs in which they feel they can have confidence, as it is also a time when the leader of this province needs to feel that he has the confidence of the people of Ontario.

In my belief, it will be to the advantage of good government, sound and progressive administration, and effective, decisive leadership if the election on October 21 results in a clear and decisive mandate.

As proud as I am of past achievements, I am confident of our capacity to accomplish even more in the years ahead. No province in Canada could provide its people with greater opportunities for productive and rewarding lives. It will be the task of future leadership and government to maintain the momentum of our history. It is in our interest, and in Canada's interest, that Ontario continue to be an example of the achievements of a free and enterprising people, proud of their heritage, sensitive in their concern for social justice, prudent in the care and control of their resources, devoted to the strength and vitality of our Confederation, steadfast in their faith in their institutions, and confident of their future.

During the past six months, my colleagues and I have sought to provide Ontario with a government responsive to the public interest, willing to listen, and able to act. We have been, and we intend to be, a government of decision. If the people of Ontario wish us to proceed, that decision is now theirs to make.

APPENDIX 5:

CONSTITUTIONAL CONFERENCE (1981)

Closing Speech to the 1981 First Ministers' Conference on Constitutional Renewal

Mr. Prime Minister and fellow Premiers: to say this is something of an emotional moment for all of us, certainly for myself, is something of an understatement. I think it is fair to state, Mr. Prime Minister, that there were some around this table, myself included, who wondered on Monday morning if this, in fact, would ever happen. I don't want to get emotional but I was talking to some of the media when I came in and — as is their custom and as is their responsibility — they started to sort of ask about winners and losers. I would only make this observation, Mr. Prime Minister, that from my standpoint, there's only one winner on this occasion, and that's our country. The compromise, the agreement that has been signed, I think indicates clearly that we can as Canadian political leaders show that flexibility, that ingenuity, on occasion, that stubbornness, that brings about a document that has eluded us for a lot of years.

I guess, Mr. Prime Minister, that there will be those in the academic world and the legal community and the critics who will analyze this agreement. They will note its shortcomings, its deficiencies, and that I'm prepared to accept. I guess all of us try to achieve perfection — I never have. I'm sure the rest of you may have, but I've never been able to do it. But I say to you, sir, that while this does not represent perfection — it doesn't represent exactly everything that our own province or that I would have liked to have achieved it does represent something that — not only in terms of this symbolism, in terms of what is actually going to be written — it represents a feeling amongst the people around this table that there is something to this nation, there is something to being a Canadian, this is fundamental to the future well-being of this country.

Mr. Prime Minister, I'm a partisan politician, and I suspect that tomorrow morning I will find some reason, sir, to remind you of other issues. I may even be so provocative as to challenge your Minister of Finance. But I have to say to you, sir, as chairman of this meeting and Prime Minister of this country, that you have in the past three days demonstrated a measure of flexibility which some of your critics might not have expected, a willingness to compromise where some said it could not be done. And, Mr. Prime Minister, as I say, tomorrow is another day, there will be other issues, but I could not in conscience say to the people of this country anything other than while we have argued with you, while sometimes we disagree with you, that, in fact, sir, you have demonstrated what is essential in this country: the ability to compromise and to accept the diversity and the views of so many others.

I look around this table, Mr. Prime Minister, and I see men who had the same passionate feelings about this country. We may not express them as well as Premier Hatfield and some others, but we have those feelings. I think of how far some of them have come, Mr. Prime Minister, in the past three days. I'm thinking of the Premier of Alberta. He may not want to acknowledge it but he has moved — a little bit. He has moved a little bit. I look at the Premier of Newfoundland and, you know, it's interesting. A lot will be written about this conference but — I mentioned it in the closed session when the public wasn't there and where the media weren't there to portray all of this — the consensus that has now appeared was presented by the Premier of the province that last entered Confederation. I think that has some interesting historical perspectives.

— William G. Davis, Premier of Ontario, November 5, 1981

APPENDIX 6:

FULL FUNDING FOR SEPARATE SCHOOLS
(1984)

Statement by Premier William G. Davis Regarding Roman Catholic Secondary Schools, June 12, 1984

Honourable Mr. Davis: Mr. Speaker, I wish to inform members of the Legislature that the government has undertaken a careful and fresh review of the outstanding issues surrounding public support for the Roman Catholic school system, and this afternoon I wish to outline a new course we have decided to pursue.

As colleagues on both sides of the Legislature will appreciate, this has been a subject of long and heartfelt controversy in the development of our province, ever since we assumed the burdens and choices that go with responsible government in 1842.

In an open and dynamic society such as ours, basic issues are not resolved or sincere differences settled in silence. However, we have managed to grow together because we have respected each other and from time to time we have reconciled long-standing differences and then moved forward. Progress is made not by opening old wounds but by healing old grievances. In that spirit, I believe we have an opportunity now to put one of these difficult issues behind us as we seek to continue the progressive and harmonious development of our province.

The architects of Confederation, John A. Macdonald and George Brown, were Protestants who preferred the development of a nonsectarian educational system. However, in order to secure their national vision, they accepted and advocated the protection of denominational "common" schools in the British North America Act.

All Ontario provincial governments since that time have interpreted the "common" schools of that day as the elementary Roman Catholic and public education systems have been maintained and equitably funded across this province.

Historically, it has been possible for elementary schools to continue through to the 10th grade and, in recent years, many Roman Catholic school boards have organized their programs with public support to enrol pupils at the Grades 9 and 10 level. In keeping with the understood interpretation of the Canadian Constitution, secondary Roman Catholic schools have not been provided public funds beyond Grade 10. Roman Catholic families have seen and continue to see such a limitation on public funds beyond this level as arbitrary and inequitable.

In considering at this time whether the government of Ontario should extend financial support to secondary Roman Catholic schools, as has been requested by the Roman Catholic community for over half a century, we have been guided in our deliberations by three fundamental principles, all of which must be respected in the resolution of this matter.

First, we must not only respond to the claims of the moment, but we must also work to honour those contracts and obligations that were struck to create a united Canada in 1867. Second, we must not undertake a course of action that by its nature or in its execution would cripple or limit the viability of our non-denominational public secondary school system, which is accessible to all and universally supported and which will always remain the cornerstone of our education system. Third, we are not mere hostages to old arrangements, so we have a contemporary responsibility to be sure our answer on this question strengthens rather than fragments the social fabric of this province.

While men and women of courage and conviction have been divided on this issue, up to now no Ontario government has felt it was able to discharge its duty according to these fundamental principles while at the same time granting public funds to a complete Roman Catholic secondary school system. I now believe this can be responsibly undertaken and therefore, it is our obligation to resolve the issue.

The new direction is not compelled by or founded upon a reinterpretation of old statutes or jurisprudence. The letter of the old law cannot substitute for common sense. Further, we must all appreciate that historic benefits must keep pace with changing conditions. Roman Catholic families do not object to paying their share of the cost of an extensive universal nondenominational educational system, however, they cannot at the same time accept a logic that argues their taxes should be up to date but their historic benefits should be locked in.

Since the beginning of our parliamentary democracy, freedom and therefore diversity and pluralism have been fundamental values. Our public school system has always been fundamentally important and our commitment in this regard must not be diminished. The strength of Ontario's educational heritage rests in the general merit and the value of a universally accessible, publicly supported school system. Experience has now taught us, however, that a limitation on public funding which confines it to the public secondary school system is no longer required to sustain the viability of public education in our province.

Implementing a dual secondary system will necessitate wise administration, which I will address in a moment. Yet I am confident our secondary system, in which we can all take considerable pride, will not be jeopardized. For some time, a third of the students in our dual elementary school system have been enrolled in our Roman Catholic schools. Through the administration of core curriculum and proper funding, our public elementary school system certainly has remained viable and, indeed, second to none.

With more stable enrolments at this time, along with appropriate funding, core curriculum changes and soon province-wide testing, there is no reason to believe our public secondary school system will perform any less effectively in the future.

Members should be aware of the fact that to protect our public education system, while assuming some costs which are now carried privately by Roman Catholic families, will require additional public funding. While some of this can be accomplished through appropriate redistribution, our ultimate objective will remain one of providing high-quality education at the lowest possible cost to the taxpayers.

In practical terms I do not believe we could or should create a separate public system or a small segment of our community that wishes to isolate itself, but we are addressing today the aspirations of a good third of our families, who have demonstrated their competence and determination to provide contemporary education for their children.

Above all, I wish to address a concern I have always held and which has been honourably put forward by many others. In all our endeavours we must seek to build fellowship and common values, not segregation and mutual suspicion, but dualism today surely does not mean upholding advancing or legitimizing the ancient idea of a separate Protestant Ontario and a separate Roman Catholic Ontario.

Clearly, our Roman Catholic citizens want to maintain their own school system for their children, but our community is not, as tragically some other parts of the world still are, divided on religious grounds. Roman Catholics, regardless of their educational backgrounds, work equally within our society and are every bit as ambitious to share fully in the life and progress of Ontario.

If we are to serve the spirit and the realities of 1867, we should acknowledge that basic education was what was recognized then and that today basic education requires a secondary, as well as an elementary, education. As the nondenominational system has evolved to meet society's needs, so too has the Roman Catholic school system.

The extension of financing to separate school Grades 9 and 10 demonstrates that financial and operational arrangements can evolve over time and honour the intentions of the original constitution. If we work co-operatively and prudently, we can complete this task without compromising the quality of our public schools, while demonstrating the essential justice and good faith of our society.

It is, therefore, the government's intention to permit the Roman Catholic school boards to establish a full range of elementary and secondary education and, as a part of the public system, to be funded accordingly. This new program will be introduced at the rate of one year of secondary education for each school year, beginning September 1, 1985. This process will be accomplished in much the same way we are implementing the new special education provisions and will parallel the revised secondary school structure. Some flexibility will be included to allow for a phase-in period that is in keeping with the capacity of the individual board in question.

Our first step will be to set up a planning and implementation commission to guide and advise all parties on the implementation of this change. It will receive and adjudicate the plans submitted by the Roman Catholic school boards. It will advise the government on required changes in the Education Act and, most important, it will conduct arbitrations that may well be required in some instances arising out of the sharing or the transfer of schools and school locations, as well as other matters related to the transition.

This commission will be vital to the effective execution of this program and will be made up of representatives of the Ministry of Education, the educational community at large and the Roman Catholic community.

It is not the expectation of the government, and I trust the separate school systems across Ontario will recognize this clearly, to expend large sums on new capital grants to accommodate demands for new secondary school facilities. Rather, the commission will ensure that our abundant existing capital stock is effectively employed to provide a full range of programs. I underline this point because I think it is very important. As my predecessor, John Robarts, indicated, a duplication of facilities caused by such a policy would be impractical and indefensible. The first planning task is to make maximum use of existing school plants.

Equally, we must consider the interests of our secondary school teachers. It has been a long-established practice for elementary Roman Catholic school boards to have Roman Catholics constitute the large majority of the teachers they employ. In the light of declining enrolments in our secondary system, it would be unacceptable and unfair to extend this practice to the new Roman Catholic secondary school system. Consequently, for a period of 10 years, Roman Catholic school boards will employ non-Catholic teachers in their secondary schools who, once hired, will be permitted to earn tenure — the proper words would be "seniority" — religion notwithstanding.

The planning and implementation commission will work with the Ontario Teachers' Federation, the Education Relations Commission and others to assure that all teacher personnel matters are addressed in an equitable fashion. Further, while the essence of this new policy is to enrich the education resources available to Roman Catholic families in Ontario, it is my hope the new Roman Catholic school boards will consider granting to all students and their families in the most positive way universal access to publicly supported Roman Catholic schools, should such access be desired, limited only by the availability of space and the designation of assessment support.

I should also like to take this opportunity to state that it is still the wish of the government, pending the response to questions now before the courts, to create within certain boards of education panels of trustees elected by Franco-Ontarian electors who will have defined powers governing classes in schools where French is the language of instruction.

While my hope today is to resolve a historic issue in our traditional public education structure, what we have decided to do legitimately raises questions about the place of independent schools in our province. While rights are not at issue, the diversity and quality of our society are affected and served by these schools. The government believes it is timely and useful to review the role of these schools in educating our children. Thus, a commission of inquiry will be established by the Ministry of Education, first, to document and comment on the role of independent schools; second, to assess whether public funding and its attendant obligations would be desirable and could be compatible with the nature of their independence; and, third, to identify possible alternative forms of governance for these schools and make recommendations for changes deemed to be appropriate.

Finally, I would like to take this opportunity to address briefly our responsibility in funding education generally. The current formula for calculating general legislative grants has been in place since 1969. There is also the public concern about the costs of education and the ability of our school boards to contain such costs.

Given these considerations, along with the statement of policy I referred to at the beginning of my statement, the government intends to set up a commission to inquire into the financing of elementary and secondary education in Ontario. This examination is appropriate in order to ensure efficiency, economy, effectiveness and equity. It is also timely as the province moves to extend support for the Roman Catholic school system.

Both the commission on independent schools and the commission on the financing of elementary and secondary education will report in May 1985, and responses to their recommendations will be concluded by January 1986.

Before I close, may I return for a moment to the basic decision upon which we seek the understanding and acceptance of the community at large — the extension of public funding for our Roman Catholic secondary school system. Of course, there will be difficulties and, clearly, as with all changes in the order of things, some advantages that may seen to be found in the status quo will be given up in securing new benefits. I am convinced, however, that our secure and vibrant school system is not threatened and the majority of our citizens who support our nonsectarian school system will not be hurt.

As Sir John A. Macdonald explained the accommodations of his time to the majority over a century ago: "We do not want to stand on the extreme limits of our rights. We are ready to give and take. We can afford to be just, we can afford to be generous, because we are strong."

It is neither my hope nor my expectation to settle all differences today. No one enjoys the last word in any democracy. However, as has been the case in nation building and constitutional reform, it is my strong conviction that the path we have chosen is worthy of broad agreement and will serve our common interests.

It is time to put behind us any lingering doubts about our regard for one another and to rededicate ourselves to the bright hopes of our future.

[Mr. Bob Rae, leader of the New Democratic Party, stands on a point of order.]

Mr. Rae: Mr. Speaker, on a point of order: In the light of the historic statement the Premier has just made, I wonder if it would be appropriate for the leaders of other parties to be allowed to respond to a statement I think is one that does a great deal to unite this province. It is certainly one I would like to respond to on behalf of my party.

Mr. Speaker: I ask the direction of the House.

Honourable Mr. Davis: Mr. Speaker, can I suggest because I go back in history a little, that there have been three occasions in my time as a member of the House when statements were made by the then Premier, at which time the leaders of the opposition parties made some observations. I appreciate the suggestion from the member for York South [Bob Rae].

I recall it at the time Mr. [Leslie] Frost made certain observations and I recall it at the introduction of the foundation tax plan when [Liberal leader]

Mr. [John] Wintermeyer — I think I am correct in this and the member for Brant-Oxford-Norfolk [Mr. Robert Nixon] can correct me — and the then leader of the New Democratic Party, made certain observations. On an issue of this nature, I would have no objection to accepting that as precedent.

[Mr. David Peterson, leader of the official opposition, responds for the Liberal Party of Ontario.]

Mr. Peterson: Mr. Speaker, this is indeed a historic day and I think all members of this Legislature recognize it as such.

When the Premier's assistant phoned my office at roughly one minute to two this afternoon to say there would be a major announcement, knowing the Premier as we do I must confess we thought it would be about the dome and not about so significant an issue in the history of this province.

We unreservedly support this statement. I am sure the Premier is aware of that. With the Premier's strong sense of history, which he revealed today in his statement, and his acute memory for what has transpired in this province, I am sure he would be the first to stand with me in applauding the member for Brant-Oxford-Norfolk for the strong stand he took on this issue when he was leader of the Liberal Party.

It is no secret that in the history of this province many people have given blood — some real and some symbolic — over this issue. On behalf of my party, I am proud today to identify myself and my colleagues with the statement of the Premier on this major advance in position. I am not one of those who is going to ask why. I am only going to say "hurrah." It is long overdue. It has been too divisive an issue for too many years in the past.

I take this occasion to celebrate the Road-to-Damascus conversion of the government on this issue. We are committed to trying to work with the government in any way we can to bring forward a successful, speedy and easy facilitation of these policies. We will work through a select committee, if that is one of the ways chosen. We will use our good offices to make sure these historical injustices are rectified as quickly and expeditiously as possible.

[Mr. Bob Rae, leader of the New Democratic Party, responds for the NDP.]

Mr. Rae: Mr. Speaker, few issues in our public life are as difficult or as divisive as issues surrounding religion and language. It is a curiosity to me that this is true. Ever since I went into politics, I have been surprised by it struck by it, and sometimes appalled by it. Anything any government can do to bring the people of this province together on an issue that has proved to be as difficult and as divisive as this particular one is a tremendous contribution to decency and to our sense of civility as a province.

I would be wrong not to be generous today to the Premier, as he has, I think been generous to the people of this province in making this policy clear today. It would also be wrong if I did not pay tribute to the courage of many members of my own party who made this case and, indeed, made several parts of the Premier's speech before it became popular or before it became easier to do so. I pay tribute to some members of my own party who, at considerable personal cost, have participated in various election campaigns on this particular issue.

I say this not in a spirit of partisanship but simply in the sense that sometimes those who are prepared to say things 10 or 20 years in advance do pay a certain price. I think it would be wrong for us not to pay tribute to members in all parties who have taken the position that it was time — I believe some time ago, but certainly today — to recognize that we have fundamentally two public systems at work in the province, that they have to be funded fairly and equally and that we have to recognize the claim of a very substantial minority to genuine equality in educational funding.

It is going to take a great deal of goodwill, it is going to take a great deal of give and take and it is going to take a great deal of understanding to make this policy work.

When I raised this matter with the Premier in his estimates six months ago, I was hoping for an answer. I am very pleased with the answer we have received. I did not receive one at the time I asked for it. I am delighted to have received it today.

We will be coming back with some questions about implementation, some questions about how the policy can be made to work and some questions about overcrowding still in the elementary system; there are a number of problems that are still outstanding. But I want to say the Premier has made a very important contribution to a sense of fairness in this province by making this statement today. We congratulate him for it. We look forward to working with his government in seeing that it can work on a nonpartisan basis. All of us in this House have an obligation to make it work. The Premier has my personal commitment and the commitment of our party that we will make it work.

The time was right. We are delighted the move has been made. Equality has made an important advance in Ontario today.

APPENDIX 7:

RETIREMENT PRESS CONFERENCE (1984)

William Grenville Davis (WGD): For those of you who don't know, I, uh, I have invited my wife, Kathy, and our eldest son, Neil, to join us today. Kathy declined to sit up here with me, as is her custom.

I have written today to the President of the Ontario Progressive Conservative Association, Mr. David McFadden, and I informed him of my decision, a very difficult decision, to step down as leader of our party, effective the next leadership convention, which I have asked Mr. McFadden to arrange for the earliest appropriate date, hopefully in January of 1985.

By that time, I will have had the privilege of serving as premier of this province for almost 14 years and as a member of the legislature for, initially, the great riding of Peel, now the City of Brampton, for nearly 26 years.

For the opportunities that all of those years have provided to me, I am deeply grateful to the people of my constituency, and to all of the people of our province. The enduring support which they have extended both to me and to the party under my leadership is something for which I will always be thankful. There's no more honoured or significant way to spend the better part of one's life than in the service of one's fellow citizens. And I feel deeply honoured to have had the opportunity to serve this province and its people. I have learned from them over these past 25 years. I've learned about decency, I've learned about tolerance and understanding. The people of our province are capable of tremendous progress and goodwill as they have repeatedly demonstrated during the past quarter century. In almost every area of life in this province, the past 14 years has seen change, it's seen progress, and a quality of life in terms of opportunity. We have welcomed hundreds of thousands of citizens from beyond the borders of our province, people who have chosen, of their own free will, to make Ontario their home. They have contributed so much to our province's well-being.

We are now, Mr. President of the gallery, the home for almost nine million people, and I think in anybody's assessment, we are a splendid home as well. Economically, we have faced some very difficult challenges, particularly in the last couple of years but, the resilience of the recovery, the new investments taking place in the auto sector, in high technology, aeronautics, and other industries, will over the long term bring further health and prosperity to our way of life.

I would like to believe that humane and competent government has created a significant role in creating the framework in which individual Ontarians have been able to achieve progress for themselves and for their communities. And I believe in order for that to continue, it is time for new leadership for the Progressive Conservative Party, together with the new ideas and new perspectives that such a change will bring.

Fortunately, as a party, as an organization, it has never been stronger. As a result, many people have urged me, you're all aware of this, to seek another mandate at this moment, confident that we would receive strong endorsement from the people. I have been deeply touched by the expressions of confidence and loyalty which have caused me to reflect, somewhat longer than I had expected, on my decision. But having decided to leave political life, it would be less than honourable and certainly less than honest for me to seek a mandate unless I was personally committed to serving a full term.

For Kathleen and me, we now look forward to more time together. I'm not sure that a couple of months from now she will be quite as enthused! More time for our children and as you will see in the text, grandchildren is not quite right yet, it is only a grandchild but, it will be grandchildren in roughly another month and a half.

Perhaps it will give me an opportunity to pursue another career. I've always thought I might like journalism as a profession. Twenty-six years is a long time for any one assignment in anyone's life. And if that's true for me, it's certainly more than true for Kathleen who has soldiered through the many sacrifices with a devotion and a sense of commitment which has made her as much a servant of the people of this province and to the party, as really anyone holding elected office.

As for the future, in case any of you ask, for that matter, in case any of you are that interested, I have not engaged in any serious thought as to what I might do but, I do intend after a period of some reflection, to become actively involved in some pursuit which will be both challenging and demanding.

It is my intention to continue to represent the people and the constituency of Brampton until the next general election and to offer every possible assistance and counsel to my successor, when he or she is chosen by the membership of the party at a convention in the next few months.

As I looked around the cabinet table last Wednesday and again, just a few moments ago, as I look across our caucus and the broad membership of our party, I see a great wealth of ability, skill, talent, and perhaps even ambition, which must now be used to both seek and to maintain the leadership of our party and a continuing mandate from the people of our province.

It has always been my wish, as a relatively competitive person, to leave the party and the government in a strong and as a dynamic a circumstance as possible. With both the party in my view, and the government in, I believe, good standing with the public, with the great strength of our organization and with the support and co-operation we can expect to receive from the new Progressive Conservative government in Ottawa, I believe our party is extremely strong.

It would've been easy to simply continue with that kind of strength behind us but, I believe in the long run, it is more responsible for me to pass on the leadership of what I believe to be a popular and dynamic party to my successor, who will then have ample time to offer new leadership and eventually choose a new election date sometime before the spring of '86.

I will leave politics with few regrets. Throughout my career I have remained constantly and sincerely committed to achieving national reconciliation. And that goal was realized, in part at least, at the time of the signing of the Constitutional Accord. We have always done our very best to demonstrate good faith and a firm commitment to minority language rights. The spirit which lay at the foundation of our actions was one through which we sought to achieve balance and opportunity for all Ontarians of both language groups in this province.

While there will always be times when passions and partisan excess produce words and circumstances that are regrettable, I have always tried to treat opponents, I'm sure not always with success, as well as my friends, with respect and a sense of fairness. Certainly, I feel that I in turn have been treated that way by the vast majority of those with whom I've been associated in public life, including members of your own profession.

This is not the end of an era in Ontario politics, because eras are never shaped by any single human being. This will be the beginning of a new approach, new personalities and perhaps some new directions. But there always is, in any democratic society, the importance of continuity. The problem solved by one administration, produce opportunities for the next. And the opportunities missed by one administration, provide the challenges for its successors. It is because my confidence in the capacity of the Ontario Progressive Conservative Party to meet those challenges and opportunities and to do so in a humane and competent fashion, that I feel confident in passing on the leadership of this dynamic and humane party.

[Bill Davis's prepared remarks end here. What follows are the premier's extemporaneous comments.]

I also want to, because I don't get this opportunity too often, to digress a moment and express a personal word of support and thanks not just to my cabinet and caucus colleagues but members of the party across this province. People who are not members of any political party, who have been so kind and so supportive and also to, and this is always hazardous, thank a few individuals in particular.

I have already mentioned Kathleen, as well as the members of my family. Neil, who's here today, is what, 28? His first entrance into political life, it was the greatest campaign picture of the 1959 campaign. He probably doesn't even remember it. He was fishing up at the Albion Hills Conservation Area with his father. Widely distributed in the local press. I thought the three-year-old was probably getting more support in that constituency than was his father. And Neil has, uh, I don't say he's unique, but he has been in every political campaign that I've been in.

There is a person here who I sometimes facetiously, but not always facetiously, say runs the Government of Ontario. Miss [Helen] Anderson, who has been with me since October of 1962. Clare Westcott, who sometimes has his own view of things, who has been invaluable for the same length of time, who never really wanted his boss to get too far ahead of him, and who has subtly already said he was retiring before I said I was!

And, of course, Dr. [Ed] Stewart, my deputy, and Mr. [John] Tory, Mr. [Michael] Danaher, Laird [Saunderson], and Hughie Segal who was with the office for a number of years. There are just so many, but I cannot in any way include all of those who have been so helpful, but I could not lose this opportunity as well to mention a number of those who have been so supportive and so important to me. I don't know what Mr. Tory is going to do because he is a great young man with a tremendous future, who is a bit of a partisan, but, John, uh —

[Premier Davis is emotionally overcome, and after several seconds of silence, observers in the media studio begin to applaud.]

I also am going to exercise a prerogative that never existed for any premier of this province: I intend to play for the premier's office, next June, when we meet in that annual event, whether I'm invited or not.

[The above is a reference to the annual baseball game between MPPs and the Queen's Park Press Gallery. Premier Davis now begins taking questions, most of which are inaudible on the recording. Paul Rhodes asks the first question about what Premier Davis considers his single most important accomplishment.]

WGD: Paul, it's very difficult. I, uh, I'm sure that when historians write of this period of history, to the extent that 13 years will find its way into the history books of Canada, I just hope that some author gives it more than two paragraphs. I don't know what single accomplishment. I'm sure that some historians will look at the constitutional discussions and probably in terms of a single item that would stand out in the minds of some people, and perhaps myself. I guess I look back at the last 13-plus years in a different way. Not what single event, what single, in quotes, "accomplishment," or what have you. I look on it as a 13-year period where with a group of men and women in cabinet and caucus that we made a conscientious effort to give leadership and direction to the people of this province, and I'm not trying to make life difficult for anyone, but I try to look at it as 13 years of good government, not without the odd mistake, which you won't get me to acknowledge here today, but sure, there were some. And I know that under our system where people focus on the premier or the leader of a party, we're all caught up in this sort of presidential leadership-style of politics, and I can't change that, but I like to think that as a government we've done a lot of things. A lot of things right, a lot of things good, and I share all of those with my colleagues, because we were all a part of it.

[Bruce Stewart from the *Hamilton Spectator* asks when Premier Davis actually made the decision to retire.]

WGD: Bruce, ah, that's a very difficult question to answer. It might've been two weeks ago, could've been last May or June, but I think that most people would understand that to have a provincial Conservative leadership convention going on the same time as a national leadership convention for the Liberal Party, might have sort of fragmented people's ... I'm teasing a little bit. I was very anxious to play a role in the federal campaign. That to me was important both for the country

I believed in what I was doing, and I believed it for the party. Why now? I wish you had been with all of us yesterday at Thanksgiving dinner, because there is no good time. I don't think there is any right time. I'm leaving when there's some things I'd still like to see done. If I were to stay another three years, it would not be any easier, the decision would not be any less difficult. Apart from my family and my known affection for the Toronto Argonauts, public life has been my life for 25 years. And I guess when you are sort of caught up in that, you really don't have an answer as to "why now?" Why not three years from now or why not three years ago?

[Bruce Stewart follows up with an inaudible question.]

WGD: Bruce, none in this room. There are some, a few cynics out there. I've never said this to, uh, anyone publicly, but my late father, probably more than anyone else, encouraged me to get into public life. Father was a past chairman of the hospital board, a past chairman of the district high school board, past chairman of the public school board, recording steward at Grace United Church, member of the Lions Club, member of the Rotary Club, and one who, for 30 years, was in public life in his own way as Crown attorney for our county and probably, if he'd had his health — we're all prejudiced about our fathers — would've been perhaps a member of either the House here, or the House of Commons. My mother was very much the same way. And they impressed upon me the obligation, as they saw it, not obligation, that's not the right way of describing it, the opportunity, I guess, that we should all seek, if we feel we have something to contribute, to serve in some respects in the public domain. I can't tell you, Bruce, what six months from now I might do, bu I guess public service has been my life. I've been committed to it, but I guess I'll go back to a phrase which was true then and is even more true now — I haven't made any plans to make any plans, to create any plans. I, uh, I don't know.

[Claire Hoy of the *Toronto Sun* asks Premier Davis to be more specific in answering when, specifically, he actually made the decision to resign.]

WGD: Kathy just said: "We'll have another press conference tomorrow to discuss that." Claire, how do I answer that? When did I actually decide? When did I start thinking about it? Listen, I'm influenced tremendously by what journalists write and you've been predicting now for several months. And I certainly now, with your move to the major leagues, I didn't want to prove you wrong. No, Claire, I guess that I was in the process of coming to this decision 10 days, two weeks, who knows? Perhaps the night of the federal election [**September 4, 1984**]. I've been thinking about it for some period of time. I said quietly to myself, and not so quietly to a few others after the March election of '81, that I felt then that that was the last provincial election I probably would run. As to the exact date, I guess for those who want to write a chronicle of this, I was very moved last Wednesday at cabinet. I thought further about what I wanted to do. I wouldn't hide from you that that was the route I wanted to go last Wednesday, but I, um, have a very great sense of loyalty to those men and women in cabinet and in caucus who wished me to continue. The decision I guess, for historical purposes, really was finally made yesterday when we had all the family there.

[**Claire Hoy asks a follow-up question, whether Premier Davis's family agreed with his decision.**]

WGD: No, that was at the cottage. Well, I think, Claire, that anybody in public life cannot expect a great deal of privacy. That goes with the territory. I can only tell you that my family has always supported what I've decided to do and I hope you will understand if I don't tell you in great detail what when on yesterday.

[**Someone asks whether Premier Davis's resignation may negatively affect plans to build a domed stadium in Toronto.**]

WGD: Well, if Kathy will not ever forgive me because some two years ago I mentioned in my view, Southern Ontario should have a multi-purpose cultural facility and that matter will still be left up in the air. But Kathleen reminded me that cultural facilities also included an opera house and I had been persuaded by Kathleen that that is something that should not be set aside. Alan, I can't answer that. I'm sure tonight at midnight or whenever, I'll say to myself, "Gosh, I won't be around when A, B, C, and D may take place." Joanie will still be around and she'll tell you she's been great.

[**Someone asks when Premier Davis told his cabinet and caucus of his plans.**]

WGD: Well, I told the members of my staff somewhat late yesterday afternoon to call for a cabinet meeting this afternoon.

[**Lorrie Goldstein of the *Toronto Sun* asks if Premier Davis will miss the media.**]

WGD: What's it going to be like being a columnist, Lorrie? A new career, I mean, there are two of us here! You won't believe this, but one of the things that I will miss around this place are not press conferences per se but those quiet, genteel discussions as we go in and out of … yes, Lorrie, I'm sorry.

[Someone asks if Premier Davis intends to support any of the candidates seeking to succeed him.]

WGD: No, it will be a total neutrality. I will not take, or at least I will not be obviously supporting any candidate. I just feel fortunate that there are a number of able men and women who have that capacity and I … listen, they're all friends and colleagues. I, I shan't be. And I would never presume to speak for Kathy, but I hope she doesn't either, but I can't guarantee this! Neil, I'm almost … yes.

WGD: Oh, that is outside my area of responsibility, Lorrie. I don't know.

[Colin Vaughan from Citytv asks about funding for the proposed domed stadium.]

WGD: Colin, I can't answer that. I mean, the public knows my views. No tax money. **[Funding from]** lottery funds, private sector, Government of Canada, Metropolitan Toronto. That this is something that I think over a period of time is going to happen. Whether it will come to me before I start checking on the local lacrosse teams and softball teams in Brampton, hockey teams, I honestly don't know.

WGD: Well, this will come as a great surprise to you, but Kathy and I haven't decided yet. Although I should tell you that … listen, my weaknesses are known! And Kathy sometimes shares in my weaknesses and don't misunderstand that, but her favourite NFL team is on television tonight — the 49ers are playing!

[Someone asks Premier Davis if he'd accept a seat in the Senate from newly elected Prime Minister Brian Mulroney.]

WGD: Robert, listen, I am always prepared to consider anything that could be helpful, but I think if you asked yourself whether after being premier for 13 years, trying to be pleasant most days, et cetera, et cetera, would you?

[Someone yells] What do you say? What do you mean? **[Much laughter follows.]**

WGD: I mean, if I want a change, it's not what I would consider a change.

WGD: Listen, I feel just a little relaxed now, not totally. This has not been the easiest day for me. So I'm going to offer you some advice. I think it's always unwise for journalists to try and relate one set of events with another set of events, because history will record that, those sets of events, while they may have certain similarities, in fact, produce totally opposite results. You understand what I'm saying? No? Well, things haven't changed!

[Orland French asks if Ontarians can expect, in the dying days of the Davis administration, another blockbuster decision such as full funding for separate schools.]

WGD: I don't expect another announcement like the separate school one, Orland, no. Listen, the government will continue to function. I caution my cabinet colleagues, a number of whom are here, that because I was retiring, they should not forget who's boss until that actually occurs, because there's nothing to preclude me from shuffling the cabinet. I'll disclose this to you: I invited two people into cabinet today who'd never been there before — Kathleen and Neil, and I said, "We're gonna have a shuffle," and some of them almost believed it for a minute! No, they didn't really. But, Orland, I can't tell you whether there'll be anything the equivalent of the separate school decision. I don't foresee something of that nature on the horizon, but the government will continue to function.

WGD: No, I will be there until **[inaudible]**. I may take a few days off for you know ...

[Someone asks if the government will be able to implement the full funding for Catholic schools decision without Premier Davis there, given the controversy about the policy still "swirling."]

WGD: Well, I'm not sure that the fallout is swirling. I keep pretty close eye on these things and it's a very significant policy change and the policy is there. And while I know it's easy to go to a trustee there or a teacher here, you can always find somebody who will create some degree of swirling. Is that what you said? Swirling about? With great respect, I know the educational community in this province. I know that on issues of this nature, there is never total unanimity. But they're also pretty dedicated people and I am completely confident that the goodwill, the understanding, the sensitivity, will, in fact, be there. It's not all going to happen. I could stay for another three years and you will still have some measures of differences because that's the nature. But I am very confident that that change will be effective, and it will be done with a minimum amount of difficulty, in spite of the fact that you will find somebody tomorrow morning, six months from now, five years from now who might offer some controversial comment, too.

[Someone asks if Premier Davis has any regrets about not making Ontario officially bilingual.]

WGD: There will be some journalists who will write about this, I expect. I guess as I have watched things in this province and in Canada, there will be some who will say this is something this premier might've done. It was an issue and is an issue of sensitivity, but I genuinely believe that there is a growing awareness and understanding in other parts of Canada, particularly in our sister province of Quebec, of the facts of what we have accomplished. And I think that the route that we have taken as a government, the pattern established some years ago, has been effective, it has worked, it has been accepted, and I think there's a growing awareness and understanding of this fact. I am comfortable with my own conscience in terms of that issue.

[Orland French asks, with Premier Davis resigning, if his beloved hometown of Brampton will now slip into obscurity.]

WGD: Brampton will never slip into obscurity! How do you like that for an unequivocal answer? Orland, you never had that kind of luck?

WGD: The executive, not the president of the association is, and will be, conveying this to the members of the executive.

[Someone asks if Premier Davis has a preferred candidate in mind to run for the PC nomination in Brampton. There had been rumours his son, Neil, might run.]

WGD: I intend to be neutral in terms of my successor in Brampton unless … unless Kathleen decides to become the candidate!

[Rosemary Speirs of the *Toronto Star* asks about Premier Davis's immediate plans.]

WGD: No, I will be in the House tomorrow, Rosemary, and I am gonna be at the Premier's Dinner, to which you are all invited, Wednesday night. But I may just, well, I never disappear, but you may find me hard to reach for three or four days. Kathy and I feel like just a bit of a change, but I'll be there tomorrow.

WGD: No, I don't expect so. Dr. Stewart and I thought we might just take the government aircraft and fly to San Diego to see … [**uproarious laughter**]. And you're all invited!

[**Someone asks if Premier Davis is inadvisably leaving the PC Party, given his current irreplaceable standing with the Ontario public.**]

WGD: No. No one is irreplaceable, indispensable, et cetera. I can tell you that the party is not … I can be relatively objective, not totally, but with all this talk about possibilities of elections, people have been doing a little homework, and anyway, the party is in excellent standing in the province and what cabinet were saying to me is something I will always treasure. I've not been in any other cabinet and I guess I can't categorically say that the cabinet of this province is unique, but I don't think there are too many more like it, where I've had the same degree of loyalty and support from my colleagues than I've enjoyed. We've struggled through a lot of issues together. We've worked well together and I think what cabinet was saying to me was based on what we've accomplished together. And I, uh, listen, some of them may be a little upset, but I tell you, they're pretty tremendous people and they'll make it work.

[**Someone asks if Premier Davis intends to represent Ontario at the next first ministers' meeting.**]

WGD: I guess that will all depend on whether I'll have some good ideas for a first ministers' meeting. I can't answer that. You see, we're meeting in Ottawa, what, on the 13th is it, of November, to discuss a date, where technically, oh, I don't say technically, whether it's practically possible to have a full-fledged Premiers' Conference before Christmas is problematic, I guess. So then you're into January in any event. But certainly, I'll not seek a delay, because I don't think a delay would be a wise thing, but it may be that it will turn out that the best, or most optimum date, would be after convention, in any event. It may turn out that way.

[**Colin Vaughan of Citytv asks if Premier Davis thinks he'll actually have to hustle for a new job or whether the offers will simply fly in.**]

WGD: Colin, if I were as fortunate as you, the answer would be yes. But in that I am not, the answer is no. I will have to seek gainful employment. I say that with a modest degree of regret maybe. No, I don't! Colin, I guess you don't say no to any suggestion, but if whether I might quietly indicate I would like …

[The recording fades out at this point.]

APPENDIX 8:

BOARDS OF DIRECTORS

When Bill Davis retired from politics more than three decades ago, he became a much-desired member of many boards of directors.

Past Boards
Algoma Steel (steel manufacturer, based in Sault Ste. Marie).
BPO Properties (Brookfield Office Properties).
Canadian Football League.
CIBC (one of Canada's "Big Five" chartered banks).
Corel (Canadian software company headquartered in Ottawa).
Cosma (subsidiary of Magna International Inc., the international auto parts company).
Credit Suisse First Boston (investment banker).
Dylex (one of Canada's largest clothing retailers, defunct since 2001).
First American Corporation (financial services company).
Fleet Aerospace (Canadian aerospace subcontractor).
Ford of Canada (Canadian arm of the multinational automaker).
Hemlo (gold mine, now owned by Barrick Gold).
Honeywell (computer consumer products, aerospace systems).
ICP — International Comfort Products (manufacturer of HVAC systems and gas and oil furnaces).
Magna Entertainment (gambling and horse-racing company).

Magna International (international auto parts manufacturer).

MID Developments (a real estate investment trust).

Nike (athletic shoe apparel and sports equipment manufacturer).

O&Y — Olympia & York (international property development firm).

Power Corporation (diversified international management and Canadian holding company).

RRREIT (Retirement Residences Real Estate Investment Trust; became Revera).

Seagram (alcohol beverages company).

St. Lawrence Cement (distributes cement via trucks throughout Toronto).

Current Boards
FCT — First Canadian (title insurance company).

Home Capital Group (provides Canadians with mortgages, credit cards, and deposit services).

Magellan Aerospace (Canadian manufacturer of aerospace systems and components; formerly called Fleet Aerospace).

Non-Profit Boards
Brampton's Blue Ribbon Exploratory Panel (chair of the panel looking into securing a university in Brampton).

University of Toronto Governing Council.

Fundraising Committees
Peel Memorial Hospital.

University of Toronto.

APPENDIX 9:

LONGEST-SERVING CANADIAN PREMIERS BY TENURE

1. George Henry Murray	Nova Scotia	26 years, 6 months, 4 days
2. Ernest Manning	Alberta	25 years, 6 months, 11 days
3. Oliver Mowat	Ontario	23 years, 8 months, 17 days
4. Joey Smallwood	Newfoundland	22 years, 9 months, 17 days
5. John Bracken	Manitoba	20 years, 5 months, 6 days
6. W.A.C. Bennett	British Columbia	20 years, 1 month, 14 days
7. Maurice Duplessis	Quebec	18 years, 2 months, 30 days
8. Tommy Douglas	Saskatchewan	17 years, 3 months, 28 days
9. Richard Hatfield	New Brunswick	16 years, 11 months, 15 days
10. L.A. Taschereau	Quebec	15 years, 10 months, 3 days
11. Angus L. Macdonald	Nova Scotia	15 years, 3 months, 10 days
12. Lomer Gouin	Quebec	15 years, 3 months, 15 days
13. Robert Bourassa	Quebec	14 years, 7 months, 13 days
14. Rodmond Roblin	Manitoba	14 years, 6 months, 13 days
15. Peter Lougheed	Alberta	14 years, 1 month, 22 days
16. Ralph Klein	Alberta	14 years
17. William G. Davis	Ontario	13 years, 11 months, 7 days
18. Leslie Frost	Ontario	12 years, 6 months, 4 days
19. Alexander Campbell	Prince Edward Island	12 years, 1 month, 21 days
20. John Buchanan	Nova Scotia	11 years, 11 months, 7 days

APPENDIX 10:

ONTARIO PREMIERS BY TENURE

1. Oliver Mowat	23 years, 270 days	1872–96
2. William G. Davis	13 years, 344 days	1971–85
3. Leslie Frost	12 years, 188 days	1949–61
4. James P. Whitney	9 years, 229 days	1905–14
5. John P. Robarts	9 years, 113 days	1961–71
6. Dalton McGuinty	9 years, 111 days	2003–13
7. Mitchell Hepburn	8 years, 103 days	1934–42
8. G. Howard Ferguson	7 years, 152 days	1923–30
9. Mike Harris	6 years, 292 days	1995–2002
10. George W. Ross	5 years, 110 days	1899–1905
11. David Peterson	5 years, 97 days	1985–90
12. George Drew	5 years, 63 days	1943–48
13. William Hearst	5 years, 43 days	1914–19
14. Bob Rae	4 years, 268 days	1990–95
15. John S. Macdonald	4 years, 157 days	1867–71
16. Ernest C. Drury	3 years, 244 days	1919–23
17. Kathleen Wynne	3 years, 233 days	2013– (as of October 1, 2016)
18. George S. Henry	3 years, 207 days	1930–34
19. Arthur Hardy	3 years, 92 days	1896–99
20. Ernie Eves	1 year, 190 days	2002–03

21. Edward Blake	310 days	1871–72
22. Gordon Conant	209 days	1942–43
23. Thomas L. Kennedy	197 days	1948–49
24. Frank Miller	138 days	1985
25. Harry Nixon	91 days	1943

BIBLIOGRAPHY

All of the following books were helpful in the writing of this one.

Boyer, Patrick. *The Big Blue Machine: How Tory Campaign Backrooms Changed Canadian Politics Forever*. Toronto: Dundurn, 2015.

Clarkson, Adrienne. *Heart Matters: A Memoir*. Toronto: Penguin Canada, 2008.

Crosbie, John. *No Holds Barred: My Life in Politics*. Toronto: McClelland & Stewart, 1997.

Dixon, Robert. *William Davis and the Road to Completion in Ontario's Catholic High Schools, 1971–1985*. Toronto: Canadian Catholic Historical Association, 2003.

English, John. *Just Watch Me: The Life of Pierre Elliott Trudeau 1968–2000*. Toronto: Knopf Canada, 2009.

Freeman, Neil B. *The Politics of Power: Ontario Hydro and Its Government, 1906–1995*. Toronto: University of Toronto Press, 1996.

Gidney, R.D. *From Hope to Harris: The Reshaping of Ontario's Schools*. Toronto: University of Toronto Press, 1999.

Goodman, Eddie. *Life of the Party: The Memoirs of Eddie Goodman*. Toronto: Key Porter Books, 1988.

Gotlieb, Allan. *The Washington Diaries, 1981–1989*. Toronto: McClelland & Stewart, 2006.

Ibbitson, John. *Promised Land: Inside the Mike Harris Revolution*. Toronto: Prentice Hall, 1997.

Jackman, Hal. *The Letters and Diaries of Henry Newton Rowell Jackman, 1982–85*. Toronto: Harmony Printing Ltd., 2009.

Kolber, Leo. *Leo: A Life*. Montreal and Kingston: McGill-Queen's University Press, 2003.

MacDonald, L. Ian. *Mulroney: The Making of the Prime Minister*. Toronto: McClelland & Stewart, 1984.

Manthorpe, Jonathan. *The Power and the Tories: Ontario Politics, 1943 to the Present*. Toronto: Macmillan of Canada, 1974.

Martin, Lawrence. *Chrétien: The Will to Win, Volume 1*. Toronto: Lester Publishing, 1995.

McCallion, Hazel. *Hurricane Hazel: A Life with Purpose*. Toronto: HarperCollins Canada, 2014.

McGuinty, Dalton. *Dalton McGuinty: Making a Difference*. Toronto: Dundurn, 2015.

McMurtry, Roy. *Memoirs and Reflections*. Toronto: The Osgoode Society, 2013.

Mulroney, Brian. *Memoirs*. Toronto: McClelland & Stewart, 2007.

Rae, Bob. *From Protest to Power: Personal Reflections on a Life in Politics*. Toronto: Viking Canada, 1996.

Savage, Larry. *Socialist Cowboy: The Politics of Peter Kormos*. Winnipeg: Roseway Publishing, 2014.

Scott, Ian. *To Make a Difference: A Memoir*. Toronto: Stoddart, 2001.

Segal, Hugh. *In Defence of Civility: Reflections of a Recovering Politician*. Toronto: Stoddart, 2000.

_____. *The Long Road Back: The Conservative Journey, 1993–2006*. Toronto: HarperCollins Canada, 2006.

_____. *No Surrender: Reflections of a Happy Warrior in the Tory Crusade*. Toronto: HarperCollins Canada, 1996.

_____. *The Right Balance: Canada's Conservative Tradition*. Vancouver: Douglas & McIntyre, 2011.

Smith, Cameron. *Unfinished Journey: The Lewis Family*. Toronto: Summerhill Press, 1989.

Stevens, Geoffrey. *The Player: The Life & Times of Dalton Camp*. Toronto: Key Porter Books, 2003.

Stewart, Edward E. *Cabinet Government in Ontario: A View from Inside*. Halifax: Institute for Research on Public Policy, 1989.

Zajda, Joseph I., ed. *International Handbook on Globalisation, Education and Policy Research: Global Pedagogies and Policies*. Dordrecht, Netherlands: Springer, 2005.

DR. ROBERTO GROSSO BURSARY

Given Bill Davis's lifelong connection to education, my wife, Francesca, and I put our heads together to think about how we could use this book project to further some educational goals. We came up with what we thought was a pretty neat idea, and fortunately, many of Mr. Davis's friends and business colleagues agreed.

My late father-in-law, Dr. Roberto Grosso, was chairman of the board of Laurentian University in Sudbury. Furthermore, two of my sisters-in-law and one brother-in-law attended the university as students. Because of those connections to Laurentian, and my frequent visits to the Nickel City, the former Laurentian board chair, Floyd Laughren, and current president, Dominic Giroux, asked me to serve as the university's second chancellor. It's been a tremendous honour to hold that position since 2013.

As a result, Francesca and I started the Dr. Roberto Grosso Bursary at Laurentian in the hope of raising enough money to help fund the education for one medical student per year at the Northern Ontario School of Medicine (NOSM), which Francesca's father helped get off the ground. To our delight, many of Mr. Davis's friends and colleagues have made contributions to that bursary to honour the former premier and his commitment to education. Thanks to their generosity, Northern Ontario will have more doctors in the future, providing more care, and saving lives to an underserved part of our province. I thank Francesca for pursuing and following up with the donors listed here, to whom we are truly grateful.

CORPORATIONS

CIBC: "CIBC was honoured to have Bill Davis serve on our Board of Directors from 1985 to 1999. As a member of the Nominating Committee, he helped attract strong talent to the board to ensure progressive success for many years to come. Whether in politics, business, or academia, Ontario's history rightfully includes the outstanding contributions of Premier Davis to our province." — Victor G. Dodig, President and CEO, CIBC

Magna International Inc.: "As a former member and chairman of the Magna Board, Bill Davis made significant contributions to the Magna family. During his tenure, he helped guide the company through some of its most challenging economic times as well as a period of dramatic growth. Bill played a key role in positioning the company to be the global leader it is today. On a personal note, I always valued Bill's counsel and respected his ability to look at the big picture when dealing with issues." — Don Walker, CEO

Power Corporation: "Power Corporation of Canada is proud to support this fine biography of the Right Honourable Bill Davis. Bill served on our Board of Directors for more than 20 years during which we were privileged to benefit from his good judgment, his vision, and his quiet good humour. His advice was and is always thoughtful and was sought both by the corporation and its controlling family. While he has left his mark in recent decades on corporate Canada, his greatest contribution is the vital ongoing role he plays in the public life of Ontario and Canada." — Paul and André Desmarais, Co-Chief Executive Officers, Power Corporation of Canada

Revera Living: "As chair emeritus of Revera's Board of Directors, Bill Davis has provided thoughtful and forward-looking leadership to support the company through tremendous growth. He has generously shared his wit and wisdom and has given me excellent advice over the years. He has made a distinct contribution to public life and remains an inspiration to those looking to make a difference in our world." — Thomas G. Wellner, President and CEO

INDIVIDUALS

Douglas G. Bassett, OC, OOnt: "Bill Davis is truly a great Canadian and an outstanding gentleman."

Isabel Bassett and Ernie Eves: "Premier Davis had a progressive, compassionate, conservative approach to public service that championed public education and broadened social justice, while advancing human rights and freedoms. He played a pivotal role in building consensus among the provinces to help achieve the patriation of our Constitution from the British Parliament in 1982. A leader with tremendous integrity, humility, wit, and wisdom, he had a deep sense of duty and made a real difference in the lives of others. We are proud to consider Bill Davis a friend and to support his commitment to public education and community service through the Dr. Roberto Grosso Bursary."

Allan Broadbent, Chairman and CEO, Avana Capital Corporation; Chairman and Founder, Maytree Foundation: "Bill Davis was an effective Ontario premier at an important time in Canadian history. Steve Paikin combines his clear affection for politicians with his critical eye to help us understand the man and his times, as he has previously done with a penetrating biography of John Robarts."

Michael Decter, former Cabinet Secretary, Manitoba, and Deputy Minister of Health, Ontario: "I first met Premier Davis at Premiers' Conferences and First Ministers' Conferences in the 1970s and later with Manitoba Premier Howard Pawley in the 1980s. When I served as a deputy minister in the Ontario government and for two decades afterward, I would encounter Premier Davis. He was at every such occasion unfailingly constructive, thoughtful, humorous, and wise. Premier William Grenville Davis stands as an outstanding Canadian leader and a role model for a generation of Canadian politicians."

Jim Fleck, former CEO, Office of the Premier (1972–74): "Premier Davis has my eternal gratitude for embracing the report of the Committee on Government Productivity (COGP) and taking on, as his chief of staff, a businessman academic with no political background to help ensure its implementation. I was privileged to observe his calm demeanour as he listened carefully, probed deeply, and when he had to, made the tough decisions. His base was Ontario, but his influence was national. A great premier."

Honourable Jerry Grafstein, QC: "There are two fathers of the new Constitution of 1982 and the Charter of Rights and Freedoms. Without these two individuals — Pierre Elliott Trudeau and William Grenville Davis — neither would have been realized. It is important that Premier Davis's crucial role is formally recognized in the pages of this book."

Ignat (Iggy) Kaneff, OOnt, LL.D. (Hon.): "William Davis has been a most inspirational leader for our great Province of Ontario, as well as for Canada. For the past 60 years, he has advised and guided Ontarians and Canadians in building a stronger, more productive, and more successful society. William Davis, also known as the father of the Ontario education system, made groundbreaking changes to the post-secondary education system through the creation of many new public schools, universities, and the establishment of 22 community colleges. In recent years, his advisory role to the Kaneff Group of Companies is highly regarded, and we are proud and honoured to be associated with Mr. Davis, a pillar of our community, province, and country."

Tom Kierans, Retired Investment Banker and CEO of the C.D. Howe Institute: "Bill Davis has been my friend and my mentor."

Peter Munk, Chairman Emeritus of Barrick Gold Corporation: "Bill Davis is a personal friend and one of the finest civil servants and premiers we have been fortunate to have in Ontario. He has my greatest admiration, as he does from most people from Ontario. He was selfless, committed, straight — I must say a typical, high-quality Canadian patriot. It was these kinds of people who created the country so that all of us immigrants could be part of this magnificent experiment."

Andrew and Valerie Pringle: "Bill Davis is a public servant we admire and respect who made a great contribution to Ontario. He is also, not surprisingly, a wonderful human being from whom we can all learn a great deal."

Hugh Segal, Master, Massey College: "Bill Davis defined modern compassionate and civil conservatism through every one of his deeds, actions, and commitments as no Canadian ever has or ever will. Canada and Ontario are stronger, more humane, and free because of his work."

Dr. Calvin and Angie Stiller: "Premier Davis has been a role model for us for most of our adult lives. His demonstration of caring for others is the hallmark of his life. We are pleased that such a talented writer as Steve Paikin has generously documented for posterity this remarkable man and his consistent 'old-school' nobility. He has impacted more than five generations and given us a sterling example of a life, of a 'certain philosophical persuasion,' lived by principle, always for others. It's unlikely that Canada will see the likes of him again!"

Larry Tanenbaum, OC: "Bill Davis is one of our truly great Canadians. As premier for 14 years, he was devoted to helping build a more progressive and inclusive Ontario, and he continues his important work to this day. He has achieved a rarity in politics — he has the ability to transcend political boundaries for the greater good. Bill is an outstanding public servant, an enthusiastic and loyal Argos fan, and most important, my good and valued friend."

His Worship, John Tory, the Mayor of Toronto: "Premier Davis has been and is my mentor, my political role model, and is like a second father to me. We have worked together in politics and in law and most of all we are friends."

The Gage Family
The Grosso Family
The Paikin Family
The Rennie Family

ACKNOWLEDGEMENTS

Let me start with a word about source materials for this book. Fortunately for historians, the people who worked in Bill Davis's premier's office kept excellent scrapbooks. There are literally hundreds, maybe thousands of files, at the Archives of Ontario filled with newspaper articles, government and private correspondence, audiotapes of speeches and interviews, and memorabilia covering the more than eight and a half decades of Bill Davis's life. Rachel Barton and her team at the archives were hugely helpful, professional, and quick off the mark to assist me with whatever I needed. Thank you, Rachel. Many of the documents at the archives are still off limits to the public for many more years because of cabinet secrecy laws. But Mr. Davis gave me access to it all to help make this book more comprehensive and offer a fuller picture of his life to the reader. For that decision alone, I owe him a debt of gratitude. But there's more to say on the subject of this book later.

Other archivists were also of tremendous assistance: David Bogart and Fiona Watson at the Queen's Park Legislative Library, Kyle Neill at the Peel Art Gallery Museum and Archives, and David Pond at the legislative research service. Our archives are the receptacles of our collective historic memory. They do an important job for which I'm grateful.

I'm enormously indebted to Michael Carroll, who served as the editor on this project. Michael did yeoman's work cleaning up my scruffy prose and made the manuscript much better than it otherwise would have been.

He also caught, to my embarrassment, more mistakes than I'd like to admit. Michael, thank you for all of your efforts to make Bill Davis's story a better read. Naturally, whatever mistakes or problems that remain in the text are my fault, not his.

In a section of this book called "Dr. Roberto Grosso Bursary," you'll see more information about how several of Mr. Davis's friends and colleagues significantly contributed to a bursary in my late father-in-law's name in recognition of the former premier's contribution to education in Ontario. Dr. Cal Stiller of London, Ontario, was the driving force behind that mission, and I can't thank him enough for his tireless efforts. Thanks to him and many others, several students in Northern Ontario, who otherwise might not be able to, are going to become doctors. Bravo, Dr. Stiller.

I'm also thankful to those friends and colleagues of Mr. Davis's who spoke to me for this book, recalling in some cases memories that were many decades in their rearview mirrors. It's simply a fact of life that people can be more honest about yesteryear in part because they've had more time to figure out what's truly important, or also because there really aren't any political consequences for telling the truth 40 years after the fact. I hope the younger interviewees won't mind my singling out a few of the more senior political figures for special mention.

Clare Westcott is 92 years old, still speaks to Bill Davis on the phone almost every day, and remains a great storyteller about days of yore. As I type this, Robert Nixon is now 87 years old and is still breathing fire over that 1971 election he and his Liberals lost to Mr. Davis. One of the most enjoyable things on my calendar is my annual visit to his farm in St. George to celebrate his birthday over lunch with our pals, Mark Littell and Howard Brown. Mr. Nixon still writes a daily blogpost, sharing his views on politics and the meaning of life, and I love listening to his stories from back in the day. Margaret Birch, Ontario's first-ever female cabinet minister, welcomed me into her son Randy's home in Pickering, where she now lives, with a big hug, even though we hadn't seen each other since she left public life more than 30 years ago. She is in astonishingly good health for a woman who just turned 95 years old. Despite four stents in her heart from a procedure four years ago, she looks wonderful and still drives a car. She has three grandchildren and five great-grandchildren. It was a pleasure to spend time with her and get her take on the Davis years. And Dr.

Bette Stephenson, sadly, has been fighting ill health for many years. But, fortunately, that didn't stop her from twice welcoming me into her home in Richmond Hill to reminisce about her time in Bill Davis's cabinet. I'm so grateful to these four stalwarts of politics for making time for me.

I also drew upon hours and hours of tape-recorded interviews conducted in the 1990s by former *London Free Press* reporter George Hutchison. "Hutch," who was also press secretary to Premier David Peterson, came to my TVO office one day with a treasure trove of interviews he did with first-hand witnesses and participants of the past half century of Ontario history. He had hoped to use them himself one day for a project he was working on, but for whatever reason, that project never came together, so George simply handed the boxes and boxes of tapes to me with a "maybe they'll be of some use to you some day." It was a selfless and generous thing for him to have done. Those interviews helped give me significant added insight for this book, particularly the interviews of those who have since died, such as Frank Miller, Thomas Wells, and Norman Atkins. Thank you so much, George.

Of course, the most significant thank-you needs to go to the man who is at the centre of this story. It is impossible for me to adequately express my gratitude to Ontario's 18th premier for trusting me to tell his story. True, I wish the green light had come sooner, but I won't be the only person in Bill Davis's life who has said that. Speaking candidly, given his occasional health challenges, I have always feared Mr. Davis might not make it to the finish line to see this book published. His long-standing joke has always been: "I can't die. I've still got five children and 12 grandchildren to support." Thankfully, we are both still around to enjoy seeing his life story finally make it into print. Bill Davis became premier of Ontario when I was 10 years old and remained in that job until I turned 24. His most formative years in politics coincided with my most formative years of growing up. As a result, he was basically the only premier I had any awareness of for the first quarter century of my life. He was the premier at the dawn of my career in journalism, and there is a certain appropriate symmetry in being fortunate enough to be able to tell his story as my career in journalism heads toward dusk.

Let me also pay tribute to a woman who might not get the credit she deserves because one can only imagine how difficult it is to live alongside a legend. Kathleen Davis is simply one of the most generous and loving people I've ever met. Everyone calls her husband "Premier" or "Mr. Davis." Now that Norman Atkins is no longer with us, she's the only one who calls him "Billy." As a product of his generation, Mr. Davis might not easily be given to complimenting his wife in public. But anyone who has watched this couple over the past half century knows Bill Davis could never have become Premier Davis without Kathleen Davis. Although not a big fan of politics, she has been indispensable to his success. Thank you, Mrs. Davis, for our conversations for this book and, of course, for taking such good care of this book's subject.

Thanks, as well, to the second and third generations of Davis family members: the five children and their spouses: Neil and Ruth, Nancy and Michael, Catherine and Abraham, Ian and Rose, and Meg and Paul; and the 12 grandchildren: Christine, Kathleen, Jr., Meg, Michael, Noah, Emmett, Spencer, William, Robert, Kerr, Molly, and Jack. Of that group, I know Kathleen the best, since she's been a helpful family contact doing fact-checking along the way and was once a guest on *The Agenda*, talking about her human rights advocacy work. It was a pleasure to have her on the program and *not* mention her grandfather until the last few minutes of the interview!

I confess that covering stories at Queen's Park as a reporter in my early twenties and participating in scrums with Premier Davis meant reminding myself not to let the awe I felt for him manifest itself. "Poker face," I kept telling myself, "poker face." By the time I began covering the Ontario legislature, Premier Davis was truly at the top of his political prowess. It was a great time to be in one's twenties, watching the master at work. Luckily, I had the good fortune of watching legendary reporters such as CBC-TV's Robert Fisher and Citytv's Colin Vaughan treat Davis with respect but not reverence. In fact, as much as they obviously liked the man personally, they showed me that affection didn't need to get in the way of doing the job professionally. Both Robert and Colin loved nothing more than to get into a good cut and thrust with Davis, who just kept chewing on his pipe, smiling, and fending off their hard-hitting questions with aplomb. Frankly, it was difficult to determine who enjoyed those scrums more. Probably the premier — he was so good at them.

Colin, alas, is now gone, but I was fortunate indeed to learn from the likes of Robert Fisher, who just retired last year after a superb nearly five decades in journalism, most of them at CBC. It remains one of the highlights of my career to have been asked by Robert back in 1985 to be a guest panellist on his *Dateline Ontario* program on CBC-TV. It was *the* Queen's Park show of its day, and I have no doubt that much of my interest and passion for Ontario politics has happened because Robert so kindly took me under his wing 30 years ago and showed me the way it was done.

And while I'm thanking former journalists, I also need to acknowledge the singular role Fraser Kelly has played in my career and my life. In the 1980s, he anchored (with Hilary Brown) the six o'clock evening newscast on CBC-TV, and I was one of his reporters. It was another of my life's highlights to hear him read the intro to one of my pieces, followed by: "Steve Paikin reports." He was (and is) a mentor to me. A decade ago when I wrote a biography about Bill Davis's predecessor, John Robarts, Fraser gave me the single most important piece of advice I needed to hear in writing that book. Not surprisingly, he did it again for this book. The advice will stay between the two of us, but just know that it was indispensable.

Speaking of indispensable, my assistant at TVO (or as I like to call her, my "co-pilot"), Sue Beres, was that and more. Trying to get *The Agenda* on the air five nights a week, writing columns for the TVO website, adequately performing my role as chancellor at Laurentian University, doing some visiting professor lectures for journalism and broadcasting students at Ryerson University, while writing this book was a bit of a load. Sue was invaluable in setting up interviews for this book, transcribing many of those interviews, researching various facts that needed nailing down, and offering the occasional wise piece of advice that made this book better than it might otherwise have been. Thanks, CP. You're awesome.

This is the seventh book I've written, but the first in which Dan Dunsky hasn't been my teammate at TVO. Dan left the provincial broadcaster last year after 19 wonderful years of producing some excellent television programs. We worked together on TVO's first-ever nightly current affairs program *Studio 2*, then co-created a weekly foreign affairs program called *Diplomatic Immunity*, and finally co-created *The Agenda with Steve Paikin* in 2006. It was he as executive producer, not I as anchor, who insisted my name be part of the program's title. For nine years *The Agenda* was a delightful partnership between the two of us. I don't mind saying that I was the face of the show, but Dan was the brains of it. To his credit, Dan also understood that it was a good thing for *The Agenda* to give me permission to write books "on the side" or during my summer vacations, because it all contributed to making me a better informed, more useful host for the show. For all your support and friendship through the years, Dan, thank you.

And while I'm at it, thanks as well to the great folks at TVO where I've had the pleasure of working since 1992. Mr. Davis likes to kid me that without his creation of TVO when he was minister of education I'd have been out of work for the past quarter century. I've never contradicted him when he's said that, since I fear he might be right. I've been blessed to work for and with some extraordinary people: from Peter Herrndorf to Isabel Bassett, to the current dynamic duo of board chair Peter O'Brian and CEO Lisa de Wilde, and my immediate boss, John Ferri, vice-president of current affairs and documentaries, and *The Agenda*'s new executive producer, Stacey Dunseath, our very own *khaleesi* (if you don't get that reference, you're obviously not watching *Game of Thrones*). Yes, I've been at Ontario's public broadcaster and digital pioneer for a long time now. But that's because I still believe in its mission of treating our audience as *citizens*, not potential consumers to be delivered to advertisers. The private sector does a great job of the latter. I'm just grateful that successive Ontario governments of all political stripes have seen the value in having just one property on the media landscape with a different mission.

Some of Mr. Davis's colleagues from back in the day were also most helpful with their time and efforts to convince the former premier to participate in this project after so many years of my entreaties falling on deaf ears. At the top of that list belongs the name John Tory, the current mayor of Toronto. I first met Mayor Tory when he was one of Premier Davis's principal advisers and I was a cub reporter at CHFI Radio. All these years later I not only need to thank His Worship for helping persuade Mr. Davis to do this book but also for being part of one unforgettable moment I had the privilege to witness. At a time when it's so easy to be cynical about public life I'll always remember one time in particular at Mayor Tory's swearing-in ceremony in 2014. Louise Russo is a well-known anti-crime crusader and victims' advocate because she had the misfortune of being in the wrong place at the wrong time. In 2004 she walked into a shop to buy her daughter a sandwich when she was hit by a stray bullet during the commission of a crime. The bullet shattered her spine, and Louise, a mother of three, became a paraplegic. John Tory befriended her, checked in on her over the years, and stayed in touch with her even after he left politics. Now, with Bill Davis standing alongside and watching his swearing-in as Toronto's 65th mayor, Tory wanted her to put the chain of office around his neck. Louise made two attempts to do so, but because of her injuries, couldn't raise her arms high enough to perform the task. So Mayor Tory, completely unscripted, got down on his knees in front of her as she sat in her wheelchair so that she could reach his neck and put the chain around it. In nearly three and a half decades of covering public life, I've never seen a single image that so brilliantly encapsulated what politics ought to be about: the powerful, on bended knee, serving the powerless. It says a lot about Mayor Tory that his instincts told him to get on his knees rather than take the chain from Louise and put it on himself. And, of course, we know where he learned those values of public service: from his then 85-year-old mentor who was standing right beside him at that ceremony. While I am, of course, scrupulously neutral concerning the mayor's policies and how successfully he has implemented them, I do want to thank him for that indelible image, and for his efforts to persuade Mr. Davis to co-operate with this book.

I also want to thank Mr. Davis's other wunderkind from three and four decades ago. Hugh Segal has also tried numerous times over the years to persuade his former boss to let someone — *anyone* — write his biography. Occasionally, he would taunt Mr. Davis with lines such as "You'd better do this soon before you start losing your marbles and then it'll be too late!" Thank you, Hugh Segal, for helping to put that full-court press on this book's subject, for answering all my fact-checking emails, and for writing so many good books of your own along the way. They were a valuable resource for this one.

Books don't get written without a lot of understanding from one's family, because instead of spending time with them, you're sitting by yourself in the Archives of Ontario on a beautiful Saturday afternoon, or in your office at home banging away at your laptop computer until the wee hours of the morning. So thanks to my parents, Marnie and Larry Paikin. I never buy lottery tickets. I figure I already won the lottery being your kid, so what are the odds of winning again? My younger brother, Jeff, is what every older brother wants — a younger brother who looks older than I do. But I jest. The reality is: he's still the "funnest" guy I know, I couldn't be prouder of his success, and there's no one's company I enjoy more.

My four kids are the pride and joy of my life. I'm at the stage of life when 75 percent of my kids are living outside Toronto, and thankfully the one who still lives in Toronto continues to take my calls. Mind you, that one just turned 13, so I hear from others that might soon stop. I hope not. I love that my daughter, Giulia, is the only girl on her all-boys' baseball team and enjoys cheering for the Boston Red Sox along with her old man. My boys — Zachary, Henry, and Teddy — continue to dazzle me with their interests, their talents, and their plans. Zach is doing his Ph.D. in international relations at the University of Kent in Canterbury, U.K.; Henry is the first of my offspring who's off the payroll: after attending three different universities in France, England, and Spain, he just got hired by the Senate of Canada to do communications and provide digital content to its website; and Teddy is doing his undergrad in politics, history, and economics at Sciences Po in Rheims, France. They are truly citizens of the world, and I have no doubt they'll all make their marks wherever their journeys take them. Already I'm enjoying what every parent wants to experience — meeting people who ask, "Aren't you the father of …?" I couldn't be prouder of you all.

Finally, I need to thank my wife, Francesca Grosso. She undoubtedly had no clue what she was signing up for when she married me. She got a husband who loves his job too much, loves writing books too much, loves taking his kids to plays, concerts, and sporting events too much, and loves hanging out with friends and family too much. It has often meant there is less of me left over for her than she'd prefer (or maybe I'm overestimating that). But I rejoice in and marvel at her accomplishments, whether it's running her successful health-care consultancy with our pal, Mike McCarthy; writing two excellent books herself (*Navigating Canada's Health Care* and *The History of Sunnybrook Hospital: Battle to Greatness*), or creating our modest little home-away-from-home on Manitoulin Island. Every time I write a book, Francesca becomes a kind of "literary widow" for a year or two at a time, as all my "free time" disappears into, as she calls it, "another damn book." So, Fra, I promise, this is my last one. (Mind you, I've made that promise on six previous occasions. But I mean it this time … I think.) In any event, Fra, you are amazing. *Grazie mille, e sono multo lieto di fare la sua conoscenza.*

INDEX